BLACK THEATRE USA

THE FREE PRESS
New York   London   Toronto   Sydney

BLACK THEATRE USA

PLAYS BY AFRICAN AMERICANS

The Early Period
1847–1938

Revised and Expanded Edition

Edited by

JAMES V. HATCH
TED SHINE

THE FREE PRESS
A Division of Simon & Schuster Inc.
1230 Avenue of the Americas
New York, NY 10020

THE FREE PRESS and colophon are trademarks
of Simon & Schuster Inc.

Designed by Carla Bolte

Manufactured in the United States of America

10 9 8 7 6 5

Library of Congress Cataloging-in-Publication Data

Black theatre USA : plays by African Americans from 1847 to today /
    [edited by] James V. Hatch, Ted Shine. —Rev. and expanded ed.
        p.   cm.
    Rev. ed. of: Black theater, U.S.A.
    Paperback ed. issued in 2 vols. Vol. 1: The early period,
    1847–1938; v. 2: The recent period, 1937–today.
    Includes bibliographical references and index.
    ISBN 0–684–82306–3 (cloth).—ISBN 0–684–82308–X (pbk. : v. 1).—
    ISBN 0–684–82307–1 (pbk. : v. 2)
        1. American drama—Afro-American authors.   2. Afro-Americans—
    Drama.   I. Hatch, James Vernon.   II. Shine, Ted.
    III. Title: Black theater, U.S.A.
    PS628.N4B56   1996
    812.008' 03520396073—dc20   95–40329
                                                           CIP
    ISBN-13: 978-1-4516-3650-5

This book is dedicated to James "Beanie" Butcher, Owen Vincent Dodson, Winona Lee Fletcher, Errol Gaston Hill, Thomas D. Pawley III, and Anne Cooke Reid. Their scholarship, integrity, and devotion to preparing students to excel in the theatre arts made them giants in the American theatre.

CONTENTS

Foreword   *Margaret B. Wilkerson*   ix

Acknowledgments   xiii

THOSE WHO LEFT AND THOSE WHO STAYED

THE BLACK DOCTOR *Ira Aldridge* (1847)	3
THE BROWN OVERCOAT *Victor Séjour* (1858)	25
THE ESCAPE; OR, A LEAP FOR FREEDOM *William Wells Brown* (1858)	35

YES WE CAN

IN DAHOMEY *Paul Laurence Dunbar and Jesse A. Shipp* (1902)	63
STAR OF ETHIOPIA *W.E.B. Du Bois* (1912)	86
WHY WE ARE AT WAR *United States Food Administration* (1918)	92
APPEARANCES *Garland Anderson* (1925)	95

EARLY PLAYS BY BLACK WOMEN

RACHEL *Angelina Grimké* (1916)	133
MINE EYES HAVE SEEN *Alice Dunbar-Nelson* (1918)	169
AFTERMATH *Mary Burrill* (1919)	175
THEY THAT SIT IN DARKNESS *Mary Burrill* (1919)	182
FOR UNBORN CHILDREN *Myrtle Smith Livingston* (1926)	188
THE CHURCH FIGHT *Ruth Gaines-Shelton* (1925)	193
UNDERTOW *Eulalie Spence* (1929)	197
THE PURPLE FLOWER *Marita Odette (Occomy) Bonner* (1928)	206

FOLK PLAYS OF THE 1920s

THE DEACON'S AWAKENING   *Willis Richardson* (1920)   216

BALO   *Jean Toomer* (1922)   223

A SUNDAY MORNING IN THE SOUTH   *Georgia Douglas Johnson* (1925)   231

'CRUITER   *John Matheus* (1926)   238

OLD MAN PETE   *Randolph Edmonds* (1934)   246

FROM THE DEPRESSION

JOB HUNTERS   *H. F. V. Edward* (1931)   259

DON'T YOU WANT TO BE FREE?   *Langston Hughes* (1937)   266

BIG WHITE FOG   *Theodore Ward* (1938)   284

LEGEND AND HISTORY

THE FIRST ONE   *Zora Neale Hurston* (1927)   327

GRAVEN IMAGES   *May Miller* (1929)   334

NATURAL MAN   *Theodore Browne* (1937)   342

A SOLDIER'S PLAY   *Charles Fuller* (1981)   364

LIBERTY DEFERRED   *John D. Silvera and Abram Hill* (1938)   394

Bibliographies   409

About the Editors   415

FOREWORD

Black Theatre USA is a classic. No other anthology captures the grand sweep and surge of theatre created by African Americans since its beginnings in the early nineteenth century. Now expanded and issued in two volumes, this collection of plays is a unique mirror of the history and perspectives of a people whose history both defines and complicates the meaning of the American Dream.

In a society whose popular culture is shaped by corporate dollars and mass media, the theatre still offers a space where the individual artist can speak out of the intimacy of community. Many of the playwrights represented in Volume I, most of whom wrote prior to and during the Great Depression, had little hope or likelihood of having their work presented in the professional theatre or on Broadway. In small, local theatres supported by churches, community centers, and social organizations, these playwrights retained control of their work and were not subject to the political agendas and cultural ignorance of monied interests. Thus these plays represent authentic voices that address the complexities of African American life in the United States, from chattel slavery of pre-Emancipation days to the economic slavery of the Depression and beyond. Alongside these works stand the few that made it to the professional stage, but are nevertheless rooted in the rich soil of Black life and thought from the first decades of this century.

Most of the volume is organized chronologically up to the Great Depression of the 1930s, with each section pursuing a theme and opening with an enlightening discussion of the period and the plays. The first section, "Those Who Left and Those Who Stayed" immediately confronts the reader with the plays of two Black men who spent most of their years in Europe and a third who wrote from his experience as a slave in the United States. Their views of race and color, culture and politics are necessarily shaped by their individual circumstances. Yet all wrote at a time when slavery was still the law of the land in the United States, and the stereotypes of Black people were becoming imbedded in the American psyche. While Victor Séjour's *The Brown Overcoat* follows its Parisian forebears in its removal from nineteenth-century realities, and Ira Aldridge's *The Black Doctor* is a romantic story of an interracial marriage, William Wells Brown writes in *The Escape; or, A Leap for Freedom*, a compelling play drawn from his experiences as a slave, replete with subtle challenges to society's construction of the slave as Black buffoon. These plays are poignant counterpoints to the blackface minstrels portrayed by whites and inherited by Blacks on the American stage during this period.

"Any man can do what he desires to do, can become anything he desires to be." Carl, the bellhop-hero in Garland Anderson's *Appearances* who is typical of America's "can-do" attitude, articulates the theme of the next set of plays and their authors. Black and uneducated, he imagines himself a playwright and creates a drama within a drama in which a Black bellhop is falsely accused of rape, but is exonerated at the end. Anderson, along with W.E.B. Du Bois, Jesse A. Shipp, and Paul Laurence Dunbar, is part of a generation of so-called "self-made men"—"firsts" who refused to be limited by societal definitions of race. Anderson became the first Black to have a full-length play produced on Broadway. W.E.B. Du Bois, who was the first Black to receive a Ph.D. from Harvard University, parades the achievements of African Americans in his play, *Star of Ethiopia*. Shipp's and Dunbar's *In Dahomey* was one of the early original Black musicals produced on Broadway.

"Early Plays by Black Women" is one of the eternal treasures of this volume. Proving Anna Julia Cooper's statement, "When and where I enter, the whole race enters with me," these writers address a range of social and political issues that affect Black communities during the first three decades of the twentieth century. The quandaries posed by World War I are explored in *Mine Eyes Have Seen* as Black men are forced to decide whether to fight for a nation that still lynches them at home; the plight of women denied knowledge of birth control is movingly told in *They That Sit In Darkness*; Black women's anger at Black male–white female miscegenation spills onto the stage in *For Unborn Children*, while *The Church Fight* and *Undertow* pursue domestic themes of jealousy and personal rivalry. Two of the jewels in this section, like book ends, begin and end this set of plays. *Rachel* by Angelina Grimké shows the devastating impact of racism on a sensitive, young Black woman who rejects the "feminine" expectations of marriage and motherhood rather than love a Black man and children who are always at risk. Written in 1916, it stands in sharp contrast to *The Purple Flower*, an allegory that portrays the final revolution when Blacks forcibly claim equality by overthrowing their oppressors. Since most of these plays were not published or were produced in very local circumstances, their publication opens a window into some of the most profound and difficult problems of the period as seen through the eyes of Black women.

The early years of the twentieth century witnessed a growing interest in the "Negro" as research subject, as scholars of the young social science disciplines began to study the "exotic" or the "folkways" of their own country. The dialect of African Americans had always been the dialogue of choice of white playwrights. But it was left to Black playwrights to capture the idiom of their people in fresh ways and to reflect the life and ways of rural Blacks. In "Folk Plays of the 1920s," the subject matter ranges from the horrors of lynching in *A Sunday Morning in the South* to the religious ecstasy of *Balo*, from the pain of separation caused by northern migrations in *'Cruiter*, all told through the language and perspective of the folk. Also among these authors is that group of committed teachers who built the concept of Black drama in Southern schools and who left a body of work based on their knowledge and study of Black life.

Out of the Depression Era came two of the most distinguished playwrights in this volume and two frequently produced works. *Don't You Want To Be Free?* adds Black music to some of Langston Hughes' most poignant poetry, giving historical and political context to the plight of workers and the poor, both Black and white. *Big White Fog* by Theodore Ward puts human faces on the Black community's political debates questioning Garveyism, capitalism, and socialism and their ability to be socially responsive systems. This section is rounded out by *Job Hunters*, a short play based on H.F.V. Edward's experience with the New York State Employment Service as a job locator and an interviewer of Harlem's unemployed. The impact of this devastating period is movingly documented in these works.

While all of the plays in the volume have some historical value, the works in the last section, "Legend and History," interpret myth and legend, or imaginatively reconstruct actual situations. May Miller's *Graven Images*, a children's play based on a Biblical reference, represents the efforts by many Black playwrights to let young audiences know that they are a part of world history. Theodore Browne captures one of the great, popular legends of Black culture—*John Henry*, a larger-than-life figure who has inspired numerous songs, stories, poetry, paintings, plays. While *Liberty Deferred* from the Federal Theatre Project chronicles the history of African Americans, a popular form of Black theatre, *A Soldier's Play*, focuses on Black soldiers in World War II and their complex responses to an oppressive military that segregates and demeans them. A controversial Pulitzer Prize-winning work of the 1980s, it raises disturbing questions about justice in an unjust society.

The plays in this volume represent only a small portion of the great body of Black dramatic literature. Each is a microcosm of reflections, perspectives, and ideas growing out of Black life and culture, and each represents hundreds of other equally challenging works. Some of these playwrights are known primarily for achievements in other fields. For example, Du Bois was a philosopher and educator, Ira Aldridge was an actor honored by European royalty, and Paul Laurence Dunbar a prolific and beloved poet. Others, such as Victor Séjour, Mary Burrill, Marita Bonner, Willis Richardson, Randolph Edmonds, and Charles Fuller, have produced their own body of work worthy of discussion and production. The editors' bibliography guides the reader to other important sources.

This book is not only a unique collection of plays, but a large slice of American life and history. A treasure trove of research leads for students of theatre, history and culture; an unusual entry to the face behind the mask of civility characteristic of this century's early decades; a compelling collection of dramatizations that illuminate the spirit, resilience, and complexity of the only unwilling immigrants to America, *Black Theatre USA* is a unique anthology that will never lose its savor.

—MARGARET B. WILKERSON

ACKNOWLEDGMENTS

The editors are grateful to Vanessa Jackson and Judy Blum for secretarial assistance; to Celia Knight, Ellen Simon, and Lori Williams for copy editing; to Whitney LeBlanc, Thomas Pawley, Robert West, Tisch Jones, Freda Scott Giles, Leo Hamalian, and John Graziano for editorial and critical analysis; to Beth Anderson, our chief editor, for steering us safely though this book's voyage; and finally to Dr. Oscar Brockett, who was our mentor in history and research at the University of Iowa.

THOSE WHO LEFT AND THOSE WHO STAYED

Ira Aldridge • Victor Séjour • William Wells Brown

I n William Dunlap's play *A Trip to Niagara*, which opened in 1828, the Black
gentleman, Job Jerryson, tells a fellow servant, "If you would like to see our
theatre, I can give you an order. I am one of the managers. We rehearse every
club night—the Shakespeare Club." In all likelihood, Jerryson is referring to the
African Grove Theatre. Thanks to recent and careful scholarship of George A.
Thompson, Jr., we now know that in the season of 1820–21, William A[lexander]
Brown, an actor, playwright, and sometime ship's steward, founded the African
Grove Theatre—which was also a tea garden—at 38 Thompson Street in lower
Manhattan, for the pleasure of free persons of color on their leisure day. When
the neighbors complained about the noise, he moved "uptown" to Bleecker and
Mercer Streets, which was then on the northern edge of the city. Discovering
that he had moved too far away from his audience, Brown moved back to Houston and Mercer where he built a building not far from the Park Theatre, a popular white establishment.

The drama *King Shotaway*, written by Brown himself and based on "the In-
surrection of the Caravs on the Island of St. Vincents [San Domingo]" was performed in the African Grove Theatre. The script is not extant, but *King Shotaway*
is the first play known to be written and performed by an African American. Also
in this theatre, the West Indian actor James Hewlett performed. Here Ira
Aldridge saw his first Shakespeare production. However, the African Grove was
closed in 1822 by the constable after white rowdies "out for a lark brought disorder and wanton mischief." There is some evidence that the disorder was deliberately provoked by the owner of the Park Theatre, who feared the competition of
a Black company performing Shakespeare.

For the next seventy years the major commercial opportunity for Black actors

1

was blackface minstrelsy. Before the Civil War, William Henry Lane, professionally named "Juba," performing with a white minstrel troupe in the United States and England, became the most famous African American dancer. After the war, Charles Hicks organized the Georgia Minstrels, the first of several companies of African American minstrels. To obtain bookings, however, they had to have white managers. They also were required to wear minstrel makeup—the face covered with burnt cork and the eyes and mouth circled in red and/or white. By the 1890s, some Black actors had stopped wearing this disguise and a number turned to writing and producing their own musicals, such as *In Dahomey* (printed here).

Several talented African American women also took the stage after the Civil War. Pauline Elizabeth Hopkins, a popular novelist and short fiction writer, wrote three musical dramas: *Aristocracy* (1877), *Winona* (1878), and *Slaves Escape; or The Underground Railroad* (also entitled *Peculiar Sam*) (1879). The Hyers Sisters, Emma and Annie, mounted and toured a half a dozen shows including *Out of Bondage* (1880). Matilda Sisseretta Jones toured in 1896 with her own company, the Black Patti Troubadours, which for their finale presented scenes from *Lucia, Martha,* and *Il Trovatore.*

Faced with limited opportunity, some talents—Morgan Smith, Louis Gottschalk, Ira Aldridge, and Victor Séjour—left to work in Europe. Others—William Wells Brown, Pauline Hopkins, the Hyers Sisters, Paul Laurence Dunbar, William Easton, Sisseretta Jones, Bob Cole, Will Marion Cook, Sam Lucas, Ada Overton, Bert Williams, and George Walker—elected to work in the United States. The decision to stay in America may often have depended on whether the artist could adapt to ministrelsy or not. If the artists were "serious"—that is, if they wished to write or perform drama or concert music *sans* blackface—their hopes lay outside the country. Nearly all who stayed relied in some way upon musical comedy and dance. Serious drama remained a dream.

In 1893, playwright William Easton wrote in the introduction to his militant verse play *Dessalines,* "Indeed we have had excellent caricaturists of the Negro in his only recognized school of legitimate drama, i.e., buffoonery. But the author of this work hopes to see a happier era inaugurated by the constant production of legitimate drama written exclusively for Negro players." However, the "happier era" he hoped for did not begin to develop for another thirty years.

THE BLACK DOCTOR
1847

Ira Aldridge (1807–1867)

The white handkerchief in the dark hand of the Moor, the dark face in a cloak of white marble, the eyes fastened on the linen—this is the Pietro Calvi bust of Othello that stands inside the entrance of the Schomburg Research Library in Harlem.

Of the visitors who pause to glance at the statue, a few recognize the bronze plaque's legend: Ira Aldridge, the Tragedian. The names, if not the accomplishments, of great nineteenth-century actors (Booth, Kean, Bernhardt) are familiar to many Americans. Ira Aldridge, whom Herbert Marshall calls "a dark star whose brilliance has been dimmer by the sins of omission and commission of the white world," was remembered through a hundred years of silence by a few writers who would remind America during Negro History Week that Aldridge was the first Black American honored by the Republic of Haiti for service to his race. They remembered also that he had received the Prussian Gold Medal for Arts and Science from King Frederick, and that he had been awarded the Medal of Ferdinand from Franz Joseph of Austria for his performance of *Othello*.

Aldridge claimed descent from the Fulah princes of Senegal; however, the evidence indicates he was born on July 24, 1807, in New York City, where he attended the African Free School on Mulberry Street. In 1820–21, Aldridge saw plays at the African Grove Theatre and watched the fine West Indian actor James Hewlett perform.

At age seventeen, Aldridge faced the same choices that other Black men and women who wished to be theatre artists faced: to stay and find some kind of work in blackface song and dance, or to leave America. By October 17, 1825, he had renamed himself "Mr. Keane" and was acting in London as "the Celebrated Tragedian of Colour from the African Theatre, New York." Not until 1835 did he list himself as "Mr. Aldridge" in his playbills.

The story of his life in England and on the European continent is one of struggle, recognition, and success. Billing himself as "The African Roscius, a native of Senegal," he established himself not only in the Black roles of Othello and Titus Andronicus, but also as King Lear, Macbeth, Shylock, and Richard III.

Nor did he limit himself to Shakespeare. His repertoire included *The Padlock*, a comedy in which he played Mungo, a dis-

3

obedient servant; the role of Ginger Blue, a waiter, in a farce entitled *The Virginia Mummy;* and the lead role, Fabian, in *The Black Doctor.* This play, originally written in French by Anicet-Bourgeois, opened in London in 1846. The version printed here was adapted for the English stage by Aldridge.

The plot is a romantic tale of the Black physician who heals, falls in love with, and marries (secretly) the daughter of a French aristocrat. The inevitable family conflict, imprisonment, insanity, and denouement predictably follow. However, the racial statement made by the play's main character presents the doctor with dignity—a dignity marred by his acceptance of European standards of culture at the expense of his own color.

As described by Aldridge, Fabian "is not a black man, but a handsome Mulatto, yellow and brown." This description may have been intended as a portrait of the au-thor. (One critic compared Aldridge to "a new half penny.") Quite possibly he was also indicating to white audiences that the term "black" included shades other than charcoal.

Ira Aldridge's color irritated those English critics who could not endure to see a "slave" perform Shakespeare. Other critics came to the actor's defense. Perhaps the tragedian's situation was akin to the Black doctor's in the play: his color sometimes provoked hostility, but his talent was so in evidence that his detractors could not hold the field. Like Fabian, he married a white Englishwoman, had children (several by other women), and enjoyed honors, property, and British citizenship. Although he opened negotiations to perform in New York, he never returned to America. While on tour, he died in Lodz, Poland, where he is buried. Whatever Europe's prejudices, they had not prevented the artist from developing and living by his talent.

The Black Doctor

CAST OF CHARACTERS

(IN ORDER OF APPEARANCE)

HANNIBAL GRIMAUD, *wine shop owner*
LIZETTE GRIMAUD, *his wife*
SUSANNE GRIMAUD, *his daughter*
PIERRE BRIQUET, *valet to St. Luce*
JACQUES FILS, *suitor to Susanne*
CHRISTIAN, *old Negro servant to Fabian*
FABIAN, *the black doctor*
PAULINE REYNERIE, *beloved of Fabian*
LIA, *mulatto servant to Pauline*
CHEVALIER ST. LUCE *cousin and fiancé to Pauline*
MARCHIONESS DE LA REYNERIE, *Pauline's mother*
ANDRE, *loyal friend to Fabian*
AURELIA, *sister to St. Luce*
LORDS, LADIES, SOLDIERS, JAILORS, *etc.*

ACT ONE

Scene One

(The Wine-shop of HANNIBAL GRIMAUD, *at the town of St. Louis, in the Isle of Bourbon.—Enter* GRIMAUD, LIZETTE, *and* SUSANNE, *right)*

GRIMAUD   Don't talk, woman, but hear me! I'm Commander-in-Chief: as the great Louis said, "I'm France"—which means, I'm every-thing and everybody.
LIZETTE   But now, husband, consider—
GRIMAUD   Don't waste your breath by hus-banding me! I'm firm, inflexible! A solid square! There's no breaking through me.
SUSANNE   But, dear father—
GRIMAUD   Don't father me you jade; or rather, don't get anybody else to father me. I tell you, when you do marry, it shall be to a man of my choosing. Do you imagine that I,

Hannibal Grimaud, who have served seventeen campaigns, will condescend to marry my daughter to a common barber?

LIZETTE   Pierre Briquet isn't a common barber; he keeps as good a shop as any in the town, and is well to do in the world beside.

GRIMAUD   Not a common barber! Look at my chin; how dare you contradict me? Didn't he shave me yesterday with his own hand?

SUSANNE   That was out of friendship; for, you know, your own hand shook so with—

GRIMAUD   Silence, you impudent baggage, or I'll shake you. Once for all, I tell you I'm not to be shaved into any such connections; and as for that other suitor of yours—that threadpaper fellow, Jacques Fils, why, he's a fool.

LIZETTE   He's as good a young man as any in town.

GRIMAUD   Good! Good for nothing.

LIZETTE   Sober, steady and industrious.

SUSANNE   And an excellent workman.

LIZETTE   Two such suitors are not to be despised.

SUSANNE   And I'm sure men are scarce enough in the colony, unless you'd have me marry a blackamoor.

GRIMAUD   You shall marry whom I please, you jade, and he shall be as black as I like. I tell you Pierre Briquet and Jacques Fils are very well in their way; but be prudent, girl; give your best smiles to the best customers. Remember you're a soldier's daughter; and though your post may be a wine-shop, let your heart be surrounded with a *chevaux de frize* of pride, which shall render it impervious to the puffs of a barber, or all the finedrawn compliments of a tailor.

LIZETTE   I'm sure Susanne has all the proper pride of her mother's family.

GRIMAUD   Lather and soapsuds, what do you mean? Why, you were only a laundress when I raised you to the honorable distinction of a soldier's wife! Her mother's family indeed—she has little to boast of on that score.

LIZETTE   Score, indeed! Your washing-score was long enough when I married you, and you were only a—

GRIMAUD   Silence, woman! *(looking round)* Here comes some neighbors; order, to your post. And remember, I'm commander. *(enter* PIERRE BRIQUET *and* JACQUES FILS, *left)* Welcome neighbors, welcome.

BRIQUET   Good morning, friend Grimaud; I've some news for you; so just step in, though I'm in a terrible hurry.

GRIMAUD   Ay; good, I hope?

BRIQUET   For me, at any rate; but first, some wine; my throat's as dry as the high road.

JACQUES   And so is mine.

GRIMAUD   Susanne, some wine. Ah, this is a fine country.

BRIQUET   Do you say so?

GRIMAUD   Ay, for wine's cheap, and one's always thirsty—ha, ha!

ALL   Ha, ha! very cool. (SUSANNE *brings wine*)

GRIMAUD   Well, Master Briquet, now for your news.

BRIQUET   Well, first and foremost, my shop's to let.

SUSANNE   Your shop?

BRIQUET   Yes, my shop, pretty one; I'm this very day engaged by the Chevalier St. Luce, as his valet and confidential attendant.

SUSANNE   What! Mademoiselle de la Reynerie's cousin, and who they say is to be her husband?

BRIQUET   So they say; and now she's her own mistress, the death of her mother having removed all restraint.

GRIMAUD   But is the death of the Marchioness authenticated?

BRIQUET   Why, seeing the vessel she was to have sailed to France in was wrecked, and every soul has perished, there's very little doubt of the matter. Ah, poor Mademoiselle de la Reynerie! She has had two narrow escapes, for grief and anxiety had nearly killed her.

GRIMAUD   Ay, but the Black Doctor saved her both times.

LIZETTE   Only, to think now, that a mulatto, and a slave, should have become the most eminent physician in all the island!

GRIMAUD   The Black Doctor isn't a slave.

LIZETTE   Well, but he was before he was free.

GRIMAUD   Don't you run down people, wife of mine. Remember what you were before I married you.

BRIQUET   But the strangest thing of all is, that after the Black Doctor had saved the life of Mademoiselle de la Reynerie, and become domiciled in the family, he should suddenly disappear, and now nearly six months have elapsed since he was seen here in St. Louis, though some of the negroes say he has been observed wandering on the cliffs, but always avoiding anyone who appeared to seek him.

GRIMAUD   Well, everybody likes the Black Doctor, and so they should, if it were only for the services he has rendered Mademoiselle de la Reynerie; she'll be a treasure to the man that wins her.

BRIQUET   And she's so rich, too, plenty of gold and jewels; plantations here, and estates in France.

GRIMAUD   Unexceptionable and desirable plunder, friend Briquet, and worth leading a forlorn hope for.

SUSANNE   I suppose we may look soon, then for a wedding?

BRIQUET   Why, can't exactly say, though the Chevalier will shortly honor me with his entire confidence, and I'll let you know as soon as we arrange affairs.

GRIMAUD (*goes upstage;* LIZETTE *follows*) We, indeed.

BRIQUET   I say, Susanne, what pleasure I should have in curling you up for a cetain day.

SUSANNE   Curling me up, indeed! What do you mean?

BRIQUET   Though art couldn't improve you, Susanne. Macassar oil, bergamot, and eau de Cologne would be only adding perfumery to the violet

SUSANNE   La! Briquet, how you do talk.

JACQUES(*aside, very melancholy*)   I see my suit cut on the cross; soft soap carries it.

SUSANNE   What's the matter, Jacques? You seem dull today.

JACQUES (*very spoony*)   Not particular.

BRIQUET   It's only the thoughts of losing my company, Susanne; quite natural, you know! The needle always inclines to the pole—but I must be off.

JACQUES (*joyfully*)   What! Are you going?

BRIQUET   Yes, and I'm going to take you with me; you don't think I'd leave you here with Susanne?

JACQUES (*going up*)   Heigho!

BRIQUET   Besides, I must attend the Chevalier; he will be expecting me. Good bye, Susanne, I shall see you again soon; good day, Grimaud; good day Madame Grimaud.

GRIMAUD   If you hear any news of the Black Doctor, mind you let us know.

BRIQUET   It's likely I shall; for little Lia, the foster sister of Mademoiselle de la Reynerie, is very ill, and as he can't have left the island, no doubt he'll be found to attend upon her; but I must say goodbye once more, Susanne. (*aside*) I shall see you again this evening. Come along, Jacques.

JACQUES (*sorrowfully*)   Goodbye all. (*looking at* SUSANNE) Heigho! (*exit at the door*)

GRIMAUD   That Briquet's a greater puppy than ever; and as for the other, why he's a perfect idiot. Come hustle about, it's near dinner time.

SUSANNE   Puppy, indeed! I'm sure Briquet's not at all a puppy.

LIZETTE   Nor poor Jacques half such a fool as he looks to be; but nobody is good enough for you.

GRIMAUD   Yes, you're good enough for me, but don't dare dispute with me; I'll teach you to mutiny; to the right about, march! (*they go off, he follows, right*)

Scene Two

(*Fabian's Hut, constructed of bamboo, an opening right, facing the audience, and leading to a garden. In the garden is seen a green bank, another opening at the back, which is the entrance to the hut, from which wild rocky scenery is visible. Second-entrance, left, a door leading to the interior of the hut; at the back, right, of the entrance, a small trunk, a hatchet hanging on a nail just over it. Rude couch, covered with tiger skin—a few wooden chairs left, and facing the audience. As scene opens,* CHRISTIAN, *an old Negro, is seen watching at the entrance as if looking for someone*)

CHRISTIAN   How long he stays! Well, I must prepare his meal, though I fear he will not taste it. (*looking out*) Ah! he comes at last; how unhappy he looks; when he's that way, my presence here seems to oppress him; so I'll retire, and wait till he calls me. (*exit, left*)

(*Enter* FABIAN, *slowly, right, holding in his hand a little cross of gold, hanging from his neck; places his hat on the little trunk, and his gun near the entrance*)

FABIAN   Sacred relic, worn by my mother, and which, after I had closed her eyes in death, I took from her cold breast—when evil thoughts cross me, I press you to my lips, and all my anger is absorbed in tears. Can this little relic, so powerful against evil, avail nothing to my sufferings? In vain I place it on my burning heart; it cannot quench the passion that consumes it. To it alone I breathe my fearful secret; that I, a mulatto, and late a slave, dare to love the daughter of a white man—the daughter of him who was my master! It is madness—madness! *(falls on his knees, his hand on the foot of the couch)* Pray for me, my mother!

(CHRISTIAN appears at the entrance, looks in, and signs to PAULINE to enter. She enters with LIA, who is leaning on her arm, and appears ill; places her on a seat near the entrance, and comes down alone)

PAULINE *(after an effort to speak)*   Monsieur Fabian.

FABIAN *(quickly turning at the sound of her voice)*   Heavens! *(rises)*

PAULINE *(advancing)*   Monsieur Fabian!

FABIAN   Is it indeed you, mademoiselle, and here?

PAULINE *(with great gentleness)*   When death threatened, you came to my assistance; when life and health returned, you left me; but you did not impose on me forgetfulness nor ingratitude. *(offers a purse)*

FABIAN *(with emotion)*   And it is for this you are here? Oh, mademoiselle, I thought you were good—generous—

PAULINE   The gold I have brought you, I wish you to distribute among your poor patients—

FABIAN *(taking the purse)*   You are an angel. *(looking at LIA with happiness)* I bless heaven for seconding my endeavors; again I see you, whom death has twice so nearly snatched away—I am happy, I am proud!

PAULINE   Good Fabian! But this mystery that cause me to—

FABIAN   Mystery!

PAULINE   Yes, which perhaps you can help me to unravel. Since you have ceased to come to the Reynerie, a man has been seen at night wandering about the dwelling, near my window; he has eluded all search—all pursuit; one night the negro on duty fired at him quite at random, and next morning, at the foot of a large tree, traces of blood were found. Fabian, I cannot tell you my feelings at the sight of that blood. *(looking earnestly at him)* You had not always that scar on your forehead.

FABIAN   That scar? A fall I had on the rock.

PAULINE *(aside, agonized)*   'Twas his blood!

FABIAN   Mademoiselle, what is the matter?

PAULINE   Fabian, the desire to thank you was not the only motive that brought me here; I have come to claim your assistance for my poor foster-sister, Lia.

FABIAN   Lia! Once so happy and so gay!

PAULINE   But now so ill, so spirit-broken! Yes, Fabian, poor Lia is sinking beneath sorrows I am ignorant of; she will die if you do not save her. *(brings LIA forward)* Look at her. Courage, dear Lia; he restored me, and will give you health and strength.

FABIAN *(gives her a seat, takes her hand, and looks at her)*   What is the matter, Lia?

LIA *(without raising her head)*   Nothing.

PAULINE   Dear Lia, tell Fabian the cause of your suffering.

LIA   I do not suffer.

PAULINE *(to FABIAN)*   Always the same answer; you cannot assist, if she persists in the silence; she will die, and none will ever know the grief that killed her.

FABIAN   Yes, I know it.

LIA *(alarmed)*   Heavens!

FABIAN   I know her malady, but cannot save her.

PAULINE *(alarmed)*   What do you say?

FABIAN   The sickness that oppresses her is of the heart.

LIA *(rising in terror)*   Fabian, Fabian! Oh, be silent. *(falls back in her seat)*

PAULINE *(aside)*   This mystery!

FABIAN   You love.

LIA   Oh, no, no, no, no, no.

FABIAN   Do not try to deceive me; the budding passion which brightened to your eyes during your mistress's convalescence, since then I see has grown, and consumed the heart in which you strived to stifle it.

LIA *(hiding her face in her hand)*   Have pity, Fabian, have pity!

FABIAN   And this love, pure and chaste, you would hide from all, as if it were a shame for you to love one whom you have no right to love, and who despises you.

PAULINE   Oh no! 'Tis impossible.

FABIAN   Because he is not of your accursed race; because he is a European.

PAULINE   What do I hear?

FABIAN   And yet is Monsieur Bertrand a good and worthy young man.

LIA   Do not mention that name.

PAULINE   Bertrand, the young Frenchman? Mr. Barbantine's clerk?

FABIAN   Yes, mademoiselle, yes! He is a good and worthy young man; but his skin is white *(to LIA)* and yours is dark, as mine; therefore you have not the right to love him. Suffer, poor sister, suffer and despair, for yours is a malady for which there is no remedy.

PAULINE   Oh, heavens! Ought I to understand?

LIA *(weeping)*   I wish to die; 'tis all I desire.

PAULINE   Unhappy girl, but you must not, shall not; I will save you. *(looking at FABIAN)* You say he is not of her race; what is that to me, since she loves him—would die for him? You hear me, Fabian; I say she shall live, she shall be his wife.

LIA *(joyfully)*   His wife!

FABIAN *(astonished)*   'Tis impossible.

PAULINE   It shall be my work, my secret care, known only to us three; he loves you?

LIA   But if he marries me, he is lost.

FABIAN   Yes, he will be proscribed, driven out by the man who has fostered him.

PAULINE   No matter, I am rich; I know it now, and for the first time feel proud of it. He shall be free, and you shall be happy. *(looking at FABIAN)* I know not what gives me strength and resolution, before unknown to me; by-and-by we will go to Barbantine's residence; I will see Bertrand, he shall hear me, he will understand; but you, Lia, weak and suffering, must not go with me, and I will not confide our secret to another; *(with firmness)* I will go alone.

FABIAN *(sorrowfully)*   Alone!

PAULINE *(with gentleness)*   No, Fabian, you shall go with me; when it strikes three at St. Louis, be at the end of the avenue of palms. Come, Lia, my sister, look cheerfully, all will be well. Look, Fabian, she is better already; her eyes are brighter; thanks to you, she feels the blessings of hope, and hope is life. Come, Lia, come. *(exit hurriedly: LIA kisses his hand, and exits after her)*

FABIAN   He is of another race—what is that to me? She loves him—would die for him! She said so, here but now, and to me, who would die for her. Oh, mother, mother, bless you; I asked you, you prayed for me, and in an instant heaven has sent me a moment of joy—of bliss. *(the report of a gun heard, and ST. LUCE calling without)*

ST. LUCE *(without)*   Help! Help!

(CHRISTIAN appears at the entrance, and points, left)

CHRISTIAN   Master! Master! Yonder a hunter! A Serpent! *(takes down hatchet, is going)*

FABIAN   You are not strong enough; give me the weapon. *(takes hatchet from him, and rushes out)*

CHRISTIAN *(following to entrance)*   No, master, no, let me go; my life is worthless, but your— *(enter ST. LUCE, conducted by FABIAN)* Ha, he was in time.

FABIAN *(to ST. LUCE)*   Lean on me, sir.

ST. LUCE *(a gun in his hand)*   No thank you, Doctor; I am not much hurt. *(CHRISTIAN takes ST. LUCE's hat and gun and places them in a corner)*

FABIAN *(gives hatchet to CHRISTIAN, who replaces it)*   Some water. *(exit CHRISTIAN. FABIAN gives ST. LUCE a seat)*

ST. LUCE   I have many times seen death as near, but have never been on such intimate terms with a serpent before; 'tis an indigenous produce which does little honor to your country. *(CHRISTIAN returns with coconut-shell full of water and gives it to FABIAN, who hands it to ST. LUCE)*

ST. LUCE *(returns it to FABIAN after drinking)* Thank you.

FABIAN *(looking at his left hand)*   You are wounded.

ST. LUCE   O, 'tis nothing.

FABIAN   Allow me. *(taking from the little trunk the necessaries to dress the wound)* What could bring you to this isolated spot? *(exit CHRISTIAN, who returns immediately with more water; FABIAN washes and dresses ST. LUCE's wounded hand)*

ST. LUCE   Only curiosity! You must know I was stretched out under a banana tree, enjoying that dreamy repose, which, while it transports us to an ideal world, still allows us to hear what is passing in this. I dreamt I was hunting at Marly, when suddenly the foliage near me became agitated, and thinking it was a rabbit, I seized my gun, and fired, as near as I could judge, upon the spot of his hiding place, when all of a sudden I saw the grey head of an enormous serpent rise up before me; so I called out lustily for help, and my kind stars sent you to my assistance, when there was no more space between me and my enemy than just enough for your hatchet. By my faith, Doctor, you are a wonderful man, and your exact manner of amputation is complete.

FABIAN   Sir, if you ever seek rest, this miserable dwelling is at your service; but if you desire to return to St. Louis, allow me to offer a guide.

ST. LUCE (*rising*)   A thousand thanks for your proffered hospitality; but I must not give my sister time to be uneasy at my absence; therefore, will only accept the guide you offer.

FABIAN (*to* CHRISTIAN)   Prepare to conduct the Chevalier by the road through St. Hane.

ST. LUCE   Doctor, you are decidedly the good genius of our family; without your assistance, lovely eyes might this night have been drowned in tears; yes, my cousin would again have hid her sweet face in the grief of mourning, which is soon to smile on her affianced husband.

FABIAN (*at the back of the stage, turns suddenly round*)   Affianced husband: of whom do you speak?

ST. LUCE   Of my cousin, who is to—

FABIAN   Of Mademoiselle de la Reynerie?

ST. LUCE   Certainly.

FABIAN   No, it is impossible.

ST. LUCE   Impossible: and why?

FABIAN (*embarrassed*)   Because I know no one in Bourbon worthy to possess such a treasure.

ST. LUCE   True; but then I do not belong to the Isle.

FABIAN   You!

ST. LUCE   Yes, I am in love, my dear sir—seriously in love; you are astonished to hear it, they would not believe it at Versailles; but I repeat it, I'm in love, and intend to marry; our union was first projected by Madame de la Reynerie, and Pauline but waited the end of her mourning, in order to obey her mother's wish.

FABIAN (*overpowered*)   She!

ST. LUCE   And though the aristocracy of Bourbon should blame me ever so, I shall insist on your presence at my marriage, which, but for you, death had twice prevented. Farewell, Doctor, or rather, goodbye for the present. (*to* CHRISTIAN, *who is standing at the entrance, and presents* CHEVALIER *with hat and gun*) Go on before me friend, and heaven protect us from sun and serpents. Goodbye, Fabian. (*exit* ST. LUCE *and* CHRISTIAN)

FABIAN (*with a sudden burst*)   She loves that man, he will be her husband! And yet but now I have saved him! I have allowed him to go from me with life. (*seizes his gun, is about to rush out, and suddenly stops*) Kill him! Assassinate him! No, no, 'tis not he who should die! It is, ah——I; water! Air! I shall suffocate! (*falls at the end of the couch, his hand falls on his chest, he seizes the little cross suspended round his neck*) Again that dreadful idea crossed my brain, and my hand unintentionally falls on this little relic——O, my mother, 'tis your voice I hear, 'tis heaven commands I should avoid a crime, and still drag on this wretched life of suffering! (*three o'clock strikes*) Three o'clock; she is waiting for me—she, St. Luce's bride! (*rises with a sudden burst*) No, no, it shall not be! I will not die alone. (*throws away cross*) Mother, I hear you not, you shall not save her——together, together, we will die together! (*rushes out*)

Scene Three

(*The High Road near Reynerie. Enter* BRIQUET *and* JACQUES, *right; they are both a little elevated*)

BRIQUET   Capital stuff that, wasn't it, Jacques? That's the house to live in! Long life to the Chevalier and his intended bride. I say, Jacques, my boy, why don't you laugh?

JACQUES   I can't laugh, Briquet: I'm melancholy.

BRIQUET   It's a professional failing; tailors are naturally melancholy; sedentary employment produces thoughts, therefore it's natural.

JACQUES   You've called me a natural three times.

BRIQUET   Don't interrupt me Jacques, but listen,—what was I saying? O, I remember; long life to the Chevalier and his intended bride! Talking of brides I intend to be married myself shortly.

JACQUES   You be married! And pray who is to be the bride?

BRIQUET   Who's to be the bride? Why, whom do you think but Susanne, the lovely charming little Susanne?

JACQUES   Have you got her consent?

BRIQUET   Not yet.

JACQUES   Have you got her father's consent?

BRIQUET   Not exactly, but I've got the consent of one party.

JACQUES   What, her mother?

BRIQUET   No (*hiccup*) myself.

JACQUES   Well, that's something towards it, but I should like to see you propose it to old Grimaud, he'd——

BRIQUET   What do I care about old Grimaud? Do you think I'm afraid of old Grimaud? I'm afraid of nobody, when my blood's up. I fear neither man nor—(*turning round*) the devil! (*enter* CHRISTIAN, *the old negro, right*)

CHRISTIAN   Your master waits for you at the Reynerie.

BRIQUET   What do you know about my master?

CHRISTIAN   But little! I have just acted as his guide—he met with a slight accident in the woods.

BRIQUET   An accident?

CHRISTIAN   Yes, which delayed him beyond the time appointed to his return. But all danger is past, thanks to the timely assistance of my master.

BRIQUET   And who is your master?

CHRISTIAN   The Black Doctor. (*exit, right*)

BRIQUET (*turns from him as he speaks*)   I say, Jacques, (*looks round, finds* CHRISTIAN *gone*) Why, he's gone; so the Black Doctor's come to hand at last. I was going down to Grimaud's, but as my new master wants me I can't, so do you tell him. Do you hear that the Black Doctor's still in the land of the living? None of your nonsense now with Susanne. I feel rather queer, but the Chevalier will attribute that to my anxiety on his account. Good-bye Jacques; keep steady, my boy; I shall see you tomorrow; keep steady—and keep me always in your eyes as an example. (*they exit differently*)

Scene Four

(*Enormous rocks, left. A rock, right forming a grotto; near which, on one side is a stone bench, a rock in which steps are rudely cut, descending to the sea in the center of the stage; with a rock in which a seat appears rudely cut. A pathway, left, a little elevated, and overhanging the steep cliffs. The whole scene is wild and gloomy in the extreme; the sea at back. As the scene opens* PAULINE *and* FABIAN *appears at the very top of the rock, right*)

PAULINE   This path seems unfrequented; why have we come this way?

FABIAN   The inhabitants rarely visit this bay, which they have called the mulatto's grotto; there is a popular legend attached to it.

PAULINE   Shall we reach the Reynerie before Bertrand? I wish to be first, to tell Lia of the success of our enterprise.

FABIAN   He is going round in the boat; the wind and tide will be against him, so we have the advantage. Rest yourself here a moment to recruit your strength.

PAULINE (*sits on rock, center of stage*)   This is a wild and gloomy spot.

FABIAN   Did you not desire me to take the most retired route? Mademoiselle de la Reynerie wished to avoid anyone whilst walking beside the mulatto Fabian. 'Twas otherwise in your childhood; then you did not disdain to lean on my arm.

PAULINE (*after a moment's silence as if to change the conversation*)   Fabian, I think you have my fan.

FABIAN (*takes it from his bosom, and presents it to her respectfully*)   'Tis here, Mademoiselle.

PAULINE   But, you too must be tired, Fabian, for your hand trembles so as it did just now; are you ill?

FABIAN   No, lady.

PAULINE   Ah, I shall be so happy to tell Lia the obstacles that separated her from Bertrand no longer exist; in a month she shall leave the colony with her affianced husband; they shall live in a country where prejudice will not condemn their union——will not crush their mutual affection; Lia, my sister you at least shall be happy. (*sighing*)

FABIAN   Happy! Yes, in the love of her husband! For without his love of what avail would have been my penetration or your generous friendship?

PAULINE   Bertrand has a noble heart.

FABIAN   He loves her.

PAULINE   He was not born under your sky; had he been a creole, he would have hid his passion in the utmost depths of his heart.

FABIAN   And Lia would have perished; and had Bertrand been a creole he dared not have shed one tear to her memory; is it not so?

PAULINE (*rising with calm dignity*)   Fabian, we will continue our walk; the Countess and her brother will be waiting for me.

FABIAN (*endeavoring to contain himself*)   He loves you, lady.

PAULINE (*embarrassed*)   He has told me so.

FABIAN   He is to be your husband.

PAULINE   'Twas my mother's dearest wish. (FABIAN *staggers against the rock, right;* PAULINE *is going, turns round and looks at him*) Fabian, I am waiting for you. (*he passes his hand across his forehead, appears to be looking attentively at two crosses carved in one of the rocks*)

FABIAN   Those two crosses carved in the rock, and which appertain to the legend I told you of just now.

PAULINE   What legend?

FABIAN   Shall I tell you?

PAULINE   Yes, tell me the history of this legend.

FABIAN   (*goes back, looks at the sea which is seen gradually to rise, then returns to* PAULINE) Listen, then. There lived in St. Louis, a poor mulatto—a slave, who (I have forgotten for what good service rendered to his master) received his freedom! The generous gift should have made him happy, but it was otherwise; for once free he was compelled to leave his master's dwelling, and under that roof dwelt his better angel. At length he went forth, more wretched in his freedom than in his slavery! For he loved—yes madly loved—adored that master's daughter. (*wind heard*)

PAULINE   (*alarmed*)   How dreadfully the wind howls.

FABIAN   (*not heeding her*)   He would have buried his love in his heart, though it had crushed it; but the young and noble lady, who used to converse with him, in few kind words, completed the delusion. He thought himself beloved—and though respect to the pride of her race forbade her to be his, he thought at least she would never be another's. The fool was dreaming; one word awoke him, she was about to marry—to marry! She had deceived him, had sported with his agony; she should not have done so—it was imprudent for then the wretched man took an oath to unite himself to her by the solemn, dreadful, awful tie of death.

PAULINE   (*rising agitated, looks at the sea, which is gradually surrounding them*)   Fabian! Fabian! Not now; the sea rises. (*going*) Let us go. Come, come, Fabian!

FABIAN   (*detains her*)   Go! (*smiles*) No, the mulatto had calculated every chance; in his turn he had deceived the young girl—he had led her into a snare—they both stood here—on the spot we now occupy; the tide was rising fast, only one path was free—but the sea continued to gain on them. (*seizes both her hands*) The young girl entreated the mulatto to try to save her; but he, without pity for her terror or her tears, held her with hands of iron. At last he told her he loved her. (*looking round*) Still the sea was gaining ground; every chance of escape was gone, and yet death has less of horror for the young girl than the mulatto's love.

PAULINE   (*in much terror*)   Fabian, for pity's sake, save me!

FABIAN   Save you! And is it not possible you guess I love you?

PAULINE   (*struggling with her feelings*)   No, no! You are deceiving me; you would not—could not see me die here before your eyes!

FABIAN   (*pointing to sea*)   Look, Pauline, before we should reach the rocks which we now but descended together, the sea would dash us to atoms against their rugged points! I feared my own weakness, and closed every avenue to the road of repentance or pity; death surrounds us, but we shall perish together! How! You no longer tremble, will you not call down heaven's curses on your destroyer's head?

PAULINE   (*solemnly*)   Fabian!

FABIAN   (*pointing to sea*)   No earthly power can save us!

PAULINE   (*rushing to pathway, which the sea has not yet reached*)   Then let me beg my mother's forgiveness and pray to heaven for you. (*falls on her knees against the rock*)

FABIAN   For me!

PAULINE   Yes, for you! Now I am sure of death, I may acknowledge, without shame or remorse, that I understand you, Fabian, and I forgive you, for I have long, long loved you!

FABIAN   Did I hear aright? Love me! And I—I am her murderer! Oh, heavens, (*rushes to her and supports her in his arms*) you will not allow it! Kill me! But save her! (*looks around*) Ah! 'Tis too late! She is already dying. (*carries her up the rock, lays her down, takes off his vest, waves it, shouting for help. The sea reaches them, curtain falls as he is still struggling with her in the water. Bertrand is seen at the back in a boat, Curtain*)

ACT TWO

Scene One

(*A handsome drawing-room in the Marchioness's Home in Paris, elegantly furnished. At the back, large folding doors, opening to a gallery; on each side, at the back, a large window, with hangings, a door left and right; handsome bookcase and bureau on each side; canopy, left, arm chairs right and left: a handbell on the bookcase. Enter* BRIQUET *and* JACQUES, *very handsomely and foppishly dressed, and rather grotesquely*)

BRIQUET   And so, friend Jacques, you have followed us to Paris?

JACQUES   Yes, I felt so dull when you left, that I made up my mind to come too; but what a grand house to be sure!

BRIQUET (*offers snuff*)   Yes, we are pleasantly situated. Do you still operate? (*makes sign of cutting with shears*)

JACQUES   Yes, I cut out.

BRIQUET   Ah, you rogue, you have cut me out; and how does Madame Fils?

JACQUES   Oh, she's quite well.

BRIQUET   Delighted to hear it—shall be still more delighted to see her. I bear no ill-will; but how the deuce you managed it, I never could guess.

JACQUES   Why, you see, I didn't talk of marrying until I got more than my own consent in the business.

BRIQUET   Ha, ha, I recollect; but really, in Paris, a wife is rather an incumbrance, and you see my situation brings me so much in contact with the fashionable world, that one don't miss the little comforts, as they are termed, of matrimony; strange things have happened since we rusticated in St. Louis.

JACQUES   Strange, indeed, to think that the Marchioness, whom we all supposed drowned, should be alive after all.

BRIQUET   Yes, and she is gone to Versailles, to present her daughter, Madame Pauline, to her Majesty, the Queen, upon her return from the colonies; she'll be back in an hour.

JACQUES   And the Black Doctor?

BRIQUET   Oh, he's with us—couldn't do without him; though, by-the-by, the Marchioness doesn't much relish his being here; but the circumstance of his having twice saved her daughter's life, and her still delicate health, in some way reconcile her to his presence.

JACQUES   That was a fearful business, too, when Monsieur Bertrand saved them both; there was a sort of mystery in that affair!

BRIQUET   No doubt, no doubt, friend Jacques; there are more mysteries than we can fathom in this world; it was, as you say, a close shave.

JACQUES   Rather too fine-drawn an affair for me, I own; and the marriage with the Chevalier!

BRIQUET   Why, there seems some reluctance on her part, but the Marchioness is positive. I suppose, eventually, she must marry; but come into my room, and we will take a glass to old times, and our future acquaintance. (*as they are going, enter* ANDRE *at the door in back, which is open*) And what do you want, friend?

ANDRE   The Doctor, if you please.

BRIQUET   This is not a doctor's shop, friend; you are in the house of the Marchioness de la Reynerie.

ANDRE   Yes, I know; but he I seek lives here.

BRIQUET   Who is it you mean?

ANDRE   The Doctor; the good worthy man I have come to thank; he's well-known in our quarter, ever since he attended my poor mother; everybody gave her up, even the hospital doctors; and today, thanks to him, she's quite well again! Oh, he's got plenty of practice; but he always gives the poor the preference; and when he passes our way, men, women, and children bless the Black Doctor.

BRIQUET   The Black Doctor! Oh, now I know who you mean. He means Fabian.

ANDRE   Is that his name?

BRIQUET   Yes, he's a mulatto, an enfranchised slave, whom Mademoiselle de la Reynerie brought over from Bourbon, a curiosity.

(*Fabian appears at door, dressed in court suit, sword, etc.*)

ANDRE   A curiosity, indeed! Goodness and charity are, no doubt, a curiosity to you; take care how you speak about him before me!

FABIAN (*comes down*)   Noble heart!

ANDRE   Ah, is that you, Doctor?

BRIQUET   Come along, Jacques.

ANDRE   Why, Doctor, how dares that powdered monkey—

FABIAN (*calmly*)   How is your mother, today, Andre?

ANDRE   Well, quite well; she sent me, though strong enough to come herself, but she was afraid—

FABIAN   Afraid!

ANDRE   This is how it is, Doctor; we took it into our heads that, as everybody must live by their trade, a doctor can't give away his time to everybody for nothing; so I worked double tides, and have brought you a fortnight's wages; it isn't much, but such as it is there it is.

FABIAN   I accept your offer, good friend, but you must be my banker, and when you meet with a fellow-creature who needs it more than yourself, give it to him.

ANDRE   From you?

FABIAN   As you please.

ANDRE   I'll do as you desire! Farewell, Mr. Fabian; don't forget Andre. In a few months I am going to my brother in Bretagne—'tis our country.

FABIAN   Bretagne?

ANDRE   Yes, if you should ever come there you shall have the best place at our fireside, as you already have in our hearts. Farewell, Mr. Fabian. *(exit at door, first shaking* FABIAN's *hand)*

FABIAN   *(seats himself, and finishes reading a letter, which he has in his hand)* "Yes, Fabian, with Bertrand, my husband, who loves me more than ever, in the bosom of his family, who welcomed me as another child; I am happy, very happy; when you hear of this, ah, let us hear of your happiness, too." *(refolds the letter ironically)* Happy! yes, my good Lia, I live in a noble house, am head lackey to the Marchioness de la Reynerie—distinguished honor! True, I am waited on by my fellow servants, in my own apartment. Oh, yes, I am happy, very happy! *(rising)* Heavens! Whence comes this patience, this resignation? For six long months have I endured this, and yet I have not roused my sleeping energies, and cried aloud to them all. She whom you surround with such homage, such flattery, she is mine, my own, my wife! No, I am silent. Shut up the livelong day, I endeavor to forget my condition in study, and only when I hear the carriage which conveys the Marchioness from the door, do I venture to exchange a look—a word with Pauline, then a stranger comes, and I must needs retire, a smile and a tear—*(noise of carriage, he runs to window and looks out)* 'Tis

she! I shall see her, I shall see her. Oh, this is the secret of my resignation. *(a servant opens the folding doors, the* CHEVALIER, *in court-dress enters, conducting* PAULINE, *who is also in court-dress.* ST. LUCE *does not notice* FABIAN, *who stands aside, and is not seen by* PAULINE. *Aside)* Still that man forever at her side!

ST. LUCE   Now, cousin! Cannot the gracious reception you met with at Versailles, raise a smile in that beautiful face? For my part, like the Marchioness, I was delighted as I observed the looks of our charming Queen wander from yourself to rest on me—she doubtless guessed what I could poorly conceal.

PAULINE   Your pardon, Chevalier, my mother, I believe, is waiting for you.

ST. LUCE   May I not be excused for forgetting her, when by your side? *(aside)* Ever cold and constrained! I cannot understand it. Adieu, for the present my lovely cousin! Do try to think a little of me until I see you again, I shall think of no one else. *(he is about to kiss her hand, she withdraws it, he signifies his mortification; as he is going, stops on seeing* FABIAN*)* So, you were here, were you?

PAULINE   *(surprised)*   Fabian!

ST. LUCE   In the drawing room, we may readily discern we are not in Bourbon, and are making rapid strides towards equality, as the commons have it. *(aside)* This is very strange, but doubtless you have come for mademoiselle's order—you should have knocked sir. If there are no longer slaves in Paris, I believe we still have lackeys. *(exit at door)*

FABIAN   True, a slave in Bourbon! here a lackey.

PAULINE   *(in a supplicating voice)*   But the slave! The lackey! Is he not my lord—my husband in the sight of heaven, and in mine, who lives for him? Is he not great, is he not noble, has he not a right to be proud of himself? Do you not bear next your heart a sacred deed, signed by a minister of heaven—a deed that plainly says "That the lackey—the slave—is my master?"

FABIAN   Our marriage, blessed by an unknown minister, in an isolated corner in the Isle of Bourbon, your mother will have power to break, by a simple motion of her fan. *(drawing a paper from his breast)* Since this may not be the passport of business for either, at least it can be made the instrument of revenge.

PAULINE (*calmly*)   Yes, Fabian, you can show it to my mother; you can say to her, your daughter has changed her proud name of La Reynerie for that of Fabian; your daughter has even given herself to me. You can do all this, and I should forgive you; but my mother would curse the memory of her child!

FABIAN   Oh, forgive me, Pauline, forgive me; you know not what I suffer, you know not my wretchedness; but fear not, I will bear up against the grief that is killing me, against the jealousy that consumes me.

PAULINE   What, Fabian, jealousy?

FABIAN   No, no doubt ever entered my heart, it would kill me at once. Pauline, I will be confiding, calm! I shall see you daily go to those fetes where so many temptations surround you, but I will be silent; you will accept his arm for your escort, that man who is ever at your side, that man who loves you, I shall see him, as I did but now, gaze on you with admiration, raise that hand to his lips, which is mine—I say, I shall see all this, and yet I shall be silent.

MARCHIONESS (*without*)   Pauline, 'tis I, open the door.

PAULINE   My mother, and she will find me here, and with you.

FABIAN (*rushes to window*)   No, though I should be dashed to atoms on the pavement below.

PAULINE   Stay! (*pointing to the chamber*) There, in that room, by the back staircase, hasten.

MARCHIONESS (*without*)   Pauline! Pauline, I say!

FABIAN (*going by direction, right*)   You see I am obedient. I am going; I shall be silent. (*Exit*)

(*Enter the* MARCHIONESS, *center*)

MARCHIONESS (*looking round*)   Were you alone, Pauline?

PAULINE (*embarrassed*)   Yes, yes, mother, alone.

MARCHIONESS   When the Chevalier left you, Fabian was here.

PAULINE   He was.

MARCHIONESS   How did the man presume to enter here, without your express order?

PAULINE (*hesitating*)   He came to tell me of a visit he had paid to some poor pensioners of mine, as I had desired him.

MARCHIONESS (*haughtily*)   And I desire you may have no such explanations in the future; tomorrow he shall leave this house, and in three days quit France.

PAULINE   He! Fabian?

MARCHIONESS   I am about to send him back to the colony, there he will henceforth enjoy independence. I will reward him, as I ought, for his faithful servitude to you; but let us speak no more of the man, but come at once to the business that brings me here now. The Queen was pleased with you, my daughter, and in order to have you one of her ladies of honor, her Majesty wishes you to marry.

PAULINE   What do I hear?

MARCHIONESS   The Chevalier St. Luce will this evening receive letters patent that will confer on him the title of Count, and tomorrow the King will add to the obligations I already owe him, by himself signing your contract.

PAULINE   No, no, I did not hear aright; mother, 'tis impossible!

MARCHIONESS   Impossible! Listen to me, Pauline; I have determined to have you a noble protector, and a defender; I could not confide my child to one more noble or more worthy than St. Luce, already almost my son. I repeat, 'tis my determination you should marry him, and by the memory of your father, it shall be as I say. (*goes to bookcase and rings bell*)

PAULINE (*aside*)   Then 'tis heaven's will I should die! (*enter servant, center*)

MARCHIONESS   Tell Fabian I have an important command for him; show all visitors into this apartment, I will receive him here. (*exit servant. To* PAULINE)   You will for the future receive the Chevalier as your intended husband. (PAULINE *knees to her, kisses her hand, and weeps*) Pauline, you cannot make me alter my determination! Your resistance would be as useless as your prayers.

PAULINE   Mother, heaven is my witness, I would have devoted to you the life you gave me. I asked, I sought, but to live in your heart, and you drive me from you!

MARCHIONESS   To give you to the arms of a husband.

PAULINE   Before your will excludes me and separates us, my mother, gaze on me as you used to do; when a child I looked for and found all, all my joys in your eyes; bless me as you used to do, when I prayed to heaven that I might live and die for my mother's love.

MARCHIONESS (*raising her*)　Tomorrow, Pauline, at the altar, I will bless both my children.

PAULINE (*aside*)　Tomorrow you will have no daughter! (*servant opens door at back*)

MARCHIONESS　Calm yourself, Pauline; we are no longer alone.

(*Servant announces the following ladies and gentlemen:* COUNTESS DE RESADEUC, MDLLE. *and* CHEVALIER DE ST. LUCE, MADAME DE BEAUOMEAL, MONSIEUR *and* MADAME DE LA FRERAGE, MARCHIONESS L'AMBERVILLE, COUNCIL-LOR OMMISSOR. *All the company is received by the* MARCHIONESS, *who presents them to* PAULINE *as they enter; she curtsies to them all; the* MAR-CHIONESS *conducts the ladies to the canopy, and places herself in an armchair beside it;* PAULINE, *struggling with emotion, conducts one of the ladies right; one chair remains unoccupied between her and the lady; the gentlemen remain standing in groups behind the ladies right and left; the* COUNT-ESS DE RESADEUC *alone remains standing for a moment by the* MARCHIONESS)

AURELIA ST. LUCE　My good aunt, at length the dearest wish of my heart will be fulfilled. St. Luce has just told me—

MARCHIONESS (*smiling*)　That I am a very humble and obedient subject. It is my intention it should be known at Versailles this very evening, that I have presented the Countess de St. Luce, lady of honor to her Majesty, the Queen, to all my friends.

ALL　Lady of honor! (*the gentlemen compli-ment* ST. LUCE)

AURELIA ST. LUCE　At length, then you are my sister. (*taking* PAULINE's *hand*)

PAULINE (*aside*)　Heaven! Give me one hour more of strength and courage!

ST. LUCE　My dear aunt, I know not how to thank you; but believe me, I will prove worthy of the treasure you confide to me. (*kisses the hand of* REYNERIE, *approaches* PAULINE, *who re-mains motionless*) How! not one look? (*enter servant, center*)

SERVANT　Monsieur Fabian, Madam.

PAULINE　Fabian!

ST. LUCE　She starts at the name!

MARCHIONESS　Very well, tell him to wait.

AURELIA ST. LUCE (*to* MARCHIONESS *de la Reynerie*)　Poor Fabian, I have scarcely seen

him since his arrival, and I have talked so much about him to these ladies that they are as anxious to see him as I was at the Isle of Bourbon.

MARCHIONESS　In this apartment! You for-get.

AURELIA (*laughing*)　O, they won't know of it in Bourbon.

PAULINE (*aside*)　Before so many he will be-tray himself.

ST. LUCE (*aside*)　Pale, trembling. 'Twas the same this morning, and always so at the ques-tion of his name! By heaven! I will know how far she is interested in this man. My dear aunt, allow me to join in my sister's entreaty; be-sides, I owe Fabian a debt.

MARCHIONESS　You!

ST. LUCE　Yes, of honor.

MARCHIONESS　Well, dear Count, today I cannot refuse you anything. (*to servant*) Tell Fabian he may come in. (*exit servant*)

PAULINE (*aside*)　We are lost!

ST. LUCE (*laughing*)　Quite a presentation, I declare.

(*Enter* FABIAN: *at sight of company he stops; upon a sign from the* MARCHIONESS *bows and ad-dresses her*)

FABIAN　You sent for me, madam; what are your commands?

AURELIA (*to a lady*)　What do you think of him?

MARCHIONESS　You are about to quit my house to leave France.

AURELIA　Why? Where is he going?

MARCHIONESS　To Bourbon.

FABIAN (*quickly*)　Madam, I— (*catches* PAULINE's *eye, stops*)

ST. LUCE (*aside*)　How she watches him!

FABIAN　When am I to depart, madam?

MARCHIONESS　Tomorrow; the steward has received my orders. You will find that I have not forgotten past services, nor been unmind-ful of your future welfare; you may now retire.

ST. LUCE (*to* MARCHIONESS)　Not yet, my dear aunt; you must allow me to beg you will delay his departure for a few days. Fabian, we are no longer at Bourbon; therefore I can and will reward you for the service you there ren-dered me; the invitation I there gave you I hold good here, and repeat, I wish you to be present at my marriage with Mademoiselle de la Reynerie, (*looks from* FABIAN *to* PAULINE) which will be celebrated in three days.

(FABIAN *suddenly starts.* PAULINE *instantly rises, and takes her eyes from him.* FABIAN, *struggling with his feelings, endeavours to be calm and silent. Aside)* Again! At all hazard I will know the worst.

AURELIA   You will grant my brother's request, will you not, dear aunt? Fabian, you do not thank my brother.

ST. LUCE (*smiles contemptuously)*   No, I remember; 'tis very natural; he does not like to own himself so bad a prophet. Fabian has declared all marriage impossible for Mademoiselle de la Reynerie.

MARCHIONESS   He!

ST. LUCE   Yes, my dear aunt; doubtless he was afraid of losing so profitable and unexpected a source of patronage and favor. (*looks at* PAULINE) What other motive could there be? I am afraid our cousin's protection has been thoughtless, and perhaps may be fatal to our Doctor.

MARCHIONESS   How?

ST. LUCE   No doubt, in Bourbon 'twill be necessary to duff these trappings of a gentleman which appear rather strange; here 'tis only laughed at, but in Bourbon 'twould be otherwise; there his insolence would be chastised, particularly the sword, which sits but ill on a mulatto, who could not dare to raise it even to ward off the planter's whip!

PAULINE (*without taking her eyes from* FABIAN) Ah!

AURELIA   Brother, you are cruel!

ST. LUCE (*haughtily)*   No, sister; 'tis not I, but reason that says every man in his station. Look! Fabian already pays dearly for the ridiculous dreams to which an imputed benevolence has given birth; he suffers, for he cannot forget what he was—what he is! See how he plays with the hilt of the sword! That hand, which still wears the impression of the chain—

FABIAN (*in a fury)*   Ah! (*draws the sword and with a sudden expression breaks it, throws it at his feet, and covering his face with his hands, weeps)*

ST. LUCE   Why, what's the matter?

AURELIA (*coming between them)*   Brother, you are very cruel; you have wounded his feelings.

PAULINE (*rushing forward)*   I can endure this no longer; 'tis cowardly—infamous! (*goes to her mother and speaks in a voice choked with pas-sion and sobs)* Mother, dismiss these people; I must speak to you alone!

MARCHIONESS (*rising)*   This agitation!

PAULINE   Have pity on me—on yourself! Dismiss them!

MARCHIONESS (*aside to her)*   You alarm me, Pauline! Friends, my daughter is ill; it alarms me!

AURELIA   Indeed! (*to* PAULINE) Are you ill?

MARCHIONESS   Leave us to ourselves! Chevaliers, adieu until tomorrow! (*exit guests)*

ST. LUCE (*aside)*   If you have indeed favored this unruly rival, cousin, I have at least paid your insult by insult. Come, sister. (*takes her hand; as he is leading her off gives a look of scorn at* FABIAN, *who is following him)*

PAULINE   No, no—stay, Fabian!

MARCHIONESS   Why do you detain him?

PAULINE   Because if you drive him forth, you must also drive me forth; because if he goes, 'tis my duty to follow him.

MARCHIONESS   To follow Fabian!

PAULINE   Yes, mother, my love—my lord—my husband!

MARCHIONESS   He!

PAULINE (*to him)*   Look up, loved and injured Lord; heaven, that gives you resignation, has at last given me courage; can you forgive me?

MARCHIONESS   Fabian's wife! No, you did not say that?

PAULINE   I have said it, mother, and my husband shall not be dishonoured.

MARCHIONESS   Wretched girl, take then—

FABIAN (*coming between them)*   Be not in such haste to curse, lady! Your malediction would be impious and could not reach to heaven. She, who now humbles herself, who weeps, is pure as the angels. True, she loved me, a poor slave—because I had staked my life to save her mother's; but I tell you your blood runs in her veins. She was ashamed of her love, and only on the brink of a precipice, death surrounding us, when help appeared impossible, as with her last breath, her secret escaped her.

MARCHIONESS   Heavens, was I restored to life but to be witness of this dishonor? This infamous marriage shall be dissolved.

FABIAN   Dissolve my marriage! You cannot do it, madam; call your servants—they shall make way for your daughter's husband; recall the Chevalier St. Luce, who so insolently crushed me with his aristocracy, and whom but for Pauline's imploring look, I would have annihilated as I did that weapon; call him, and I will tell my insolent rival 'tis now his turn to feel the torments of jealousy and rage, for his betrothed is my lawful wedded wife!

MARCHIONESS   I will invoke the judge, the magistrate, the King himself!

FABIAN   All slaves who set foot on European ground are free; therefore am I, before affranchised, now doubly so; and the law makes no distinction of rank or colony.

MARCHIONESS *(to PAULINE)*   You hear him—you hear this man proclaim our shame! If your father could rise from his grave, he would strike you dead! He would rather see you in your grave than so degraded, so dishonored!

PAULINE *(takes a small phial from her bosom)* Then let him judge me! Father, I come! *(FABIAN rushes to her, seizes phial, throws it away)*

FABIAN   Pauline!

MARCHIONESS   What does this mean?

FABIAN   It means, madam, that she was about to swallow poison.

MARCHIONESS   Poison!

FABIAN   Yes, which she had concealed, that your curse might fall upon her corpse!

MARCHIONESS *(sinking overpowered into a chair)*   Pauline!

PAULINE *(kneeling)*   I cannot live under my mother's malediction.

FABIAN   Then 'tis for me to complete this act of devotion. What neither your King nor your laws can do, Fabian himself will act. This marriage—consecrated by a holy minister of heaven, who will reveal the secret to no one—this inviolable—this indissoluble marriage, I myself will annul.

PAULINE   You!

MARCHIONESS   How say you?

FABIAN *(struggling with his grief)*   Madam, I restore to you your daughter. Pauline, this one act has repaid me hours of grief and misery, and anguish; you would have died for me, you shall live for your mother! *(forces her to Marchioness)* Farewell, Pauline; you cannot be mine till we meet again in heaven! *(at the door)* Not mine, Pauline, but never another's! Farewell! *(exit)*

PAULINE   Mother, he leaves me but to seek comfort in death! *(tries to follow him. MARCHIONESS detains her)*

MARCHIONESS *(to servants, who enter)*   Follow Fabian, see you do not let him leave the house. Should it be necessary, use force; but on no account let him depart.

ACT THREE

Scene One

(The stage is divided horizontally in two parts, each part again divided into two portions. The portion right, above, forms a well-lighted apartment, splendidly furnished; at back, a window with curtains; left, a toilet-table, dressing-glass, center, a table with an arm-chair on each side; a door leading to staircase, which forms left of upper portion; at foot of staircase, a trap-door leading to dungeon below. The staircase is not seen, but forms left lower portion; lower portion, right, is the dungeon; a large stone pillar, behind which, is straw; in front of and right of pillar, a stone bench; left of pillar, at back, a window, with iron bars; on front pillar, on block of stone, a lighted lamp. BRIQUET is discovered in the upper apartment reading a newspaper.)

BRIQUET   Eleventh of July—then I have been as an inhabitant of the Royal Chateau, the Bastille, two months and six days exactly, and why? "Briquet," said my master, Monsieur de St. Luce, "you are my valet, I give you twelve hundred francs a year to wait upon me, shave me, dress me and powder my wig, in whatever corner of France I may be. The King sends me to the Bastille, therefore you must follow me, to dress, shave, and powder me, in the Bastille." *(rises)* And here we are, lodged in the tower of the chapel, just above the moat. This apartment is not so bad, nor the bedroom either; the furniture is good, I may say, elegant; in short, 'tis a gentlemanly prison, but still it is a prison! *(drums without)* Hallo! What does that mean? First time I've heard them since we've been here; perhaps the King's coming to see us and give us our liberty. *(drums again)* Enter ST. LUCE, *in drawing-gown)*

ST. LUCE   Briquet! What, rascal! Didn't you hear me?

BRIQUET   Yes sir; did you say the carriage, sir?

ST. LUCE   Eh?

BRIQUET   I beg your pardon, sir; I'm always forgetting we are in "status quo."

ST. LUCE *(laughing)*   We must accustom ourselves to it, Briquet. *(sits)* Come, dress my hair.

BRIQUET (*getting comb, etc.*)   But sir, aren't you going to try to get out of here?

ST. LUCE (*looking in a hand mirror*)   I beg pardon? Never! I've done the King great service and he has punished me! So much the worse for him.

BRIQUET (*combing his hair*)   And me too! I beg your pardon, but it seems to me you did—

ST. LUCE   My duty, sir! I was breakfasting at the "cafe de joie"; facing me were three citizens. I should have known the plebians a mile off, by the smell of them. (Take care what you are about.) They were members of the new assembly of deputies of the States General, chatting on public affairs. (*looks in glass*) A little more powder on that side. At the mention of a proposition, which I did not approve of, I rose and addressed them, and flatly told them I thought everything of the aristocracy, very little of the clergy, and nothing of the people; so we warmed upon the subject until we quarreled. I offered to fight one of them; he accepted! "My name," said I, "is the Chevalier de St. Luce." "Sir," says the fellow, "my name is Barnaby." "Never heard of it," said I. Then the bystanders threw themselves between us, and separated Barnaby and me; but the adventure reached the ears of the court. Well, thinks I, Barnaby will be arrested; but instead of that they arrested me.

BRIQUET   Yes, sir, I understand; but I never offended Barnaby, so I—

ST. LUCE   What do complain of? The lodging's well enough, the table is well served, the wine excellent, and the air of captivity a fine thing for the appetite. Ring for my dinner.

BRIQUET (*taking glass from* ST. LUCE)   Yes, sir, but then you didn't leave your heart at the gate of the Bastille, while I—but, perhaps I haven't told you I was just going to be married?

ST. LUCE   Oh, yes, you did; I thought it a capital joke.

BRIQUET   Not for my intended, though— poor little Runnette, I appointed to meet her by the third tree on the left-hand side of the park, and she's been waiting there two months and six days exactly; how impatient she must be.

ST. LUCE   Oh, don't make yourself uneasy; she's found amusements, I dare say; a great many of the national guards pass through the park.

BRIQUET   Sir, don't talk in that way, or I shall be capable of setting fire to the Bastille.

ST. LUCE   Well, I won't prevent you; but first see after the dinner.

BRIQUET   Yes, sir, I'll get the table ready. Poor Runnette, how tired she must be. (*exit*)

ST. LUCE   Poor fellow! He also is jealous. My suspicion is right. Pauline loved Fabian, and must have owned it to her mother; for when I presented myself at the house I was informed he had departed for the Isle of Bourbon and would never return to France. The Marchioness had left Paris, taking Pauline with her; she was to become a nun! By my faith, to be trifled with, deceived, and sacrificed for a mulatto! I know not where to hide my shame; fortunately the King came to my assistance, and hid me and my blushes in the Bastille. (*drums heard*) What the devil's the matter today? Briquet!

BRIQUET   Perhaps it is some fete day. (*heavy bell heard*) Hark to the bell of Notre Dame! (*both look out of window*)

(*Enter* JAILOR, *left, followed by* COOK *with the dinner. They place it on the table.* COOK *exits, and* JAILOR *locks the door*)

ST. LUCE (*at window*)   Oh, here's my dinner. (*to* JAILOR) What have you brought me?

JAILOR (*giving* BRIQUET *a basket*)   Everything we could get of the best, Chevalier, and, as usual, wine from the governor's cellar.

ST. LUCE   You are a capital fellow, and full of little delicate attentions. (*looks into basket*) What! No ice? I must have some ice, or I shall send a complaint to the King.

BRIQUET   Dine without ice! Impossible!

JAILOR   It isn't our fault, sir; an express was sent off this morning to procure some, but it isn't come yet. The parks and public places are crowded with people, and every place is very difficult of access.

ST. LUCE   What's their difficulty of movement to me?

BRIQUET   Certainly not, we see not so much room to move about. (*exit right with basket.* JAILOR *goes to window*)

ST. LUCE   They ought to have an ice house in the place, but they have no consideration for state prisoners. By-the-by, I sent a request to the ministers; I have asked for a room where I can have better air. Can anything be more scandalous than to lodge a gentleman even with the moat, in the very cellar, for I suppose there can be nothing underneath us!

JAILOR (*at window*)   No sir, nothing underneath.

ST. LUCE   What are you staring at, eh?

JAILOR (*leaving window quickly*)   Me, sir!

ST. LUCE (*at window*)   I am not mistaken—they are arranging cannon on the rampart, to the left.

JAILOR   Possibly.

ST. LUCE   Can these plebeians have begun their system? (*drum*) Yes, that's the call to arms! By heaven, if I were but free, I could wish for nothing better than the command of a company of musketeers to sweep the path clean of these rascals!

BRIQUET (*at door*)   Dinner, ready, sir.

SIR LUCE   Bravo! Let but the King give these gentlemen of Paris a good lesson, and the minister send them a few leaden sugar plums, I'll forgive them both for making me dine without ice! (*exit. Enter* SECOND JAILOR *from staircase*)

SECOND JAILOR   The storm threatens! They are only waiting for the cannon from the Invalides, to attack the Bastille. The governor fears the insurgents may gain some communication with the prisoners! come, quick! (*exit both, left door, and lock it*)

(*The straw behind the pillar in dungeon, compartment right, is seen to move, and* FABIAN *pale and haggard, raises himself, passes his hand over his forehead, and rises with difficulty; takes the lamp, approaches window, looks out, listens, then retires discouraged; puts lamp on stone*)

FABIAN (*shaking his head*)   Nothing! Still nothing! (*shivering*) The damp has penetrated my very limbs! I asked them for a little fresh straw, and they said it would cost too much! Straw! Your hatred and revenge are well obeyed here, proud Marchioness! it would have been more merciful to let me die than bury me alive. While I thought to purchase Pauline's pardon by my exile, they threw me into this tomb! Why should I complain? Death will come quicker here; but Pauline, what has become of her? (*warms his hands over lamp*) My limbs are frozen, but here, (*places hand on heart*) here I am on fire! Kind heaven, preserve my reason till Andre's return; but why should I expect him? May not what I

fancy to be recollection, be but a dream? For now I doubt everything! My memory, my thoughts, my existence; and yet, no, I remember well, yesterday I was sitting there—there, when a voice struck upon my ear, and that voice was Andre's; yes, Andre, who was at work in that gloomy gallery. I called, whispered my name, but he could not understand that the voice of a man proceeded from the bowels of the earth! (*listens again*) Nothing! Nothing! (*falls, overwhelmed*) Andre will not come! (*a stone falls at this moment through the window, a letter attached to it*) What's that? (*picks up letter*) A letter from him; yes, yes, it is; thanks Andre! Thank heaven! (*weeps, at last he opens letter. At this moment,* JAILOR *is seen, descending staircase; he opens trap, carries a loaf of bread and a jug of water.* FABIAN *reads letter by lamp, while* JAILOR *descends into left division, below*) "My dear benefactor, I know not if I shall be fortunate enough to see you; all Paris is in arms, and they are firing on all who approach the Bastille; but you shall have the letter, though they take my life." My good Andre! "I have been to the Marchioness's house, and it was filled with mourning; the hall was hung with black. (*he is almost choked with emotion*) A priest was in prayer beside an escutcheoned coffin, covered with velvet. I asked who was dead in the house, and they answered—(*enter* JAILOR *quickly;* FABIAN *has just time to hide the letter*)

JAILOR (*puts bread and water on stone*) Here!

FABIAN   Thank you.

JAILOR   Yesterday, while a man was at work in that gallery (*pointing to window*) you approached that opening; the sentinel saw the light from your lamp and also your signs. (*seizes lamp*) You won't do it again!

FABIAN   What are you going to do?

JAILOR   Take away the lamp; 'tis the governor's order.

FABIAN (*on his knee*)   O, no, no, not now, for mercy's sake!

JAILOR   We know nothing here but obedience. (*puts out lamp, exits, and locks door*)

FABIAN (*still on his knees*)   Heavens! I cannot see, and my letter! (*goes to window, and then to place where lamp stood*) All is darkness, all is night; the coffin—those mourners; who, who could it be? (*with a cry of despair*) Ah, she—she is dead! (*falls senseless on the straw.*

The cannonading begins; noise of musketry.
JAILOR *appears through trap—gets on staircase)*

JAILOR   They have commenced the attack!
Luckily the Bastille is impregnable. *(goes upstairs, and exits, left door. Reports of cannon at
end of scene)*

(Enter BRIQUET, *right)*

BRIQUET   The cannon! Merciful powers!
Why, it's the cannon. *(enter* ST. LUCE, *right)*

ST. LUCE *(going to window)*   Yes, the artillary
of the fortress are firing on the Place St. Antoine; but, by heaven; the Place St. Antoine
answers them in their own way!

BRIQUET   Heavens! Is it possible? *(shouts
without)*

ST. LUCE   This is becoming serious! Listen!
Those confused cries—that dreadful clamor!

BRIQUET *(at window)*   And yonder on the
ramparts, what a crowd! O, sir, they are no
longer soldiers—it is the people!

(Shouts without, "Victory! Victory!")

ST. LUCE   'Tis impossible; why they'll never
take the Bastille like a cockle-shell! *(shouts
without, "Victory! Victory!" Last discharge of
musketry; and the doors are bent in with hatchets;
the one at top of stairs falls—several men and soldiers hurry in, some carrying torches, all shouting
"Victory!" Listening at door)* They are coming
at us! *(the doors are broken in, and several persons enter the* CHEVALIER's *apartments; a soldier
of the French Guard is at the head of them)*
What is this?

ALL   Liberty! Liberty!

ST. LUCE   How long has it been the fashion
to enter the Bastille thus?

SOLDIER   There is no longer a Bastille; tomorrow it will be levelled to the ground; citizen, you are free!

ST. LUCE *(astonished)*   Nonsense!

BRIQUET *(quickly)*   Free! The people fought
for us; hurrah for the people!

SOLDIER   Citizens, you are free!

ALL   Liberty! Liberty! *(all leave room and remain outside)*

ST. LUCE   Certainly, I shall go out, but not
this figure! Briquet, quick, my coat and hat!
(BRIQUET enters inner room. ST. LUCE *takes off
dressing gown;* BRIQUET *reenters with necessaries
for toilet)*

BRIQUET   Here they are, sir. *(dresses him)*

(Enter ANDRE *down staircase, gets amongst
crowd, looks about)*

ANDRE   Yes, I'm sure it was in this tower.

SOLDIER   Who are you looking for?

ANDRE   A poor prisoner.

SOLDIER   There is no one else here; there's
nothing beneath. Come, let us go.

ALL   Ay, ay.

ANDRE   Nay, stay; I'm sure I'm not mistaken; I am sure beneath our feet a wretched
man is perishing, for whom but now I risked
my life.

SOLDIER   Look yourself and be satisfied.

ANDRE *(pointing to trap)*   This trap, perhaps
it may be raised; let us try.

ALL   Yes, yes. *(they all assist with hatchets,
etc.)*

ANDRE   Pull it up. *(they raise it)* There, look!

SOLDIER   And do you mean to say there is a
living being down there?

ANDRE   Yes, a fellow-creature; a good and
worthy man. *(goes down followed by others; one
bears a torch)*

ST. LUCE   Now my gloves and my hat. *(BRI-
QUET gives them)* My sword—ha! I haven't
one. Now then, I'll soon to Versailles.

BRIQUET   And I to the Park. *(both exit up
staircase;* BRIQUET *shouting "Hurrah for the people!" At this moment* ANDRE *and others break
into dungeon below, and, by the torchlight, discover* FABIAN)

ANDRE   Fabian! Fabian! 'Tis I, Andre!
(raises him)

FABIAN *(reviving)*   Andre! Andre! Are you,
too, a prisoner?

ANDRE   No, no; you are free.

FABIAN *(joyfully)*   Free! *(rises, is rushing out,
suddenly returns to* ANDRE) Fool that I am! If
they have restored my liberty it is because she
is dead—Pauline is dead!

ANDRE   No, no; it was not she—'tis the
Marchioness.

FABIAN   And I am free?

ALL   Yes, you are—you are! *(shouts)* Liberty!
Liberty!

*(FABIAN rushes to staircase, then stops suddenly,
looks at* ANDRE *and those who surround him; then
breaks into a loud fit of laughter; they look sorrowfully at him. 'Tis apparent his reason is gone. At
last he falls senseless and exhausted. He is raised
by* ANDRE. *Cannon again. The whole back of up-*

per part of scene falls in, and discovers the city, the ramparts, and various groups with torches, etc. Women, citizens, soldiers; red fire, etc.)

ACT FOUR

Scene One

(An immense gothic apartment in the old Castle of Resadeuc in Bretagne; at the back, a high and vast fireplace; left of fireplace, a large window, opening on a balcony; right of fireplace, a gallery, which is lighted by two painted windows; doors right and left, two each, by side of which hang portraits of the Marquis and Marchioness de la Reynerie, that of the Marchioness is right; left, a small table with writing materials, beside it an armchair; right, a sofa; at back, by fireplace, a gothic stool. BRIQUET watching at window, ST. LUCE standing by fireplace; AURELIA and PAULINE seated, warming themselves)

ST. LUCE (to BRIQUET)   Do you see anything strange or suspicious about the chateau?

BRIQUET   No, sir, I see nothing but the snow and ice. (through open window snow is seen falling) If you will allow me, sir, I'll close the window. (shuts it) Oh, dear! What a precious year is the year 1793!

ST. LUCE   Go, hasten to the fisherman who promised to let me have his boat to cross to Noman-Mere. Once at sea, either by his own will or by force, he shall take us to England. My sister and my cousin Pauline will not be safe until then. Quick! Quick!

BRIQUET   I'm gone, sir. (exit)

AURELIA (rising)   Why take us from this asylum, which the devotion of our tenentry has hitherto rendered so secure.

PAULINE (rising)   My dear friends, why did you expose yourselves for me? Why did you not leave me to die?

AURELIA   Pauline, we may await death in a cell or at the foot of the cross; but to die on a scaffold, exposed to insult from an enraged mob—to die by the hand of the executioner—O, 'tis too dreadful to think of!

PAULINE   Those tortures would be but momentary, and my life is one continued agony—you know that my dying mother never forgave poor Fabian, who suddenly disappeared, since when we could never learn if he still lived or had ceased to suffer.

ST. LUCE   When my sister confided your secret to me, I did all in my power to discover him; I wrote to Bourbon, but none had seen or heard of him; the enraged people disbelieve your marriage, and consider Fabian was sacrificed through your connivance.

AURELIA   Oh, could the late Marchioness see death thus hovering around you, she would call on Fabian to preserve her child; for the proof of the marriage, which is in his possession, would now save her life!

ST. LUCE   Yes, that certificate, signed by the Abbe L'Audrey, who performed the ceremony, would prove her innocence. (Enter BRIQUET)

BRIQUET   I could not find the fisherman, sir; but I have brought his brother, who knew all about it.

ST. LUCE (to AURELIA)   'Till I have test of this man's fidelity, it would be imprudent to let him see our cousin.

AURELIA (pointing to door)   We will wait in the library. Come, Pauline.

ST. LUCE   Bring the man in. (exit BRIQUET)

PAULINE (looking at portrait)   Mother, mother! Why should we separate again? Here, at the foot of this dear but dreadful image, I would be content to die. (exit with AURELIA, right door. Enter BRIQUET with ANDRE; he points to ST. LUCE)

BRIQUET   There is the gentleman. (exit at back)

ST. LUCE (at table with papers)   Why is it your brother has not come?

ANDRE   He is on a jury at Nantz; I am informed of the business. Bless you, sir, I soon got my hand in again to the old trade; I'll take you quite as safely as my brother.

ST. LUCE   Are you sure of that?

ANDRE   I shall have a steady comrade.

ST. LUCE   Discreet and silent.

ANDRE   Poor fellow, he never speaks to anyone, never remembers anyone! His complaint is all in his brain, and in his heart—so, at least, the doctor says, but his arms are stiff and strong, and the sea breeze does him good. He often spends whole days in the boat, and loves to be rocked by the waves in the clear sunshine; it brings his own country to recollection. He is very wretched, and I have often heard him mention the names of those who have caused all his sorrows. Then at times he weeps over, and hides again in his bosom, a timeworn discolored paper, which he treasures as a precious relic.

ST. LUCE (*busy with papers and scarce hearing the latter part of Andre's speech*)   You will be answerable for this man?

ANDRE   As for myself, sir.

ST. LUCE (*putting papers in pocket*)   'Tis well; have you brought him with you?

ANDRE   Yes sir; he was delighted when he saw me prepare the boat, and I told him we were going for a sail as soon as the tide served.

ST. LUCE   Where is he?

ANDRE   Sitting yonder, under the chestnut tree.

ST. LUCE   Now I'll give you the sum agreed for by your brother.

ANDRE   I am at your service, sir.

ST. LUCE   Follow me, then. (*exit left door, followed by* ANDRE)

(*Enter* FABIAN, *from gallery, right, walks slowly, looking on all sides*)

FABIAN   Andre! Andre! The tide is up; we must go. It is still rising—rising! (*fancying himself surrounded by the waves*) O, save her! Save her! Leave me to perish, I ought to perish— the Abbe L'Audrey! Yes, the poor mulatto will love you—cherish you, even as the mariner does his distant home! (*sees portrait of* MAR- CHIONESS) There—there is your mother! (*supplicating*) Do not curse! No—no, do not curse her! I will go, I will leave her! (*holds out his arms*) Take her, bind me—send me to a dungeon—to the Bastille, ha! (*a pause*) Hark! The cannon—they are coming! Free! Yes—yes, I am free—free! (*puts hand to head, closes his vest*) How I tremble! I am very cold—ha! Some fire, fire! (*sits by fire. Enter* ST. LUCE *and* ANDRE, *left door*)

ST. LUCE   Well, then, now we understand each other, I'll fetch the ladies.

ANDRE   And I'll bring my comrade. (*going, sees* FABIAN) Ha! There he is, poor fellow! (*speaks kindly to him*) We are coming on board—don't you hear me? Ha! I see, he has forgotten me again. Come, 'tis I, Andre!

(*Enter* AURELIA *and* PAULINE, *right door*)

AURELIA   Courage, Pauline, courage! (*enter* ST. LUCE, *right door*)

ST. LUCE   Come, let us be quick. (*enter* BRI- QUET, *in terror*)

BRIQUET   O, sir! O, my lady!

ST. LUCE   What's the matter?

BRIQUET   It's all over with us!

ALL   What?

BRIQUET   I was keeping a lookout as you desired me, sir, when on a sudden, I saw a number of armed men coming by the Nantz road.

ALL   Nantz!

BRIQUET   They are led on by two ill-looking fellows, one of whom I heard say to the rest, pointing to the chateau, "'Tis there she is hid—there you will find the *ci-devant* Marchioness de la Reynerie!"

ANDRE (*suddenly*)   Reynerie!

ST. LUCE   They cannot enter but by force. Come, come—we may yet escape! (*they are going*)

ANDRE (*aside*)   'Tis she then, the Marchioness, I was about to save!

ST. LUCE (*to* ANDRE)   Why do you pause?

ANDRE (*comes down center*)   Take back your money—I recall my promise!

ST. LUCE   How say you?

ANDRE (*throws down purse*)   I say that for a million of gold I would not guide you!

PAULINE   Heavens! What do you mean?

ANDRE   I mean, lady, I will not aid in the escape of Mademoiselle de la Reynerie—I will not save her whom I have denounced!

ST. LUCE   You wretch!

ANDRE   Justice is for all.

PAULINE   What have I ever done to you?

ANDRE   To me, lady, nothing; had you been my enemy, I could have forgiven you; but you and your family consigned my friend, and benefactor, the best of men, to the foul dungeons of the Bastille!

ST. LUCE   Dare you accuse her?

ANDRE   Yes, and to prove my accusation, I had the jailor's book in my hand, from which I tore a leaf, and there read these words following after my friend's name: "At the request of the family of de Reynerie this man is to be forgotten." I kept that leaf, and have placed it in the hands of the tribunal of Nantz.

ST. LUCE   Wretch! (*places hand on sword*)

ANDRE   Take my life, but I will not be your guide.

AURELIA (*to* ANDRE)   This is a dreadful error; believe me when I swear she is innocent—O, have pity on her.

ANDRE   Pity for her; look at her victim! (*points to* FABIAN)

ALL   Here!

ANDRE   Yes, there is the martyred victim to the pride of the de la Reynerie.

PAULINE   *(with energy, and looking at* FABIAN*)* Why does he not, then accuse me? Why does he not look at me? I am Pauline de la Reynerie, and before Heaven declare I never injured you. *(*FABIAN *raises his head, she recognizes him)*

PAULINE   Fabian! *(chord)*

ANDRE   You know him, then?

PAULINE   Fabian!

ANDRE   Yes, look at him; see what the Bastille has done for him.

ALL   The Bastille.

PAULINE   *(looking at portrait)*   O, mother, mother.

ANDRE   I brought him from there myself; and when I told him he was free, he no longer understood me—his reason had fled. *(*FABIAN *comes down, right)*

ALL   Mad.

PAULINE   No, no, I'll not believe it; he will know me. My friend, my husband. Heaven has had pity on us—if but for a day, an hour, it has united us. Heavens! Not one look of joy—not an expression of love in his eyes.

AURELIA   The Bastille, he was in the Bastille.

ANDRE   Yes. When I brought him away they wanted to put him in the madhouse; but then he would but have exchanged his prison; so I took him, and I have shared my crust with him ever since.

PAULINE   Did you do this? *(takes his hand)* O, may heaven bless you for it. If riches are still left to us, all shall be yours. If I am permitted to live, you shall be our friend, our brother! And if I am to die, my last prayer upon the scaffold shall be for you and for him. *(turns to* FABIAN*)*

ANDRE   What says she? Was Fabian, then—

ST. LUCE   Her husband.

ANDRE   Her husband.

AURELIA   When Fabian was in the Bastille, she too was a prisoner; and now you have destroyed her!

ANDRE   You are not deceiving me? No, no; falsehood has not such accents. Sir, when you are ready we will go. *(distant shouts)*

AURELIA   *(to* ST. LUCE*)*   Come, come.

ANDRE   Nay, 'tis too late! But fear not, lady, fear not! *(goes to window)* My brother is amongst them. *(to* AURELIA*)* Come with me, lady; you are known and respected by all here; they will hear you, and believe you; and you can assist me to repair the wrong I have done.

AURELIA   Yes, yes. Come brother, come. *(exit all but* PAULINE *and* FABIAN*)*

PAULINE   *(looking at* FABIAN*)*   Still that dreadful insensibility—still dumb! Heavens! Cannot my tears, my grief, find a way to his heart. *(falls on her knees before him)*

FABIAN   *(looking at her)*   Poor Lia! You suffer much! Why do you weep?

PAULINE   *(quickly)*   You remember Lia! O, then you cannot forget Pauline!

FABIAN   Pauline! Yes—the affianced wife of the Chevalier St. Luce. *(clock strikes three—he rises)* Three o'clock—she is waiting for me.

PAULINE   Where are you going?

FABIAN   To the Palmtree walk. I will not suffer and die alone. I'll—hush—yes—I'll take her to the Grotto by the sea—we will die together!

PAULINE   Horrible thought.

FABIAN   Hush, the tide is up—at five o'clock. *(shouts without)*

PAULINE   *(rushes to window)*   They are here—they do not believe Andre.

FABIAN   *(to himself)*   I know the way.

PAULINE   They are coming—they will soon force an entrance. *(returns to* FABIAN*)* Fabian! One effort to restore his reason—the moment is propitious. You remember the Grotto by the sea?

FABIAN   *(to himself)*   The tide was rising.

PAULINE   I was resigned, for I thought to die with you, and for you.

FABIAN   *(still the same)*   The tide was higher. *(shouts without)*

PAULINE   They approach. Fabian, do you hear those shouts; today, as in Bourbon, the tempest surrounds us, but much more terrible than the ocean. It is a dreadful mob, thirsting for human blood. *(now nearer, and she clings to him)* O, Fabian! Save me! Save me!

FABIAN   Now, now, it rises higher, higher.

PAULINE   *(looking at him)*   Still the same! Heaven, thy will be done. Fabian, when at Bourbon I believed myself dying. I owned I loved you! Fabian, my husband, I love you now. Death is indeed at hand, and my last sigh shall breathe a blessing on your name.

FABIAN   *(half recollecting)*   Yes, yes; you are Pauline.

PAULINE (*falls on knees*)   Merciful heaven, receive my thanks.

(*Noise. Enter* AURELIA *and* ST. LUCE)

AURELIA   They are here, Pauline, they are here.

ST. LUCE   They will see Fabian.

PAULINE (*joyfully*)   He has recognized me.

FABIAN (*recognizing* ST. LUCE, *and relapsing immediately*)   Still that man forever at her side. (*enter* ANDRE, *followed by Citizens, armed, from balcony and garden*)

PAULINE   Andre! Andre! He has recognized me.

ANDRE (*to all*)   Look: brother! See, all, I have not deceived you.

FABIAN (*wildly*)   What do these men mean?

AURELIA   Speak, Fabian; tell them Mademoiselle de la Reynerie was ignorant of your captivity in the Bastille.

FABIAN (*in a low voice*)   In the Bastille. (*movement in crowd*)

ANDRE   Tell them she is your wife.

FABIAN (*looking at* MARCHIONESS's *portrait*) No, no, the Marchioness would kill her; 'tis false, I am not her husband. (*murmurs of indignation from mob*)

PAULINE   O, heaven, (*to* FABIAN) you will destroy me.

FABIAN   No, no, hush; I will save you.

PIERRE (*fiercely*)   You hear him; he himself accuses her! To Nantz with the aristocrat!

ALL   To Nantz! to Nantz!

ANDRE (*restraining them.—to* PIERRE) Brother, brother! (*a man in gallery, armed with gun, steps forward*)

MAN   We may as well settle it here. (*he fires at* PAULINE, FABIAN *rushes forward, receives the shot, staggers, and falls*)

ANDRE   Wretch, what have you done?

PAULINE (*falls on her knees beside* FABIAN) Murdered—murdered him! (*people retire confused.* FABIAN *is raised by* CHEVALIER *and* ANDRE; *his reason is returning*)

FABIAN   Pauline, dear Pauline, it is indeed you? (*trying to recollect*) Ha, ha, again I—

PEOPLE (*rushing forward*)   Death to the house of Reynerie.

ANDRE (*in terror*)   They will kill her!

FABIAN (*struggling to his feet*)   Kill her! (*his reason returns*) Stand off! She is my wife!

ALL   His wife!

ST. LUCE   Yes, his wife.

PIERRE (*advancing*)   Show us the proof.

ALL   Ay, ay; the proof.

FABIAN   The proof? 'tis here. (FABIAN *is supported by* ST. LUCE, ANDRE *holding* PAULINE *before him;* AURELIA *is on right hand; he opens his vest and produces the marriage certificate, gives it to* PIERRE, *who shows it to people, and they retire up, expressing silent regret. As he opens his vest, blood flows*)

PAULINE (*shuddering*)   Ha! There is blood upon his breast! (*falls on his neck*) They have murdered him!

FABIAN (*sinking fast*)   Pauline, the blow that struck me, was intended for you, and I—I bless heaven, who has granted me to die for—you, for—you! (*dies in their arms*)

(*Curtain*)

THE BROWN OVERCOAT
1858

Victor Séjour (1817–1874)

Born in New Orleans on June 2, 1817, of a Creole quadroon mother and a free Black man from Santo Dominigo, Juan Victor Séjour Marcon et Ferrand demonstrated a talent for writing poetry early on, at Saint Barbe Academy. At age seventeen, to complete his education, Victor was sent to Paris to remove him from the humiliation imposed upon men of color, even freed men. For the remaining thirty-eight years of his adult life, Séjour acted in plays and wrote dramas for the Parisian theatre. "Tall, handsome and distinguished, with sparkling brown eyes and a complexion too dark and lips too large for him to be mistaken for Caucasian, Séjour was an impressive figure in Paris in the heyday of his glory."[1] Within two years, he had published a novella, "Le Mulatre" ("The Mulatto"), but it was his long poem about the return of Emperor Napoleon's body to Paris, *Le Retour de Napoléon*, published in 1824, that brought the young man his fame.

Popular with important literary figures of the day—among them Alexander Dumas père, and the playwright Emile Augier—Séjour began his theatre career in 1844 with a verse drama, *Diégarias*, at the Théâtre Français. Over the following years he wrote twenty other produced plays, many of them full-length romantic historical dramas in the manner of Victor Hugo, whom he admired. In his plays Séjour "dwells on love of parents and their children, and on the beauty of romantic and marital love. Amid his successes, he dutifully and devotedly brought his parents to Paris, where they lived out their last years. In spite of his plays' high appreciation for marriage and their attractive portrayal of fidelity, Séjour fathered three sons of three mothers out of wedlock."[2]

The reports that Séjour wrote one play with Blacks as characters, *Le Volunteers of 1814*, are false. The play does not concern itself with the siege of New Orleans, but with Napoleon in Europe. He did, however, write a play in 1858, *Le Martyre du Coeur (The Martyrdom of the Heart)*, with

1. Charles Rousseve, *The Negro in Louisiana* (New Orleans: Xavier Press, 1937.)

2. Charles Edwards O'Neill, *Directory of American Negro Biography* (New York: W. W. Norton, 1982.)

one Black character, a Jamaican. It was reported he wrote a five-act drama entitled *L'Esclave (The Slave)*, but the script has never been found.

Séjour penned *The Brown Overcoat* the same year that William Wells Brown published *The Escape* (1858), and it was produced the following year. It is a typical artificial comedy in what was then the degenerated tradition of Molière and Beaumarchais. The dialogue is sometimes witty, often relying on puns that cannot be duplicated in translation. The play has nothing to do with race and little to do with the world.[3]

Yet the play is significant in a collection of this kind, for it was written by a Black American playwright who led a successful nonracial artist's life. Unlike Aldridge, he seems to have left the "problem" of racism behind. He integrated into French society and was honored with the title Chevalier and made a member of the Légion d'Honneur. On September 10, 1874, he fulfilled the nineteenth-century's image of the artist by dying in a charity hospital of tuberculosis.

Few of Séjour's plays have been produced, although *The Brown Overcoat*, translated by Townsend Brewster, was produced Off-Broadway on December 6, 1972. The centenary of his death was commemorated with a Séjour production at Loyola University in New Orleans, and at Southern University his likeness appears in a mural of "great Negroes of Louisiana." Along with Ira Aldridge, Séjour pioneered the tradition that if an African American artist could achieve in Europe, that artist might then find some respect at home. Paris in particular became the mecca for many, including Josephine Baker, Chester Hines, Richard Wright, and James Baldwin.

The Brown Overcoat

CAST OF CHARACTERS

ANNA, *servant to the Countess*
THE COUNTESS
THE BARON, *her lover*

Translated by PAT HECHT, *1970*

SCENE   *A small elegant drawing room with a table in the middle; a window on the right, opening out onto the street; flowers in vases on the fireplace.*

Scene One

THE COUNTESS, ANNA

(ANNA *is tidying up. The* COUNTESS *is stretched out on a chaise longue, a bouquet of flowers in her hand*)

ANNA (*indicating a book*)   Yes, Madame, a book entitled *Love* by Monsieur de Stendhal.

COUNTESS   Put it there. Madame de Montville claims that it is a ridiculous book.

ANNA   Perhaps she is no longer young enough to believe in it.

COUNTESS   So, the Baron came . . .

ANNA   Yes, madame, yesterday, after dark . . .

COUNTESS (*indicating the mantelpiece*)   Take away those flowers; they must be wilted.

ANNA   Wilted? . . . no, not at all, Madame, they are the ones the Baron brought.

COUNTESS   You are unaware, I imagine, that

certain flowers wilt more quickly than others . . . Take them away.

ANNA (*aside*) That poor baron . . . Can it be the beginning of the end already? (*she leaves*)

COUNTESS (*alone*) To break off a relationship is nothing; it is the manner of going about it that is everything. A man who could guess the exact moment when he inspires indifference would be indeed precious. Yes, but where can you find this phoenix . . . The least conceited imagines himself adored—adored! A day, a year passes, but always . . . (*she shrugs her shoulders, smiling.* ANNA *returns*)

ANNA (*aside*) The execution is complete.

COUNTESS I will dine at six o'clock.

ANNA Yes, Madame.

COUNTESS Have the carriage harnessed, I am going out this evening.

ANNA (*straightening*) Yes, Madame.

COUNTESS (*aside*) That young man thinks about me, I know it. Why else should I encounter his large eyes every time I go to the window . . . especially in such weather! (*at the window*) George . . . a lovely name! George Duroi . . . a great artist . . . however, I can't shout at him across the rooftops, nor make signals to him like a frustrated virgin . . .

ANNA (*to the* COUNTESS) Madame is going to catch cold. (*aside*) She doesn't hear me . . . my word, that's astonishing . . . is it because of the little musician across the way? Oh, no, she doesn't like music. (*aloud*) If Madame believes me, she will come in, the wind is cold.

COUNTESS (*angrily*) Cold . . . then close the window. (*a bell outside rings*) Someone is ringing. (ANNA *exits*) That girl sees everything . . . Bah! I am a widow, thank God, and free. (*picking up her bouquet*) Dear little bouquet! . . . everyday, on my window or on the seat of my carriage, I find one like it. Certainly the Baron would not take such pains . . . he is becoming dull. (*to* ANNA, *who returns*) Well?

ANNA It's the seamstress delivering Madame's negligees.

COUNTESS What sort of air do they have?

ANNA A babbling and coquettish air, which should please Madame.

A VALET (*from the upstage door*) Monsieur the Baron of Precy, Madame? . . .

COUNTESS (*aside*) He is certainly tactful, this time. Usually he enters unannounced. . . .

I have half a mind to say I am not in . . . no, I would make an enemy . . . I prefer to strangle him with kid gloves. (*aloud*) Show him in. (*to* ANNA) I must look like an escaped prisoner . . .

ANNA Madame the Countess has never been more beautiful.

COUNTESS Flatterer. (*aside*) In fact, so much the better, at least I will not frighten him when I send him away. (*the* BARON *enters;* ANNA *exits*)

Scene Two

THE BARON, THE COUNTESS

BARON (*kissing her hand*) Good day, Countess! . . .

COUNTESS Good day, Baron. . . .—But why are you here, it's only two o'clock?

BARON I've come too early?

COUNTESS My word! . . . How are you?

BARON Very well.

COUNTESS And your horses?

BARON Poorly: my little mare broke her knee this morning.

COUNTESS You have had your hair cut?

BARON No.

COUNTESS You have a curious air about you. . . . Ah, it's your collar. It's not flattering.

BARON The time of Adonises is past. (*offering her a bouquet*) Countess?

COUNTESS You couldn't be more gallant. (*she stuffs it into one of the vases on the mantel*)

BARON How cold it is.—Have you been out?

COUNTESS (*sitting*) No. Why?

BARON It's freezing here . . . the fire must have been allowed to go out.

COUNTESS (*picking up a newspaper*) I haven't stirred, I have letters to write. (*she reads*)

BARON It's amazing.

COUNTESS Oh, how awful! . . . A young girl has just killed her father!

BARON (*warming himself*) I saw that. . . . Turn the page, you'll see a man who was hacked up like a piece of beef.

COUNTESS What did you think of Frezzolini?

BARON The same as everyone else—ravishing!

COUNTESS And that lovely big family of bourgeois we had in front of us?

BARON   Which ones?

COUNTESS   In wedding clothes, piled on top of each other like a stack of sheets; they had red hands, were ecstatic about everything, and stuffed their bouquets between their legs so they could applaud.

BARON   Ah, that's true—Yesterday I was at Madame de Montville's. . . . I spent my night chasing after seats.

COUNTESS   I would love to have seen you, you who love to take your time . . . then, what are you doing?

BARON   *(taking off his overcoat)*   I don't want to make you lie, Countess. *(he throws it on a piece of furniture)*

COUNTESS   That's it, act like you're at an inn, don't bother yourself, do as you like. She visited me this morning.

BARON   Who? The inn?*

COUNTESS   Charming. A little French lesson which you give me in passing. . . . What is the price?

BARON   I will tell you later, Countess.

COUNTESS   *(shrugging her shoulders)*   I had a visit from Madame de Montville. Her blond hair was blazing.

BARON   *(sitting)*   A beautiful incendiary . . . a real forest fire.

COUNTESS   That woman is flighty, don't you think so? She seemed as startled as a lark.

BARON   Oh, good God . . . why? . . . does she have problems of the heart?

COUNTESS   She came from the sea, it's possible. Oh, by the way . . . Ah, but is it possible?

BARON   Some gossip, tell me?

COUNTESS   She noticed that Paul had brown eyes, she thought they were black until now, and she broke off their relationship.

BARON   Paul expected it.

COUNTESS   For a long time?

BARON   For six months.

COUNTESS   But they've only known each other three.

BARON   What do you expect, he's a cautious man.

COUNTESS   *(indicating the overcoat)*   Baron, just what is that?

BARON   That? It's my overcoat.

COUNTESS   Ah! Yes, your maroon overcoat.

BARON   Yes, my brown overcoat. . . .

---

*A play on words based on the use of the possessive in French. It does not translate well into English.

COUNTESS   How can you like maroon? You bought it?

BARON   Someone might have given it to me, who knows. *(aside)* She has her nerve.

COUNTESS   You were saying?

BARON   Nothing, nothing. *(he takes a few steps toward the mantel)*

COUNTESS   Are you bored?

BARON   Once a week, Countess.

COUNTESS   Is this your day?

BARON   Perhaps tomorrow.

COUNTESS   You know, your friend Paul is a generous man. At least he has enough pride to anticipate certain things.

BARON   Unless one is conceited, one always does. It is in good taste to save a woman the confusion and embarrassment of those things.

COUNTESS   But still, must one guess them?

BARON   A witty woman shows them in her attitude.

COUNTESS   You think so?

BARON   A timid or false woman in her opinions.

COUNTESS   Look at me Baron—what do you see?

BARON   That new coiffeur suits you.

COUNTESS   And?

BARON   You are charming!

COUNTESS   That's all? . . .

BARON   *(kissing her hand)*   A thousand pardons, Countess, you are adorable.

COUNTESS   *(aside)*   My attitude says nothing, it seems. I'll have to open his eyes.

BARON   *(taking the book)*   Love! *(throwing it on the table)* . . . These authors are delightful. . . . They find a thousand little things in love. . . . Me, I would compare love to a box of matches. That's not poetic, but it's true—and the termination of a relationship to a railway system; that's even less poetic, but no less true. There are trains and trains, I tell you, convoys and convoys—of certain women—you've seen them go by. You say to them: "I know everything!" . . . they turn their back laughing . . . rupture at full speed. . . . Others . . . you encounter them when you are attired any old way, with your cravat badly tied; they look at you over their fans as if you were a curiosity, and there they are, cured . . . a pleasure train! As for those frantic virgins, it's different:—three o'clock strikes, you arrive with a story which I've heard told twenty times with success. You have lost on the rise or the fall of the stock exchange. She opens her eyes wide, shaking. . . . But you slowly take out the most elegant little wallet in Russian leather . . . emotion stifled. . . . You delicately reveal the five or six thousand franc notes that you have slipped inside . . . her eyes soften . . . and you offer it all, crying: I am ruined; arrange to live your life with this, or find another lover. She throws her arms around your neck, which means she has already made her choice, and, after all is said, you are the right sort of man.

COUNTESS   At a cheap price.

BARON   At the current price—a merchandise train.

COUNTESS   You are in the mood for absurdities, Baron, continue. . . .

BARON   I'm finished.

COUNTESS   Then your train has no branch lines?

BARON   To where?

COUNTESS   Why, to the country of love which is true, profound, eternal.

BARON   Ah! Heroines of novels. They are deadly; they have hollow eyes, a pale complexion; little hands which have claws, little teeth which bite, little knives which kill, little cups of tea which poison. But you are loved for yourself alone—to be a slave, it's nothing; a galley slave, it's little. . . . "Don't complain, silly, you are loved for yourself." Finally the chain is broken . . . you breathe . . . but too late! Unhappy creature! . . . She was jealous, and you have swallowed arsenic without suspecting it . . . thus the victim pants, his teeth chatter, his eyes roll, his hair falls, he is going to die, he dies; the locomotive explodes! . . .

COUNTESS   You have been loved like that, Baron?

BARON   Perhaps by you, Countess.

COUNTESS   What time is it?

BARON (*taking out his watch*)   My watch has stopped! . . . look, your clock too!

COUNTESS (*yawning*)   And if we did the same, Baron?

BARON (*sitting down*)   I'm agreeable.

COUNTESS (*aside*)   He's settling in!

BARON (*reading a newspaper*)   Ah! What a comment! . . . Arthur has a genius for flexible relationships. You think of putting him out the door, it's too late, he has already jumped out the window.

COUNTESS   But that's very shrewd!

BARON   You think so? . . . It's possible! . . . In fact, why not? . . . I am of that school myself! I always jump out the window.

COUNTESS (*offering her hand*)   Goodbye, Baron.

BARON (*astonished*)   Are you going out?

COUNTESS   Me? No, I'm staying. (*she sits*)

BARON (*rising, aside*)   What's the matter with her? (*leaning on her chair*) Shall we dine together?

COUNTESS   I had a little bouquet . . . What have you done with it?

BARON   A bouquet?

COUNTESS   Look for it, I'm attached to it.

BARON   Flowers, Countess, none . . . (*as if remembering*) But wait . . .

COUNTESS   You sat on them?

BARON   Ah, Countess . . . But what is the matter with you today?

COUNTESS   The Marquis of Lorman sat in a wash basin. He never noticed it until the water started running down his legs.

BARON   The Marquis is sixty years old.

COUNTESS   Age has nothing to do with it. Well, my flowers, where are they? They couldn't have flown away.

BARON   I thought I saw them under my overcoat.

COUNTESS   My poor flowers . . . Why, your overcoat is a monument! They must be crushed.

BARON (*producing the flowers*)   It's true. See here, Countess, it's a little thing.

COUNTESS   A little thing! And do you also undress in a drawing room! . . . You have no respect for anything! Baron, I already told you that I was irritated by your overcoat, your abominable maroon overcoat . . . what more do you want?

BARON   Brown, Countess!

COUNTESS   You know very well that that maroon fades.

BARON   But brown, Countess, brown?

COUNTESS   It's ugly and heavy!

BARON   Heavier than gray?

COUNTESS   Well, just because you were in the Crimea and at the assault of Sebastopol, you think you can do anything . . . you were a zouave! . . . Oh, how well I understand Madame de Montville, who hated her husband's outfit with yellow buttons . . . there are certain things that get on your nerves and you wish they were a hundred miles away.

BARON *(laughing)*   Poor Montville! . . . Ah! Let us speak of him . . . it was neither his outfit nor his buttons she detested, it was him.

COUNTESS   Well, Madame de Montville fled green, I flee maroon.

BARON *(picking up his overcoat)*   There, there, Countess. . . . Yes, my overcoat is maroon . . . yes, it has faded . . . but I'll have your furniture recovered . . . is that agreed?

COUNTESS *(aside, exasperated)*   Oh! *(aloud)* But you are not going to have my furniture recovered—you sit on it, that's all . . . Save that for your little dancers from the Opera.

BARON   I'll take my overcoat away, I'll hang my overcoat elsewhere. *(striking his forehead with his hand)* Ah! *(he fumbles through all his pockets)*

COUNTESS   What is the matter with you? What? Are you going to assassinate me, like in Antony?*

BARON *(emphatically, gesturing with his overcoat)*   If she resists me, I have her . . . but no, that would not be appropriate. . . .

COUNTESS *(aside)*   Conceited!

BARON   Besides, you are a widow. Your ticket for the box, I forgot it.

COUNTESS   What box?

BARON   The box you asked me to get for the Théâtre Français. Today is Friday.

COUNTESS   I asked you for a box at the Théâtre Français? But what can you be thinking of? I have known all their idiocies for the past ten years. I am going to the concert.

BARON   To the concert? You?

COUNTESS   Yes, me. So?

BARON   You hate music, you've told me so twenty times.

COUNTESS   Military music, yes.

BARON   Bravo. Then when the evenings are long and you become bored, we can play together. I love my dear violin . . . but I didn't dare tell you about it . . . I have neglected it, that dear friend; it has been in its case for the past ten months.

COUNTESS   What . . . what are you saying . . . you have your friends in cases?

BARON *(laughing)*   Why, no, countess . . . I'm speaking of my violin.

COUNTESS   Fine, you will play for me . . . from a distance. *(piano music is heard in the dis-*

tance) Here, listen . . . there, that passage . . . oh, how beautiful, how admirable!

BARON *(warming himself)*   I believe Litz or Thalberg whipped through their melodies in a much different manner.

COUNTESS   Vandal! But listen! That's genius!

BARON   Genius! Nowadays everyone has genius, even my porter. He has the genius to bring me my newspapers and my letters.

COUNTESS   Go ahead, scoff! but in the field of art you are as advanced as a Chinaman.

BARON   The Chinese, Countess, invented gunpowder before us.

COUNTESS   Yes, but they are Chinese.

BARON   If the whole world became ecstatic about a note of music, that would be quite a concert.

COUNTESS   To be brief, tonight I am going to Hertz's.

BARON   You have tickets?

COUNTESS   No! . . . I counted on you to find them for me. . . . But, truly, am I asking too much, Baron?

BARON   How many seats?

COUNTESS   Two . . . as close to the orchestra as possible. . . . Run quickly, and thank you in advance. When you decide to be amiable, you do it better than anyone.

BARON *(putting on his overcoat)*   You'll hear Monsieur George Duroi . . . a talented man, that one.

COUNTESS   Ah!

BARON   Very talented . . . do you want me to take you?

COUNTESS   You know him?

BARON   Not at all, but should I meet him so I may introduce you?

COUNTESS   You are too kind.

BARON   I shall return. *(he leaves)*

Scene Three

THE COUNTESS (alone)

COUNTESS   At last! . . . *(the sound of a carriage is heard)* Bon voyage! . . . At least he'll exercise his horses. . . . *(she opens the window)* He is at his window! . . . It is his eyes that please me most of all! . . . How different they are from the Baron's dull, dead eyes. Ah! these artists, their breath embraces the air, the habit of fame illuminates them, near or far, they dazzle like the sun. (ANNA *enters and gives*

---

*Probably a reference to *Julius Caesar,* with confusion about both the title and the assassin.

the COUNTESS *a letter and a bouquet on a silver platter)*

Scene Four

THE COUNTESS, ANNA

COUNTESS *(turning)* What is it?

ANNA A letter, Madame!

COUNTESS *(opening the letter, aside)* It's from him! . . . *(while reading)* What a charming thought . . . he asks me to attend his concert and sends me tickets. . . . Oh, yes, I'll go . . . and he will see in my eyes the certainty and the pride of his triumph! . . . I am going to thank him! . . . *(she sits at her table and searches . . . looking at a paper)* An old draft of a letter to the Baron . . . *(throwing it away)* Two months already! Was I such a fool then? *(she finds her pen)* Ah! *(as soon as she begins to write, she stops)* No! . . . he will see me, that will be enough—Anna!

ANNA *(coming nearer)* Madame?

COUNTESS Straighten my hair. Has my gown come?

ANNA Yes, Madame.

COUNTESS My blue gown?

ANNA Yes, Madame.

COUNTESS What do you think of it?

ANNA It is the most beautiful blue. Madame will make more than one person jealous, they will be so envious of the Baron.

COUNTESS Ah! *(aside)* It's true, he loves blue . . . they'll think it's for him. *(aloud)* Arrange my hair with fresh violets . . . with these, for instance. *(she indicates the bouquet which accompanied the letter)* I'll wear my white gown.

ANNA Perhaps these violets won't be sufficient; if Madame wants more, she can choose from the ones the Baron brought.

COUNTESS Why no . . . they are already faded, see . . .

ANNA *(aside, finishing the coiffeur)* Already! . . . she must have boiled them . . . *(aloud)* There, it's done, Madame.

COUNTESS *(primping in front of her mirror)* Not too bad. *(the BARON enters)*

Scene Five

THE BARON, THE COUNTESS

BARON *(entering)* It's me, Countess . . . I have been gone a long time . . . but you must blame only the congestion of the streets . . . the road thronged with curious spectators . . . they were pushing about the wheels of my carriage, and all that for a mere chimney fire. *(he removes his overcoat and starts to put it on the chair)*

COUNTESS Again?

BARON Oh, pardon me, I forgot. . . . Habit, what can you expect? *(he goes toward the room on the right)*

COUNTESS Where are you going?

BARON Nurtured in the seraglio. . . .

COUNTESS Into my bedroom? . . . Is this a bet, Baron?

BARON Is there nothing left but the anteroom?

COUNTESS And so? Isn't that enough for the maroon?

BARON *(his overcoat in his hand)* You know the proverb, Countess. . . .

COUNTESS *(indicating the overcoat)* Get rid of that furnishing.

BARON A brutal but true proverb. . . .

COUNTESS You haven't left?

BARON When you want to kill your dog. . . . * Never mind. I'll take my "furnishing" away. *(he exits)*

COUNTESS *(alone, irritated)* He will never understand! Oh! Men! Until they are twenty, they are idiots, after thirty, they are absurd! . . . *(to the BARON, who returns)* How old are you, Baron?

BARON Thirty-two.

COUNTESS *(aside)* That's it.

BARON Why?

COUNTESS I am twenty-eight, and you are younger than I am.

BARON How do you make that out?

COUNTESS Me? I don't. *(she sits)*

BARON *(aside)* But what is the matter with her today? *(aloud)* Here are your tickets for the concert.

COUNTESS *(aside, with irritation)* He found some. *(aloud)* I am going to write to Madame de Montville, we will go together.

BARON I will pick you up.

COUNTESS No, don't bother. *(she writes)*

---

*Here one of the Countess' lines has been omitted. In the original there is a play upon the word *maroon*, which has multiple meanings. The English *maroon*, lacks this richness and the joke is therefore not translatable.

BARON   Say what you like, I'm freezing in your house.

COUNTESS   That's an idea.

BARON   *(warming himself)*   Yes, it's also the thermometers' idea, they all show fifteen degrees below zero.

COUNTESS   In Russia?

BARON   In Paris.

COUNTESS   Along the waterfront? . . .

BARON   In this room.

COUNTESS   *(rising)*   Last year's thermometer, it might have frozen in this weather, that's possible. *(she rings for* ANNA, *who enters)* Have this note taken to Madame de Montville immediately; I would like an answer.

BARON   Now I have it on my legs. *(stamping)*

COUNTESS   What?

BARON   The wind . . . no wonder, the window is open.

COUNTESS   Oh, that's right . . . it was smoky.

BARON   *(going to close the window)*   Undoubtedly it was also smoky at your neighbor's, his window is yawning wide open.

COUNTESS   That's because it's bored.

BARON   *(closing the window)*   And yours too . . . is bored?

COUNTESS   That's its prerogative . . . isn't that permitted? . . . your overcoat really exasperates me!

BARON   Women are strange, admit it. I am not speaking about swollen women who chew charcoal . . . that only proves one thing, that swelling is an unnatural condition.*

COUNTESS   *(laughing)*   There is a singularly idiotic paradox.

BARON   Paradox is the fertilizer of truth. There is a world down there, said Columbus, paradox; the world turns, cried Galileo, paradox. . . . Who would dare to think and say the contrary today?

COUNTESS   What are you getting at?

BARON   As for wit, it's an exercise for hunchbacks. I have been told Voltaire wasn't one. Who knows. Who will prove to me that he didn't have Aesop's hump inside himself and that one was not the cover of the other.

COUNTESS   Conclude, Baron . . . what are you getting at, finally?

BARON   What am I getting at? Well, Countess, in asking you have done me a service . . . I have lost my train of thought.

COUNTESS   You are irritating. You speak of the strangeness of women. But be brief. You have wit, I agree; but you act too much as if you know it and are waiting to be admired.

BARON   I must be as stupid as a goose to justify the description you've given of me.

COUNTESS   Women are strange, you say . . . which women?

BARON   You, for example! . . . Yes, you! My overcoat is brown, and you know it; for three months I have had the bad habit, I admit, to put that garment on this chair; for three months that thing has come and gone without horrifying you . . . and today, all of a sudden, my overcoat attracts your attention . . . you become edgy when you see it . . . it becomes maroon . . . it is ugly, it is heavy, it fades . . . and all that for a wicked little cheap bouquet of violets that I touched by mistake! . . .

COUNTESS   Crushed!

BARON   Crushed, so be it! But that, come now—

COUNTESS   There, your friend Paul is passing under my window on horseback.

BARON   Invite him up, he will judge us.

COUNTESS   Do you believe that someone can look without seeing, Baron?

BARON   Yes, blind men.

COUNTESS   Listen without hearing? . . .

BARON   Yes, deaf men.

COUNTESS   Very well! I know such a man, who neither sees nor hears, although he has eyes as open as doors, and ears . . . well! . . . I wouldn't say that about your friend, Paul. No, he is basically Parisian from head to foot. And in addition, he has something about him which assures you that he will never care for you more than is appropriate. His whole personality is arranged for that. He spies your looks, observes your bearing, convinced that a woman will always know that he is willing to guess her thoughts. A smile, it's enough; half a word, it's too much. He enters a boudoir as one does a mechanized theater. He fears what is underneath. You might pity him if he ignored the fact that that is where the mysterious mirror of our dreams, I might even say the inventory of our weaknesses, is found. This Chinese curio is there, why? this faded bouquet, why? this tear drop on the leaf of a half-opened book, why? yesterday you like blue, today you

---

*The French word *grosse* means not only swollen, but both fat and pregnant. The play on words in the original is a clever one.

like pink, why? And finally, this window is open when it ought to be closed, why?

BARON *(laughing)* But on that account, Amelie, your window was open and I asked you why.

COUNTESS What a curious thing man is! You invent an entire mass of delicate revelations to enlighten him; half lights to show your soul; muted colors to betray your thoughts. . . . But bah! the former man of wit looks at you through his past triumphs. His vanity is eternal, he considers your love eternal. Here the comparison becomes absurd. Rupture at full speed,* that's false: nothing is more torturous and less prompt . . . the ties tighten with the efforts you make to break them. However, what is more painful to say than: "I no longer love you," or else, "I love another," or yet "I have been unfaithful to you." At the confessional, it is good, you have a grill in between, and, if necessary, little curtains that you can close . . . but to have there, under your eyes, in front of you, near you, a man you have forgotten and whom you must make understand, it, it's horrible! Oh, what a stupid thing vanity is. I am furious with these conceited idiots who have a triple blindfold over their eyes. Unless you put a hundred guards at your door to keep them from coming in, they will never understand. Don't you agree?

BARON It's possible.

COUNTESS I am going to dress. *(aside)* I believe he has understood. *(she exits)*

Scene Six

THE BARON (alone)

BARON Have I been anticipated? I am afraid I have. It seems I am beginning to decrease in value. Now the important thing is to salvage an honorable retreat . . . a retreat of illusions. *(he looks at himself in the mirror)* Still, I'm not getting too much of a stomach yet. . . . *(ANNA enters and starts towards the mantel)*

Scene Seven

THE BARON, ANNA

BARON Come here, Anna.

ANNA *(aside)* Here comes the critical moment, my girl, you are going to be questioned.

*A reference to the Baron's earlier train analogy. The connection is no clearer in the original.

BARON Will your mistress be ready soon?

ANNA In ten minutes, Baron.

BARON I have acted like a fool here; thinking too much of the Countess and not enough of you. We have an account to settle, here! . . .

ANNA Five louis! Baron, here are five louis which could, if necessary, be very eloquent.

BARON You are mistaken . . . and just in case you want to speak, here is another louis to keep you silent. Go on, go.

ANNA Funny man! *(she takes the bouquet and exits)*

Scene Eight

THE BARON (alone)

BARON I am satisfied with myself. I would also like to teach the Countess a little lesson. *(noticing the draft of the letter)* What is this? *(he picks it up)* A draft of a letter, from the Countess. . . . Perhaps this will tell me more than I want to know. Bah! For what purpose. *(he throws the paper on the table)* But it is always good to know these things, if only to be the first to laugh. *(he picks up the letter and reads)* "Dear Baron!" She is writing to me . . . to announce my disaster. At least she is courteous about it. *(reading)* "I was in a state of despair because they didn't have you wait yesterday evening." Yesterday evening? . . . *(he reads)* "Like an idiot, that stupid Anna let you leave." It's true, she didn't say anything to me. *(reading)* "I have a thousand things in my heart," A thousand things leading up to a dismissal; she is charming! *(reading)* "A thousand things in my heart. First, I love you like a madwoman . . ." *(looking)* Like a madwoman! Dear Amelie! *(reading)* "Next . . ." Nothing more! . . . next . . . like a madwoman, that's certain! I too am amazed! . . . that poor Countess! Here she is! . . . *(the COUNTESS enters in evening dress)*

Scene Nine

THE COUNTESS, THE BARON

COUNTESS *(aside)* Still here!

BARON *(looking at her hair. Aside)* My violets! . . . I must not mention them to her, she would be capable of persuading me that they are not mine! . . . *(aloud)* Do you know you are charming to no longer be angry with me, Countess.

COUNTESS   From what do you conclude that?

BARON   From what? . . . from nothing! . . . You are angry at me, so be it. Then I beg your pardon on my knees! *(he kneels at her feet)*

COUNTESS   This is the first time I have ever seen you like that.

BARON *(trying to kiss her hand)*   There is a beginning to everything, Countess.

COUNTESS *(withdrawing her hand)*   No!

BARON *(rising, wounded)*   Ah! . . . has my overcoat bitten you this time?

COUNTESS   It's as if . . . it sprawls out in this anteroom as if it were at an old clothes shop . . . one might even say it swells.*

BARON   Perhaps it is sick . . . you must send your doctor to cure it.

COUNTESS *(dryly)*   Ah! charming.

BARON   It does annoy you, doesn't it.

COUNTESS   It irritates me.

BARON   It is, however, close to the door . . . but perhaps not close enough.

COUNTESS   Not at all . . . however . . .

BARON   However, it ought to be on my shoulders, shouldn't it?

COUNTESS   I didn't say that.

BARON   Come, I agree that I am a fool, Countess. Here we have been strolling for two hours, my overcoat and me, me and my over-coat, from room to room, and I didn't notice it until just now. *(six o'clock strikes)* Six o'clock! *(kissing her hand)* Your dinner hour, Countess, farewell!

COUNTESS   Your place is set, you know.

BARON   Yes . . . yes . . . later . . . tomorrow. *(the piano is heard)*

COUNTESS *(aside, happily)*   Ah! *(the BARON observes her)*

BARON *(aside)*   What, music impassions her to this degree? Her? . . . But wait! the musician, perhaps! *(he goes to the window and looks. Softly)* Countess?

COUNTESS   What?

BARON   But your neighbor, that's George Duroi!

COUNTESS   Really?

BARON   You didn't know? . . . Well! I've told you . . . His overcoat is handsome.

COUNTESS   And?

BARON *(kissing her hand)*   It is blue.

COUNTESS   What do you mean by that?

BARON   In two months, Countess, let me know if blue fades.—Farewell, Countess, farewell! *(he exits. A moment of silence;—then, the COUNTESS rings; to ANNA who appears)*

COUNTESS   Have dinner served!

---

*In French the word for overcoat is masculine. Thus, in the original the possessive pronoun in this speech and the next few lines could refer to the Baron as well as the overcoat.

THE ESCAPE; OR, A LEAP FOR FREEDOM
1858

William Wells Brown (1814–1884)

In 1857, the United States Supreme Court, in the Dred Scott Decision, held that a man once defined as property could not shed the title of property merely by walking about in "free territory," but had to be returned to his original owner. Two years later, John Brown, angered and impatient with federal law and order, attacked Harper's Ferry in what he hoped would be the beginning of protracted guerrilla warfare—protracted until the conscience of America could distinguish property from people.

The Black abolitionist writer William Wells Brown confronted the idea of people as property with *The Escape*, published in 1858. This play was based on personal experience, an experience as inhumane as it was common: birth into slavery.

> I was born in Lexington, Ky. The man who stole me as soon as I was born recorded the birth of all the infants which he claimed to be born his property. . . . My father's name as I learned from my mother, was George Higgins. He was a white man, a relative of my master, and connected with some of the first families in Kentucky.

With these sentences, Brown begins his autobiography, *Narrative of William Wells Brown, a Fugitive Slave* (1847), a story that traces his life from his unhappy childhood to his escape in 1834 at the age of twenty. His rage against the humiliations of slavery began early:

> My master, Dr. Young, had no children of his own, but had a nephew, the son of his brother. When this boy was brought to Dr. Young, his name being William, the same as mine, my mother was ordered to change mine to something else. This, at the time, I thought to be one of the most cruel acts that could be committed upon my rights; and I received several very severe whippings for telling people that my name was William.

Later the author not only reassumed his given name, but also chose his own surname, Wells Brown, after the Ohio Quaker who befriended him on his last flight for freedom. His two previous attempts at escape had failed. His first recapture resulted in "Virginia play," a punishment in which the slave was tied in the smokehouse, flogged, and then "smoked" by setting piles of tobacco stems afire. After the slave had coughed to the point of asphyxiation, he was untied and sent back to work.

In *The Escape*, relentlessly, through humor and pathos, Brown records "rottened" virtue in those he remembered from his childhood: his master, the clergyman, the overseer ("the Yankees were the most cruel"), and the slave speculator who claimed virtue but had none. *The Escape* is a documentary, not only of key instances in Brown's life, but also of the thesis that *power corrupts*.

During his twenty years as a slave, Brown had served as a house servant, a waiter in a tavern, a field hand, a handyboy in a printing shop, an assistant in a medical office, a helper to a slave trader, and a worker on a Mississippi River steamboat. The "melodramatic" ending in the play, where Glen and Melinda fight off their pursuers to jump into the boat as it leaves the shore for Canada, is more than a theatrical climax. As an employee on a steamboat in 1842, he safely conveyed sixty-nine fugitive slaves across Lake Erie to Canada.

Brown lectured frequently for antislavery societies in New England until 1849, when he traveled to France for the International Peace Conference. For the next five years, he remained in Britain delivering over a thousand lectures on the evils of slavery. He completed his autobiography and a novel, *Clotel; or, The President's Daughter*, about Thomas Jefferson's daughter by his slave Sally Hemings. In his later years, Brown published several histories of Black achievements in America.

The Escape, written for the abolitionists of the North, deserves to be read for more than the gratuity that "William Wells Brown was the first Negro to . . . ." The play is a well-structured melodrama conceived in the style of *Uncle Tom's Cabin* (1852), the single most popular drama of that time. The "box" set had not yet made its appearance; painted scenic drops, dioramas, and sliding wings mounted on tracks enabled such epics to move forward at a cinematic pace. Brown also included Cato, a darkey dialect comic, taken directly from minstrelsy, America's most popular mass entertainment of the 1850s. Cato's stupidity in pretending to be a dentist made his audience feel comfortably superior. However, when he sees his opportunity, Cato makes his leap for freedom—an action no white playwright of that period would have ever considered for a low comedy character.

Brown read his play aloud for the first time on Wednesday, February 4, 1857, in the town hall of Salem, Massachusetts, as he would read it aloud on many other occasions. Some reviewers liked the play.

> Mr. Brown's Drama is, in itself, a masterly refutation of all apologies for slavery, and abounds in wit, satire, philosophy, arguments and facts, all ingeniously interwoven into one of the most interesting dramatic compositions of modern times. (Auburn, N.Y., *Daily Advertiser*)

Or again,

> Mr. Brown exhibits a dramatic talent possessed by few who have under the best instructions, made themselves famous on the stage. (*Seneca Falls Courier*)

Why then was the play not produced? Brown, like the mythic Icarus, may have flown his play too near the sun. His puritanical abolitionist audiences may have wavered before Brown's blunt portrayal of the slave owner's sexual license. There is some evidence that Brown wrote and read from a second play, *Experience; or, How to Give a Northern Man a Backbone* (1856), the tale of a white man mistakenly sold into slavery; however, no copy has ever been found.

Despite the North's victories in battle, Black playwrights were still not admitted onto the American stage. After the Civil War the play was neglected. James Weldon Johnson states in *Black Manhattan* (1930) that Brown's career was "in no degree a direct factor in the Negro's theatrical development." In 1937, Sterling Brown noted in his book *Negro Poetry and Drama* that *The Escape* was a "hodge-podge with some humor and satire and much melodrama." Playwright Loften Mitchell, in his history *Black Drama* (1967), writes "[Brown's] scenes, unfortunately, are close to blackface minstrelsy, much more so than the author's personal slave experiences should have permitted." In her study *Negro Playwrights in the American Theater, 1925–1959* (1969), Doris Abramson, who uncovered a printed copy of the play in the Boston Athenaeum Library, summarizes her evaluation by calling it "an interesting document both from a social and theatrical point of view."

The Escape was finally produced in December 1971 at Emerson College in Boston. An adaptation by Phil Blackwell and directed by Professor Tisch Jones received three productions in the eighties at the University of Iowa, Stoneycreek in Connecticut, and Penumbra Theatre in Minneapolis.

The Escape; or, A Leap for Freedom

PLAYWRIGHT'S PREFACE

This play was written for my own amusement, and not with the remotest thought that it would ever be seen by the public eye. I read it privately, however, to a circle of my friends, and through them was invited to read it to a Literary Society. Since then, the drama has been given in various parts of the country. By the earnest solicitation of some in whose judgment I have the greatest confidence, I now present it in a printed form to the public. As I never aspired to be a dramatist, I ask no favor for it, and have little or no solicitude for its fate. If it is not readable, no word of mine can make it so; if it is, to ask favor for it would be needless.

The main features in the drama are true. Glenn and Melinda are actual characters, and still reside in Canada. Many of the incidents are drawn from my own experience of eighteen years at the South. The marriage ceremony, as performed in the second act, is still adhered to in many of the southern states, especially in the farming districts.

The ignorance of the slave, as seen in the case of Big Sally, is common wherever chattel slavery exists. The difficulties created in the domestic circle by the presence of beautiful slave women, as found in Dr. Gaines's family is well understood by all who have ever visited the valley of the Mississippi.

The play, no doubt, abounds in defects, but as I was born in slavery, and never had a day's schooling in my life, I owe the public no apology for errors.

—W. W. B.

CHARACTERS REPRESENTED

DR. GAINES, *proprietor of the farm at Muddy Creek*
MR. CAMPBELL, *a neighboring slave owner*
REV. JOHN PINCHEN, *a clergyman*
DICK WALKER, *a slave speculator*
MR. WILDMARSH, *neighbor to Dr. Gaines*
MAJOR MOORE, *a friend of Dr. Gaines*
MR. WHITE, *a citizen of Massachusetts*
BILL JENNINGS, *a slave speculator*
JACOB SCRAGG, *overseer to Dr. Gaines*
MRS. GAINES, *wife of Dr. Gaines*
MR. AND MRS. NEAL, AND DAUGHTER, *Quakers, in Ohio*
THOMAS, *Mr. Neal's hired man*
GLEN, *slave of Mr. Hamilton, brother-in-law of Dr. Gaines*
CATO, SAM, SAMPEY (BOB), MELINDA, DOLLY, SUSAN, AND BIG SALLY, *slaves of Dr. Gaines*
PETE, NED, BILL, AND TAPIOCA, *slaves*
OFFICERS, LOUNGERS, BARKEEPER, *etc.*

ACT ONE

Scene One

(*A Sitting-Room.* MRS. GAINES, *looking at some drawings*—SAMPEY, *a white slave, stands behind the lady's chair. Enter* DR. GAINES, *right*)

DR. GAINES   Well, my dear, my practice is steadily increasing. I forgot to tell you that neighbor Wyman engaged me yesterday as his family physician; and I hope that the fever and ague, which is now taking hold of the people, will give me more patients. I see by the New Orleans papers that the yellow fever is raging there to a fearful extent. Men of my profession are reaping a harvest in that section this year. I would that we could have a touch of the yellow fever here, for I think I could invent a medicine that would cure it. But the yellow fever is a luxury that we medical men in this climate can't expect to enjoy; yet we may hope for the cholera.

MRS. GAINES   Yes, I would be glad to see it more sickly here, so that your business might prosper. But we are always unfortunate. Everybody here seems to be in good health, and I am afraid that they'll keep so. However, we must hope for the best. We must trust in the Lord. Providence may possibly send some disease among us for our benefit.

(*Enter* CATO, *right*)

CATO   Mr. Campbell is at de door, massa.
DR. GAINES   Ask him in, Cato.

(*Enter* MR CAMPBELL, *right*)

DR. GAINES   Good morning, Mr. Campbell. Be seated.

MR. CAMPBELL   Good morning, doctor. The same to you, Mrs. Gaines. Fine morning, this.

MRS. GAINES   Yes, sir; beautiful day.

MR. CAMPBELL   Well, doctor, I've come to engage you for my family physician. I am tired of Dr. Jones. I've lost another very valuable nigger under his treatment; and, as my old mother used to say, "change of pastures makes fat calves."

DR. GAINES   I shall be most happy to become your doctor. Of course, you want me to attend to your niggers, as well as to your family?

MR. CAMPBELL   Certainly, sir. I have twenty-three servants. What will you charge me by the year?

DR. GAINES   Of course, you'll do as my other patients do, send your servants to me when they are sick, if able to walk?

MR. CAMPBELL   Oh, yes; I always do that.

DR. GAINES   Then I suppose I'll have to lump it, and say $500 per annum.

MR. CAMPBELL   Well, then, we'll consider that matter settled; and as two of the boys are sick, I'll send them over. So I'll bid you good day, doctor. I would be glad if you would come over some time, and bring Mrs. Gaines with you.

DR. GAINES   Yes, I will; and shall be glad if you will pay us a visit, and bring with you Mrs. Campbell. Come over and spend the day.

MR. CAMPBELL   I will. Good morning, doctor. (*exit* MR CAMPBELL, *right*)

DR. GAINES   There, my dear, what do you think of that? Five hundred dollars more added to our income. That's patronage worth having! And I am glad to get all the negroes I can to doctor, for Cato is becoming very useful to me in the shop. He can bleed, pull teeth, and do almost anything that the blacks require. He can put up medicine as well as any one. A valuable boy, Cato!

MRS. GAINES   But why did you ask Mr. Campbell to visit you, and to bring his wife? I am sure I could never consent to associate with her, for I understand that she was the daughter of a tanner. You must remember, my dear, that I was born with a silver spoon in my mouth. The blood of the Wyleys runs in my veins. I am surprised that you should ask him to visit you at all; you should have known better.

DR. GAINES   Oh, I did not mean for him to visit me. I only invited him for the sake of compliments, and I think he so understood it; for I should be far from wishing you to associate with Mrs. Campbell. I don't forget, my dear, the family you were raised in, nor do I overlook my own family. My father, you know, fought by the side of Washington, and I hope some day to have a handle to my own name. I am certain Providence intended me for something higher than a medical man. Ah! by-the-by, I had forgotten that I have a couple of patients to visit this morning. I must go at once. (*exit* DR. GAINES, *right*)

(*Enter* HANNAH, *left*)

MRS. GAINES Go, Hannah, and tell Dolly to kill a couple of fat pullets, and to put the biscuit to rise. I expect brother Pinchen here this afternoon, and I want everything in order. Hannah, Hannah, tell Melinda to come here. (*exit* HANNAH, *left*) We mistresses do have a hard time in this world; I don't see why the Lord should have imposed such heavy duties on us poor mortals. Well, it can't last always. I long to leave this wicked world, and go home to glory. (*enter* MELINDA) I am to have company this afternoon, Melinda. I expect brother Pinchen here, and I want everything in order. Go and get one of my new caps, with the lace border, and get out my scolloped-bottomed dimity petticoat, and when you go out, tell Hannah to clean the white-handled knives, and see that not a speck is on them; for I want everything as it should be while brother Pinchen is here. (*exit* MRS. GAINES, *left*, MELINDA, *right*)

Scene Two

(*Doctor's shop*—CATO *making pills. Enter* DR. GAINES, *left*)

DR. GAINES Well, Cato, have you made the batch of ointment that I ordered?

CATO Yes, massa; I dun made de intment, an' now I is making the bread pills. De tater pills is up on the top shelf.

DR. GAINES I am going out to see some patients. If any gentlemen call, tell them I shall be in this afternoon. If any servants come, you attend to them. I expect two of Mr. Campbell's boys over. You see to them. Feel their pulse, look at their tongues, bleed them, and give them each a dose of calomel. Tell them to drink no cold water, and to take nothing but water gruel.

CATO Yes, massa; I'll tend to 'em. (*exit* DR. GAINES, *left*) I allers knowed I was a doctor, an' now de ole boss has put me at it, I muss change my coat. Ef any niggers comes in, I want to look suspectable. Dis jacket don't suit a doctor; I'll change it. (*exit* CATO—*immediately returning in a long coat*) Ah! now I looks like a doctor. Now I can bleed, pull teef, or cut off a leg. Oh! well, well, ef I aint put de pill stuff an' de intment stuff togedder. By golly,

dat ole cuss will be mad when he finds it out, won't he? Nebber mind, I'll make it up in pills, and when de flour is on dem, he won't know what's in 'em; an' I'll make some new intment. Ah! yonder comes Mr. Campbell's Pete an' Ned; dems de ones massa sed was comin'. I'll see ef I looks right. (*goes to the looking-glass and views himself*) I em some punkins, ain't I? (*knock at the door*) Come in.

(*Enter* PETE *and* NED, *right*)

PETE Whar is de doctor?

CATO Here I is; don't you see me?

PETE But whar is de ole boss?

CATO Dat's none you business. I dun tole you dat I is de doctor, an dat's enuff.

NED Oh! do tell us whar de doctor is. I is almos dead. Oh me! oh dear me! I is so sick. (*horrible faces*)

PETE Yes, do tell us; we don't want to stan here foolin'.

CATO I tells you again dat I is doctor. I larn de trade under massa.

NED Oh! well, den, give me somethin' to stop dis pain. Oh dear me! I shall die. (*he tries to vomit, but can't—ugly faces*)

CATO Let me feel your pulse. Now put out your tongue. You is berry sick. Ef you don't mine, you'll die. Come out in de shed, an' I'll bleed you. (*exit all—re-enter*) Dar, now take dese pills, two in de mornin' and two at night, and ef you don't feel better, double de dose. Now, Mr. Pete, what's de matter wid you?

PETE I got de cole chills, an' has a fever in de night.

CATO Come out, an' I'll bleed you. (*exit all—re-enter*) Now take dese pills, two in de mornin' and two at night, an' ef dey don't help you, double de dose. Ah! I like to forget to feel your pulse and look at your tongue. Put out your tongue. (*feels his pulse*) Yes, I tells by de feel ob your pulse dat I is gib you de right pills. (*enter Mr. Parker's* BILL, *left*) What you come in dat door widout knockin' for?

BILL My toof ache so, I didn't tink to knock. Oh, my toof! my toof! Whar is de doctor?

CATO Here I is; don't you see me?

BILL What! you de doctor, you brack cuss! You looks like a doctor! Oh, my toof! my toof! Whar is de doctor?

CATO I tells you I is de doctor. Ef you don't

believe me, ax dese men. I can pull your toof in a minnit.

BILL   Well, den, pull it out. Oh, my toof! how it aches! Oh, my toof! (CATO *gets the rusty turnkeys*)

CATO   Now lay down on your back.

BILL   What for?

CATO   Dat's de way massa does.

BILL   Oh, my toof! Well, den, come on. (*lies down,* CATO *gets astraddle of* BILL's *breast, puts the turnkeys on the wrong tooth, and pulls*—BILL *kicks, and cries out*)—Oh, do stop! Oh! oh! oh! (CATO *pulls the wrong tooth*—BILL *jumps up*)

CATO   Dar, now, I tole you I could pull your toof for you.

BILL   Oh, dear me! Oh, it aches yet! Oh me! Oh, Lor-e-massy! You dun pull de wrong toof. Drat your skin! ef I don't pay you for this, you brack cuss! (*they fight, and turn over table, chairs and bench*—PETE *and* NED *look on. Enter* DR. GAINES, *right*)

DR. GAINES   Why, dear me, what's the matter? What's all this about? I'll teach you a lesson, that I will. (*the* DOCTOR *goes at them with his cane*)

CATO   Oh, massa! he's to blame, sir. He's to blame. He struck me fuss.

BILL   No, sir; he's to blame; he pull de wrong toof. Oh, my toof! oh, my toof!

DR. GAINES   Let me see your tooth. Open your mouth. As I live, you've taken out the wrong tooth. I am amazed. I'll whip you for this; I'll whip you well. You're a pretty doctor. Now lie down, Bill, and let him take out the right tooth; and if he makes a mistake this time, I'll cowhide him well. Lie down, Bill. (BILL *lies down, and* CATO *pulls the tooth*) There now, why didn't you do that in the first place?

CATO   He wouldn't hole still, sir.

BILL   He lies, sir. I did hole still.

DR. GAINES   Now go home, boys; go home. (*exit* PETE, NED *and* BILL, *left*)

DR. GAINES   You've made a pretty muss of it, in my absence. Look at the table! Never mind, Cato; I'll whip you well for this conduct of yours today. Go to work now, and clear up the office. (*exit* DR. GAINES, *right*)

CATO   Confound dat nigger! I wish he was in Ginny. He bite my finger and scratch my face. But didn't I give it to him? Well, den, I reckon I did. (*he goes to the mirror, and discovers that his coat is torn*—*weeps*) Oh, dear me! Oh, my coat—my coat is tore! Dat nigger has

tore my coat. (*he gets angry, and rushes about the room frantic*) Cuss dat nigger! Ef I could lay my hands on him, I'd tare him all to pieces,— dat I would. An' de ole boss hit me wid his cane after dat nigger tore my coat. By golly, I wants to fight somebody. Ef ole massa should come in now, I'd fight him. (*rolls up his sleeves*) Let 'em come now, ef dey dare—ole massa, or any body else; I'm ready for 'em.

(*Enter* DR. GAINES, *right*)

DR. GAINES   What's all this noise here?

CATO   Nuffin', sir; only jess I is puttin' things to rights, as you tole me. I didn't hear any noise except de rats.

DR. GAINES   Make haste, and come in; I want you to go to town. (*exit* DR. GAINES, *right*)

CATO   By golly, de ole boss like to cotch me dat time, didn't he? But wasn't I mad? When I is mad, nobody can do nuffin' wid me. But here's my coat, tore to pieces. Cuss dat nigger! (*weeps*) Oh, my coat! oh, my coat! I rudder he had broke my head den to tore my coat. Drat dat nigger! Ef he ever comes here agin, I'll pull out every toof he's got in his head—dat I will. (*exit, right*)

Scene Three

(*A room in the quarters. Enter* GLEN, *left*)

GLEN   How slowly the time passes away. I've been waiting here two hours, and Melinda has not yet come. What keeps her, I cannot tell. I waited long and late for her last night, and when she approached, I sprang to my feet, caught her in my arms, pressed her to my heart, and kissed away the tears from her moistened cheeks. She placed her trembling hand in mine, and said, "Glen, I am yours; I will never be the wife of another." I clasped her to my bosom, and called God to witness that I would ever regard her as my wife. Old Uncle Joseph joined us in holy wedlock by moonlight; that was the only marriage ceremony. I look upon the vow as ever binding on me, for I am sure that a just God will sanction our union in heaven. Still, this man, who claims Melinda as his property, is unwilling for me to marry the woman of my choice, because he wants her himself. But he shall not have her. What he will say when he finds that we are married, I cannot tell; but I am determined to protect my wife or die. Ah! here comes Melinda. (*enter* MELINDA, *right*) I am glad to see you, Melinda. I've been waiting long, and feared you would not come. Ah! in tears again?

MELINDA   Glen, you are always thinking I am in tears. But what did master say today?

GLEN   He again forbade our union.

MELINDA   Indeed! Can he be so cruel?

GLEN   Yes, he can be just so cruel.

MELINDA   Alas! alas! how unfeeling and heartless! But did you appeal to his generosity?

GLEN   Yes, I did; I used all the persuasive powers that I was master of, but to no purpose; he was inflexible. He even offered me a new suit of clothes, if I would give you up; and when I told him that I could not, he said he would flog me to death if I ever spoke to you again.

MELINDA   And what did you say to him?

GLEN   I answered, that, while I loved life better than death, even life itself could not tempt me to consent to a separation that would make life an unchanging curse. Oh, I would kill myself, Melinda, if I thought that, for the sake of life, I could consent to your degradation. No, Melinda, I can die, but shall never live to see you the mistress of another man. But, my dear girl, I have a secret to tell you, and no one must know it but you. I will go out and see that no person is within hearing. I will be back soon. (*exit* GLEN, *left*)

MELINDA   It is often said that the darkest hour of the night precedes the dawn. It is ever thus with the vicissitudes of human suffering. After the soul has reached the lowest depths of despair, and can no deeper plunge amid its rolling, fetid shades, then the reactionary forces of man's nature began to operate, resolution takes the place of despondency, energy succeeds instead of apathy, and an upward tendency is felt and exhibited. Men then hope against power, and smile in defiance of despair. I shall never forget when first I saw Glen. It is now more than a year since he came here with his master, Mr. Hamilton. It was a glorious moonlight night in autumn. The wide and fruitful face of nature was silent and buried in repose. The tall trees on the borders of Muddy Creek waved their leafy branches in the breeze, which was wafted from afar, refreshing over hill and vale, over the rippling water, and the waving corn and wheat fields. The starry sky was studded over with a few light, flitting clouds, while the moon, as if rejoicing to witness the meeting of two hearts that should be cemented by the purest love, sailed triumphantly along among the shifting vapors.

Oh, how happy I have been in my acquaintance with Glen! That he loves me, I do well believe it; that I love him, it is most true. Oh, how I would that those who think the slave incapable of the finer feelings, could only see our hearts, and learn our thoughts,—thoughts that we dare not utter in the presence of our masters! But I fear that Glen will be separated from me, for there is nothing too base and mean for master to do, for the purpose of getting me entirely in his power. But, thanks to Heaven, he does not own Glen, and therefore cannot sell him. Yet he might purchase him from his brother-in-law, so as to send him out of the way. But here comes my husband.

(*Enter* GLEN, *left*)

GLEN   I've been as far as the overseer's house, and all is quiet. Now, Melinda, as you are my wife, I will confide to you a secret. I've long been thinking of making my escape to Canada, and taking you with me. It is true that I don't belong to your master, but he might buy me from Hamilton, and then sell me out of the neighborhood.

MELINDA   But we could never succeed in the attempt to escape.

GLEN   We will make the trial, and show that we at least deserve success. There is a slave trader expected here next week, and Dr. Gaines would sell you at once if he knew that we were married. We must get ready and start, and if we can pass the Ohio river, we'll be safe on the road to Canada. (*exit, right*)

Scene Four

(*Dining-room.* REV. MR. PINCHEN *giving* MRS. GAINES *an account of his experience as a minister*—HANNAH *clearing away the breakfast table*—SAMPEY *standing behind* MRS. GAINES' *chair*)

MRS. GAINES   Now, do give me more of your experience, brother Pinchen. It always does my soul good to hear religious experience. It draws me nearer and nearer to the Lord's side. I do love to hear good news from God's people.

MR. PINCHEN   Well, sister Gaines, I've had great opportunities in my time to study the heart of man. I've attended a great many camp-meetings, revival meetings, protracted meetings, and death-bed scenes, and I am satisfied, sister Gaines, that the heart of man is full of sin, and desperately wicked. This is a wicked world, sister Gaines, a wicked world.

MRS. GAINES   Were you ever in Arkansas, brother Pinchen? I've been told that the people out there are very ungodly.

MR. PINCHEN   Oh, yes, sister Gaines. I once spent a year at Little Rock, and preached in all the towns round about there; and I found some hard cases out there, I can tell you. I was once spending a week in a district where there were a great many horse thieves, and one night, somebody stole my pony. Well, I knowed it was no use to make a fuss, so I told brother Tarbox to say nothing about it, and I'd get my horse by preaching God's everlasting gospel; for I had faith in the truth, and knowed that my Savior would not let me lose my pony. So the next Sunday I preached on horse-stealing, and told the brethren to come up in the evenin' with their hearts filled with the grace of God. So that night the house was crammed brim full with anxious souls, panting for the bread of life. Brother Bingham opened with prayer, and brother Tarbox followed, and I saw right off that we were gwine to have a blessed time. After I got 'em pretty well warmed up, I jumped on to one of the seats, stretched out my hands, and said, "I know who stole my pony; I've found out; and you are in here tryin' to make people believe that you've got religion; but you ain't got it. And if you don't take my horse back to brother Tarbox's pasture this very night, I'll tell your name right out in meetin' tomorrow night. Take my pony back, you vile and wretched sinner, and come up here and give your heart to God." So the next mornin', I went out to brother Tarbox's pasture, and sure enough, there was my bob-tail pony. Yes, sister Gaines, there he was, safe and sound. Ha, ha, ha.

MRS. GAINES   Oh, how interesting, and how fortunate for you to get your pony! And what power there is in the gospel! God's children are very lucky. Oh, it is so sweet to sit here and listen to such good news from God's people! You Hannah, what are you standing there listening for, and neglecting your work? Never

mind, my lady, I'll whip you well when I am done here. Go at your work this moment you lazy huzzy! Never mind, I'll whip you well. (*aside*) Come, do go on, brother Pinchen, with your godly conversation. It is so sweet! It draws me nearer and nearer to the Lord's side.

MR. PINCHEN   Well, sister Gaines, I've had some mighty queer dreams in my time, that I have. You see, one night I dreamed that I was dead and in heaven, and such a place I never saw before. As soon as I entered the gates of the celestial empire, I saw many old and familiar faces that I had seen before. The first person that I saw was good old Elder Pike, the preacher that first called my attention to religion. The next person I saw was Deacon Billings, my first wife's father, and then I saw a host of godly faces. Why, sister Gaines, you knowed Elder Goosbee, didn't you?

MRS. GAINES   Why, yes; did you see him there? He married me to my first husband.

MR. PINCHEN   Oh, yes, sister Gaines, I saw the old Elder, and he looked for all the world as if he had just come out of a revival meetin'.

MRS. GAINES   Did you see my first husband there, brother Pinchen?

MR. PINCHEN   No, sister Gaines, I didn't see brother Pepper there; but I've no doubt but that brother Pepper was there.

MRS. GAINES   Well, I don't know; I have my doubts. He was not the happiest man in the world. He was always borrowing trouble about something or another. Still, I saw some happy moments with Mr. Pepper. I was happy when I made his acquaintance, happy during our courtship, happy a while after our marriage, and happy when he died. (*weeps*)

HANNAH   Massa Pinchen, did you see my ole man Ben up dar in hebben?

MR. PINCHEN   No, Hannah; I didn't go amongst the niggers.

MRS. GAINES   No, of course brother Pinchen didn't go among the blacks. What are you asking questions for? Never mind, my lady, I'll whip you well when I'm done here. I'll skin you from head to foot. (*aside*) Do go on with your heavenly conversation, brother Pinchen; it does my very soul good. This is indeed a precious moment for me. I do love to hear of Christ and Him crucified.

MR. PINCHEN   Well, sister Gaines, I promised sister Daniels that I'd come over and see her this morning, and have a little season of prayer with her, and I suppose I must go. I'll tell you more of my religious experience when I return.

MRS. GAINES   If you must go, then I'll have to let you; but before you do, I wish to get your advice upon a little matter that concerns Hannah. Last week, Hannah stole a goose, killed it, cooked it, and she and her man Sam had a fine time eating the goose; and her master and I would never have known a word about it, if it had not been for Cato, a faithful servant, who told his master. And then, you see, Hannah had to be severely whipped before she'd confess that she stole the goose. Next Sabbath is sacrament day, and I want to know if you think that Hannah is fit to go to the Lord's supper after stealing the goose.

MR. PINCHEN   Well, sister Gaines, that depends on circumstances. If Hannah has confessed that she stole the goose, and has been sufficiently whipped, and has begged her master's pardon, and begged your pardon, and thinks she'll never do the like again, why then I suppose she can go to the Lord's supper; for

> While the lamp holds out to burn,
> The vilest sinner may return.

But she must be sure that she has repented, and won't steal any more.

MRS. GAINES   Now, Hannah, do you hear that? For my own part, I don't think she's fit to go to the Lord's supper, for she had no occasion to steal the goose. We give our niggers plenty of good wholesome food. They have a full run to the meal tub, meat once a fortnight, and all the sour milk about the place, and I'm sure that's enough for anyone. I do think that our niggers are the most ungrateful creatures in the world, that I do. They aggravate my life out of me.

HANNAH   I know, missis, dat I steal de goose, and massa whip me for it, and I confess it, and I is sorry for it. But, missis, I is gwine to de Lord's supper, next Sunday, kase I ain't agwine to turn my back on my bressed Lord an' Massa for no old tough goose, dat I ain't. (*weeps*)

MR. PINCHEN   Well, sister Gaines, I suppose I must go over and see sister Daniels; she'll be waiting for me. (*exit* MR. PINCHEN, *center*)

MRS. GAINES   Now, Hannah, brother Pinchen is gone, do you get the cowhide and follow me to the cellar, and I'll whip you well for aggravating me as you have today. It seems as if I can never sit down to take a little comfort with the Lord, without you crossing me. The devil always puts it into your head to disturb me, just when I am trying to serve the Lord. I've no doubt but that I'll miss going to heaven on your account. But I'll whip you well before I leave this world, that I will. Get the cowhide and follow me to the cellar. (*exit* MRS. GAINES *and* HANNAH, *right*)

ACT TWO

Scene One

(*Parlor.* DR. GAINES *at a table, letters and papers before him. Enter* SAMPEY, *left*)

SAMPEY   Dar's a gemman at de doe, massa, dat wants to see you, seer.

DR. GAINES   Ask him to walk in, Sampey. (*exit* SAMPEY, *left*)

(*Enter* WALKER)

WALKER   Why, how do you do, Dr. Gaines? I em glad to see you, I'll swear.

DR. GAINES   How do you do, Mr. Walker? I did not expect to see you up here so soon. What has hurried you?

WALKER   Well, you see, doctor, I comes when I em not expected. The price of niggers is up, and I em gwine to take advantage of the times. Now, doctor, ef you've got any niggers that you wants to sell, I em your man. I am paying the highest price of anybody in the market. I pay cash down, and no grumblin'.

DR. GAINES   I don't know that I want to sell any of my people now. Still, I've got to make up a little money next month, to pay in bank; and another thing, the doctors say that we are likely to have a touch of the cholera this summer, and if that's the case, I suppose I had better turn as many of my slaves into cash as I can.

WALKER   Yes, doctor, that is very true. The cholera is death on slaves, and a thousand dollars in your pocket is a great deal better than a nigger in the field, with cholera at his heels. Why, who is that coming up the lane? It's Mr. Wildmarsh as I live! Jest the very man I wants to see. (*enter* MR. WILDMARSH) Why, how do you do, Squire? I was jest a thinkin' about you.

WILDMARSH   How are you, Mr. Walker? and how are you, doctor? I am glad to see you both looking so well. You seem in remarkably good health, doctor?

DR. GAINES   Yes, Squire, I was never in the enjoyment of better health. I hope you left all well at Licking?

WILDMARSH   Yes, I thank you. And now, Mr. Walker, how goes times with you?

WALKER   Well, you see, Squire, I em in good spirits. The price of niggers is up in the market, and I am lookin' out for bargains; and I was jest intendin' to come over to Lickin' to see you, to see if you had any niggers to sell. But it seems as ef the Lord knowed that I wanted to see you, and directed your steps over here. Now, Squire, ef you've got any niggers you wants to sell, I em your man. I am payin' the highest cash price of anybody in the market. Now's your time, Squire.

WILDMARSH   No, I don't think I want to sell any of my slaves now. I sold a very valuable gal to Mr. Haskins last week. I tell you, she was a smart one. I got eighteen hundred dollars for her.

WALKER   Why, Squire, how you do talk! Eighteen hundred dollars for one gal? She must have been a screamer to bring that price. What sort of a lookin' critter was she? I should like to have bought her.

WILDMARSH   She was a little of the smartest gal I've ever raised; that she was.

WALKER   Then she was your own raising, was she?

WILDMARSH   Oh, yes; she was raised on my place, and if I could have kept her three or four years longer, and taken her to the market myself, I am sure I could have sold her for three thousand dollars. But you see, Mr. Walker, my wife got a little jealous, and you know jealousy sets women's heads a teetering, and so I had to sell the gal. She's got straight hair, blue eyes, prominent features, and is almost white. Haskins will make a spec, and no mistake.

WALKER   Why, Squire, was she that pretty little gal that I saw on your knee the day that your wife was gone, when I was at your place three years ago?

WILDMARSH   Yes, the same.

WALKER   Well, now, Squire, I thought that was your daughter; she looked mightily like you. She was your daughter, wasn't she? You need not be ashamed to own it to me, for I am mum upon such matters.

WILDMARSH   You know, Mr. Walker, that people will talk, and when they talk, they say a great deal; and people did talk, and many said the gal was my daughter; and you know we can't help people's talking. But here comes the Rev. Mr. Pinchen; I didn't know that he was in the neighborhood.

WALKER   It is Mr. Pinchen, as I live; jest the very man I wants to see. (*enter* MR. PINCHEN, *right*) Why, how do you do, Mr. Pinchen? What in the name of Jehu brings you down here to Muddy Creek? Any camp-meetins, revival meetins, death-bed scenes, or anything else in your line going on down here? How is religion prosperin' now, Mr. Pinchen? I always like to hear about religion.

MR. PINCHEN   Well, Mr. Walker, the Lord's work is in good condition everywhere now. I tell you, Mr. Walker, I've been in the gospel ministry these thirteen years, and I am satisfied that the heart of man is full of sin and desperately wicked. This is a wicked world, Mr. Walker, a wicked world, and we ought all of us to have religion. Religion is a good thing to live by, and we all want it when we die. Yes, sir, when the great trumpet blows, we ought to be ready. And a man in your business of buying and selling slaves needs religion more than anybody else, for it makes you treat your people as you should. Now, there is Mr. Haskins,—he is a slave-trader, like yourself. Well, I converted him. Before he got religion, he was one of the worst men to his niggers I ever saw; his heart was as hard as stone. But religion has made his heart as soft as a piece of cotton. Before I converted him, he would sell husbands from their wives, and seem to take delight in it; but now he won't sell a man from his wife, if he can get any one to buy both of them together. I tell you, sir, religion has done a wonderful work for him.

WALKER   I know, Mr. Pinchen, that I ought to have religion, and I feel that I am a great sinner; and whenever I get with good pious people like you and the doctor, and Mr. Wildmarsh, it always makes me feel that I am a desperate sinner. I feel it the more, because I've got a religious turn of mind. I know that I would be happier with religion, and the first spare time I get, I am going to try to get it. I'll go to a protracted meeting, and I won't stop till I get religion. Yes, I'll scuffle with the Lord till I gets forgiven. But it always makes me feel bad to talk about religion, so I'll change the subject. Now, doctor, what about them thar niggers you thought you could sell me?

DR. GAINES   I'll see my wife, Mr. Walker, and if she is willing to part with Hannah, I'll sell you Sam and his wife, Hannah. Ah! here comes my wife; I'll mention it. (*enter* MRS. GAINES, *left*) Ah! my dear, I am glad you've come. I was just telling Mr. Walker, that if you were willing to part with Hannah, I'd sell him Sam and Hannah.

MRS. GAINES   Now, Dr. Gaines, I am astonished and surprised that you should think of such a thing. You know what trouble I've had in training up Hannah for a house servant, and now that I've got her so that she knows my ways, you want to sell her. Haven't you niggers enough on the plantation to sell, without selling the servants from under my very nose?

DR. GAINES   Oh, yes, my dear; but I can spare Sam, and I don't like to separate him from his wife; and I thought if you could let Hannah go, I'd sell them both. I don't like to separate husbands from their wives.

MRS. GAINES   Now, gentlemen, that's just the way with my husband. He thinks more about the welfare and comfort of his slaves, than he does of himself or his family. I am sure you need not feel so bad at the thought of separating Sam from Hannah. They've only been married eight months, and their attachment can't be very strong in that short time. Indeed, I shall be glad if you do sell Sam, for then I'll make Hannah *jump the broomstick* with Cato, and I'll have them both here under my eye. I never will again let one of my house servants marry a field hand—never! For when night comes on, the servants are off to the quarters, and I have to holler and holler enough to split my throat before I can make them hear. And another thing: I want you to sell Melinda. I don't intend to keep that mulatto wench about the house any longer.

DR. GAINES   My dear, I'll sell any servant from the place to suit you, except Melinda. I can't think of selling her—I can't think of it.

MRS. GAINES   I tell you that Melinda shall leave this house, or I'll go. There, now you have it. I've had my life tormented out of me by the presence of that yellow wench, and I'll stand it no longer. I know you love her more than you do me, and I'll—I'll—I'll write—

write to my father. (*weeps*). (*Exit* MRS. GAINES, *left*)

WALKER   Why, doctor, your wife's a screamer, ain't she? Ha, ha, ha. Why, doctor, she's got a tongue of her own, ain't she? Why, doctor, it was only last week that I thought of getting a wife myself; but your wife has skeered the idea out of my head. Now, doctor, if you wants to sell the gal, I'll buy her. Husband and wife ought to be on good terms, and your wife won't feel well till the gal is gone. Now, I'll pay you all she's worth, if you wants to sell.

DR. GAINES   No, Mr. Walker; the girl my wife spoke of is not for sale. My wife does not mean what she says; she's only a little jealous. I'll get brother Pinchen to talk to her, and get her mind turned upon religious matters, and then she'll forget it. She's only a little jealous.

WALKER   I tell you what, doctor, ef you call that a little jealous, I'd like to know what's a heap. I tell you, it will take something more than religion to set your wife right. You had better sell me the gal; I'll pay you cash down, and no grumblin'.

DR. GAINES   The girl is not for sale, Mr. Walker; but if you want two good, able-bodied servants, I'll sell you Sam and Big Sally. Sam is trustworthy, and Sally is worth her weight in gold for rough usage.

WALKER   Well, doctor, I'll go out and take a look at 'em, for I never buys slaves without examining them well, because they are sometimes injured by over-work or underfeedin'. I don't say that is the case with yours, for I don't believe it is; but as I sell on honor, I must buy on honor.

DR. GAINES   Walk out, sir, and you can examine them to your heart's content. Walk right out, sir.

Scene Two

(*View in front of the Great House. Examination of* SAM *and* BIG SALLY.——DR. GAINES, WILDMARSH, MR. PINCHEN *and* WALKER *present*)

WALKER   Well, my boy, what's your name?

SAM   Sam, sir, is my name.

WALKER   How old are you, Sam?

SAM   Ef I live to see next corn plantin' time, I'll be 27, or 30, or 35, or 40—I don't know which, sir.

WALKER   Ha, ha, ha. Well, doctor, this is

rather a green boy. Well, mer feller, are you sound?

SAM   Yes, sir, I spec I is.

WALKER   Open your mouth and let me see your teeth. I allers judge a nigger's age by his teeth, same as I does a hoss. Ah! pretty good set of grinders. Have you got a good appetite?

SAM   Yes, sir.

WALKER   Can you eat your allowance?

SAM   Yes, sir, when I can get it.

WALKER   Get out on the floor and dance; I want to see if you are supple.

SAM   I don't like to dance; I is got religion.

WALKER   Oh, ho! you've got religion, have you? That's so much the better. I likes to deal in the gospel. I think he'll suit me. Now, mer gal, what's your name?

SALLY   I is Big Sally, sir.

WALKER   How old are you, Sally?

SALLY   I don't know, sir; but I heard once dat I was born at sweet pertater diggin' time.

WALKER   Ha, ha, ha. Don't know how old you are! Do you know who made you?

SALLY   I hev heard who it was in de Bible dat made me, but I dun forget de gentman's name.

WALKER   Ha, ha, ha. Well, doctor, this is the greenest lot of niggers I've seen for some time. Well, what do you ask for them?

DR. GAINES   You may have Sam for $1000, and Sally for $900. They are worth all I ask for them. You know I never banter, Mr. Walker. There they are; you can take them at that price, or let them alone, just as you please.

WALKER   Well, doctor, I reckon I'll take 'em; but it's all they are worth. I'll put the handcuffs on 'em, and then I'll pay you. I likes to go accordin' to Scripter. Scripter says ef eatin' meat will offend your brother, you must quit it; and I say, ef leavin' your slaves without the handcuffs will make 'em run away, you must put the handcuffs on 'em. Now, Sam, don't you and Sally cry. I am of a tender heart, and it ollers makes me feel bad to see people cryin'. Don't cry, and the first place I get to, I'll buy each of you a great big *ginger cake*,—that I will. Now, Mr. Pinchen, I wish you were going down the river. I'd like to have your company; for I allers likes the company of preachers.

MR. PINCHEN   Well, Mr. Walker, I would be much pleased to go down the river with you, but it's too early for me. I expect to go to Natchez in four or five weeks, to attend a camp-meetin', and if you were going down then, I'd like it. What kind of niggers sells best in the Orleans market, Mr. Walker?

WALKER   Why, field hands. Did you think of goin' in the trade?

MR. PINCHEN   Oh, no; only it's a long ways down to Natchez, and I thought I'd just buy five or six niggers, and take 'em down and sell 'em to pay my travellin' expenses. I only want to clear my way.

Scene Three

(Sitting-room—table and rocking-chair. Enter MRS. GAINES, *right, followed by* SAMPEY)

MRS. GAINES   I do wish your master would come; I want supper. Run to the gate, Sampey, and see if he is coming. (*exit* SAMPEY, *left*) That man is enough to break my heart. The patience of an angel could not stand it.

(Enter SAMPEY, *left*)

SAMPEY   Yes, missis, master is coming.

(Enter DR. GAINES, *left. The Doctor walks about with his hands under his coat, seeming very much elated)*

MRS. GAINES   Why, doctor, what is the matter?

DR. GAINES   My dear, don't call me *doctor*.

MRS. GAINES   What should I call you?

DR. GAINES   Call me Colonel, my dear— Colonel. I have been elected Colonel of the Militia, and I want you to call me by my right name. I always felt that Providence had designed me for something great, and He has just begun to shower His blessings upon me.

MRS. GAINES   Dear me, I could never get to calling you Colonel; I've called you Doctor for the last twenty years.

DR. GAINES   Now, Sarah, if you will call me Colonel, other people will, and I want you to set the example. Come, my darling, call me Colonel, and I'll give you anything you wish for.

MRS. GAINES   Well, as I want a new gold watch and bracelets, I'll commence now. Come, Colonel, we'll go to supper. (*aside*) Ah! now for my new shawl. Mrs. Lemme was here today, Colonel, and she had on, Colonel, one of the prettiest shawls, Colonel, I think, Colonel, that I ever saw, Colonel, in my life, Colonel. And there is only one, Colonel, in

Mr. Watson's store, Colonel; and that, Colonel, will do, Colonel, for a Colonel's wife.

DR. GAINES   Ah! my dear, you never looked so much the lady since I've known you. Go, my darling, get the watch, bracelets and shawl, and tell them to charge them to Colonel Gaines; and when you say "Colonel," always emphasize the word.

MRS. GAINES   Come, Colonel, let's go to supper.

DR. GAINES   My dear, you're a jewel,—you are! (*exit, right*)

(*Enter* CATO, *left*)

CATO   Why, whar is massa and missis? I tought dey was here. Ah! by golly, yonder comes a mulatter gal. Yes, its Mrs. Jones's Tapioca. I'll set up to dat gal, dat I will. (*enter* TAPIOCA, *right*) Good ebenin', Miss Tappy. How is your folks?

TAPIOCA   Pretty well, I tank you.

CATO   Miss Tappy, dis wanderin' heart of mine is yours. Come, take a seat! Please to squze my manners; love discommodes me. Take a seat. Now, Miss Tappy, I loves you; an ef you will jess marry me, I'll make you a happy husband, dat I will. Come, take me as I is.

TAPIOCA   But what will Big Jim say?

CATO   Big Jim! Why, let dat nigger go to Ginny. I want to know, now, if you is tinkin' about dat common nigger? Why, Miss Tappy, I is surstonished dat you should tink 'bout frowin' yourself away wid a common, ugly lookin' cuss like Big Jim, when you can get a fine lookin', suspectable man like me. Come, Miss Tappy, choose dis day who you have. Afore I go any furder, give me one kiss. Come, give me one kiss. Come, let me kiss you.

TAPIOCA   No you shan't—dare now! You shan't kiss me widout you is stronger den I is; and I know you is dat. (*he kisses her. Enter* DR. GAINES, *right, and hides*)

CATO   Did you know, Miss Tappy, dat I is de head doctor 'bout dis house? I beats de ole boss all to pieces.

TAPIOCA   I hev hearn dat you bleeds and pulls teef.

CATO   Yes, Miss Tappy; massa could not get along widout me, for massa was made a doctor by books; but I is a natral doctor. I was born a doctor, jess as Lorenzo Dow was born a preacher. So you see I can't be nuffin' but a

doctor, while massa is a bunglin' ole cuss at de bissness.

DR. GAINES (*in a low voice*)   Never mind; I'll teach you a lesson, that I will.

CATO   You see, Miss Tappy, I was gwine to say—Ah! but afore I forget, jess give me anudder kiss, jess to keep company wid de one dat you give me jess now,—dat's all. (*kisses her*) Now, Miss Tappy, duse you know de fuss time dat I seed you?

TAPIOCA   No, Mr. Cato, I don't.

CATO   Well, it was at de camp-meetin'. Oh, Miss Tappy, dat pretty red calliker dress you had on dat time did de work for me. It made my heart flutter—

DR. GAINES (*low voice*)   Yes, and I'll make your black hide flutter.

CATO   Didn't I hear some noise? By golly, dar is teves in dis house, and I'll drive 'em out. (*takes a chair and runs at the* DOCTOR, *and knocks him down. The* DOCTOR *chases* CATO *round the table*) Oh, massa, I didn't know 'twas you!

DR. GAINES   You scoundrel! I'll whip you well. Stop! I tell you. (*curtain falls*)

ACT THREE

Scene One

(*Sitting-room.* MRS. GAINES, *seated in an arm chair, reading a letter. Enter* HANNAH, *left*)

MRS. GAINES   You need not tell me, Hannah, that you don't want another husband, I know better. Your master has sold Sam, and he's gone down the river, and you'll never see him again. So, go and put on your calico dress, and meet me in the kitchen. I intend for you to *jump the broomstick* with Cato. You need not tell me that you don't want another man. I know that there's no woman living that can be happy and satisfied without a husband.

HANNAH   Oh, missis, I don't want to jump de broomstick wid Cato. I don't love Cato; I can't love him.

MRS. GAINES   Shut up, this moment! What do you know about love? I didn't love your master when I married him, and people don't marry for love now. So go and put on your calico dress, and meet me in the kitchen. (*exit* HANNAH, *left*) I am glad that the Colonel has sold Sam; now I'll make Hannah marry Cato, and I have them both here under my eye. And

I am also glad that the Colonel has parted with Melinda. Still, I'm afraid that he is trying to deceive me. He took the hussy away yesterday, and says he sold her to a trader; but I don't believe it. At any rate, if she's in the neighborhood, I'll find her, that I will. No man ever fools me. (*exit* MRS. GAINES, *left*)

Scene Two

(*The kitchen—slaves at work. Enter* HANNAH, *right*)

HANNAH   Oh, Cato, do go and tell missis dat you don't want to jump de broomstick wid me,—dat's a good man! Do, Cato; kase I nebber can love you. It was only las week dat massa sold my Sammy, and I don't want any udder man. Do go tell missis dat you don't want me.

CATO   No, Hannah, I ain't a gwine to tell missis no such think, kase I dose want you, and I ain't a-gwine to tell a lie for you ner nobody else. Dar, now you's got it! I don't see why you need to make so much fuss. I is better lookin' den Sam; an' I is a house servant, an' Sam was only a fiel hand; so you ought to feel proud of a change. So go and do as missis tells you. (*exit* HANNAH, *left*) Hannah needn't try to get me to tell a lie; I ain't a-gwine to do it, kase I dose want her, an' I is bin wantin' her dis long time, an' soon as massa sold Sam, I knowed I would get her. By golly, I is gwine to be a married man. Won't I be happy! Now, ef I could only jess run away from ole massa, an' get to Canada wid Hannah, den I'd show 'em who I was. Ah! dat reminds me of my song 'bout ole massa and Canada, an' I'll sing it fer yer. Dis is my moriginal hyme. It comed into my head one night when I was fass asleep under an apple tree, looking up at de moon. Now for my song:—

AIR—"*Dandy Jim*"

Come all ye bondmen far and near,
Let's put a song in massa's ear,
It is a song for our poor race,
Who're whipped and trampled with disgrace.

[CHORUS]
My old massa tells me, Oh,
This is a land of freedom, Oh;
Let's look about and see if it's so,
Just as massa tells me, Oh.

He tells us of that glorious one,
I think his name was Washington,
How he did fight for liberty,
To save a threepence tax on tea.

(*Chorus*)

But now we look about and see
That we poor blacks are not so free;
We're whipped and thrashed about like fools,
And have no chance at common schools.

(*Chorus*)

They take our wives, insult and mock,
And sell our children on the block,
They choke us if we say a word,
And say that "niggers" shan't be heard.

(*Chorus*)

Our preachers, too, with whip and cord,
Command obedience in the Lord;
They say they learn it from the big book,
But for ourselves, we dare not look.

(*Chorus*)

There is a country far away,
I think they call it Canada,
And if we reach Victoria's shore,
They say that we are slaves no more.

Now haste, all bondmen, let us go,
And leave this *Christian* country, Oh;
Haste to the land of the British Queen,
Where whips for negroes are not seen.

Now, if we go, we must take the night,
And never let them come in sight;
The bloodhounds will be on our track,
And wo to us if they fetch us back.

Now haste all bondmen, let us go,
And leave this *Christian* country, Oh;
God help us to Victoria's shore,
Where we are free and slaves no more!

(*Enter* MRS. GAINES, *left*)

MRS. GAINES   Ah! Cato, you're ready, are you? Where is Hannah?

CATO   Yes, missis; I is bin waitin' dis long time. Hannah has bin here tryin' to swade me to tell you dat I don't want her; but I telled her dat you sed I must jump de broomstick wid her, an' I is gwine to mind you.

MRS. GAINES   That's right, Cato; servants should always mind their masters and mistresses, without asking a question.

CATO   Yes, missis, I allers dose what you and massa tells me, an' axes nobody.

(*Enter* HANNAH, *right*)

MRS. GAINES   Ah! Hannah; come, we are waiting for you. Nothing can be done till you come.

HANNAH   Oh, missis, I don't want to jump de broomstick wid Cato; I can't love him.

MRS. GAINES   Shut up, this moment. Dolly, get the broom. Susan, you take hold of the other end. There, now hold it a little lower—there, a little higher. There, now, that'll do. Now Hannah, take hold of Cato's hand. Let Cato take hold of your hand.

HANNAH   Oh, missis, do spare me. I don't want to jump de broomstick wid Cato.

MRS. GAINES   Get the cowhide, and follow me to the cellar, and I'll whip you well. I'll let you know how to disobey my orders. Get the cowhide, and follow me to the cellar. (*exit* MRS. GAINES *and* HANNAH, *right*)

DOLLY   Oh, Cato, do go an' tell missis dat you don't want Hannah. Don't you hear how she's whippin' her in de cellar? Do go an' tell missis dat you don't want Hannah, and den she'll stop whippin' her.

CATO   No, Dolly, I ain't a-gwine to do no such a thing, kase ef I tell missis dat I don't want Hannah, den missis will whip me; an' I ain't a-gwine to be whipped fer you, ner Hannah, ner nobody else. No, I'll jump de broomstick wid every woman on de place, ef missis wants me to, before I'll be whipped.

DOLLY   Cato, ef I was in Hannah's place, I'd see you in de bottomless pit before I'd live wid you, you great big wall-eyed, empty-headed, knock-kneed fool. You're as mean as your devilish old missis.

CATO   Ef you don't quit dat busin' me, Dolly, I'll tell missis as soon as she comes in, an' she'll whip you, you know she will.

(*Enter* MRS. GAINES *and* HANNAH, *right*. MRS. GAINES *fans herself with her handkerchief, and appears fatigued*)

MRS. GAINES   You ought to be ashamed of yourself, Hannah, to make me fatigue myself in this way, to make you do your duty. It's very naughty in you, Hannah. Now, Dolly, you and Susan get the broom, and get out in the middle of the room. There, hold it a little lower—a little higher; there, that'll do. Now, remember that this is a solemn occasion; you are going to jump into matrimony. Now, Cato, take hold of Hannah's hand. There, now, why couldn't you let Cato take your hand before? Now get ready, and when I count three, do you jump. Eyes on the *broomstick!* All ready. One, two, three, and over you go. There, now you're husband and wife, and if you don't live happy together, it's your own fault; for I am sure there's nothing to hinder it. Now, Hannah, come up to the house, and I'll give you some whiskey, and you can make some apple toddy, and you and Cato can have a fine time. (*exit* MRS. GAINES *and* HANNAH, *left*)

DOLLY   I tell you what, Susan, when I get married, I is gwine to have a preacher to marry me. I ain't a-gwine to jump de broomstick. Dat will do for fiel' hands, but house servants ought to be 'bove dat.

SUSAN   Well, chile, you can't speck any ting else from ole missis. She come from down in Carlina, from 'mong de poor white trash. She don't know any better. You can't speck nothin' more dan a jump from a frog. Missis says she is one of de akastocacy; but she ain't no more of an akastocacy dan I is. Missis says she was born wid a silver spoon in her mouf; ef she was, I wish it had a-choked her, dat's what I wish. Missis wanted to make Linda jump de broomstick wid Glen, but massa ain't a-gwine to let Linda jump de broomstick wid anybody. He's gwine to keep Linda fer heself.

DOLLY   You know massa took Linda 'way las' night, an' tell missis dat he has sold her and sent her down de river; but I don't b'lieve he has sold her at all. He went ober towards de poplar farm, an' I tink Linda is ober dar now. Ef she is dar, missis'll find it out, fer she tell'd massa las' night, dat ef Linda was in de neighborhood, she'd find her. (*exit* DOLLY *and* SUSAN)

Scene Three

(*Sitting room—chairs and table. Enter* HANNAH, *right*)

HANNAH   I don't keer what missis says; I don't like Cato, an' I won't live wid him. I always love my Sammy, an' I loves him now.

(*knock at the door—goes to the door. Enter* MAJ. MOORE, *center*) Walk in, sir; take a seat. I'll call missis, sir; massa is gone away. (*exit* HANNAH, *right*)

MAJ. MOORE   So I am here at last, and the Colonel is not at home. I hope his wife is a good-looking woman. I rather like fine-looking women, especially when their husbands are from home. Well, I've studied human nature to some purpose. If you wish to get the good will of a man, don't praise his wife, and if you wish to gain the favor of a woman, praise her children, and swear that they are the picture of their father, whether they are not not. Ah! here comes the lady.

(*Enter* MRS. GAINES, *right*)

MRS. GAINES   Good morning, sir!

MAJ. MOORE   Good morning, madam! I am Maj. Moore, of Jefferson. The Colonel and I had seats near each other in the last Legislature.

MRS. GAINES   Be seated, sir. I think I've heard the Colonel speak of you. He's away, now; but I expect him every moment. You're a stranger here, I presume?

MAJ. MOORE   Yes, madam, I am. I rather like the Colonel's situation here.

MRS. GAINES   It is thought to be a fine location. (*enter* SAMPEY, *right*) Hand me my fan, will you, Sampey?

(SAMPEY *gets the fan and passes near the* MAJOR, *who mistakes the boy for the Colonel's son. He reaches out his hand*)

MAJ. MOORE   How do you do, Bob? Madam I should have known that this was the Colonel's son, if I had met him in California; for he looks so much like his papa.

MRS. GAINES (*to the boy*)   Get out of here this minute. Go to the kitchen. (*exit* SAMPEY, *right*) That is one of the niggers, sir.

MAJ. MOORE   I beg your pardon, madam; I beg your pardon.

MRS. GAINES   No offence, sir; mistakes will be made. Ah! here comes the Colonel.

(*Enter* DR. GAINES, *center*)

DR. GAINES   Bless my soul, how are you, Major? I'm exceedingly pleased to see you. Be seated, be seated, Major.

MRS. GAINES   Please excuse me, gentlemen; I must go and look after dinner, for I've no doubt that the Major will have an appetite for dinner, by the time it is ready. (*exit* MRS. GAINES, *right*)

MAJ. MOORE   Colonel, I'm afraid I've played the devil here today.

DR. GAINES   Why, what have you done?

MAJ. MOORE   You see, Colonel, I always make it a point, wherever I go, to praise the children, if there are any, and so today, seeing one of your little servants come in, and taking him to be your son, I spoke to your wife of the marked resemblance between you and the boy. I am afraid I've insulted madam.

DR. GAINES   Oh! don't let that trouble you. Ha, ha, ha. If you did call my son, you didn't miss it much. Ha, ha, ha. Come, we'll take a walk, and talk over matters about old times. (*exit, left*)

Scene Four

(*Forest scenery. Enter* GLEN, *left*)

GLEN   Oh, how I want to see Melinda! My heart pants and my soul is moved whenever I hear her voice. Human tongue cannot tell how my heart yearns toward her. Oh, God! thou who gavest me life, and implanted in my bosom the love of liberty, and gave me a heart to love, Oh, pity the poor outraged slave! Thou, who canst rend the veil of centuries, speak, Oh, speak, and put a stop to this persecution! What is death, compared to slavery? Oh, heavy curse, to have thoughts, reason, taste, judgment, conscience, and passions like another man, and not have equal liberty to use them! Why was I born with a wish to be free, and still be a slave? Why should I call another man master? And my poor Melinda, she is taken away from me, and I dare not ask the tyrant where she is. It is childish to stand here weeping. Why should my eyes be filled with tears, when my brain is on fire? I will find my wife—I will; and wo to him who shall try to keep me from her!

Scene Five

(*Room in a small cottage on the Poplar Farm, ten miles from Muddy Creek, and owned by* DR. GAINES. *Enter* MELINDA, *right*)

MELINDA   Here I am, watched, and kept a prisoner in this place. Oh, I would that I could escape, and once more get with Glen. Poor

Glen! He does not know where I am. Master took the opportunity, when Glen was in the city with his master, to bring me here to this lonely place, and fearing that mistress would know where I was, he brought me here at night. Oh, how I wish I could rush into the arms of sleep!—that sweet sleep, which visits all alike, descending, like the dews of heaven, upon the bond as well as the free. It would drive from my troubled brain the agonies of this terrible night.

(*Enter* DR. GAINES, *left*)

DR. GAINES   Good evening, Melinda! Are you not glad to see me?

MELINDA   Sir, how can I be glad to see one who has made life a burden, and turned my sweetest moments into bitterness?

DR. GAINES   Come, Melinda, no more reproaches! You know that I love you, and I have told you, and I tell you again, that if you will give up all idea of having Glen for a husband, I will set you free, let you live in this cottage, and be your own mistress, and I'll dress you like a lady. Come, now, be reasonable!

MELINDA   Sir, I am your slave; you can do as you please with the avails of my labor, but you shall never tempt me to swerve from the path of virtue.

DR. GAINES   Now, Melinda, that black scoundrel Glen has been putting these notions into your head. I'll let you know that you are my property, and I'll do as I please with you. I'll teach you that there is no limit to my power.

MELINDA   Sir, let me warn you that if you compass my ruin, a woman's bitterest curse will be laid upon your head, with all the crushing, withering weight that my soul can impart to it; a curse that shall cling to you throughout the remainder of your wretched life; a curse that shall haunt you like a spectre in your dreams by night, and attend upon you by day; a curse, too, that shall embody itself in the ghastly form of the woman whose chastity you will have outraged. Command me to bury myself in yonder stream, and I will obey you. Bid me do anything else, but I beseech you not to commit a double crime,—outrage a woman, and make her false to her husband.

DR. GAINES   You got a husband! Who is your husband, and when were you married?

MELINDA   Glen is my husband, and I've been married four weeks. Old Uncle Joseph married us one night by moonlight. I see you are angry; I pray you not to injure my husband.

DR. GAINES   Melinda, you shall never see Glen again. I have bought him from Hamilton, and I will return to Muddy Creek, and roast him at the stake. A black villain, to get into my way in that manner! Here I've come ten miles tonight to see you, and this is the way you receive me!

MELINDA   Oh, master, I beg you not to injure my husband! Kill me, but spare him! Do! do! he is my husband!

DR. GAINES   You shall never see that black imp again, so good night, my lady! When I come again, you'll give me a more cordial reception. Good night! (*exit* DR. GAINES, *left*)

MELINDA   I shall go distracted. I cannot remain here and know that Glen is being tortured on my account. I must escape from this place,—I must,—I must!

(*Enter* CATO, *right*)

CATO   No, you ain't a-gwine to 'scape, nudder. Massa tells me to keep dese eyes on you, an' I is gwine to do it.

MELINDA   Oh, Cato, do let me get away! I beg you, do!

CATO   No; I tells you massa told me to keep you safe; an' ef I let you go, massa will whip me. (*exit* CATO, *left*)

(*Enter* MRS. GAINES, RIGHT)

MRS. GAINES   Ah, you trollop! here you are! Your master told me that he had sold you and sent you down the river, but I knew better; I knew it was a lie. And when he left home this evening, he said he was going to the city on business, and I knew that was a lie too, and determined to follow him, and see what he was up to. I rode all the way over here tonight. My side-saddle was lent out, and I had to ride ten miles bare-back, and I can scarcely walk; and your master has just left here. Now deny that, if you dare.

MELINDA   Madam, I will deny nothing which is true. Your husband has just gone from here, but God knows that I am innocent of anything wrong with him.

MRS. GAINES   It's a lie! I know better. If you are innocent, what are you doing here, cooped up in this cottage by yourself? Tell me that!

MELINDA   God knows that I was brought here against my will, and I beg that you will take me away.

MRS. GAINES   Yes, Melinda, I will see that you are taken away, but it shall be after a fashion that you won't like. I know that your master loves you, and I intend to put a stop to it. Here, drink the contents of this vial,—drink it!

MELINDA   Oh, you will not take my life,— you will not!

MRS. GAINES   Drink the poison this moment!

MELINDA   I cannot drink it.

MRS. GAINES   I tell you to drink this poison at once. Drink it, or I will thrust this knife to your heart! The poison or the dagger, this instant! (*she draws a dagger;* MELINDA *retreats to the back of the room, and seizes a broom.*)

MELINDA   I will not drink the poison! (*they fight;* MELINDA *sweeps off* MRS. GAINES,—*cap, combs and curls. Curtain falls*)

ACT FOUR

Scene One

(*Interior of a dungeon*—GLEN *in chains*)

GLEN   When I think of my unmerited sufferings, it almost drives me mad. I struck the doctor, and for that, I must remain here loaded with chains. But why did he strike me? He takes my wife from me, sends her off, and then comes and beats me over the head with his cane. I did right to strike him back again. I would I had killed him. Oh! there is a volcano pent up in the hearts of the slaves of these Southern States that will burst forth ere long. When that day comes, wo to those whom its unpitying fury may devour! I would be willing to die, if I could smite down with these chains every man who attempts to enslave his fellow-man.

(*Enter* SAMPEY, *right*)

SAMPEY   Glen, I jess bin hear massa call de oberseer, and I spec somebody is gwine to be whipped. Anudder ting: I know whar massa took Linda to. He took her to de poplar farm, an' he went away las' night, an' missis she follow after massa, an' she ain't come back yet. I tell you, Glen, de debil will be to pay on dis place, but don't you tell anybody dat I tole you. (*exit* SAMPEY, *right*)

Scene Two

(*Parlor.* DR. GAINES, *alone*)

DR. GAINES   Yes, I will have the black rascal well whipped, and then I'll send him. It was most fortunate for me that Hamilton was willing to sell him to me. (*enter* MR. SCRAGG, *left*) I have sent for you, Mr. Scragg. I want you to take Glen out of the dungeon, take him into the tobacco house, fasten him down upon the stretcher, and give him five hundred lashes upon his bare back; and when you have whipped him, feel his pulse, and report to me how it stands, and if he can bear more, I'll have you give him an additional hundred or two, as the case may be.

SCRAGG   I tell you, doctor, that suits me to a charm. I've long wanted to whip that nigger. When your brother-in-law came here to board, and brought that boy with him, I felt bad to see a nigger dressed up in such fine clothes, and I wanted to whip him right off. I tell you, doctor, I had rather whip that nigger than go to heaven, any day,—that I had!

DR. GAINES   Go, Mr. Scragg, and do your duty. Don't spare the whip!

SCRAGG   I will, sir; I'll do it in order. (*exit* SCRAGG, *left*)

DR. GAINES   Everything works well now, and when I get Glen out of the way, I'll pay Melinda another visit, and she'll give me a different reception. But I wonder where my wife is? She left word that she was going to see her brother, but I am afraid that she has got on my track. That woman is the pest of my life. If there's any place in heaven for her, I'd be glad if the Lord would take her home, for I've had her too long already. But what noise is that? What can that be? What is the matter?

(*Enter* SCRAGG, *left, with face bloody*)

SCRAGG   Oh, dear me! oh, my head! That nigger broke away from me, and struck me over the head with a stick. Oh, dear me! Oh!

DR. GAINES   Where is he, Mr. Scragg?

SCRAGG   Oh! sir, he jumped out of the window; he's gone. Oh! my head; he's cracked my skull. Oh, dear me, I'm kilt! Oh! oh! oh!

(*Enter* SLAVES, *right*)

DR. GAINES   Go, Dolly, and wash Mr. Scragg's head with some whiskey, and bind it up. Go at once. And Bob, you run over to Mr. Hall, and tell him to come with his hounds; we must go after the rascal. (*exit all except the* DOCTOR, *right*) This will never do. When I catch the scoundrel, I'll make an example of him; I'll whip him to death. Ah! here comes my wife. I wonder what she comes now for? I must put on a sober face, for she looks angry. (*enter* MRS. GAINES, *left*) Ah! my dear, I am glad you've come, I've been so lonesome without you. Oh! Sarah, I don't know what I should do if the Lord should take you home to heaven. I don't think that I should be able to live without you.

MRS. GAINES   Dr. Gaines, you ought to be ashamed to sit there and talk in that way. You know very well that if the Lord should call me home to glory tonight, you'd jump for joy. But you need not think that I am going to leave this world before you. No; with the help of the Lord, I'll stay here to foil you in your meanness. I've been on your track, and a dirty track it is, too. You ought to be ashamed of yourself. See what promises you made me before we were married; and this is the way you keep your word. When I married you, everybody said that it was a pity that a woman of my sweet temper should be linked to such a man as you. (*she weeps and wrings her hands*)

DR. GAINES   Come, my dear, don't make a fool of yourself. Come, let's go to supper, and a strong cup of tea will help your head.

MRS. GAINES   Tea help my head! tea won't help my head. You're a brute of a man; I always knew I was a fool for marrying you. There was Mr. Comstock, he wanted me, and he loved me, and he said I was an angel, so he did; and he loved me, and he was rich; and mother always said that he loved me more than you, for when he used to kiss me, he always squeezed my hand. You never did such a thing in your life. (*she weeps and wrings her hands*)

DR. GAINES   Come, my dear, don't act so foolish.

MRS. GAINES   Yes; everything I do is foolish. You're a brute of a man; I won't live with you any longer. I'll leave you—that I will. I'll go and see a lawyer, and get a divorce from you—so I will.

DR. GAINES   Well, Sarah, if you want a divorce, you had better engage Mr. Barker. He's the best lawyer in town; and if you want some money to facilitate the business, I'll draw a check for you.

MRS. GAINES   So you want me to get a divorce, do you? Well, I won't have a divorce; no, I'll never leave you, as long as the Lord spares me. (*exit* MRS. GAINES, *right*)

Scene Three

(*Forest at night—large tree. Enter* MELINDA, *left*)

MELINDA   This is indeed a dark night to be out and alone on this road. But I must find my husband, I must. Poor Glen! if he only knew that I was here, and could get to me, he would. What a curse slavery is! It separates husbands from their wives, and tears mothers from their helpless offspring, and blights all our hopes for this world. I must try to reach Muddy Creek before daylight, and seek out my husband. What's that I hear?—footsteps? I'll get behind this tree.

(*Enter* GLEN, *right*)

GLEN   It is so dark, I'm afraid I've missed the road. Still, this must be the right way to the poplar farm. And if Bob told me the truth, when he said that Melinda was at the poplar farm, I will soon be with her; and if I once get her in my arms, it will be a strong man that shall take her from me. Aye, a dozen strong men shall not be able to wrest her from my arms. (MELINDA *rushes from behind the tree*)

MELINDA   Oh, Glen! It is my husband,—it is!

GLEN   Melinda! Melinda! it is, it is. Oh God! I thank Thee for this manifestation of Thy kindness. Come, come, Melinda, we must go at once to Canada. I escaped from the overseer, whom Dr. Gaines sent to flog me. Yes, I struck him over the head with his own club, and I made the wine flow freely; yes, I pounded his old skillet well for him, and then jumped out of the window. It was a leap for freedom. Yes, Melinda, it was a leap for freedom. I've said "master" for the last time. I am free; I'm bound for Canada. Come, let's be off, at once, for the negro dogs will be put upon our track. Let us once get beyond the Ohio river, and all will be right. (*exit, right*)

ACT FIVE

Scene One

(Bar-room in the American Hotel—travellers lounging in chairs, and at the bar. Enter BILL JENNINGS, *right)*

BARKEEPER   Why, Jennings how do you do?

JENNINGS   Say Mr. Jennings, if you please.

BARKEEPER   Well, Mr. Jennings, if that suits you better. How are times? We've been expecting you, for some days.

JENNINGS   Well, before I talk about the times, I want my horses put up, and want you to tell me where my niggers are to stay tonight. Sheds, stables, barns, and everything else here, seems pretty full, if I am a judge.

BARKEEPER   Oh! I'll see to your plunder.

FIRST LOUNGER   I say, Barkeeper, make me a brandy cocktail, strong. Why, how do you do, Mr. Jennings?

JENNINGS   Pretty well, Mr. Peters. Cold evening, this.

FIRST LOUNGER   Yes, this is cold. I heard you speak of your niggers. Have you got a pretty large gang?

JENNINGS   No, only thirty-three. But they are the best that the country can afford. I shall clear a few dimes, this trip. I hear that the price is up.

(Enter MR. WHITE, *right)*

WHITE   Can I be accommodated here tonight, landlord?

BARKEEPER   Yes, sir; we've bed for man and beast. *(to the waiter)* Go, Dick, and take the gentleman's coat and hat. You're a stranger in these parts, I rec'on.

WHITE   Yes, I am a stranger here.

SECOND LOUNGER   Where mout you come from, ef it's a far question?

WHITE   I am from Massachusetts.

THIRD LOUNGER   I say, cuss Massachusetts!

FIRST LOUNGER   I say so too. There is where the fanatics live; cussed traitors. The President ought to hang 'em all.

WHITE   I say, landlord, if this is the language that I am to hear, I would like to go into a private room.

BARKEEPER   We ain't got no private room empty.

FIRST LOUNGER   Maybe you're mad 'bout what I said 'bout your State. Ef you is, I've

only to say that this is a free country, and people talks what they please; an' ef you don't like it, you can better yourself.

WHITE   Sir, if this is a free country, why do you have slaves here? I saw a gang at the door, as I came in.

SECOND LOUNGER   He didn't mean that this was a free country for niggers. He meant that it's free for white people. And another thing, ef you get to talkin 'bout freedom for niggers, you'll catch what you won't like, mister. It's right for niggers to be slaves.

WHITE   But I saw some white slaves.

FIRST LOUNGER   Well, they're white niggers.

WHITE   Well, sir, I am from a free State, and I thank God for it; for the worst act that a man can commit upon his fellow-man, is to make him a slave. Conceive of a mind, a living soul, with the germs of faculties which infinity cannot exhaust, as it first beams upon you in its glad morning of existence, quivering with life and joy, exulting in the glorious sense of its developing energies, beautiful, and brave, and generous, and joyous, and free,—the clear pure spirit bathed in the auroral light of its unconscious immortality,—and then follow it in its dark and dreary passage through slavery, until oppression stifles and kills, one by one, every inspiration and aspiration of its being, until it becomes a dead soul entombed in a living frame!

THIRD LOUNGER   Stop that; stop that, I say. That's treason to the country; that's downright rebellion.

BARKEEPER   Yes, it is. And another thing,— this is not a meeting-house.

FIRST LOUNGER   Yes, if you talk such stuff as that, you'll get a chunk of cold lead in you, that you will.

(Enter DR. GAINES *and* SCRAGG, *followed by* CATO, *right)*

DR. GAINES   Gentlemen, I am in pursuit of two valuable slaves, and I will pay five hundred dollars for their arrest. *(exit* MR. WHITE, *left)*

FIRST LOUNGER   I'll bet a picayune that your niggers have been stolen by that cussed feller from Massachusetts. Don't you see he's gone?

DR. GAINES   Where is the man? If I can lay my hands on him, he'll never steal another nigger. Where is the scoundrel?

FIRST LOUNGER   Let's go after the feller. I'll

go with you. Come, foller me. (*exit all, left, except* CATO *and the* WAITER)

CATO   Why don't you bring in massa's saddle-bags? What de debil you standin' dar for? You common country niggers don't know nuffin', no how. Go an' get massa's saddle-bags and bring 'em in. (*exit* SERVANT, *right*) By golly! ebry body's gone, an' de bar-keeper too. I'll tend de bar myself now; an' de fuss gemman I waits on will be dis gemman of color. (*goes behind the counter, and drinks*) Ah, dis is de stuff fer me; it makes my head swim; it makes me happy right off. I'll take a little more.

(*Enter* BARKEEPER, *left*)

BARKEEPER   What are you doing behind the bar, you black cuss?

CATO   I is lookin' for massa's saddle-bags, sir. Is dey here?

BARKEEPER   But what were you drinking there?

CATO   Me drinkin'! Why, massa, you muss be mistaken. I ain't drink nuffin'.

BARKEEPER   You infernal whelp, to stand there and lie in that way!

CATO   Oh, yes, seer, I did tase dat coffee in dat bottle; dat's all I did.

(*Enter* MR. WHITE, *left, excited*)

MR. WHITE   I say, sir, is there no place of concealment in your house? They are after me, and my life is in danger. Say, sir, can't you hide me away?

BARKEEPER   Well, you ought to hold your tongue when you come into our State.

MR. WHITE   But, sir, the Constitution gives me the right to speak my sentiments, at all times and in all places.

BARKEEPER   We don't care for Constitutions nor nothin' else. We made the Constitution, and we'll break it. But you had better hide away; they are coming, and they'll lynch you, that they will. Come with me; I'll hide you in the cellar. Foller me. (*exit* BARKEEPER *and* WHITE, *left*)

(*Enter the mob, right*)

DR. GAINES   If I can once lay my hands on that scoundrel, I'll blow a hole through his head.

JENNINGS   Yes, I say so too; for no one knows whose niggers are safe, now-a-days. I must look after my niggers. Who is that I see

in the distance? I believe it's that cussed Massachusetts feller. Come, let's go after him. (*exit the mob, right*)

Scene Two

(*Forest at night. Enter* GLEN *and* MELINDA, *right*)

MELINDA   I am so tired and hungry, that I cannot go further. It is so cloudy that we cannot see the North Star, and therefore cannot tell whether we are going to Canada, or further South. Let's sit down here.

GLEN   I know that we cannot see the North Star, Melinda, and I fear we've lost our way. But, see! the clouds are passing away, and it'll soon be clear. See! yonder is a star; yonder is another and another. Ah! yonder is the North Star, and we are safe!

Star of the North! though night winds drift
    The fleecy drapery of the sky
Between thy lamp and me, I lift,
    Yea, lift with hope my sleepless eye,
To the blue heights wherein thou dwellest,
And of a land of freedom tellest.

Star of the North! while blazing day
    Pours round me its full tide of light,
And hides thy pale but faithful ray,
    I, too, lie hid, and long for night:
For night: I dare not walk at noon,
Nor dare I trust the faithless moon—

Nor faithless man, whose burning lust
    For gold hath riveted my chain,—
Nor other leader can I trust
    But thee, of even the starry train;
For all the host around thee burning,
Like faithless man, keep turning, turning.

I may not follow where they go:—
    Star of the North! I look to thee
While on I press; for well I know,
    Thy light and truth shall set me free:—
Thy light, that no poor slave deceiveth;
Thy truth, that all my soul believeth.

Thy beam is on the glassy breast
    Of the still spring, upon whose brink
I lay my weary limbs to rest,
    And bow my parching lips to drink.
Guide of the friendless negro's way,
I bless thee for this quiet ray!

In the dark top of southern pines
    I nestled, when the Driver's horn

Called to the field, in lengthening lines,
    My fellows, at the break of morn.
And there I lay till thy sweet face
Looked in upon "my hiding place."

The tangled cane-brake, where I crept
    For shelter from the heat of noon,
And where, while others toiled, I slept,
    Till wakened by the rising moon,
As its stalks felt the night wind free,
Gave me to catch a glimpse of thee.

Star of the North! in bright array
    The constellations round thee sweep,
Each holding on its nightly way,
    Rising, or sinking in the deep,
And, as it hangs in mid heaven flaming,
The homage of some nation claiming.

This nation to the Eagle cowers;
    Fit ensign! she's a bird of spoil:—
Like worships like! for each devours
    The earnings of another's toil.
I've felt her talons and her beak,
And now the gentler Lion seek.

The Lion, at the Monarch's feet
    Crouches, and lays his mighty paw
Into her lap!—an emblem meet
    Of England's Queen, and English law:
Queen, that hath made her Islands free!
Law, that holds out its shield to me!

Star of the North! upon that shield
    Thou shinest,—Oh, for ever shine!
The negro, from the cotton field
    Shall, then, beneath its orb recline,
And feed the Lion, crouched before it,
Nor heed the Eagle, screaming o'er it!

With the thoughts of servitude behind us, and the North Star before us, we will go forward with cheerful hearts. Come, Melinda, let's go on. (*exit, left*)

Scene Three

(*A street. Enter* MR. WHITE, *right*)

MR. WHITE   I am glad to be once more in a free State. If I am caught again south of Mason and Dixon's line, I'll give them leave to lynch me. I came near losing my life. This is the way our constitutional rights are trampled upon. But what care these men about Consti-

tutions, or anything else that does not suit them? But I must hasten on. (*exit, left*)

(*Enter* CATO, *in disguise, right*)

CATO   I wonder if dis is me? By golly, I is free as a frog. But maybe I is mistaken; maybe dis ain't me. Cato, is dis you? Yes, seer. Well, now it is me, an' I em a free man. But, stop! I muss change my name, kase ole massa might foller me, and somebody might tell him dat dey seed Cato; so I'll change my name, and den he won't know me ef he sees me. Now, what shall I call myself? I'm now in a suspectable part of de country, an' I muss have a suspectable name. Ah! I'll call myself Alexander Washington Napoleon Pompey Caesar. Dar, now, dat's a good long, suspectable name, and everybody will suspect me. Let me see; I wonder ef I can't make up a song on my escape! I'll try.

AIR—*"Dearest Mae"*

Now, freemen, listen to my song, a story I'll relate,
It happened in de valley of de ole Kentucky State:
Dey marched me out into de fiel', at every break of day,
And work me dar till late sunset, widout a cent of pay.

    Dey work me all de day,
    Widout a bit of pay,
    And thought, because dey fed me well,
    I would not run away.

Massa gave me his ole coat, an' thought I'd happy be,
But I had my eye on de North Star, an' thought of liberty;
Ole massa lock de door, an' den he went to sleep,
I dress myself in his bess clothes, an' jump into de street.

[CHORUS]
    Dey work me all de day,
    Widouta bit of pay,
    So I took my flight, in the middle of de night,
    When de sun was gone away.

Sed I, dis chile's a freeman now, he'll be a slave no more;
I travell'd faster all dat night, dan I ever did before.

I came up to a farmer's house, jest at de break of
    day,
And saw a white man standin' dar, sed he, "You
    are a runaway."

(*Chorus*)

I tole him I had left de whip, an' bayin' of de
    hound,
To find a place where man is man, ef sich dar can
    be found;
Dat I had heard, in Canada, dat all mankind are
    free,
An' dat I was going dar in search of liberty.

(*Chorus*)

I've not committed any crime, why should I run
    away?
Oh! shame upon your laws, dat drive me off to
    Canada.
You loudly boast of liberty, an' say your State is
    free,
But ef I tarry in your midst, will you protect me?

(*Chorus*)

Scene Four

(*Dining-room.—table spread.* MRS. NEAL *and*
CHARLOTTE)

MRS. NEAL   Thee may put the tea to draw,
Charlotte. Thy father will be in soon, and we
must have breakfast. (*enter* MR. NEAL, *left*) I
think, Simeon, it is time those people were
called. Thee knows that they may be pursued,
and we ought not to detain them long here.

MR. NEAL   Yes, Ruth, thou art right. Go,
Charlotte, and knock on their chamber door,
and tell them that breakfast is ready. (*exit*
CHARLOTTE, *right*)

MRS. NEAL   Poor creatures! I hope they'll
reach Canada in safety. They seem to be worthy persons.

(*Enter* CHARLOTTE, *right*)

CHARLOTTE   I've called them, mother, and
they'll soon be down. I'll put the breakfast on
the table.

(*Enter* NEIGHBOR JONES, *left*)

MR. NEAL   Good morning, James. Thee has
heard, I presume, that we have two very interesting persons in the house?

JONES   Yes, I heard that you had two fugi-
tives by the Underground road, last night; and
I've come over to fight for them, if any persons
come to take them back.

(*Enter* THOMAS, *right*)

MR. NEAL   Go, Thomas, and harness up the
horses and put them to the covered wagon,
and be ready to take these people on, as soon
as they get their breakfast. Go, Thomas, and
hurry thyself. (*exit* THOMAS, *right*) And so thee
wants to fight, this morning, James?

JONES   Yes; as you belongs to a society that
don't believe in fighting, and I does believe in
that sort of thing, I thought I'd come and re-
lieve you of that work, if there is any to be
done.

(*Enter* GLEN *and* MELINDA, *right*)

MR. NEAL   Good morning, friends. I hope
thee rested well, last night.

MRS. NEAL   Yes, I hope thee had a good
night's rest.

GLEN   I thank you, madam, we did.

MR. NEAL   I'll introduce thee to our neighbor, James Jones. He's a staunch friend of thy
people.

JONES   I am glad to see you. I've come over
to render assistance, if any is needed.

MRS. NEAL   Come, friends, take seats at the
table. (*to* GLEN *and* MELINDA) Thee'll take seats
there. (*all take seats at the table*) Does thee
take sugar and milk in thy tea?

MELINDA   I thank you, we do.

JONES   I'll look at your *Tribune*, Uncle
Simeon, while you're eating.

MR. NEAL   Thee'll find it on the table.

MRS. NEAL   I presume thee's anxious to get
to thy journey's end?

GLEN   Yes, madam, we are. I am told that
we are not safe in any of the free States.

MR. NEAL   I am sorry to tell thee, that that
is too true. Thee will not be safe until thee
gets on British soil. I wonder what keeps
Thomas; he should have been here with the
team.

(*Enter* THOMAS, *left*)

THOMAS   All's ready; and I've written the
prettiest song that was ever sung. I call it "The
Underground Railroad."

MR. NEAL   Thomas, thee can eat thy breakfast far better than thee can write a song, as thee calls it. Thee must hurry thyself, when I send thee for the horses, Thomas. Here lately, thee takes thy time.

THOMAS   Well, you see I've been writing poetry; that's the reason I've been so long. If you wish it, I'll sing it to you.

JONES   Do let us hear the song.

MRS. NEAL   Yes, if Thomas has written a ditty, do let us hear it.

MR. NEAL   Well, Thomas, if thee has a ditty, thee may recite it to us.

THOMAS   Well, I'll give it to you. Remember that I call it, "The Underground Railroad."

AIR—*"Wait for the Wagon"*

Oh, where is the invention
    Of this growing age,
Claiming the attention
    Of statesman, priest, or sage,
In the many railways
    Through the nation found,
Equal to the Yankees'
    Railway under-ground?

[CHORUS]
No one hears the whistle,
    Or rolling of the cars,
While negroes ride to freedom
    Beyond the stripes and stars.

On the Southern borders
    Are the Railway stations,
Negroes get free orders
    While on the plantations;
For all, of ev'ry color,
    First-class cars are found,
While they ride to freedom
    By Railway under-ground.

(*Chorus*)

Masters in the morning
    Furiously rage,
Cursing the inventions
    Of this knowing age;
Order out the bloodhounds,
    Swear they'll bring them back,
Dogs return exhausted,
    Cannot find the track.

(*Chorus*)

Travel is increasing,
    Build a double track,

Cars and engines wanted,
    They'll come, we have no lack.
Clear the track of loafers,
    See that crowded car!
Thousands passing yearly,
    Stock is more than par.

(*Chorus*)

JONES   Well done! That's a good song. I'd like to have a copy of them verses. (*knock at the door.* CHARLOTTE *goes to the door, and returns. Enter* CATO, *left, still in disguise*)

MR. NEAL   Who is this we have? Another of the outcasts, I presume?

CATO   Yes, seer; I is gwine to Canada, an' I met a man, an' he tole me dat you would give me some wittals an' help me on de way. By golly! ef dar ain't Glen an' Melinda. Dey don't know me in dese fine clothes. (*goes up to them*) Ah, chillen! I is one wid you. I golly, I is here too! (*they shake hands*)

GLEN   Why, it is Cato, as I live!

MELINDA   Oh, Cato, I am so glad to see you! But how did you get here?

CATO   Ah, chile, I come wid ole massa to hunt you; an' you see I get tired huntin' you, an' I am now huntin' for Canada. I leff de ole boss in de bed at de hotel; an' you see I thought, afore I left massa, I'd jess change clothes wid him; so, you see, I is fixed up,— ha, ha, ha. Ah, chillen! I is gwine wid you.

MRS. NEAL   Come, sit thee down, and have some breakfast.

CATO   Tank you, madam, I'll do dat. (*sits down and eats*)

MR. NEAL   This is pleasant for thee to meet one of thy friends.

GLEN   Yes, sir, it is; I would be glad if we could meet more of them. I have a mother and sister still in slavery, and I would give worlds, if I possessed them if by so doing I could release them from their bondage.

THOMAS   We are all ready, sir, and the wagon is waiting.

MRS. NEAL   Yes, thee had better start.

CATO   Ef anybody tries to take me back to ole massa, I'll pull ebry toof out of dar heads, dat I will! As soon as I get to Canada, I'll set up a doctor shop, an' won't I be poplar? Den I rec'on I will. I'll pull teef fer all de people in Canada. Oh, how I wish I had Hannah wid me! It makes me feel bad when I tink I ain't a-gwine to see my wife no more. But, come, chillen, let's be makin' tracks. Dey say we is most to de British side.

MR. NEAL   Yes, a few miles further, and you'll be safe beyond the reach of the Fugitive-Slave Law.

CATO   Ah, dat's de talk fer dis chile. (*exit, center*)

Scene Five

(*The Niagara River—a ferry.* FERRYMAN, *fastening his small boat*)

FERRYMAN (*advancing, takes out his watch*)   I swan, if it ain't one o'clock. I thought it was dinner time. Now there's no one here, I'll go to dinner, and if anybody comes, they can wait until I return. I'll go at once. (*exit, left*)

(*Enter* MR. WHITE, *right, with an umbrella*)

MR. WHITE   I wonder where that ferryman is? I want to cross to Canada. It seems a little showery, or else the mist from the Falls is growing thicker. (*takes out his sketch-book and pencils,—sketches*)

(*Enter* CANE PEDLAR, *right*)

PEDLAR   Want a good cane today, sir? Here's one from Goat Island,—very good, sir,—straight and neat,—only one dollar. I've a wife and nine small children,—youngest is nursing, and the oldest only three years old. Here's a cane from Table Rock, sir. Please buy one! I've had no breakfast today. My wife's got the rheumatics, and the children's got the measles. Come, sir, do buy a cane! I've a lame shoulder, and can't work.

MR. WHITE   Will you stop your confounded talk, and let me alone? Don't you see that I am sketching? You've spoiled a beautiful scene for me, with your nonsense.

(*Enter* SECOND PEDLAR *right*)

SECOND PEDLAR   Want any bead bags, or money purses? These are all real Ingen bags, made by the Black Hawk Ingens. Here's a pretty bag, sir, only 75 cents. Here's a money purse, 50 cents. Please, sir, buy something! My wife's got the fever and ague, and the house is full of children, and they're all sick. Come, sir, do help a worthy man!

MR. WHITE   Will you hold your tongue? You've spoiled some of the finest pictures in the world. Don't you see that I am sketching?

(*exit* PEDLARS, *right, grumbling*)   I am glad those fellows have gone; now I'll go a little further up the shore, and see if I can find another boat. I want to get over. (*exit, left*)

(*Enter* DR. GAINES, SCRAGG, *and an* OFFICER)

OFFICER   I don't think that your slaves have crossed yet, and my officers will watch the shore below here, while we stroll up the river. If I once get my hands on them all the Abolitionists in the State shall not take them from me.

DR. GAINES   I hope they have not got over, for I would not lose them for two thousand dollars, especially the gal.

(*Enter* FIRST PEDLAR)

PEDLAR   Wish to get a good cane, sir? This stick was cut on the very spot where Sam Patch jumped over the falls. Only 50 cents. I have a sick wife and thirteen children. Please buy a cane; I ain't had no dinner.

OFFICER   Get out of the way! Gentlemen, we'll go up the shore. (*exit, left*)

(*Enter* CATO, *right*)

CATO   I is loss fum de cumpny, but dis is de ferry, and I spec dey'll soon come. But didn't we have a good time las' night in Buffalo? Dem dar Buffalo gals make my heart flutter, dat dey did. But, tanks be to de Lord, I is got religion. I got it las' night in de meetin'. Before I got religion, I was a great sinner; I got drunk, an' took de name of de Lord in vain. But now I is a conwerted man; I is bound for hebben; I toats de witness in my bosom; I feel dat my name is rote in de book of life. But dem niggers in de Vine Street Church las' night shout an' make sich a fuss, dey give me de headache. But, tank de Lord, I is got religion, an' now I'll be a preacher, and den dey'll call me de Rev. Alexander Washinton Napoleon Pompey Caesar. Now I'll preach and pull teef, bofe at de same time. Oh, how I wish I had Hannah wid me! Cuss ole massa, fer ef it warn't for him, I could have my wife wid me. Ef I hadn't religion, I'd say "Damn ole massa!" but as I is a religious man, an' belongs to de church, I won't say no sich a thing. But who is dat I see comin'? Oh, it's a whole heap of people. Good Lord! what is de matter?

(*Enter* GLEN *and* MELINDA, *left, followed by* OFFICERS)

GLEN   Let them come; I am ready for them. He that lays hands on me or my wife shall feel the weight of this club.

MELINDA   Oh, Glen, let's die here, rather than again go into slavery.

OFFICER   I am the United States Marshal. I have a warrant from the Commissioner to take you, and bring you before him. I command assistance.

(*Enter* DR. GAINES, SCRAGG, *and* OFFICER, *right*)

DR. GAINES   Here they are. Down with the villain! down with him! but don't hurt the gal!

(*Enter* MR. WHITE, *right*)

MR. WHITE   Why, bless me! these are the slaveholding fellows. I'll fight for freedom! (*takes hold of his umbrella with both hands.— The fight commences, in which* GLEN, CATO, DR. GAINES, SCRAGG, WHITE, *and the* OFFICERS, *take part.—*FERRYMAN *enters, and runs to his boat.—* DR. GAINES, SCRAGG *and the* OFFICERS *are knocked down,* GLEN, MELINDA *and* CATO *jump into the boat, and as it leaves the shore and floats away,* GLEN *and* CATO *wave their hats, and shout loudly for freedom.—Curtain falls*)

YES WE CAN

Paul Laurence Dunbar • Jesse A. Shipp • W.E.B. Du Bois

Garland Anderson

At the close of the Civil War in 1865, Black illiteracy exceeded 90 percent; by 1880, 30 percent had learned to read; by 1890, half the population read; and by 1910, the percentage was two-thirds. This newfound literacy created a demand for Black newspapers and periodicals, which in turn opened access to political and economic opportunities, as well as ushering in new aspirations and cultural tastes. Ex-slaves and their descendants joined an ebullient America that was intoxicated with the belief that hard work and initiative equaled success, a doctrine that had received continuous enunciation from such writers as Elbert Hubbard, whose pamphlet, *Message to Garcia*, sold forty million copies by propounding that "the world bestows its big prizes both in money and honors, for but one thing, and this is initiative." In this atmosphere of unopposed capitalism, it is not surprising to find African Americans who believed that once they were free of slavery, they could do whatever they set their hearts to.

Perhaps this optimism explains why Blacks, even though lynching was at its peak, took to the professional stage in considerable numbers with their own music, dance, and verbal styles. The operetta—a popular European musical form—and the infectious music of ragtime were the vehicle and engine of a new American musical form that in the 1890s began to supplant the minstrel show.

The first Black musical comedy to break with the old minstrel pattern was Bob Cole and William "Billy" Johnson's *A Trip to Coontown* (1897), a takeoff on the popular white show, *A Trip to Chinatown*. During the next ten years, nearly ninety African American musicals appeared, initiated by an amazingly talented group of writers and musicians: Paul Laurence Dunbar, the Whitman Sisters, James Weldon and Rosamund Johnson, Jesse A. Shipp, Bob Cole, Sisseretta

Jones, Bert Williams, George Walker, Ada Overton, Will Marion Cook, Lottie Walker, and the duo of Tutt and Whitney. Among the most popular shows, performed mostly for white audiences, were *Clorindy, The Origin of the Cakewalk* (1898), *Senegambian Carnival* (1898), *Jes' Lak White Fo'ks* (1900), *The Sons of Ham* (1900–1902), *The Smart Set* (1901), *In Dahomey* (1902), *The Shoo-Fly Regiment* (1905), *Abyssinia* (1906), *The Man from 'Bam* (1906), and *Bandana Land* (1907). By 1910, even the *Ziegfeld Follies* employed the comic talents of Bert Williams, who dreamed of roles in serious drama: "Let us have a Negro drama such as Shakespeare might have written. . . . And let us raise a Negro Booth to interpret it."

In those "optimistic" years, many African Americans succeeded in some businesses and professions that had been previously closed to them, including the theatre. The pessimism of *No Place to Be Somebody* had not yet infected Black America.

IN DAHOMEY
1902

Jesse A. Shipp, book (c.1869–1934)
Will Marion Cook, music (1869–1944)
Paul Laurence Dunbar, lyrics (1872–1906)

Soon after the end of slavery, African American singers and dancers began to perform in theatrical companies. Frequently they would appear in "colored" minstrel shows that toured the country from coast to coast, or would perform their specialities in dime museum vaudeville shows. One troupe, the Hyers Sisters Combination, toured with a different kind of show: a full-length musical. The sisters, managed by their father, presented, with some success, several full-length shows during the 1870s and 1880s, including *Out of Bondage, The Underground Railroad,* and *Urlina, The African Princess.* In 1890, a white Chicago theatre owner, Sam Jack, and the Black minstrel and vaudevillian, Sam Lucas, developed a minstrel show that included women performers in its song and dance. Their show, *The Creole Burlesque Show,* was so successful that it played in Chicago for nine weeks during the 1893 Columbian Exposition, and in

1896 was still on the road playing to mixed audiences.

By 1896, several more musical shows were crisscrossing the country. The most important of these were *South Before the War* (produced by Whalen and Martell) and *The Octoroons* and *Oriental America* (produced by John W. Isham). Many of the young Black performers of the period polished their routines in these touring shows, as well as in the vaudeville and minstrel shows in which they appeared during the off-season.

One successful team of singing and dancing comedians, Egbert (Bert) Williams (1876–1921) and George Walker (1872–1911), appeared at Koster and Bial's Music Hall in New York City—one of the first Black acts to do so—where they received accolades from many critics. From 1898 to 1901, they starred in several full-length touring shows: *A Lucky Coon* (1898), *The Policy Players* (1899), and *Sons of Ham*

(1900–01). All of these shows revolved around low comedy plot situations, and included opportunities for the entire cast to perform their specialities. In *Sons of Ham*, for example, Williams and Walker, in an attempt to fleece a rich Black man, impersonate two college students, Annie and Jennie, whom they assume, on the basis of the names, to be his daughters. When his real children show up, they are revealed to be sons whose names are really Aniesta Babdola and Jenarusha Hassambad. Furthermore, they are jugglers, since the parts were originally played by a team of jugglers, the Reese brothers.

In 1902, Williams and Walker teamed up with writer Jesse A. Shipp, composer Will Marion Cook, and lyricist Paul Laurence Dunbar to produce a new show, *In Dahomey*. As was the theatre practice in those days, the creators reused lyrics from their earlier songs, brought in other composers to assemble a script that combined low comedy, ethnic jokes, and references to current social and political events. The names of the characters are drawn from minstrelsy. Reading through the program, one meets Shylock Homestead, a detective of sorts, whose name is certainly derived from Sherlock Holmes, the most famous fictional detective of the day. "Dr. Straight (in name only), street fakir," who is a faker, that is, a con man who runs a fraudulent lotion and cream scam; "George Reeder, proprietor of an intelligence office," who is literate (a reader) and can sift through official documents; "Leather, a bootblack," and so on.

During the opening scene, Dr. Straight is attempting to persuade the crowd that his products, "Straightaline" and "Oblicutucus," are the best hair straighteners and skin lighteners, respectively, on earth. To African Americans in the audience, this scene was a satire of the many advertisements that appeared in Black newspapers of the day. Similarly, in act 2, scene 2, Shy-

lock's friend, Rareback, tells of the exploits of Nick Carter and Old Sleuth. The satirical references here refer to the dime-novel detective, Nick Carter, whose Indiana Jones-like adventures were read by large segments of the audience that attended those shows, and to the pseudonymous author of mystery novels, "Old Sleuth." Rareback's story is so incredible that Shylock has difficulty in accepting it, and forgoes hearing the conclusion. In act 2, scene 3, in a more serious vein, the playwright Jesse Shipp recounts some of the difficulties faced by ex-slaves in their dealings with whites, when Mr. and Mrs. Lightfoot voice their feelings over whether their benefactor should be called "Master (or Mars') John" or "Mr. Goodman."

During its four-year run, *In Dahomey* was altered significantly. Several of the songs mentioned in this script were dropped in favor of new songs, and the final act, a pantomimed transformation scene (the version printed here) that left audiences somewhat confused was moved to the beginning of the show to serve as a prologue. Although Paul Laurence Dunbar and Will Marion Cook are named as lyricist and composer, respectively, they were not the only writers of the songs that were performed during the run of the show. Some songs, such as Harry Von Tilzer's "I Wants to be a Actor Lady," were interpolated, and others were written by the musicians who replaced Cook as conductor when he moved on to new projects.

At the turn of the century, the most popular songs from musicals were published as sheet music. A few composers, including Victor Herbert, were lucky enough to have all the music to some of their shows published in piano-vocal score. From all the Black musicals produced before 1920, *In Dahomey* is the only one that had a relatively complete score published. Surprisingly, it was not published in the United States, but in Great Britain, where the show, with Williams and Walker starring, played for eight months and gave a command performance before the royal family. Although this score represents only one early version of *In Dahomey*, it is still an important artifact since it is the most complete extant version.[1]

The songs in *In Dahomey* are characteristic of the many popular tunes around 1900. Some of Cook's songs reflect his training as a classical composer and violinist; for the close of the first scene of act 2, for example, he wrote "Society" in Viennese high operetta style. Others came from more popular genres. The finale, "The Czar of Dixie," was in the latest American vernacular style, ragtime. Similarly, the lyrics display a variety of styles. But Cook and Dunbar also use dialect as a device to represent class distinctions. Thus, in the opening of act 1, the chorus sings in dialect to reflect on the status of the "new Negro":

> Swing along chillun, swing along de lane,
> Lif' yo' head an' yo' heels mighty high.
> Swing along chillun, 'tain't a goin' to rain,

Sun's as red as de rose, in de sky,
Come along Mandy, come along Sue,
White fo'ks awatchin' an' seein' what yo' do,
White fo'ks jealous when you'se walkin' two by two.

For the educated daughter of Cicero Lightfoot, however, the lyric is high art:

> Love looks not at estate, oh No!
> 'Twere folly one should think it so.
> The beggar maid become a queen
> Who through her lover's eyes is seen.

Although some earlier Black shows and their stars caught the public's attention, *In Dahomey* was the first full-length Black musical to make its stars, Bert Williams and George Walker, household names. It was also the first African American show that synthesized successfully the various genres of American musical theatre popular at the beginning of the twentieth century—minstrelsy, vaudeville, comic opera, and musical comedy.

—*John Graziano*

In Dahomey, a Negro Musical Comedy

Songs published in England in the 1902 edition

In Dahomey, a Negro Musical Comedy
Book by Jesse A. Shipp
Lyrics by Paul L. Dunbar and others
Music by Will Marion Cook
Keith, Prowse & Co. Ltd., 48 Cheapside, London, E.C.
Copyright 1903 by W. M. Cooke, New York

Time: Three months before beginning of play.
Place: Dahomey.

Characters

Je-Je-, a Caboceer . . . Charles Moore
Menuki, messenger of the king . . . Wm. Elkins
Moses Lightfoot, agent of Dahomey Colonization Society . . . Wm. Barker
Shylock Homestead, called "Shy" by his friends . . . Bert A. Williams
Rareback Punkerton, "Shy's" personal friend and adviser . . . Geo. W. Walker
Cicero Lightfoot, President of a Colonization Society . . . Pete Hampton

---

1. Several songs in the English score are not identified in this version of the book. See addendum at the end of the play for the texts of additional songs, which at some later or earlier point were in the play.

Dr. Straight . . . in name only, street fakir . . . Fred Douglas

George Reeder, proprietor of an intelligence office . . . Alex Rogers

Henry Stampfield, letter carrier, with an argument against immigration . . . Walter Richardson

Me Sing, a Chinese cook . . . Geo. Catlin

Hustling Charley, promoter of Get-the-Coin Syndicate . . . J. A. Shipp

Leather, a bootblack . . . Richard Connors

Officer Still . . . J. Leubrie Hill

White Wash Man . . . Green Tapley

Messenger Rush, but not often . . . Theodore Pankey

Pansy, daughter of Cecilia Lightfoot, in love with Leather . . . Abbie Mitchell

Cecilia Lightfoot, Cicero's wife . . . Mrs. Hattie McIntosh

Mrs. Stringer, dealer in forsaken patterns, also editor of fashion notes in *Beanville Agitator* . . . Mrs. Lottie Williams

Rosetta Lightfoot, a troublesome young thing . . . Aida Overton Walker

Colonists, Natives, etc.

Synopsis

Prologue. Scene . . . Garden of Caboceer, governor of a province

Act I . . . Public Square, Boston

Act II . . . Scene 1 . . . Exterior of Lightfoot's home, Gatorville, Florida

Scene 2 . . . Road, one and a half miles from Gatorville

Scene 3 . . . Interior of Lightfoot's home

CONTENTS

Overture . . . "The Attuck's March"

No. 1 song . . . My Dahomian Queen

No. 2 chorus . . . Caboceers' Entrance

Act I

No. 3 Opening Chorus . . . Swing Along

No. 4 song . . . Molly Green

No. 5 song . . . On Broadway in Dahomey Bye and Bye

Act II

No. 6 song . . . I Wants to be a Actor Lady

No. 7 song . . . Brown Skin Baby Mine

No. 8 song . . . Leader of the Colored Aristocracy

No. 9. Solo & Chorus . . . Society

No. 10 song . . . I'm a Jonah Man

No. 11 Chorus and Solo . . . The Czar

No. 12 song . . . On Emancipation Day, Song

No. 13 song . . . On Emancipation Day, March

No. 14 Cake Walk . . . Chocolate Drops

No. 15 Jig . . . Jig

No. 16 Cake Walk . . . Happy Jim

No. 17. song . . . That's How the Cake Walk's Done

No. 18. March (two-step & a cake walk) . . . Ragtime Drummer

ACT I

SCENE 1:

(Public Square with a house doorway. Above the door is a sign: "Intelligence Office." A crowd is assembled around a medicine show pitchman. Applause at rise of curtain. A banjo player acts as an interlocutor as Tambo, and Bones tell one or two jokes. The banjoist sings a song. Dr. Straight, the pitchman, addresses the crowd.)

DR. STRAIGHT   After listening to great attempts at beautiful strains of melodious music and a pyrotechnical display of humorous humorosities, quintessence of brevity rather than prolix verbosity, will best accomplish the purpose for which I appear here this evening. Now that I've made everything so plain that even a child can understand, I'll proceed with business. I hold here in my hand a preparation made from roots, herbs, barks, leaf grasses, cereals, vegetables, fruits and chemicals warranted, by myself, to do all that I claim, even more. I'm not here to sell this article but simply to advertise the greatest boon that mankind has ever known. I will forfeit one thousand dollars to—hold up the money so that they can see it *(attendants hold up a large sack marked $1000)*—or I will take the same amount from any dark skin son or daughter of the genius [1] Africanus that I cannot immediately transform into an Apollo or Cleopatra with a hirsute appendage worthy of a Greek goddess.

VOICE *(interrupting)* Look here, Mr. Medicine man, if you 'specs to sell any of dem bottles of whatever you've got there to anybody in this crowd, you'd better bring your language down to the limitations of a universal understanding. I've been standin' here ten minutes tryin' to figger out what you're talkin' about and I tell you as the old maxim says, "Patience ceases to be virtuous."

DR. S. Your patience shall be rewarded. I'll come to the point at once. This compound known as Straightaline is the greatest hair tonic on earth. What will Straightaline do? Why it cures dandruff, tetter itch, and all scalp diseases at once and forever. It makes hair grow on bald-headed babies. It makes curly hair as straight as a stick in from one to ten days. Straightaline straightens kinky hair in from ten to thirty days and most wonderful of all, Straightaline straightens knappy or knotty hair. *(he hesitates)*

VOICE Well?

DR. S. In three days.

VOICE I'll take a bottle of dat.

DR. S. Wait, wait, wait, this is not all. I have another preparation, Oblicuticus, "Obli"—in this case, being an abbreviation of the word "obliterate." "Cuti"—taken from the word "cuticle," the outer skin, and "cuss" is what everybody does when the desired results are not obtained, but there is no such word as "fail." This wonderful face bleach removes the outer skin and leaves in its place a peachlike complexion that can't be duplicated—even by peaches. Changing black to white and vice versa. I am going to spend only one day in your city, but I am going to convince you by exhibiting a living evidence of my assertions that these two grand preparations, *Straightaline* and *Obliquities* are the most wonderful discovery of modern times. *(attendant stands up)*[2] This young man is a martyr to science. Here you have the work of nature. Here the work of art. Here is the kinky hair here. *(stage business with hair and skin color)* The long, silky straight hair, here the bronze of nature, here the peachlike complexion. Remember, I leave here tomorrow for Gatorville, Florida.

VOICES Give me a bottle, give me a bottle.

DR. S. Wait a minute—I'm not here to sell, I'm only advertising these two grand articles, *Straightaline* and *Obliticus,* and after dispensing with a few coin of the realm, if you will accompany me to Skinners, I will place a few bottles of Straightaline and Obliticus at your disposal. Mind you, I'm not here to sell but to advertise. I'm not here to make money, but to give it away. *(he throws coins and exits. A quartet—The Barbers Society of Philosophical Research—enters and sings "Annie Laurie")*[3]

> Maxwelton's braes are bonnie, Where early fa's the dew,
> And 'twas there that Annie Laurie gave me her promise true.
> Which ne'er forgot will be, and for bonnie Annie Laurie
> I'd lay me doon and dee.

MOSE LIGHTFOOT *(calcium artist[4] in the summer, member of the B.S. of P.R. in winter)* I do think the colored race is the biggest set of fools I ever cast my optics against.

(Enter HENRY STAMPFIELD, *letter carrier, from the door of the Intelligence Office.)*

STAMPFIELD Hello. Mose, what are you kicking about?

MOSE Ain't kickin' at all. Got both feet restin' right on the ground whar they belong. I'se just naturally disgusted with the frivolities of the colored population of dis country.

STAMP You shouldn't let trifles annoy you. I'll dare say you'll find the population of Dahomey quite as much a source of annoyance as the colored population of this country. Your exalted opinion of the ideal life to be found in a barbarous country is beyond my comprehension.

MOSE It's all right for you, son, to argue that way, 'cause you 'specs to live and die amongst these white folks here in the United States, but the colonization society that leaves this country for Dahomey takes a different view of the matter. In the first place, we've

---

1. The authors frequently pun on words by using malapropisms.

2. The attendant is possibly made up to be half white and half black.

3. A Scots ballad popular with quartets because of possibilities for harmony.

4. "Calcium artist" may refer to the man who puts a solution of calamine on his skin to make it appear white. Several years later, a film starring Bert Williams features a group credited as the "Calomine Artists."

'vestigated the country and found out just what's what.

STAMP   In other words, the existing conditions.

MOSE   *(doubtfully)* Yes. Everything points to success. They tell me that gold and silver in Dahomey is plentiful, as the whiskey is on election day in Bosting [Boston]. The climate's fine—just the right thing for raisin' chickens and watermelons. It never snows so you don't need no clothes *(pauses)* such as the people wear here, and who know but what you can get a few franchises from the king to start street cars, 'lectric lights and saloons to running.

STAMP   You've fine, big ideas, but suppose the natives suddenly don't take kindly to the new order of things and refuse to be electric lighted, salooned and otherwise fixed up with blessings of civilization. Suppose they look upon you as intruders and instead of receiving you with open arms *(pause)* make war on you.

MOSE   *(slowly)* If it comes to that, we'll arrange with dem gentlemen like Uncle Sam did with the Indians.

STAMP   How is that?

MOSE   Kick the stuffin' out of dem and put them on a reservation.

(GEORGE REEDER, who runs the Intelligence Office, enters and crosses as if to enter the office.)

STAMP   Hello, there Reeder. I've got a registered letter for you. I was just in the office, but didn't like to leave it. *(business of signing receipts, etc.)*

REEDER   I suppose you and Mose were having one of your regulation arguments about Dahomey, eh?

STAMP   Bye the bye, when does the Colonization Society leave for Dahomey?

REEDER   They don't go direct from here to Dahomey. They leave here tomorrow for Gatorville, Florida, where they join the main body. I don't know when they start for Dahomey. I may go along myself. The fact of the matter is, they are in session in my office at this moment.

MOSE   *(STAMP starts to exit but MOSE interrupts)* Just wait a minute, Stampfield. I forgot to give you this letter. It's for my brother. You know he's the fountain head of this whole scheme to go to Dahomey. It's the only thing we ever did agree on. *(voices inside as if quarreling)* That's the first argument I've missed since I've been a member of the Society. *(exit MOSE)*

STAMP   Well, Reeder, if you do go to Dahomey, accept my best wishes for success. So long.

(He exits. Enter the quartet singing "Annie Laurie." They cross the stage and exit, the singing dying out by degrees.)

REEDER   Well, that's a jolly crowd. *(looking in the direction of the singers. Enter MRS. STRINGER, a widow and a clothes dealer in forsaken patterns).*

MRS. STRINGER   Yes, they couldn't help but be jolly. They haven't got anything on their mind but their hair.

REEDER   Mrs. Stringer. *(bows politely)*

MRS. S.   Has anyone asked for me during my absence?

REEDER   Only Mrs. Waite.

MRS. S.   It's a wonder she wouldn't get tired of that.

REEDER   Of what?

MRS. S.   Of calling when I'm out, and keeping me waiting for that little bill that's been standing nearly two months. She owes me for the biggest bargain that ever slipped through my fingers. I sold her a silk dress worth three dollars and twenty-five cents a yard that belonged to Mrs. Mountine for a beggarly twelve dollars, and she still owes me ten dollars and ninety-eight cents of that. A bargain debt. I don't see what service a dress that Mrs. Mountine could wear would be to a tiny little woman like Mrs. Waite.

REEDER   Why, Mrs. Mountine weights 250 pounds if she weighs an ounce and Mrs. Waite not more than 115 pounds or twenty pounds at the most.

MRS. S.   Yes, but Mrs. Waite has three children—all girls. *(if audience doesn't catch on, add the following)* And there's enough goods in that dress to make them all dresses. Don't you know, Mrs. Reeder, I've got a notion to take advantage of the cheap rate that the Dahomian Colonization Society is getting from here to Gatorville, Florida. I've got a lot of dresses of good material but ancient as to style I might dispose of. You know they are still wearing *(name something fashionable about eight or ten years ago)* in Florida.

REEDER   Not a bad idea at all. I'm thinking of going myself. If you make up your mind, let me know.

MRS. S.   *(starting to enter the office)* Mr. Reeder. *(coquettish)*

REEDER   Mrs. Stringer *(bowing. Exit* MRS. STRINGER*)* Clever woman *(opens letter)* Now we'll see who this is from. *(reads aloud)* Mr. intelligence man . . . *(turns letter over and looks at address)* Send to my address at once two detectives Box 13, Gatorville, Florida. I lost last Friday, which was the thirteenth of the month, a silver casket with a cat drawed on the outside and a cat's eyes on the inside. A friend of mine give me your address and said you could furnish anything from a Chinese laundry to a bull pup, and that is why I write to you for a couple of detectives. Inclosed find second-class fare for detectives and two dollars extra if they find the cat's eye, as it is very valuable. P.S. Don't forget to send the detectives. Respectfully yours, Cicero Lightfoot, Box 13, Gatorville, Florida. *(laughs)* Alright, Mr. Lightfoot, I'll try and look out for your case. *(exits)*

(Salvation Army in the distance sing "There's a Land . . ." Enter cross stage from left to right; exits for about ten seconds, then enters with bass drum large enough to obscure view of SHYLOCK HOMESTEAD, singing and beating drum. Business. Enter RAREBACK. Business. Laughs)[5]

RAREBACK   What are you doing, ah, ah *(laughs)* What's the . . . what's the . . . *(laughs)* What's the matter? Where'd you get that suit of clothes and what are you doing with that drum? *(stops laughing by degrees)*

SHYLOCK   Ha, ha, it's funny, ain't it?

RARE   Don't get mad because I laugh, but on the level, you're a sight . . . *(laughs)* that coat . . . *(laughs)* but you know, I'm your friend. *(extends hand as if to shake hands. SHYLOCK refuses)*

SHY   Go on away, go on away. Every dog has his day, and you've had more 'n' your share,

and I've figured out your case to a focus. The more days a dog has, the more days a dog wants, and you've jest naturally got dog enough in you to want every day.

RARE   You ain't mad sure enough, are you, Shy? See, I call you by the name that Mother used to call you, Shy. You ain't mad are you, Sherry? *(burlesque pathos)*

SHY   No, I ain't mad. I've been laughing every since we got off that boat we come up on from down south. Ha, ha, ha. *(sarcastically)* I'm laughing 'cause I worked all the winter and then got worked for every cent I made while I was on the boat coming up here. I'm laughing 'cause three days after I git in town after workin' all the winter, I've got to blow the bass drum in the Salvation Army to keep from starving to death.

RARE   Well, it ain't my fault that you've got that drum. Neither is it my fault that you worked all the winter and haven't got anything now. I told you not to speculate with your money.

SHY   Spec-a-late! Spec-a-late! Den I didn't lose my money shootin' craps? I lost it speculatin'?

RARE   It won't do any good for you and I to squabble over what can't be helped. I'm in just as bad a fix as you are, and I believe all our bad luck came through the silver box I got hold of just about three hours before we struck the wharf.

SHY   I don't know nothin' about *our* bad luck, but I do know all about *my* bad luck, when the man came on board the boat with that rusty lookin' coat on and wanted to sell that silver box, I was the fust man that reached out my hand to get it, but jist as soon as I seen dat a cat was scratched on the back, I turned round three times, walked backwards four steps, throwed a hand full of salt over my left shoulder, and I give him back that box so quick, if I was superstitious, I'd a swore I seen that cat's whiskers move.

RARE   Shy, did you see inside that box?

SHY   No sah, the outside was enough for me.

RARE   There was a cat's eye in that box and it looked as if the eye was alive.

SHY   You know a cat's got nine lives anyhow, and if that cat's eye ain't been dead but once, it's got eight more chances. Look here,

---

5. Lyrics for Salvation Army song were not provided. Any reference to "business" means comic improvisation.

you ain't got that thing in your pocket now have you?

RARE   No, I just left the fellow that I sold it to just before we got off the boat. Do you remember how many times that box changed hands before I got hold of it?

SHY   Yes, fust that man with the rusty yaller coat offered to sell it for a dollar and six bits, then I come purty near havin' it. Say, don't you know every time I think of how near I come to havin' that box, it gives me the shivers.

RARE   Why? You ain't superstitious.

SHY   Not excruciatingly, but then cats is bad luck, and that's all there is to it, but to get back to the subject, he finally sold the box for six bits and that bowlegged cook that bought it had that box just thirteen minutes when he got broke, and the man he sold it to had thirteen dollars, and after speculatin' with a cross-eyed barber about four minutes, the thirteen dollars and the box changed hands again. Jist about that time I begun speculatin' myself, and I lost sight of it until I saw you with it jist before the boat landed. After the boat landed, it was a case of root hog or die til I struck a job blowin' the drum.

RARE   You don't blow a drum, you beat a drum.

SHY   If you carried this drum far as I did, you'd know there's a lot of blowin' attached to this job. Yes, I'm blowing this drum.

RARE   Well, we won't argue whether you beat or blow the drum. The financial question interests me more than anything else. You haven't got a cent. Neither have I. What are we going to do?

SHY   I'm goin' to keep my job in the Salvation Army.

RARE   (*pathetically*) Shy, I don't like to hear you talk that way. We've been with each other all our lives. It's been a little rocky at times, I'll admit, but we've always managed to pull through our good luck and our bad luck, our sunshine and our rain, but we've shared them all alike (*pauses*) together.

SHY   (*about to cry*) You knowed I didn't have a cent when I got off that boat and to-day's the fust time in three days I've put my feet under a table. (*pauses to wipe away a tear. RAREBACK also wipes a tear away*) Then I didn't have nothin' but pork and beans. (*business*)

REEDER   (*Enters from Intelligence Office, letter in hand. He starts as if to leave, but stops and meditatively notices SHYLOCK and RAREBACK*) I wonder if . . . by Joe, I'll ask them anyway. (*RARE and SHY start to leave*) Gentlemen, just a minute. Are you looking for work?

SHY   Not if we can find anything else to do.

RARE   (*pushing SHY back*) Yes (*slowly*), we would like to have a job.

SHY   Yes, we'd like to have a job, but we weren't lookin' for no work.

RARE   Shut up! Let me talk to the gentleman. We are not engaged at the present time and wouldn't mind something light.

REEDER   My name is Reeder.

RARE   And mine is Rareback Punkerton. Allow me to introduce my friend, Shylock.

REEDER   A strange coincidence. One might almost say your names were synonyms with the position I'm about to offer you.

SHY   If the job's as heavy as the language, excuse me.

RARE   Go ahead, Mr. Reeder.

REEDER   I want a little private detective work done in connection with this letter I hold here in my hand. I'll explain. An old gentleman living in Gatorville, Florida, being a little superstitious (*business for RARE and SHY*) has lost an insignificant article to which he sets great store. He considers the article of inestimable value and has offered a reward of five hundred dollars for its return. Now, I've come to the conclusion that the old man in question has not lost the article, but being overcareful, he has hidden the aforesaid article from himself, as it were. So I think by careful search you would very likely find the article among some of his effects that he had overlooked; however, he imagines it has been stolen.

RARE   I guess we could handle the case, eh, Sherry?

SHY   Well, I hope so, John.

REEDER   The lost article is a silver casket.

SHY   What's he talkin' about, a coffin?

REEDER   The casket in this instance happens to be a little silver box. Beautifully ornamented on the center of a perfectly smooth and highly polished surface is engraved a cat. (*SHY funny fall business*) What's the matter with your friend?

RARE   He has cat-aleptic fits.

REEDER   If you will step in the office, we will talk the matter over. (*starts inside*)

SHY   You go on and be a detective. I'll keep my job in the Salvation Army. *(picks up drum)*

REEDER   How's that?

RARE   Go right ahead, Mr. Reeder. We'll join you in a few minutes. *(exit* REEDER. RAREBACK *snatches the drum from* SHY *and joyfully exclaims)* You don't want that drum now. You don't know when you're in good luck. The silver box he's talking about is the one I sold the fellow that I just left down in Graball's saloon. We'll go down there, bring him up here. You go in and borrow three dollars from Reeder, buy the box, but we won't tell Reeder we've got it. Then we'll go down to Gatorville, Florida, for a bluff, live a week in clover, then give the old man the box and get the five hundred, eh? *(slaps* SHY *on the shoulder)*

SHY   Get the money first. The way you tell that sounds so natural. I could feel myself separatin' that old man from that five hundred . . . if it wasn't for that cat.

RARE   Instead of being bad luck, a cat turns out to be the best friend we ever had. After this you ought to hug and kiss every cat you run across.

SHY   I've got to admit if it wasn't for that cat's picture, you couldn't tell that box from no other silver box; therefore, I'm bound to respect cats but no fust-class detective ain't goin' round huggin' and kissin' cats, no matter how much he respects them. *(*RAREBACK *starts to exit just before* SHYLOCK *finishes: Song "Ambulance")*[6]

MRS. STRINGER   *(from a window to a passerby)* Excuse me, but would you please knock on that Chinaman's door for me.[7]

PASSERBY   *(knocking on the door of the Chinese restaurant)* Say! *(the door opens. Chink [sic] singing inside doesn't answer at once. Passerby calls again loudly)* Say, if you've got time to stop hitting that pipe, there's a lady across the street that wants you!

ME SING   *(Chink [sic]* ME SING *appears with pipe [Chinese tobacco] in hand)* You get away. I call policeman.

PASSERBY   Get out, you pigtail. You've got rats in your kitchen.[8] *(exit laughing. Chinaman continues quarreling in dialect)*

MRS. S.   *(calling loudly)* Me Sing, Me Sing! Never mind the man. Bring me something to eat. I'm starving.

ME SING   What do you want?

MRS. S.   Bring me some Chinese ham and eggs. *(addressing friends)* What do you want? *(to* ME SING) One order of bird's nest soup. *(addressing friend number two)* and you? *(to* ME SING) And one order of shark fins. Be sure and bring over sugar for the tea and above all things, hurry.

ME SING   *(repeats the orders in dialect and exits. "Song of the Colonization Society")*[9]

MOSE   The five minute recess has been revoked, and your presence is requested on the inside. *(After song, enter* RAREBACK, SHYLOCK, *and* HUSTLING CHARLIE, *arm in arm boisterously)*

HUSTLING CHARLIE   Why there's nothin' to it. I'm goin' to join this Colonization Society, blow over to Africa with them and get the money. Just imagine reading this over the door, "Hustling Charlie, Keeper of the Royal Dice Box to his Majesty Ruben, the First King of Dahomey," eh, boys?

RARE   I never heard of this scheme before. Tell us about it. *(business of* RAREBACK *and* SHY *looking for box)*

SHY   Yes, explain the circumstances.

HUSTLING C.[10]   Well, there's a society down in Florida that's been pilin' up coin for years. Now that they're flush, they're goin' to go blow. They ain't satisfied to see their noodles ain't swelled on account of their dough, but they figure this country's a dead one. Some bloke tipped off Dahomey as the original Klondike and they're goin' against the brace, hook, line, and sinker. I'm goin' to steer the gang down to Gatorville where the main Gazaboo of the whole push hangs out. Say, fellows, I get two dollars a head from the captain of the dugout that snatches 'em away from this burg, and I've got a contract with a medicine shark, in all cases of sea sickness, we split the purse fifty-fifty. If anybody pegs out on the trip, I've got an undertaker waitin' at the wharf that gives me 35 percent of the net. Am I asleep at the switch, ask me?

---

6. The lyrics for "Ambulance" were not included in this version.

7. Racial slurs used in minstrelsy were commonly against the Chinese, Jews, Dutch (Germans), and Italians.

8. Chinese eating rats was a Westerner's stereotype of Asians.

9. The lyrics for "Colonization Society" were not included in this text.

10. Hustling Charlie's speech may be the first printed record of Black urban slang on stage.

RARE   Shy and me are going down to Gatorville on a little business ourselves. If you'll let us in on that graft of yours, we might make that trip to Dahomey.

HUSTLING C.   *(starting to leave the office)* Well, I'll think it over. I've got some business inside, boys.

SHY   Wait a minute, Hustler, I've got a little business with you outside. You remember that box with a cat scratched on the back?

HUSTLING C.   Yes, what about it?

SHY   I was just thinkin'. I was just thinkin'. *(business)*

HUSTLING C.   Thinkin' what?

SHY   I'd like to have that box for a watch charm and I'll give you three dollars for it, cash money. *(RAREBACK laughs)* What you laughin' at? You sich a fine detective, I guess you kin get it for two dollars. *(RAREBACK continues to laugh)*

HUSTLING C.   I'm sorry I haven't got it, boys. I just sold it to a fellow that was going aboard on a ship that was about to sail. He just got there as they was pullin' in the gang plank.

SHY   Is you sure the fellow that went up that gang plank is the one you sold the box to that had the cat scratched on the back?

HUSTLING C.   No chance to be mistaken.

SHY   When he went up the gang plank, did he have this box with the cat scratched on the back—in his hand?

HUSTLING C.   Say, since I come to think of it, he had a big satchel in one hand, he was fishin' around in his pockets with the other hand, and the box in his mouth. Say, I'm goin' inside. I'll see you when I come out.

RARE   What in the world did you ask all those questions for?

SHY   What's the use of being a detective if you can't ask questions even if you do know it won't do no good.

RARE   Well, Sherry, we'll have to keep up our bluff anyway, so we'll go down to Gatorville, Florida, make old man Lightfoot think we are looking for the box he lost, and if we're lucky, we may get a chance to go to Dahomey with this emigration society.

SHY   Say, man, have you got any idea how fast you'se carryin' me through life. Ten minutes ago, I was a soldier in the Salvation Army. Five minutes after that I'm a detective, and now you want me to be an emigrant.

RARE   *(laughing)* Stick to me and after we're in Dahomey six months if you like it, I'll buy it for you. I'll tell the King over there that I'm a surveyor, and you're a contractor. If he asks for a recommendation, I'll tell him to go over to New York City and take a look at Broadway— it's the best job the firm ever did, and if he don't mind, we'll build him a Broadway in the jungle. *(song)*

Broadway in the Jungle[11]

If we went to Dahomey, suppose the King would say
We want a Broadway built for us, we want it right away.
We'd git a bunch of natives, say ten thousand or more
Wid banyan trees, build a big department store.
We'd sell big Georgia possums, some water melons, too
To get the coin for other things we'd like to do.
If we couldn't have real horse cars, we'd use zebras for awhile
On the face of the Broadway clock, use a crock-o-(dial).

[CHORUS]
On Broadway in Dahomey bye and bye
We'll build a Bamboo Railway to the sky.
You'll see on the sides of the rocks and hills,
"Use Carter's Little Liver Pills."[12]
On Broadway in Dahomey bye and bye.

We'd git some large Gorillas and use them for police,
then git a Hippopotamus for Justice of the Peace.
We'd build a nice roof garden somewhere along the line,
Serve Giraffe Highballs and real Cokenut wine.
We'd use Montana Diamonds to make Electric light,
And then have Wagner sung by parrots ev'ry night.
We'd have a savage festival, serve Rhine-os-e-rus stew,
Have pork chops and U-need-a Biscuit too.

(Chorus)

---

11. Words by Alex Rogers and music by Al Johns, this song appears in the published score but not the text of the play.

12. Carter's Little Liver Pills was one of the first big national advertising campaigns for a patented medicine in America. In the second verse, "U-need-a Biscuit" was another widely advertised product.

On Broadway in Dahomey bye and bye,
None but the Royal blood can qualify.
Mister Noah wid de ark and all his guests,
Will p'rade each night sixteen abreast,
On Broadway in Dahomey bye and bye.

(*Curtain*)

ACT II

Scene 1:

(*Exterior of* LIGHTFOOT *home, garden of the summer house. Chorus sings "For Florida."*)

For Florida our home so bright.
Our voices ring with true delight.
From verdant vale to arid stand,
She is for 'ere a summer land.
Her tree, her rocks, her streamlets clear,
To all our loyal hearts are dear.
So let us sing it loud and long,
For Florida, a song, a song.

We are the children of the sun.
Upon our brows His work is done.
Tho' rude and black our faces be,
Our hearts are brave, our hands are free.
And as we sing, so shall we strive,
As long as loyalty's alive.
Our hearts, our arms, our souls, hurrah,
For Florida! For Florida!

(*Enter from the house,* CICERO LIGHTFOOT *in shirt sleeves and apron, spoon in hand*)

CICERO Dat song expresses my sentiments to the letter. After all, there ain't no place like Florida.

MOSE 'Ceptin' Dahomey, but outside of Dahomey and Boston, I endorse your statements.

CICERO I don't know nothin' about no other place 'cept Florida. It might be the worse place in the world, but whether it's worst or best, it's home, and, Mose (*cautiously*), if Dahomey pulls up shy, I'm comin' back here. (*loudly*) Now folks, jist make yourself at home. I got a little business to 'tend to. Come on, Moses, I want to show you the first possum that ever greased his face with a persimmon.

MOSE Go on, Cicero, you ain't got a possum, have you?

CICERO I jest this minute got through basting him.

MOSE Did you press a few sweet potatoes around his ribs?

CICERO Come on, man, you wastin' your breath. Did I press a few sweet potatoes around his ribs? Why no respectable possum wouldn't stay in a pan where there wasn't no sweet potatoes. Come on, man.

MOSE (*addressing friends*) Excuse me, folks. I'm gwine to inspect the leading feature of this birthday party.

CHORUS What's that?

MOSE (*loudly*) A possum.

(*Exit all in a rush—"We want to see, etc." Introduce Rosetta Lightfoot with song*[13] *as she enters with wheelbarrow. There's a looking glass in barrow. Whistling, she removes looking glass and rolls the barrow behind the summer house. Business with looking glass*)[14]

I Wants to be a Actor Lady[15]
Mad about the stage was Carrie Brown,
She served at a draper's shop in town;
Each new piece they play'd,
There you'd find this maid
First night in the gall'ry sitting down.
Carrie could recite, "The Soldier's Dream";
All the shopgirls held her in esteem,
For in the dining hall
She would entertain them all,
And, when applauded, she would almost scream:

[CHORUS]
I wants to be a actor lady
Playing, you know,
Star in the show;
Spotlight for me; no back row shady;
I'm the real thing;
I dance and sing;

---

13. In the text, there is no indication for the name of this song. As the role of Rosetta was played by Ada Overton Walker, she may have sung "Vassar Girl," a song she had made famous in *Sons of Ham,* and which was published in the London *In Dahomey* score. Another song for which she was known, "I Wants to be a Actor Lady," was published in the London score. At different times, she may have sung either, or a third song, "She's Dancing Sue." Here, the editors print the first two.

14. Her pantomime with the mirror was widely praised by critics.

15. The lyrics with their English stage references clearly indicate that the song was in the London production where it was sung with great success by Ada Overton Walker. Words by Vincent Bryan. English version by Arthur Trevelyen. Music by Harry von Tilzer.

Miss Terry may make Shakespeare go,
But she can't sing, "Flo from Pimlico,"
And I wants to be a actor lady too—indeed I do!
Carrie said that Shakespeare was an ass,
Barrie wasn't bad, but still no class;
"If George Sims," said she,
"Wrote a play for me,
You to see me act could get no pass."
"Over my dead body first, you cur!
Death to life with you, I much prefer!"
"Farewell, Claude, we must part!
You have broke my trusting heart!"
With lines like them I'd make all London stir.

(Chorus)

I wants to be a actor lady
Playing you know,
Star in the show;
Spotlight for me, no back row shady,
I'm the real thing,
I dance and sing;
Miss Mary Moore is splendid truly,
But she can't warble "Mister Dooley;"
I wants to be a actor lady too—indeed I do!

Carrie wrote to Mister Beerbohm Tree:
"Though to you I may a stranger be,
When your season starts,
Of the ladies' parts
Give the most important one to me;
Olga Nethersole is very fine,
But her acting can't compare with mine;
I'm just about her height;
Herbert, don't forget to write,
And say a five years' contract I may sign!"

(Chorus)

I wants to be a actor lady
Playing you know,
Star in the show;
Spotlight for me, no back row shady,
I'm the real thing,
I dance and sing;
Miss Nethersole beguiles and smiles,
But she can't teach this gal "Varmer Giles;"
And I wants to be a actor lady too—indeed I do!

Vassar Girl[16]

Have you heard the latest news they tell?
It's startling all the nation.

(Chorus)

It's startling all the nation,
If you haven't heard the news, ah well
Just listen to my song.

(Chorus)

Just listen to her song.
There once was a school that was so very rare.

(Repeat chorus)

That a poor dusky maid couldn't breathe its very
air.

(Repeat chorus)

You couldn't enter if you dad were not a million-
aire.

(Repeat chorus)

To be ought but a blueblood or a swell you didn't
dare.

(Chorus)

I am the first dark belle who ever went to Vassar.
I play my part so well—I came from Madagas-
car—
They thought I was a swell, and the boys—they
did adore.
And if I gave a smile, they quickly asked for
more.
They sent bouquets galore to the elegant
brunette.
I've got a stock in store of their billet doux as yet
They did know sufficient to come in from out the
wet.

(Girl)

They had never seen my dark papa,
And I didn't have to show him.

(Repeat chorus)

Till I bade the others all ta-ta!
Then I didn't mind at all.

(Repeat chorus)

---

16. Word and music were by V. Bryan and H. Von Tilzer. That
the song *Vassar Girl* does not fit the continuity, is hardly an argument that it was not sung by Ada Overton Walker (Rosetta).
Because the song was based on an actual incident where a
"colored" girl passed for white at the all-girls school, it was a
popular topic, and may well have been interpolated into the
show.

Oh, the papers howled and said it was a shame,
And they really thought that I was to blame.
They thought that I had played an awful little
    game,
But they had to own that I got there just the
    same.

(Repeat chorus)

ROSETTA   *(referring to her mirror)* I guess this is big enough for Mrs. Stringer, the lady that's coming from Boston to see whether she's got her mole on the right or left side of her expression? Mama says as the customs of polite society in Boston are so entirely different from those of Gatorville, you and your father, during this lady's sojourn here, will make it convenient to retire as often as is possible to the rear of the domicile. Mama always looks out for our comfort. Mrs. Stringer, Mama says, in addition to her regular business, writes the fashion notes in the *Beanville Agitator,* the leading colored paper of Boston. I wonder if she was to see me *(business)* would she mention my costume.

MRS. LIGHTFOOT   *(calling loudly from inside)* Rosetta! Rosetta! (ROSETTA *picks up glass and rushes into the house. Loud crash follows. Enter* DR. STRAIGHT, REEDER, *and* HUSTLING CHARLIE)

HUSTLING C.   Come on, fellows. This is the place. Ain't it a daisy?

DR. STRAIGHT   I reckon we have to make him a member of the Syndicate, eh, Reed?

REEDER   Mr. Lightfoot must be worth considerable money?

HUSTLING C.   You've got the right dope. He's got plenty of dough. I guess you're wondering how an old hayseed like Lightfoot bumped into this layout. Well, the old duffer that built this joint back in the "Wish I was in Dixie" days had the biggest free labor plant in the district, so old Lightfoot says. Old Goodman—that's the guy's name you know—lost his graft along in the halcyon days of get the money without a struggle, and got tapped. Now old Lightfoot, with the instinct of a politician, stuck to the wreck. Goodman got lucky, blowed himself for this hangout, and in grateful remembrance of the stick to the bridge sentiments of old Lightfoot, he willed him the place. Shortly after he got groggy, and after playing the "seven ages" to a finish, he cashed in his chips.

REEDER   It's a wonder that Lightfoot could be induced to give up his home even to go to Dahomey. According to your story, old man Goodman and Lightfoot were inseparable friends. Notwithstanding one was the master and the other the slave. When reverses came to old man Goodman, though no longer a slave, Lightfoot remained in his service, and when Dame Fortune smiled on old man Goodman again, he showed his appreciation by willing Lightfoot this place, and he, out of pure sentiment, ought to cling . . .

DR. STRAIGHT   *(interrupting)* Say, Reeder, you'd make a first-class medicine spieler. I want to see this old man you're talking about. I might straighten his hair for him. If I had his money, I'd stay right here in Florida, and the things I'd do with it would astonish the natives.

HUSTLING C.   Say, Cull, it makes you feel good to think of the mazuma, eh?

REEDER   Yes, money's the thing. Horses, carriages, wining and dining. I can see it all floating before me.

HUSTLING C.   You can see things floating, eh? Do you know what they call your complaint up in the foolish factory?

DR. S.   In the language of medicine. He has visionary derangement of the intellect.

HUSTLING C.   In the Bowery, where I was raised, they'd call his disease "roaming in the garden." *(unidentified song here.[17] Enter* MRS. STRINGER *accompanied by* ME SING *with boxes and bundles, etc., also chorus and* MRS. LIGHTFOOT *from the house)*

MRS. LIGHTFOOT   *(after greetings)* I've been looking every minute for you. I sent the wagon down to the landing, but I suppose John didn't know you.

MRS. STRINGER   No, but I can't conceive of your having a man about the place mean enough to let a woman walk two miles over a newly macadamized road with a new pair of number threes on a number four foot, if he had recognized her as the person to be delivered bag and baggage to Mr. and Mrs. Lighthead—I mean Lightfoot's residence. *(business of looking startled)*

---

17. This unidentified song, sung by the trio of Dr. Straight, Reeder, and Hustling Charlie, was probably "I May Be Crazy But I Ain't No Fool."

CHORUS   What's the matter?

MRS. S.   I've lost something. *(everybody looks around searchingly)*

MRS. L.   *(excitedly)* What is it?

MRS. S.   *(as if suddenly remembering. Smiling)* My cook.

MRS. L.   Your cook? *(enter* ME SING*)*

MRS. S.   Yes, there he is. Come here, Me Sing.

MRS. L.   For heaven sake. He's a Chinaman.

MRS. S.   Don't get excited. He won't bite you. My doctor's put me on a chop suey diet and I'm compelled to have him.

MRS. L.   *(calling loudly)* Rosetta, Rosetta.

ROSETTA   *(entering from house, answering)* Yes, M'am.

MRS. L.   Show Mr. Chop Suey to Mrs. Stringer's room.

(Enter MRS. LIGHTFOOT, DR. STRAIGHT, MOSES LIGHTFOOT, HUSTLING CHARLIE, *and* REEDER*)*

CICERO   Ladies and gentlemen, allow me to introduce my friends, Dr. Straight, Mr. Reeder, and Mr. Hustler. These is high society gentlemen from the North wid great reputations.

MRS. L.   Well, they don't look it. But I might be mistaken.

CICERO   You certainly is 'cause dey know all the secrets.

(Finale for Act I)

Society

Cicero

> To get in high society
> You need a great reputation,
> Don't cultivate sobriety
> But rather ostentation,
> A lot of gold lay'd by in gilt-edged stocks,
> A few town lots, let's say a dozen blocks,
> A high-toned house that builded upon rocks,
> Then you're in society!

> To get in high society
> I've always had an ambition,
> And since I've got the brass, now we
> Are sure to have position.
> A royal prince my little girl shall wed,
> For since the days of lords and dukes have sped,
> It takes a prince to put you at the head
> Of the best society!

Pansy

> Surely you're only mocking,
> Such levity is simply shocking
> Your prince for me would be too far above
> A royal prince is he I love.
> Besides where is this prince for me to love?

(Chorus)

Cicero

> Just to think of a house on some big avenue,
> (South Fifth will do.)
> And a prince who would spend all his time woo-
>   ing you,
> (And your money too!)

Pansy

> Love looks not at estate. Oh No!
> T'were folly one should think it so.
> The beggar maid becomes a queen
> Who through her lover's eyes is seen.

Pansy and Leather

> We care not for the world of fools
> Love dignifies the soul—it rules.
> The pomp of kings the pride of state
> Are naught when love o'er-takes the great.
> The humble cot becomes a throne
> Whose dwelling place love makes his own,
> So all man's heart and being makes his own,
> So all man's heart and being sing
> Love is the King! Love is the King!

(Curtain)

Scene 2:

(Road a short distance from Gatorville. Enter RAREBACK *and* SHYLOCK *disguised)*

RARE   Come on, Shy, we're on the right road. Here's a sign post. "Gatorville One . . . one . . .

SHY   What's that? Gatorville, one hundred miles yet?

RARE   No, no, Gatorville. One mile and some more.

SHY   Some more miles.

RARE   Come on. It can't be much further. Look, you can already see the house tops.

SHY   I've been having that same bird's eye view of dem houses ever since I got off dat train.

RARE   A detective is never supposed to get tired. Why Nick Carter or Old Sleuth would laugh at the idea of a detective wanting rest. At the rate we're going, it will be plumb dark before we get into the town.

SHY   I ain't worryin' about gittin' into the town. If those people find out we ain't no regular detectives, the thing to figure on is how to get out of town.

RARE   You're just as much a detective as you're ever going to be. I can see now that you'll never be a Nick Carter or an Old Sleuth.

SHY   You always castin' up reflections. I never heard of dis man Nick Carter or old Hoof either.

RARE   Never heard of Nick Carter and Old Sleuth? Why, Shy, they're the greatest detectives in the world. Nick Carter is the only man living that's been shot through the heart forty-one times, and Old Sleuth's been knocked in the head with his arms tied behind him and a gag in his mouth and throwed in every sewer in the country.

SHY   With that kind of treatment as a regular diet, how long is a man supposed to last?

RARE   Why say, Shy, that ain't nothin'. Old Sleuth and Nick Carter were both sent out to a western town to trace up some bankrobbers. The robbers got word of it somehow and waylaid the train about thirty miles from town. Imagine a mountain pass about fifty thousand feet above the level of the sea, a bridge suspended in mid-air over a chasm one thousand feet deep. A stormy night. The snow falling thick and fast and not a ship to be seen. The robbers, after removing the middle span of the bridge, fled like specters down the track to a curve a hundred yards away, and there behind a huge boulder lay in wait for the train. On rushed the fast mail. Every passenger was asleep excepting Nick Carter and Old Sleuth, and they were playing pinochle in the smoking apartment of the car. Crack, crack, crack and the whiplike report of a gatling gun rang out on the midnight air. Nick Carter was seen to rise suddenly to his feet and take from the hat rack a bottle of rye whiskey, take a drink and light a cigar and coolly raise the window to prevent the broken glass from entering the wounds made by the bullets of the bandits. Old Sleuth, always on the alert, threw a keg of

beer out of window, and the robbers ceased firing long enough to secure the beer, by which time the train was well on its way to the deadly bridge, little dreaming of the danger ahead. Nick Carter sat down to trim his corns, when Old Sleuth whose hearing was wonderfully acute said: "Nick, the middle span is out of that bridge ahead. I can hear the air sucking the broken rails. Something must be done and at once. Quick as a flash, Nick cut the bell cord with his corn knife, plunged through the window, caught the telegraph wire, which broke with his weight and swung him over the chasm. Letting go the wire, he dropped to the bottom, attached the bell cord to the span that had been removed, which fortunately had landed on a bed of marsh and remained intact, passed the other end to Old Sleuth, who had by this time reached the cow catcher of the engine and with superhuman effort, the span was snatched in place, the lives of the sleeping passengers saved.

SHY   How deep did you say that chasm was?

RARE   One thousand feet.

SHY   Then I suppose this Nick Carter having rubber soles on his shoes, hit himself on top de head and bounced back in de smoking department of de car and played pinochle till he got to town.

RARE   Nothing so unreasonable as that occurred. An artificial lake at the head of the gap used as a reservoir became flooded and burst its banks, the torrent of water swept through the chasm and carried Nick Carter to the town thirty miles away and landed him on the platform of the depot just as the train pulled in with Old Sleuth standing on the cab of the engine smoking a Child's cigar.

SHY   I know it's taking advantage of good nature to ask any more questions, but would you kindly let me know if the robbers was apprehended.

RARE   (*laughing*) Now I can see that you are improving. Only a first-class detective would use that word "apprehended." Yes, they were caught after a number of even more bloodcurdling incidents that I've related to you.

SHY   Jist the finishing incidentals'll do.

RARE   The robbers, after securing the beer that Old Sleuth threw out the windows, descended to a valley twenty-six thousand two hundred and six feet below.

SHY   By actual measurement?

RARE   Yes, by actual measurement, and after drinking the beer, lay down to collect their thoughts.

SHY   How many robbers was there?

RARE   Three.

SHY   I believe that part of the story.

RARE   What part?

SHY   The part where the three robbers after drinking a whole keg of beer between them—laid down.

RARE   Nick Carter opened his satchel on the platform of the depot and took out an airship while Old Sleuth, unscrewing the top of his walking cane, removed a large electric light plant.

SHY   *(interrupting)* Never mind. You needn't explain no more. I can see them robbers was up against it.

RARE   Come on, Shy, I'll tell you the rest of the story as we go along.

SHY   You ain't going to tell me the rest, 'cause I'm jist naturally ashamed to listen to you. *(exit RARE laughing, followed by SHY)*

Scene 3:

(Interior with transparent windows showing a porch. CICERO LIGHTFOOT and wife are busy getting the room in order)

MRS. LIGHTFOOT   *(to MR. L., who is gazing vacantly at the lights)* Mr. Lightfoot, if you have no objections, would you mind telling me why you are standing there totally oblivious of your surroundings. You look like you are in a trance.

MR. LIGHTFOOT   I was jest standin' here thinkin' what a shame it was that Master John died so soon after he built this house. You know he traveled all over the world, and it seems to me he had everything put in this house that he had seen in anybody else's house, even these 'lectum lights, and then after all the trouble he went to, make everything so comfortable, he dropped out and didn't have a chance to enjoy it.

MRS. L.   Well, if he hadn't dropped out, you wouldn't have dropped in. Of course, it was very nice of old man Goodman to will you this property, and you ought to be very grateful to him for no other reason than that he outlived all his heirs. But I lose my temper when you say Mars John. Why don't you say Mr. Goodman?

MR. L.   Well, I 'pose I could say Mr. Goodman jest to please you, but when I think of the many kind things Mars John done for me . . .

MRS. L.   *(interrupting)* There, there, you needn't go over all that stuff again. I know it by heart—you're as obstinate about this as you are to the faults of that dear daughter of ours.

MR. L.   You see, if you had been raised down here, you wouldn't feel so bad about the customs of the country. Of course, up there in Boston where you come from, it's different, and poor Rosetta, that chile's jest growed up like a wild weed. She means well.

MRS. L.   *(interrupting)* She might mean well, but she never does well and . . . *(sound of crash)* Heavens! What is she done? *(rushes of calling)* Rosetta!

MRS. L.   Dat's Rosetta clearing the dishes off the table. *(pause. Crash outside)* I wonder if there's anything broke? *(exit. Enter RAREBACK climbing over porch rail burglar fashion. He enters the room, examines the doors, and blows out lights. SHY from outside whistles mysteriously two or three times, then calls for RAREBACK)*

SHY   What's the matter with that light? *(pauses for answer. No answer comes, then he whistles. RAREBACK goes to the porch and leans over the rail, looks down to the ground and says)*

RARE   Get a move on, you down there. Climb over the fence. Look out. That's a dog house. That's right. Come around the path. There you are. Now climb up this post.

SHY   It's so dark down here I can't see no post.

RARE   Pssst. *(pointing to the post)* Here's the post. There's a ladder over there. Use that.

SHY   I told you once it was dark down here. How you 'spect me to see a ladder. *(loud noise)*

RARE   *(indicating the spot)* That's it. Now pick it up. Place it here and hurry up.

SHY   Never mind me hurryin' up. When I get up there, don't you let me find you trying to hurry down.

RARE   *(impatiently)* Stop that noise and come on. *(leaves porch, comes inside, examines doors. SHYLOCK enters)*

SHY   Look here, Rareback, ain't we takin' a mighty long chance comin' in these people's house this way?

RARE   Pssh, don't talk so loud. There must be a mystery surrounding everything we do.

SHY   Yes, and if we keep down these kind of tricks, we'll be surrounded all right enough, and it won't be with no mystery either.

RARE   Shut your mouth and listen to me. You know that that cat's eye ain't here in this place, and I know it ain't here. Now we've got to tell this old man some sort of a fish story to keep up our reputation as detectives.

SHY   I don't know nothing about no fish.

RARE   Psh . . . I have it! (*whispers to* SHY, *who laughs*)

SHY   I know that yarn backwards.

RARE   Someone's coming. Stand still (*enter* CICERO LIGHTFOOT *singing softly. On entering the room, he stops suddenly*)

CICERO   I thought I left them lights lit. (*turns on light*)

RARE   Is your name Cicero Lightfoot?

CICERO   Dat's my name, but who is you?

RARE   Tell him who we are, Shy.

SHY   We're a couple of detectives.

RARE   From Boston.

CICERO   (*mysteriously closes the door*) Den you'se the gentlemen I sent for. I'm awful glad you come. If you don't find that cat's eye fore I leave, I want you to go right along with us to Dahomey, 'cause I kinda think I know who's got it.

RARE AND SHY   (*very loud*) Good. (*business for old man as* RARE *and* SHY *take out notebooks and write*)

RARE   When did you first lose this cat's eye?

SHY   He didn't lose it but once.

CICERO   Last Friday a week ago.

R&S   Good. (*business with notebooks*)

SHY   What was your father's first name?

CICERO   Ephriham Lightfoot.

R&S   Good. (*business with notebooks*)

RARE   Do you drink gin?

CICERO   I takes a drop now and then.

SHY   Have you any in the house now?

CICERO   A gallon jugfull.

R&S   Awful good. (RARE *pulls* SHY's *sleeve*)

SHY   (*to* CICERO) Excuse me. (RARE *and* SHY *hold consultation*)

RARE   We've got a surprise for you, ain't we Shy?

SHY   (*to* RARE) I'm ashamed to look him in the face.

RARE   Do you know Captain Kidd?

---

18. Possibly borrowed from Williams and Walker's first show *The Gold Bug.*

CICERO   What's that got to do with me?

SHY   Do you think that he'll stand for it?

RARE   We'll tell him anyway. (*song Captain Kidd*)[18]

Hurrah for Captain Kidd

There was once a bold pilot who sailed on the
   sea,
And he was wicked as wicked can be.
He never thought nothin' of cuttin' a throat,
Or when it came handy of sinkin' a boat.
His name it was Kidd, though no youngster was
   he,
He was like a tax gatherer who sailed on the sea.
An' 'tis plain that by pirating, stealing, and sich,
This Captain did grow most tremendously rich.

[CHORUS]
Then hurrah for Captain Kidd,
What he did, of course, he did.
But from all his potted treasures
I have lifted up the lid.
Then hurrah for Captain Kidd,
For I've found the gold he hid.
And the money's proves a quid
For the sins of Captain Kidd.
But the Captain was cautious and going alone,
He sank a big pot in a hole by a stone.
Then potted his treasure and put on the lid,
And said, "Now my money is certainly hid."
But went out to sail on the same evil tack
And alas, I should tell it, he never came back.
And so while a diggin' down there in my lot,
I chanced on unearthing the Captain's old pot.

(*Repeat Chorus*)

Spread the news!
Spread the news!
Spread the news!
Mistah Johnsin's found de gol'
Found de gol' dat once was hid,
By de pirate Captain Kidd.
Spread de news!
Spread de news!
Let de people all be told
Mistah Johnsin's found de gold,
Everybody spread de news.

(*exit* RARE *and* SHY *and* CICERO. *Enter* MRS. STRINGER, *accompanied by a bunch of girls, all talking at once.*)

MRS. STRINGER   I'm awfully well pleased that my ideas met with your approval. (*all girls talk-*

ing at once) It is very likely that all of you are right, but the trouble is your argument is bunched. Now listen, girls, and I'll show you what an advantage you have in dealing with me. I have the most fashionable dresses in stock to be seen in Gatorville, all of them made, with one exception, of imported silks, satins, and laces of the best quality and workmanship. Now (*selecting a girl*), I've got a dark green satin (*describes old-fashioned dress*) that would just suit you.

THE GIRL   (*indignantly*) Suit me!

MRS. S.   Yes, if you were going to a Colonial ball.

CHORUS   Oh!

MRS. S.   (*to another girl*) And I've the most beautiful mourning costume, and mourning would be so becoming to you, your hair, your eyes.

THE GIRL   And my feet and my hands.

MRS. S.   You have got charming feet and hands.

THE GIRL   Yes, but there's nobody dead in my family.

MRS. S.   That's too bad. I . . . I mean you're fortunate. Remember, if I sell any of these dresses, they will be described in the fashion notes of the *Beanville Agitator*. The original price and the make's name will also be mentioned. Will you look at the dresses, my room is here. (*pointing to the door, girls exit talking. After exit*) That last shot was the one that hit the mark. (*exit* MRS. S. *Enter* ROSETTA)

Leader of the Colored Aristocracy

To be the leader of the color'd aristocracy,
Is my ambition.

CHORUS: Is her ambition,
    I have a longing just the same as all the quality,
    For recognition.

CHORUS: For recognition,

Solo: To have folks say as I pass by,
    She moves on a social plane, so very high.
    To get up on her level you needn't ever try.
    She's the leader of the colored aristocracy.

CHORUS: She's the leader of the colored aristocracy.

(Refrain)

And then I'll drill these darkies till
They're up in high society's hypocracy.
They'll come my way,
To gain entree
To the circles of the color'd aristocracy.
Now to establish swell society for colour'd folks,
I have a yearning,

CHORUS: She has a yearning

And from the high ton'd 'ristocratic white folks
    how to lead,
ROSETTA: I have been learning.

CHORUS: She has been learning.

ROSETTA: All I need is lots of dough,
For that regulates the social scale, you know.
'Twill put me in position to make the proper
    show,
As leader of the color'd aristocracy.

CHORUS: As the leader of the color'd aristocracy.

(Repeat chorus)

(*Exit* ROSETTA. *Enter* SHYLOCK, *who opens* MRS. STRINGER's *door. Girls scream, he closes door quickly*)

SHY   Dem women must a thought I was a mouse. (MRS STRINGER *comes to the door*)

MRS. S.   (*angrily*) What do you mean by opening my door without knocking?

SHY   Excuse me. (*stuttering*) Is . . . is Mr. Rareback Punkerton in there?

MRS. S.   (*indignantly*) Sir!

SHY   I was looking for Mr. Rareback Punkerton.

MRS. S.   What would Mr. Anybody be doing in a room where I was fitting dresses on a lot of young ladies?

SHY   I don't know, ma'm, but Rareback ain't very bashful.

MRS. S.   Indeed! Well sir, if you come to this door again, I shall have Mr. Lightfoot eject you from the premises, do you understand, eject you from the premises, do you understand, do you understand, eject you from the premises. (*exits and slams door*)

SHY   I got a right to have her arrested for threatening my personal safety. Rareback's fixin' to git me and him both in jail. He's got that old man down there in the yard diggin' up the whole place looking for a chest of gold, and—*(outside everybody "Hurrah, Hurrah!"* SHYLOCK *goes to porch and looks down in the yard)* Dem people's down thar jumpin' up and down like they're crazy. I wonder if dem people found out Rareback ain't no detective. *(enter* MOSE LIGHTFOOT *excitedly dancing and yelling)*

MOSE   Hurrah, hurrah, hurrah, now for Dahomey. *(sings)*

> Hurrah, hurrah, we bring the jubilee
> Hurrah, hurrah, wese going you and me
> Soon we'll be sailing far across the sea.
> Riding to the land of Dahomey.

(Dance and funny step as if he had pain in his side)

SHY   What's the matter down there?

MOSE   Cicero's found a chest of gold. *(continues singing "Hurrah" and exits)*

SHY   I must find Rareback. *(singing mockingly "Hurrah" he exits. Chorus sings out from the side. "Spread the News" and enters. Hold for tableau.* CICERO *enters last with chest)*

CICERO   Now dat I've got this gold, I'm goin' to have my pedigree wrote. There's a gentleman down in Cheaterville dat can find the Royal ancestors for anybody dat got fifty dollars to spare for his trouble. In fact, he said there was a time when every darkey was a king. *(song)*

Evah Darkey Is a King

> Dar's a mighty curious circumstance
> Dat's a botherin' all de nation.
> All de yankees is dissatisfied
> Wid a deir untitled station.
> Dey is huntin' after title
> Wid a golden net to snare 'em!
> But dey ain't got all de title
> For it is a 'culiar ting.
> When a dahkey stahts to huntin'
> He is sho' to prove a king.

(Chorus)

> Evah darkey is a king!
> Royalty is jes' de ting.
> If yo' social life's a bungle,
> Jes you go back to yo' jungle,
> And remember dat your daddy was a king.

> Scriptures say dat Ham was de first black man.
> Ham's de father of our nation.

> All de black folks to dis very day
> B'longs right in de Ham creation.
> Ham, he was a king in ancient days,
> An' he reigned in all his glory.
> So ef we is all de Sons of Ham,
> Natcherlly dat tells de story.
> White folks what's got dahkey servants
> Try an' get dem every thing.
> You must nevah speak insulting
> You may be talking to a king.

(Repeat chorus)

ROSETTA   Now Uncle Cicero, where is that picture that came from Paris that you was going to show us?

CICERO   I almost forgot that of all his pictures, dat was Mars John's favorite. *(looks at wife sheepishly. She turns away disgusted)* I show it to you. *(exposes picture)*

ROSETTA   What the name of the picture, Uncle Cicero?

CICERO   The Czar of Dixie. *(song)*

The Czar

> There's a man who's mighty grand
> Who rules supreme in Dixie land,
> He's President, the Mayor, and the Governor,
> He's the citizen's private counsellor,
> You will find if you engage him in a social chat,
> He's a gentlemman, a scholar, and a diplomat,
> 'Mongst the leaders of his race he is the brightest
>   star,
> And throughout the whole of Dixie, he is called
>   the Czar.

> [CHORUS]
> He is the greatest thing,
> And known afar,
> The Black folks always sing,
> He is the Czar.
> His style is superfine,
> He's always right in line,
> He says the world is mine,
> He is the Czar.
> The Black folks always sing
> He is the Czar.

> This great man's a modern man
> And does things on a modern plan
> He's the idol of his subjects, he's their guiding
>   light
> And they all obey be he wrong or right,

In the world of fashion he is called the Beau
    Brummell,
For his manners like his clothes proclaim the per-
    fect swell,
When they held the coronation there were rulers
    from afar,
Who were dazzled by the glory of this Dixie Czar.

(Repeat chorus)

(Curtain)

ACT III

Scene 1:

(Dark stage at rise of curtain. Swamp near the
capitol Dahomey[19] with a practical moonrise effect
over a small body of water in perspective. Light
gradually works up to medium moonlight. Fireflies
are seen. Ballet or chorus are costumed as frogs;
the color scheme of costumes and scenery is the
same. The chorus or ballet of ten girls and four
men are posed beside a stream with backs to audience. Their backs are covered with leaves to look
like foliage of the swamp until they turn and dance.
The song "My Lady Frog" is sung by two idealized
lovers in frog costumes who float down the stream
in a canoe. The refrain is taken up by chorus. At
the finish of the refrain, the ballet/chorus turn and
face the audience to form a picture and they dance)

My Lady Frog

(sung by chorus)

Where the water-lilies cluster
'Neath drooping willows;
When the moon so soft and tender
Peeps through the trees;
Where the vines of brilliant lustre,
Find mossy pillows;
Where the ferns so tall and slender
Sway with the breeze,
There lived a lady frog, green pollywog was she;
Her lover tho' was one of brown.
Throughout the whole night long a little song
    sang he,
And whispered for the moon was looking down.

---

19. In this version, registered with the Library of Congress, the
third act is written as a scenario (outline) with no dialogue and
three song titles in the prologue.

(sung by male frog)

My lady frog of opal hue,
Here on this log,
I sing to you.
Bright as the flies
That light this bog,
So are your eyes,
My lady frog.

(sung by chorus)

As the lovers sat a-waiting,
From o'er the way
Came a frog with chest a swelling,
A bull frog green.
Told he of a palace waiting,
In grand array,
How the lady of his dwelling,
Would be a queen.
And tho' 'tis sad to say, he took away this
    maid.
The frog of brown now croaks with pain,
And when the night is still, from o'er the hill, 'tis
    said
You hear in mournful tones the old refrain.

(Repeat male solo)

(Exit Chorus and lights out. Change to Garden of
the King of Dahomey)

My Dahomian Queen

In Dahomey so grand,
Just along side the strand,
Lives a Moorish maid so near and dear to
    me.
When I sought her heart and hand,
She made me understand
That if I wish'd my little bride she'd be.
When the moon is brightly beamin',
From the azure skies a streamin',
In my cottage I'm a dreamin',
A dreamin' of our weddin' day.
Natives of exalted station,
Potentates from ev'ry nation.
Will be there to hear me when I say—

[CHORUS]
My Dahomian queen,
My dusky turtle dove,
What a beautiful scene,
Me and my lady love.
She's so sweet and serene,
Fresh from the jungle green,

She is my Kai-o-ka-lo-nian,[20]
Royal Dahomian queen,

My Dahomian queen.
When I become a king,
All the jingle bells will ring,
While through the streets on palanquins we're
    borne.
'Twill be the grandest thing,
Just to hear the natives sing,
As loyally they fall before my throne.
Caboceers will be our sentry,
'Rabian knights will be our gentry,
The wonder of the twentieth century.
A-makin' even sunlight fade.
Seems the breezes will be sighin'
Nature with itself be a-vieing
A-singin' while my babe and I parade—

(Repeat chorus)

(A women's drill team, costumed as Amazons, enters and executes a precision marching drill. They exit, and a Dahomian explains their behavior as a local custom. Then the Caboceers march in singing)[21]

Caboceers Entrance

We are the loyal subjects of King Eat-Em-All,
The ruler over all our states both great and small.
Great is his name, more great his fame,
Before his Majesty all nations prostrate fall.
Forward with chargers dashing,
Their armor brightly flashing,
With bayonets a clashing
Like demons they hunt the fray.
The Caboceers! We greet with cheers!
The Caboceers, long be their years!
The Caboceers! We greet with cheers!
The Caboceers, long be their years!
Mighty their reign and glorious,
Their power all victorious,
Like gods of light before us
They come, the world to sway, to sway, to sway.

[CHORUS]
Brightest vision of the morning,
Deign to glad our longing eyes.
Come and with thy wonderous coming,
Dim the lustre of the skies.
Mighty ruler of our nation,
Hail we thee with loud acclaim,
Great thy name and great thy station,
Caboceers, long may ye reign.

(Chorus enters as African chiefs, soldiers, natives, dancing girls. After march, chorus comes to front of stage, kneels and sings choral descriptive of glories of Cannibal King and Caboceers. At the middle of the choral, they rise at the words "Mighty ruler of our nation" and sway to and fro with swinging palm leaves. At the end, the chorus falls prostrate to the floor on their faces to greet SHYLOCK HOMESTEAD and RAREBACK PUNKERTON dressed as Caboceers. Song: "Every Darkey Is a King." Dialogue follows in which the box with cat's eye is found. CICERO LIGHTFOOT is disgusted with Dahomey and announces his return to America. The musical concludes with two rousing numbers: "Emancipation Day," and a triumphant cakewalk—most popular dance of the era—a production number that lasted twenty minutes.)

On Emancipation Day

Streets are gay,
On dey way,
All de alleys done turn'd out.
Mistah Giles
Wid Miss Liles make a figure widout doubt.
Hyeah dey come,
Lord dat drum
In de black ban' holds de sway.
'Cept the brass,
Give it sass, on Emancipation Day.
Darkies standin' on tip toe,
Makin' goo-goos at de show.

[CHORUS]
On Emancipation Day,
All you white fo'ks clear de way.
Brass ban' playin' sev'ral tunes,
Darkies eyes look jes' lo'k moons,
Marshall of de day a struttin',
Lord but he is gay.
Coons dress'd up lak masqueraders,
Porters arm'd lak rude invaders.
When dey hear dem ragtime tunes,
White fo'ks try to pass fo' coons on Emancipation Day.

---

20. The Queen of Hawaii, Liliuokalani, had been deposed by American planters in 1893. She came to the United States where she remained in the news because she sued the federal government for her property losses. She also wrote the popular song, "Aloha Oe," known as "Farewell to Thee."

21. Precision drilling in exotic costumes was popular theatre and circus entertainment at the turn of the century.

Heah um cry,
My oh my,
When de'cession shows it head.
Majors brown
Ridin' down on cart hosses deck'd in red.
Teeth lak pearls,
Greet the girls standin' dere lak dusky storms.
Oh! my pet,
What a set of owdacious uniforms.
Generals stiff as hick'ry sticks
In de dress of seventy-six.

(Repeat chorus)

That's How the Cake Walk's Done

Cake-walking craze, it's a fad nowadays
With black folks and white folks too,
And I really declare it's done ev'rywhere,
Though it may be something new to you.
'Twas introduced years ago down in Dixie you
    know,
By Black folks in Tennessee.
So just to show you,
I'm going to do
A cake walk of a high degree.

[CHORUS]
Bow to the right, bow to the left,
Then you proudly take your place.
Be sure to have a smile on your face,
Step high with lots of style and grace.
With a salty prance do a ragtime dance,
Step way back and get your gun.
With a bow, look wise, make goo-goo eyes,
For that's the way the cake walk's done.

My Grandmother told me that she used to be
The best cake walker in the state,
When she walk'd down the line, lord, chile she
    did shine.
But of course her style is out of date;
The Parisians, you know, they all walk just so,
They call it ze cake walk dance.
But with me you'll agree,
That the folks from Paree
In this cake walk would have no chance.

(Repeat chorus)

Many long years ago there was poor Old Black
    Joe;
Use to walk just like this for a prize.
There was big Jasper Brown, the cake walker
    clown,

Walk'd like this with his best gal Miss Lize.
Old Tildy Snow, and Bill Jones, with his
    rheumatic bones,
To see them walk was fun.
With that old-style prance, they have no chance
When this late-style cake walk is done.

(Repeat chorus)

Swing Along[22]

Swing along chillun, swing along de lane;
Lif' yo' head and yo' heels mighty high.
Swing along chillun, 'taint a-goin' to rain,
Sun's as red as de rose in de sky.
Come along Mandy, come along Sue,
White fo'ks a-watchin' an' seein' what you do,
White fo'ks jealous when you'se walkin' two by
    two,
So swing along chillun, swing along.
We'll a swing along . . . yes a swing along,
An' a lif' a' yo' heads up high,
Wif' pride an' gladness beamin' from yo' eye.
We'll a swing along . . . yes a swing along,
From a early morn till night,
Lif' yo' head an' yo' heels mighty high
An' a swing both lef' an' right

(Repeat)

Molly Green

There's a bright ray of sunshine, Molly Green,
Pure as the light of daytime,
She's a dream.
Eyes like the stars of nighttime
Has my queen,
Tender as buds in springtime
Just sixteen.

[CHORUS]
Molly, Molly,
Dear little dark-eyed Molly,
Always so gay and so jolly.
Who can help loving you,
Molly, Molly,
My heart is pledg'd to Molly.
If Cholly loves Molly,
I don't think it folly to love her too.
Down where the sad wavers murmur
To the sea,

22. Although not found in this Library of Congress version of
the text, other songs were known to have been interpolated
into the snow. Some of those are printed here.

On pleasant nights in summer
Oft were we,
Strolling along together,
Moll and me,
Whisp'ring that lovers ever we would be.

Brown-Skin Baby Mine[23]

Dar's a charmin' dark-eyed little lassie dat I
    know,
Who wid' tender teasin' glances sets my heart
    aglow.
Lafin' eyes an' lips lak' cherries,
Long in pickin' time,
Browner den de huckleberries
Ripenin' on de vine.

[CHORUS]
She ain't no violet,
She ain't no red, red rose,
An' tho' the lily of de valley's sweet,
She's sweeter yet I knows.
She ain't no tulip rare,
Nor mornin' glory fine,
But 'mongst de flowers fair,
Kaint none compare
Wid Brown-skin baby mine.
When we wed we won't go travellin' to no for-
    eign lan',
We doan' want no high-tone mansion, or no
    palace gran',
What I keer bout sunny It'ly, or de river Rhine?
All I wants is jes' a home an' brown-skin baby
    mine.

(Repeat chorus)

I'm a Jonah Man[24]

My hard luck started when I was born, leas' so
    the old folks say.

Dat same hard luck been my bes' fren' up to dis
    very day.
When I was young my mamma's frens to find a
    name they tried.
They named me after Papa and the same day
    Papa died.
For I'm a Jonah,
I'm an unlucky man.
My family for many years would look on me and
    then shed tears,
Why am I dis Jonah I sho' can't understand,
But I'm a good substantial full-fledged real first-
    class Jonah man.
A fren' of mine gave me a six-month meal ticket
    one day.
He said, "It wont do me no good, I've got to go
    away."
I thanked him as my heart wid joy and gratitude
    did bound.
But when I reach'd the restaurant the place had
    just burn'd down.
For I'm a Jonah,
I'm a unlucky man.
It sounds just like that old, old tale,
But sometimes I feel like a whale.
Why am I dis Jonah I sho' can't understand,
But I'm a good substantial full-fledged real first-
    class Jonah man.
My brother once walk'd down the street and fell
    in a coal hole.
He sued the man that owned the place and got
    ten thousand cold.
I figured this was easy so I jump'd in the same
    coal hole.
Broke both my legs and the Judge give me one
    year for stealin' coal.
For I'm a Jonah,
I'm an unlucky man.
If it rain'd down soup from morn till dark,
Instead of a spoon I'd have a fork.
Why am I dis Jonah I sho' can't understand,
But I'm a good substantial full-fledged first-class
    Jonah man.

---

23. "Brown-Skin Baby Mine" was sung by Abbie Mitchell, Will
Marion Cook's wife.

24. "Jonah Man," and "Nobody," written and performed by
Bert Williams, became his trademark songs. Other songs listed
for the show but the lyrics are not printed here: "Chocolate
Drops," "Happy Jim," "Dat Girl of Mine," "Dear Luzon,"
"Good Evenin'," "I May Be Crazy But I Ain't No Fool," "My
Castle on the Nile," "Me and De Minstrel Ban'," "A Rich
Coon's Babe," "Returned," "She's Dancing Sue," "When Sousa
Comes to Town," "Who Dat Say Chicken in Dis Crowd," and
"Why Adam Sinned."

STAR OF ETHIOPIA
1912

WHY WE ARE AT WAR
1918

African American Pageants

Too pictorial to be a parade, but not dramatic enough to be a play, pageants—with their music, costume, dance, narration, and tableaux—reenacted historical events. Sometimes held out of doors in stadiums, sometimes passing in front of the community seated in bleachers or, in the case of small celebrations, presented in auditoriums, the citizenry assembled to acknowledge an anniversary by reenacting its history. Through pageantry, the citizens told themselves who they were, an important function to a nation of diverse immigrants. In 1914, a pageant in St. Louis used a cast of 7,000 people and played to an audience of 100,000 at each performance.

America's romance with pageantry began in 1876 with the centennial Fourth of July celebration, and in Philadelphia eleven years later with the hundredth anniversary of the United States Constitution. African Americans were nearly invisible in the lat-ter. Black residents had been asked to ride on three floats depicting their progress from slavery to freedom. While a number of African Americans appeared on the last float, none would ride the wagon for slavery, even when offered money to do so.[1]

Five Black colleges produced pageants to honor race progress and their founders: *The Masque of Colored America, Pageant of Progress in Chicago, Culture of Color, A Constellation of Women,* and *The Milestones of the Race.* Willis Richardson included four pageants in his anthology *Plays and Pageants from the Life of the Negro* (1930). Because pageants contained little dialogue and minimum narration, they were printed in outline or scenario form, as *The Star of Ethiopia* (1913) and *Why We Are at War* (1918), appear here.

---

1. David Glassberg, *American Historical Pageantry, The Uses of Tradition In the Early Twentieth Century,* (Chapel Hill: University of North Carolina Press, 1990).

STAR OF ETHIOPIA
1913

W.E.B. Du Bois (1868–1963)

Pageantry, extremely popular during the first quarter of the twentieth century, was viewed by some as a precursor to a national theatre, which became an intensely sought-after goal at a time when dramatists were turning away from European models toward reflections of American life in a uniquely American form, primarily through the study of American folkways. W.E.B. Du Bois was acutely aware of this national enthusiasm and saw in it an opportunity, and in the August 1916 issue of *The Crisis* he wrote: "It seemed to me that it might be possible . . . to get people interested in this development of Negro drama to teach on the one hand the colored people themselves the meaning of their history and their rich, emotional life through a new theatre, and on the other, to reveal the Negro to the white world as a human, feeling thing."

Du Bois loved the theatre, but it was much more than an interest or avocation to him; he encouraged its development in the African American community as a valuable weapon in its cultural and political propaganda arsenal. Much has been written about his encouragement of playwrights through the contests sponsored by *The Crisis*, the journal he edited under the auspices of the NAACP, as well as of his founding of the Krigwa (Crisis Guild of Writers and Artists) Players, a Little Theatre company. Less has been said of the ground-breaking pageant he wrote and produced, *The Star of Ethiopia*.

Du Bois started the first of several drafts of *The Star of Ethiopia* in 1911. At first he called the work *The Jewel of Ethiopia: A Masque in Episodes* (there were six in the first draft). Since the masque is more allegorical than commemorative, he began with a scene in which Shango, the god of thunder, gives the Jewel of Freedom to Ethiopia, a land often chosen as a symbol of the longed-for homeland of the Black Diaspora, in return for her soul. The jewel finally reaches the United States after being lost and found several times. The masque ends with a celebratory tableau, which includes the Queen of Sheba, Nat Turner, Toussaint L'Ouverture, Mohammed Askia, and other heroic historical figures. In subsequent drafts, *The Jewel of Freedom* became *The Star of Faith,* and some of the allegorical elements of the masque were blended into a historical panorama. By 1913, the title had become *The People of People and Their Gifts to Men* and was published in *The Crisis* after its presentation at the National Emancipation Exposition, which was held to mark the fiftieth anniversary of the Emancipation Proclamation, at the Twelfth Regiment Armory in New York from October 22 through 31, 1913.

It was reported that over 14,000 people viewed the pageant, in which 350 performers and musicians participated under the direction of Charles Burroughs, one of Du Bois's former students from Wilberforce

University. It was Burroughs who provided the continuity and put the pageant into stageable form as a prelude followed by six episodes, which told "the tale of the oldest and strongest of the races of mankind, whose faces be Black." Each episode would illustrate the gifts of this race to the world: the Gift of Iron, the Gift of Civilization, the Gift of Faith, the Gift of Humiliation (slavery), the Gift of Struggle Toward Freedom, and the Gift of Freedom, following a chronology of historical events, underscored by African American music and dance, from prehistory through the present.

In 1915, Du Bois, through the producing organization he had formed, the Horizon Guild, raised the funds needed to repeat the pageant in Washington, D.C. This time, on October 11, 13, and 15, 1915, in the American League Baseball Park, there were 1,200 participants, including a chorus of 200 singers, who subsequently performed *The Star of Ethiopia*, as it would now be known. The Superintendent of Colored Education threw his entire system into the effort, and the Colored District Militia was enlisted for the battle episodes. J. Rosamond Johnson served as Director of Music. This production was a resounding critical and artistic success, though not a financial one. Du Bois had hoped to reproduce the pageant at least ten more times, but could only realize production twice more: with 1,000 participants in Philadelphia on May 16, 18, and 20, 1916; and with 300 participants at the Hollywood Bowl in Los Angeles on June 15 and 18, 1925. Du Bois's dreams of establishing an independent producing organization and of gaining recognition by the American Pageant Association, which studiously ignored his efforts, remained unfulfilled.

There are several manuscripts of unproduced pageants among Du Bois's papers, and he did publish one of them, *George Washington and Black Folk*, which commemorated the bicentenary of Washington's birth and chronicled his attitude toward and treatment of Black people at various stages of his life and career. Like *The Star of Ethiopia*, this pageant reflects Du Bois's extensive knowledge of classical literature and his love of fable, parable, and allegory.

The Star of Ethiopia stands as a nearly phenomenal achievement. Tens of thousands witnessed it; several thousand were involved in its preparation and execution. This was truly a communal effort, a source of social cohesiveness and artistic pride, which inspired inquiries from all over the country, as well as the production of subsequent local pageants in Washington and Cincinnati. There is no way to measure what this effort must have meant in terms of audience development and interest in African American drama and theatre, but it must be acknowledged as a factor in sustaining the hope for a national Black theatre and as a seminal event in the development of African American drama and theatre during the Harlem Renaissance period.

—*Freda Scott Giles*

Star of Ethiopia

The pageant of Negro history as written by W.E.B. Du Bois and produced by Charles Burroughs, Master; Daisy Tapley, Dora Cole Norman, Marie Stuart Jackson, Augustus G. Dill and 350 others, during the exhibition, and entitled "The People of Peoples and Their Gifts to Men."

PRELUDE

The lights of the Court of Freedom blaze. A trumpet blast is heard and four heralds, Black and of gigantic stature, appear with silver trumpets and standing at the four corners of the temple of beauty cry:

"Hear ye, hear ye! Men of all the Americas, and listen to the tale of the eldest and strongest of the races of mankind, whose faces be Black. Hear ye, hear ye, of the gifts of Black men to this world, the Iron Gift and Gift of Faith, the Pain of Humility and the Sorrow Song of Pain, the Gift of Freedom and of Laughter, and the undying Gift of Hope. Men of the world, keep silence and hear ye this!"

Four banner bearers come forward and stand along the four walls of the temple. On their banners is written:

"The First Gift of the Negro to the world, being the Gift of Iron. This picture shall tell how, in the deep and beast-bred forests of Africa, mankind first learned the welding of iron, and thus defense against the living and the dead."

What the banners tell the heralds solemnly proclaim.

FIRST EPISODE. THE GIFT OF IRON:

The lights grow dim. The roar of beasts is heard and the crash of the storm. Lightnings flash. The dark figure of an African savage hurries across the foreground, frightened and cowering and dancing. Another follows defying the lightning and is struck down; others come until the space is filled with 100 huddling, crowding savages. Some brave the storm, some pray their Gods with incantation and imploring dance. Mothers shield their children, and husbands their wives. At last, dimly enhaloed in mysterious light, the Veiled Woman apears, commanding in stature and splendid in garment, her dark face faintly visible, and in her right hand Fire, and Iron in her left. As she passes slowly round the Court the rhythmic roll of tomtoms begins. Then music is heard; anvils ring at the four corners. The arts flourish, huts arise, beasts are brought in and there is joy, feasting and dancing.

A trumpet blast calls silence and the heralds proclaim

THE SECOND EPISODE, SAYING:

"Hear ye, hear ye! All of them that come to know the Truth, and listen to the tale of the wisest and gentlest of the races of men whose faces be Black. Hear ye, hear ye, of the Second Gift of Black men to this world, the Gift of Civilization in the dark and splendid valley of the Nile. Men of the world, keep silence and hear ye this." *The banners of the banner bearers change and read:*

"The Second Gift of the Negro to the world, being the Gift of the Nile. This picture tells how the meeting of Negro and Semite in ancient days made the civilization of Egypt the first in the world."

There comes a strain of might music, dim in the distance and drawing nearer. The 100 savages thronged round the whole Court rise and stand listening. Slowly there come fifty veiled figures and with them come the Sphinx, Pyramid, the Obelisk and the empty Throne of the Pharaoh drawn by oxen. As the cavalcade passes, the savages, wondering, threatening, inquiring , file by it. Suddenly a Black chieftain appears in the entrance, with the Uraeus in one hand and the winged Beetle in the other. The Egyptians unveil and display Negroes and mulattoes clothed in the splendor of the Egyptian Court. The savages salaam; all greet him as Ra, the Negro. He mounts the throne and the cavalcade, led by posturing dancers and Ra, and fol-

lowed by Egyptians and savages, pass in procession around to the right to the thunder of music and tomtoms. As they pass, Ra is crowned as Priest and King. While the Queen of Sheba and Candace of Ethiopia join the procession at intervals.

Slowly all pass out save fifty savages, who linger examining their gifts. The lights grow dim as Egyptian culture dies and the fifty savages compose themselves to sleep. As they sleep the light returns and the heralds proclaim

THE THIRD EPISODE, SAYING:

"Hear ye, hear ye! All them that come to see the light and listen to the tale of the bravest and truest of the races of men, whose faces be Black. Hear ye, hear ye, of the Third Gift of black men to this world—a Gift of Faith in Righteousness hoped for but unknown; men of the world, keep silence and hear ye this!" The banners change and read:

"The Third Gift of the Negro to the world, being a Gift of Faith. This episode tells how the Negro race spread the faith of Mohammed over half the world and built a new culture thereon."

There is a sound of battle. The savages leap to their feet. Mohammed and fifty followers whirl in and rushing to the right beat the savages back. Fifty Songhay enter and attack the Mohammedans. Fifty other Mohammedans enter and attack the Songhay. Turning, the Songhay bear the last group of Mohammedans back to the left where they clash with the savages. Mohammedan priests strive and exhort among the warriors. At each of the four corners of the temple a priest falls on his face and cries: "God is God! God is God! There is no God but God, and Mohammed is his prophet!" Four more join, others join until gradually all is changed from battle to the one universal cry: "God is God! God is God! There is no God but God, and Mohammed is his prophet!" In each corner, however, some Mohammedans hold slaves in shackles, secretly.

Mansa Musa appears at the entrance with entourage on horseback, followed by Black Mohammedan priests and scholars. The procession passes around to the right with music and dancing, and passes out with Mohammedans and Songhay, leaving some Mohammedans and their slaves on the stage.

The herald proclaims

THE FOURTH EPISODE, SAYING:

"Hear ye, hear ye! All them that know the sorrow of the world. Hear ye, hear ye, and listen to the tale of the humblest and the mightiest of the races of men whose faces be Black. Hear ye, hear ye, and learn how this race did suffer of Pain, of Death and Slavery and yet of this Humiliation did not die. Men of the world, keep silence and hear ye this!" The banners change again and say:

"The Fourth Gift of the Negro to the world, being a Gift of Humiliation. This gift shows how men can bear even the Hell of Christian slavery and live."

The Mohammedans force their slaves forward as European traders enter. Other Negroes, with captives, enter. The Mohammedans take gold in barter. The Negroes refuse gold, but are seduced by beads and drink. Chains rattle. Christian missionaries enter, but the slave trade increases. The wail of the missionary grows fainter and fainter until all is a scene of carnage and captivity with whip and chain and only a frantic priest, staggering beneath a cross and crowned with bloody thorns, wanders to and fro in dumb despair.

There is silence. Then a confused moaning. Out of the moaning comes the slave song, "Nobody Knows the Trouble I've Seen," and with it and through the chained and bowed forms of the slaves as they pass out is done the Dance of Death and Pain.

The stage is cleared of all its folk. There is a pause, in which comes the Dance of the Ocean, showing the transplantation of the Negro race over seas.

Then the heralds proclaim

THE FIFTH EPISODE, SAYING:

"Hear ye, hear ye! All them that strive and struggle. Hear ye, hear ye, and listen to the tale of the stoutest and the sturdiest of the races of men whose faces be Black. Hear ye, hear ye, and learn how this race did rise out of slavery and the valley of the shadow of death. Men of the world, keep silence and hear ye this!" The banners change again and read:

"The Fifth Gift of the Negro to the world, being a Gift of Struggle Toward Freedom. This picture tells of Alonzo, the Negro pilot of Columbus, of

Stephen Dorantes who discovered New Mexico, of the brave Maroons and valiant Haytians, of Crispus Attucks, George Lisle and Nat Turner."

Twenty-five Indians enter, circling the Court right and left, stealthily and watchfully. As they sense the coming of the whites, they gather to one side of the temple, watching.

Alonzo, the Negro, enters and after him Columbus and Spaniards, in mail, and one monk. They halt at the other side of the temple and look about searchingly, pointing at the Indians. Slaves follow. One of the slaves, Stephen Dorantes, and the monk seek the Indians. The monk is killed and Stephen returns, circling the Court, tells his tale and dies. The Spaniards march on the Indians. Their slaves—the Maroons—revolt and march to the left and meet the Indians on the opposite side. The French, some of the mulattoes and Negroes, enter with more slaves. They march after the Spanish. Their slaves, helped by mulattoes and Toussaint, revolt and start back. The French follow the Spaniards, but the returning Haytians meet oncoming British. The Haytians fight their way through and take their place next to the Maroons. Still more slaves and white Americans follow the British. The British and Americans dispute. Attucks leads the Americans and the British are put to flight. Spanish, French and British, separated by dancing Indians, file around the Court and out, while Maroons, Haytians and slaves file around in the opposite direction and meet the Americans. As they pass, the French, by guile, induce Toussaint to go with them. There is a period of hesitation. Some slaves are freed, some Haytians resist aggression. George Lisle, a freed Negro, preaches the true religion as the masters listen. Peace ensues and the slaves sing at their tasks. Suddenly King Cotton arrives, followed by Greed, Vice, Luxury and Cruelty. The slaveholders are seduced. The old whips and chains appear. Nat Turner rebels and is killed. The slaves drop into despair and work silently and sullenly. The faint roll of tomtoms is heard.

The heralds proclaim

THE SIXTH EPISODE, SAYING:

"Hear ye, hear ye! citizens of New York, and learn of the deeds of eldest and strongest of the races of men whose faces be Black. Hear ye, hear ye, of the Sixth and Greatest Gift of Black men to the world,

the Gift of Freedom for the workers. Men of New York, keep silence and hear ye this." The banners change and say:

"The sixth and last episode, showing how the freedom of Black slaves meant freedom for the world. In this episode shall be seen the work of Garrison and John Brown; of Abraham Lincoln and Frederick Douglass, the marching of Black soldiers to war and the hope that lies in little children."

The slaves work more and more dejectedly and drivers force them. Slave music comes. The tomtoms grow louder. The Veiled Woman appears with fire and iron. The slaves arise and begin to escape, passing through each other to and fro, confusedly. Benezet, Walker and Garrison enter, scattering their writings, and pass slowly to the right, threatened by slave drivers. John Brown enters, gesticulating. A knot of Negroes follow him. The planters seize him and erect a gallows, but the slaves seize his body and begin singing "John Brown's Body."

Frederick Douglass enters and passes to the right. Sojourner Truth enters and passes to the left. Sojourner Truth cries: "Frederick, is God dead?" Voices take up the cry, repeating: "Frederick, is God dead?" Douglass answers: "No, and therefore slavery must end in blood." The heralds repeat: "Slavery must end in blood."

The roll of drums is heard and the soldiers enter. First, a company in blue with Colonel Shaw on horseback.

A single voice sings "O Freedom." A soprano chorus takes it up.

The Boy Scouts march in.

Full brasses take up "O Freedom."

Little children enter, and among them symbolic figures of the laborer, the Artisan, the Servant of Men, the Merchant, the Inventor, the Musician, the Actor, the Teacher, Law, Medicine and Ministry, the All-Mother, formerly the Veiled Woman, now unveiled in her chariot with her dancing brood, and the bust of Lincoln at her side.

With burst of music and blast of trumpets, the pageant ends and the heralds sing:

"*Hear ye, hear ye, men of all the Americas, ye who have listened to the tale of the oldest and strongest of the races of mankind, whose faces be Black. Hear ye, hear ye, and forget not the gift of Black men to this world—the Iron Gift and Gift of Faith, the Pain of Humility and Sorrow Song of Pain, the* Gift of Freedom and Laughter and the undying Gift of Hope. Men of America, break silence, for the play is done.*"

Then shall the banners announce:

"*The play is done!*"[2]

WHY WE ARE AT WAR
1918

United States Food Administration

Why We Are At War is pageantry for patriotic propaganda, in this case, to persuade African Americans to support their nation's entry into World War I. Initially, W.E.B. Du Bois had questioned the rationale for a segregated army. The training of Negro officers at Fort Des Moines and the drafting of African Americans to fight in Europe for freedoms denied at home, did not satisfy his sense of fairness. Nevertheless, two years later, in the hope of achieving some equality, he published an editorial, "Close Ranks" in *Crisis* Magazine in which he recommended that Negroes join the military and fight for democracy.

During the war, two Black Americans, Arthur Ulysses Craig and E. T. Atwell, heads of the Negro Press Section in the Educational Division of the United States Food Administration, dispatched letters to towns and cities where African Americans lived in large numbers. Their aim was to reach every possible group of Blacks through the Black press, schools, moving picture theatres, fraternal institutions, and churches. After ascertaining the names and number of local theatres (Chicago listed 104) and their seating capacities, the Food Administration sent each a pageant supporting the war efforts, with instructions that it be performed on July 4th by the local Black citizens. The introductory letter and pageant outline with speeches is printed below.[3]

United States Food Administration

Washington, D.C.
May 27, 1918

Dear Sir:

Enclosed herewith you will find suggestive plans for having the Negro celebrate July 4th by having appropriate exercises of a win-the-war nature.

The County Food Administrator, with your approval, will have charge of the celebration for which

---

2. *The Crisis* (November 1913).

3. James V. Hatch uncovered these pageant materials in the files of the U.S. Food Administration in the National Archives. Produced here are (1) the introductory letter, (2) the outline for the pageant, (3) instructions on how to organize the pageant, and (4) the text of the major speech (edited version) to be delivered.

you will find suggestive plans for the guidance of the Food Administrator. If these suggestive plans meet with your approval, we shall send at your request programs and directions for all you county food administrators [see below].

It is further suggested that in case of an all-day celebration, the Department of Agriculture, the Department of Labor, the Council of National Defense, the Red Cross, etc., be given an opportunity to take part in the exercises of the day and have exhibits.

—Negro Press Section
Educational Division

Fourth of July Celebration

(Time 1½ to 2 hours)

PRAYER—Short Prayer. (4 min.)

MUSIC—"Star Spangled Banner" by band, orchestra or sung by audience. If not known, a choir or a quartet to sing one stanza. (2 min.)

INTRODUCTORY REMARKS—(Message from the President)—"Mr. Hoover's Appeal to the Twelve Million Negroes in the United States," read by the Colored Federal Administrator, the Mayor or a member of the State Legislature, etc. (5 min.)

"WHY WE ARE AT WAR"—Address furnished by the Negro Press Section. Children with American flags and Allies' flags march on stage and stand in line side by side. The speaker then takes his place in front of the children, and delivers his address. (15 min.) [See text below]

MUSIC—"Onward, Christian Soldiers" by band, choir, quartet or audience. (5 min.)

"Food Will Win the War." Notes furnished by the Negro Press Section. Demonstrated with talks by a teacher of domestic science in the U.S. Food Administration uniform. Picture of costume furnished. (30 min.)

CONSERVATION AND CANNING—By War Kitchen.

MUSIC—"Over There."

ADDRESS—"Labor for Victory."—Furnished by Negro Press Section from the Bureau of Negro Economics, Department of Labor. (15 min.)

MUSIC—"Before I'd Be a Slave," or "Work for the Night Is Coming." (5 min.)

ADDRESSES—Two-minute talks by visitors, or if the chairman wishes, A Red Cross talk. (6 min.)

MUSIC—"Keep the Home Fires Burning." Children (5 min.)

REMARKS—By Chairman.

MUSIC

BENEDICTION

Notes for County Food Administrator

re 4th of July Celebration

The County Food Administrator is to appoint a committee who will carry out the Fourth of July Celebration according to his directions. It is important for the success of the celebration that all members of the committee are in harmony. A good plan is to select three or more Negroes of good character and ability, having the respect of both white and Black citizens, and have them assist in the selection of the committee.

Do not let the program extend over two hours. Meetings fail of their purpose by being too long. When people begin to leave, cut your program. Be sure the meeting accomplishes its object.

In arranging for this celebration, see that every group of Negroes, such as ministers of the different denominations, day and Sunday School teachers, lodges, physicians, businessmen, farmers, editors of Negro papers, etc., have a representative on the program, or have something to do with the celebration.

Decorations: Red, white and blue and American flags and flags of Allies.

If children take part, be sure that they talk loudly enough to be heard. Have a second child to learn a part, so that in case the first child is sick, the second child can take the part.

The program may be printed by a colored printer as a patriotic donation.

You may find that a union or one meeting cannot be held; then allow the separate meetings to be held.

The celebration may be held on school grounds, in a grove, fair grounds, in a large hall or theatre. The cooperation of the white citizens is desired and may secure the use of a theatre for the purpose of the celebration.

Have the sheriff appoint colored men to assist in keeping order. No intoxicants to be allowed on the grounds.

The point of the celebration to reflect the serious conditions of the war and the celebration to be not for pleasure, except for the children; the men and women are to be present that they may learn what they can do to help stop the destruction of their liberty, as well as the liberty of all free men—or to keep from being slaves.

Why We Are at War[4]

"You have just learned how great, grand and glorious your country is, and when you see the Stars and Stripes floating in the sky, you have a right to feel proud because you are an American citizen. Your country may be wrong at times, but it is your country just the same, and the best on earth. If you think your country is wrong, you as American citizens know how to correct the wrong. Americans today are not trying to make their country perfect, they have a more important duty and task, which is to save their country, or make the world safe for democracy. Lincoln considered that man a traitor who in time of war merely expresses doubt as to his country's winning the war.

"Today we celebrate the birth of our beloved country or nation, but with a heavy heart, ready to give our life's blood that we may continue to live as free men and not as slaves. For over 3,000 years men of different nations have been trying to make laws so that the people could live as free men and not as slaves. Today Germany is trying to destroy the government of free people, and all men everywhere will be put into slavery by Germany, which has never felt the spirit of freedom.

"Germany, while enjoying all the confidence and good will of the people of the earth, has been using all its scientific knowledge to find a way to be pre-

pared that it might rule the nations of the earth. Germany has tried to make her task of conquest easy by every way she can and especially by breaking whatever bonds of union there are in a nation. For instance, in this country the German Government has created with more or less success a bad feeling between the different classes of people by lies well told. The stories which you heard last year that our government was going to take your canned fruit or your money from the banks are evidence of this. These statements were circulated that you might lose confidence in your country. We may quarrel among ourselves, but like the case of the peacemaker who takes part in the quarrel between husband and wife, we will both jump on the third party, and so those who tried to make the Negro disloyal found that the Negro could not be persuaded to do anything against his country.

"This is a world religious war, to settle for all time whether man shall be governed by the law that might is right or by the law of justice, freedom, and equality. Does the Kaiser believe in God? No. If the Kaiser believed in God he would not destroy the large churches of Europe, the first thing at which the Germans aim their big guns. Can the Kaiser love God and at the same time murder defenseless men, women, and children, or seek by lies to make one class of people hate the other?

"No! The Kaiser's god is not our God of perfect love, justice, and perfect goodness. Shall the world be governed by Germany, or shall all nations be free to improve their governments, as they have been doing now for over 3,000 years? This nation under Lincoln said that men should never be made slaves; so today we fight for the freedom of our nation and the nations of the earth—or, to make the world safe for democracy. There is no future for men and women, Black or white, until the world is safe for democracy. We have a present duty, which is to do all we can to win the war. We cannot remain a free people—we do not deserve to be free—unless in all things we stand by our government together with all free people who are fighting to make the world safe for democracy. For us, Black and white, it is freedom or slavery."

---

4. The central address by the government has been edited to save space; however, all its original points remain intact.

APPEARANCES

1925

Garland Anderson (1886–1939)

Garland Anderson may be best remembered in England as the Black man who introduced Nu-Snack, the cold malted milk, there in the 1930s. In America he was the first Black to have a full-length play produced on Broadway, which he accomplished through persistence, talent, and willpower. His spirit was that of the time—"Yes, I can." Anderson's boyhood was nearly as dramatic as the plot of his play. Born in Wichita, Kansas, the fourth of twelve children, he had completed four years of schooling before his father moved to take a job as a janitor in the Sacramento, California, Post Office. When he was eleven, his mother died and he ran away from home. After knocking about for a time hawking newspapers and serving as a dining car waiter on the railroad, in 1917 he became a bellboy and sometime switchboard operator at the Braeburn Hotel Apartments in San Francisco.

Anderson reputedly never drank, smoked tobacco, or used crude language, and for two years he studied Christian Science, admiring the possibilities it offered for controlling one's own destiny. One day, given a free ticket to the theatre by a hotel resident, he saw the morality drama, *The Fool* (1922), by Channing Pollock. Immediately he realized that to tell the world his own message, he must write a play.

> At first, the idea seemed absurd. . . . No one realized more than myself that though I wanted to write this play, I had no training in the technique of dramatic construction; but I also realized that to shirk what I wanted to do could be likened to the outer shell of the acorn after it was planted in the ground saying to the inner stir of life for expression, "What are you stirring for? Surely you don't expect to become a great oak tree?" With this firm conviction I determined to write a play.

In three weeks of writing between calls at the switchboard, he had completed the story of Carl, a Black bellhop, falsely accused of rape. He entitled his three-act drama *Don't Judge by Appearances*, later abbreviated to *Appearances*. At a friend's suggestion, he sent the play to the actor Al Jolson, who gave the novice playwright a trip to New York to seek his fortune. A backers' audition was arranged at the Waldorf; the name of Governor Al Smith appeared on the invitation. Richard Harrison (De Lawd in *Green Pastures*, 1930) read *Appearances* to 600 guests while Anderson sat nearby in his bellhop uniform. One hundred and forty dollars was raised, nearly enough to pay for the rental of the hall.

He wrote to President Coolidge, and when an appointment was refused, he went directly to the White House and persuaded the president's secretary to allow him to meet the president (possibly as part of a group). Whatever the case, it was a publicity coup. Anderson reported, "It was due in no small measure to President Coolidge's interest in my work that my play was produced in New York."

On June 19, Lester A. Sagar, manager of the Central Theatre, took over the production of *Appearances* with its cast of fourteen. Sagar cast Black actors as the "three colored characters": Lionel Monagas, Evelyn Mason, and Doe Doe Green. It was a bold move. Broadway policy in 1925 was to have white actors play "colored" roles in blackface to avoid mixed casts and controversy like the one caused by the interracial casting of Eugene O'Neill's *All God's Chillun Got Wings* in the year previous, 1924, when the press had demanded that the Off-Broadway production be banned because Paul Robeson kissed the hand of the white actress.

Rehearsals had hardly begun when a headline appeared in a New York daily: "Nedda Harrigan Quits Play with Negro in the Cast." But Broadway was in transition. Because *Appearances* succeeded with a mixed cast, David Belasco took courage and produced *Lulu Belle* (1926) with white actors as mulattos, but the rest of the company was Black.

Appearances opened at the Frolic Theater on October 13, 1925, and ran twenty-three performances. Then, for two years, the play toured Los Angeles, Seattle, Chicago, and San Francisco, playing several weeks or months in each city. On April 1, 1929, *Appearances* opened again in New York at the Hudson Theater. This time it ran twenty-four performances.

Critical reception to the first opening had been kind; the white critics were amazed that a Negro bellhop with a fourth-grade education had written a play. Four years later, they were less kind, faulting the structure and finding Anderson's drama more amateurish. Black critics, with their own political agenda, saw Anderson as a white creation, an image that Anderson himself did little to dispel when he made such statements as,

> The White race is the superior race of this age. In making this statement I do not feel that it is any reflection on my own race. The White race has centuries of civilization behind it, while the Negro race has less than a hundred years since its slavery in America in which it can lay claim to any civilized status.

Undaunted, the production traveled to London in March 1930, where the Black comedian Doe Doe Green (in the role of Rufus) so delighted the English that he became a *succès de curiosité* and was given billing larger than the play's title. Despite the fact that Rufus became the star, the theme of *Appearances*—"as a man thinketh, so is he"—is clearly personified by Carl, the bellhop. This sober, hardworking, cheerful, and very self-possessed man was certainly an advance in dignity over any Black image on the professional stage at that time and was a sharp contrast to the minstrel-like Rufus.

While in London, Anderson met the queen and the popular authors of the day, including John Galsworthy. He was the first Black man to become a member of the international writers' organization P.E.N. He also met Doris Sequirra, daughter of a prominent physician, whom he later brought to America and married. She recorded their experiences as a racially mixed couple in her book *Nigger Lover*.

Anderson's play was a brave one for presenting in 1925 a Black man *falsely* accused by a white woman. How could he dare present a white woman whose virtue was inferior to that of a Black man? To account for this plot revelation, he had to manufacture a denouement for Broadway's satisfaction, and he did.

Garland Anderson had little or no influence on the subsequent Black theatre, although he claimed to have written three other plays. One, *Extortion*, a seven-character play, was optioned by David Belasco but was never produced. The last years of

Anderson's life were spent as an ordained minister of Constructive Thinking at the Truth Center. He traveled widely, lecturing, and published a book on his beliefs, *Uncommon Sense*.

A newspaper in Regina, Canada, reporting on one of Anderson's lectures in 1936, wrote: "He is the first Negro since Booker T. Washington to tour the country speaking to white people only. Seldom, he admitted, does a Negro ever appear to hear him. 'They are not interested,' he said rather sadly." But to make moral judgments about Anderson and his play is perhaps to lose sight of a trait that has been typically American: those who believe that personal hard work can triumph over all obstacles.

Appearances

CAST OF CHARACTERS

FRANK THOMPSON
CARL
MRS. GLADYS THOMPSON
FRED KELLARD
ELSIE BENTON
LOUISE THORNTON
JUDGE THORNTON
RUFUS JONES
ELLA
JACK WILSON
POLICE OFFICER
JUDGE ROBINSON
CLERK OF COURT
COURT STENOGRAPHER
GERALD SAUNDERS
HIRAM MATTHEWS
A. A. ANDREWS
BAILIFF

PROLOGUE

(SCENE: *lobby of the Hotel Mount Shasta. A small residential hotel in San Francisco. There is a desk, a partition left of the desk that partially masks door to an office. In centre of left wall is a staircase going up and off left. The main entrance is right. Entrance back of desk by lifting section of desk. Service phone back of desk, a cigar, cigarette case. Left and below stairs door to service quarters. Other furniture to suit.*

TIME: *7:30 evening.*

DISCOVERED: *at rise:* JUDGE ROBINSON *and* JUDGE THORNTON *both seated. Lights up)*

JUDGE ROBINSON   Same old topics, nothing new. Can't find anything in the paper.
JUDGE THORNTON   Tell me, Judge Robinson, do you believe this man whom you were forced to sentence to-day was guilty.
JUDGE ROBINSON   Why—yes, I do.
JUDGE THORNTON   Sorry I can't agree with you, but I don't think he was.

JUDGE ROBINSON   How can you say that, Judge Thornton, when you were in court yourself, for surely you could see that all the appearances were against him.

JUDGE THORNTON   I know, but I have come to believe we cannot judge entirely by appearances.

JUDGE ROBINSON   You're getting sentimental in your old age. Why not only the appearances, but the testimony, the evidence, in fact everything was against him.

JUDGE THORNTON   Admitting all of that, it was only circumstantial at the best and all during this trial to-day there was going over in my mind something which Carl (the bell-boy here) told me the other day. He described to me the most beautiful and realistic dream I ever heard. In this dream there was a trial scene which in many ways was similar to the case before you to-day.

JUDGE ROBINSON   The bell-boy. Oh, yes, he is the one who thinks a man can do anything he believes he can. What is he delving in, some kind of creed or religion?

JUDGE THORNTON   Oh, he says it is just simple faith and no particular creed or religion.

JUDGE ROBINSON   If he believes a man can do anything, then why don't he make something of himself? Why is he working as a bell-hop?

JUDGE THORNTON   That is just what I was going to tell you, he believes that his dream is coming true, for he intends to work it out himself and in doing it he will prove that any man can do what he believes he can, if his purpose is right.

JUDGE ROBINSON   How will this prove his point?

JUDGE THORNTON   He reasons this way. That if he, with color, lack of education, lack of money and all against him, can work his dream out in real life, it will prove that other people with greater advantages can naturally do greater things.

JUDGE ROBINSON   What is this dream all about?

JUDGE THORNTON   I wouldn't want to spoil the effect by trying to tell you. I'd like him to tell it to you just as he did to me, for his description is so realistic that you can almost see and hear each character.

JUDGE ROBINSON   Well, you have me interested now. I want to hear it.

(Enter CARL)

JUDGE THORNTON   Carl! I want you to tell Judge Robinson your unusual dream just as you told it to me.

CARL   Judge, it would take too long, and maybe Judge Robinson wouldn't want to listen.

JUDGE ROBINSON   Go right ahead, Carl, I haven't a thing in the world to do.

CARL   It's all so wonderful that when I think of it I just fill up, but I believe it will come true. You know my dream began right here in the lobby of this hotel, and both you, Judge Robinson and Judge Thornton were in it, and a lot of other people you both know. There was Mrs. Thornton, Mr. Wilson, Mrs. Thompson, Mr. Thompson, Mr. Kellard, and other people. Do you know I seem to see it now, just as real, just as plain . . . first I heard the telephone ring, then I saw someone appear in the distance, not so plain at first, but it seemed to grow clearer and clearer until I heard Mr. Thompson say:

(Fade out into Act One)

ACT ONE

(Scene: same as Prologue. Discovered at rise: CARL standing center. MR. THOMPSON answering phone)

THOMPSON   Yes sir . . . Mr. Morie wants his mail, Carl.

CARL   Yes, sir. I'll take it right up, sir.

(MRS. THOMPSON comes down stairs. Goes to desk)

THOMPSON *(as she passes him)*   Still angry, my dear?

MRS. THOMPSON   Who? I?—What's the use of being angry?

THOMPSON   I know I have my faults, but I don't deserve this.

MRS. THOMPSON   Maybe it's because of your faults, you still keep up the semblance. A wife sometimes is a very good protection.

THOMPSON   It's a good thing I've got a sense of humor.

(FRED KELLARD enters from swing doors)

KELLARD *(goes to desk)*   How d'ye.

THOMPSON   How do you do, sir. *(turns register and offers pen)* Nice evening, isn't it?

KELLARD   Yeh—fine—oh, I ain't expecting to stay here. I'm looking for Mr. Jack Wilson.

(CARL *enters down stairs*)

THOMPSON   Mr. Wilson's out. (*to* CARL) Did Mr. Wilson leave any message?

CARL   He said if a gentleman named Kellard called to tell him he would be back by eight o'clock. (*sits on bench*) He had to go to his office. It's almost that now.

KELLARD   Thank you. That's me. I'm Kellard. (*takes out watch*) Guess my Ingersoll's mite fast.

THOMPSON   Won't you take a seat and wait?

KELLARD   Thanks. (*sits on settee*) Great city, this.

THOMPSON   Ah, yes. San Francisco is the greatest city on the Pacific Coast, bar none.

KELLARD   Did you say bar one?

THOMPSON   I said bar none—guess you're from the East.

KELLARD   Well I was born in England, but I've been a cowpuncher so long I've almost forgotten it, the place I come from now is known as Hell's Hole, and it is. (*rises*) You got seegars there?

THOMPSON   Yes, sir.

KELLARD (*turns to* MRS. THOMPSON)   Does the lady mind if I smoke?

MRS. THOMPSON   Not at all.

KELLARD   Thanks. (*goes to desk*) I got a particular good taste in cigars.

THOMPSON (*takes a box of cigars from case*) Yes. Well, here's one I can recommend.

KELLARD (*reaches in box*)   Yes, sir. A particular good taste.

THOMPSON   Three for a dollar.

KELLARD (*takes hand away suddenly*)   Yeh— but my pocketbook limits my taste to about two for a quarter.

THOMPSON (*gets another box and offers it*) Here you are. A very good cigar.

KELLARD (*takes two. Puts one in pocket, lights other*)   Business rushin'.

THOMPSON   Saturday night is our off night. Most of our guests spend a week end in the country.

KELLARD   Must be nice to be rich. (*to* CARL) What's that you're reading, son? (CARL *stands up*) Oh! Kinder deep, ain't it?

CARL   No, sir. I don't find it so.

KELLARD   Yeh! I tried to read it, once, couldn't make a thing out of it.

CARL   You read it, sir?

KELLARD   Yes, sir. A school teacher we had up our way from Los Angeles had this book among others. Well, she was a nice cheerful little body, but somehow I couldn't get interested in her.

(THOMPSON *goes across, looks at* MRS. THOMPSON, *then looks out door left, then exits office door*)

CARL   Her. Oh!! I see! I suppose if you could have got interested in her, you might have worked up an interest in *her* books.

KELLARD (*goes to chair right of table, sits*)   You said a mouthful, son. But she certainly was a nice cheerful little body.

(ELSIE *enters door left, hesitates, then goes to desk*)

ELSIE   I beg your pardon, but do you have cigarettes?

CARL (*goes behind desk*)   Yes, ma'am. Any particular brand?

ELSIE   Have you the Deities with the cork tips?

CARL   Yes, miss.

ELSIE (*pays for cigarettes, looks all round lobby*)   So sorry to trouble you, but I forgot to get a package in town and I thought you might possibly keep them. It's nice to know a place where a lady may purchase cigarettes without going into a regular tobacco shop.

CARL (*offers coin*)   Your change, miss.

ELSIE   Keep the change. (*exits door left*)

(CARL *returns to bench*. THOMPSON *enters, looks out door left*)

KELLARD   Yes, sir. Must be plum embarrassing for that lady to go into a real tobacco shop. Yes, sir. Say don't you serve meals here?

THOMPSON   Yes, sir, but dinner's over.

KELLARD   Only asked ya to make talk. I had dinner down the street, in the Oriental Cafe. That boy's got a mighty good head on him. I tried that book he's reading. Someways I think I'm plain thick.

THOMPSON   Carl not only understands it, but I am sure he practices it, eh, Carl?

CARL   Yes, sir.

KELLARD (*sits*)   And it works?

CARL   Yes, sir.

KELLARD   Yeah, always?

CARL   It has never failed me yet.

KELLARD   As I remember it, it worked mighty well for that little school teacher, exceptin' it was kinder slow in one thing.

THOMPSON   What was that?

KELLARD   She was trying to get a husband.

THOMPSON   A husband? Wouldn't a single man do? *(both laugh)*

MRS. THOMPSON   Apparently not nowadays.

(THOMPSON exits office)

KELLARD   Well, you know what I mean.

CARL   Did she get one, sir?

KELLARD   Married the biggest crook and liar in the country.

CARL   Crook?

KELLARD   Yes, sir, and made him so durned honest, that cheatin' him is like stealing candy from a baby. He's still a right smart liar. We call him A. A. Alias Ananias.

CARL   Who was Ananias?

KELLARD   Ananias? Why, he's the grand-daddy of all the liars. Yes, sir! He could lie . . .

(LOUISE THORNTON enters stairs right, looks at KELLARD, goes to desk)

LOUISE   Stamp, Carl?

CARL   *(goes behind desk)*   Yes, Miss Thornton. How many, Miss, one, one two. I mean one two-cent stamp?

KELLARD   *(removes hat)*   I beg your pardon, ma'am. I really have better manners than to stare at a lady that way. I beg your pardon.

(THOMPSON enters)

THOMPSON   The man is waiting to see Mr. Wilson.

KELLARD   Yes, ma'am! Kellard is the name, miss, Fred Kellard.

LOUISE   *(goes to KELLARD)*   Oh, yes. Mr. Wilson spoke of you. You have a mine or something that he is interested in.

KELLARD   Yes, miss. That's just what it is. A mine or something.

THOMPSON   This is Miss Louise Thornton, daughter of Judge Thornton—and a—well, a close friend of Mr. Wilson.

(They shake hands)

KELLARD   I am pleased to meet you, miss.

CARL   *(comes from behind desk)*   Shall I mail it for you Miss Louise?

LOUISE   No. Thank you, Carl. *(starts to door left)* I'll mail it myself. It's only a little way and I'll enjoy the walk.

(CARL goes back to seat)

KELLARD   Gosh! I just thought of something.

THOMPSON   What?

KELLARD   I was so interested talking to the proprietor of that Capital Cafe, that I plum forgot to tip the waiter.

THOMPSON   Oh, I guess it'll be all right.

KELLARD   No, sir. My conscience wouldn't let me sleep. I just gotta go to put myself right with that waiter.

LOUISE   Oh, well, the mailbox is on the way to the Cafe.

KELLARD   *(goes to door left)*   Yeh, I was hoping it was.

THOMPSON   But how about Mr. Wilson?

KELLARD   Tell him we'll be back shortly. *(exit)*

THOMPSON   Mr. Jack Wilson better look out with that chap around.

MRS. THOMPSON   It might be a good thing for him. It isn't good for a man to be too sure.

THOMPSON   What do you mean by that?

MRS. THOMPSON   Oh . . . Just what I said.

THOMPSON   Wait a minute.

MRS. THOMPSON   Well?

THOMPSON   Just what did you mean by that?

MRS. THOMPSON   I said, "It isn't good for a man to be too sure"; if you don't understand, I can't explain. *(exits)*

THOMPSON   *(sits on settee)*   Carl!

CARL   Yes, sir.

THOMPSON   You know pretty nearly everything that goes on in this hotel.

CARL   Yes, sir.

THOMPSON   You must know that everything isn't as it should be between Mrs. Thompson and myself.

CARL   I'm sorry to say I do.

THOMPSON   I've heard you talk about these ideas you have and I've seen some of them work. Now what would you do, if you were in my place? Forget your color, what would you do?

CARL   *(looks at book)*   This little book says, first put myself right, sir, and everything else would be right.

THOMPSON   Suppose *she's* wrong?

CARL   I'd put myself right, sir, and everything else would be all right.

THOMPSON   Easier said than done.

CARL   No, sir, it's just as easy to do if you believe and know you can. Mrs. Thompson is a very fine lady, sir.

THOMPSON   *(goes back of desk)*   You bet she is. None better.

(JUDGE THORNTON enters. Goes directly to stairs)

JUDGE   Hello!

CARL   Good evening, Judge.

THOMPSON   Miss your dinner, Judge?

JUDGE   No, I had it at the Club. Where is Louise?

THOMPSON   She went to mail a letter. I had a bite put up in your room.

JUDGE   Oh, thanks, you're not only a good manager, Thompson, you're a fine host.

THOMPSON   The customer is always right, even when he praises us.

JUDGE   I guess you're right. Well, tell Louise when she returns that I'm up in my room. *(exits)*

(RUFUS enters)

RUFUS   Please, Mister, can I use your telephone?

THOMPSON   Go ahead. (RUFUS *looks at phone, holding it at several angles)* What's the matter?

RUFUS   I'se looking to see where I drops the nickel.

THOMPSON   That's all right, make your call and pay me after.

RUFUS   Yes, sir. Thank you, Boss. Hello, Central, I want Main 806, yes, Ma'm, that's it. Hello, is dis Main 806? Mrs. Harper, please. I see you had an ad in the paper Tuesday for a colored boy. Did you get the boy? Is he satisfactory? No, he isn't satisfactory? What's the matter with that boy? Lody me. Could a boy be as bad as that. What's that? You say you're going to fire that boy to-morrow morning? Yes, ma'm, I'll be there to-morrow morning. Sure you can depend on me. *(starts for door left)*

THOMPSON   Well, Sam, it looks as though you would get that job.

RUFUS   Get it—I just lost it. I had my suspicion, I was going to get fired. Now I know it, yes, sir, I knows it. *(goes back to desk. Hands*

THOMPSON *coin)* But here's your nickel. Thank you, boss.

THOMPSON   Just a minute. What's your name?

RUFUS   My name is Rufus George Washington Jones.

THOMPSON   And what kind of work are you doing for Mrs. Harper?

RUFUS   Mrs. Harper's running a boarding house. And I was hired as janitor, but I spent most of my time washing dishes and scrubbing floors.

THOMPSON   What did she pay you?

RUFUS   Fourteen dollars a week is all I get.

THOMPSON   Well, Rufus, I need a porter and if you are willing to work I'll give you eighteen to work for me.

(Phone rings)

RUFUS   How much did you say, boss?

THOMPSON   Fifteen dollars a week.

RUFUS   I heard you the first time, boss.

THOMPSON   *(at phone)*   Hello! Sure! Delighted. *(crosses to stairs)* Take care of this boy, Carl, and look after the desk. Judge wants to see me.

CARL   Yes, sir.

(THOMPSON exits stairs right)

RUFUS   Did he say "Judge?"

CARL   Yes.

RUFUS   Jest call him Judge. He ain't a regular honest-to-goodness Judge is he?

CARL   Oh, yes, he's a regular Judge. Why?

RUFUS   I just wanted to know, in case sometime I have to say *good morning,* Judge.

CARL   That's no way to think. Don't think about the thing you don't want to happen. Only think about what you want.

RUFUS   Think! What has "thinking" got to do with what I get?

CARL   Everything, because what you think most about is what you get the most of.

RUFUS   Oh, yes. I see! What you thinking about, Master Carl?

CARL   Oh, I have a great theory. I believe a man can become anything he thinks he can. You wouldn't understand. Are you ready to start work? *(crosses to door right and rings bell)*

RUFUS   Nothin' else but!

CARL   I've rung for Miss Buford. She'll show you your *duties.*

RUFUS   Show me what . . .

CARL   Your *duties*. Your *work*.

RUFUS   Work? Oh, yes. When you said "show me my duties," I thought you meant something else entirely different.

(ELLA BUFORD *enters service door*. CARL *rises*)

ELLA   You rang, Carl?

RUFUS   Look at that, a colored girl, and a high yaller.

CARL   Yes, Miss Ella. I wish to introduce you to Mr. Rufus George Washington Jones. Have I the right name?

RUFUS   You sure has, but I'se generally called jest Rufus.

ELLA (*comes to* RUFUS)   How do you do, Rufus?

RUFUS (*shakes hands with her*)   I'm very well, Miss, and I thanks yuh for asking.

CARL   This is Miss Ella Buford, who is the acting housekeeper. Mrs. Thompson herself being the regular one.

RUFUS   Buford! Did you say Buford?

CARL   Yes.

RUFUS   I know some Bufords. It wouldn't be that you is relations to the Bufords of Gadsden, Alabama, ma home town?

ELLA   No, sir, my family came from Ohio.

RUFUS   Oh, which reminds me of a story, if I may exude. Well, one darkey meets another darkey and says, "Ain't you the darkey I met in Chicago last spring?" And the other darkey says, "I ain't never been in Chicago my whole life." Then the first darkey says, "I ain't never been in Chicago my own self," so it must have been two other darkeys.

CARL (*comes between* ELLA *and* RUFUS) What was the name of that *story-telling* porter we had about a year ago, Ella?

ELLA   Oh, you mean Mr. Percival Caldwell.

CARL   That boy just *storied* himself right out of his job, Rufus.

RUFUS   I perceive your point, Mr. Carl, yes, sir, I perceive it clearly.

CARL   Miss Buford is a law student at the University. Mrs. Thompson allows her off for her classes.

RUFUS   A law student! If I ever gets in trouble and use a lawyer, I suttinly avail myself of your professional proclivities. No jury could ever resist the charms of such a delightful defender.

CARL   Miss Ella and I are also engaged to be married, Rufus.

RUFUS   I gives yuh my firmest condemnations. I gives 'em for both of you each.

(WILSON *enters door left*)

WILSON   What is this? A colored convention?

CARL   I beg your pardon, Mr. Wilson, I didn't hear you come in. Miss Ella will show you your duties.

ELLA   This way, Rufus . . .

RUFUS   Show me my duties? Yes, sir, I know what you mean. First time he tells me duties, I think it's something entirely different. (*exit with* ELLA *service door*)

WILSON   Did anyone call?

CARL (*goes behind desk*)   Yes, sir, a Mr. Fred Kellard. He forgot something and went to attend to it. Said he would be right back.

WILSON   What did he forget? His gun?

CARL   No, sir, he forgot to tip the waiter at the Capital Cafe and he went back to attend to it.

WILSON (*goes to desk*)   Miss Louise in?

CARL   No, sir. Her father, the Judge, is in. Miss Louise went to mail a letter.

WILSON   Give me a package of Melachrinos.

CARL (*gives him cigarettes*)   Yes, sir. Charge them?

WILSON   Yes. Carl, give me a light. Hurry up Carl . . . (CARL *gives him a light*)

CARL   Yes, sir.

WILSON   About three weeks ago you and I had a heart-to-heart talk about Miss Louise.

CARL   Yes, sir.

WILSON   I told you to cut out this bunk that you have been handing her.

CARL   Yes, sir.

WILSON   The stuff you read in those books. This good in everyone and God within everything comes to pass as a result of the law. And I promised something bad would happen to you if you didn't cut it out.

CARL   Yes, sir.

WILSON   Some of the people around here seem to think you're all right. But to me you're just a slick proposition. Repeating a lot of stuff that you don't believe in yourself in order to put yourself in *good* with a lot of fool white folks.

CARL   Yes, sir.

WILSON   And I'll tell the world you seem to be getting away with it.

CARL   Yes, sir.

WILSON   Now, for some reason Miss Louise is trying to postpone our wedding for a year. "Something from within" tells her to wait, "an inner voice," and I know where she got that "inner voice" and "something from within," because I've heard you use it.

CARL   Yes, sir.

WILSON   And the thought struck me—this is a slick nigger. And naturally the big thing he's after is money.

CARL   Yes, sir. It would be natural for *you* to think that.

WILSON   (*rises and goes to* CARL)   Now, last time I threatened, but I didn't seem to scare you at all.

CARL   No, sir, you didn't scare me.

WILSON   Oh, figured you were in so solid there wasn't anything I could do that would bother you?

CARL   Nothing you could do would bother me, sir.

WILSON   Yeh? Well . . . er . . . here's a better proposition. If Miss Louise changes her mind and the wedding takes place, say within a month, there's five hundred dollars in it for you.

CARL   Yes, sir.

WILSON   And you'll do it?

CARL   No, sir.

WILSON   You won't?

CARL   No, sir, I will not.

WILSON   (*back to settee, sits*)   Oh! All right, we'll see what happens.

CARL   You call me a "slick nigger" and say these things I work so hard to believe in are "bunk." You're wrong, Mr. Wilson. You're wrong when you say I'm slick, wrong when you call my ideas "bunk." Mr. Wilson, I'll admit that I'm just a negro servant, a good servant to everyone, even to you.

WILSON   I was wrong, Carl. You're not a slick nigger. You're just a damn fool nigger.

CARL   But there's no color in words, in ideas, Mr. Wilson. They belong to anyone who asks for them.

THOMPSON   (*comes downstairs*)   Hello Jack!

WILSON   Hello, Frank!

THOMPSON   Just up having a little drink—

"Apollinaris Water" with your future father-in-law. He has a good brand.

WILSON   Oh, yes. Come over and sit down.

THOMPSON   Sure! (*to* CARL) Anything?

CARL   No, sir.

WILSON   That damned nigger gets my goat.

THOMPSON   Don't do that, Wilson! He can hear you. If you knew how hard it is to get as good a boy as he is . . . you think of me, damn it. You're always picking on him. Sometimes I think because you *know* he won't fight back.

WILSON   All anybody has to do to get a rise out of you is to say something against Carl. Forget it. I was just kidding. (*phone rings*) Listen, this chap Kellard, I told you about.

(CARL *answers phone*)

THOMPSON   Yes, he was in.

WILSON   Well, he has a selenium mine.

THOMPSON   Yes.

WILSON   And there's a lot of money in it for someone to get out.

CARL   (*from phone*)   Mr. Thompson!

THOMPSON   What is it?

CARL   Mrs. Thompson says to send up the porter. The bathroom door is stuck in Mrs. French's room. (*goes to service door right*)

THOMPSON   All right. Attend to it . . . and . . . check up those grocery bills, Carl.

CARL   I'll do it, sir. (*exits service door*)

THOMPSON   All right, now, shoot!

WILSON   This chap, Kellard, has been working this mine called "Hell's Hole" and he needs about a hundred and fifty thousand dollars to develop it.

THOMPSON   And he's here to try and get it?

WILSON   Yeh. The minute he came to me I wired East and I've got an offer of one hundred thousand dollars for the property as it stands.

THOMPSON   Good boy.

WILSON   Yes, but the damn fool won't sell.

THOMPSON   Did you show him the offer?

WILSON   I did *not*. I sounded him out and found he was dead set, that he wouldn't sell for—for half a million.

THOMPSON   I see.

WILSON   You want a piece of it?

THOMPSON   What, the mine?

WILSON   No, the cash offer.

THOMPSON   I don't get yuh!

WILSON   I've got a contract drawn up, that he's going to sign giving me power of attorney to handle everything with no time limit. Now if you've got ten thousand to spare, I'll declare you in.

THOMPSON   Say! Have you stopped to think how this guy Kellard might act if he got riled?

WILSON   Handling roughnecks like him is one of the best things I do. Well, how about it?

THOMPSON   I haven't got the money.

WILSON   Your wife has.

THOMPSON   Yes, but there's a slight coldness there.

WILSON   What about?

THOMPSON   I don't exactly know, but I think that someone has tipped her off about something.

WILSON   You think she's wise about Elsie?

THOMPSON   No, I guess her suspicions are just general, but I wish you'd suggest to Elsie to keep away from here.

WILSON   Has she been here?

THOMPSON   Came in here to-night. Pulled a bum story about forgetting to buy some cigarettes. You gotta tell her to keep away from here.

WILSON   I'll do that all right. But did your wife see her?

THOMPSON   No. She was sitting there writing a letter, but she didn't look up.

WILSON   Oh, I see. So this doesn't interest you.

(JUDGE THORNTON *comes downstairs*)

THOMPSON   No, unless I can fix up things with Gladys.

JUDGE   Did I understand you to say that Louise went out to mail a letter?

THOMPSON   Yes.

JUDGE   She must have gone to Oakland to do it.

WILSON   Was she alone?

THOMPSON   No. She left here with Mr. Kellard.

WILSON   With whom?

THOMPSON   Kellard, she came in while he was here and I presented her.

JUDGE   Kellard! Who is Mr. Kellard?

WILSON   A client of mine. Hardly a chap I would introduce to Louise, however, a roughneck miner.

(*Phone rings*)

THOMPSON   That's so? He didn't strike me that way.

JUDGE   No?

(*Enter* CARL *from service door. Crosses to desk at once to answer phone*)

THOMPSON   No. A rough, breezy sort of a chap. From the height of his heels I should say an ex-cowpuncher.

CARL (*at phone*)   Yes, ma'am. Someone for you Mr. Wilson.

WILSON   Thanks.

JUDGE   Maybe that's Louise.

WILSON (*at phone.* JUDGE *goes to writing desk*)   Hello! Yes! Yes! Well, all you've got to do is to go through with it. Do as you're told! If there's any trouble I'll take care of you. (*goes down to* JUDGE)

(RUFUS *comes downstairs*)

THOMPSON (*from behind desk*)   Did you fix that bathroom door, Rufus?

RUFUS   Yes, sir. Sure did! She gives me thirty cents to get some ice cream for my own self. . . . (RUFUS *starts to door*)

THOMPSON   All right, Rufus, you can go and get it. And Rufus . . .

RUFUS (*stops*)   Yes, sir.

THOMPSON   Be sure you get *ice cream.*

RUFUS   Yes, sir, boss. I know what you mean, but the place I could get that dun got raided by the government. I'se going to get me a strawberry nut sundae just drippin' with chocolate juice. (*exits*)

LOUISE (*enters left*)   Hello, Jack. Daddy.

(KELLARD *enters*)

WILSON   Where were you?

KELLARD (*to* WILSON)   She was with me. But don't shoot me until you hear the end of it. It is all my fault.

LOUISE   Oh, it was not your fault.

KELLARD   Mr. Wilson, to set your mind at rest, before I had time to tell her that her eyes were like the skies over Mount Shasta or that her hair was like the sun-kissed wheat tossed in the wind, she held up her hand so that I could see that she had been corralled by a better man.

LOUISE   Oh, er . . . Daddy, this is Mr. Kellard, a friend of Jack's. Mr. Kellard, my father, Judge Thornton.

KELLARD I throw myself on the mercy of the Court, your Honor.

JUDGE Perhaps it isn't the first time, Mr. Kellard.

KELLARD Well, I will admit that good luck and smart lying has saved me several times.

WILSON Where were you?

KELLARD May I explain?

WILSON (*to* KELLARD) No, no, thank you. (*to* LOUISE) I think you should explain. Your father and I were worried and we were just going out to find you.

JUDGE Jack, being an ardent young lover, may have been worried, my dear, but I can hardly say I was.

WILSON You left to mail a letter—the mail box is two blocks from here and you're away nearly half an hour.

KELLARD I can explain everything, Mr. Wilson, and when I have you will see it was all my fault.

LOUISE It was not your fault any more than it was mine.

WILSON (*to* KELLARD) You'll understand my feelings, Kellard, when I tell you that there have been several attacks recently around this neighborhood on young and unprotected women.

JUDGE Is that so? I haven't heard of it.

WILSON (*to* JUDGE) The police have kept it out of the papers.

JUDGE Well, you're the District Attorney, you'd have to prosecute these cases, so you ought to know.

WILSON (*to* KELLARD) The girls claim it was a colored man who annoyed them. So naturally, you understand, Kellard.

KELLARD Certainly, but I can't figure out what danger Miss Louise would be in from anybody if she was with me.

THOMPSON Well, perhaps he thinks you're the danger!

KELLARD I beg your pardon, sir, but that remark might be interpreted several ways.

THOMPSON I meant that you're young and not hard to look at and haven't any trouble expressing yourself.

KELLARD That last crack of yours—that no trouble in expressing yourself, sometimes referred to by my friends as gabbing, that really is what delayed Miss Louise.

WILSON Miss Thornton. You'll pardon my calling your attention to your little slip—Miss Thornton, not Miss Louise.

LOUISE I like the way he drawls "Miss Louise," and when he corrected himself I told him not to.

WILSON I suppose he liked the way you said Fred and that's what you call him.

LOUISE Oh, don't be silly!

JUDGE Now suppose we change the subject. Mr. Kellard, I understand that you are a miner, or an owner of a mine.

KELLARD Yes, I have a selenium mine. (*takes document from pocket*) Here's the prospectus.

LOUISE If you want to know he started telling me about his mine and your interest in it, and that was why I was so interested and didn't notice how far we were walking.

WILSON All right, I accept your apology.

LOUISE But I'm not apologizing. I have nothing to apologize for. Really, Jack, you're awfully aggravating!

JUDGE Reckon my way of changing the subject wasn't a happy one. I'll try again.

KELLARD Better not, Judge. I'm sorry and I'll ease myself right out.

(KELLARD *starts for door* WILSON *goes up and stops him*)

WILSON I have that contract here for you to sign, Kellard.

KELLARD Yeah? I reckon it can wait. Yes, sir. I reckon I'd rather let it wait.

WILSON (*takes a hold of* KELLARD) Just a minute. You have me wrong, Kellard. Listen, just a minute. In the first place I'm very much in love and perhaps a little jealous, and as Thompson says—you're young and not hard to look at. You understand.

LOUISE It is because you're angry at me for something else that you're scolding me for this.

WILSON All right. I'm sorry, I apologize.

LOUISE You should.

WILSON Well, I do.

(KELLARD *goes to* CARL *and takes book he's reading*)

KELLARD Reckon I'll try changing the subject, Judge. Once some cowboys nursing a grudge decided to settle it, and set to. It was a cruel wicked fight . . . when suddenly a little school marm from Los Angeles with ideas like is in this book, hove in sight. . . .

WILSON   Oh, I see, one of those good stories you heard.

KELLARD   No, sir. I was there.

LOUISE   You were in the fight?

KELLARD   Yes, ma'am. I was in the middle of it and on the bottom. Well, the first thing I know . . . I see that little school marm on with a hose and she said, "If you galouts will stand where you are, still, and close your eyes I'll demonstrate peace." Well, there wasn't much choice so we did as she said. Everything was quiet for about a minute, then she said "Amen."

THOMPSON   Did it stop you?

KELLARD   Sure did. We got laughing so much, we just laughed all the fight out of us, and the little school marm laughed with us.

JUDGE   (*picks up book and looks at it*)   That's one of Carl's books, isn't it?

KELLARD   Yes, sir.

JUDGE   Carl.

CARL   Yes, Judge.

JUDGE   Could anybody do that?

CARL   Yes, Judge.

JUDGE   Well, we seem to be trying to have a battle royal.

CARL   Yes, Judge.

JUDGE   Could I do it?

CARL   Yes, Judge, that is if you believe you can.

JUDGE   Well, I believe, I believe I can!

WILSON   Darn silly bunk!

LOUISE   I don't think it bunk!

WILSON   All right, my eyes are closed.

JUDGE   Now, everybody who has rancour in their hearts, close their eyes until I say "Amen." (LOUISE *motions to* WILSON *to close his eyes. Pause. Everyone laughs*) Amen!

WILSON   Darned silly bunk.

LOUISE   Yes, but it worked. I couldn't look at you without laughing to save my life.

JUDGE   Well, Carl. Its manner of working rather surprised me but as Louise says—"It worked."

KELLARD   The fact is, Wilson, this young lady and I started in the same general direction from here and in an unguarded or thoughtless moment she asked me about the selenium mine, and you know how it is when I get going. Did you say you had those contracts?

WILSON   Yes. Want to look them over?

KELLARD   Sure I do.

WILSON   Oh, Frank, can we use your office?

THOMPSON   Of course. Go through here, Mr. Kellard.

(WILSON *exits*)

KELLARD   Sure does work, don't it?

CARL   Yes, sir.

KELLARD   Wish I could understand the darned thing. (*exits*)

(JUDGE *takes out cigar and matches and lights match*)

JUDGE   Explain yourself young lady. Explain this playing fast and loose with a young man's affections.

LOUISE (*runs to* JUDGE, *blows out match, and runs to bottom of stairs. Turns to* THOMPSON) Yes, I will. Is Mrs. Thompson in her room?

THOMPSON   Yes.

LOUISE   Anyone with her?

THOMPSON   I don't think so.

LOUISE   I'll go up and explain to her.

JUDGE   But, Louise, you listen to me . . .

LOUISE (*goes up a step*)   But . . . we walked so far that we had to get a taxi to get us back. (*step*) And the waiter is still waiting for his tip! (*step*) And here is the letter I went out to mail. (*exits*)

WILSON (*comes from office*)   Judge Thornton, will you witness this signature?

JUDGE   Why, certainly (*they exit*)

(MRS. THOMPSON *and* LOUISE *come downstairs.* THOMPSON *sees them and goes into office.*

MRS. THOMPSON (*goes to settee*)   Carl, will you ask Ella to make some lemonade?

CARL   Yes, madam, I will. (*exits*)

LOUISE (*runs up to office door, listens, then comes back*)   Yes, he's with them.

MRS. THOMPSON   Who, Jack?

LOUISE   Oh, yes, Jack's there too. Did you notice the drawly way he has?

MRS. THOMPSON   All I noticed was . . . that he seemed to be rather a fast worker.

LOUISE   Fast. Why, he's chain lightning! He has mentioned every nice thing about me that I know of and a lot more I never thought of. (*looks at office door*) He said my giggle sounded like the silvery mountain stream laughing its way over moss-covered rocks. Now . . . you . . . listen to it. Do you hear any silvery mountain stream?

MRS. THOMPSON No, it would seem to me that your drawling gentleman has had a lot of practice at that kind of conversation.

LOUISE Certainly. But how do you explain the fact that one of the ones he has practiced on hasn't gobbled him up?

MRS. THOMPSON Perhaps one of them has.

LOUISE There you go trying to spoil it all, but I don't think so. Help me find out.

MRS. THOMPSON Of course I will.

WILSON (*coming from office*) Well, that's that.

LOUISE Is . . . your . . . business finished?

(KELLARD *comes from office.* WILSON *takes* KELLARD'S *hand, shakes it and tries to start him to door*)

WILSON Signed, sealed, and delivered. Now, we won't keep you any longer, Kellard!

MRS. THOMPSON Mr. Kellard surely has no desire to tear himself away so quickly?

(KELLARD *stops. Throws hat down on sofa*)

KELLARD No, ma'am. I never give going away a thought.

MRS. THOMPSON You're probably thirsty, after your long, dry talk. I've ordered some lemonade.

KELLARD Lemonade? Lady, you saved my life! Anything I adore . . . is a nice cold glass of lemonade. (*to* LOUISE) Don't you?

LOUISE I love it!

MRS. THOMPSON *Mrs. Kellard* probably prepares it nicely.

KELLARD There ain't no Mrs. Kellard yet, but I hope Mrs. Kellard when I get her likes lemonade the way you do, Miss Thornton.

WILSON Sounds to me like a put-up job. (*goes up to desk*)

LOUISE (*to* WILSON) What do you mean dear?

WILSON You know what I mean.

LOUISE No, I don't really.

(Enter ELLA *and* CARL *from service door*)

MRS. THOMPSON Put it there, Carl. Sit down, Mr. Kellard.

KELLARD (*sits on settee*) Yes, ma'am.

MRS. THOMPSON Interrupt your studies, Ella?

ELLA No, ma'am. Shall I serve it?

(LOUISE *gives* KELLARD *a glass of lemonade*)

MRS. THOMPSON No, Ella. We'll serve ourselves.

WILSON I beg your pardon, Kellard, but real gentlemen do not seat themselves while ladies stand.

KELLARD No? Well . . . Perhaps you're right, but I learned my manners in England from my grandma, and when a lady invites me to sit, I jest naturally sit.

WILSON Oh, I didn't understand. Sorry.

ELLA Will that be all, Mrs. Thompson?

MRS. THOMPSON Yes, that's all. Good-night.

(ELLA *goes upstairs*)

CARL Good night, Ella.

ELLA Good night, Carl.

LOUISE (*turns to* CARL) Oh, Carl, aren't you and Ella engaged?

CARL Yes, Miss Louise, why?

LOUISE Is that the way you say good-night?

CARL We said good night before we came in.

ELLA (*from head of stairs*) That's why it took so long to make the lemonade. (*exits*)

CARL (*to* THOMPSON) Albert is here. May I go?

THOMPSON Of course. And if you see that boy Rufus tell him to hurry with that ice cream. He must be freezing it. Good night, Carl. (*exits*)

CARL I will, sir. Good night. (*exits*)

(JUDGE THORNTON *enters.* WILSON *goes up to phone and makes a call*)

MRS. THOMPSON Here we are, won't you have a glass of lemonade, Judge?

JUDGE Thanks.

LOUISE Jack, here's your lemonade. Here, dad.

JUDGE Business all settled up, Mr. Kellard.

KELLARD Yes, sir. I figure a month from now I ought to have enough money to start operations.

WILSON (*from phone*) I hope to interest the Judge, Kellard.

JUDGE Perhaps. Just a little. Speculation is bad at my time of life.

KELLARD See here, Judge. You're not speculating when you invest your money in my mine. No, sir, I'd rather like to tell you about it.

JUDGE   And I'd like to hear about it.

KELLARD   (*talks very fast*)   Well, this is a selenium mine up here at Hell's Hole, the ore is about 90 per cent real stuff. . . .

JUDGE   But not to-night . . . some other time.

KELLARD   Just as you say, Judge. I reckon it *is* getting late.

(*Phone rings*)

JUDGE   No, not late for young folks, but I guess I'll wander upstairs. Good night.

(THOMPSON *comes from office and answers phone*)

LOUISE   Good-night, dad.

THOMPSON   Oh, yes, Mrs. French. Why, I don't know. Should have been back long ago? I'll send him up with the ice cream the minute he comes. (*exits office*)

JUDGE   Mr. Kellard, if you are not otherwise engaged, I should be pleased to have you come here to-morrow and have dinner with me.

KELLARD   Thank you, sir.

WILSON   Fine! Be company for *you*, Judge. Louise and I are going to spend the day motoring.

LOUISE   Oh, I've forgotten that.

WILSON   I haven't.

KELLARD   You wouldn't.

WILSON   What?

KELLARD   I didn't say anything.

WILSON   Thought you did.

KELLARD   No, sorry.

JUDGE   Well, good night. (*exits*)

MRS. THOMPSON   Now, Mr. Kellard, you told Miss Thornton all about your mine. Mr. Wilson knows all about it, suppose you and I go out on the verandah and you tell me all about it.

KELLARD   Yes, ma'am.

LOUISE   Oh, I think I can stand hearing it again myself.

MRS. THOMPSON   Yes, but you can hardly expect Jack to, and I want to hear. You do want to tell me, don't you? (*exits*)

KELLARD   Yes, ma'am, sure do. (*to* LOUISE) Well, do we say good night now, Miss Thornton.

LOUISE   Good night, sir. I'm really, really glad to have met you.

KELLARD   Yeah, I'll probably be in town for two or three weeks.

WILSON   Thought you said you were going right back after we signed up?

KELLARD   I won't lie. I did say that, but since then something very, very important has come up. Something I hope will detain me. Good-night, Miss Louise. I beg your pardon, Miss Thornton. (*exits right*)

LOUISE   Good night.

WILSON   What's the idea?

LOUISE   If you are going to start that sort of talk I'm going right upstairs.

WILSON   I suppose I haven't any right to talk this way? I suppose I haven't any reason to feel hurt or abused?

LOUISE   I don't know whether you have or not, yet.

WILSON   Just when I should be feeling happy; just when I close the deal that would make me a barrel of money, so I can marry you and support you, you turn on me and act this way. Do you think you are giving me a square deal?

LOUISE   No, I don't. And I know I ought to be ashamed of myself, but I'm not.

WILSON   What have I done?

LOUISE   Perhaps it's the things you haven't done. I don't know, but for quite a while now you seem to enjoy rubbing me the wrong way. First you didn't like the way I combed my hair, then my skirts might have been longer.

WILSON   Oh, I say! You didn't take me seriously.

LOUISE   You didn't say it, but you might just as well have, and then when I became interested in Carl's books you not only made fun of them, but you tried to make fun of me and developed a positive hatred of Carl.

(WILSON *has been pacing up and down center all during this speech. He stops and almost yells*)

WILSON   That damn nigger is back of it all! He's got you hypnotized.

LOUISE   Don't talk like an idiot and for goodness' sake sit down. Pacing up and down like a bear in its cage.

(*Woman screams offstage*).

WILSON   My God! What was that? (*runs to door right. Looks out*)

(*Enter* MRS. THOMPSON *and* KELLARD. KELLARD *exits.*)

LOUISE   That's a woman screaming.

(*Offstage:* "HELP . . . HELP")

MRS. THOMPSON   Louise, there's some woman in trouble.

LOUISE   Where's Mr. Kellard?

(*Enter* THOMPSON *from office*)

THOMPSON   What's the matter? Guess I'll go and find out. (*exits*)

LOUISE   I'm going.

MRS. THOMPSON   You can do no good there. People are running from every direction.

(JUDGE *comes downstairs*)

JUDGE   I saw a mob forming. What's the matter?

MRS. THOMPSON   We don't know.

LOUISE   We heard a woman scream.

MRS. THOMPSON   There is someone coming this way, running. He's coming in here.

(RUFUS *enters door left*)

RUFUS   I didn't do nothin'. I didn't do nothin', Carl called me. They ain't going to lynch me. I didn't do nothin'. 'Fore God, I didn't. Let me go.

WILSON   What's the matter?

RUFUS   Get out of my way! Get out of my way! . . . They ain't going to get me. They ain't going to lynch me. And . . . (*rushes off*)

JUDGE   We should have held him.

(*Cries offstage:* "Lynch him. String him up. Lynch him. Lynch the damn nigger. Get a rope," etc.)

THOMPSON   The mob is coming this way. Bring the lady here.

(ELSIE BENTON *is brought in by* SAUNDERS *and* MATTHEWS. ELLA *enters*)

MRS. THOMPSON   A glass of water.

(THOMPSON *exits*)

ELLA   What is it? What is it, Miss Louise?

LOUISE   We don't know.

ELLA   Carl! (CARL *is dragged on by a Policeman,* ELLA *kneels by* CARL) Carl, boy, what have they done to you?

MRS. THOMPSON   Mrs. Benton!

JUDGE   I'm Judge Thornton, Officer, what happened?

ELSIE (*hysterically*)   I was walking along the street when this Negro attacked me and when I fought him off he called another Negro, but that's the one . . . look, he almost tore my waist off my body!

ELLA   What have they done to you? What is it, boy? Tell your Ella.

WILSON   So they got you at last, did they, Carl? This is a good chance to try that "bunk" of yours.

CARL   Bunk, that bunk, as you call it, is always with me. I've done nothing wrong and have nothing to fear.

(*Curtain*)

ACT TWO

(*A courtroom, one week later*)

JUDGE   Is that all?

WILSON   That's all.

JUDGE (*to witness*)   Then step down.

CLERK   Next witness.

WILSON   Mrs. Elsie Benton . . .

(*General murmur from witnesses, saying* "Now the case will start. So that's the woman," etc.)

CLERK (*to bailiff*)   Mrs. Elsie Benton.

BAILIFF (*calls*)   Mrs. Elsie Benton. (ELSIE BENTON *rises and goes to witness stand*)

CLERK   Name?

ELSIE   Elsie Benton.

CLERK   Address?

ELSIE   869 Pine Street.

CLERK   Raise your right hand. Do you solemnly swear that the evidence you are about to give will be the truth, the whole truth, and nothing but the truth, so help you, God?

ELSIE   I do. (*she sits*)

WILSON   Mrs. Benton, will you please explain in your own words, just what happened.

ELSIE   About nine o'clock on the evening of the sixteenth. . . .

JUDGE   Mrs. Benton, you will kindly address your remarks to the jury.

ELSIE   On the evening of the sixteenth about 9 o'clock I was going to post a letter. Just as I was walking past a vacant lot this . . . the Negro stepped out behind me, then turned suddenly and said to me "White girl, I want you to go with me." I told him to go along about his business or I would scream and started to hurry along as it was dark and I was afraid, then he took hold of me and tried to put his hand over my mouth. I screamed, trying to get away, when I heard him call "Rufus, Rufus, come help me," and I twisted in his grasp long enough to see another man come out of the vacant lot. I fought, fought desperately, fought as any woman will fight in defense of her honor, but I could feel myself being drawn nearer and nearer to that vacant lot, then I heard shouts; and before the other Negro could help, men came and rescued me.

JUDGE   Then what happened?

ELSIE   They captured the first man . . . but the other one . . . after a fight . . . got away. What happened directly after that I don't know. Everything went black. When I came to . . . two men were supporting me . . . and the first man . . . the one who accosted me . . . was in the hands of the police. . . . Everything after that is a sort of blur. . . . All I know is I awoke in my own apartment in the care of a nurse.

WILSON   Is that all you remember, Mrs. Benton?

ELSIE   Yes, sir.

WILSON   That's all, your Honor.

JUDGE ROBINSON   Does the defendant's lawyer care to question the witness?

CLERK   Your Honor, the attorney for the defendant is not present.

JUDGE ROBINSON   (*to* CARL)   Where is your attorney?

CARL   Your Honor, I have no attorney. I do not feel that one is necessary.

JUDGE ROBINSON   Young man, you are here charged with a very serious offence. If you are convicted it means a long term of imprisonment.

CARL   Your Honor, I am innocent of this charge. I shall tell nothing but the truth, and the truth needs no defense.

ELLA   Your Honor, I am here to defend Carl Sanderson.

WILSON   I object.

ELLA   But your Honor.

JUDGE ROBINSON   The objection sustained. The defendant has waived his rights to an attorney.

JUDGE THORNTON   Your Honor.

JUDGE ROBINSON   Judge Thornton.

JUDGE THORNTON   Your Honor, the defendant, Carl Sanderson, has certain ideas regarding the power of truth that we, of perhaps more mature experience, do not have, having met the power of lies. I did not know until yesterday that the defendant intended to take this stand. In fact I had been led, or perhaps misled, into the idea that his defense had been taken care of. As Carl Sanderson doesn't wish Counsel I shall respect his belief—but his co-defendant, Rufus Jones, hasn't any such scruples and it is as his attorney that I appear in the case.

JUDGE ROBINSON   It has been many years since you have been in this court, Judge Thornton. A court whose bench you so ably graced. I welcome you.

JUDGE THORNTON   I thank you, Judge Robinson.

WILSON   (*rises. To* JUDGE THORNTON)   Well, now the usual courtesies from one Judge to another having been attended to, do you wish to question the witness?

JUDGE THORNTON   No. (ELSIE *rises*)

WILSON   One moment before you leave the stand, Mrs. Benton. (*looks at papers, then to stand*) Mrs. Benton, are you a native of California?

ELSIE   No, sir. I was born in Utah.

WILSON   You are a married woman?

ELSIE   A widow, sir.

WILSON   A widow? Have you been a widow long?

ELSIE   About two years. Please don't ask me how my husband died; if he'd been alive this couldn't have happened. . . .

WILSON   One moment. (*goes to table. Picks up dress. Back to stand*) Is this the garment you wore on the night of the attack?

ELSIE   Yes.

WILSON   And it was damaged in this manner during the assault?

ELSIE   Yes.

WILSON   Your Honor, I wish to offer this in evidence.

JUDGE ROBINSON   Mark it for identification, Exhibit A.

(CLERK *takes dress, marks it, then gives it to a stenographer*)

WILSON   That is all, Mrs. Benton.

(WILSON *sits.* ELSIE *leaves stand, back to seat*)

CLERK   Next witness.

WILSON   Arresting officer.

CLERK   Officer Calahan.

BAILIFF   Officer Calahan.

(CALAHAN *rises and takes the stand*)

CLERK   Do you solemnly swear the evidence you are about to give to be the truth, the whole truth, and nothing but the truth, so help you God?

POLICEMAN   I do.

WILSON   State to the Court what you know of the case.

OFFICER   I was walking along Howard Street about 9 o'clock on Saturday evening, the sixteenth, when my attention was attracted by people running on Seventh Street. I immediately ran and arrived just in time to rescue the prisoner from the mob.

JUDGE ROBINSON   Then what happened?

OFFICER   I had considerable trouble keeping the crowd under control. They were shouting "Lynch him" and, "Get a rope." The complainant identified the prisoner and I made the arrest, charging him with assault.

JUDGE ROBINSON   Is that all you know about the case?

OFFICER   There was talk of another Negro who was concerned in the assault, but I didn't see him.

JUDGE ROBINSON   But the other man was apprehended?

OFFICER   Well, your Honor, I was so hot on his trail that he gave himself up. He knew he didn't have a chance. He's here in court.

WILSON   That's all, your Honor.

JUDGE ROBINSON   Do you wish to question the witness?

CARL   No, your honor.

JUDGE ROBINSON   You, Judge Thornton?

JUDGE THORNTON   No questions, your Honor.

JUDGE ROBINSON   That's all.

(CALAHAN *goes back to seat*)

CLERK   Next witness.

WILSON   Gerald Saunders.

CLERK   Gerald Saunders.

BAILIFF   Gerald Saunders.

(WILSON *beckons to* SAUNDERS, *who points to himself, as though to ask* "You mean me?" WILSON *nods and* SAUNDERS *beams an acknowledgment.* SAUNDERS *takes stand*)

CLERK   Your name?

SAUNDERS   Gerald Saunders.

STENOGRAPHER   I didn't get that.

CLERK   Sanders.

SAUNDERS   I beg your pardon, but the name is pronounced "Sawnders."

CLERK   All right . . . Your address?

SAUNDERS   Number eleven Poinsettia Place.

CLERK   Raise your right hand! Do you solemnly swear that the evidence you are about to give shall be the truth, the whole truth and nothing but the truth, so help you God?

SAUNDERS   I certainly do! (*sits*)

WILSON   State to the Court just what you know about the case.

SAUNDERS   Well, it was about 9 o'clock on the evening of the sixteenth. . . .

JUDGE ROBINSON (*gavel*)   A little louder, please.

SAUNDERS   Well, it was about 9 o'clock on the evening of the sixteenth; while strolling along Seventh Street I was going to make whoopee, I was startled by a woman's scream about a block away. I turned and saw a woman struggling to free herself from a man and heard her screams. Always responding to the calls of the weaker sex when in danger (*loud laugh. Gavel*), I turned and rapidly ran to the rescue. As I approached I saw another man going to join the struggle. Then other men came, but I . . . I . . . was the first on the scene.

JUDGE ROBINSON   Yes, yes, go on.

SAUNDERS   But when . . . this other man . . . this other black fellow saw me, he turned and ran away, but this one . . . was still struggling with the lady . . . the charming lady who is sitting there. I immediately launched myself into the fray and struck the Negro. Others joined me and only the arrival of the Officer, saved the man from the expression of my just wrath.

CLERK   Your Honor, I didn't get that.

JUDGE ROBINSON   His just wrath. Is that all you know?

SAUNDERS   Yes, your Honor.

JUDGE ROBINSON   I thought so. (*to* CARL) Do you wish to question the witness?

CARL   No, your Honor.

JUDGE ROBINSON   You, Judge Thornton?

JUDGE THORNTON   No, your Honor.

JUDGE ROBINSON   That's all. (*gavel*) Step down!

SAUNDERS   Oh, but your Honor, no matter what may be said here. . . .

CLERK   His Honor said "That's all."

WILSON   Hiram Matthews.

CLERK   Hiram Matthews.

BAILIFF   Hiram Matthews.

(MATTHEWS *takes stand*)

CLERK   Your name?

MATTHEWS   Hiram Matthews.

CLERK   Your address?

MATTHEWS   425 Bush Street.

CLERK   Raise your right hand. Do you solemnly swear that the evidence you are about to give shall be the truth, the whole truth, and nothing but the truth, so help you God?

MATTHEWS   Well, yes . . .

CLERK   Say "I do."

MATTHEWS   Well, well, I do.

WILSON   State to the court anything that you may know about this case.

MATTHEWS   Well, about 9 o'clock in the evening, on the evening of the sixteenth . . .

JUDGE ROBINSON   (*gavel*)   We can hear you.

MATTHEWS   Oh, well! I was going along Seventh Street, on my way home . . . having been to see Mr. Lewis on Eighth Street about a job of work . . . being a first-class painter . . . as you know, Judge.

JUDGE ROBINSON   Proceed.

MATTHEWS   Well, I was walking along when I heard a woman scream. And looking up the street I saw a man and a woman struggling.

JUDGE ROBINSON   Proceed.

MATTHEWS   Well, I immediately started running and I passed this feller Sanders, as I run.

SAUNDERS   (*rises*)   Saunders!

(BAILIFF *puts him down*)

JUDGE ROBINSON   I trust you run faster than you can talk, Matthews.

MATTHEWS   Well if Sanders can run as fast as he can talk he'd a beat me to it.

JUDGE ROBINSON   Proceed.

MATTHEWS   Well, as I got close, I could see what the trouble was. I see the complaintiff a-strugglin' to free herself from the grasp of the prisoner.

JUDGE ROBINSON   Proceed.

MATTHEWS   Well, getting up (*rises*), I

grabbed the prisoner and separated him from the complaintiff and took a healthy punch at him like this (*takes wild punch at air*) and I caught him on the nose! (*sits*)

JUDGE ROBINSON   Did you see the other defendant, Rufus Jones?

MATTHEWS   Well, yes and no. Ya see I was too busy helpin' the crowd, with the one that I punched to notice much, but seems to me as there was another one for somebody give me a hell . . . a hell (*gavel*) healthy kick and I got the bruise to show for it yit, but I ain't swearing to nothin' I ain't sure of, and I ain't *sure* I seen him.

JUDGE ROBINSON   Is that all?

MATTHEWS   Well, yes, your Honor.

JUDGE ROBINSON   Do you wish to question the witness?

CARL   (*rises*)   No, your Honor. (*sits*)

JUDGE ROBINSON   Judge Thornton?

JUDGE   (*rises*)   Mr. Matthews, there seems to be some difference of opinion between you and Mr. Saunders.

SAUNDERS   (*rises*)   Thank you. (*sits*)

MATTHEWS   Well, to tell you the truth, I never seen this man Sanders in the mix-up until after it was all over, and then I see he was the man who was trying to help me support her when she fainted.

JUDGE THORNTON   That's all. (*sits*)

JUDGE ROBINSON   Questions? (WILSON *shakes head negative*) Step down.

CLERK   Next witness.

WILSON   (*rises. To Judge*)   If it pleases the court we rest here. I have thirty witnesses who will testify as to the later events of the assault, but . . . it seems to be wasting the time of your Honor, and members of the jury to put them on the stand. (*sits*)

JUDGE ROBINSON   Witnesses for the defense.

CARL   (*rises*)   May I take the stand, your Honor?

JUDGE ROBINSON   Certainly. (CARL *takes the stand*)

CLERK   Your name?

CARL   Carl Sanderson.

CLERK   Your address?

CARL   861 Sutter Street.

CLERK   Raise your right hand. Do you solemnly swear that the evidence you are about to give shall be the truth, the whole truth, and nothing but the truth?

CARL   I swear that what I am about to say is the truth and nothing else but the truth, so help me God!

CLERK   Say "I do."

CARL   I do.

JUDGE ROBINSON   Will you tell this court what you know about what happened on the night in question?

CARL   May I be allowed to tell my story in my own way, Judge?

JUDGE ROBINSON   Certainly.

CARL (*sits*)   Thank you . . . Members of the Jury, I firmly believe that when a man tells the truth, the whole truth and nothing but the truth, knowing in his heart that it will be re-acted to as the truth, no other result possibly can follow. I am speaking now simply to tell the truth. . . . On the night of Saturday the sixteenth, about 9 o'clock, I was walking up Seventh Street when I noticed a lady. . . . Just as I passed her she said, "Just a minute" . . . I looked round, and as there was no one else in sight, I asked her if she was speaking to me, and she replied "I certainly am," and added, "Give me that ten dollars you owe me." I in-sisted that she must be mistaken, as I was cer-tain that she had never laid eyes on me until that night.

JUDGE ROBINSON   Just a minute. You admit then that you were on Seventh Street that night?

CARL   Yes, your Honor.

JUDGE ROBINSON   And you admit that you saw this woman, Mrs. Benton?

CARL   Yes, your Honor.

JUDGE ROBINSON   You also admit that you spoke to her?

CARL   Yes, your Honor, but only after . . .

JUDGE ROBINSON   That's enough, go on with your story.

CARL   She said: "I just got out of jail, and I don't mind going back. If you don't give me that ten dollars now I will scream and say that you assaulted me" . . . I tried to reason with her . . . but she insisted . . . and said: "I'll give you just one second to produce the money"; then I tried to walk away from her, but she stayed right even with me. She took a firm grip on my coat. At that time we were just be-side the vacant lot, and she let out a piercing scream, and I tried to free myself from her, then I pulled myself away—I turned and saw

Rufus Jones and I called him, then someone hit me and I was knocked down; then some-one kicked me and jumped on me. Then someone pulled me up on my feet and pushed me back to the fence. It was Kellard, and he held the crowd off, till the Officer came up and put me under arrest.

ELSIE (*rises*)   He's a liar, your Honor. How dare he say I held his coat!

(*Gavel.* BAILIFF *puts* ELSIE *down*)

JUDGE ROBINSON   Have you any witnesses to verify what you have told the court?

CARL   Your Honor the truth is the only evi-dence I need.

JUDGE ROBINSON   Young man, you are here charged with a terrible crime. It has been en-tered as assault. It might have been entered under another name that would have meant, if convicted, the penitentiary for practically your life. At best, conviction will mean a long sentence. You may believe that truth has the power you think it has, but your belief doesn't coincide with the facts as they appear to a Judge sitting in court. I admit it should, but I am sorry to say it does not.

CARL   It must stand with me, your Honor. It's my most treasured possession. It's all I have, and I stake my all on it.

WILSON (*rises*)   Your Honor, this man is just a clever crook.

JUDGE THORNTON (*rises*)   I object, your Honor.

WILSON   You're not appearing for this defen-dant, Judge Thornton.

JUDGE ROBINSON   There has been nothing here introduced as evidence that the defen-dant is a crook, and even though Judge Thornton is not this boy's lawyer the Court, in the interests of law, and its proper administra-tion, must order your statement to be stricken from the record.

WILSON   Exception, your Honor.

(WILSON *and* JUDGE THORNTON *sit*)

JUDGE ROBINSON   Note the exception. Is that all?

CARL   Yes, your Honor.

JUDGE ROBINSON   Step down.

(CARL *goes to seat.* JUDGE THORNTON *rises, comes to bench*)

JUDGE THORNTON   Your Honor, I appreciate the wisdom of your statement to the defendant, Carl Sanderson, regarding the truth, and I could wish with you that it would prevail, especially in our courts, but I have also seen the power of truth exemplified by the defendant whom I have known for the last two years, and such has been his proof that I feel he has a certain right to his faith. In defending Rufus Jones, my client, naturally my defenses must include Carl Sanderson, but such is my respect for him and his philosophy of life that if I could I would limit my defense solely to that of my client, but that is impossible. *(back to table. Looks through papers. Calls)* Mr. Frederick Kellard, will you take the stand?

CLERK   Frederick Kellard.

BAILIFF   Frederick Kellard.

(KELLARD takes stand)

CLERK   Your name?

KELLARD   Frederick L. Kellard.

CLERK   Your address?

KELLARD   I'm stopping at the Hotel Mount Shasta now.

CLERK   Raise your right hand. Do you solemnly swear that the evidence you are about to give shall be the truth, the whole truth, and nothing but the truth, so help you God?

KELLARD   I do.

JUDGE THORNTON   Mr. Kellard, will you tell the court what you know about the case?

KELLARD   Yes, sir. On the evening of the trouble, and at the time it happened, I was sittin' talking to Mrs. Thompson, wife of the proprietor of the Hotel Mount Shasta, on the porch of that hotel. I heard a scream and lookin' down the street, which I could see from where I was sittin', I saw a man and a woman . . . now—it seems to me the *man* was tryin' to get away from the woman.

ELSIE *(rises)*   How can you tell such a lie.

JUDGE ROBINSON   You must not interrupt, Madam.

ELSIE   But when I hear him say . . .

MATTHEWS *(rises)*   That wasn't nothing like it at all.

SAUNDERS *(rises)*   No such thing happened, I swear.

ELSIE   But when I hear . . .

JUDGE ROBINSON *(gavel)*   Order in court. Proceed Mr. Kellard.

(Everyone quiet immediately)

KELLARD   Yes, your Honor. Then I saw another man approach, then the lady cried "Help, help, murder," and I jumped off the porch and started on my way there, but before I could reach them quite a crowd had assembled and there was a fight goin' on. I found this man Matthews sittin' on the back of a man on the ground and the other gentleman, Mr. Sanders, heroically kickin' the fallen man in the face.

SAUNDERS *(rises)*   Certainly I kicked him, and I'd do it again.

(Gavel—BAILIFF puts him down)

KELLARD   Yes, Ma'am, I reckon you would, if he was lyin' down with somebody on his back.

WILSON *(rises)*   I object.

JUDGE ROBINSON   Object! One of your own witnesses started it. Proceed Mr. Kellard.

(WILSON sits)

KELLARD   Yes, your Honor. Well, there was Sanders. . .

SAUNDERS *(rises)*   Saunders is my name.

(BAILIFF puts him down)

KELLARD   . . . and Matthews and six or seven more tryin' to join 'em. I knocked the heroic Mr. Sanders down and Mr. Matthews is mistaken about the colored boy kickin' him. It was me.

MATTHEWS   I don't believe it.

KELLARD   I can tell you the exact place I landed, if you want me to.

(General laugh. Gavel)

JUDGE ROBINSON   Proceed, Mr. Kellard.

KELLARD   Well, then, I lifted the man to his feet, for he was hurt, and for the first time realized it was Carl, the colored boy from the hotel. I pushed him back against the fence and battled with the mob till the police officer came, and then stood by with the officer as he took him to the hotel to wait for the wagon.

JUDGE ROBINSON   Is that all?

KELLARD   Yes, your Honor.

JUDGE THORNTON *(rises—to WILSON)*   Your witness. *(sits)*

WILSON (*rises—to bench*)   Your Honor, Mr. Kellard and I are friends and interested in business. I wish you would explain to him that our friendship and business relationship must not be allowed to interfere with my professional duties.

JUDGE ROBINSON   I'm quite sure Mr. Kellard will understand. Proceed with your examination.

WILSON   Mr. Kellard, in your description of things, aren't you sometimes inclined to . . . well . . . er . . . amplify them a bit?

KELLARD   Well . . . I'm rather fond of using what you might term "a little local color."

WILSON   Exactly! And isn't your inclination to do that likely to cause you to use a little "color" in your description of the assault?

KELLARD   No—sir! When a feller man is facin' a long term in prison I take no chance on "color"—I speak the facts, facts as I see 'em.

WILSON   In your testimony you stated that "the *man* seemed to be tryin' to get away from the *lady*."

KELLARD   Yes, sir.

WILSON   And you heard the witnesses, Saunders and Matthews, testify under oath. Now they say the lady was struggling to get away from the man.

KELLARD   Yeah, I heard 'em.

WILSON   Have you good eyesight, Mr. Kellard?

KELLARD   Ain't takin' to wearin' specks yet.

SAUNDERS (*rises*)   Oh, is that so?

JUDGE ROBINSON   Kindly remove the witness Saunders from the Court. (*loud laugh from* MATTHEWS) Also Mr. Matthews. (BAILIFF *takes each one to door right and policeman puts them out*)

WILSON   Perhaps you only "seemed" to see this to keep from testifying to what you really saw.

KELLARD   The inference bein'?

WILSON   Never mind about the inference. Isn't it a fact that you really saw the same as the other witnesses?

KELLARD   No, sir, I did not.

WILSON   And these two witnesses *saw* and you only "seemed to see."

KELLARD   They didn't see.

WILSON   Are you sure of that?

KELLARD   Yes, sir.

WILSON   And why are you so sure, Mr. Kellard?

KELLARD   Because I can see in the dark better than either of 'em. And I couldn't see.

WILSON   Oh, you can see in the dark, can you? Are you a "Nictolops?"

KELLARD   Well, if you'll tell me what that is, I'll tell you if I am.

WILSON   It's the technical name for a person who sees in the dark.

KELLARD   Oh—there's lots of them where I come from. But I never heard them called that.

WILSON   What do you call them?

KELLARD   Night herders. We herd thousands of cattle night after night, an' ye learn to see mighty well in the dark, an' I'm particular good at it. And that's why I say they didn't see what they claimed; when we get a herder that's *sure* he sees things in the dark, we generally bed him down in the booby hatch.

WILSON   You have heard this lady testify? Now you wouldn't infer that she lies, you're a man, aren't you?

KELLARD   Yes, sir.

WILSON   With a man's heart? And a man's respect for women?

KELLARD   Yes, sir.

WILSON   Then why do you sit there and lie—what can be your object?

KELLARD   That's what's worrying me—and somethin' I can't git through my head.

WILSON (*quickly*)   You mean you can't understand your object in telling this lie?

KELLARD   No, sir. I can't understand *hers*.

WILSON (*pause—then to bench*)   I object to that answer.

JUDGE ROBINSON   If I strike out this answer from the record I'll have to strike out all the matter you have used in leading up to it.

WILSON (*goes back to table*)   Withdraw the objection.

JUDGE ROBINSON   Through with the witness?

WILSON   Yes, your Honor. (*sits*)

JUDGE THORNTON (*rises*)   Mr. Kellard, did you ever see my defendant Rufus Jones?

KELLARD   I couldn't swear to that, but I did see something black pass me on the way to the fight!

JUDGE THORNTON   When did you first meet the defendant, Carl Sanderson?

KELLARD   In the early part of the evening on which the trouble took place.

JUDGE THORNTON   How did you meet him?

KELLARD   He was the bell-hop at the hotel and seein' him around I spoke to him.

JUDGE THORNTON   You were not a friend of his?

KELLARD   No, sir, never laid eyes on him till that night.

JUDGE THORNTON   Then your interest in coming here is purely to see justice done?

KELLARD   Yes, Judge.

(JUDGE THORNTON *goes back to table*)

JUDGE ROBINSON   Is that all?

JUDGE THORNTON   Yes, your Honor. All right, Mr. Kellard. (JUDGE ROBINSON *motions* KELLARD *to step down*) Mr. Frank Thompson.

CLERK   Frank Thompson.

BAILIFF   Frank Thompson.

(THOMPSON *takes stand*)

CLERK   Your name?

THOMPSON   Frank Thompson.

CLERK   Your address?

THOMPSON   Hotel Shasta.

CLERK   Raise your right hand. Do you solemnly swear that the evidence you are about to give shall be the truth, the whole truth, and nothing but the truth, so help you God?

THOMPSON   I do. (*sits*)

JUDGE THORNTON (*rises and comes to stand*) Do you know the other defendant? My client Rufus Jones?

THOMPSON   Yes, sir. He came in the night of the trouble, he wanted work and I liked his looks and hired him as porter.

JUDGE THORNTON   The defendant, Carl Sanderson, is in your employ is he not?

THOMPSON   Yes, sir.

JUDGE THORNTON   Will you tell the court what you know about him?

THOMPSON   Carl Sanderson has been in my employ for the past two years and a half and I've always found him conscientious and faithful in the discharge of his duty, truthworthy, and honest. I never had or heard any complaint regarding his conduct while in my employ.

JUDGE THORNTON   That's all.

JUDGE ROBINSON   Any questions?

WILSON (*rises*)   No questions. (*sits*)

JUDGE ROBINSON   Step down.

JUDGE THORNTON   Rufus Jones.

CLERK   Rufus Jones.

BAILIFF   Rufus Jones.

(RUFUS *rises, starts to put hat on.* JUDGE THORNTON *stops him.* RUFUS *then starts for stand, sees* JUDGE ROBINSON, *stops*)

RUFUS   Good morning Judge. (*finally gets to stand*) You ain't goin' to leave me, Judge?

JUDGE THORNTON   No, no, Rufus.

CLERK   Name?

RUFUS   My name is . . . my name is . . . where is my name?

CLERK   Yes?

RUFUS   Yes, sir.

JUDGE ROBINSON   Just give him your full name Rufus.

RUFUS   My full name is Rufus George Washington Jones, sir.

CLERK   Address?

RUFUS   Sir?

CLERK   Where . . . are . . . you . . . staying?

RUFUS   I'm in jail now.

CLERK   All right . . . Raise your right hand. (RUFUS *raises left hand*) [JUDGE THOMPSON Other hand, Rufus] . . .

CLERK   Do you solemnly swear that the evidence you are about to give shall be the truth, the whole truth, and nothing but the truth, so help you God?

RUFUS   I don't know what the gentleman says he says it so fast.

JUDGE ROBINSON   He is asking you to tell the truth on the Bible, Rufus.

RUFUS   Sure I tell the truth, so help me God.

JUDGE ROBINSON   Proceed with your examination, Judge Thornton.

(RUFUS *goes to sit down, keeping tight grip on* Bible. CLERK *pulls it away from him*)

JUDGE THORNTON   Will you tell the court anything you know about this alleged assault?

RUFUS   Sir?

JUDGE THORNTON   About the trouble.

RUFUS   Oh. Well, the night of the trouble, I goes in the hotel to telephone. And the boss man there, Mr. Thompson, he tell me he has got a job of work for me, as porter, and he introduces me to Mr. Carl and Mr. Carl introduces me to Miss Ella Buford. I thought she was related to some Bufords I knows in Gadsden, Alabama, but she says she came from . . . oh . . .

JUDGE ROBINSON (*gavel*) Just a minute. Is this necessary?

JUDGE THORNTON (*up to bench*) I have tried to get this witness down to facts. I have tried leading him a little, but the minute I interrupt, while he is trying to figure out the meaning of my question he loses all idea of any answer. It was a night of horror to this boy and every little incident of that night stands out to him doubly magnified.

JUDGE ROBINSON All right, go ahead.

(JUDGE THORNTON *back to stand*)

RUFUS Yes, sir. Judge, your Honor—where was I, Mr. Judge?

JUDGE THORNTON Miss Ella Buford didn't come from Gadsden, Alabama.

RUFUS No, siree, she come from Ohio. Well, Miss Buford she explains to me my duties. That means my work, your Honor.

JUDGE ROBINSON Proceed.

RUFUS Yes, your Honor, I is proceeding. Where was I at, Mr. Judge?

JUDGE THORNTON Miss Ella Buford had explained your duties.

RUFUS Yes, Judge. Well, the first thing in my duties was—the surface bell rings and Mr. Thompson, the gentleman sittin' there he says—"Boy go to room forty-eight—Mrs. French—her bathroom door is dum stuck— you go fix it!" Well, I goes up . . .

JUDGE THORNTON All right, Rufus. Now after you fixed Mrs. French's bathroom door, what did she say to you?

RUFUS But Mr. Judge, I ain't fixed that door yet.

JUDGE THORNTON I know, but omit the fixing and come to what she said to you *after* you had fixed it.

RUFUS She couldn't say nothing to me, Judge, till after I fixed that door . . . and I ain't fixed it yet.

JUDGE THORNTON All right, Rufus.

JUDGE ROBINSON Why is this necessary? And what bearing does it have on the case?

JUDGE THORNTON (*to bench*) It explains the movement of the witness and will *prove* that there could not have been collusion between this boy and Carl Sanderson as inferred in the charge.

JUDGE ROBINSON All Right. Proceed.

(JUDGE THORNTON *back to stand*)

RUFUS Yes, Judge. Well I . . . Where was I, Judge?

JUDGE THORNTON Mrs. French was giving you money.

RUFUS Yes, Judge, No, Judge. She ain't givin' me no money yet.

JUDGE THORNTON All right then; you went up to Mrs. French's room—go ahead.

RUFUS Yes, sir, Judge. Well I'se goes up to room foorty-eight and I knocks on the door, and I can't hear nothin', then I knocks again. Then I hears a voice, my . . . way off. And it says "Come in—the outside door is unlocked." Well I goes in. Then a voice says: "I'm here in the bathroom and the door is stuck," and I could tell by the lady's voice that the lady is real mad. And I says, "Lady, jes' a minute, and I bust this door right ofen its hingus." Well, before I can bust, that lady says, "Boy, I got this cake of soap in my hand and it's a big one and if you bust in that door, I'll bust you in the head." Well I does! I turns the knob way round and the door loosens . . . she had done forgot to turn the knob . . . And the lady laughs and says, "Boy, I'd give a dollar for a plate of ice-cream," and I says "Give me the dollar and I get it for you," and she gives me thirty cents to buy some ice cream for my ownself, then I comes downstairs, tell the boss man, Mr. Thompson, and he says I can go and get the ice cream.

JUDGE THORNTON About what time was that, Rufus?

RUFUS About 8:30, Judge.

JUDGE THORNTON Will you tell the court where you were between that time and 9 o'clock, the time of the alleged assault?

RUFUS Yes, sir, Judge. I knows these places around here don't sell ice cream to no colored folks, so I goes way down South, take me ten minutes on the car and I go to Carlins drug store. (*to* JUDGE ROBINSON) That's the colored drug store, your Honor.

JUDGE THORNTON Yes, go on.

RUFUS And I gets myself a strawberry nut sundae with chocolate juice. It costs me fifteen cents. And it tastes so good I gets myself a coffee nut sundae smothered in with more chocolate juice. Then I comes back, to Drews, that big store on Howard Street, that place just jammed and packed and them clerks all busy, so I sees the boss man in the back and I tells him, and he gits it for me his ownself all done up in a box; so I starts for the hotel. I'se hurrying. When somebody says: "Rufus—Rufus," and I sees it's Carl, and I see the lady's got hold of him and he's trying to get away. And I starts towards him. Then it seems that the ground opens up and there's nothin' but white folks all around me, and I gets a club on the back of my head and I falls down and somebody jumps on me. So I pulls myself up and I fights myself out. I jumps a fence, goes through the hotel, gets to the next street. I goes down a block, then down Seventh Street. I'se all in, so I lands in a hole in the street where's they is fixing a colvert. A big piece of the drain pipe, just big enough for I can crawl in, and I does lie there.

JUDGE THORNTON   How long did you lie there, Rufus?

RUFUS   I *don't* know, Judge. A long time. Then I hear folks come to that hole, and I sees lights flashin'— . . . and I hear somebody say, they is tryin' to get dogs. When I hears them say dogs—I jus' like to die.

JUDGE THORNTON   You have been chased by dogs, Rufus?

RUFUS   Yes, sir, Mr. Judge.

JUDGE ROBINSON   Does the fact of him being chased by dogs have any bearing on *this* case?

JUDGE THORNTON   Only that it shows the blind hatred that seems to inflame certain types of white minds where a Negro is concerned; and will explain to the jury why some of the testimony may have been influenced by this hatred.

JUDGE ROBINSON   You wouldn't wish to infer that the *Court* has been influenced by that, Judge?

JUDGE THORNTON (*to bench*)   No, your Honor, but the *jury* have to decide this case on *evidence* perhaps influenced by this prejudice.

JUDGE ROBINSON   All right, proceed.

JUDGE THORNTON   Come, Rufus, I want you to tell the court all about those dogs.

RUFUS (*terrified*)   Dogs?

JUDGE THORNTON (*quietly*)   Yes, Rufus, the dogs.

RUFUS   Well, I was workin' for a lady back home and she 'cused me of stealin' a ring, so they takes and locks me in the smoke house till the Constable can come. So I digs myself out and gets away an' into a swamp and hides myself. In the middle of the night the baying of the dogs wakes me up and I knows they got the scent by the way they bays, and I starts travellin', but 'taint no use, so I climbs a big old stump and soon the dogs is all round me, then the white folks come and they want to string me up, but the constable wouldn't let them; and they drags me back to the house, when we gets there, the lady she finds her ring where she lost it, and tell the folks I didn't steal it at all.

JUDGE ROBINSON   Did they arrest her?

RUFUS   No, sir. She gave me two dollars and give me my job back agin.

JUDGE ROBINSON   And you took them?

RUFUS   Yes, sir. First time I ever had a whole two dollars in my whole life.

JUDGE THORNTON   Your witness. (RUFUS *rises*) Stay right there, Rufus.

WILSON (*rises, comes to center*)   I congratulate Judge Thornton. Altho' he has not been practicing in court for years he has lost none of his ability to keep one eye on the jury. So members of the jury if Rufus suddenly develops an inability to understand or answer any questions, the Judge has prepared you to believe that it is ignorance and not his desire to evade the questions I put to him.

JUDGE ROBINSON   Time enough to talk of that when the witness fails to answer.

WILSON   Because his Honor seems to reprove me at times, doesn't mean that his Honor wishes *you* to confuse *me* with the case I'm prosecuting.

JUDGE ROBINSON (*gavel*)   You will ask me to strike that off the record of this court, Wilson, or I'll hold you in contempt.

WILSON   Will your Honor have my remark stricken from the record?

JUDGE ROBINSON   Strike it out.

(STENOGRAPHER *does so*)

WILSON   You say that no store in the neighborhood or near the place of the assault will serve a colored man with ice cream?

RUFUS   No, sir, I didn't say that.

WILSON   Don't you know that it's against the law to refuse to serve a colored person?

RUFUS   I never said they refused to serve you, sir.

WILSON   Oh, then, you could have bought the ice cream around there?

RUFUS   Yes, sir.

WILSON   Then why didn't you?

RUFUS   Well, they will serve you, sir, but they put some flavor on that ice cream that just spoils it for eatin', sir.

(*Laugh*—WILSON *walks away right, disgusted*)

WILSON   That's preposterous.

RUFUS   Is that so, sir? I never hears with what they calls it before. It sure taste worse than it sounds—

WILSON   Don't try to be funny.

RUFUS   Lord God, boss, I ain't tryin' to be funny. This ain't no place for me to try to be funny in.

WILSON (*back to stand*)   How near were you to Sanderson when he *claimed* he called to you?

RUFUS   Well, Ah I think it was—

WILSON   How near were you to Carl Sanderson when he claimed he called to you?

RUFUS   Well, I think . . .

WILSON   Don't think. Answer my question.

RUFUS   Boss, I gotta think, I ain't no lawyer.

WILSON   Don't try to evade my question. How near were you to Carl Sanderson when he claimed he called to you?

RUFUS   About thirty-five or forty yards, sir.

WILSON   Didn't you testify to the police court that you were fifty or sixty yards away?

RUFUS   I don't remember what I said—I was too scared.

WILSON   You mean you don't want to remember?

RUFUS   No, sir.

WILSON   And because you don't want to remember you're unable to remember? Answer yes or no.

RUFUS   Yes or no.

WILSON   What do you mean by "yes or no"?

RUFUS   I don't know, sir—you *told* me to say "yes or no" and I does it.

WILSON   Your Honor, this isn't a dumb or ignorant witness, but a smart or instructed witness trying to evade the questions I put to him.

JUDGE ROBINSON   I think his answers are made in all seriousness; proceed.

WILSON   You say you saw the defendant, Carl Sanderson, and the lady struggling? And the lady was screaming—now then, wasn't it because the lady's screams had interfered with your dastardly intentions that Carl Sanderson was trying to get away?

RUFUS   Sir?

WILSON   Didn't you hear me?

RUFUS   Yes, sir.

WILSON   Then answer me.

RUFUS   I hears you talking, sir, but I don't know what you say.

WILSON (*to bench*)   I appeal to your Honor.

JUDGE ROBINSON   Mr. Wilson, would you *like* the court to conduct the case for you?

WILSON (*back to stand*)   Wasn't Carl Sanderson trying to get away, because the lady's screams had frightened him?

RUFUS   I don't know, sir. All I know is he sure was trying to get away.

WILSON   You're certain of that?

RUFUS   Yes, sir. *Certain sure.*

WILSON   And wasn't it the same reason you tried to get away?

RUFUS   No, sir, I didn't run till I gets hit in the head and kicked.

WILSON   Ah! If you are innocent as you claim you are, why did you run?

RUFUS   What did you say?

WILSON   I said, if you are innocent, why did you run?

RUFUS   Because you're innocent ain't goin' ter do yer no good if you're hangin' from a telegram pole.

WILSON (*walks away right*)   You don't mean to say that in a civilized city like San Francisco that you were afraid of being lynched?

RUFUS   When I hears somebody say "lynch"—I knows that ain't no place for me to be in.

WILSON (*back to stand*)   You admit that it was after the lady screamed that Carl Sanderson tried to get away?

RUFUS   When I sees him, he sure was tryin' to git away from that lady.

WILSON   And she was screaming and calling for help?

RUFUS   Yes, sir.

WILSON   That's all. (*back to seat*)

JUDGE THORNTON (*rises*)   That's all Rufus, you may step down.

(RUFUS *back to table*)

JUDGE THORNTON   Louise Thornton.

CLERK   Louise Thornton.

BAILIFF   Louise Thornton.

CLERK   Name?

LOUISE   Louise Thornton.

CLERK   Address?

LOUISE   Hotel Shasta.

CLERK   Raise your right hand. Do you solemnly swear that the evidence you are about to give shall be the truth, the whole truth, and nothing but the truth, so help you God?

LOUISE   I do. (*sits*)

JUDGE THORNTON (*rises—comes to center*) Will you tell the court what you know about this case?

LOUISE   The morning after the trouble I remembered that Rufus said he had a package containing ice cream. After this I walked down to the place where the trouble happened and found—

(JUDGE *goes to table. Gets ice cream box, comes back to stand*)

JUDGE   This?

LOUISE   Yes. On it is printed "Drew's Confectionery and Ice Cream Store." I took this down to Mr. Drew and asked him if he remembered the colored boy purchasing the ice cream and he said he did, that he himself had waited on the boy and the time was about 9 o'clock. That's all.

JUDGE THORNTON (*holds the box up*)   I desire to offer this in evidence, your Honor.

JUDGE ROBINSON   Mark it for identification—Exhibit A for the defense. Is that all?

(CLERK *takes box. Marks it*)

JUDGE THORNTON   That's all, your Honor.

JUDGE ROBINSON   Do you care to question the witness?

WILSON   No questions. (*rises and goes to stand to help* LOUISE *down. She walks right by him.* WILSON *back to table, sits*)

JUDGE THORNTON   Your Honor, inasmuch as there has been no evidence introduced in this case which in any way connects my client, Rufus Jones, with the alleged assault, I move that he is discharged.

WILSON (*rises*)   I object.

JUDGE ROBINSON   Overruled. I find no evidence against Rufus Jones and order his discharge. Rufus Jones . . .

RUFUS   Sir?

JUDGE ROBINSON   Rufus Jones, you may go.

RUFUS   Yes, sir. Alabama Bound. (*exits right*)

(JUDGE THORNTON *goes to table, sits*)

WILSON (*rises*)   Your client having been discharged, Judge Thornton, that ends your connection with this case. (*sits*)

JUDGE THORNTON (*rises*)   Your Honor, I throw myself on the mercy of the court and beg that I be allowed to remain.

JUDGE ROBINSON   Your request is granted.

WILSON (*rises*)   But your Honor . . .

JUDGE ROBINSON   Judge Thornton, will you join me on the Bench?

JUDGE THORNTON   I thank you, your Honor.

(WILSON *sits*)

JUDGE ROBINSON   How long will it take the prosecution to prepare its case for the jury?

WILSON   I'm ready now, your Honor.

JUDGE ROBINSON   Proceed.

(WILSON *rises—goes to center of stage*)

WILSON   Your Honor and members of the Jury. There are many crimes committed by hypocrites who mask their crimes under the cloak of religion. In my brief career before the courts I have found most criminals claim innocence, even those caught redhanded, as the defendant in this case was. Imagine, members of the jury, a young woman leaves her apartment in the city at 9 o'clock to mail a letter, when suddenly out of the dark of a vacant lot a Black man jumps. And taking hold of her he tries to drag her into the lot. A place covered with great high weeds. She resists, screaming, and is rescued from this man who would have despoiled her. The law says there must be one law for white and the same law for the Black, and I subscribe to the law, but there is something that the law cannot control and that is the honor of a white woman when attacked by a Black man. Some of you have wives and daughters; all of you have had mothers; just imagine a woman, a widow; does not your blood boil at this dastardly attack, this dastardly thing that happened to her? The defendant has made no defense; he has refused counsel. Why? Do I need to ask why? You know why he refused to defend himself; because he had no defense to offer. Don't believe this nonsense about good, and truth, the greatest criminal tried in the courts of this city quoted that holy book, the Bible, every time he opened his mouth. You know who I mean, and the only reason this man doesn't stand charged with rape and murder was because he was interrupted before he could put into execution his fiendish desire. In his own testimony on the stand, he admits he was on Seventh Street the night of the attack. He admits he saw Mrs. Benton, he admits he *spoke* to her. Those were his admissions,—you know the rest. Now I ask you, Members of the Jury, to bring in a verdict of guilty, for that's the only verdict you, as men, can bring in, for by it you will prove your humanity; by it you will prove your protection of your own homes, your daughters, your wives, your sweethearts. . . . So I ask you Members of the Jury to bring in a verdict of guilty. (*back to table. Sits*)

JUDGE ROBINSON   Carl Sanderson. Do you wish to address the jury? It's your right.

CARL (*rises*)   Yes, your Honor. Your Honor, and Members of the Jury, I have made no defense because I need none. I have done no wrong and that's why I believe harm cannot come to me. Even if you find me guilty and send me to prison I will still believe that good will still be good and truth more powerful than prison bars. I feel nothing but good to this lady who has so falsely accused me and in my heart there is a great sorrow for her; for as good will come from good, so evil comes from evil; it is as one thinks in his heart. I have told the truth—there is nothing more to say. (*sits*)

JUDGE ROBINSON (*rises*)   Members of the Jury, it is now my duty to charge you as to the law or the laws governing this case. Laws are made for the protection of the people, with suitable penalties for those who break these laws. Everyone is entitled to this protection and anyone breaking them must be punished. The plaintiff claims that the defendant wantonly attacked her on the public highway. The defendant claims that he was the one attacked. Therefore you must seek among the evidence for a motive—for back of every action there must be a motive. You will weigh the evidence carefully. The defendant has the same rights in this court as the plaintiff . . . The attorney for the plaintiff has tried to infer that the rulings of this court were induced by some personal animus on the part of the court. This you will take no cognizance of . . . It is a trick some lawyers descend to just for

that purpose . . . that is to give you the impression that the court bears malice. (MRS. THOMPSON *writes note, gives it to* LOUISE, *who starts for bench.* BAILIFF *stops her, then takes note and gives it to* JUDGE THORNTON) I merely tell you this so that you may judge impartially. You will now retire to the Jury Room and report to me when you have reached a verdict.

(JUDGE THORNTON *leaves bench, comes down center*)

JUDGE THORNTON   Your Honor, I move that this case be re-opened on the ground of new evidence.

WILSON (*rises*)   I object. This is a trick to confuse the court and the jury.

JUDGE THORNTON   Your Honor knows me well enough to know that I would not ask this without some powerful reason.

WILSON   You cannot interfere with the rules of the law in this way. The court cannot allow it. This case has gone to the jury.

JUDGE THORNTON   If your Honor please, the jury can retire while this evidence is being submitted and your Honor decides its bearing on this case.

JUDGE ROBINSON   Your request is granted.

WILSON   I object.

JUDGE ROBINSON   Over-ruled.

WILSON   Your client has been discharged. You have no rights in this case.

JUDGE THORNTON (*turns to Wilson*)   I have the right of every man to see justice done.

JUDGE ROBINSON   Members of the Jury. I request that you do not start your deliberations until you hear from me.

WILSON   I object.

JUDGE ROBINSON   Over-ruled.

WILSON   This is a trick to confuse you, Members of the Jury.

JUDGE ROBINSON   Mr. Bailiff, you will place under arrest anyone holding speech with the jury.

WILSON   I object to the whole proceeding.

JUDGE ROBINSON   Over-ruled.

WILSON   I take exception to that ruling. (*sits*)

JUDGE ROBINSON   Note the exception—proceed, Judge Thornton.

JUDGE THORNTON   Mrs. Thompson, will you take the stand?

(MRS. THOMPSON *takes stand*)

CLERK   Your name?

MRS. THOMPSON   Gladys Thompson.

CLERK   Your address?

MRS. THOMPSON   Hotel Mount Shasta.

CLERK   Raise your right hand. Do you solemnly swear that the evidence you are about to give shall be the truth, the whole truth, and nothing but the truth, so help you God?

MRS. THOMPSON   I do. (*sits*)

JUDGE ROBINSON   Mrs. Thompson, if you have testimony to offer which has a vital bearing on this case, as your action suggests, you will state to the court why you waited until this time to introduce it.

MRS. THOMPSON   I was hoping against hope that I wouldn't have to tell, but when I heard what your Honor said to the jury about "motive," I knew what the jury's verdict would be, and some irresistible force compelled me to write this note, and hand it to Louise, and she had it passed to her father.

JUDGE ROBINSON   You have not given me a motive yet, Mrs. Thompson.

MRS. THOMPSON   I knew that it would let someone who is very near to me and very dear to me know something that I didn't want him to know.

JUDGE ROBINSON   Yes.

MRS. THOMPSON   I am speaking of my husband.

(THOMPSON *rises*)

JUDGE ROBINSON   What has your husband to do with it?

MRS. THOMPSON   Oh, nothing directly . . . but I found that he was spending a great deal of his time with another woman and I engaged a detective to watch him.

WILSON (*rises*)   I object.

JUDGE ROBINSON   Over-ruled. (WILSON *sits*) Proceed, Mrs. Thompson.

MRS. THOMPSON   And I asked the detective to find out for me all he could about that woman.

WILSON (*rises*)   This is immaterial, and irrelevant, and I object to it.

JUDGE ROBINSON   Over-ruled.

WILSON   Exception.

JUDGE ROBINSON   Noted. (WILSON *sits*) Proceed.

MRS. THOMPSON   Mrs. Elsie Benton is not a widow. Her husband is alive and lives in Provo City, Utah, with her little boy whom she deserted nearly two years ago.

(ELSIE *rises, startled, comes down to table*)

WILSON (*rises*)   Which, even if true, has nothing to do with the fact that she was assaulted.

JUDGE ROBINSON (*gavel*)   Quiet! Proceed.

MRS. THOMPSON   She has been enamored and living with another man ever since that time.

ELSIE   Stop her, for God's sake, can't you stop her?

(WILSON *quiets her*)

MRS. THOMPSON   Six months ago, in Oakland, where she and this man had an apartment, she accused another man of practically the same thing that she has charged Carl with, but this man suspected and instead of having him arrested, he had her arrested, charging blackmail.

ELSIE   Can't you stop her?

(WILSON *quiets her again*)

MRS. THOMPSON   Her counsel made such a fine plea for her that the Judge remanded her in custody. And another thing—Mrs. Benton is not a white woman. I have positive proof that she is a Negress. If Mr. Wilson wants me to go on I will.

WILSON (*comes to bench*)   Wait, wait. Your Honor knows that all I have ever asked from the Court was justice and if Mrs. Thompson can prove these things, I'll be only too . . .

MRS. THOMPSON   The detective with the affidavits is waiting.

JUDGE ROBINSON   Who is the detective?

MRS. THOMPSON   Ex-chief McAuliffe. Shall I go on, your Honor?

WILSON   No, no, your Honor . . . all I asked was justice. I am quite satisfied. The plaintiff has misled me. (*back to table*)

ELSIE (*rises*)   But you said . . . you promised.

WILSON   Shut up or you'll end in prison yourself.

ELSIE   I won't shut up. You said . . .

WILSON   Quiet!

ELSIE   Wait! It wasn't my fault, he planned it all—he wanted to get rid of Carl. It's all his fault.

WILSON   Will you be still?

ELSIE   I don't want to go to jail again.

WILSON   Quiet! Your Honor.

ELSIE   He made me do it, your Honor. He wanted to get rid of Carl. He planned it all.

WILSON   Your Honor, I can explain . . .

JUDGE ROBINSON (*rises*)   *You* will explain to the Bar Association—The witness, Mrs. Benton, will remain in the custody of this court. Carl Sanderson . . .

(ELSIE *collapses*)

CARL   Yes, sir.

JUDGE ROBINSON   It is evident from the testimony of Mrs. Thompson and the quarrel between Attorney Wilson and Mrs. Benton that you have been the victim of a plot . . . What its objects were, and why it was planned, this court will find out. You will pass out of this court completely exonerated. The case against you is dismissed. *You are discharged.*

(*Gavel. Curtain*)

ACT THREE

(*At rise:* CARL, *behind hotel desk in uniform. Short pause. Enter* RUFUS *from porch*)

RUFUS (*goes to desk. Gives mail to* CARL) Mail, Mr. Carl.

CARL   Thanks.

RUFUS   If you're busy on your work, Mr. Carl, I can rack 'em for you.

CARL   That's all right, Rufus, I'm finished writing for the time being. I've got to dream some more.

RUFUS   Ever since we 'scapes from bein' put in jail you does nothin' but write. Does it all come out of your own head?

CARL   It all comes from the source of infinite supply.

RUFUS   Sometimes I got dreams too.

CARL   Yes?

RUFUS   Oh yes, sur, but they's all about chicken and gin.

CARL   If you would dream something good for you, Rufus, you would realize that dream, if you have faith in yourself.

RUFUS   Faith! What is that?

CARL   I believe I read something in the Bible about "Faith being the substance of the thing hoped for, the evidence of the thing not seen."

RUFUS   That 'minds me of when I was a pickaninny runnin' around our cabin in Alabama.

CARL   How's that?

RUFUS   We never had much *ham*, but I always dreamed and hoped that one day we get a lot.

CARL   Did you get it?

RUFUS   Sure, one night my pappy came home with two whole pounds.

CARL   Where did he get it?

RUFUS   I reckon he got it from the source of infinite supply . . . when the store-keeper had his back turned . . . Well, my mammy ate one pound and my pappy ate the other and when I gets the dish there's nothing left but faith . . .

CARL   Faith?

RUFUS   No! I means gravy.

CARL   Why do you call faith "gravy," Rufus?

RUFUS   'Cause it's the substance of the thing hoped for and the evidence of the thing not seen.

CARL   Go 'way from here, boy!

(RUFUS *exits left.* THOMPSON *enters from stairs*)

THOMPSON (*goes back of desk*)   Is the mail in, Carl?

CARL   Yes, sir.

THOMPSON   I suppose I deserve all I am getting, eh Carl?

CARL   You know better than I do, sir.

THOMPSON   Mrs. Thompson might write and let me know where she is.

CARL (*sits on bench*)   No news is good news, sir.

(*Enter* ANDREWS)

THOMPSON   Good evening. Want your key, Mr. Andrews?

ANDREWS (*goes directly to stairs*)   I have it, thank you.

THOMPSON   Here is a letter for you.

ANDREWS (*he stops and takes letter from* THOMPSON)   Thanks.

(LOUISE *enters*)

LOUISE   Good evening, Mr. Andrews.

ANDREWS   How do you do?

THOMPSON   Oh, you two have met?

ANDREWS   Oh, yes indeed. (*exit upstairs*)

LOUISE (*goes to desk left, picks up papers*) Oh, yes, indeed . . . Did Fred get back?

THOMPSON   Carl, did you see Mr. Kellard?

CARL   Yes, sir. He said he had a date with a policeman and went out.

LOUISE   He wandered off with my vanity case . . . put it in his pocket and walked off with it.

THOMPSON   That is a tragedy, isn't it?

LOUISE   It will be for him when I get my hands on him.

THOMPSON   Do you know, I wouldn't be surprised if Wilson is trying to frame Fred Kellard with this fellow's assistance. There is nothing too rotten for that bird to try.

LOUISE   You think that Andrews may be helping Jack Wilson?

THOMPSON   I think he will stand watching.

LOUISE   Tell me when Fred gets back. I'll talk to him.

THOMPSON   Everything is all right?

LOUISE (*crosses to stairs*)   I promised Ella that I would look over her accounts.

THOMPSON   I don't know what I should have done if you hadn't helped out, Miss Louise, since Gladys went away.

(*Phone rings*)

LOUISE   It is no more than Gladys would have done for me. Besides I am glad for the chance to learn a little something about housekeeping.

(LOUISE *exits upstairs*)

CARL   Hello! Yes ma'am. No, Mrs. French, no mail. Nothing but your bill. No, ma'am. It isn't due till the fifteenth.

(THOMPSON *goes to desk left, sits.* CARL *exits service door.* ELSIE *appears at door left. Crosses to right*)

THOMPSON (*rises, sees* ELSIE)   What are you doing here?

ELSIE   Your wife asked me to come.

THOMPSON (*goes over to her*)   My wife wouldn't have anything to do with a woman like you.

ELSIE   Your wife has had a great deal to do with a woman like me. If you'll listen, perhaps you'll understand. You know your wife's story at the trial was true . . . Do you know who the man was? . . . Jack Wilson . . . I came here on a visit about two years ago . . . met him . . . fell madly in love with him, and finally went to

live with him, sending word to my husband that I had gone to Los Angeles.

THOMPSON   What has all this to do with Mrs. Thompson?

ELSIE   After that trial Wilson lied himself out of it . . . he's clever . . . he put it all on me . . . and that judge simply tore me to bits . . . then let me go on the condition that I leave San Francisco at once.

THOMPSON   But you are here.

ELSIE   Ella told your wife of my trouble. I was sick, body and soul. When I was strong enough she urged me to go back to my husband and boy . . . and she even went with me—back home.

THOMPSON   Where *is* my wife? Will you take me to her?

ELSIE   I can't. I'd like to speak to Carl.

THOMPSON (*goes to service door*)   Carl? (CARL *enters*) Mrs. Benton wishes to speak to you. (THOMSPON *exits to office*)

ELSIE   Carl, when you realize that great dream of yours and you're famous . . .

(*Enter* WILSON)

CARL   Famous; my dream hasn't anything in it about being famous, all I ask is to realize it for the good it will bring to others.

ELSIE   Carl, here's a letter from Mrs. Thompson. She asked me to give it to you secretly.

CARL   From Mrs. Thompson? Oh, thank you.

(THOMPSON *enters from office*)

WILSON   Well? What are you doing here?

THOMPSON   None of your damn business.

WILSON   I'll make it my business.

THOMPSON (*steps between* WILSON *and phone*) You keep away from that phone.

(CARL *exits*)

WILSON   The police have an order to pick up this woman any time she is found in San Francisco.

THOMPSON   She came to see me. She is under my protection, and nobody is going to touch her.

(RUFUS *enters*)

WILSON (*starts for door, left*)   I don't need your phone. I'll get a policeman.

THOMPSON   If this man tries to leave here, Rufus, you stop him.

RUFUS   Yes, sir. Sure will.

WILSON   Before you go out of this town I'll have the police after you, and your husband no doubt will be also glad to know where you are.

ELSIE   And my husband, who is waiting for me in Oakland, will be after you, Mr. Jack Wilson. He is crazy to meet you, for he knows everything you did to me.

WILSON   How interesting?

THOMPSON   Rufus. I am going to take Mrs. Benton out and put her in a taxi. If Wilson tries to phone or follow us, I leave you to stop him.

(THOMPSON *goes to door, waits*)

RUFUS   Yes, sir, Mr. Boss, I sure will.

ELSIE (*starts for door, and stops near* WILSON) I *am* glad to see you again, Jack.

WILSON   Yes?

ELSIE   Yes. They say Love is blind, after seeing you again I'll tell the world it is not only blind, but deaf and dumb . . . particularly dumb. (*exit with* THOMPSON)

WILSON   Get away from that phone.

RUFUS   No, sir. Mr. Boss man says you shouldn't use it.

WILSON   Give me that phone before I take it away from you.

RUFUS   Mr. Wilson, did you ever hear of Alabama Jones—the prize-fighter?

WILSON   Yes, why?

RUFUS   My name's Jones, and I come from Alabama.

WILSON   Give me that phone.

RUFUS   Now, wait a minute, the Boss man says you can't use it. This one is named "lightnin'." And this one's named "dynamite." When Lightnin' jabs . . . Dynamite crosses over and busts . . . Ooze away from me white man . . . ooze on away.

WILSON   You can't bluff me.

RUFUS   Lord God, man, I ain't tryin' to bluff you. I'se just stating facts. If you think I'm bluffin', just call my bluff.

WILSON   You wouldn't dare to strike a white man.

RUFUS   Ain't never did it yet, outside the ring, but the Boss man told me to watch that phone.

WILSON (*starts for phone*)   Get out of my way.

RUFUS (*stops him*)   Mr. Wilson, if you like your face don't start nothing, because if you does you ain't going to recognize you' own self for months and months.

WILSON (*sits*)   You damn orang-outang, you!

RUFUS   What's that you called me?

WILSON   An orang-outang.

RUFUS   I don't know what that is, but if you don't take it back I'se going to lam you one for luck. Now is I what you said, or isn't I? Answer yes or no.

WILSON   No.

RUFUS   What? What you say?

WILSON   No, I mean—yes.

RUFUS   What you mean—No, I mean yes.

WILSON   You stay in your place!

RUFUS   One of the rules of the prize ring is . . . never hit a man when he's down . . . and you're safe while you're setting . . . But don't rise, white boy . . . don't rise.

(THOMPSON *enters*)

THOMPSON   All right, Rufus.

RUFUS   Oh Boss; don't never give me no more job like that.

THOMPSON   Why?

RUFUS   He's nervous and I'm scared to death.

THOMPSON   Did you have your dinner yet?

RUFUS   No, sir, but God and this gentleman has given me a fine appetite.

THOMPSON   Then run along and eat.

RUFUS   Yes, sir. If they is one word in the English language that spells more to me than any other, it is that one word. E. T. E. Eat. (*exit*)

THOMPSON   Now, Wilson, you can get out. And God help you if anyone interferes with Mrs. Benton.

WILSON   I came here to see Mr. Andrews. He is a guest here, and I have the right to call on him.

THOMPSON   He can get out with you. I am running this hotel.

(ANDREWS *enters*)

ANDREWS   Oh, Wilson.

WILSON   Andrews, I came here to see you.

ANDREWS   What's the matter?

WILSON   This fool, Thompson, is trying to put me out.

THOMPSON   Mr. Andrews, you are a guest here. It is none of my business what my guests do or with whom they associate, but this man Wilson is a crook.

ANDREWS   I guess I can take care of myself. I don't need a wet nurse yet.

THOMPSON   All right. Your week is up to-morrow. I should need your room.

ANDREWS   All right. You'll get it.

(THOMPSON *exits to office*)

WILSON   I offered him a chance to come in on the selenium mine, and he is sore because he didn't.

ANDREWS   Some people are that way, aren't they?

WILSON   World's full of them.

ANDREWS   Well, the check arrived. Here it is. (*shows check*) "Pay to the Order of John Wilson" . . . pay to you personally . . . that's right, isn't it? You own the property?

WILSON   Yes.

ANDREWS   You have the bill of sale—assign-ments and everything with you?

WILSON   Yes.

ANDREWS   You bought this mine from Kel-lard, didn't you?

WILSON   Yes, sure.

ANDREWS   Well that's O.K. Well, I'm going down the street. Like to come?

WILSON   Yes.

ANDREWS   All right! Wait 'til I get my hat and I'll go with you. (*exit upstairs*)

(CARL *enters service door, goes up to desk*)

WILSON   You're a pretty slick proposition, but you've slipped a cog this time.

CARL   What do you mean, sir?

WILSON   You know what I mean—How long has this little affair been going on . . . Oh, don't look so dumb. (*grabs letter from* CARL's *pocket. Enter* THOMPSON) The affair between you and Mrs. Thompson.

THOMPSON   Wilson, will you please leave my wife's name out of your discussion.

WILSON   Perhaps you would rather let your bell-hop discuss her. He is apparently on more intimate terms with her.

THOMPSON (*rushes at* WILSON)   Damn you— you . . .

WILSON (*stops him*)   Wait a minute! Ask your little "good-within" boy to explain the letter Elsie Benton gave him from your wife.

THOMPSON   Letter! Did you receive a letter from Mrs. Thompson?

CARL   Nothing personal, sir.

WILSON   Not personal! Listen to this. "Carl, I have decided to do what you asked. Al-though I didn't think I could ever bring myself to it. . . . By all means let no one at the hotel know of our plans, especially my husband," and it is signed "Gladys Thompson."

THOMPSON   And I trusted you—you dirty rat. Corresponding with my wife. (*grasps Carl by neck, chokes him, throws him down.* ELLA *en-ters right*)

ELLA (*rushes to* THOMPSON, *takes his arm*) Mr. Thompson, Mr. Thompson! What are you doing? You are killing him, please . . .

THOMPSON   He's been secretly correspond-ing with my wife.

ELLA   Oh, I know, I know! Carl has been corresponding with Mrs. Thompson. Why, only to-night Mrs. Benton brought him a letter from your wife saying she would return to you.

THOMPSON   Return . . . to me?

ELLA   Why, yes, Mr. Thompson. She came in through the servants entrance. We had planned to surprise you. Your wife is upstairs now waiting for you.

(THOMPSON *looks at* CARL, *then exits upstairs*)

WILSON   As somebody once said, "The Devil can quote Scripture." If anybody wants me, I'll be in Mr. Andrews' room. (*exit upstairs*)

ELLA (*helps* CARL *get up*)   Carl—Carl boy! (RUFUS *enters*) Rufus!

RUFUS   Yes, Miss Ella.

ELLA   Take this laundry up to Room 48.

RUFUS   Yes, ma'am.

CARL   What was that song you were singing, Rufus?

RUFUS   Song? Oh! That was a spiritual—an old convict song.

CARL   Sing some more.

RUFUS   Sure. (*sings until off upstairs.* CARL *sits*)

ELLA (*kneels beside* CARL)   Carl.

CARL   Yes, dear!

ELLA   Have you thought of where you are going and what you are going to do when you've realized your great ambition?

CARL   You mean, where are *we* going, and what are *we* going to do, don't you, dear? We are going back among our own people. For I realize now how much we need them, and they need us.

ELLA   Oh, I'm so proud of you. You're going up and up—and will take your place along with Frederick Douglass and Booker T. Washington.

CARL   We are going up together dear. For any success I might attain will be due to the inspiration I receive from you. For I firmly believe that any man who ever succeeded must have been inspired by some good woman.

ELLA   It makes me so happy to hear that I've been an inspiration to you.

CARL   You've been that, and more dear. I have a wonderful idea——(THOMPSON *and* MRS. THOMSPON *enter down stairs*) Now when we get back to Savannah, we are first going to . . .

THOMPSON   *Ella!* Check up that new linen.

ELLA   Yes sir. (*they jump up*)

CARL   I didn't hear him come in, did you?

ELLA   Nugh-nugh! (*exits right. Enter* JUDGE THORNTON *from stairs*)

JUDGE   Has anyone seen Mr. Kellard?

CARL   Yes, sir. He's out on the porch with Miss Louise. Shall I look for him?

JUDGE   No, don't look for him . . . better page him.

CARL   Yes, sir . . . Paging Mr. Fred Kellard . . . Paging Mr. Fred Kellard . . . (*exits door left*)

JUDGE   Well, Mrs. Thompson, I suppose we'll get some service now you're back. This good man of yours has been wandering round like a ghost with a silent sorrow. Mighty glad to see you back and so will everyone else be.

(THOMPSON *exits office*)

MRS. THOMPSON   I know about everything. Louise has been writing to me.

(CARL *enters, paging* "Mr. Frederick Kellard," *and exits to office. Enter* KELLARD *left*)

KELLARD   Who's paging me? Look who's here! (*goes down to* MRS. THOMPSON) Glad to see you.

(*Enter* LOUISE)

JUDGE   I want to see you, Fred.

LOUISE   Gladys, when did you get back?

JUDGE   You're in this too, Louise.

(*They go to porch entrance*)

LOUISE   I'm busy.

JUDGE   I've been all over your case, Fred. You gave Wilson Power of Attorney to practically do as he likes, but who gave you the right to give that Power of Attorney?

KELLARD   Why, my partners did.

JUDGE   Did they give it to you in writing?

KELLARD   No, sir. There isn't a speck of writing between us. Share and share alike three ways.

JUDGE   But legally, that doesn't count, without their written signatures. Mr. Wilson hasn't a leg to stand on.

KELLARD   Listen, Judge, they gave me the right—told me whatever I did would go with them.

JUDGE   I know. But you got tied up with a crook.

KELLARD   You see, Judge, it's like this; one of my partners has been East and he's trying to work it another way. He's got a customer who will take over the whole thing, promote it on the same terms, but absolutely refuses to let Wilson have anything to do with it. Now if this partner fails, we'll see if we can work it out some other way.

JUDGE   Well, you don't mind if I go after him, do you?

KELLARD   No, sir, you go just as far as you like.

(WILSON *and* ANDREWS *come down stairs talking*)

WILSON   But I can't see the necessity of it.

ANDREWS   (*goes to above table*)   No doubt, but you must remember we are an old Boston firm, and do business accordingly.

WILSON   Ah! The two-handed gunman.

KELLARD   Who told you that Wilson?

WILSON   My friend, Mr. Andrews.

KELLARD   Did he tell you I was a good two-handed gunman?

WILSON   Yes.

KELLARD   And did he tell you I was a good shot with either hand?

WILSON   He did.

KELLARD   Well, I'm sorry he told you that Wilson, because if you don't settle that business pretty quick, you're going to learn it personally.

WILSON   You can't get away with that rough stuff here.

KELLARD   I can't, eh? Now you listen to me, and you wait 'til I'm through. I worked for two whole years in Hell's Hole, and believe me it was Hell without any drinking water. But you can get out of there, but no man yet has ever come out of the Hell I'll send you to.

ANDREWS   Aw! This stuff doesn't get us anywhere. Let's get our business over with. Oh, Judge Thornton!

JUDGE   Yes.

ANDREWS   Pardon me, but will you witness a little business transaction for me?

JUDGE   Why not?

ANDREWS   (*shows* JUDGE *check*)   Thank you. I want you to witness that I have passed to Mr. Wilson a certified check for one hundred thousand dollars.

JUDGE   I will.

ANDREWS   And here, Mr. Wilson, is the check.

WILSON   (*starts for door*)   Thanks. I'm late. You'll have to excuse me.

JUDGE   (*stops him*)   Just a minute, Jack. I have a little business to transact with you.

(KELLARD *goes in front of door left*)

WILSON   Some other time.

JUDGE   Some other time won't do, it's now.

WILSON   (*walks by Judge*)   You can't detain me if I want to go.

KELLARD   Perhaps I can.

JUDGE   First, the assignment, signed by Fred Kellard, assigning the property to you isn't worth the paper it's written on.

ANDREWS   What's that you say, Judge?

WILSON   It's good enough for me.

JUDGE   It happens he has two partners.

WILSON   That's a lie.

JUDGE   Have you their signatures in your Incorporation papers?

ANDREWS   Do you mean that Wilson doesn't own the property?

JUDGE   He never owned it. He was only empowered to incorporate, issue and sell the stock.

ANDREWS   Wilson, you sold me something you do not own. You received our money under false pretenses. That's criminal, isn't it, Judge?

JUDGE   Yes, sir.

WILSON   (*comes to center*)   Well, if you are going to make a fuss, here's your check. Give me back those contracts.

ANDREWS   But we want the mine! You were a witness, Judge.

WILSON   (*starts back to door*)   Well, if you won't take the check, I'll keep it.

KELLARD   Just a minute. Payment on that check is stopped.

WILSON   Why? It's certified.

KELLARD   Obtained under false pretenses. And, before you cash it in the morning, I'll get out an injunction and every bank in California will know about it.

WILSON   What do you mean?

KELLARD   That is what I mean. Meet my partner, Andrew Andrews——better known as Alias Ananias Andrews.

LOUISE   He's your partner?

KELLARD   Yes, ma'am.

WILSON   It's a frameup. You can't get away with it.

JUDGE   You'll be lucky Wilson if these men don't telephone to the police and put you under arrest as a common swindler.

WILSON   Yes, perhaps you're right, Judge. I say, perhaps you're right. Looks as though I'm in a bit of a mess, all through this damned check. (*gives check to* CARL) Carl, here's a tip for you for the black page in your book of converts. Something to talk about from me. It isn't worth anything, you might have it framed. I'll remember the time I gave a bellboy a certified check for one hundred grand, but it does look like a jam. Doesn't it, Judge?

JUDGE   Certainly does, Wilson.

WILSON   (*turns to* ANDREWS)   So you're Mr. Andrews from Boston are you?

ANDREWS   I never even saw Boston.

WILSON   And I thought you were from the East.

ANDREWS   Sure I been East . . . all the way to Omaha. Carl, will you ask that gentleman outside to step in?

(CARL *exits*)

WILSON   Well, you certainly put it over.

(POLICEMAN *enters left*)

ANDREWS   Yes, sir. We planned this little party for your special benefit, and just so you won't forget it, here is a little souvenir for you.

(POLICEMAN *hands* WILSON *a warrant*)

WILSON   Well, what's this?

ANDREWS   It's a warrant for your arrest for taking money under false pretenses and other things . . . issued by Judge Robinson.

WILSON   I never did like that Judge.

OFFICER   Reckon you remember me, Mr. Wilson. I'm the policeman that arrested that colored boy you framed.

WILSON   Oh, yes, I remember you perfectly.

OFFICER   Will you come quietly, or shall I use these? (*shows a pair of handcuffs*)

WILSON   Quietly—very—very quietly. Well, things seem to have broken pretty badly for me, folks.

ANDREWS   So Wilson, you turned out to be a first-class crook.

WILSON   Crook, yes—but not first class. I was caught.

CARL   You can't fight good, sir.

WILSON   Good . . . hell. The only good that any of you have that I haven't is good luck. Well, don't do anything till you hear from me. (*exits with* OFFICER)

CARL   But what will I do with this check?

JUDGE   Too bad it isn't any good, Carl. If it was you'd be rich and able to realize any ambition you might have.

CARL   But I have realized my ambition, Judge.

LOUISE   Realized it, how?

KELLARD   What is the ambition you realized?

CARL   You don't know—but you, even Mr. Wilson and Mrs. Benton and Judge Robinson, you've all helped me to realize it.

KELLARD   How come?

(*Lights start dimming*)

CARL   A few years ago I dreamed I was going to do something big in life. It seemed too wonderful to be true, but that dream was with me night and day; it would give me no rest, so I said, "If God has given me this dream, he'll give me the power and knowledge by which to realize it, for its message was good, good for my own people, good for everyone it could reach."

LOUISE   I'm dying to know what it is. Aren't you, Fred?

KELLARD   Just jumpin' right out of my skin.

CARL   I dreamed a play; first, it was just a jumble of thoughts that gradually straightened itself out, then characters came into being and they began to think and then to talk, and as they talked I put it down on paper. For all my thoughts and all they said were filled with a big message.

JUDGE   What's the message, Carl?

CARL   If a Black bell-boy with not much schooling could imagine himself a playwright; that by believing and working he could write a play that was interesting and entertaining enough to hold an audience, it would prove to the world beyond the shadow of a doubt that any man can do what he desires to do, can become anything he desires to be. For you see you are all characters that I have dreamt.

(*All lights out, but blues and overhead spot*)

KELLARD   How come? Wait a minute. You mean I'm a dream? And not real?

CARL   No. You're real now.

LOUISE   Am I engaged to marry him?

(*Blues dim out slowly*)

CARL   Yes.

LOUISE   Oh . . . then that's all right.

THOMPSON   What about me? Am I a dream hotel manager or a real one?

CARL   You're all real now.

ALL   Real! Real!

CARL   (*steps into spot. Blues out*)   And as my dream came to an end, I could hear Mr. Kellard say, "Wait a minute! You mean to say I'm a dream?" And then Miss Thornton said, "Am I engaged to marry him?" Then Mr. Thompson spoke—all I could hear was "Real—Real"—Then I knew my dream had ended in a wonderful reality, for they were dreams, and now they are real people. And I thank God my dream has come true.

(*Their voices became fainter and fainter. Curtain*)

EARLY PLAYS
BY BLACK WOMEN

Angelina Weld Grimké · Alice Dunbar-Nelson · Mary Burrill

Myrtle Smith Livingston · Ruth Gaines-Shelton · Eulalie Spence

Marita Odette Occomy Bonner

T he decade of the 1920s was variously called the Harlem Renaissance, the Negro Awakening, the Jazz Era, and the Decade of the New Negro; in that decade, African Americans defined *themselves* for the first time, and indeed, they went about this self-searching consciously, with a great deal of discussion and insight. Poetry, fiction, music, arts, and theatre flourished. While the end of World War I saw Black rebellions in the streets of Omaha, Chicago, Knoxville, Tulsa, and Washington, D.C., it also introduced a spate of all-Black musicals on Broadway: *Shuffle Along, From Dixie to Broadway, Blackbirds of 1928, Blackberries, Rang Tang, Chocolate Dandies*, and *Running Wild*. Five dramas written by African Americans also graced the Great White Way: *The Chipwoman's Fortune, Appearances, Meek Mose, Fools' Errand*, and *Harlem*. Yet W.E.B. Du Bois, a tireless promoter of Black artists and the editor of *The Crisis*, wrote in 1926:

> If a man writes a play and a good play, he is lucky if he earns first class postage upon it. Of course he may sell it commercially to some producer on Broadway, but in that case it would not be a Negro play or if it is a Negro play it will not be about the kind of Negro you and I know or want to know. If it is a Negro play that will interest us and depict our life, experience, and humor, it can not be sold to the ordinary theatrical producer, but it can be produced in our churches and lodges and halls.

The six one-act plays and the one full-length play gathered here were published between April 1918 and April 1929—from the end of World War I to the stock market crash. All were written by women; all saw production on the stages of school, church, and lodge; all were written by school teachers. Six appeared in periodicals: *Birth Control Review, Carolina Magazine, The Crisis,* and *Opportunity.* All were original voices that were unwelcome in the commercial theatre of the 1920s, voices that "depict our life, experience, and humor." With the increasing awareness of women's history and the rise of the feminist movement, these African American plays have been "rediscovered." A careful reading will reveal that these are not the products of club women amusing themselves. The dramas confront major issues for Black women: voting, birth control, miscegenation, lynching, child rearing, and patriotism.

RACHEL

1916

Angelina Weld Grimké (1880–1958)

In 1915, the NAACP published a request for plays concerning race propaganda: "The Drama Committee of the NAACP, the authorized national body for the purpose of studying ways and means of utilizing the stage in the service of our cause, had been at work for several weeks. The committee was anxious to have race plays submitted for examination."[1]

It was understandable that *The Crisis* would place such a call. Throughout the United States, the lynching of Black people had reached an all-time high. The film *Birth of a Nation* had become a box-office hit, causing race protests in many cities. While the NAACP launched a national protest of the film's showing, the membership rolls of the Ku Klux Klan increased. In the midst of this domestic struggle between the races, America prepared for her first "Great War to Save Civilization." Blacks from the rural south migrated to the industrial centers of the north in search of freedom as well as economic security.

Around the same time, a play by Angelina Weld Grimké, *Blessed Are the Barren*, was already in process. She believed that perhaps the blight of racism might be obliterated if she could just touch the hearts of white mothers. Though well-published as a poet and writer of short stories, this was her first play. Her script, eventually entitled *Rachel*, was submitted and accepted by the Drama Committee of the NAACP. Produced originally in Washington, D.C., in 1916 at the Myrtill Miner School, with a subsequent production in 1917 at the Neighborhood Playhouse in New York and then again in Cambridge, Massachusetts, the play remains a major classic by a Black playwright, and it is the earliest extant full-length drama written by a Black female.

Angelina Weld Grimké, born in 1880, was the only daughter of Archibald Grimké and Sarah E. Stanley. This was an interracial marriage that was unique in that it was a legal marriage. Little is known about her mother's heritage, but her paternal grandfather was the brother of the famous South Carolina abolitionists,

---

1. *The Crisis* (March 1915).

Sarah Grimké and Angelina Grimké Weld.

Her grandmother, Nancy Weston, had been a slave and had three sons by her master. One son, Angelina's father, Archibald, in spite of his slave origins, received an outstanding education and became a prominent leader of his time. The Black Grimkés represented the "Talented Tenth" that W.E.B. Du Bois referred to when he wrote: ". . . in the early part of the century came other exceptional men. Some were natural sons of unnatural fathers and were often given a liberal training and thus a race of educated mulattos sprang up to plead for Black men's rights."[2]

There are many similarities between the drama's author and the title character of the play. According to Gloria Hull, Angelina Weld Grimké was brought up in a "liberal, aristocratic society of old Boston, and was educated at the finest private schools where she was probably the only black student."[3] Their fathers shared similar occupations; Rachel and Angelina were both teachers, and the choice to never have children, which Rachel makes at the end of the play, was Angelina's vow to the grave. A noteworthy difference between Rachel and Angelina is the fact that Angelina grew up without her mother, who died when she was eight. Reared by her father, motherhood became a major theme in many of Angelina's literary works.

Rachel was the first attempt by a Black woman to use the stage for race propaganda in order "to enlighten the American people relative to the lamentable condition of the millions of Colored citizens in this free republic." Receiving very few reviews, the play, unfortunately, was not seen by mass audiences. As Eulalie Spence noted, white audiences didn't wish to be reminded about their sins, and Black audiences already were very well aware of the "lamentable condition of the million of Colored citizens." With the play's 1920 publication, however, *Rachel* reached a larger female audience and became the subject of the ongoing debate among critics of the theatre and other literary forums. In particular, the original Drama Committee that produced the work had already divided opinions on the function of drama: should drama be propaganda or art? A minority of the Drama Committee dissented from a propaganda platform and were instrumental in founding the Howard Players, which promoted the largely artistic approach encouraged by Alain Locke.[4] W.E.B. Du Bois represented the opposing point of view, the same one reflected in a letter to Angelina from H.G. Wells. "Many thanks for your play, a most moving one, that has stirred me profoundly. I have long felt the intensity of the tragedy of the educated coloured people. Some day I hope I may find a way to help your folk."[5]

Stylistically, *Rachel* is caught "betwixt and between." The language is poetic and on the edge of artificiality. This flowery romantic dialogue tugs the play toward sentimentalism, while Miss Grimké's experimentation with the new style of her day—realism/naturalism—tugs the play in the opposite direction. Because Ibsen and Chekhov were among her favorite authors, one cannot help, when one sees phrases such as "my chickabiddy," of thinking of *A Doll's House*. One cannot ignore the Chekhovian "inactivity" of her characters, who at the same time demonstrate strong personal development through their internal motivation for change.

2. Howard Brotz. *Negro Social and Political Thought, 1850–1920* (NY: Basic Books, 1966).

3. Gloria Hull, *Color, Sex, and Poetry: Three Women Writers of the Harlem Renaissance* (New York: W.W. Norton, 1984).

4. Alain Locke and Montgomery Gregory, *Plays of Negro Life* (New York: Harper & Brothers, 1927).

5. Robert Fehrenbach, "An Early Twentieth-Century Problem Play of Life in Black America: Angelina Grimké's *Rachel* (1916)," in *Wild Women in the Whirlwind* (New Brunswick, NJ: Rutgers University Press, 1990).

In 1990, after a half century of neglect, Tisch Jones directed *Rachel* at Spelman College in Atlanta, Georgia. The production proved the play to be a voice from the past that still spoke to audiences today. *Rachel* is a study of the consequences of racial oppression in a society that declares that life, liberty, and the pursuit of happiness are available to all. Its treatment of the problems of unemployment, institu-tionalized racism, and poverty, as well as issues surrounding love, marriage, and motherhood, still render the play timely. For students who find *Rachel* unbelievable or exaggerated, a perusal through issues of *The Crisis* during the play's era will remind the reader how very realistic the play was in its time.

Tisch Jones

Rachel

CAST OF CHARACTERS

MRS. LOVING, *mother*
RACHEL LOVING, *her daughter*
TOM LOVING, *her son*
JOHN STRONG, *Tom's friend*
JIMMY, *the neighbor's small boy*
MRS. LANE, *a black woman*
ETHEL, LOUISE, NANCY, MARY, MARTHA, JENNY, *children*

ACT ONE

(*The scene is a room scrupulously neat and clean and plainly furnished. The walls are painted green, the woodwork white. In the rear at the left [left and right are from the spectator's point of view] an open doorway leads into a hall. Its bare green wall and white baseboard are all that can be seen of it. It leads into the other rooms of the flat. In the center of the rear wall of the room is a window. It is shut. The white sash curtains are pushed to right and left as far as they will go. The green shade is rolled up to the top. Through the window can be seen the red bricks of a house wall, and the tops of a couple of trees moving now and then in the wind. Within the window, and just below the sill, is a shelf upon which are a few potted plants. Between the window and the door is a bookcase full of books and above it, hanging on the wall, a simply framed, inexpensive copy of Millet's "The Reapers." There is a run extending from the right center to just below the right upper entrance. It is the vestibule of the flat. Its open doorway faces the left wall. In the right wall near the front is another window. Here the sash curtains are drawn together and the green shade is partly lowered. The window is up from the bottom. Through it street noises can be heard. In front of this window is an open, threaded sewing-machine. Some frail, white fabric is lying upon it. There is a chair in front of the machine and at the machine's left a small table covered with a green cloth. In the rear of the left wall and directly opposite to the entrance to the flat is the doorway leading into the kitchenette, dishes on shelves can be seen behind glass doors.*

In the center of the left wall is a fireplace with a grate in it for coals; over this is a wooden mantel painted white. In the center is a small clock. A pair of vases, green and white in coloring, one at each end, complete the ornaments. Over the mantel is a narrow mirror; and over this, hanging on the wall Burne-Jones' "Golden Stairs" simply framed. Against the front end of the left wall is an upright piano with a stool in front of it. On top is music neatly piled. Hanging over the piano is Raphael's "Sistine Madonna." In the center of the floor is a green rug, and in the center of this, a rectangular dining-room table, the long side facing front. It is covered with a green table-cloth. Three dining-room chairs are at the table, one at either end and one at the rear facing front. Above the table is a chandelier with four gas jets enclosed by glass globes. At the right front center is a rather shabby arm-chair upholstered in green.*

Before the sewing-maching, MRS. LOVING *is seated. She looks worried. She is sewing swiftly and deftly by hand upon a waist in her lap. It is a white, beautiful thing and she sews upon it delicately. It is about half-past four in the afternoon; and the light is failing.* MRS. LOVING *pauses in her sewing, rises and lets the window-shade near her go up to the top. She pushes the sash-curtains to either side, the corner of a red brick house wall being thus brought into view. She shivers slightly, then pushes the window down at the bottom and lowers it a trifle from the top. The street noises become less distinct. She takes off her thimble, rubs her hands gently, puts the thimble on again, and looks at the clock on the mantel. She then reseats herself, with her chair as close to the window as possible and begins to sew. Presently a key is heard, and the door opens and shuts noisily.* RACHEL *comes in from the vestibule. In her left arm she carries four or five books strapped together; under her right, a roll of music. Her hat is twisted over her left ear and her hair is falling in tendrils about her face. She brings into the room with her the spirit of abounding life, health, joy, youth.* MRS. LOVING *pauses, needle in hand, as soon as she hears the turning key and the banging door. There is a smile at each other. Then* RACHEL *throws her books upon the dining-room table, places the music there also, but with care, and rushing to her mother, gives her a bear hug and a kiss)*

RACHEL   Ma dear! dear, old Ma dear!

MRS. LOVING   Look out for the needle, Rachel! The waist! Oh, Rachel!

RACHEL, *(on her knees and shaking her finger directly under her mother's nose),*   You old, old fraud! You know you adore being hugged. I've a good mind . . .

MRS. LOVING   Now, Rachel, please! Besides, I know your tricks. You think you can make me forget you are late. What time is it?

RACHEL *(looking at the clock and expressing surprise)*   Jiminy Xmas! *(whistles)* Why, it's five o'clock!

MRS. LOVING *(severely)*   Well!

RACHEL *(plaintively)*   Now, Ma dear, you're going to be horrid and cross.

MRS. LOVING *(laughing)*   Really, Rachel, that expression is not particularly affecting, when your hat is over your ear, and you look, with your hair over your eyes, exactly like some one's pet poodle. I wonder if you are ever going to grow up and be ladylike.

RACHEL   Oh! Ma dear, I hope not, not for the longest time, two long, long years at least. I just want to be silly and irresponsible, and have you to love and torment, and, of course, Tom, too.

MRS. LOVING *(smiling down at Rachel)*   You'll not make me forget, young lady. Why are you late, Rachel?

RACHEL   Well, Ma dear, I'm your pet poodle, and my hat is over my ear, and I'm late, for the loveliest reason.

MRS. LOVING   Don't be silly, Rachel.

RACHEL   That may sound silly, but it isn't. And please don't "Rachel" me so much. It was honestly one whole hour ago when I opened the front door down stairs. I know it was, because I heard the postman telling some one it was four o'clock. Well, I climbed the first flight, and was just starting up the second when a little shrill voice said, "Lo!" I raised my eyes, and there, half-way up the stairs, sitting in the middle of a step, was just the dearest, cutest, darlingest little brown baby boy you ever saw. "Lo! yourself," I said. "What are you doing, and who are you anyway?" "I'm Jimmy; and I'm widing to New York on the choo-choo tars." As he looked entirely too young to be going such a distance by himself, I asked him if I might go too. For a minute or two he considered the question and me very seriously, and then he said, "Es," and made room for me on the step beside him. We've been everywhere: New York, Chicago, Boston, London, Paris and Oshkosh. I wish you could have heard him say that last place. I suggested going there just to hear him. Now, Ma dear, is it any wonder I am late? See all the places we have been in just one "teeny, weeny" hour? We would have been traveling yet, but his horrid, little mother came out and called him in. They're in the flat below, the new people. But before he went, Ma dear, he said the "cunningest" thing. He said, "Will you tum out an' p'ay wif me aden in two minutes?" I nearly hugged him to death, and it's a wonder my hat is on my head at all. Hats are such unimportant nuisances anyway!

MRS. LOVING   Unimportant nuisances! What ridiculous language you do use, Rachel! Well, I'm no prophet, but I see very distinctly what is going to happen. This little brown baby will be living here night and day. You're not happy unless some child is trailing along in your rear.

RACHEL (*mischievously*)   Now, Ma dear, who's a hypocrite? What? I suppose you don't like children! I can tell you one thing, though, it won't be my fault if he isn't here night and day. Oh, I wish he were all mine, every bit of him! Ma dear, do you suppose that "she woman" he calls mother would let him come up here until it is time for him to go to bed? I'm going down there this minute. (*rises impetuously*)

MRS. LOVING   Rachel, for Heaven's sake! No! I am entirely too busy and tired today without being bothered with a child romping around in here.

RACHEL (*reluctantly and a trifle petulantly*) Very well, then. (*for several moments she watches her mother, who has begun to sew again. The displeasure vanishes from her face*) Ma dear!

MRS LOVING   Well.

RACHEL   Is there anything wrong today?

MRS. LOVING   I'm just tired, chickabiddy, that's all.

RACHEL (*moves over to the table. Mechanically takes off her hat and coat and carries them out into the entryway of the flat. She returns and goes to the looking glass over the fireplace and tucks in the tendrils of her hair in rather a preoccupied manner. The electric doorbell rings. She returns to the speaking tube in the vestibule. Her voice is heard answering*) Yes!—Yes!—No, I'm not Mrs. Loving. She's here, yes!—What? Oh! come right up! (*appearing in the doorway*) Ma dear, it's some man, who is coming for Mrs. Strong's waist.

MRS. LOVING (*pausing and looking at Rachel*) It is probably her son. She said she would send for it this afternoon. (*RACHEL disappears. A door is heard opening and closing. There is the sound of a man's voice. Rachel ushers in* MR. JOHN STRONG)

STRONG (*bowing pleasantly to* MRS. LOVING) Mrs. Loving? (MRS. LOVING *bows, puts down her sewing, rises and goes toward* STRONG) My name is Strong. My mother asked me to come by and get her waist this afternoon. She hoped it would be finished.

MRS. LOVING   Yes, Mr. Strong, it is all ready. If you'll sit down a minute, I'll wrap it up for you. (*she goes into hallway leading to other rooms in flat*)

RACHEL (*manifestly ill at ease at being left alone with a stranger; attempting, however, to be the po-lite hostess*)   Do sit down, Mr. Strong. (*they both sit*)

RACHEL (*nervously after a pause*)   It's a very pleasant day, isn't it, Mr. Strong?

STRONG   Yes, very. (*he leans back composedly, his hat on his knee, the faintest expression of amusement in his eyes*)

RACHEL (*after a pause*)   It's quite a climb up to our flat, don't you think?

STRONG   Why, no! It didn't strike me so. I'm not old enough yet to mind stairs.

RACHEL (*nervously*)   Oh! I didn't mean that you are old! Anyone can see you are quite young, that is, of course, not too young, but,— (STRONG *laughs quietly*) There! I don't blame you for laughing. I'm always clumsy just like that.

MRS. LOVING (*calling from the other room*) Rachel, bring me a needle and the sixty cotton, please.

RACHEL   All right, Ma dear! (*rummages for the cotton in the machine drawer, and upsets several spools upon the floor. To* STRONG) You see! I can't even get a spool of cotton without spilling things all over the floor. (STRONG *smiles*, RACHEL *picks up the spools and finally gets the cotton and needle*) Excuse me! (*goes out door leading to other rooms.* STRONG, *left to himself, looks around casually. The "Golden Stairs" interests him and the "Sistine Madonna"*)

RACHEL (*reenters, evidently continuing her function of hostess*)   We were talking about the climb to our flat, weren't we? You see, when you're poor, you have to live in a top flat. There is always a compensation, though; we have bully—I mean nice air, better light, a lovely view, and nobody "thud-thudding" up and down over our heads night and day. The people below have our "thud-thudding," and it must be something *awful*, especially when Tom and I play "Ivanhoe" and have a tournament up here. We're entirely too old, but we still play. Ma dear rather dreads the climb up three flights, so Tom and I do all the errands. We don't mind climbing the stairs, particularly when we go up two or three at a time,—that is—Tom still does. I can't, Ma dear stopped me. (*sighs*) I've got to grow up it seems.

STRONG (*evidently amused*)   It is rather hard being a girl, isn't it?

RACHEL   Oh, no! It's not hard at all. That's the trouble, they won't let me be a girl. I'd love to be.

MRS. LOVING (*reentering with* parcel. *She smiles*)   My chatterbox, I see, is entertaining you, Mr. Strong. I'm sorry to have kept you waiting, but I forgot, I found, to sew the ruching in the neck. I hope everything is satisfactory. If it isn't, I'll be glad to make any changes.

STRONG (*who has risen upon her entrance*) Thank you, Mrs. Loving, I'm sure everything is all right.

(*He takes the package and bows to her and* RACHEL. *He moves towards the vestibule,* MRS. LOVING *following him. She passes through the doorway first. Before leaving,* STRONG *turns for a second and looks back quietly at* RACHEL. *He goes out too.* RACHEL *returns to the mirror, looks at her face for a second, and then begins to touch and pat her hair lightly and delicately here and there.* MRS. LOVING *returns*)

RACHEL (*still at the glass*)   He was rather nice, wasn't he Ma dear?—for a man? (*laughs*) I guess my reason's a vain one,—he let me do all the talking. (*pauses*) Strong? Strong? Ma dear, is his mother the little woman with the sad, black eyes?

MRS. LOVING (*resuming her sewing; sitting before the machine*)   Yes. I was rather curious, I confess, to see this son of hers. The whole time I'm fitting her she talks of nothing else. She worships him. (*pauses*) It's rather a sad case, I believe. She is a widow. Her husband was a doctor and left her a little money. She came up from the South to educate this boy. Both of them worked hard and the boy got through college. Three months he hunted for work that a college man might expect to get. You see he had the tremendous handicap of being colored. As the two of them had to live, one day, without her knowing it, he hired himself out as a waiter. He has been one now for two years. He is evidently goodness itself to his mother.

RACHEL (*slowly and thoughtfully*)   Just because he is colored! (*pauses*) We sing a song at school, I believe, about "the land of the free and the home of the brave." What an amusing nation it is.

MRS. LOVING (*watching* RACHEL *anxiously*) Come, Rachel, you haven't time for "amusing nations." Remember, you haven't practised any this afternoon. And put your books away; don't leave them on the table. You didn't practice any this morning either, did you?

RACHEL   No, Ma dear,—didn't wake up in time. (*goes to the table and in an abstracted manner puts books on the bookcase; returns to the table; picks up the roll of sheet music she has brought home with her; brightens; impulsively*) Ma dear, just listen to this lullaby. It's the sweetest thing. I was so "daffy" over it, one of the girls at school lent it to me. (*she rushes to the piano with the music and plays the accompaniment through softly and then sings, still softly and with great expression, Jessie Gaynor's "Slumber Boat"*)

Baby's boat's the silver moon;
        Sailing in the sky,
Sailing o'er the sea of sleep,
        While the clouds float by.

Sail, baby, sail,
        Out upon that sea,
Only don't forget to sail
        Back again to me.

Baby's fishing for a dream,
        Fishing near and far,

His line a silver moon beam is,
        His bait a silver star.

Sail, baby, sail,
        Out upon that sea,

Listen, Ma dear, right here. Isn't it lovely? (*plays and sings very softly and slowly*)

        Only don't forget to sail
        Back again to me.

(*pauses; in hushed tones*) Ma dear, it's so beautiful—it—it hurts.

MRS. LOVING (*quietly*)   Yes, dear, it is pretty.

RACHEL (*for several minutes watches her mother's profile from the piano stool. Her expression is rather wistful*)   Ma dear!

MRS. LOVING   Yes, Rachel.

RACHEL   What's the matter?

MRS. LOVING (*without turning*)   Matter! What do you mean?

RACHEL   I don't know. I just *feel* something is not quite right with you.

MRS. LOVING   I'm only tired—that's all.

RACHEL   Perhaps. But—(*watches her mother a moment or two longer; shakes her head; turns back to the piano. She is thoughtful; looks at her hands in her lap*) Ma dear, wouldn't it be nice if we could keep all the babies in the world—always little babies? Then they'd be always little, and cunning, and lovable; and they could never grow up, then, and—and—be bad. I'm so sorry for mothers whose little babies—grow up—and—and—are bad.

MRS. LOVING (*startled; controlling herself, looks at Rachel anxiously, perplexedly. Rachel's eyes are still on her hands. Attempting a light tone*) Come, Rachel, what experience have you had with mothers whose babies have grown up to be bad? You—you talk like an old, old woman.

RACHEL (*without raising her eyes, quietly*) I *know* I'm not old; but, just the same I know that is true. (*softly*) And I'm so sorry for the mothers.

MRS. LOVING (*with a forced laugh*) Well, Miss Methuselah, how do you happen to know all this? Mothers whose babies grow up to be bad don't, as a rule, parade their faults before the world.

RACHEL That's just it—that's *how* you know. They don't talk at all.

MRS. LOVING (*involuntarily*) Oh! (*ceases to sew; looks at RACHEL sharply; she is plainly worried. There is a long silence. Presently RACHEL raises her eyes to Raphael's "Madonna" over the piano. Her expression becomes rapt; then, very softly, her eyes still on the picture, she plays and sings Nevin's "Mighty Lak' a Rose"*)

Sweetest li'l feller,
    Ev'rybody knows;
Dunno what to call him,
    But he mighty lak' a rose!
Lookin' at his Mammy
    Wid eyes so shiny blue,
Mek' you think that heav'n
    Is comin' clost ter you!

W'en his dar a sleepin'
    In his li'l place
Think I see de angels
    Lookin' thro' de lace.
W'en de dark is fallin',
    W'en de shadders creep,
Den dey comes on tip-toe,
    Ter kiss him in his sleep.

Sweetest li'l feller, etc.

(*with head still raised, after she has finished, she closes her eyes. Half to herself and slowly*) I think the loveliest thing of all the lovely things in this world is just (*almost in a whisper*) being a mother!

MRS. LOVING (*turns and laughs*) Well, of all the startling children, Rachel! I am getting to feel, when you're around as though I'm shut up with dynamite. What next? (*RACHEL rises, goes slowly to her mother, and kneels down beside her. She does not touch her mother*) Why so serious, chickabiddy?

RACHEL (*slowly and quietly*) It is not kind to laugh at sacred things. When you laughed, it was as though you laughed—at God!

MRS. LOVING (*startled*) Rachel!

RACHEL (*still quietly*) It's true. It was the best in me that said that—it was God! (*pauses*) And, Ma dear, if I believed that I should grow up and not be a mother, I'd pray to die now. I've thought about it a lot, Ma dear, and once I dreamed, and a voice said to me—oh! it was so real—"Rachel, you are to be a mother to little children." Wasn't that beautiful? Ever since I have known how Mary felt at the "Annunciation." (*almost in a whisper*) God spoke to me through some one, and I believe. And it has explained so much to me. I know now why I just can't resist any child. I have to love it—it calls me—it—draws me. I want to take care of it, wash it, dress it, live for it. I want the feel of its little warm body against me, its breath on my neck, its hands against my face. (*pauses thoughtfully for a few moments*) Ma dear, here's something I don't understand: I love the little black and brown babies best of all. There is something about them that—that—clutches at my heart. Why—why—should they be—oh!—pathetic? I don't understand. It's dim. More than the other babies, I feel that I must protect them. They're in danger, but from what? I don't know. I've tried so hard to understand, but I can't. (*her face radiant and beautiful*) Ma dear, I think their white teeth and the clear whites of their big black eyes and their dimples everywhere—are—are—(*breaks off*) and, Ma dear, because I love them best, I pray God every night to give me, when I grow up, little black and brown babies—to protect and guard. (*wistfully*) Now, Ma dear, don't you see why you must never laugh at me again? Dear, dear, Ma dear? (*buries her head in her mother's lap and sobs*)

MRS. LOVING (*for a few seconds, sits as though dazed, and then instinctively begins to caress the head in her lap. To herself*) And I suppose my experience is every mother's. Sooner or later—of a sudden she finds her own child a stranger to her. (*to* RACHEL, *very tenderly*) Poor little girl! Poor little chickabiddy!

RACHEL (*raising her head*)   Why do you say, "Poor little girl," like that? I don't understand. Why, Ma dear, I never saw tears in your eyes before. Is it—is it—because you know the things I do not understand? Oh! It *is* that.

MRS. LOVING (*simply*)   Yes, Rachel, and I cannot save you.

RACHEL   Ma dear, you frighten me. Save me from *what*?

MRS. LOVING   Just life, my little chick-abiddy!

RACHEL   Is life so terrible? I had found it mostly beautiful. How can life be terrible, when the world is full of little children?

MRS. LOVING (*very sadly*)   Oh, Rachel! Rachel!

RACHEL   Ma dear, what have I said?

MRS. LOVING (*forcing a smile*)   Why, the truth, of course, Rachel. Life is not terrible when there are little children—and you—and Tom—and a roof over our heads—and work—and food—and clothes—and sleep at night. (*pauses*) Rachel, I am not myself today. I'm tired. Forget what I've said. Come, Chick-abiddy, wipe your eyes and smile. That's only an imitation smile, but it's better than none. Jump up now, and light the lamp for me, will you? Tom's late, isn't he? I shall want you to go, too, for the rolls and pie for supper.

RACHEL (*rises rather wearily and goes into the kitchenette. While she is out of the room* MRS. LOVING *does not move. She sits staring in front of her.* MRS. LOVING *can just be seen when* RACHEL *reenters with the lamp. She places it on the small table near her mother, adjusts it, so the light falls on her mother's work, and then lowers the window shades at the windows. She still droops.* MRS. LOVING, *while* RACHEL *is in the room, is industrious.* RACHEL *puts on her hat and coat listlessly. She does not look in the glass*) Where is the money, Ma dear? I'm ready.

MRS. LOVING   Before you go, Rachel, just give a look at the meat and see if it is cooking all right, will you, dearie?

RACHEL (*goes out into the kitchenette and presently returns*)   It's all right, Ma dear.

MRS. LOVING (*while* RACHEL *is out of the room, she takes her pocket book out of the machine-drawer, opens it, takes out money and gives it to* RACHEL *upon her return*)   A dozen brown rolls, Rachel. Be sure they're brown! And, I guess,—an apple pie. As you and Tom never seem to get enough apple pie, get the largest she has. And here is a quarter. Get some candy—any kind *you* like, chickabiddy. Let's have a party tonight, I feel extravagant. Why, Rachel! Why are you crying?

RACHEL   Nothing, dear Ma dear. I'll be all right when I get in the air. Goodbye! (*rushes out of the flat.*) MRS. LOVING *sits idle. Presently the outer door of the flat opens and shuts with a bang, and* TOM *appears.* MRS. LOVING *begins to work as soon as she hears the banging door*).

TOM   'Lo, Ma! Where's Sis,—out? The door's off the latch. (*kisses his mother and hangs hat in entryway*)

MRS. LOVING (*greeting him with the same beautiful smile with which she greeted* RACHEL.) Rachel just went after the rolls and pie. She'll be back in a few minutes. You're late, Tommy

TOM   No, Ma—you forget—it's pay day. (*with decided shyness and awkwardness he hands her his wages*) Here, Ma!

MRS. LOVING (*proudly counting it*)   But, Tommy, this is every bit of it. You'll need some.

TOM   Not yet! (*constrainedly*) I only wish——. Say, Ma, I hate to see you work so hard. (*fiercely*) Some day—some day——. (*breaks off*)

MRS. LOVING   Son, I'm as proud as though you have given me a million dollars.

TOM (*emphatically*)   I may some day,—you see. (*abruptly changing the subject*) Gee! Ma, I'm hungry. What's for dinner? Smell's good.

MRS. LOVING.   Lamb and dumplings and rice.

TOM   Gee! I'm glad I'm living—and a pie too?

MRS. LOVING   Apple pie, Tommy.

TOM   Say, Ma, don't wake me up. And shall "muzzer's" own little boy set the table?

MRS. LOVING   Thank you, Son.

TOM (*folds the green cloth, hangs it over the back of the arm-chair, gets white table-cloth from kitchenette and sets the table. The whole time he is whistling blithely a popular air. He lights one of the gas jets over the table*)   Ma!

MRS. LOVING   Yes, Son.

TOM   I made "squad" today,—I'm quarterback. Five other fellows tried to make it. We'll all have to buy new hats, now.

MRS. LOVING (*with surprise*)   Buy new hats! Why?

TOM (*makes a ridiculous gesture to show that his head and hers are both swelling*) Honest, Ma, I had to carry my hat in my hand tonight,—couldn't even get it to perch aloft.

MRS. LOVING (*smiling*) Well, I for one, Son, am not going to say anything to make you more conceited.

TOM You don't *have* to say anything. Why, Ma, ever since I told you, you can almost look down your own back your head is so high. What? (MRS. LOVING *laughs. The outer door of the flat opens and shuts.* RACHEL's *voice is heard*)

RACHEL (*without*) My! That was a "drefful" climb, wasn't it? Ma, I've got something here for you. (*appears in the doorway carrying packages and leading a little boy by the hand. The little fellow is shy but smiling*) Hello, Tommy! Here, take these things for me. This is Jimmy. Isn't he a dear? Come, Jimmy. (TOM *carries the packages into the kitchenette.* RACHEL *leads* JIMMY *to* MRS. LOVING) Ma dear, this is my brown baby. I'm going to take him right down stairs again. His mother is as sweet as can be, and let me bring him up just to see you. Jimmy, this is Ma dear. (MRS. LOVING *turns expectantly to see the child. Standing before her, he raises his face to hers with an engaging smile. Suddenly, without word or warning, her body stiffens; her hands grip her sewing convulsively; her eyes stare. She makes no sound*)

RACHEL (*frightened*) Ma dear! What is the matter? Tom! Quick! (TOM *reenters and goes to them*)

MRS. LOVING (*controlling herself with an effort and breathing hard*) Nothing, dears, nothing. I must be—I am—nervous tonight. (*with a forced smile*) How do-you-do, Jimmy? Now, Rachel—perhaps—don't you think—you had better take him back to his mother? Goodnight, Jimmy! (*eyes the child in a fascinated way the whole time he is in the room.* RACHEL, *very much perturbed, takes the child out*) Tom, open that window, please! There! That's better! (*still breathing deeply*) What a fool I am!

TOM (*patting his mother awkwardly on the back*) You're all pegged out, that's the trouble—working entirely too hard. Can't you stop for the night and go to bed right after supper?

MRS. LOVING I'll see, Tommy dear. Now I must look after the supper.

TOM Huh! Well, I guess not. How old do you think Rachel and I are anyway? I see; you think we'll break some of this be-au-tiful Hav-i-land china, we bought at the "Five and Ten Cent Store." (*to* RACHEL *who has just reentered wearing a puzzled and worried expression. She is without hat and coat*) Say, Rachel, do you think you're old enough?

RACHEL Old enough for what, Tommy?

TOM To dish up the supper for Ma.

RACHEL (*with attempted sprightliness*) Ma dear thinks nothing can go on in this little flat unless she does it. Let's show her a thing or two. (*they bring in the dinner.* MRS. LOVING *with trembling hands tries to sew.* TOM *and* RACHEL *watch her covertly. Presently she gets up*)

MRS. LOVING I'll be back in a minute, children. (*goes out the door that leads to the other rooms of the flat.* TOM *and* RACHEL *look at each other*)

RACHEL (*in a low voice keeping her eyes on the door*) Why do you suppose she acted so strangely about Jimmy?

TOM Don't know—nervous, I guess,—worn out. I wish—(*breaks off*)

RACHEL (*slowly*) It may be that; but she hasn't been herself this afternoon. I wonder— Look out! Here she comes!

TOM (*in a whisper*) Liven her up. (RACHEL *nods.* MRS. LOVING *reenters. Both rush to her and lead her to her place at the right end of the table. She smiles and tries to appear cheerful. They sit down,* TOM *opposite* MRS. LOVING *and* RACHEL *at the side facing front.* MRS. LOVING *asks grace. Her voice trembles. She helps the children bountifully, herself sparingly. Every once in a while she stops eating and stares blankly into her plate; then, remembering where she is suddenly, looks around with a start and goes on eating.* TOM *and* RACHEL *appear not to notice her*)

TOM Ma's "some" cook, isn't she?

RACHEL Is she! Delmonico's isn't in it.

TOM (*presently*) Say, Rachel, do you remember that Reynolds boy in the fourth year?

RACHEL Yes. You mean the one who is flatnosed, freckled, and who squints and sneers?

TOM (*looking at* RACHEL *admiringly*) The same.

RACHEL (*vehemently*) I hate him!

MRS. LOVING Rachel, you do use such violent language. Why hate him?

RACHEL I do—that's all.

TOM Ma, if you saw him just once, you'd understand. No one likes him. But, then, what can you expect? His father's in "quod" doing time for something, I don't know just what.

One of the fellows says he has a real decent mother, though. She never mentions him in any way, shape or form, he says. Hard on her, isn't it? Bet I'd keep my head shut too;—you'd never get a yap out of me. (RACHEL *looks up quickly at her mother;* MRS. LOVING *stiffens perceptibly, but keeps her eyes on her plate.* RACHEL *catches* TOM's *eye; silently draws his attention to their mother; and shakes her head warningly at him*)

TOM (*continuing hastily and clumsily*) Well, anyway, he called me "nigger" today. If his face isn't black, his eye is.

RACHEL Good! Oh! Why did you let the other one go?

TOM (*grinning*) I knew he said things behind my back; but today he was hopping mad, because I made quarter-back. He didn't!

RACHEL Oh, Tommy! How lovely! Ma dear, did you hear that? (*chants*) Our Tommy's on the team! Our Tommy's on the team!

TOM (*trying not to appear pleased*) Ma dear, what did I say about er—er "capital" enlargements?

MRS LOVING (*smiling*) You're right, Son.

TOM I hope you got that "capital," Rachel. How's that for Latin knowledge? Eh?

RACHEL I don't think much of your knowledge, Tommy dear; but (*continuing to chant*) Our Tommy's on the team! Our Tommy's on the team! Our—(*breaks off*) I've a good mind to kiss you.

TOM (*threateningly*) Don't you dare.

RACHEL (*rising and going toward him*) I will! I will! I will!

TOM (*rising, too, and dodging her*) No, you don't, young lady. (*a tremendous tussle and scuffle ensues*)

MRS. LOVING (*laughing*) For Heaven's sake! children, do stop playing and eat your supper. (*they nod brightly at each other behind her back and return smiling to the table*)

RACHEL (*sticking out her tongue at Tom*) I will!

TOM (*mimicking her*) You won't!

MRS. LOVING Children! (*they eat for a time in silence*)

RACHEL Ma dear, have you noticed Mary Shaw doesn't come here much these days?

MRS. LOVING Why, that's so, she doesn't. Have you two quarreled?

RACHEL No, Ma dear. (*uncomfortably*) I—think I know the reason—but I don't like to say, unless I'm certain.

TOM Well, I know. I've seen her lately with those two girls who have just come from the South. Twice she bowed stiffly, and the last time made believe she didn't see me.

RACHEL Then you think—? Oh! I was afraid it was that.

TOM (*bitterly*) Yes—we're "niggers"—that's why.

MRS. LOVING (*slowly and sadly*) Rachel, that's one of the things I can't save you from. I worried considerably about Mary, at first—you do take your friendships so seriously. I knew exactly how it would end. (*pauses*) And then I saw that if Mary Shaw didn't teach you the lesson—some one else would. They don't want you, dearies, when you and they grow up. You may have everything in your favor—but they don't *dare* to like you.

RACHEL I know all that is generally true—but I had hoped that Mary—(*breaks off*)

TOM Well, I guess we can still go on living even if people don't speak to us. I'll never bow to *her* again—that's certain.

MRS. LOVING But, Son, that wouldn't be polite, if she bowed to you first.

TOM Can't help it. I guess I can be blind, too.

MRS. LOVING (*wearily*) Well—perhaps you are right—I don't know. It's the way I feel about it too—but—but I wish my son always to be a *gentleman*.

TOM If being a *gentleman* means not being a *man*—I don't wish to be one.

RACHEL Oh! well, perhaps we're wrong about Mary—I hope we are. (*sighs*) Anyway, let's forget it. Tommy guess what I've got. (*rises, goes out into entryway swiftly, and returns holding up a small bag*) Ma dear treated. Guess!

TOM Ma, you're a thoroughbred. Well, let's see—it's—a dozen dill pickles?

RACHEL Oh! stop fooling.

TOM I'm not. Tripe?

RACHEL Silly!

TOM Hog's jowl?

RACHEL Ugh! Give it up—quarter-back.

TOM Pig's feet?

RACHEL (*in pretended disgust*) Oh! Ma dear—send him from the table. It's CANDY!

TOM Candy? Funny, I never thought of that! And I was just about to say some nice, delicious chitlings. Candy! Well! Well! (RACHEL *disdainfully carries the candy to her mother, returns to her own seat with the bag and helps herself. She ignores* TOM)

TOM (*in an aggrieved voice*) You see, Ma, how she treats me. (*in affected tones*) I have a good mind, young lady to punish you, er—er corporeally speaking. Tut! Tut! I have a mind to master thee—I mean—you. Methinks that if I should advance upon you, apply, per-chance, two or three digits to your glossy locks and extract—aha!—say, a strand—you would no more defy me. (*he starts to rise*)

MRS LOVING. (*quickly and sharply*) Rachel! give Tom the candy and stop playing. (RACHEL *obeys. They eat in silence. The old depression re-turns. When the candy is all gone,* RACHEL *pushes her chair back, and is just about to rise, when her mother, who very evidently nerving herself for something, stops her*) Just a moment, Rachel. (*pauses, continuing slowly and very seriously*) Tom and Rachel! I have been trying to make up my mind for some time whether a certain thing is my duty or not. Today—I have de-cided it is. You are old enough, now,—and I see you ought to be told. Do you know what day this is? (*both* TOM *and* RACHEL *have been watching their mother intently*) It's the sixteenth of October. Does that mean anything to either of you?

TOM and RACHEL (*wonderingly*) No.

MRS. LOVING (*looking at both of them thought-fully, half to herself*) No—I don't know why it should. (*slowly*) Ten years ago—today—your father and your half-brother died.

TOM I do remember, now, that you told us it was in October.

RACHEL (*with a sigh*) That explains—today.

MRS. LOVING Yes, Rachel. (*pauses*) Do you know—how they—died?

TOM and RACHEL Why, no.

MRS. LOVING Did it ever strike you as strange—that they—died—the same day?

TOM Well, yes.

RACHEL We often wondered, Tom and I; but—but somehow we never quite dared to ask you. You—you—always refused to talk about them, you know, Ma dear.

MRS. LOVING Did you think—that—per-haps—the reason—I—I—wouldn't talk about them—was—because, because—I was ashamed—of them? (TOM *and* RACHEL *look un-comfortable*)

RACHEL Well, Ma dear—we—we—did—wonder.

MRS. LOVING (*questioningly*) And you thought?

RACHEL (*haltingly*) W-e-l-l—

MRS. LOVING (*sharply*) Yes?

TOM Oh! come, now, Rachel, you know we haven't bothered about it at all. Why should we? We've been happy.

MRS. LOVING But when you have thought—you've been ashamed? (*intensely*) Have you?

TOM Now, Ma, aren't you making a lot out of nothing?

MRS. LOVING (*slowly*) No. (*half to herself*) You evade—both—of you. You *have* been ashamed. And I never dreamed until today you *could* take it this way. How blind—how al-most criminally blind, I have been.

RACHEL (*tremulously*) Oh! Ma dear, don't! (TOM *and* RACHEL *watch their mother anxiously and uncomfortably.* MRS. LOVING *is very evidently nerving herself for something*)

MRS. LOVING (*very slowly, with restrained emo-tion*) Tom—and Rachel!

TOM Ma!

RACHEL Ma dear! (*a tense, breathless pause*)

MRS. LOVING (*bracing herself*) They—they—were lynched!!

TOM and RACHEL (*in a whisper*) Lynched!

MRS. LOVING (*slowly, laboring under strong but restrained emotion*) Yes—by Christian peo-ple—in a Christian land. We found out after-wards they were all church members in good standing—the best people. (*a silence*) Your fa-ther was a man among men. He was a fanatic. He was a Saint!

TOM (*breathing with difficulty*) Ma—can you—will you—tell us—about it?

MRS. LOVING I believe it to be my duty. (*a silence*) When I married your father I was a widow. My little George was seven years old. From the very beginning he worshiped your father. He followed him around—just like a little dog. All children were like that with him. I myself have never seen anybody like him. "Big" seems to fit him better than any other word. He was big-bodied—big-souled. His loves were big and his hates. You can imagine, then, how the wrongs of the Negro—ate into his soul. (*pauses*) He was utterly fear-less. (*a silence*) He edited and owned, for several years, a small Negro paper. In it he said a great many daring things. I used to plead with him to be more careful. I was always afraid for him. For a long time, nothing hap-pened—he was too important to the community. And then—one night—ten years ago—a mob made up of the respectable people in the town lynched an innocent black man—and what was worse—they knew him to be innocent. A white man was guilty. I never saw your father so wrought up over anything: he couldn't eat; he couldn't sleep; he brooded night and day over it. And then—realizing fully the great risk he was running, although I begged him not to—and all his friends also—he deliberately and calmly went to work and published a most terrific denunciation of that mob. The old prophets in the Bible were not more terrible than he. A day or two later, he received an anonymous letter, very evidently from an educated man, calling upon him to retract his words in the next issue. If he refused his life was threatened. The next week's issue contained an arraignment as frightful, if not more so, than the previous one. Each word was white-hot, searing. That night, some dozen masked men came to our house.

RACHEL *(moaning)*   Oh, Ma dear! Ma dear!

MRS. LOVING *(too absorbed to hear)*   We were not asleep—your father and I. They broke down the front door and made their way to our bedroom. Your father kissed me—and took up his revolver. It was always loaded. They broke down the door. *(a silence. She continues slowly and quietly)* I tried to shut my eyes—I could not. Four masked men fell—they did not move any more—after a little. *(pauses)* Your father was finally overpowered and dragged out. In the hall—my little seventeen-year-old George tried to rescue him. Your father begged him not to interfere. He paid no attention. It ended in their dragging them both out. *(pauses)* My little George—was—a man! *(controls herself with an effort)* He never made an outcry. His last words to me were: "Ma, I am glad to go with Father." I could only nod to him. *(pauses)* While they were dragging them down the steps, I crept into the room where you were. You were both asleep. Rachel, I remember, was smiling. I knelt down by you—and covered my ears with my hands—and waited. I could not pray—I couldn't for a long time—afterwards. *(a silence)* It was very still when I finally uncovered my ears. The only sounds were the faint rustle of leaves and the "tap-tapping of the twig of a tree" against the window. I hear it still—sometimes in my dreams. *It was the tree—where they*

were. (a silence) While I had knelt there waiting—I had made up my mind what to do. I dressed myself and then I woke you both up and dressed you. *(pauses)* We set forth. It was a black, still night. Alternately dragging you along and carrying you—I walked five miles to the house of some friends. They took us in, and we remained there until I had seen my dead laid comfortably at rest. They lent me money to come North—I couldn't bring you up—in the South. *(a silence)* Always remember this: There never lived anywhere—or at any time—any two whiter or more beautiful souls. God gave me one for a husband and one for a son and I am proud. *(brokenly)* You — must—be—proud—too. *(a long silence. MRS. LOVING bows her head in her hands. TOM controls himself with an effort. RACHEL creeps softly to her mother, kneels beside her and lifts the hem of her dress to her lips. She does not dare touch her. She adores her with her eyes)*

MRS. LOVING *(presently raising her head and glancing at the clock)*   Tom, it's time, now, for you to go to work. Rachel and I will finish up here.

TOM *(still laboring under great emotion goes out into the entryway and comes back and stands in the doorway with his cap. He twirls it around and around nervously)*   I want you to know, Ma, before I go—how—how proud I am. Why, I didn't believe two people could be like that—and live. And then to find out that one—was your own father—and one—your own brother.—It's wonderful! I'm—not much yet, Ma, but—I've—I've just got to be something now. *(breaks off. His face becomes distorted with passion and hatred)* When I think—when I think—of those devils with white skins—living somewhere today—living and happy—I—see—red! I—I—goodbye! *(rushes out, the door bangs)*

MRS. LOVING *(half to herself)*   I was afraid—of just that. I wonder—if I did the wise thing—after all.

RACHEL *(with a gesture infinitely tender, puts her arm around her mother)*   Yes, Ma dear, you did. And, hereafter, Tom and I share and share alike with you. To think, Ma dear, of ten years of this—all alone. It's wicked! *(a short silence)*

MRS. LOVING   And, Rachel, about that dear little boy, Jimmy.

RACHEL   Now, Ma dear, tell me tomorrow. You've stood enough for one day.

MRS. LOVING   No, it's better over and done with—all at once. If I had seen that dear child suddenly any other day than this—I might have borne it better. When he lifted his little face to me—and smiled—for a moment—I thought it was the end—of all things. Rachel, he is the image of my boy—my George!

RACHEL   Ma dear!

MRS. LOVING   And, Rachel—it will hurt—to see him again.

RACHEL   I understand, Ma dear. (*a silence. Suddenly*) Ma dear I am beginning to see—to understand—so much. (*slowly and thoughtfully*) Ten years ago, all things being equal, Jimmy might have been—George? Isn't that so?

MRS. LOVING   Why—yes, if I understand you.

RACHEL   I guess that doesn't sound very clear. It's only getting clear to me, little by little. Do you mind my thinking out loud to you?

MRS. LOVING   No, chickabiddy.

RACHEL   If Jimmy went South now—and grew up—he might be—a George?

MRS. LOVING   Yes.

RACHEL   Then, the South is full of tens, hundreds, thousands of little boys, who, one day may be—and some of them with certainty—Georges?

MRS. LOVING   Yes, Rachel.

RACHEL   And the little babies, the dear, little, helpless babies, being born today—now—and those who will be, tomorrow, and all the tomorrows to come—have *that* sooner or later to look forward to? They will laugh and play and sing and be happy and grow up, perhaps, and be ambitious—just for *that*?

MRS. LOVING   Yes, Rachel.

RACHEL.   Then, everywhere, everywhere, throughout the South, there are hundreds of dark mothers who live in fear, terrible, suffocating fear, whose rest by night is broken, and whose joy by day in their babies on their hearts is three parts—pain. Oh, I know this is true—for this is the way I should feel, if I were little Jimmy's mother. How horrible! Why—it would be more merciful—to strangle the little things at birth. And so this nation—this white Christian nation—has deliberately set its curse upon the most beautiful—the most holy thing in life—motherhood! Why—it—makes—you doubt—God!

MRS. LOVING   Oh, hush! little girl. Hush!

RACHEL (*suddenly with a great cry*)   Why, Ma dear, *you know*. You were a mother, George's mother. So, this is what it means. Oh, Ma dear! Ma dear! (*faints in her mother's arms*)

ACT TWO

(TIME: *October sixteenth, four years later; seven o'clock in the morning.*

SCENE: *The same room. There have been very evident improvements made. The room is not so bare; it is cosier. On the shelf, before each window, are potted red geraniums. At the windows are green denim drapery curtains covering fresh white dotted Swiss inner curtains. At each doorway are green denim portieres. On the wall between the kitchenette and the entrance to the outer rooms of the flat, a new picture is hanging, Millet's "The Man With the Hoe." Hanging against the side of the run that faces front is Watts's "Hope." There is another easy-chair at the left front. The table in the center is covered with a white table-cloth. A small asparagus fern is in the middle of this. When the curtain rises there is the clatter of dishes in the kitchenette. Presently RACHEL enters with dishes and silver in her hands. She is clad in a bungalow apron. She is noticeably all of four years older. She frowns as she sets the table. There is a set expression about the mouth. A child's voice is heard from the rooms within*)

JIMMY (*still unseen*)   Ma Rachel!

RACHEL (*pauses and smiles*)   What is it, Jimmy boy?

JIMMY (*appearing in rear doorway, half-dressed, breathless, and tremendously excited over something. Rushes toward RACHEL*)   Three guesses! Three guesses! Ma Rachel!

RACHEL (*her whole face softening*)   Well, let's see—maybe there is a circus in town .

JIMMY   No sirree! (*in a sing-song*) You're not right! You're not right!

RACHEL   Well, maybe Ma Loving's going to take you somewhere.

JIMMY   No! (*vigorously shaking his head*) It's—

RACHEL (*interrupting quickly*)   You said I could have three guesses, honey. I've only had two.

JIMMY   I thought you had three! How many are three!

RACHEL (*counting on her fingers*)   One! Two! Three! I've only had one! two!—See? Perhaps Uncle Tom is going to give you some candy.

JIMMY (*dancing up and down*)   No! No! No! (*catches his breath*) I leaned over the bath-tub, way over, and got hold of the chain with the button on the end, and dropped it into the little round place in the bottom. And then I runned lots of water in the tub and climbed over and fell in splash! just like a big stone; (*loudly*) and took a bath all by myself alone.

RACHEL (*laughing and hugging him*)   All by yourself, honey? You ran the water, too, boy, not "runned" it. What I want to know is, where was Ma Loving all this time?

JIMMY   I stole in "creepy-creep" and looked at Ma Loving and she was awful fast asleep. (*proudly*) Ma Rachel, I'm a "nawful," big boy now, aren't I? I are almost a man, aren't I?

RACHEL   Oh! Boy, I'm getting tired of correcting you—"I am almost a man, am I not?" Jimmy, boy, what will Ma Rachel do, if you grow up? Why, I won't have a little boy any more! Honey, you mustn't grow up, do you hear? You mustn't.

JIMMY   Oh, yes, I must; and you'll have me just the same, Ma Rachel. I'm going to be a policeman and make lots of money for you and Ma Loving and Uncle Tom, and I'm going to buy you some trains and fire-engines, and little, cunning ponies, and some rabbits, and some great 'normous banks full of money— lots of it. And then, we are going to live in a great, big castle and eat lots of ice cream, all the time, and drink lots and lots of nice pink lemonade.

RACHEL   What a generous Jimmy boy! (*hugs him*) Before I give you "morning kiss," I must see how clean my boy is. (*inpsects teeth, ears and neck*) Jimmy, you're sweet and clean enough to eat. (*kisses him; he tries to strangle her with hugs*) Now the hands. Oh! Jimmy, look at those nails! Oh! Jimmy! (JIMMY *wriggles and tries to get his hands away*) Honey, get my file off of my bureau and go to Ma Loving; she must be awake by this time. Why, honey, what's the matter with your feet?

JIMMY   I don't know. I thought they looked kind of queer, myself. What's the matter with them?

RACHEL (*laughing*)   You have your shoes on the wrong feet.

JIMMY (*bursts out laughing*)   Isn't that most 'normously funny? I'm a case, aren't I—(*pauses thoughtfully*) I mean—am I not, Ma Rachel?

RACHEL   Yes, honey, a great big case of molasses. Come, you must hurry now, and get dressed. You don't want to be late for school, you know.

JIMMY   Ma Rachel! (*shyly*) I—I have been making something for you all the morning— ever since I waked up. It's awful nice. It's— stoop down, Ma Rachel, please—a great, big (*puts both arms about her neck and gives her a noisy kiss.* RACHEL *kisses him in return, then pushes his head back. For a long moment they look at each other; and, then, laughing joyously, he makes believe he is a horse, and goes prancing out of the room.* RACHEL, *with a softer, gentler expression, continues setting the table. Presently,* MRS.LOVING, *bent and worn-looking, appears in the doorway in the rear. She limps a trifle*)

MRS. LOVING   Good morning dearie. How's my little girl, this morning? (*looks around the room*). Why, where's Tom? I was certain I heard him running the water in the tub, sometime ago. (*limps into the room*)

RACHEL (*laughing*)   Tom isn't up yet. Have you seen Jimmy?

MRS. LOVING.   Jimmy? No. I didn't know he was awake, even.

RACHEL (*going to her mother and kissing her*) Well! What do you think of that! I sent the young gentleman to you, a few minutes ago, for help with his nails. He is very much grown up this morning, so I suppose that explains why he didn't come to you. Yesterday, all day, you know, he was a puppy. No one knows what he will be by tomorrow. All of this, Ma dear, is preliminary to telling you that Jimmy boy has stolen a march on you, this morning.

MRS. LOVING   Stolen a march! How?

RACHEL.   It appears that he took his bath all by himself and, as a result, he is so conceited, peacocks aren't in it with him.

MRS. LOVING.   I heard the water running and thought, of course, it was Tom. Why, the little rascal! I must go and see how he has left things. I was just about to wake him up.

RACHEL   Rheumatism's not much better this morning, Ma dear. (*confronting her mother*) Tell me the truth now, did you or did you not try that liniment I bought you yesterday?

MRS. LOVING. (*guiltily*)   Well, Rachel, you see—it was this way, I was—I was so tired, last night,—I—I really forgot it.

RACHEL   I thought as much. Shame on you!

MRS. LOVING   As soon as I walk around a bit it will be all right. It always is. It's bad, when I first get up—that's all. I'll be spry enough in a few minutes. *(limps to the door; pauses)* Rachel, I don't know why the thought should strike me, but how very strangely things turn out. If any one had told me four years ago that Jimmy would be living with us, I should have laughed at him. Then it hurt to see him; now it would hurt not to. *(softly)* Rachel, sometimes—I wonder—if, perhaps, God—hasn't relented a little—and given me back my boy,—my George.

RACHEL   The whole thing was strange, wasn't it?

MRS. LOVING.   Yes, God's ways are strange and often very beautiful; perhaps all would be beautiful—if we only understood.

RACHEL.   God's ways are certainly very mysterious. Why, of all the people in this apartment-house, should Jimmy's father and mother be the only two to take the smallpox, and the only two to die. It's queer!

MRS. LOVING   It doesn't seem like two years ago, does it?

RACHEL   Two years, Ma dear! Why it's three the third of January.

MRS. LOVING   Are you sure, Rachel?

RACHEL *(gently)*   I don't believe I could ever forget that, Ma dear.

MRS. LOVING   No, I suppose not. That is one of the differences between youth and old age—youth attaches tremendous importance to dates,—old age does not.

RACHEL *(quickly)*   Ma dear, don't talk like that. You're not old.

MRS. LOVING   Oh! yes, I am, dearie. It's sixty long years since I was born; and I am much older than that, much older.

RACHEL   Please, Ma dear, please!

MRS. LOVING *(smiling)*   Very well, dearie, I won't say it any more. *(a pause)* By the way,—how—does Tom strike you, these days?

RACHEL *(avoiding her mother's eye)*   The same old, bantering, cheerful Tom. Why?

MRS. LOVING   I know he's all that, dearie, but it isn't possible for him to be really cheerful. *(pauses; goes on wistfully)* When you are little, we mothers can kiss away all the trouble, but when you grow up—and go out—into the world—and get hurt—we are helpless. There is nothing we can do.

RACHEL   Don't worry about Tom, Ma dear, he's game. He doesn't show the white feather.

MRS. LOVING.   Did you see him, when he came in, last night?

RACHEL   Yes.

MRS. LOVING   Had he had—any luck?

RACHEL   No. *(firmly)* Ma dear, we may as well face it—it's hopeless, I'm afraid.

MRS. LOVING   I'm afraid—you are right. *(shakes her head sadly)* Well, I'll go and see how Jimmy has left things and wake up Tom, if he isn't awake yet. It's the waking up in the mornings that's hard. *(goes limping out rear door. RACHEL frowns as she continues going back and forth between the kitchenette and the table. Presently TOM appears in the door at the rear. He watches RACHEL several moments before he speaks or enters. RACHEL looks grim enough).*

TOM *(entering and smiling)*   Good-morning, "Merry Sunshine"! Have you, perhaps, been taking a—er—prolonged draught of that very delightful beverage—vinegar? *(RACHEL, with a knife in her hand, looks up unsmiling. In pretended fright)* I take it all back, I'm sure. May I request, humbly, that before I press my chaste, morning salute upon your forbidding lips, that you—that you—that you—er—in some way rid yourself of that—er—knife? *(bows as RACHEL puts it down).* I thank you. *(he comes to her and tips her head back; gently)* What's the matter with my little Sis?

RACHEL *(her face softening)*   Tommy dear, don't mind me. I'm getting wicked, I guess. At present I feel just like—like curdled milk. Once upon a time, I used to have quite a nice disposition, didn't I, Tommy?

TOM *(smiling)*   Did you, indeed! I'm not going to flatter you. Well, brace yourself, old lady. Ready, One! Two! Three! Go! *(kisses her, then puts his hands on either side of her face, and raising it looks down into it).* You're a pretty, decent little sister, Sis, that's what T. Loving thinks about it; and he knows a thing or two. *(abruptly looking around)* Has the paper come yet?

RACHEL   I haven't looked, it must have, though, by this time. *(TOM, hands in his pockets, goes into the vestibule. He whistles. The outer door opens and closes, and presently he saunters back, newspaper in hand. He lounges carelessly in the arm-chair and looks at RACHEL)*

TOM   May T. Loving be of any service to you?

RACHEL   Service! How?

TOM   May he run, say, any errands, set the table, cook the breakfast? Anything?

RACHEL *(watching the lazy figure)*   You look like working.

TOM *(grinning)*   It's at least—polite—to offer.

RACHEL.   You can't do anything; I don't trust you to do it right. You may just sit there, and read your paper—and try to behave yourself.

TOM *(in affectedly meek tones)*   Thank you, ma'am. *(opens the paper, but does not read.* JIMMY *presently enters riding around the table on a cane.* RACHEL *peeps in from the kitchenette and smiles.* TOM *puts down his paper)* 'Lo! Big Fellow, what's this?

JIMMY *(disgustedly)*   How can I hear? I'm miles and miles away yet. *(prances around and around the room; presently stops near TOM, attempting a gruff voice)* Good-morning!

TOM *(lowering his paper again)*   Bless my stars! Who's this? Well, if it isn't Mr. Mason! How-do-you-do, Mr. Mason? That's a beautiful horse you have there. He limps a trifle in his left, hind, front foot, though.

JIMMY   He doesn't!

TOM   He does!

JIMMY *(fiercely)*   He doesn't!

TOM   *(as fiercely)* I say he does!

MRS. LOVING *(appearing in the doorway in the rear)*   For Heaven's sake! What is this? Good-morning, Tommy.

TOM *(rising and going toward his mother,* JIMMY *following astride of the cane in his rear)*   Good-morning, Ma. *(kisses her; lays his head on her shoulder and makes believe he is crying; in a high falsetto)* Ma! Jimmy says his horse doesn't limp in his hind, front right leg, and I say he does.

JIMMY *(throws his cane aside, rolls on the floor and kicks up his heels. He roars with laughter)*   I think Uncle Tom is funnier than any clown in the "Kickus."

TOM *(raising his head and looking down at* JIMMY; RACHEL *stands in the kitchenette doorway)* In the *what,* Jimmy?

JIMMY   In the "kickus," of course.

TOM   "Kickus"! "Kickus"! Oh, Lordy! *(TOM and RACHEL shriek with laughter;* MRS. LOVING *looks amused;* JIMMY, *very much affronted, gets upon his feet again.* TOM *leans over and swings* JIMMY *high in the air)* Boy, you'll be the death of me yet. Circus, son! Circus!

JIMMY *(from on high, soberly and with injured dignity)*   Well, I thinks "kickus" and circus are very much alike. Please put me down.

RACHEL *(from the doorway)*   We laugh, honey, because we love you so much.

JIMMY *(somewhat mollified, to* TOM)   Is that so, Uncle Tom?

TOM   Surest thing in the world! *(severely)* Come, get down, young man. Don't you know you'll wear my arms out? Besides, there is something in my lower vest pocket, that's just dying to come to you. Get down, I say.

JIMMY (laughing)   How can I get down? *(wriggles around)*

TOM   How should I know? Just get down, of course. *(very suddenly puts* JIMMY *down on his feet.* JIMMY *tries to climb up over him).*

JIMMY   Please sit down, Uncle Tom?

TOM *(in feigned surprise)*   Sit down! What for?

JIMMY *(pummeling him with his little fists, loudly)*   Why, you said there was something for me in your pocket.

TOM *(sitting down)*   So I did. How forgetful I am!

JIMMY *(finding a bright, shiny penny, shrieks)* Oh! Oh! Oh! *(climbs up and kisses* TOM *noisily).*

TOM   Why, Jimmy! You embarrass me. My! My!

JIMMY   What is 'barrass?

TOM   You make me blush.

JIMMY   What's that?

MISS LOVING   Come, come, children! Rachel has the breakfast on the table. *(TOM sits in* JIMMY's *place and* JIMMY *tries to drag him out).*

TOM   What's the matter, now?

JIMMY   You're in *my* place.

TOM   Well, can't you sit in mine?

JIMMY *(wistfully)*   I wants to sit by my Ma Rachel.

TOM   Well, so do I.

RACHEL   Tom, stop teasing Jimmy. Honey, don't you let him bother you; ask him please prettily.

JIMMY   Please prettily, Uncle Tom.

TOM   Oh! well then. *(gets up and takes his own place. They sit as they did in Act I only* JIMMY *sits between* TOM, *at the end, and* RACHEL)

JIMMY *(loudly)*   Oh, goody! goody! goody! We've got sau-sa-ges.

MRS. LOVING.   Sh!

JIMMY (*silenced for a few moments;* RACHEL *ties a big napkin around his neck, and prepares his breakfast. He breaks forth again suddenly and excitedly*) Uncle Tom!

TOM Sir?

JIMMY I took a bath this morning, all by myself alone, in the bath-tub, and I ranned, no (*doubtfully*) I runned, I think—the water all in it, and got in it all by myself; and Ma Loving thought it was you; but it was *me*.

TOM (*in feignedly severe tones*) See here, young man, this won't do. Don't you know I'm the only one who is allowed to do that here? It's a perfect waste of water—that's what it is.

JIMMY (*undaunted*) Oh! no, you're not the only one, 'cause Ma Loving and Ma Rachel and me—alls takes baths every single morning. So, there!

TOM You 'barrass me. (JIMMY *opens his mouth to ask a question;* TOM *quickly*) Young gentleman, your mouth is open. Close it, sir; close it.

MRS. LOVING Tom, you're as big a child exactly as Jimmy.

TOM (*bowing to right and left*) You compliment me. I thank you, I am sure.

(*They finish in silence*)

JIMMY (*sighing with contentment*) I'm through, Ma Rachel.

MRS. LOVING Jimmy, you're a big boy, now, aren't you? (JIMMY *nods his head vigorously and looks proud*) I wonder if you're big enough to wash your own hands, this morning?

JIMMY (shrilly) Yes, ma'am.

MRS. LOVING Well, if they're beautifully clean, I'll give you another penny.

JIMMY (*excitedly to* RACHEL) Please untie my napkin, Ma Rachel! (RACHEL *does so*) "Excoose" me, please.

MRS. LOVING AND RACHEL. Certainly.
(JIMMY *climbs down and rushes out of the rear doorway*)

MRS. LOVING (*solemnly and slowly; breaking the silence*) Rachel, do you know what day this is?

RACHEL (*looking at her plate; slowly*) Yes, Ma dear.

MRS. LOVING Tom.

TOM (*grimly and slowly*) Yes, Ma.

(*A silence*)

MRS. LOVING (*impressively*) We must never—as long—as we live—forget this day.

RACHEL No, Ma dear.

TOM No, Ma.

(*Another silence*)

TOM (*slowly; as though thinking aloud*) I hear people talk about God's justice—and I wonder. There, are you, Ma. There isn't a sacrifice—that you haven't made. You're still working your fingers to the bone—sewing—just so all of us may keep on living. Rachel is a graduate in Domestic Science; she was high in her class; most of the girls below her in rank have positions in the schools. I'm an electrical engineer—and I've tried steadily for several months—to practice my profession. It seems our educations aren't of much use to us: we aren't allowed to make good—because our skins are dark. (*pauses*) And, in the South today, there are white men—(*controls himself*) They have everything; they're well-dressed, well-fed, well-housed; they're prosperous in business; they're important politically; they're pillars in the church. I know all this is true—I've inquired. Their children (our ages, some of them) are growing up around them; and they are having a square deal handed out to them—college, position, wealth, and best of all, freedom, without galling restrictions, to work out their own salvations. With ability, they may become—anything; and all this will be true of their children's children after them. (*a pause*) Look at us—and look at them. We are destined to failure—they, to success. Their children shall grow up in hope; ours, in despair. Our hands are clean;—theirs are red with blood—red with the blood of a noble man—and a boy. They're nothing but low, cowardly, bestial murderers. The scum of the earth shall succeed.—God's justice, I suppose.

MRS. LOVING (*rising and going to* TOM; *brokenly*) Tom, promise me—one thing.

TOM (*rises gently*) What is it, Ma?

MRS. LOVING That—you'll try—not to lose faith—in God. I've been where you are now—and it's black. Tom, we don't understand God's ways. My son, I know, now—He is beautiful. Tom, won't you try to believe, again?

TOM (*slowly, but not convincingly*) I'll try, Ma.

MRS. LOVING (*sighs*) Each one, I suppose, has to work out his own salvation. (*after a pause)* Rachel, if you'll get Jimmy ready, I'll take him to school. I've got to go down town shopping for a customer, this morning.

(RACHEL *rises and goes out the rear doorway;* MRS. LOVING, *limping very slightly now, follows. She turns and looks back yearningly at* TOM, *who has seated himself again and is staring unseeingly at his plate. She goes out.* TOM *sits without moving until he hears* MRS. LOVING's *voice within and* RACHEL's *faintly; then he gets the paper, sits in the arm-chair and pretends to read)*

MRS. LOVING *(from within)*   A yard, you say, Rachel? You're sure that will be enough. Oh! you've measured it. Anything else?—What?—Oh, all right. I'll be back by one o'clock, anyway. Good-bye. *(enters with* JIMMY. *Both are dressed for the street.* TOM *looks up brightly at* JIMMY)

TOM   Hello! Big Fellow, where are you taking my mother, I'd like to know? This is a pretty kettle of fish.

JIMMY *(laughing)*   Aren't you funny, Uncle Tom! Why, I'm not taking her anywhere. She's taking me. *(importantly)* I'm going to school.

TOM   Big Fellow, come here. (JIMMY *comes with a rush)*. Now, where's that penny I gave you? No, I don't want to see it. All right. Did Ma Loving give you another? *(vigorous noddings of the head from* JIMMY) I wish you to promise me solemnly—Now, listen! Here, don't wriggle so! not to buy—Listen! too many pints of ice-cream with my penny. Understand?

JIMMY *(very seriously)*   Yes, Uncle Tom, cross my "tummy"! I promise.

TOM   Well, then, you may go. I guess that will be all for the present. (JIMMY *loiters around looking up wistfully into his face)* Well?

JIMMY   Haven't you—aren't you—isn't you—forgetting something?

TOM *(grabbing at his pockets)*   Bless my stars! what now?

JIMMY   If you could kind of lean over this way. (TOM *leans forward)* No, not that way. (TOM *leans toward the side away from* JIMMY) No, this way! *(laughs and pummels him with his little fists)* This way!

TOM *(leaning toward* JIMMY)   Well, why didn't you say so, at first?

JIMMY *(puts his arms around* TOM's *neck and kisses him)*   Good-bye, dear old Uncle Tom. (TOM *catches him and hugs him hard)* I likes to be hugged like that—I can taste—sau-sa-ges.

TOM   You 'barrass me, son. Here, Ma, take your boy. Now remember all I told you, Jimmy.

JIMMY   I 'members.

MRS. LOVING   God bless you, Tom, Good luck.

JIMMY *(to* TOM)   God bless you, Uncle Tom. Good luck!

TOM *(much affected, but with restraint, rising)* Thank you—Good-bye. (MRS. LOVING *and* JIMMY *go out through the vestibule.* TOM *lights a cigarette and tries to read the paper. He soon sinks into a brown study. Presently* RACHEL *enters humming.* TOM *relights his cigarette; and* RACHEL *proceeds to clear the table. In the midst of this, the bell rings three distinct times)*

RACHEL and TOM   John!

TOM   I wonder what's up—It's rather early for him.—I'll go. *(rises leisurely and goes out into the vestibule. The outer door opens and shuts. Men's voices are heard.* TOM *and* JOHN STRONG *enter. During the ensuing conversation* RACHEL *finishes clearing the table, takes the fern off, puts on the green table-cloth, places a doily carefully in the centre, and replaces the fern. She apparently pays no attention to the conversation between her brother and* STRONG. *After she has finished, she goes to the kitchenette. The rattle of dishes can be heard now and then)*

RACHEL *(brightly)*   Well, stranger, how does it happen you're out so early in the morning?

STRONG   I hadn't seen any of you for a week, and I thought I'd come by, on my way to work, and find out how things are going. There is no need of asking how you are, Rachel. And the mother and the boy?

RACHEL   Ma dear's rheumatism still holds on.—Jimmy's fine.

STRONG   I'm sorry to hear that your mother is not well. There isn't a remedy going that my mother doesn't know about. I'll get her advice and let you know. *(turning to* TOM) Well, Tom, how goes it? (STRONG *and* TOM *sit)*

TOM *(smiling grimly)*   There's plenty of "go," but no "git there."

(There is a pause)

STRONG   I was hoping for better news.

TOM   If I remember rightly, not so many years ago, you tried—and failed. Then, a colored man had hardly a ghost of a show;—now he hasn't even the ghost of a ghost.

STRONG   That's true enough. *(a pause)* What are you going to do?

TOM (*slowly*) I'll do this little "going act" of mine the rest of the week; (*pauses*) and then, I'll do anything I can get to do. If necessary, I suppose, I can be "white-wing."

STRONG Tom, I came—(*breaks off; continuing slowly*) Six years ago, I found I was up against a stone wall—your experience, you see, to the letter. I couldn't let my mother starve, so I became a waiter. (*pauses*) I studied waiting; I made a science of it, an art. In a comparatively short time, I'm a head-waiter and I'm up against another stone wall. I've reached my limit. I'm thirty-two now, and I'll die a head-waiter. (*a pause*) College friends, so-called, and acquaintances used to come into the restaurant. One or two at first—attempted to commiserate with me. They didn't do it again. I waited upon them—I did my best. Many of them tipped me. (*pauses and smiles grimly*) I can remember my first tip, still. They come in yet; many of them are already powers, not only in this city, but in the country. Some of them make a personal request that I wait upon them. I am an artist, now, in my proper sphere. They tip me well, extremely well—the larger the tip, the more pleased they are with me. Because of me, in their own eyes, they're philanthropists. Amusing, isn't it? I can stand their attitude now. My philosophy—learned hard, is to make the best of everything you can, and go on. At best, life isn't so very long. You're wondering why I'm telling you all this. I wish you to see things exactly as they are. There are many disadvantages and some advantages in being a waiter. My mother can live comfortably; I am able, even, to see that she gets some of the luxuries. Tom, it's this way—I can always get you a job as a waiter; I'll teach you the art. If you care to begin the end of the week—all right. And remember this, as long as I keep my job—this offer holds good.

TOM I—I— (*breaks off*) Thank you. (*a pause; then smiling wryly*) I guess it's safe enough to say, you'll see me at the end of the week. John you're—(*breaking off again. A silence interrupted presently by the sound of much vigorous rapping on the outer door of the flat. RACHEL appears and crosses over toward the vestibule*)

RACHEL Hear the racket! My kiddies gently begging for admittance. It's about twenty minutes of nine, isn't it? (TOM *nods*). I thought so.

(*Goes into the entryway; presently reappears with a group of six little girls ranging in age from five to about nine. All are fighting to be close to her; and all are talking at once. There is one exception: the smallest tot is self-possessed and self-sufficient. She carries a red geranium in her hand and gives it her full attention*).

LITTLE MARY It's my turn to get "Morning kiss" first, this morning, Miss Rachel. You kissed Louise first yesterday. You said you'd kiss us "alphabetically." (*ending in a shriek*) You promised! (RACHEL *kisses* MARY, *who subsides*)

LITTLE NANCY (*imperiously*) Now, me. (RACHEL *kisses her, and then amid shrieks, recriminations, pulling of hair, jostling, etc., she kisses the rest. The small tot is still oblivious to everything that is going on*).

RACHEL (*laughing*) You children will pull me limb from limb and then I'll be all dead; and you'll be sorry—see, if you aren't. (*they fall back immediately.* TOM *and* JOHN *watch in amused silence.* RACHEL *loses all self-consciousness, and seems to bloom in the children's midst*) Edith! come here this minute, and let me tie your hair-ribbon again. Nancy, I'm ashamed of you, I saw you trying to pull it off. (NANCY *looks abashed but mischievous*). Louise, you look as sweet as sweet, this morning; and Jenny, where did you get the pretty, pretty dress?

LITTLE JENNY (*snuffling, but proud*) My mother made it. (*pauses with more snuffles*) My mother says I have a very bad cold. (*there is a brief silence interrupted by the small tot with the geranium*)

LITTLE MARTHA (*in a sweet, little voice*) I—have—a—pitty—'ittle flower.

RACHEL Honey, it's beautiful. Don't you want "Morning kiss" too?

LITTLE MARTHA Yes, I do.

RACHEL Come, honey. (RACHEL *kisses her*) Are you going to give the pretty flower to Jenny's teacher? (*vigorous shakings of the head in denial*) Is it for—mother? (*more shakings of the head*) Is it for—let's see—Daddy? (*more shakings of the head*) I give up. To whom are you going to give the pretty flower, honey?

LITTLE MARTHA (*shyly*) "Oo."

RACHEL You, darling!

LITTLE MARTHA Muzzer and I picked it—for "oo." Here 't is. (*puts her finger in her mouth, and gives it shyly*)

RACHEL Well, I'm going to pay you with three big kisses. One! Two! Three!

LITTLE MARTHA   I can count, One! Two! Free! Tan't I? I am going to school soon; and I wants to put the flower in your hair.

RACHEL *(kneels)*   All right, baby. (LITTLE MARTHA *fumbles and* RACHEL *helps her*)

LITTLE MARTHA *(dreamily)*   Miss Rachel, the little flower loves you. It told me so. It said it wanted to lie in your hair. It is going to tell you a pitty 'ittle secret. You listen awful hard—and you'll hear. I wish I were a fairy and had a little wand. I'd turn everything into flowers. Wouldn't that be nice, Miss Rachel?

RACHEL   Lovely, honey!

LITTLE JENNY *(snuffling loudly)*   If I were a fairy and had a wand, I'd turn you, Miss Rachel, into a queen—and then I'd always be near you and see that you were happy.

RACHEL   Honey, how beautiful!

LITTLE LOUISE   I'd make my mother happy—if I were a fairy. She cries all the time. My father can't get anything to do.

LITTLE NANCY   If I were a fairy, I'd turn a boy in my school into a spider. I hate him.

RACHEL   Honey, why?

LITTLE NANCY.   I'll tell you sometime—I hate him.

LITTLE EDITH   Where's Jimmy, Miss Rachel?

RACHEL   He went long ago; and chickies, you'll have to clear out, all of you, now, or you'll be late. Shoo! Shoo! *(she drives them out prettily before her. They laugh merrily. They all go into the vestibule)*

TOM *(slowly)*   Does it ever strike you—how pathetic and tragic a thing—a little colored child is?

STRONG   Yes.

TOM   Today, we colored men and women, everywhere—are up against it. Every year, we are having a harder time of it. In the South, they make it as impossible as they can for us to get an education. We're hemmed in on all sides. Our one safeguard—the ballot—in most states, is taken away already, or is being taken away. Economically, in a few lines, we have a slight show—but at what a cost! In the North, they make a pretense of liberality: they give us the ballot and a good education, and then—snuff us out. Each year, the problem just to live, gets more difficult to solve. How about these children—if we're fools enough to have any? (RACHEL *reenters. Her face is drawn and pale. She returns to the kitchenette*)

STRONG *(slowly, with emphasis)*   That part—is damnable! *(a silence)*

TOM *(suddenly looking at the clock)*   It's later than I thought. I'll have to be pulling out of here now, if you don't mind. *(raising his voice)* Rachel! (RACHEL *still drawn and pale, appears in the doorway of the kitchenette. She is without her apron*) I've got to go now, Sis. I leave John in your hands.

STRONG   I've got to go, myself, in a few minutes.

TOM   Nonsense, man! Sit still. I'll begin to think, in a minute, you're afraid of the ladies.

STRONG   I am.

TOM   What! And not ashamed to acknowledge it?

STRONG   No.

TOM   You're lots wiser than I dreamed. So long! *(gets hat out in the entry-way and returns; smiles wryly)* "Morituri Salutamus." *(they nod at him—*RACHEL *wistfully. He goes out. There is the sound of an opening and closing door.* RACHEL *sits down. A rather uncomfortable silence, on the part of* RACHEL, *ensues.* STRONG *is imperturbable)*

RACHEL *(nervously)*   John!

STRONG   Well?

RACHEL   I—I listened.

STRONG   Listened! To what?

RACHEL   To you and Tom.

STRONG   Well,—what of it?

RACHEL   I didn't think it was quite fair not to tell you. It—it seemed, well, like eavesdropping.

STRONG   Don't worry about it. Nonsense!

RACHEL   I'm glad—I want to thank you for what you did for Tom. He needs you, and will need you. You'll help him?

STRONG *(thoughtfully)*   Rachel, each one—has his own little battles. I'll do what I can. After all, an outsider doesn't help much.

RACHEL   But friendship—just friendship—helps.

STRONG   Yes. *(a silence)* Rachel, do you hear anything encouraging from the schools? Any hope for you yet?

RACHEL   No, nor ever will be. I know that now. There's no more chance for me than there is for Tom,—or than there was for you—or for any of us with dark skins. It's lucky for me that I love to keep house, and cook, and sew. I'll never get anything else. Ma dear's sewing, the little work Tom has been able to get, and the little sewing I sometimes get to do—keep us from the poorhouse. We live. According to your philosophy, I suppose, make the best of it—it might be worse.

STRONG (*quietly*)   You don't want to get morbid over these things, you know.

RACHEL (*scornfully*)   That's it. If you see things as they are, you're either pessimistic or morbid.

STRONG   In the long run, do you believe, that attitude of mind—will be—beneficial to you? I'm ten years older than you. I tried your way. I know. Mine is the only sane one. (*goes over to her slowly; deliberately puts his hands on her hair, and tips her head back. He looks down into her face quietly without saying anything*)

RACHEL (*nervous and startled*)   Why, John, don't! (*he pays no attention, but continues to look down into her face*)

STRONG (*half to himself*)   Perhaps—if you had—a little more fun in your life, your point of view would be—more normal. I'll arrange it so I can take you to some theatre, one night, this week.

RACHEL (*irritably*)   You talk as though I were a—a jelly-fish. You'll take me, how do you know I'll go?

STRONG   You will.

RACHEL (*sarcastically*)   Indeed! (STRONG *makes no reply*) I wonder if you know how—how—maddening you are. Why, you talk as though my will counts for nothing. It's as if you're trying to master me. I think a domineering man is detestable.

STRONG (*softly*)   If he's, perhaps, *the* man?

RACHEL (*hurriedly, as though she had not heard*)   Besides, some of these theatres put you off by yourself as though you had leprosy. I'm not going.

STRONG (*smiling at her*)   You know I wouldn't ask you to go, under those circumstances. (*a silence*) Well, I must be going now (*he takes her hand, and looks at it reverently.* RACHEL, *at first resists; but he refuses to let go. When she finds it useless, she ceases to resist. He turns his head and smiles down into her face*) Rachel, I am coming back to see you, this evening.

RACHEL   I'm sure *we'll* all be very glad to see you.

STRONG (*looking at her calmly*)   I said—*you*. (*very deliberately, he turns her hand palm upwards, leans over and kisses it; then he puts it back into her lap. He touches her cheek lightly*)

Good-bye—little Rachel. (*turns in the vestibule door and looks back, smiling*) Until tonight. (*He goes out.* RACHEL *sits for some time without moving. She is lost in a beautiful day-dream. Presently she sighs happily, and after looking furtively around the room, lifts the palm* JOHN *has kissed to her lips. She laughs shyly and jumping up, begins to hum. She opens the window at the rear of the room and then commences to thread the sewing-machine. She hums happily the whole time. A light rapping is heard at the outer door.* RACHEL *listens. It stops, and begins again. There is something insistent, and yet hopeless in the sound.* RACHEL *looking puzzled, goes out into the vestibule. . . . The door closes. Rachel, and a black woman, poorly dressed, and a little ugly, black child come in. There is the stoniness of despair in the woman's face. The child is thin, nervous, suspicious, frightened*)

MRS. LANE (*in a sharp, but toneless voice*)   May I sit down? I'm tired.

RACHEL (*puzzled, but gracious; draws up a chair for her*)   Why, certainly.

MRS LANE.   No, you don't know me—never even heard of me—nor I of you. I was looking at the vacant flat on this floor—and saw your name—on your door,—"Loving!" It's a strange name to come across—in this world.—I thought, perhaps, you might give me some information. (*the child hides behind her mother and looks around at* RACHEL *in a frightened way*)

RACHEL (*smiling at the woman and child in a kindly manner*)   I'll be glad to tell you anything, I am able Mrs.—

MRS. LANE   Lane. What I want to know is, how do they treat the colored children in the school I noticed around the corner? (*the child clutches at her mother's dress*)

RACHEL (*perplexed*)   Very well—I'm sure.

MRS. LANE (*bluntly*)   What reason have you for being sure?

RACHEL   Why, the little boy I've adopted goes there; and he's very happy. All the children in this apartment-house go there too; and I know they're happy.

MRS. LANE   Do you know how many colored children there are in the school?

RACHEL   Why, I should guess around thirty.

MRS. LANE.   I see. (*pauses*) What color is this little adopted boy of yours?

RACHEL (*gently*)   Why—he's brown.

MRS. LANE   Any black children there?

RACHEL (*nervously*) Why—yes.

MRS. LANE Do you mind if I send Ethel over by the piano to sit?

RACHEL N—no, certainly not. (*places a chair by the piano and goes to the little girl holding out her hand. She smiles beautifully. The child gets farther behind her mother*)

MRS. LANE. She won't go to you—she's afraid of everybody now but her father and me. Come Ethel. (MRS. LANE *takes the little girl by the hand and leads her to the chair. In a gentler voice*) Sit down, Ethel. (ETHEL *obeys. When her mother starts back again toward* RACHEL, *she holds out her hands pitifully. She makes no sound*) I'm not going to leave you, Ethel. I'll be right over here. You can see me. (*the look of agony on the child's face, as her mother leaves her, makes* RACHEL *shudder*) Do you mind if we sit over here by the sewing machine? Thank you. (*they move their chairs*)

RACHEL (*looking at the little, pitiful figure watching its mother almost unblinkingly*) Does Ethel like apples, Mrs. Lane?

MRS. LANE. Yes.

RACHEL Do you mind if I give her one?

MRS. LANE. No. Thank you, very much.

RACHEL (*goes into the kitchenette and returns with a fringed napkin, a plate, and a big, red apple cut into quarters. She goes to the little girl, who cowers away from her; very gently*) Here, dear, little girl, is a beautiful apple for you. (*the gentle tones have no appeal for the trembling child before her*)

MRS. LANE (*coming forward*) I'm sorry, but I'm afraid she won't take it from you. Ethel, the kind lady has given you an apple. Thank her nicely. Here! I'll spread the napkin for you, and put the plate in your lap. Thank the lady like a good little girl.

ETHEL (*very low*) Thank you. (*They return to their seats.* ETHEL *with difficulty holds the plate in her lap. During the rest of the interview between* RACHEL *and her mother, she divides her attention between the apple on the plate and her mother's face. She makes no attempt to eat the apple, but holds the plate in her lap with a care that is painful to watch. Often, too, she looks over her shoulder fearfully. The conversation between* RACHEL *and her mother is carried on in low tones*)

MRS. LANE I've got to move—it's *Ethel*.

RACHEL What is the matter with that child? It's—it's heartbreaking to see her.

MRS. LANE. I understand how you feel,—I don't feel anything, myself, any more. (*a pause*) My husband and I are poor, and we're ugly and we're Black. Ethel looks like her father more than she does like me. We live in 55th Street—near the railroad. It's a poor neighborhood, but the rent's cheap. My husband is a porter in a store; and, to help out, I'm a caretaker. (*pauses*) I don't know why I'm telling you all this. We had a nice little home—and the three of us were happy. Now we've got to move.

RACHEL Move! Why?

MRS. LANE It's Ethel. I put her in school this September. She stayed two weeks. (*pointing to* ETHEL) That's the result.

RACHEL (*in horror*) You mean—that just two weeks—in school—did that?

MRS. LANE. Yes. Ethel never had a sick day in her life—before. (*a brief pause*) I took her to the doctor at the end of the two weeks. He says she's a nervous wreck.

RACHEL But what could they have done to her?

MRS. LANE (*laughs grimly and mirthlessly*) I'll tell you what they did the first day. Ethel is naturally sensitive and backward. She's not assertive. The teacher saw that, and, after I had left, told her to sit in a seat in the rear of the class. She was alone there—in a corner. The children, immediately feeling there was something wrong with Ethel because of the teacher's attitude, turned and stared at her. When the teacher's back was turned they whispered about her, pointed their fingers at her and tittered. The teacher divided the class into two parts, divisions, I believe, they are called. She forgot all about Ethel, of course, until the last minute, and then, looking back, said sharply: "That little girl there may join this division," meaning the group of pupils standing around her. Ethel naturally moved slowly. The teacher called her sulky and told her to lose a part of her recess. When Ethel came up—the children drew away from her in every direction. She was left standing alone. The teacher then proceeded to give a lesson about kindness to animals. Funny, isn't it, *kindness to animals*? The children forgot Ethel in the excitement of talking about their pets. Presently, the teacher turned to Ethel and said disagreeably: "Have you a pet?" Ethel said, "Yes," very low. "Come, speak up, you sulky

child, what is it?" Ethel said: "A blind puppy."
They all laughed, the teacher and all. Strange,
isn't it, but Ethel loves that puppy. She spoke
up: "It's mean to laugh at a little blind puppy.
I'm glad he's blind." This remark brought
forth more laughter. "Why are you glad?" the
teacher asked curiously. Ethel refused to say.
(pauses) When I asked her why, do you know
what she told me? "If he saw me, he might not
love me any more." *(a pause)* Did I tell you
that Ethel is only seven years old?

RACHEL *(drawing her breath sharply)*   Oh! I
didn't believe any one could be as cruel as
that—to a little child.

MRS. LANE   It isn't very pleasant, is it?
When the teacher found out that Ethel
wouldn't answer, she said severely: "Take your
seat!" At recess, all the children went out.
Ethel could hear them playing and laughing
and shrieking. Even the teacher went too. She
was made to sit there all alone—in that big
room—because God made her ugly—and
Black. *(pauses)* When the recess was half over
the teacher came back. "You may go now," she
said coldly. Ethel didn't stir. "Did you hear
me!" "Yes'm." "Why don't you obey?" "I don't
want to go out, please." "You don't, don't you,
you stubborn child! Go immediately!" Ethel
went. She stood by the school steps. No one
spoke to her. The children near her moved
away in every direction. They stopped playing,
many of them, and watched her. They stared
as only children can stare. Some began whispering about her. Presently one child came up
and ran her hand roughly over Ethel's face.
She looked at her hand and Ethel's face and
ran screaming back to the others, "It won't
come off! See!" Other children followed the
first child's example. Then one boy spoke up
loudly: "I know what she is, she's a nigger!"
Many took up the cry. God or the devil interfered—the bell rang. The children filed in.
One boy boldly called her "Nigger!" before the
teacher. She said, "That isn't nice," —but she
smiled at the boy. Things went on about the
same for the rest of the day. At the end of
school, Ethel put on her hat and coat—the
teacher made her hang them at a distance
from the other pupils' wraps; and started for
home. Quite a crowd escorted her. They
called her "Nigger!" all the way. I *made* Ethel
go the next day. I complained to the authori-
ties. They treated me lightly. I was determined

not to let them force my child out of school.
At the end of two weeks—I had to take her
out.

RACHEL *(brokenly)*   Why,—I never—in all
my life—heard anything—so—pitiful.

MRS. LANE   Did you ever go to school
here?

RACHEL.   Yes. I was made to feel my color—
but I never had an experience like that.

MRS. LANE.   How many years ago were you
in the graded schools?

RACHEL   Oh!—around ten.

MRS. LANE *(laughs grimly)*   Ten years! Every
year things are getting worse. Last year wasn't
as bad as this *(pauses)* So they treat the children all right in this school?

RACHEL   Yes! Yes! I know that.

MRS. LANE   I can't afford to take this flat
here, but I'll take it. I'm going to have Ethel
educated. Although, when you think of it,—
it's all rather useless—this education! What
are our children going to do with it, when
they get it? We strive and save and sacrifice to
educate them—and the whole time—down
underneath, we know—they'll have no
chance.

RACHEL *(sadly)*   Yes, that's true, all right.—
God seems to have forgotten us.

MRS. LANE   God! It's all a lie about God. I
know.—This fall I sent Ethel to a white Sunday-school near us. She received the same
treatment there she did in the day school. Her
being there, nearly broke up the school. At
the end, the superintendent called her to him
and asked her if she didn't know of some nice
colored Sunday-school. He told her she must
feel out of place, and uncomfortable there.
That's your Church of God!

RACHEL   Oh! how unspeakably brutal. *(controls herself with an effort; after a pause)* Have
you any other children?

MRS. LANE *(dryly)*   Hardly! If I had another—I'd kill it. It's kinder. *(rising presently)*
Well, I must go, now. Thank you, for your information—and for listening. *(suddenly)* You
aren't married, are you?

RACHEL   No.

MRS. LANE   Don't marry—that's my advice.
Come, Ethel. (ETHEL *gets up and puts down the
things in her lap, carefully upon her chair. She
goes in a hurried, timid way to her mother and
clutches her hand*). Say good-bye to the lady.

ETHEL *(faintly)*   Good-bye.

RACHEL (*kneeling by the little girl—a beautiful smile on her face*)   Dear little girl, won't you let me kiss you good-bye? I love little girls. (*the child hides behind her mother; continuing brokenly*) Oh!—no child—ever did—that to me—before!

MRS. LANE (*in a gentler voice*)   Perhaps, when we move in here, the first of the month, things may be better. Thank you, again. Good-morning! You don't belie your name. (*all three go into the vestibule. The outside door opens and closes.* RACHEL *as though dazed and stricken returns. She sits in a chair, leans forward, and clasping her hands loosely between her knees, stares at the chair with the apple on it where* ETHEL LANE *has sat. She does not move for some time. Then she gets up and goes to the window in the rear center and sits there. She breathes in the air deeply and then goes to the sewing-machine and begins to sew on something she is making. Presently her feet slow down on the pedals; she stops; and begins brooding again. After a short pause, she gets up and begins to pace up and down slowly, mechanically, her head bent forward. The sharp ringing of the electric bell breaks in upon this.* RACHEL *starts and goes slowly into the vestibule. She is heard speaking dully through the tube*)

RACHEL   Yes!—All right! Bring it up! (*presently she returns with a long flower box. She opens it listlessly at the table. Within are six, beautiful crimson rosebuds with long stems.* RACHEL *looks at the name on the card. She sinks down slowly on her knees and leans her head against the table. She signs wearily*) Oh! John! John!—What are we to do?—I'm—I'm—afraid! Everywhere—it is the same thing. My mother! My little brother! Little, Black, crushed Ethel! (*in a whisper*) Oh! God! You who I have been taught to believe are so good, so beautiful how could—You permit—these—things? (*pauses, raises her head and sees the rosebuds. Her face softens and grows beautiful, very sweetly*) Dear little rosebuds!—you—make me think—of sleeping, curled up, happy babies. Dear beautiful, little rosebuds! (*pauses; goes on thoughtfully to the rosebuds*) When I look—at you—I believe—God is beautiful. He who can make a little exquisite thing like this, and this can't be cruel. Oh! He can't mean me—to give up—love—and the hope of little children. (*there is the sound of a small hand knocking at the outer door.* RACHEL *smiles*) My Jimmy!

It must be twelve o'clock. (*rises*) I didn't dream it was so late. (*starts for the vestibule*) Oh! the world can't be so bad. I don't believe it. I won't. I *must* forget that little girl. My little Jimmy is happy—and today John— sent me beautiful rosebuds. Oh, there are lovely things, yet. (*goes into the vestibule. A child's eager cry is heard; and* RACHEL *carrying* JIMMY *in her arms comes in. He has both arms about her neck and is hugging her. With him in her arms, she sits down in the armchair at the right front*).

RACHEL   Well, honey, how was school today?

JIMMY (*sobering a trifle*)   All right, Ma Rachel. (*suddenly sees the roses*) Oh! look at the pretty flowers. Why, Ma Rachel, you forgot to put them in water. They'll die.

RACHEL   Well, so they will. Hop down this minute, and I'll put them in right away. (*gathers up box and flowers and goes into the kitchenette.* JIMMY *climbs back into the chair. He looks thoughtful and serious.* RACHEL *comes back with the buds in a tall, glass vase. She puts the fern on top of the table*) There, honey, that's better, isn't it? Aren't they lovely?

JIMMY   Yes, that's lots better. Now they won't die, will they? Rosebuds are just like little "chilyun," aren't they, Ma Rachel? If you are good to them, they'll grow up into lovely roses, won't they? And if you hurt them, they'll die. Ma Rachel do you think all peoples are kind to little rosebuds?

RACHEL (*watching Jimmy shortly*)   Why, of course. Who could hurt little children? Who would have the heart to do such a thing?

JIMMY   If you hurt them, it would be lots kinder, wouldn't it, to kill them all at once, and not a little bit and a little bit?

RACHEL (*sharply*   Why, honey boy, why are you talking like this?

JIMMY   Ma Rachel, why is a "Nigger?"

(RACHEL *recoils as though she had been struck*)

RACHEL   Honey boy, why—why do you ask that?

JIMMY   Some big boys called me that when I came out of school just now. They said: "Look at the little nigger!" and they laughed. One of them runned, no ranned, after me and threw stones; and they all kept calling "Nigger! Nigger! Nigger!" One stone struck me hard in the back, and it hurt awful bad; but I didn't cry, Ma Rachel. I wouldn't let them make me cry. The stone hurts me there, Ma Rachel; but what they called me hurts and hurts here. What is a "nigger," Ma Rachel?

RACHEL (*controlling herself with a tremendous effort. At last she sweeps down upon him and hugs and kisses him*)   Why, honey, boy, those boys didn't mean anything. Silly, little, honey boy! They're rough, that's all. How *could* they mean anything?

JIMMY   You're only saying that, Ma Rachel, so I won't be hurt. I know. It wouldn't ache here like it does—if they didn't mean something.

RACHEL (*abruptly*)   Where's Mary, honey?

JIMMY   She's in her flat. She came in just after I did.

RACHEL   Well, honey, I'm going to give you two big cookies and two to take to Mary; and you may stay in there and play with her, till I get your lunch ready. Won't that be jolly?

JIMMY (*brightening a little*)   Why, you never give me but one at a time. You'll give me two?—One? Two?

RACHEL (*gets the cookies and brings them to him.* JIMMY *climbs down from the chair*)   Shoo! now, little honey boy. See how many laughs you can make for me, before I come after you. Hear? Have a good time, now.

(JIMMY *starts for the door quickly; but he begins to slow down. His face gets long and serious again.* RACHEL *watches him*)

RACHEL (*jumping at him*)   Shoo! Shoo! Get out of here quickly, little chicken. (*she follows him out. The outer door opens and shuts. Presently she returns. She looks old and worn and grey; calmly. Pauses*)   First, it's little, Black Ethel—and then's it's Jimmy. Tomorrow, it will be some other little child. The blight—sooner or later—strikes all. My little Jimmy, only seven years old poisoned! (*through the open window comes the laughter of little children at play.* RACHEL, *shuddering, covers her ears*). And once I said, centuries ago, it must have been: "How can life be so terrible, when there are little children in the world?" Terrible! Terrible! (*in a whisper, slowly*)   That's the reason it *is* so terrible. (*the laughter reaches her again; this time she listens*) And, suddenly, some day, from out of the black, the blight shall descend, and shall still forever—the laughter on those little lips, and in those little hearts. (*pauses thoughtfully*)   And the loveliest thing—almost, that ever happened to me, that beautiful voice, in

my dream, those beautiful words: "Rachel, you are to be the mother to little children." (*pauses, then slowly and with dawning surprise*)   Why, God, you were making a mock of me; you were laughing at me. I didn't believe God could laugh at our sufferings, but He can. We are accursed, accursed! We have nothing, absolutely nothing. (STRONG's *rosebuds attract her attention. She goes over to them, puts her hand out as if to touch them, and then shakes her head, very sweetly*)   No, little rosebuds, I may not touch you. Dear, little, baby rosebuds,—I am accursed. (*gradually her whole form stiffens, she breathes deeply; at last slowly*)   You God!—You terrible, laughing God! Listen! I swear—and may my soul be damned to all eternity, if I do break this oath—I swear—that no child of mine shall ever lie upon my breast, for I will not have it rise up, in the terrible days that are to be—and call me cursed. (*a pause, very wistfully; questioningly*). Never to know the loveliest thing in all the world—the feel of a little head, the touch of little hands, the beautiful utter dependence—of a little child? (*with sudden frenzy*)   You can laugh, Oh God! Well, so can I. (*bursts into terrible, racking laughter*)   But I can be kinder than You. (*fiercely she snatches the rosebuds from the vase, grasps them roughly, tears each head from the stem, and grinds it under her feet. The vase goes over with a crash; the water drips unheeded over the tablecloth and floor*)   If I kill, You Mighty God, I kill at once—I do not torture. (*falls face downward on the floor. The laughter of the children shrills loudly through the window*)

ACT THREE

(TIME: *Seven o'clock in the evening, one week later.*

PLACE: *The same room. There is a cool fire in the grate. The curtains are drawn. A lighted oil lamp with a dark green porcelain shade is in the center of the table.* MRS. LOVING *and* TOM *are sitting by the table,* MRS. LOVING *sewing,* TOM *reading. There is the sound of much laughter and the shrill screaming of a child from the bedrooms. Presently* JIMMY *clad in a flannelet sleeping suit, covering all of him but his head and hands, chases a pillow, which has come flying through the doorway at the rear. He struggles with it, finally gets it in his arms, and rushes as fast as he can through the doorway again.* RACHEL *jumps at him with a cry. He drops the pil-*

low and shrieks. There is a tussle for possession of it, and they disappear. The noise grows louder and merrier. TOM *puts down his paper and grins. He looks at his mother)*

TOM   Well, who's the giddy one in this family now?

MRS. LOVING *(shaking her head in troubled manner)*   I don't like it. It worries me. Rachel—*(breaks off)*

TOM   Have you found out, yet—

MRS. LOVING *(turning and looking toward the rear doorway, quickly interrupting him)*   Sh! *(*RACHEL, *laughing, her hair tumbling over her shoulders, comes rushing into the room.* JIMMY *is in close pursuit. He tries to catch her, but she dodges him. They are both breathless)*

MRS. LOVING *(deprecatingly)*   Really, Rachel, Jimmy will be so excited he won't be able to sleep. It's after his bedtime, now. Don't you think you had better stop?

RACHEL   All right, Ma dear. Come on, Jimmy; let's play "Old Folks" and sit by the fire. *(she begins to push the big armchair over to the fire.* TOM *jumps up, moves her aside, and pushes it himself.* JIMMY *renders assistance)*

TOM   Thanks, Big Fellow, you are "sure some" strong. I'll remember you when these people around here come for me to move pianos and such things around. Shake! *(they shake hands)*

JIMMY *(proudly)*   I am awful strong, am I not?

TOM   You "sure" are a Hercules. *(hurriedly, as* Jimmy's *mouth and eyes open wide)*. And see here! Don't ask me tonight who that was. I'll tell you the first thing tomorrow morning. Hear? *(returns to his chair and paper)*

RACHEL *(sitting down)*   Come on, honey boy, and sit in my lap.

JIMMY *(doubtfully)*   I thought we were going to play "Old Folks."

RACHEL   We are.

JIMMY   Do old folks sit in each other's laps?

RACHEL   Old folks do anything. Come on.

JIMMY *(hesitatingly climbs into her lap, but presently snuggles down and sighs audibly from sheer content;* RACHEL *starts to bind up her hair)* Ma Rachel, don't please! I like your hair like that. You're—you're pretty. I like to feel of it; and it smells like—like—oh!—like a barn.

RACHEL   My! how complimentary! I like that. Like a barn, indeed!

JIMMY   What's "complimentary"?

RACHEL   Oh! saying nice things about me. *(pinching his cheek and laughing)* That my hair is like a barn, for instance.

JIMMY *(stoutly)*   Well, that is "complimentary." It smells like hay—like the hay in the barn you took me to, one day, last summer. 'Member?

RACHEL   Yes honey.

JIMMY *(after a brief pause)*   Ma Rachel!

RACHEL   Well?

JIMMY   Tell me a story, please. It's "story-time," now, isn't it?"

RACHEL   Well, let's see. *(they both look into the fire for a space; beginning softly)* Once upon a time, there were two, dear, little boys, and they were all alone in the world. They lived with a cruel, old man and woman, who made them work hard, very hard—all day, and beat them when they did not move fast enough, and always, every night, before they went to bed. They slept in an attic on a rickety, narrow bed, that went screech! screech! whenever they moved. And, in summer, they nearly died with the heat up there, and in winter, with the cold. One wintry night, when they were both weeping very bitterly after a particularly hard beating, they suddenly heard a pleasant voice saying: "Why are you crying, little boys?" They looked up, and there, in the moonlight, by their bed, was the dearest, little old lady. She was dressed all in grey, from the peak of her little pointed hat to her little, buckled shoes. She held a black cane much taller than her little self. Her hair fell about her ears in tiny, grey corkscrew curls, and they bobbed about as she moved. Her eyes were black and bright—as bright as—well, as that lovely, white light there. No, there! And her cheeks were as red as the apple I gave you yesterday. Do you remember?

JIMMY *(dreamily)*   Yes.

RACHEL   "Why are you crying, little boys?" she asked again, in a lovely, low, little voice. "Because we are tired and sore and hungry and cold; and we are all alone in the world; and we don't know how to laugh any more. We should so like to laugh again." "Why, that's easy," she said, "it's just like this." And she laughed a little, joyous, musical laugh. "Try!" she commanded. They tried, but their laughing boxes were very rusty, and they made horrid sounds. "Well," she said, "I advise you to pack up, and go away, as soon as you can, to the Land of Laughter. You'll soon learn there, I can tell you." "Is there such a land?" they asked doubtfully. "To be sure there is," she answered the least bit sharply. "We never heard of it," they said. "Well, I'm sure there must be plenty of things you never heard about," she said just the "leastest" bit more sharply. "In a moment you'll be telling me flowers don't talk together, and the birds." "We never heard of such a thing," they said in surprise, their eyes like saucers. "There!" she said, bobbing her little curls. "What did I tell you? You have much to learn." "How do you get to the Land of Laughter?" they asked. "You go out of the eastern gate of the town, just as the sun is rising; and you take the highway there, and follow it; and if you go with it long enough, it will bring you to the very gates of the Land of Laughter. It's a long, long way from here; and it will take you many days." The words had scarcely left her mouth, when, lo! the little lady disappeared, and where she had stood was the white square of moonlight—nothing else. And without more ado these two little boys put their arms around each other and fell fast asleep. And in the grey, just before daybreak, they awoke and dressed; and, putting on their ragged caps and mittens, for it was a wintry day, they stole out of the house and made for the eastern gate. And just as they reached it and passed through, the whole east leapt into fire. All day they walked, and many days thereafter, and kindly people, by the way, took them in and gave them food and drink and sometimes a bed at night. Often they slept by the roadside, but they didn't mind that for the climate was delightful—not too hot, and not too cold. They soon threw away their ragged little mittens. They walked for many days, and there was no Land of Laughter. Once they met an old man, richly dressed, with shining jewels on his fingers, and he stopped them and asked: "Where are you going so fast, little boys?" "We are going to the Land of Laughter," they said together gravely. "That," said the old man, "is a very foolish thing to do. Come with me, and I will take you to the Land of Riches. I will cover you with garments of beauty, and give you jewels and a castle to live in and servants and horses and many things besides." And they said to him: "No, we wish to learn how to

laugh again; we have forgotten how, and we are going to the Land of Laughter." "You will regret not going with me. See, if you don't," he said; and he left them in quite a huff. And they walked again, many days, and again they met an old man. He was tall and imposing-looking and very dignified. And he said: "Where are you going so fast, little boys?" "We are going to the Land of Laughter," they said together very seriously. "What!" he said, "that is an extremely foolish thing to do. Come with me, and I will give you power. I will make you great men: generals, kings, emperors. Whatever you desire to accomplish will be permitted you." And they smiled politely: "Thank you very much, but we have forgotten how to laugh, and we are going there to learn how." He looked upon them haughtily, without speaking, and disappeared. And they walked and walked more days; and they met another old man. And he was clad in rags, and his face was thin, and his eyes were unhappy. And he whispered to them: "Where are you going so fast, little boys?" "We are going to the Land of Laughter," they answered, without a smile. "Laughter! Laughter! that is useless. Come with me and I will show you the beauty of life through sacrifice, suffering for others. That is the only life. I come from the Land of Sacrifice." And they thanked him kindly, but said: "We have suffered long enough. We have forgotten how to laugh. We would learn again." And they went on; and he looked after them very wistfully. They walked more days, and at last they came to the Land of Laughter. And how do you suppose they knew this? Because they could hear, over the wall, the sound of joyous laughter,—the laughter of men, women, and children. And one sat guarding the gate, and they went to her. "We have come a long, distance; and we would enter the Land of Laughter." "Let me see you smile, first," she said gently. "I sit at the gate; and no one who does not know how to smile may enter the Land of Laughter." And they tried to smile, but could not. "Go away and practice," she said kindly, "and come back tomorrow." And they went away, and practiced all night how to smile; and in the morning they returned, and the gentle lady at the gate said: "Dear little boys, have you learned how to smile?" and they said: "We have tried. How is this?" "Better," she said, "much better.

Practice some more, and come back tomorrow." And they went away obediently and practiced. And they came the third day. And she said: "Now try again." And tears of delight came into her lovely eyes. "Those were very beautiful smiles," she said. "Now, you may enter." And she unlocked the gate, and kissed them both, and they entered the Land—the beautiful Land of Laughter. Never had they seen such blue skies, such green trees and grass; never had they heard such birds' songs. And people men, women and children, laughing softly, came to meet them, and took them in, and made them at home; and soon, very soon, they learned to sleep. And they grew up here, and married, and had laughing, happy children. And sometimes they thought of the Land of Riches, and said: "Ah! well!" and sometimes of the Land of Power, and sighed a little; and sometimes of the Land of Sacrifice—and their eyes were wistful. But they soon forgot, and laughed again. And they grew old, laughing. And then when they died—a laugh was on their lips. Thus are things in the beautiful Land of Laughter. *(there is a long pause)*

JIMMY　I like that story, Ma Rachel. It's nice to laugh, isn't it? Is there such a land?

RACHEL　*(softly)*　What do you think, honey?

JIMMY　I thinks it would be awful nice if there was. Don't you?

RACHEL　*(wistfully)*　If there only were! If there only were!

JIMMY　Ma Rachel.

RACHEL　Well?

JIMMY　It makes you think—kind of— doesn't it—of sunshine medicine?

RACHEL　Yes, honey,—but it isn't medicine there. It's always there—just like—well—like our air here. It's *always* sunshine there.

JIMMY　Always sunshine? Never any dark?

RACHEL　No, honey.

JIMMY　*(with a big sigh)*　Oh!—Oh! I *wisht* it was here—not there. *(puts his hand up to* RACHEL's *face; suddenly sits up and looks at her)* Why, Ma Rachel dear, you're crying. Your face is all wet. Why! Don't cry! Don't cry!

RACHEL　*(gently)*　Do you remember that I told you the lady at the gate had tears of joy in her eyes, when the two, dear, little boys smiled that beautiful smile?

JIMMY　Yes.

RACHEL　Well, these are tears of joy, honey, that's all—tears of joy.

JIMMY　It must be awful queer to have tears of joy, 'cause you're happy. I never did. *(with a sigh)* But, if you say they are, dear Ma Rachel, they must be. You knows everything, don't you?

RACHEL　*(sadly)*　Some things, honey, some things. *(a silence)*

JIMMY　*(sighing happily)*　This is the beautifulest night I ever knew. If you would do just one more thing, it would be lots more beautiful. Will you, Ma Rachel?

RACHEL　Well, what, honey?

JIMMY　Will you sing—at the piano, I mean, it's lots prettier that way—the little song you used to rock me to sleep by? You know, the one about the "Slumber Boat"?

RACHEL　Oh! honey, not tonight. You're too tired. It's bedtime now.

JIMMY　*(patting her face with his little hand; wheedlingly)*　Please! Ma Rachel, please! pretty please!

RACHEL　Well, honey boy, this once, then. Tonight, you shall have the little song—I used to sing you to sleep by *(half to herself)* perhaps, for the last time.

JIMMY　Why, Ma Rachel, why the last time?

RACHEL　*(shaking her head sadly, goes to the piano; in a whisper)*　The last time. *(she twists up her hair into a knot at the back of her head and looks at the keys for a few moments; then she plays the accompaniment of the "Slumber Boat" through softly, and, after a moment, sings. Her voice is full of pent-up longing, and heartbreak, and hopelessness. She ends in a little sob, but attempts to cover it by singing, lightly and daintily, the chorus of "The Owl and the Moon," . . . Then softly and with infinite tenderness, almost against her will, she plays and sings again the refrain of "Slumber Boat")*

> Sail, baby, sail
> 　　Out from the sea,
> Only don't forget to sail
> 　　Back again to me.

(Presently she rises and goes to JIMMY, *who is lolling back happily in the big chair. During the singing,* TOM *and* MRS. LOVING *apparently do not listen; when she sobs, however,* TOM's *hand on his paper tightens;* MRS. LOVING's *needle poises for a moment in mid-air. Neither looks at* RACHEL. JIMMY *evidently has not noticed the sob)*

RACHEL (*kneeling by* JIMMY)   Well, honey, how did you like it?

JIMMY(*proceeding to pull down her hair from the twist*)   It was lovely, Ma Rachel. (*yawns audibly*) Now, Ma Rachel, I'm just beautifully sleepy. (*dreamily*) I think that p'r'aps I'll go to the Land of Laughter tonight in my dreams. I'll go in the "Slumber Boat" and come back in the morning and tell you all about it. Shall I?

RACHEL   Yes, honey. (*whispers*)

> Only don't forget to sail
> Back again to me.

TOM (*suddenly*)   Rachel! (RACHEL *starts slightly*). I nearly forgot. John is coming here tonight to see how you are. He told me to tell you so.

RACHEL (*stiffens perceptibly, then in different tones*)   Very well. Thank you. (*suddenly with a little cry she puts her arms around* JIMMY) Jimmy! honey! Don't go tonight. Don't go without Ma Rachel. Wait for me, honey. I do so wish to go, too, to the Land of Laughter. Think of it, Jimmy; nothing but birds always singing, and flowers always blooming, and skies always blue—and people, all of them, always laughing, laughing. You'll wait for Ma Rachel, won't you, honey?

JIMMY   Is there really and truly, Ma Rachel, a Land of Laughter?

RACHEL   Oh! Jimmy, let's hope so; let's pray so.

JIMMY (*frowns*)   I've been thinking— (*pauses*) You have to smile at the gate, don't you, to get in?

RACHEL   Yes, honey

JIMMY   Well, I guess I couldn't smile if my Ma Rachel wasn't somewhere close to me. So I couldn't get in after all, could I? Tonight, I'll go somewhere else, and tell you all about it. And then, some day, we'll go together, won't we?

RACHEL (*sadly*)   Yes, honey, some day— some day. (*a short silence*) Well, this isn't going to "sleepy-sleep," is it? Go, now, and say good-night to Ma Loving and Uncle Tom.

JIMMY (*gets down obediently, and goes first to* MRS. LOVING. *She leans over, and he puts his little arms around her neck. They kiss, very sweetly*) Sweet dreams! God keep you all the night!

MRS. LOVING   The sweetest of sweet dreams to you, dear little boy! Good-night! (RACHEL

watches, unwatched, the scene. Her eyes are full of yearning)

JIMMY (*going to* TOM, *who makes believe he does not see him*)   Uncle Tom!

TOM (*jumps as though tremendously startled;* JIMMY *laughs*)   My! how you frightened me. You'll put my gizzard out of commission, if you do that often. Well, sir, what can I do for you?

JIMMY   I came to say good-night.

TOM (*gathering* JIMMY *up in his arms and kissing him; gently and with emotion*)   Good-night, dear little Big Fellow! Good-night!

JIMMY   Sweet dreams! God keep you all the night! (*goes sedately to* RACHEL, *and holds out his little hand*). I'm ready, Ma Rachel, (*yawns*) I'm so nice and sleepy.

RACHEL (*with* JIMMY'S *hand in hers, she hesitates a moment, and then approaches* TOM *slowly. For a short time she stands looking down at him; suddenly leaning over him*)   Why, Tom, what a pretty tie! Is it new?

TOM   Well, no, not exactly. I've had it about a month. It is rather a beauty, isn't it?

RACHEL   Why, I never remember seeing it.

TOM (*laughing*)   I guess not. I saw to that.

RACHEL.   Stingy!

TOM   Well, I am—where my ties are concerned. I've had experience.

RACHEL (*tentatively*)   Tom!

TOM   Well?

RACHEL (*nervously and wistfully*)   Are you— will you—I mean, won't you be home this evening?

TOM   You've got a long memory, Sis. I've that engagement, you know. Why?

RACHEL (*slowly*)   I forgot; so you have.

TOM   Why?

RACHEL (*hastily*)   Oh! nothing—nothing. Come on, Jimmy boy, you can hardly keep those little peepers open, can you? Come on, honey. (RACHEL *and* JIMMY *go out the rear doorway. There is a silence*)

MRS. LOVING (*slowly, as though thinking aloud*) I try to make out what could have happened; but it's no use—I can't. Those four days, she lay in bed hardly moving, scarcely speaking. Only her eyes seemed alive. I never saw such a wide, tragic look in my life. It was as though her soul had been mortally wounded. But how? how? What could have happened?

TOM (*quietly*)   I don't know. She generally tells me everything; but she avoids me now. If we are alone in a room—she gets out. I don't know what it means.

MRS. LOVING   She will hardly let Jimmy out of her sight. While he's at school, she's nervous and excited. She seems always to be listening, but for what? When he returns, she nearly devours him. And she always asks him in a frightened sort of way, her face as pale and tense as can be: "Well, honey boy, how was school today?" And he always answers, "Fine, Ma Rachel, fine! I learned—"; and then he goes on to tell her everything that has happened. And when he has finished, she says in an uneasy sort of way: "Is—is that all?" And when he says "Yes," she relaxes and becomes limp. After a little while she becomes feverishly happy. She plays with Jimmy and the children more than ever she did—and she played a good deal, as you know. They're here, or she's with them. Yesterday, I said in remonstrance, when she came in, her face pale and haggard and black hollows under her eyes: "Rachel, remember you're just out of a sick-bed. You're not well enough to go on like this." "I know," was all she would say, "but I've got to. I can't help myself. This part of their little lives must be happy—it just must be." (*pauses*) The last couple of nights, Jimmy has awakened and cried most pitfully. She wouldn't let me go to him; said I had enough trouble, and she could quiet him. She never will let me know why he cries; but she stays with him, and soothes him until, at last, he falls asleep again. Every time she has come out like a rag; and her face is like a dead woman's. Strange isn't it, this is the first time we have ever been able to talk it over? Tom, what could have happened?

TOM   I don't know, Ma, but I feel, as you do; something terrible and sudden has hurt her soul; and, poor little thing, she's trying bravely to readjust herself to life again. (*pauses, looks at his watch and then rises, and goes to her. He pats her back awkwardly*) Well, Ma, I'm going now. Don't worry too much. Youth, you know, gets over things finally. It takes them hard, that's all—. At least, that's what the older heads tell us. (*gets his hat and stands in the vestibule doorway*) Ma, you know, I begin with John tomorrow. (*with emotion*) I don't believe we'll ever forget John. Goodnight! (*exit.* MRS. LOVING *continues to sew.*

RACHEL, *her hair arranged, reenters, through the rear doorway. She is humming*).

RACHEL.   He's sleeping like a top. Aren't little children, Ma dear, the sweetest things, when they're all helpless and asleep? One little hand is under his cheek; and he's smiling. (*stops suddenly, biting her lips. A pause*) Where's Tom?

MRS. LOVING   He went out a few minutes ago.

RACHEL (*sitting in* TOM's *chair and picking up his paper. She is exceedingly nervous. She looks the paper over rapidly; presently trying to make her tone casual*) Ma,—you—you—aren't going anywhere tonight, are you?

MRS. LOVING   I've got to go out for a short time about half-past eight. Mrs. Jordan, you know. I'll not be gone very long, though. Why?

RACHEL   Oh! nothing particular. I just thought it would be cosy if we could sit here together the rest of the evening. Can't you—can't you go tomorrow?

MRS. LOVING   Why, I don't see how I can. I've made the engagement. It's about a new reception gown; and she's exceedingly exacting, as you know. I can't afford to lose her.

RACHEL   No, I suppose not. All right, Ma dear. (*presently, paper in hand, she laughs, but not quite naturally*) Look! Ma dear! How is that for fashion, anyway? Isn't it the "limit"? (*rises and shows her mother a picture in the paper. As she is in the act, the bells rings. With a startled cry*) Oh! (*drops the paper, and grips her mother's hand*)

MRS. LOVING (*anxiously*)   Rachel, your nerves are right on edge; and your hand feels like fire. I'll have to see a doctor about you; and that's all there is to it.

RACHEL (*laughing nervously, and moving toward the vestibule*)   Nonsense, Ma dear! Just because I let out a whoop now and then, and have nice warm hands? (*goes out, is heard talking through the tube*) Yes! (*her voice emitting tremendous relief*) (Oh! bring it right up! (*appearing in the doorway*) Ma dear, did you buy anything at Goddard's today?

MRS. LOVING   Yes; and I've been wondering why they were so late in delivering it. I bought it early this morning. (RACHEL *goes out again. A door opens and shuts. She reappears with a bundle*)

MRS. LOVING   Put it on my bed, Rachel, please. (*exit* RACHEL *rear doorway; presently returns empty-handed; sits down again at the table with the paper between herself and mother; sinks in a deep revery. Suddenly there is the sound of many loud knocks made by numerous small fists.* RACHEL *drops the paper, and comes to a sitting posture, tense again. Her mother looks at her, but says nothing. Almost immediately* RACHEL *relaxes).*

RACHEL   My kiddies! They're late, this evening. *(goes out into the vestibule. A door opens and shuts. There is the shrill, excited sound of childish voices.* RACHEL *comes in surrounded by the children, all trying to say something to her at once.* RACHEL *puts her finger on her lip and points toward the doorway in the rear. They all quiet down. She sits on the floor in the front of the stage, and the children all cluster around her. Their conversation takes place in a half-whisper. As they enter they nod brightly at* MRS. LOVING, *who smiles in return)* Why so late, kiddies? It's long past "sleepy-time."

LITTLE NANCY   We've been playing "Hide and Seek," and having the mostest fun. We promised, all of us, that if we could play until half-past seven tonight we wouldn't make any fuss about going to bed at seven o'clock the rest of the week. It's awful hard to go. I *hate* to go to bed!

LITTLE MARY, LOUISE and EDITH   So do I! So do I! So do I!

LITTLE MARTHA   I don't. I love bed. My bed, after my muzzer tucks me all in, is like a nice warm bag. I just stick my nose out. When I lifts my head up I can see the light from the dining-room come in the door. I can hear my muzzer and fazzer talking nice and low; and then, before I know it, I'm fast asleep, and I dream pretty things, and in about a minute it's morning again. I love my little bed, and I love to dream.

LITTLE MARY *(aggressively)*   Well, I guess I love to dream too. I wish I could dream, though, without going to bed.

LITTLE NANCY   When I grow up, I'm never going to bed at night! *(darkly)* You see.

LITTLE LOUISE   "Grown-ups" just love to poke their heads out of windows and cry, "Child'run, it's time for bed now; and you'd better hurry, too, I can tell you." They "sure" are queer, for sometimes when I wake up, it must be about twelve o'clock, I can hear my big sister giggling and talking to some silly man. If it's good for me to go to bed early—I should think—

RACHEL *(interrupting suddenly)*   Why, where is my little Jenny? Excuse me, Louise dear.

LITTLE MARTHA   Her cold is awful bad. She coughs like this *(giving a distressing imitation)* and snuffles all the time. She can't talk out loud, and she can't go to sleep. Muzzer says she's fev'rish—I thinks that's what she says. Jenny says she knows she could go to sleep, if you would come and sit with her a little while.

RACHEL   I certainly will. I'll go when you do, honey.

LITTLE MARTHA *(softly stroking* RACHEL's *arm)* You're the very nicest "grown-up," *(loyally)* except my muzzer, of course, I ever knew. You knows all about little chil'run, and you can be one, although you're all grown up. I think you would make a lovely muzzer. *(to the rest of the children)* Don't you?

ALL *(in excited whispers)*   Yes, I do.

RACHEL *(winces, then says gently)*   Come kiddies, you must go now, or your mothers will blame me for keeping you. *(rises, as do the rest.* LITTLE MARTHA *puts her hand into* RACHEL's*)* Ma dear, I'm going to sit a little while with Jenny. I'll be back before you go, though. Come, kiddies, say good-night to my mother.

ALL *(gravely)*   Good-night! Sweet dreams! God keep you all the night.

MRS. LOVING   Good-night dears! Sweet dreams, all!

(Exeunt RACHEL *and the children.* MRS. LOVING *continues to sew. The bell presently rings three distinct times. In a few moments,* MRS. LOVING *gets up and goes out into the vestibule. A door opens and closes.* MRS. LOVING *and* JOHN STRONG *come in. He is a trifle pale but his imperturbable self.* MRS. LOVING, *somewhat nervous, takes her seat and resumes her sewing. She motions* STRONG *to a chair. He returns to the vestibule, leaves his hat, returns, and sits down)*

STRONG   Well, how is everything?

MRS. LOVING.   Oh, about the same, I guess. Tom's out. John, we'll never forget you—and your kindness.

STRONG   That was nothing. and Rachel?

MRS. LOVING   She'll be back presently. She went to sit with a sick child for a little while.

STRONG   And how is she?

MRS. LOVING   She's not herself yet, but I think she is better.

STRONG (*after a short pause*) Well, what *did* happen—exactly?

MRS. LOVING That's just what I don't know.

STRONG When you came home—you couldn't get in—was that it?

MRS. LOVING. Yes. (*pauses*) It was just a week ago today. I was down town all the morning. It was about one o'clock when I got back. I had forgotten my key. I rapped on the door and then called. There was no answer. A window was open, and I could feel the air under the door, and I could hear it as the draught sucked it through. There was no other sound. Presently I made such a noise the people began to come out into the hall. Jimmy was in one of the flats playing with a little girl named Mary. He told me he had left Rachel here a short time before. She had given him four cookies, two for him and two for Mary, and had told him he could play with her until she came to tell him his lunch was ready. I saw he was getting frightened, so I got the little girl and her mother to keep him in their flat. Then, as no man was at home, I sent out for help. Three men broke the door down. (*pauses*) We found Rachel unconscious, lying on her face. For a few minutes I thought she was dead. (*pauses*) A vase had fallen over on the table and the water had dripped through the cloth and onto the floor. There had been flowers in it. When I left, there were no flowers here. What she could have done to them, I can't say. The long stems were lying everywhere, and the flowers had been ground into the floor. I could tell that they must have been roses from the stems. After we had put her to bed and called the doctor, and she had finally regained consciousness, I very naturally asked her what had happened. All she would say was, "Ma dear, I'm too—tired—please." For four days she lay in bed scarcely moving, speaking only when spoken to. That first day, when Jimmy came in to see her, she shrank away from him. We had to take him out, and comfort him as best we could. We kept him away, almost by force, until she got up. And then, she was utterly miserable when he was out of her sight. What happened, I don't know. She avoids Tom, and she won't tell me. (*pauses*) Tom and I both believe her soul has been hurt. The trouble isn't with her body. You'll find her highly nervous. Sometimes she is very much depressed; again she is feverishly gay—almost reckless. What do you think about it, John?

STRONG (*who has listened quietly*) Had anybody been here, do you know?

MRS. LOVING No, I don't. I don't like to ask Rachel; and I can't ask the neighbors.

STRONG And the flowers were ground into the carpet?

MRS. LOVING Yes.

STRONG Did you happen to notice the box? They must have come in a box, don't you think?

MRS. LOVING Yes, there was a box in the kitchenette. It was from "Marcy's." I saw no card.

STRONG (*slowly*) It is rather strange. (*a long silence during which the outer door opens and shuts. RACHEL is heard singing. She stops abruptly. In a second or two she appears in the door. There is an air of suppressed excitement about her*)

RACHEL Hello! John. (STRONG *rises, nods at her, and brings forward for her the big arm-chair near the fire*) I thought that was your hat in the hall. It's brand new, I know—but it looks—"Johnlike." How are you? Ma! Jenny went to sleep like a little lamb. I don't like her breathing, though. (*looks from one to the other; flippantly*) Who's dead? (*nods her thanks to* STRONG *for the chair and sits down*)

MRS. LOVING Dead, Rachel?

RACHEL Yes. The atmosphere here is so funereal,—it's positively "crapey."

STRONG I don't know why it should be—I was just asking how you are.

RACHEL Heavens! Does the mere inquiry into my health precipiate such an atmosphere? Your two faces were as long, as long— (*breaks off*) Kind sir, let me assure you, I am in the very best of health. And how are you, John?

STRONG Oh! I'm always well. (*sits down*)

MRS. LOVING Rachel, I'll have to get ready to go now. John, don't hurry. I'll be back shortly, probably in three-quarters of an hour—maybe less.

RACHEL And maybe more, if I remember Mrs. Jordan. However, Ma dear, I'll do the best I can—while you are away. I'll try to be a credit to your training. (MRS. LOVING *smiles and goes out the rear doorway*) Now, let's see—in the books of etiquette, I believe, the properly reared young lady, always asks the young gentleman caller—you're young enough, aren't you, to be classed still as a "young gentleman caller?" *(no answer)* Well, anyway, she always asks the young gentleman caller sweetly something about the weather. *(primly)* This has been an exceedingly beautiful day, hasn't it, Mr. Strong? *(No answer from* STRONG, *who, with his head resting against the back of the chair, and his knees crossed is watching her in an amused, quizzical manner)* Well, really, every properly brought up young gentleman, I'm sure, ought to know, that it's exceedingly rude not to answer a civil question.

STRONG *(lazily)*   Tell me what to answer, Rachel.

RACHEL   Say, "Yes, very"; and look interested and pleased when you say it.

STRONG *(with a half-smile)* Yes, very.

RACHEL   Well, I certainly wouldn't characterize that as a particularly animated remark. Besides, when you look at me through half-closed lids like that—and kind of smile—what are you thinking? *(no answer)* John Strong, are you deaf or—just plain stupid?

STRONG   Plain stupid, I guess.

RACHEL *(in wheedling tones)*   What were you thinking, John?

STRONG *(slowly)*   I was thinking—*(breaks off)*

RACHEL *(irritably)*   Well?

STRONG   I've changed my mind.

RACHEL   You're not going to tell me?

STRONG   No.

(MRS. LOVING *dressed for the street comes in)*

MRS. LOVING   Goodbye, children. Rachel, don't quarrel so much with John. Let me see—if I have my key. *(feels in her bag)* Yes, I have it. I'll be back shortly. Good-bye. *(STRONG and RACHEL rise. He bows)*

RACHEL   Good-bye, Ma dear. Hurry back as soon as you can, won't you? *(exit* MRS. LOVING *through the vestibule.* STRONG *leans back again in his chair, and watches* RACHEL *through half-closed eyes.* RACHEL *sits in her chair nervously)*

STRONG   Do you mind, if I smoke?

RACHEL   You know I don't.

STRONG   I am trying to behave like—Reginald—"the properly reared young gentleman caller." *(lights a cigar; goes over to the fire, and throws his match away.* RACHEL *goes into the kitchenette, and brings him a saucer for his ashes. She places it on the table near him)* Thank you. *they both sit again,* STRONG *very evidently enjoying his cigar and* RACHEL) Now this is what I call cosy.

RACHEL   Cosy! Why?

STRONG   A nice warm room—shut in—curtains drawn—a cheerful fire crackling at my back—a lamp, not an electric or gas one, but one of your plain, old-fashioned kerosene ones—

RACHEL *(interrupting)*   Ma dear would like to catch you, I am sure, talking about *her* lamp like that. "Old-fashioned! plain!—You have nerve.

STRONG *(continuing as though he had not been interrupted)*   A comfortable chair—a good cigar—and not very far away, a little lady, who is looking charming, so near, that if I reached over, I could touch her. You there—and I here.—It's living.

RACHEL   Well! of all things! A compliment—and from *you!* How did it slip out, pray? *(no answer)* I suppose that you realize that a conversation between two persons is absolutely impossible, if one has to do her share all alone. Soon my ingenuity for introducing interesting subjects will be exhausted; and then will follow what, I believe, the story books call, "an uncomfortable silence."

STRONG *(slowly)*   Silence—between friends—isn't such a bad thing.

RACHEL   Thanks awfully. *(leans back; cups her cheek in her hand, and makes no pretense at further conversation. The old look of introspection returns to her eyes. She does not move)*

STRONG *(quietly)*   Rachel! (RACHEL *starts perceptibly)* You must remember I'm here. I don't like looking into your soul—when you forget you're not alone.

RACHEL   I hadn't forgotten.

STRONG   Wouldn't it be easier for you, little girl, if you could tell—some one?

RACHEL   No *(a silence)*

STRONG   Rachel,—you're fond of flowers,—aren't you?

RACHEL   Yes.

STRONG   Rosebuds—red rosebuds—particularly?

RACHEL *(nervously)*   Yes.

STRONG   Did you—dislike—the giver?

RACHEL *(more nervously; bracing herself)*   No, of course not.

STRONG   Rachel,—why—why—did you—kill the roses—then?

RACHEL *(twisting her hands)*   Oh, John! I'm so sorry, Ma dear told you that. She didn't know, you sent them.

STRONG   So I gathered (*pauses and then leans foward; quietly*) Rachel, little girl, why—did you kill them?

RACHEL (*breathing quickly*)   Don't you believe—it—a—a—kindness—sometimes—to kill?

STRONG (*after a pause*)   You—considered—it—a kindness—to kill them?

RACHEL   Yes. (*another pause*)

STRONG   Do you mean—just—the roses?

RACHEL (*breathing more quickly*)   John!—Oh! must I say?

STRONG   Yes, little Rachel.

RACHEL (*in a whisper*)   No. (*there is a long pause.* RACHEL *leans back limply, and closes her eyes. Presently* STRONG *rises, and moves his chair very close to hers. She does not stir. He puts his cigar on the saucer*)

STRONG (*leaning forward; very gently*)   Little girl, little girl, can you tell me why?

RACHEL *wearily*)   I can't.—It hurts—too much—to talk about it yet,—please.

STRONG (*takes her hand; looks at it a few minutes and then at her quietly*)   You—don't—care, then? (*she winces*) Rachel!—Look at me, little girl! (*as if against her will, she looks at him. Her eyes are fearful, hunted. She tries to look away, to draw away her hand; but he holds her gaze and her hands steadily*) Do you?

RACHEL (*almost sobbing*)   John! John! don't ask me. You are drawing my very soul out of my body with your eyes. You must not talk this way. You musn't look—John, don't (*tries to shield her eyes*)

STRONG (*quietly takes both of her hands, and kisses the backs and the palms slowly. A look of horror creeps into her face. He deliberately raises his eyes and looks at her mouth. She recoils as though she expected him to strike her. He resumes slowly*)   If—you—do—care, and I know now—that you do—nothing else, *nothing should count.*

RACHEL (*wrenching herself from his grasp and rising. She covers her ears; she breathes rapidly*)   No! No! No!—You *must* stop. (*laughs nervously; continues feverishly*) I'm not behaving very well as a hostess, am I? Let's see. What shall I do? I'll play you something, John. How will that do? Or I'll sing to you. You used to like to hear me sing; you said my voice, I remember, was sympathetic, didn't you? (*moves quickly to the piano*) I'll sing you a pretty little song. I think it's beautiful. You've never heard it, I know. I've never sung it to you before. It's Nevin's "At Twilight." (*pauses, looks down, before she begins, then turns toward him and says quietly and sweetly*) Sometimes—in the coming years—I want—you to remember—I sang you this little song.—Will you?—I think it will make it easier for me—when I—when I— (*breaks off and begins the first chords.* STRONG *goes slowly to the piano. He leans there watching intently.* RACHEL *sings*)

> The roses of yesteryear
>> Were all of the white and red;
> It fills my heart with silent fear
>> To find all their beauty fled.
>
> The roses of white are sere,
>> All faded the roses red,
> And one who loves me is not here
>> And one that I love is dead.

(*A long pause. Then* STRONG *goes to her and lifts her from the piano-stool. He puts one arm around her very tenderly and pushes her head back so he can look into her eyes. She shuts them, but is passive*)

STRONG (*gently*)   Little girl, little girl, don't you know that suggestions—suggestions—like those you are sending yourself constantly—are wicked things? You, who are so gentle, so loving, so warm—(*breaks off and crushes her to him. He kisses her many times. She does not resist, but in the midst of his caresses she breaks suddenly into convulsive laughter. He tries to hush the terrible sound with his mouth; then brokenly*) Little girl—don't laugh—like that.

RACHEL (*interrupted throughout by her laughter*)   I have to.—God is laughing.—We're his puppets.—He pulls the wires,—and we're so funny to Him.—I'm laughing too—because I can hear—my little children—weeping. They come to me generally while I'm asleep,—but I can hear them now.—They've begged me—do you understand?—begged me—not to bring them here;—and I've promised them—not to—I've promised. I can't stand the sound of their crying.—I have to laugh—Oh! John! laugh!—laugh too!—I can't drown their weeping.

(STRONG *picks her up bodily and carries her to the armchair*)

STRONG (*harshly*)   Now, stop that!

RACHEL (*in sheer surprise*)   W-h-a-t?

STRONG (*still harshly*)   Stop that!—You've lost your self-control.—Find yourself again!

(*He leaves her and goes over to the fireplace, and stands looking down into it for some little time.* RACHEL, *little by little, becomes calmer.* STRONG *returns and sits beside her again. She doesn't move. He soothes her hair back gently, and kisses her forehead—and then, slowly, her mouth. She does not resist; simply sits there, with shut eyes, inert, limp*)

STRONG   Rachel! (*pauses*) There is a little flat on 43rd Street. It faces south and overlooks a little park. Do you remember it?—it's on the top floor?—Once I remember your saying—you liked it. That was over a year ago. That same day—I rented it. I've never lived there. No one knows about it—not even my mother. It's completely furnished now—and waiting—do you know for whom? Every single thing in it, I've bought myself—even to the pins on the little bird's eye maple dresser. It has been the happiest year I have ever known. I furnished it—one room at a time. It's the prettiest, the most homelike little flat I've ever seen. (*very low*) Everything there—breathes love. Do you know for whom it is waiting? On the sitting-room floor is a beautiful, Turkish rug—red, and blue and gold. It's soft—and rich—and do you know for whose little feet it is waiting? There are delicate curtains at the windows and a bookcase full of friendly, eager, little books.—Do you know for whom they are waiting? There are comfortable leather chairs, just the right size and a beautiful piano—that I leave open—sometimes, and lovely pictures of Madonnas. Do you know for whom they are waiting? There is an open fireplace with logs of wood, all carefully piled on gleaming andirons—and waiting. There is a bellows and a pair of shining tongs—waiting. And in the kitchenette painted blue and white, and smelling sweet with paint is everything: bright pots and pans and kettles, and blue and white enamel-ware, and all kinds of knives and forks and spoons—and on the door—a roller-towel. Little girl, do you know for whom they are all waiting? And somewhere—there's a big, strong man—with broad shoulders. And he's willing and anxious to do anything—everything, and he's waiting very patiently. Little girl, is it to be—yes or no?

RACHEL (*during* STRONG's *speech life has come flooding back to her. Her eyes are shining; her face, eager. For a moment she is beautifully happy*) Oh! You're too good to me and mine, John. I—didn't dream any one—could be—so good. (*leans forward and puts his big hand against her cheek and kisses it shyly*)

STRONG (*quietly*)   Is it—yes—or no, little girl?

RACHEL (*feverishly, gripping his hands*)   Oh, yes! yes! yes! and take me quickly, John. Take me before I can think any more. You mustn't let me think, John. And you'll be good to me, won't you? Every second of every minute, of every hour, of every day, you'll have me in your thoughts, won't you? And you'll be with me every minute that you can? And, John, John!—you'll keep away the weeping of my little children. You won't let me hear it, will you? You'll make me forget everything everything—won't you—Life is so short, John. (*shivers and then fearfully and slowly*) And eternity so—long. (*feverishly again*) And, John, after I am dead—promise me, promise me you'll love me more. (*shivers again*) I'll need love then. Oh! I'll need it. (*suddenly there comes to their ears the sound of a child's weeping. It is monotonous, hopeless, terribly afraid. Rachel recoils*) Oh! John! Listen! It's my boy, again.—I—John—I'll be back in a little while. (*goes swiftly to the door in the rear, pauses and looks back. The weeping continues. Her eyes are tragic. Slowly she kisses her hand to him and disappears.* JOHN *stands where she has left him looking down. The weeping stops. Presently* RACHEL *appears in the doorway. She is haggard, and grey. She does not enter the room. She speaks as one dead might speak—tonelessly, slowly*)

RACHEL   Do you wish to know why Jimmy is crying?

STRONG   Yes.

RACHEL   I am twenty-two—and I'm old; you're thirty-two—and you're old; Tom's twenty-three—and he is old. Ma dear's sixty—and she said once she is much older than that. She is. We are all blighted; we are all accursed—all of us—, everywhere, we whose skins are dark—our lives blasted by the white man's prejudice. (*pause*) And my little Jimmy—seven years old, that's all—is blighted too. In a year or two, at best, he will be made old by suffering. (*pause*) One week ago, today, some white boys, older and larger than my little Jimmy, as he was leaving the school—called him "Nigger"! They chased him through the streets calling him, "Nigger! Nigger! Nigger!" One boy threw stones at him. There is still a bruise on his little back where one struck him. That will get well; but they bruised his soul—and that—will never—get well. He asked me what "Nigger" meant. I made light of the whole thing, laughed it off. He went to his little playmates, and very naturally asked them. The oldest of them is nine!— and they knew, poor little things—and they told him. (*pauses*) For the last couple of nights he has been dreaming—about these boys. And he always awakes—in the dark—afraid— afraid—of the now—and the future—I have seen that look of deadly fear—in the eyes—of other little children. I know what it is myself.— I was twelve—when some big boys chased me and called me names. I never left the house afterwards—without being afraid. I was afraid, in the streets—in the school—in the church, everywhere, always, afraid of being hurt. And I—was not—afraid in vain. (*the weeping begins again*) He's only a baby—and he's blighted. (*to* JIMMY) Honey, I'm right here. I'm coming in just a minute. Don't cry. (*to* STRONG) If it nearly kills me to hear my Jimmy's crying, do you think I could stand it, when my own child, flesh of my flesh, blood of my blood—learned the same reason for weeping? Do you? (*pauses*) Ever since I fell here—a week ago—I am afraid—to go—to sleep, for every time I do— my children come—and beg me—weeping— not to—bring them here—to suffer. Tonight, they came—when I was awake. (*pauses*) I have promised them again, now—by Jimmy's bed. (*in a whisper*) I have damned—my soul to all eternity—if I do. (*to* JIMMY) Honey, don't! I'm coming. (*to* STRONG) And John,—dear John—you see—it can never be—all the beautiful, beautiful things—you have—told me about. (*wistfully*) No—they—can never be—now. (STRONG *comes toward her*) No,— John dear,—you—must not—touch me—any more. (*pauses*) Dear, this—is—"Good-bye."

STRONG (*quietly*)   It's not fair—to you, Rachel, to take you—at your word—tonight. You're sick; you've brooded so long, so continuously,—you've lost—your perspective. Don't answer, yet. Think it over for another week and I'll come back.

RACHEL (*wearily*)   No,—I can't think—any more.

STRONG   You realize—fully—you're sending me—for always?

RACHEL   Yes.

STRONG   And you care?

RACHEL   Yes.

STRONG   It's settled, then for all time— "Good-bye!"

RACHEL (*after a pause*)   Yes.

STRONG (*stands looking at her steadily a long time, and then moves to the door and turns, facing her; with infinite tenderness*) Good-bye, dear, little Rachel—God bless you.

RACHEL   Good-bye, John! (STRONG *goes out. A door opens and shuts. There is finality in the sound. The weeping continues. Suddenly; with a great cry*) John! John! (*runs out into the vestibule. She presently returns. She is calm again. Slowly*) No! No! John. Not for us. (*a pause; with infinite yearning*) Oh! John,—if it only—if it only—(*breaks off, controls herself. Slowly again; thoughtfully*) No—No sunshine—no laughter—always—darkness. That is it. Even our little flat—(*in a whisper*) John's and mine—the little flat—that calls, calls us— through darkness. It shall wait—and wait—in vain—in darkness. Oh, John! (*pauses*) And my little children! my little children! (*the weeping ceases; pauses*) I shall never—see— you—now. Your little, brown, beautiful bodies—I shall never see.—Your dimples—everywhere—your laughter—your tears—the beautiful, lovely feel of you here. (*puts her hands against her heart*) Never— never—to be. (*a pause, fiercely*) But you are somewhere—and wherever you are you are mine! You are mine! All of you! Every bit of you! Even God can't take you away. (*a pause; very sweetly; pathetically*) Little children!—My little children!—No more need you come to me—weeping—weeping. You may be happy now—you are safe. Little weeping, voices, hush! hush! (*the weeping begins again. To* JIMMY, *her whole soul in her voice*) Jimmy! My little Jimmy! Honey! I'm coming.—Ma Rachel loves you so. (*sobs and goes blindly, unsteadily to the rear doorway; she leans her head there one second against the door; and then stumbles through and disappears. The light in the lamp flickers and goes out. . . . It is black. The terrible, heart-breaking weeping continues.*)

[CURTAIN]

MINE EYES HAVE SEEN
1918

Alice Dunbar-Nelson (1875–1935)

Born in New Orleans of a seamstress mother and merchant father, Alice Ruth Moore attended public schools and graduated from Straight College in 1892. Four years later, she traveled north to study English literature at Cornell University, where she wrote her thesis about the influence of Milton on Wordsworth.

In 1898, she married America's most famous Black poet, Paul Laurence Dunbar, who was pursuing his own career as a playwright and a poet, an occupation that required him to travel widely. Although their marriage began as a love match (he had seen her photograph in a newspaper), she left him after four years. In 1906, he died of tuberculosis. She remarried in 1916, this time to Bobo Nelson, a journalist and a widower with two children.

She moved to Wilmington, Delaware, to teach English at Howard High School, where *Mine Eyes Have Seen* was performed. In addition to serving as head of the English department there, Dunbar-Nelson was also a crusader for women's rights, a writer of fiction, and a poet; she edited collections of poetry (*The Dunbar Speaker and Entertainer*) and wrote columns for the Pittsburgh *Courier* and the Washington *Eagle*. A member of the American Friends Peace Committee, she traveled the nation, delivering antiwar speeches as well as addresses on women's rights.

In spite of her varied and busy career, her diaries, published by Gloria T. Hull under the title *Give Us Each Day*, reveal her frustration with the traditional role of women at that time. This is reflected in her poem "I Sit and Sew."

> The little useless seam, the idle patch;
> Why dream I here beneath my homely
>   thatch,
> When there they lie in sodden mud and
>   rain,
> Pitifully calling me, the quick ones and the
>   slain?
> You need me, Christ! It is no roseate dream
> That beckons me—this pretty futile seam,
> It stifles me—God, must I sit and sew?

Published in *The Crisis* during the last months of World War I, *Mine Eyes Have Seen* is an examination of the loyalty the Negro owes to a nation that offers no loy-

169

alty in return. This was a subject that W.E.B. Du Bois had brought militantly to the attention of the nation, with the result that he and his supporters were threatened with suppression of their magazine and possible imprisonment.

The appearance of this play during wartime certainly had a double edge. On one hand, Dunbar-Nelson is warning white America that Black soldiers will fight only for a "do right" nation. On the other hand, she is assuring America that the Black soldier will revenge German atrocities (crucifying children, raping girls)—a de-nunciation of Germany parallel to that found in *Why We Are at War*, also in this volume.

In 1973, the author's niece, Pauline Young, recalled in an interview that her aunt "taught us English in high school. She produced her play and we all took parts. The audience loved it." The ending of her play has been left open for the reader to supply. Does the young Black man join the military or not? Has the author "loaded" the play so the reader must supply the reading that the author wishes? If so, which ending is it?

Mine Eyes Have Seen

Cast of Characters

DAN, *the cripple*
CHRIS, *the younger brother*
LUCY, *the sister*
MRS. O'NEILL, *an Irish neighbor*
JAKE, *a Jewish boy*
JULIA, *Chris' sweetheart*
BILL HARVEY, *a muleteer*
CORNELIA LEWIS, *a settlement worker*

TIME   *Now*

PLACE   *A manufacturing city in the northern part of the United States.*

(SCENE *Kitchen of a tenement. All details of furnishing emphasize sordidness—laundry tubs, range, table covered with oil cloth, pine chairs. Curtain discloses DAN in a rude imitation of a steamer chair, propped by faded pillows, his feet covered with a patch-work quilt.*

LUCY *is bustling about the range preparing a meal. During the conversation she moves from range to table, setting latter and making ready the noon-day meal.*

DAN *is about thirty years old; face thin, pinched, bearing traces of suffering. His hair is prematurely* grey; nose finely chiselled; eyes wide, as if seeing BEYOND. Complexion brown.

LUCY *is slight, frail, brown-skinned, about twenty, with a pathetic face. She walks with a slight limp)*

DAN   Isn't it most time for him to come home, Lucy?

LUCY   It's hard to tell, Danny, dear; Chris doesn't come home on time any more. It's half-past twelve, and he ought to be here by the clock, but you can't tell any more—you can't tell.

DAN   Where does he go?

LUCY   I know where he doesn't go, Dan, but where he does, I can't say. He's not going to Julia's any more lately. I'm afraid, Dan, I'm afraid!

DAN   Of what, Little Sister?

LUCY   Of everything; oh, Dan, it's too big, too much for me—the world outside, the street—Chris going out and coming home nights moody-eyed; I don't understand.

DAN   And so you're afraid? That's been the trouble from the beginning of time—we're afraid because we don't understand.

LUCY (*coming down front, with a dish cloth in her hand*)   Oh, Dan, wasn't it better in the old days when we were back home—in the little house with the garden, and you and father coming home nights and mother getting supper, and Chris and I studying lessons in the dining-room at the table—we didn't have to eat and live in the kitchen then, and—

DAN (*grimly*) —And the notices posted on the fence for us to leave town because niggers had no business having such a decent home.

LUCY (*unheeding the interruption*) —And Chris and I reading the wonderful books and laying our plans—

DAN —To see them go up in the smoke of our burned home.

LUCY (*continuing, her back to* DAN, *her eyes lifted, as if seeing a vision of retrospect*) —And everyone petting me because I had hurt my foot when I was little, and father—

DAN —Shot down like a dog for daring to defend his home—

LUCY —Calling me "Little Brown Princess," and telling mother—

DAN —Dead of pneumonia and heartbreak in this bleak climate.

LUCY —That when you—

DAN —Maimed for life in a factory of hell! Useless—useless—broken on the wheel. (*his voice breaks in a dry sob*)

LUCY (*coming out of her trance, throws aside the dish-cloth, and running to* DAN, *lays her cheek against his and strokes his hair*) Poor Danny, poor Danny, forgive me, I'm selfish.

DAN Not selfish, Little Sister, merely natural.

(*Enter roughly and unceremoniously* CHRIS. *He glances at the two with their arms about each other, shrugs his shoulders, hangs up his rough cap and mackinaw on a nail, then seats himself at the table, his shoulders hunched up; his face dropping on his hand.* LUCY *approaches him timidly*)

LUCY Tired, Chris?

CHRIS No.

LUCY Ready for dinner?

CHRIS If it is ready for me.

LUCY (*busies herself bringing dishes to the table*) You're late to-day.

CHRIS I have bad news. My number was posted today.

LUCY Number? Posted? (*pauses with a plate in her hand*)

CHRIS I'm drafted.

LUCY (*drops plate with a crash.* DAN *leans forward tensely, his hands gripping the arms of his chair*) Oh, it can't be! They won't take you from us! And shoot you down, too? What will Dan do?

DAN Never mind about me, Sister. And you're drafted, boy?

CHRIS Yes—yes—but—(*he rises and strikes the table heavily with his hand*) I'm not going.

DAN Your duty—

CHRIS —Is here with you. I owe none elsewhere, I'll pay none.

LUCY Chris! Treason! I'm afraid!

CHRIS Yes, of course, you're afraid, Little Sister, why shouldn't you be? Haven't you had your soul shrivelled with fear since we were driven like dogs from our home? And for what? Because we were living like Christians. Must I go and fight for the nation that let my father's murder go unpunished? That killed my mother—that took away my chances for making a man out of myself? Look at us— you—Dan, a shell of a man—

DAN Useless—useless—

LUCY Hush, Chris!

CHRIS And me, with a fragment of an education, and no chance—only half a man. And you, poor Little Sister, there's no chance for you; what is there in life for you? No, if others want to fight, let them. I'll claim exemption.

DAN On what grounds?

CHRIS You—and Sister. I am all you have; I support you.

DAN (*half rising in his chair*) Hush! Have I come to this, that I should be the excuse, the women's skirts for a slacker to hide behind?

CHRIS (*clenching his fists*) You call me that? You, whom I'd lay down my life for? I'm no slacker when I hear the real call of duty. Shall I desert the cause that needs me—you—Sister—home? For a fancied glory? Am I to take up the cause of a lot of kings and politicians who play with men's souls, as if they are cards—dealing them out, a hand here, in the Somme—a hand there, in Palestine—a hand there, in the Alps—a hand there, in Russia— and because the cards don't match well, call it a misdeal, gather them up, throw them in the discard, and call for a new deal of a million human, suffering souls? And must I be the Deuce of Spades?

(*During the speech, the door opens slowly and* JAKE *lounges in. He is a slight, pale youth, Hebraic, thin-lipped, eager-eyed. His hands are in his pockets, his narrow shoulders drawn forward. At the end of* CHRIS' *speech he applauds softly*)

JAKE   Bravo! You've learned the patter well. Talk like the fellows at the Socialist meetings.

DAN and LUCY   Socialist meetings!

CHRIS (*defiantly*)   Well?

DAN   Oh, nothing; it explains. All right, go on—any more?

JAKE   Guess he's said all he's got breath for. I'll go, it's too muggy in here. What's the row?

CHRIS   I'm drafted.

JAKE   Get exempt. Easy—if you don't want to go. As for me—

(*Door opens, and* MRS. O'NEILL *bustles in. She is in deep mourning, plump, Irish, shrewd-looking, bright-eyed*)

MRS. O'NEILL   Lucy, they do be sayin' as how down by the chain stores they be a raid on the potatoes, an' ef ye're wantin' some, ye'd better be after gittin' into yer things an' comin' wid me. I kin kape the crowd off yer game foot—an' what's the matter wid youse all?

LUCY   Oh, Mrs. O'Neill, Chris has got to go to war.

MRS. O'NEILL   An' ef he has, what of it? Ye'll starve, that's all.

DAN   Starve? Never! He'll go, we'll live.

(LUCY *wrings her hands impotently.* MRS. O'NEILL *drops a protecting arm about the girl's shoulder*)

MRS. O'NEILL   An' it's hard it seems to yer? But they took me man from me year before last, an' he wint afore I came over here, an' it's a widder I am wid me five kiddies, an' I've niver a word to say but—

CHRIS   He went to fight for his own. What do they do for my people? They don't want us, except in extremity. They treat us like—like—like—

JAKE   Like Jews in Russia, eh? (*he slouches forward, then his frame straightens itself electrically*) Like Jews in Russia, eh? Denied the right of honor in men, eh? Or the right of virtue in women, eh? There isn't a wrong you can name that your race has endured that mine has not suffered, too. But there's a future, Chris—a big one. We younger ones must be in that

future—ready for it, ready for it—(*his voice trails off, and he sinks despondently into a chair*)

CHRIS   Future? Where? Not in this country? Where?

(*The door opens and* JULIA *rushes in impulsively. She is small, slightly built, eager-eyed, light-brown skin, wealth of black hair; full of sudden shyness*)

JULIA   Oh, Chris, someone has just told me— I was passing by—one of the girls said your number was called. Oh, Chris, will you have to go? (*she puts her arms up to* CHRIS' *neck; he removes them gently, and makes a slight gesture toward* DAN's *chair*)

JULIA   Oh, I forgot. Dan, excuse me. Lucy, it's terrible, isn't it?

CHRIS   I'm not going, Julia.

MRS. O'NEILL   Not going!

DAN   Our men have always gone, Chris. They went in 1776.

CHRIS   Yes, as slaves. Promised a freedom they never got.

DAN   No, gladly, and saved the day, too, many a time. Ours was the first blood shed on the altar of National liberty. We went in 1812, on land and sea. Our men were through the struggles of 1861—

CHRIS   When the Nation was afraid not to call them. Didn't want 'em at first.

DAN   Never mind; they helped work out their own salvation. And they were there in 1898—

CHRIS   Only to have their valor disputed.

DAN   —And they were at Carrizal, my boy, and now—

MRS. O'NEILL   An' sure, wid a record like that—ah, 'tis me ould man who said at first 'twasn't his quarrel. His Oireland bled an' the work of thim divils to try to make him a traitor nearly broke his heart—but he said he'd go to do his bit—an' here I am.

(*There is a sound of noise and bustle without, and with a loud laugh,* BILL HARVEY *enters He is big, muscular, rough, his voice thunderous. He emits cries of joy at seeing the group, shakes hands and claps* CHRIS *and* DAN *on their backs*)

DAN   And so you weren't torpedoed?

HARVEY   No, I'm here for a while—to get more mules and carry them to the front to kick their bit.

MRS. O'NEILL.   You've been—over there?

HARVEY   Yes, over the top, too. Mules, rough-necks, wires, mud, dead bodies, stench, terror!

JULIA (*horror-stricken*)   Ah—Chris!

CHRIS   Never, mind, not for mine.

HARVEY   It's a great life—not. But I'm off again, first chance.

MRS. O'NEILL   They're brutes, eh?

HARVEY   Don't remind me.

MRS. O'NEILL (*whispering*)   They maimed my man, before he died.

JULIA (*clinging to* CHRIS)   Not you, oh, not you!

HARVEY   They crucified children.

DAN   Little children? They crucified little children.

CHRIS   Well, what's that to us? They're little white children. But here our fellow-countrymen throw our little black babies in the flame—as did the worshippers of Moloch, only they haven't the excuse of a religious rite.

JAKE (*slouches out of his chair, in which he has been sitting brooding*)   Say, don't you get tired sitting around grieving because you're colored? I'd be ashamed to be—

DAN   Stop! Who's ashamed of his race? Ours the glorious inheritance; ours the price of achievement. Ashamed! I'm *proud*. And you, too, Chris, smouldering in youthful wrath, you, too, are proud to be numbered with the darker ones, soon to come into their inheritance.

MRS. O'NEILL   Aye, but you've got to fight to keep yer inheritance. Ye can't lay down when someone else has done the work, and expect it to go on. Ye've got to fight.

JAKE   If you're proud, show it. All of your people—well, look at us! Is there a greater race than ours? Have any people had more horrible persecutions—and yet—we're loyal always to the country where we live and serve.

MRS. O'NEILL   And us! Look at us!

DAN (*half tears himself from the chair, the upper part of his body writhing, while the lower part is inert, dead*)   Oh, God! If I were but whole and strong! If I could only prove to a doubting world of what stuff my people are made!

JULIA   But why, Dan, it isn't our quarrel? What have we to do with their affairs? These white people, they hate us. Only today I was sneered at when I went to help with some of their relief work. Why should you, my Chris, go to help those who hate you?

(CHRIS *clasps her to his arms, and they stand, defying the others*)

HARVEY   If you could have seen the babies and girls—and old women—if you could have—(*covers his eyes with his hand*)

CHRIS   Well, it's good for things to be evened up somewhere.

DAN   Hush, Chris! It is not for us to visit retribution. Nor to wish hatred on others. Let us rather remember the good that has come to us. Love of humanity is above the small considerations of time or place or race or sect. Can't you be big enough to feel pity for the little crucified French children—for the ravished Polish girls, even as their mothers must have felt sorrow, if they had known, for *our* burned and maimed little ones? Oh, Mothers of Europe, we be of one blood, you and I!

(*There is a tense silence.* JULIA *turns from* CHRIS, *and drops her hand. He moves slowly to the window and looks out. The door opens quietly, and* CORNELIA LEWIS *comes in. She stands still a moment, as if sensing a difficult situation*)

CORNELIA   I've heard about it, Chris, your country calls you. (CHRIS *turns from the window and waves hopeless hands at* DAN *and* LUCY) Yes, I understand; they do need you, *don't* they?

DAN (*fiercely*)   No!

LUCY   Yes, we do, Chris, we do need you, but your country needs you more. And, above that, your race is calling you to carry on its good name, and with that, the voice of humanity is calling to us all—we can manage without you, Chris.

CHRIS   You? Poor little crippled Sister. Poor Dan—

DAN   Don't pity me, pity your poor, weak self.

CHRIS (*clenching his fist*)   Brother, you've called me two names today that no man ought to have to take—a slacker and a weakling!

DAN   True. Aren't you both? (*leans back and looks at* CHRIS *speculatively*)

CHRIS (*makes an angry lunge towards the chair, then flings his hands above his head in an impatient gesture*)   Oh, God! (*turns back to window*)

JULIA   Chris, it's wicked for them to taunt you so—but Chris—it *is* our country—our race—(*outside the strains of music from a passing band are heard. The music comes faintly, gradually growing louder and louder until it reaches a crescendo. The tune is "The Battle Hymn of the Republic," played in stirring march time)*

DAN *(singing softly)*   "Mine eyes have seen the glory of the coming of the Lord!"

CHRIS *(turns from the window and straightens his shoulders)*   And mine!

CORNELIA   "As He died to make men holy, let us die to make them free!"

MRS. O'NEILL   An' ye'll make the sacrifice, me boy, an' ye'll be the happier.

JAKE   Sacrifice! No sacrifice for him, it's

those who stay behind. Ah, if they would only call me, and call me soon!

LUCY   We'll get on, never fear. I'm proud! Proud! *(her voice breaks a little, but her head is thrown back)*

(As the music draws nearer, the group breaks up, and the whole roomful rushes to the window and looks out. CHRIS remains in the center of the floor, rigidly at attention, a rapt look on his face. DAN strains at his chair, as if he would rise, then sinks back, his hand feebly beating time to the music, which swells to a martial crash. Curtain)

AFTERMATH (1919) AND
THEY THAT SIT IN DARKNESS (1919)

Mary P. Burrill (1884–1946)

Born in Washington, D.C., Mary P. Burrill, the daughter of John H. and Clara E. Burrill, graduated in 1901 from the M Street School (later Dunbar), where in 1905 she became a teacher of English and dramatics until her retirement in 1944. She specialized in speech and diction—then called elocution—and presented her own monologue *The Other Wise Man* to capacity audiences each Christmas. Few documents remain that give insight into her personal life, which she seems to have kept very private.[1] Burrill never married, and for most of her adult life, she shared a house with Howard University's first dean of women, Lucy D. Stowe.

While teaching, she wrote two one-act plays: *They That Sit in Darkness* and *Aftermath*. The latter, published in the *Liberator* (1918–1924), a white, left-wing periodical that was edited by the socialist Max Eastman, reflected the racial chaos of the "Red Summer" of 1919, when riots broke out in Omaha, Knoxville, Chicago, St. Louis, Washington, and Charleston. That summer, Black soldiers who had returned home

from service in World War I after fighting abroad for freedoms they did not have at home, were in no mood to accept second-class citizenship. In August of 1919, Ku Klux Klan memberships burgeoned and the federal government refused to pass an antilynching law. As W.E.B. Du Bois wrote in *The Crisis*, "They cheat us and mock us; they kill us and slay us. They deride our misery. When we plead for the naked protection of the law . . . they tell us to 'Go to hell!' "

Women, too, were fighting their own battles to obtain the vote (the Nineteenth Amendment), equal pay for equal work, opportunity for equal employment, and the right of birth control. In 1916, Margaret Sanger had established the first birth control clinic in Brooklyn (which the police closed down). The following year, she organized the first birth control conference in America.

They That Sit in Darkness was written for the *Birth Control Review*'s special issue (September 1919), "The Negro's Need for Birth Control as Seen by Themselves." (That issue also contained a short story by Angelina Grimké.) The *Review* was a monthly platform for the progressive men

---

1. Professor Kathy Perkins of the University of Illinois has assembled the little data that we do have.

and women who lobbied for the right of women—including poor women—to have birth control information, a struggle that did not end until 1965 when the Supreme Court struck down the last restrictive law in Connecticut. The *Review* did not, however, devote itself solely to Black birth control.

In *They That Sit in Darkness*, Burrill supports Sanger's emphasis on female education as the means to escape poverty. Although Burrill clearly favors birth control, it is the lack and loss of education that brings tragic consequences to the family in the play. The author does not blame the husband, nor does she even bring him on stage. Her targets of blame are ignorance and poverty.

After her retirement in 1944, Burrill moved to New York City, where she died in 1946. She had devoted her energies to two generations of students, three of whom went on to write plays: Willis Richardson (*The Deacon's Awakening*), May Miller (*Graven Images*), and James Butcher (*The Seer*). Butcher, who became a professor of theatre at Howard, recalled that he acted in a Spanish play, *The Bonds of Interest* for his teacher, Miss Burrill, and that she had held him to very high standards. What finer endowment could she have given him?

Aftermath

CHARACTERS

MILLIE, *a young woman*
MAM SUE, *an old woman*
REV. LUKE MOSEBY, *a clergyman*
LONNIE, *a young man*
MRS. HAWKINS, *a friend*
JOHN, *a soldier*

TIME   *The present*

PLACE   *The Thornton Cabin in South Carolina*

(*It is late afternoon of a cool day in early spring. A soft afterglow pours in at the little window of the Thornton cabin. The light falls on* MILLIE, *a slender brown girl of sixteen, who stands near the window ironing. She wears a black dress and a big gingham apron. A clothes-horse weighted down with freshly ironed garments is nearby. In the rear there is a door leading out to the road. To the left another door leads into the other room of the cabin. To the right there is a great stone hearth blackened by age. A Bible rests on the mantel over the hearth. An old armchair and a small table on which is a kerosene lamp are near the hearth. In the center of the room sits a well-scrubbed kitchen table and a substantial wooden chair. In front of the hearth, in a low rocking chair drawn close to the smouldering wood fire, sits* MAM SUE *busily sewing. The many colors in the old patchwork quilt that she is mending, together with the faded red of the bandana on her head, contrast strangely with her black dress.* MAM SUE *is very old. Her ebony face is seamed with wrinkles, and in her bleared, watery eyes there is a world-old sorrow. A service flag containing one star hangs in the little window of the cabin*)

MAM SUE (*crooning the old melody*)
O, yes, yonder comes mah Lawd,
    He is comin' dis way
Wid his sword in his han'
    O, yes, yonder comes—

(*A burning log falls apart, and* MAM SUE *suddenly stops singing and gazes intently at the fire. She speaks in deep mysterious tones to* MILLIE, *who has finished her task and has come to the hearth to put up her irons*)

See dat log dah, Millie? De one fallin' tuh de side dah wid de big flame lappin' 'round hit? Dat means big doin's 'round heah tonight!

MILLIE (*with a start*)   Oh, Mam Sue, don' you go proph'sying no mo'! You seen big doin's in dat fire de night befo' them w'ite devuls come in heah an' tuk'n po' dad out and bu'nt him!

MAM SUE (*calmly*)   No, Millie, Ah didn' see no big doin's dat night—Ah see'd *evul* doin's an' Ah tole yo' po' daddy to keep erway f'om town de nex' day wid his cotton. Ah jes knowed dat we wuz gwine to git in a row wid dem w'ite debbils—but he wou'd'n lis'n tuh his ole mammy—De good Lawd sen' me dese warnin's in dis fiah, jes lak He sen' His messiges in de fiah to Moses. Yo' chillun bettah lis'n to—

MILLIE (*nervously*)   Oh, Mam Sue, you skeers me when you talks erbout seein' all them things in de fire—

MAM SUE   Yuh gits skeered 'cause yuh don' put yo' trus' in de good Lawd! He kin tek keer o' yuh no mattuh what com'!

MILLIE (*bitterly*)   Sometimes I thinks that Gawd's done fu'got us po' cullud people. Gawd didn' tek no keer o' po' dad and *he* put *his* trus' in Him! He uster set evah night by dis fire at dis here table and read his Bible an' pray—but jes look what happen' to dad! That don' look like Gawd wuz tekin' keer—

MAM SUE (*sharply*)   Heish yo' mouf, Millie! Ah ain't a-gwine to 'ave dat sinner-talk 'roun' hyeah! (*derisively*) Gawd don't tek no keer o' yuh? Ain't yuh bin prayin' night an' mawnin' fo' Gawd to sen' yo' brudder back f'om de war 'live an' whole? An' ain't yuh git dat lettah no longer'n yistiddy sayin' dat de fightin's all done stopp't an' dat de blessid Lawd's done brung yo' brudder thoo all dem battuls live an' whole? Don' dat look lak de Lawd's done 'membered yuh?

MILLIE (*thoughtfully*)   I reckon youse right, Mam Sue. But ef anything had a-happen' to John I wuz'n evah goin' to pray no mo'!

(*MILLIE goes to the clothes-horse and folds the garments and lays them carefully into a large basket. MAM SUE falls again to her crooning*)

MAM SUE

Oh, yes, yonder comes mah Lawd,
    He's comin' dis way-a.

MILLIE   Lonnie's so late gittin' home tonight: I guess I'd bettah tek Mis' Hart's wash home tonight myse'f.

MAM SUE   Yes, Lonnie's mighty late. Ah reckons you'd bettah slip erlon' wid hit.

(*MILLIE gets her hat from the adjoining room and is about to leave with the basket when MAM SUE calls significantly*) Millie?

MILLIE   Yas, Mam Sue.

MAM SUE (*firmly*)   Don' yo' fu'git to drap dat lettah fu' John in de Pos' Awfus ez yuh goes by. Whah's de lettah?

MILLIE (*reluctantly*)   But Mam Sue, please don' lets—

(*A knock is heard. MILLIE opens the door and REV. LUKE MOSEBY enters. MOSEBY is a wiry little old man with a black, kindly face, and bright, searching eyes; his woolly hair and beard are snow-white. He is dressed in a rusty black suit with a coat of clerical cut that comes to his knees. In one hand he carries a large Bible, and in the other, a stout walking stick*)

MILLIE   Good evenin', Brother Moseby, come right in.

MOSEBY   Good eben', Millie. Good eben', Mam Sue. Ah jes drap't in to see ef you-all is still trus'in de good Lawd an'—

MAM SUE   Lor', Brudder Moseby, ain't Ah bin trus'n de good Lawd nigh onter dese eighty yeah! Whut fu' yuh think Ah's gwine to quit w'en Ah'm in sight o' de Promis' Lan'? Millie, fetch Brudder Moseby dat cheer.

MOSEBY (*drawing his chair to the fire*)   Dat's right, Mam Sue, you jes a-keep on trus'n an' prayin' and evahthing's gwine to come awright. (*observing MILLIE is about to leave*) Don' lemme 'tain yuh, Millie, but whut's all dis good news wese bin heahin' 'bout yo' brudder John? Dey say he's done won some kind o' medal ober dah in France?

MILLIE (*brightening up*)   Oh, yes, we got a lettah day befo' yestiddy f'om John tellin' us all erbout it. He's won de War Cross! He fought off twenty Germuns all erlone an' saved his whole comp'ny an' the gret French Gen'rul come an' pinned de medal on him, hisse'f!

MOSEBY   De Lawd bles' his soul! Ah know'd dat boy wud mek good!

MILLIE (*excited by the glory of it all*)   An' he's been to Paris, an' the fines' people stopp't him when they seen his medal, an' shook his han' an' smiled at him—an' he kin go evahwhere, an' dey ain't nobody all the time a'lookin' down on him, an' a-sneerin' at him 'cause he's Black; but evahwhere they's jes gran' to him!

An' he sez it's the firs' tim evah in his life he's felt lak a real, sho-nuf man!

MOSEBY   Well, honey, de Holy Book say, "De fust shill be las' and de las' shill be fust"?

MAM SUE   (*fervently*)   Dat hit do! An' de Holy Book ain't nebber tole no lie!

MOSEBY   Folks ober in Char'ston is sayin' dat some sojers is gwine to lan' dah today or tomorrer. Ah reckons day'll all be comin' 'long soon now dat de war's done stopp't.

MILLIE   I jes hates the thought of John comin' home an' hearin' 'bout dad!

MOSEBY   (*in astonishment*)   What! Yuh mean to say yuh ain't 'rite him 'bout yo' daddy, yit?

MAM SUE   Dat she ain't! Millie mus' 'ave huh way! She 'lowed huh brudder ough'n be tole, an' dat huh could keep on writin' to him jes lak huh dad wuz livin'—Millie allus done de writin'—an' Ah lets huh 'ave huh way—

MOSEBY   (*shaking his head in disapproval*)   Yuh mean tuh say—

MILLIE   (*pleading*)   But, Brother Moseby, I couldn't write John no bad news w'ilst he wuz way over there by hisse'f. He had 'nuf to worry him with death a'-starin' him in the face evah day!

MAM SUE   Yas, Brudder Moseby, Millie's bin carryin' on dem lies in huh lettahs fu' de las' six months; but today Ah jes sez to huh—Dis war done stopp't now, an' John he gwine to be comin' home soon, an' he ain't agwine to come hyeah an' fin' me wid no lie on mah soul! An' Ah med huh set down an' tell him de whole truf. She's gwine out to pos' dat lettah dis minute.

MOSEBY   (*still disapproving*)   No good nebber come—

(*The door is pushed violently open, and* LONNIE, *a sturdy Black boy of eighteen rushes in breathlessly*

LONNIE   Mam Sue! Millie! Whut'da yuh think? John's come home!

MILLIE   (*speechless with astonishment*)   John? Home? Where's he at?

MAM SUE   (*incredulously*)   What yuh sayin'? John done come home? Bles' de Lawd! Bles' de Lawd! Millie, didn' Ah tell yuh sumpin wuz gwine tuh happen?

LONNIE   (*excitedly*)   I wuz sweepin' up de sto' jes befo' leavin' an' de phone rung—it wuz John— he wuz at Char'ston—jes landid! His comp'ny's waitin' to git de ten o'clock train fu' Camp Reed, whah dey's goin' to be mustered out.

MOSEBY   But how's he gwine to get erway?

LONNIE   Oh, good evenin', Brother Moseby, Ise jes so 'cited I didn' see yuh—Why his Cap'n done give him leave to run over heah 'tell de train's ready. He ought tuh be heah now 'cause it's mos' two hours sence he wuz talkin'—

MAM SUE   Whuffo yuh so long comin' home an' tellin' us?

LONNIE   (*hesitatingly*)   I did start right out but when I git to Sherley's corner I seen a whole lot of them w'ite hoodlums hangin' 'round de feed sto'—I jes felt like dey wuz jes waitin' dah to start sumpin, so I dodged 'em by tekin' de long way home.

MILLIE   Po' Lonnie! He's allus dodgin' po' w'ite trash!

LONNIE   (*sullenly*)   Well, yuh see whut dad got by not dodgin' 'em.

MOSEBY   (*rising to go*)   Ah mus' be steppin' 'long now. Ah got to stop in to see ole man Hawkins; he's mighty sick. Ah'll drap in on mah way back fu' a word o' prayer wid John.

MAM SUE   Lonnie, yu'd bettah run erlon as Brudder Moseby go an' tote dat wash tuh Mis' Ha't. An' drap in Mis' Hawkins' sto' an' git some soap an' starch; an' Ah reckons yu'd bettah bring me a bottle o' liniment—dis ole pain done come back in mah knee. (*to* MOSEBY) Good eben, Brudder Moseby.

MOSEBY   Good eben, Mam Sue; Good eben, Millie, an' Gawd bles' yuh.

LONNIE   (*as he is leaving*)   Tell John I'll git back fo' he leaves.

(LONNIE *and* MOSEBY *leave.* MILLIE *closes the door behind them and then goes to the window and looks out anxiously*)

MILLIE   (*musingly*)   Po' John! Po' John! (*turning to* MAM SUE) Mam Sue?

MAM SUE   Yas, Millie.

MILLIE   (*hesitatingly*)   Who's goin' to tell John 'bout dad?

MAM SUE   (*realizing for the first time that the task must fall to someone*)   Dunno. Ah reckons yu'd bettah.

MILLIE   (*going to* MAM SUE *and kneeling softly at her side*)   Mam Sue, don' let's tell him now! He's got only a li'l hour to spen' with us—an' it's the firs' time fu' so long! John loved daddy so! Let 'im be happy jes a li'l longer—we kin tell 'im the truth when he comes back fu' good. Please, Mam Sue!

MAM SUE (*softened by* MILLIE's *pleading*) Honey chile, John gwine to be askin' for his daddy fust thing—dey ain't no way—

MILLIE (*gaining courage*) Oh, yes, 'tis! We kin tell 'im dad's gone to town—anything, jes so's he kin spen' these few lil'l minutes in peace! I'll fix the Bible jes like dad's been in an' been a-readin' in it! He won't know no bettah!

(MILLIE *takes the Bible from the mantel and opening it at random lays it on the table; she draws the old armchair close to the table as her father had been wont to do every evening when he read his Bible*)

MAM SUE (*shaking her head doubtfully*) Ah ain't much on actin' dis lie, Millie.

(*The soft afterglow fades and the little cabin is filled with shadows.* MILLIE *goes again to the window and peers out.* MAM SUE *falls again to her crooning*)

MAM SUE (*crooning*)
O, yes, yonder comes mah Lawd,
    He's comin' dis way
    Wid his sword in his han'—

(*to* MILLIE) Millie, bettah light de lamp; it's gittin' dark.

    He's gwine ter hew dem sinners down
        Right lebbal to de groun'
    O, yes, yonder comes mah Lawd—

(*As* MILLIE *is lighting the lamp, whistling is heard in the distance.* MILLIE *listens intently, then rushes to the window. The whistling comes nearer; it rings out clear and familiar—"Though the boys are far away, they dream of home"*)

MILLIE (*excitedly*) That's him! That's John, Mam Sue!

(MILLIE *rushes out of doors. The voices of* JOHN *and* MILLIE *are heard from without in greetings. Presently,* JOHN *and* MILLIE *enter the cabin.* JOHN *is tall and straight—a good soldier and a strong man. He wears the uniform of a private in the American Army. One hand is clasped in both of* MILLIE's. *In the other, he carries an old-fashioned valise. The War Cross is pinned on his breast. On his sleeve three chevrons tell mutely of wounds suffered in the cause of freedom. His brown face is aglow with life and the joy of homecoming*)

JOHN (*eagerly*) Where's dad? Where's Mam Sue?

MAM SUE (*hobbling painfully to meet him*) Heah's ole Mam Sue! (JOHN *takes her tenderly in his arms*) Bles' yo' heart, chile, bles' yo' heart! Tuh think dat de good Lawd's done lemme live to see dis day!

JOHN Dear old Mam Sue! Gee, but I'm glad to see you an' Millie again!

MAM SUE: Didn' Ah say dat yuh wuz comin' back hyeah?

JOHN (*smiling*) Same old Mam Sue with huh faith an' huh prayers! But where's dad? (*he glances toward the open Bible*) He's been in from de field, ain't he?

MILLIE (*without lifting her eyes*) Yes, he's come in but he had to go out ag'in—to Sherley's feed sto.'

JOHN (*reaching for his cap that he has tossed upon the table*) That ain't far. I've jes a few minutes so I'd bettah run down there an' hunt him up. Won't he be surprised!

MILLIE (*confused*) No—no, John—I fu'got; he ain't gone to Sherley's, he's gone to town.

JOHN (*disappointed*) To town? I hope he'll git in befo' I'm leavin'. There's no tellin' how long they'll keep me at Camp Reed. Where's Lonnie?

MAM SUE Lonnie's done gone to Mis' Ha't's wid de wash. He'll be back to-reckly.

MILLIE (*admiring the medal on his breast*) An' this is the medal? Tell us all erbout it, John.

JOHN Oh, Sis, it's an awful story—wait 'til I git back fu' good. Let's see whut I've got in dis bag fu' you. (*he places the worn valise on the table and opens it. He takes out a bright-colored dress pattern*) That's fu' you, Millie, and quit wearin' them black clothes.

(MILLIE *takes the silk and hugs it eagerly to her breast, suddenly there sweeps into her mind the realization that she cannot wear it, and the silk falls to the floor*)

MILLIE (*trying to be brave*) Oh, John it's jes lovely! (*as she shows it to* MAM SUE) Look, Mam Sue!

JOHN (*flourishing a bright shawl*) An' this is fu' Mam Sue. Mam Sue'll be so gay!

MAM SUE (*admiring the gift*) Who'd evah b'lieved dat yo' ole Mam Sue would live to be wearin' clo'es whut huh gran'chile done brung huh from Eu'ope!

JOHN Never you mind, Mam Sue, one of

these days I'm goin' to tek you an' Millie over there, so's you kin breathe free jes once befo' yuh die.

MAM SUE   It's got tuh be soon, 'cause dis ole body's mos' wo'e out; an' de good Lawd's gwine to be callin' me to pay mah debt 'fo' long.

JOHN   *(showing some handkerchiefs, with gay borders)*   These are fu' Lonnie. *(he next takes out a tiny box that might contain a bit of jewelry)* An' this is fu' dad. Sum'pin he's been wantin' fu' years. I ain't goin' to open it 'till he comes.

(MILLIE walks into the shadows and furtively wipes a tear from her eyes)

JOHN   *(taking two army pistols from his bag and placing them on the table)*   An' these las' are fu' youahs truly.

MILLIE   *(looking at them, fearfully)*   Oh, John, are them youahs?

JOHN   One of 'em's mine; the other's my Lieutenant's. I've been cleanin' it fu' him. Don' tech 'em—'cause mine's loaded.

MILLIE   *(still looking at them in fearful wonder)*   Did they learn yuh how to shoot 'em?

JOHN   Yep, an' I kin evah mo' pick 'em off!

MILLIE   *(reproachfully)*   Oh, John!

JOHN   Nevah you worry, li'l Sis, John's nevah goin' to use 'em 'less it's right fu' him to. *(he places the pistols on the mantel—on the very spot where the Bible has lain)* My! but it's good to be home! I've been erway only two years but it seems like two cent'ries. All that life ovah there seems like some awful dream!

MAM SUE   *(fervently)*   Ah know it do! Many's de day yo' ole Mam Sue set in dis cheer an' prayed fu' yuh.

JOHN   Lots of times, too, in the trenches when I wuz dog-tired, an' sick, an' achin' wid the cold I uster say: well, if we're sufferin' all this for the oppressed, like they tell us, then Mam Sue, an' dad, an Millie come in on that—they'll git some good ou'n it if I don't! An' I'd shet my eyes an' fu'git the cold, an' the pain, an' them old guns spittin' death all 'round us; an' see you folks settin' here by this fire—Mam Sue, noddin', an' singing'; dad a spellin' out his Bible—*(he glances toward the open book)* Let's see what he's been readin'— *(JOHN takes up the Bible and reads the first passage upon which his eye falls)* "But I say unto you, love your enemies, bless them that curse you, an' do good to them that hate you"—*(he lets the Bible fall to the table)* That ain't the

dope they been feedin' us soljers on! "Love your enemies"? It's been—git a good aim at 'em, an' let huh go!

MAM SUE   *(surprised)*   Honey, Ah hates to hyeah yuh talkin' lak dat! It sound lak yuh done fu'git yuh Gawd!

JOHN   No, Mam Sue, I ain't fu'got God, but I've quit thinkin' that prayers kin do ever'thing. I've seen a whole lot sence I've been erway from here. I've seen some men go into battle with a curse on their lips, and I've seen them same men come back with never a scratch; an' I've seen men whut read their Bibles befo' battle, an' prayed to live, left dead on the field. Yes, Mam Sue, I've seen a heap an' I've done a tall lot o' thinkin' sence I've been erway from here. An' I b'lieve it's jes like this—beyon' a certain point prayers ain't no good! The Lawd does jes so much for you, then it's up to you to do the res' fu' yourse'f. The Lawd's done His part when He's done give me strength an' courage: I got tuh do the res' fu' myse'f!

MAM SUE   *(shaking her head)*   Ah don' lak dat kin' o' talk—it don' 'bode no good!

(The door opens and LONNIE enters with packages. He slips the bolt across the door)

JOHN   *(rushing to LONNIE and seizing his hand)*   Hello, Lonnie, ole man!

LONNIE   Hello, John, Gee, but Ah'm glad tuh see yuh!

JOHN   Boy, you should 'ave been with me! It would 'ave taken some of the skeeriness out o' yuh, an' done yuh a worl' o' good.

LONNIE   *(ignoring JOHN's remark)*   Here's the soap an starch, Millie.

MAM SUE   Has yuh brung mah linimint?

LONNIE   Yassum, it's in de package.

MILLIE   *(unwrapping the package)*   No, it ain't, Lonnie.

LONNIE   Mis' Hawkins give it tuh me. Ah mus' a lef' it on de counter. Ah'll git it w'en Ah goes to de train wid John.

MILLIE   *(showing him the handkerchief)*   See whut John done brought you! An' look on de mantel! *(pointing to the pistols)*

LONNIE   *(drawing back in fear as he glances at the pistols)*   You'd bettah hide them things! No cullud man bettah be seen wid dem things down heah!

JOHN   That's all right, Lonnie, nevah you fear. I'm goin' to keep 'em an' I ain't a-goin' to hide 'em either. See them. (*pointing to the wound chevrons on his arm*) Well, when I got them wounds, I let out all the rabbit-blood 'at wuz in me! (*defiantly*) Ef I kin be trusted with a gun in France, I kin be trusted with one in South Car'lina.

MAM SUE (*sensing trouble*)   Millie, yu'd bettah fix some suppah fu' John.

JOHN (*looking at his watch*)   I don' want a thing. I've got to be leavin' in a little while. I'm 'fraid I'm goin' to miss dad after all.

(*The knob of the door is turned as though someone is trying to enter. Then there is a loud knock on the door*)

JOHN (*excitedly*)   That's dad! Don't tell him I'm here!

(JOHN *tips hurriedly into the adjoining room.* LONNIE *unbolts the door and* MRS. SELENA HAWKINS *enters*)

MRS. HAWKINS   Lonnie fu'got de liniment so I thought I' bettah run ovah wid hit, 'cause when Mam Sue sen' fu' dis stuff she sho' needs hit. Brudder Moseby's been tellin' me dat John's done come home.

JOHN (*coming from his hiding place and trying to conceal his disappointment*)   Yes, I'm here. Good evenin', Mis' Hawkins. Glad to see you.

MRS. HAWKINS (*shaking hands with* JOHN)   Well, lan' sakes alive! Ef it ain't John sho'nuf! An' ain't he lookin' gran'! Jes look at dat medal a-shining' on his coat! Put on yuh cap, boy, an' lemme see how yuh look!

JOHN   Sure! (JOHN *puts on his overseas cap and, smiling, stands at attention a few paces off, while* MAM SUE, LONNIE, *and* MILLIE *form an admiring circle around him*)

MRS. HAWKINS   Now don' he sholy look gran'! I knows yo' sistah, an' gran'-mammy's proud o' yuh! (*a note of sadness creeps into her voice*) Ef only yuh po' daddy had a-lived to see dis day!

(JOHN *looks at her in amazement.* MILLIE *and* MAM SUE *stand transfixed with terror over the sudden betrayal*)

JOHN (*looking from one to the other and repeating her words as though he can scarcely realize their meaning*)   "Ef your po' daddy had lived—" (*to* MILLIE) Whut does this mean?

(MILLIE *sinks sobbing into the chair at the table and buries her face in her hands*)

MRS. HAWKINS   Lor', Millie, I thought you'd tole him!

(*Bewildered by the catastrophe that she has precipitated,* MRS. HAWKINS *slips out of the cabin*)

JOHN (*shaking* MILLIE *almost roughly*)   Come, Millie, have you been lyin' to me? Is dad gone?

MILLIE (*through her sobs*)   I jes hated to tell you—you wuz so far erway—

JOHN (*nervously*)   Come, Millie, for God's sake don' keep me in this su'pense! I'm a brave soldier—I kin stan' it—did he suffer much? Wuz he sick long?

MILLIE   He wuzn't sick no time—them w'ite devuls come in heah an' dragged him—

JOHN (*desperately*)   My God! You mean they lynched dad?

MILLIE (*sobbed piteously*)   They burnt him down by the big gum tree!

JOHN (*desperately*)   Whut fu', Millie? Whut fu'?

MILLIE   He got in a row wid ole Mister Withrow 'bout the price of cotton—an' he called dad a liar an' struck him—an' dad he up an' struck him back—

JOHN (*brokenly*)   Didn' they try him? Didn' they give him a chance? Whut'd the sheriff do? An' the Gov-nur?

MILLIE (*through her sobs*)   They didn't do nothin'.

JOHN   Oh, God! Oh, God! (*then recovering from the first bitter anguish and speaking*) So they've come into ouah home, have they! (*he strides over to* LONNIE *and seizes him by the collar*) An' what wuz you doin' when them hounds come in here after dad?

LONNIE (*hopelessly*)   They wuz so many of 'em come an' git 'im—whut could Ah do?

JOHN   Do? You could 'ave fought 'em like a man!

MAM SUE (*pleadingly*)   Don't be too hard on 'im, John, wese ain't got no gun 'round heah!

JOHN   Then he should 'ave burnt their damn kennels ovah their heads! Who was it leadin' 'em?

MILLIE   Old man Withrow and the Sherley boys, they started it all.

(*Gradually assuming the look of a man who has determined to do some terrible work that must be done,* JOHN *walks deliberately toward the mantel where the revolvers are lying*)

JOHN (*bitterly*) I've been helpin' the w'ite man git his freedom, I reckon I'd bettah try now to get my own!

MAM SUE (*terrified*) Whut yuh gwine ter do?

JOHN (*with bitterness growing in his voice*) I'm sick o' these w'ite folks doin's—we're "fine, trus'worthy feller citizuns" when they're handin' us out guns, an' Liberty Bonds, an' chuckin' us off to die; but we ain't a damn thing when it comes to handin' us the rights we done fought an' bled fu'! I'm sick o' this sort o' life—an' I'm goin' to put an' end to it!

MILLIE (*rushing to the mantel, and covering the revolvers with her hands*) Oh, no, no, John! Mam Sue, John's gwine to kill hisse'f!

MAM SUE (*piteously*) Oh, mah honey, don' yuh go do nothin' to bring sin on yo' soul! Pray to de good Lawd to tek all dis fiery feelin' out'n yo' heart! Wait 'tel Brudder Moseby come back—he's gwine to pray—

JOHN (*his speech growing more impassioned and bitter*) This ain't no time fu' preachers or prayers! You mean to tell me I mus' let them w'ite devuls send me miles erway to suffer an' be shot up fu' the freedom of people I ain't nevah seen, while they're burnin' an' killin' my folks here at home! To Hell with 'em!

(*He pushes* MILLIE *aside, and seizing the revolvers, thrusts the loaded one into his pocket and begins deliberately to load the other*)

MILLIE (*throwing her arms about his neck*) Oh, John, they'll kill yuh!

JOHN (*defiantly*) Whut ef they do! I ain't skeered o' none of 'em! I've faced worse guns than any sneakin' hounds kin show me! To Hell with 'em! (*he thrusts the revolver that he has just loaded into* LONNIE's *hand*) Take this, an' come on here, boy, an' we'll see what Withrow an' his gang have got to say!

(*Followed by* LONNIE, *who is bewildered and speechless,* JOHN *rushes out of the cabin and disappears in the gathering darkness*)

(*Curtain*)

They That Sit in Darkness

CHARACTERS

MALINDA JASPER, *the mother*
LINDY, MILES, ALOYSIUS, MARY ELLEN, JIMMIE,
   JOHN HENRY, A WEEK-OLD INFANT, *her children*
ELIZABETH SHAW, *a visiting nurse*

The action passes in a small country town in the South in our own day.

(*It is late afternoon of a day in September. The room, which does a three-fold duty as kitchen, dining room, and living room for the Jasper family, is dingy and disorderly. Great black patches as though from smoke are on the low ceilings and the walls. To the right is a door leading into a bedroom. In the opposite wall another door leads into a somewhat larger room that serves as bedroom for six Jasper children. In the rear wall a door opens into a large yard. A window is placed to the left of the door while against the wall to the right there stands an old, battered cow-hide trunk. The furniture, which is poor and dilapidated, consists of a table in the center of the room, a cupboard containing a few broken cups and plates, a rocker, and two or three plain chairs with broken backs and uncertain legs. Against the wall to the left there is a kitchen stove on which sit a tea-kettle and a wash-boiler. Near the window, placed upon stools, are two large laundry tubs. Through open window and door one gets a glimpse of snowy garments waving and glistening in the sun.* MALINDA JASPER, *a frail, tired-looking woman of thirty-eight, and* LINDY, *her seventeen-year-old daughter, are bending over the tubs swirling their hands in the water to make sure that their task is completed. From the yard come the constant cries of children at play*)

MRS. JASPER (*straightening up painfully from the tubs*) Lor', Lindy, how my side do hurt! But thank goodnis, dis job's done! (*she sinks exhausted into the rocker*) Run git me one them tablits de doctor lef' fo' dis pain! (LINDY *hurries into the adjoining room and returns with the medicine*)

MRS. JASPER (*shaking her head mournfully*) Dis ole pain goin' to be takin' me 'way f'om heah one o' dese days!

LINDY (*looking at her in concern*) See, Ma, I tole yuh not to be doin' all this wuk! Whut's Miss 'Liz'beth goin' er say when she comes heah this evenin' an' fine out you done all this wuk after she tole yuh pertic'lar yestiddy that she wuz'n goin' let yuh out'n bed 'fo' three weeks—an' here 't'ain't been a week sence baby wuz bawn!

MRS. JASPER Ah ain't keerin' 'bout what Mis' 'Liz'beth say! Easy nuf, Lindy, fo' dese nurses to give dey advice—dey ain't got no seben children to clothe an' feed—but when dis washin' git back Ah kin nevah ketch up!

LINDY (*reprovingly*) But I could 'a done it all mys'f.

MRS. JASPER An' been all day an' night doin' it—an' miss gittn' you'se'f off in de mawnin' tuh Tuskegee—no indeedy!

LINDY (*hesitatingly*) P'rhaps I oughtn' be goin' erway an' leavin' yuh wid all dis washin' to do ever' week, an' de chillern to look af-ter—an' the baby an' all. Daddy he gits home so late he cain't be no help.

MRS. JASPER (*wearily*) Nebber you mind, Lindy, Ah'm going be gittin' aw-right bime-by. Ah ain't a-goin' be stan'in' in de way yo' gittin' dis edicashun. Yo' chance don' come, Lindy, an' Ah wants ter see yuh tek it! Yuh been a good chile, Lindy, an' Ah wants ter see yuh git mo'e out'n life dan Ah gits. Dem three yeah at Tuskegee warn't seem long.

LINDY (*her face brightening up*) Yassum, an' ef Mister Huff, the sup'inten'ent meks me county teacher lak he sez he'll do when I git back, I kin do lots mo'e fo' you an' the chillern!

(*The cry of a week-old infant comes from the ad-joining room*)

MRS. JASPER Dar now! Ah'm mightly glad he didn' wake up 'tel we git dis washin' done! Ah reckon he's hongry. Ain't Miles come back wid de milk yet? He's been gawn mos' 'en hour—see ef he's took dat guitar wid 'im.

LINDY (*going to the door and looking out*) I doan see it nowheres so I reckon he's got it.

MRS. JASPER Den Gawd knows when we'll see 'im! Lak es not he's some'airs settin' by de road thumpin' dem strings—dat boy 'ud play ef me or you wuz dyin'! Ah doan know whut's goin' com' o' 'im—he's just so lazy en shif'lis!

LINDY Doan yuh go werrin' 'bout Miles, Ma. He'll be aw-right ef he kin only learn mu-sic, an' do whut he likes. (*the cry of the infant becomes insistent*) No, Ma, you set still—I'll git his bottle an' 'tend to him. (*she goes into the bedroom*)

(*The shrieks of the children in the yard grow louder. A shrill cry of anger and pain rises above the other voices, and* MARY ELLEN, *age six, appears crying at the door*)

MARY ELLEN (*holding her head*) Ma! Ma! Mek Aloysius b'have hisse'f! He hit me on de haid wid all his might!

MRS. JASPER (*rushing to the door*) Aloysius! Yuh Aloysius! It warn't do yuh no good ef Ah 'ave to come out'n dere to yuh! John Henry, git down f'om dat tree, 'fo yuh have dem clo'es in de durt! Yo' chillern 'nuf to werry me to death!

(*As* LINDY *returns with the baby's empty bottle,* MILES *enters the rear door. He is a good-natured but shiftless looking boy of sixteen. A milk pail is swinging on his arm, leaving his hands free to strum a guitar*)

LINDY Have yuh brought the milk, Miles? An' the bread?

MILES (*setting down the milk pail*) Nup! Mister Jackson say yuh cain't have no milk, an' no nothin' 'tel de bill's paid.

MRS. JASPER Den Gawd knows we'll starve, 'cause Ah see'd yo' daddy give de doctor ebery cent o' his wages las' week. An' dey warn't be no mo'e money comin' in 'tel Ah kin git dis wash out to de Redmon's.

LINDY Well, baby's gawn back to sleep now, and p'rhaps Miss 'Liz'beth will bring some milk fo' de baby when she come in lak she did yestiddy—but they ain't nothing heah fo' de other chillern.

(*The shrieks of the children at play in the yard grow louder.*)

ALOYSIUS (*calling from without*)   Ma! Ma! John Henry done pull' down de clo'es line!

MRS. JASPER (*running again to the door*) Come in heah! Ever' single one o' yuh! Miles, run fix 'em up an' see ef any o' 'em got in de durt!

(*The Jasper children, four in number, a crestfallen, pathetic looking little group—heads unkempt, ragged, undersized, under-fed, file in terrified*)

JOHN HENRY (*terror-stricken*)   It warn't me, Ma, it was Aloysius!

MRS. JASPER   Heish yo' mouf'! March yo'se'f ever' one o' yuh an' go to baid!

MARY ELLEN (*timidly*)   We's ain't had no suppah.

MRS. JASPER   An' whut's mo'e, yuh ain't goin' git no suppah 'tel yuh larns to b'have yo'se'f!

ALOYSIUS (*in a grumbling tone*)   Cain't fool me—Ah heerd Linda say dey ain't no suppah fo' us!

MRS. JASPER (*calling to the children as they disappear in the room to the left*)   Ef Ah heahs one soun' Ah'm comin' in dere an' slap yuh into de middle o' nex' week! (*as she sinks again enhausted into the rocker*) Them chillern's goan ter be de death o' me yit!

MILES (*appearing at the door*)   De clo'es ain't dirty. I fo'git to tell yuh—I stopp't by Sam Jones an' he say he'll be 'round 'fo Lindy's trunk 'bout sun-down.

MRS. JASPER   Ah reckons yu'd bettah git yo' clo'es an' pack up 'cause it warn't be long 'fo sun-down.

LINDY (*dragging the old trunk to the center of the room*)   I ain't a-goin' less'n you git bettah, Ma. Yuh look right sick to me!

(*As* LINDY *is speaking* MISS ELIZABETH SHAW, *in the regulation dress of a visiting nurse and carrying a small black bag, appears at the rear door*)

MISS SHAW (*looking in consternation at Mrs. Jasper*)   Malinda Jasper! What are you doing out of bed! You don't mean to say that you have washed all those clothes that I see in the yard?

MRS. JASPER   Yassum, me an' Lindy done 'em.

MISS SHAW (*provoked*)   And you look completely exhausted! Come you must get right to bed!

MRS. JASPER (*leaning her head wearily against the back of the rocker*)   Lemme res' myse'f jes a minute—Ah'll be goin' 'long to-rectly.

MISS SHAW   It's a wonder in your condition that you didn't die standing right at those tubs! I don't mean to scare you but—

MRS. JASPER (*with extreme weariness*)   Lor', Mis' 'Liz'beth, it ain't *dyin'* Ah'm skeer't o', its *livin'*—wid all dese chillern to look out fo'. We ain't no Elijahs, Mis' 'Lis'beth, dey ain't no ravens flyin' 'roun' heah drappin' us food. All we gits, we has to git by wukin' hard! But thanks to be Gawd a light's dawnin'! My Lindy's gittin' off to Tuskegee to school tomorrer, Mis' 'Liz'beth!

MISS SHAW (*surprised*)   I didn't know that Lindy was thinking about going away to school.

MRS. JASPER   Thinkin' 'bout it! Lindy ain't been thinkin' an' dreamin' 'bout nothin' else sence Booker Washin'ton talked to de farmers down youder at Shady Grove some ten yeah ergo. Did yo' know Booker Washin'ton, Mis' 'Liz'beth?

MISS SHAW   I saw him once a long time ago in my home town in Massachusetts. He was a great man.

MRS. JASPER   Dat he wuz! Ah kin see him now—him an' Lindy, jes a teeny slip o' gal—after de speakin' wuz ovah down dere at Shady Grove, a-standin' under de magnolias wid de sun a-pou'in' through de trees on 'em—an' he wid his hand on my li'l Lindy's haid lak he wuz givin' huh a blessin', an' a-sayin': "When yuh gits big, li'l gal, yuh mus' come to Tuskegee an' larn, so's yuh kin come back heah an' he'p dese po' folks!" He's daid an' in his grave but Lindy ain't nevah fo'git dem words.

MISS SHAW   Just think of it! And ten years ago! How glad I am that her dream is coming true. Won't it cost you quite a bit?

MRS. JASPER   Lor', Lindy 'ud nevah git dere ef we had to sen' huh! Some dem rich folks up yonder in yo' part de world is sen'in' huh.

LINDY (*entering with her arms laden with things for her trunk*)   Good evenin', Mis' 'Liz'beth.

MISS SHAW   Well, Lindy, I've just heard of your good fortune. How splendid it is! But what will the baby do without you! How is he this afternoon?

LINDY   He's right smart, Mis' 'Liz'beth. I been rubbing his leg lack you showed me. Do yoh think it'll evah grow ez long ez the other'n?

MISS SHAW   I fear, Lindy, those little withered limbs seldom do; but with care it will grow much stronger. I have brought him some milk—there in my bag. Be careful to modify it exactly as I showed you, and give what is left to the other children.

LINDY *(preparing to fix the milk)*   Yes Mis' 'Liz'beth.

MISS SHAW *(nodding at Lindy)*   What *will you do*, Malinda, when she goes? You will have to stop working so hard. Just see how exhausted you are from this heavy work!

MRS. JASPER   Lor', Mis' 'Liz'beth, Ah'll be awright toreckly. Ah did de same thing after my li'l Tom was bawn, an' when Aloysius wuz bawn Ah git up de nex' day—de wuk had to be done.

MISS SHAW *(very gravely)*   But you must not think that you are as strong now as you were then. I heard the doctor tell you very definitely that this baby had left your heart *weaker than ever*, and that you *must* give up this laundry work.

MRS. JASPER *(pleadingly)*   'Deed, Mis' 'Liz'beth, we needs dis money whut wid all dese chillern, an' de sicknis' an' fune'ul 'spenses of li'l Tom an' Selena—dem's de chillern whut come 'tween John Henry an' dis las' baby. At'er dem bills wuz paid heah come Pinkie's trouble.

MISS SHAW   Pinkie?

MRS. JASPER *(sadly)*   Yuh nevah seed Pinkie 'cause she lef' 'fo' yuh come heah. She come 'tween Miles an' Aloysius—she warn't right in de haid—she wuked ovah tuh Bu'nett's place—Ah aint nevah been much on my gals wukin' round dese white men but Pinkie *mus' go*; an' fus thing we know Bu'nett got huh in trouble.

MISS SHAW   Poor, poor girl! What did you do to the Burnett man?

MRS. JASPER *(with deep feeling)*   Lor', Mis' 'Liz'beth, cullud folks caint's do nothin' to white folks down heah! Huh Dad went on sumpin awful wid huh ever' day, an' one mawnin' we woked up and Pinkie an' huh baby wuz gawn! We ain't nevah heerd f'om huh tuh dis day—*(she closes her eyes as if to shut out the memory of Pinkie's sorrow)* Me an' Jim 'as allus put ouah tru's in de Lawd, an' we wants tuh raise up dese chillern to be good,

hones' men en' women but we has tuh wuk so hard to give 'em de li'l dey gits dat we ain't got no time tuh look at'er dey sperrits. When Jim go out to wuk—chillern's sleepin'; when he comes in late at night—chillern's sleepin'. When Ah git through scrubbin' at dem tubs all Ah kin do is set in dis cheer an' nod—Ah doan wants tuh see no chillern! Ef it warn't fo' Lindy—huh got a mighty nice way wid 'em—Gawd he'p 'em!

MISS SHAW   Well, Malinda, you have certainly your share of trouble!

MRS. JASPER *(shaking her head wearily)*   Ah wonder whut sin we done that Gawd punish me an' Jim lak dis!

MISS SHAW *(gently)*   God is not punishing you, Malinda, you are punishing yourselves by having children every year. Take this last baby—you knew that with your weak heart that you should never have had it and yet—

MRS. JASPER   But whut kin Ah do—de chillern *come!*

MISS SHAW   You must be careful!

MRS. JASPER   *Be keerful!* Dat's all you nu'ses say! You an' de one whut come when Tom wuz bawn, an' Selena! Ah been keerful all Ah knows how but whut's it got me—ten chillern, eight livin' an' two daid! You got'a be tellin' me sumpin' better'n dat, Mis' 'Liz'beth!

MISS SHAW *(fervently)*   I wish to God it were lawful for me to do so! My heart goes out to you poor people that sit in darkness, having, year after year, children that you are physically too weak to bring into the world—children that you are unable not only to educate but even to clothe and feed. Malinda, when I took my oath as nurse, I swore to abide by the laws of the State, and the law forbids my telling you what you have a right to know!

MRS. JASPER *(with the tears trickling from her closed eyes)*   Ah ain't blamin' you, Mis' 'Liz'beth, but—

MISS SHAW   Come, come, Malinda, you must not give away like this. You are worn out—come, you must get to bed.

LINDY *(entering with more things for her trunk)*   I'm glad yuh gittin' huh to bed, Mis' 'Liz'beth, I been tryin' to all day.

MRS. JASPER *(as she walks unsteadily toward her room)*   Lindy, honey, git yo' trunk pack't. Thank Gawd yo' chance done come! Give dat *(nodding toward the partially filled bottle of milk)* to de chillern. Mis' 'Liz'beth say dey kin have it.

LINDY   All right, Ma. Mis' 'Liz'beth, ef you needs me jes call.

(MALINDA *and the* NURSE *enter the bedroom.* LINDY *is left packing her trunk.* MILES *can be heard from without strumming upon his guitar*)

MARY ELLEN *(poking her head out of the door to the children's room)*   Lindy, Lindy, whut wuz dat Ma say we all kin have?

LINDY   Some milk—it ain't much.

(The CHILDREN *bound into the room.* MARY ELLEN, *first at the table, seizes the bottle and lifts it to her lips)*

ALOYSIUS *(snatching the bottle from* MARY ELLEN*)*   Yuh got 'a be las', 'cause Mis' 'Liz'-beth say we mus'n' nebber eat or drink at'er yuh! Did'n' she, Lindy?

LINDY *(as* MARY ELLEN *begins to cry)*   Ef yo' all git to fussin' I ain't goan to bring yuh nothin' when I comes back!

MARY ELLEN *(as the children crowd about* Lindy*)*   What yuh goan 'a bring us, Lindy?

LINDY *(as she puts her things carefully into her trunk)*   When I comes back I'm goan to bring yuh all some pretty readin' books, an' some clo'es so I kin tek yuh to school ever' day where yuh kin learn to read 'em!

JOHN HENRY *(clapping his hands)*   Is we all goin', Lindy? Miles too?

LINDY   Yes indeedy! An' whut's mo'e I'm goan 'a git Miles a fine new guitar an' let him learn music. An' some day ever' body'll be playin' an' singing' his songs!

ALOYSIUS *(glowing with excitement)*   Some day he might have his own band! Might'n' he, Lindy? Lak dat big white one whut come fru heah f'om 'Lanta! Ole Miles'll come struttin' down de road.

*(*ALOYSIUS *seizes the broom, and in spite of the handicap of bow legs, gives a superb imitation of a drum major leading his band)*

LINDY *(watching* ALOYSIUS' *antics)*   An' I'm goin' tuh have Aloysius li'l legs straightened. *(as the children roll in merriment)* 'Sh! 'sh! Mus'n' mek no noise 'cause Ma ain't well! An' in de evenin' we'll have a real set-down-to-de-table suppah—Dad he won't have to wuk so hard so he kin git home early—an' after suppah we all

kin set 'round de fiah lak dey do ovah to Lawyer Hope's an' tell stories an' play games—

(The CHILDREN, *radiant as though these dreams were all realities, huddle closer about* LINDY *who, packing done, now sits enthroned upon her battered trunk)*

LINDY   'Sh—sh! Wuz that Mis' 'Liz'beth callin'? *(They listen intently but can hear nothing save the sweet, plaintive notes of an old Spiritual that* MILES *is playing upon his guitar)* Then we'll git some fine Sunday clo'es, an' a hoss an' wagun, an' when Sunday come we'll all climb in an' ride to Shady Grove to Meetin'—an' we'll set under de trees in de shade an' learn 'bout li'l Joseph an' his many-cullud coat; an' li'l Samu'l whut de Lawd called while he wuz sleepin'; an' de li'l baby whut wuz bawn in de stable an' wuz lots poor'n me an' you. An' on Sunday evenin' we'll—

MISS SHAW *(appearing at the bedroom door and speaking hurriedly)*   Send the children to bed quickly, Lindy, I need you.

(The children run into their room)

ALOYSIUS *(wistfully, at the door)*   Ef we's good, Lindy, let us git up when Sam Jones come an' see de trunk go?

LINDY *(quickly)*   Mebbe—hurry up!

MISS SHAW *(very seriously)*   Lindy, your mother's condition has grown suddenly very, very serious. The exertion of today is beginning to tell on her heart. Bring me some boiling water immediately for my hypodermic. *(calling from the rear door)* Miles, Miles! Run to the Hope's as fast as you can and ask them to telephone for the doctor—your mother is very ill. Tell him the nurse says it is urgent!

*(*MISS ELIZABETH *hurries into the bedroom, followed soon after by* LINDY *with the water. In a few minutes the sobbing of* LINDY *can be heard, and the* NURSE *re-enters the kitchen. She leans against the frame of the rear door as though exhausted and stares out into the yard at the clothes fluttering like white spirits in the gathering dusk. Then sighing deeply, she puts on her bonnet and cape and turns to go)*

MILES *(rushing in breathlessly, with his guitar under his arm)*   De Hopes ain't—

MISS SHAW *(placing her hand tenderly on his shoulder)*   Never mind, now, Miles, your mother is dead.

MILES (*his guitar crashing to the floor*)   Dead!

MISS SHAW   Yes, and you must help Lindy all you can. I would not leave but I have a case up the road that I must see tonight. I'll be back tomorrow. (*as* MILES *walks with bowed head toward his mother's room*) Come, Miles, you had better bring in the clothes before it gets dark.

(*As* MILES *follows her out,* LINDY *enters the kitchen. The light has gone from her face for she knows that the path now stretching before her and the other children will be darker even than the way that they have already known*)

MILES (*awkwardly, as he struggles in with the hamper piled high with the snowy clothes*)   Anything mo' Ah kin do, Lindy?

LINDY (*as she sits on the edge of her trunk and stares in a dazed, hopeless way at the floor*)   I reckon yu'd bettah walk up de road a piece to meet Dad an' hurry him erlong. An' stop in de Redmon's an' tell 'em dey can't have de wash tomorrer 'cause—(*gulping back her tears*) 'cause Ma's dead; but I'll git 'em out myself jes ez soon ez I kin. An', Miles, leave word fo' Sam Jones 'at he need'n' come fo' de trunk.

(Curtain)

FOR UNBORN CHILDREN

1926

Myrtle Smith Livingston (1902–1973)

Myrtle Smith Livingston, untrained in drama, wrote one play that would deliver her message to the world, and then never wrote another. *For Unborn Children* is a melodramatic plea against racially mixed marriages, or "miscegenation," as it had come to be called after the Civil War. In her play, Livingston reversed the usual stage pairing of white man (southern) and Black woman, to express how, as a Black woman, she felt betrayed. Marion, the female lead in the play, clearly voices her anger: "What is to become of us when our own men throw us down?" This anger and sense of betrayal is also reflected in the play's ending: The Black male, LeRoy, is to be lynched, yet, incredibly, he accepts his "punishment" as justice, a justice administered not by the lynch mob, but by the playwright.

Myrtle Athleen Smith Livingston, born the daughter of Issac Samuel and Lulu C. (Hall) Smith, grew up in the small town of Holly Grove, Arkansas; she attended Manual High School, graduating in 1920. To study pharmacy, she enrolled at Howard University for two years, and in 1923 she obtained a teaching certificate from Colorado Teachers College. In 1925, she married William McKinley Livingston, M.D., and taught at Lincoln College in Jefferson City, Missouri, before retiring in Hawaii, where she died in 1973.

Her theme, miscegenation, was the one racial question on which Black and white playwrights usually agreed: mixing is bad for the races, and the product will be a "tragic mulatto." The word itself originated in the late sixteenth century, derived from the Spanish and Portuguese *mulato*, the diminutive for *mule*, the product of a male jackass and a mare. *Mulatto* stigmatized persons of mixed ancestry as something less than human—as did other terms: "quadroon," "octoroon," and "half-breed."

The official white miscegenation myth—on stage and off—held that the mixing of the races was bad for whites, although it might improve the Negro genetically. On stage, persons of mixed blood, even if the Black blood be but one drop, had to die before the final curtain. The most well-known play of this genre was Dion Boucicault's *The Octoroon* (1859), which had two endings: Zoë, the mulatto, died to please American audiences, but in the British productions, she was allowed to live.

The theatre tradition of the mulatto flourished for a century, continuing through Edward Shelton's *The Nigger* (1909), where the hero is about to be elected governor when he discovers his Black past. The Black man's attempt to rape the white heroine in *Birth of a Nation* (1914) became a symbol of the nation's fear. Eugene O'Neill made a serious attempt to examine the issues of miscegenation in *All God's Chillun Got Wings* (1924). The Harlem Renaissance writer Georgia Douglas Johnson wrote two plays on the theme: *The Blue-Eyed Black Boy* (c. 1930) and *Blue Blood* (1926), both of which broke the rules and ended without a lynching, as did Joseph S. Mitchell's play *Son-Boy* (1928).

Two generations later, American audiences watched the prize-fighter Jack Johnson climb into bed with a white woman in Howard Sackler's *Great White Hope* (1968), but any objections were nicely met by her death before curtain time.

The Black tradition has been similar. Langston Hughes's first play on Broadway, *Mulatto* (1935), featured the son of a white plantation owner and his Black house servant. The son kills his father and is killed in return. Adrienne Kennedy examined a painful miscegenation with tragic consequences in *Funnyhouse of a Negro* (1964) and *The Owl Answers* (1965). An exception to this tradition of death and sorrow was Alice Childress's lovely, human play, *Wedding Band* (1966).

It is interesting to speculate why American playwrights, Black and white, denied the reality of thousands of human beings who shared white and Black gene pools, and instead elected to confirm the stage myth. Part of the answer probably lies in the historic and easy access white males had to the Black slave women and white fear of the supposedly predatory nature of Black male sexuality. As the twentieth century comes to its close, miscegenation laws have been erased, and in popular television talk shows and films, the Black male/white female shown in sexual intimacy has become a dynamic image to sell soap and movie tickets. Nevertheless, Livingston's "little" drama, *For Unborn Children*, still carries heavy freight for most Americans.

For Unborn Children

CAST OF CHARACTERS

LEROY CARLSON, *a young lawyer*
MARION CARLSON, *his sister*
GRANDMA CARLSON, *his grandmother*
SELMA FRAZIER, *a young white girl*
A MOB

(The scene of the play is somewhere in the South; the characters are all of Negro descent except the young white girl and the members of the mob. The time is in the present.

A living room is tastefully, though not richly, furnished, denoting the occupancy of a refined family, evidently of the middle class. There is a sofa to one side, a table in the center, and a leather comfort-chair in the corner; another leather chair sits in the upper part of the room. A window is in the rear. There are two entrances, one right and one left. MARION is seen sitting on the sofa reading the evening paper as the curtain rises. After perusing it quietly for a minute, she throws it down and goes to the window, peering out into the night.

Her grandmother, a gentle, well-bred, old lady enters)

GRANDMA CARLSON   Hasn't Roy come yet, Marion?

MARION   No, he hasn't, grandmother; it's almost 9 o'clock now and he said he'd be here by 6.

GRANDMA CARLSON   Did you telephone the office for him?

MARION   Yes; he left about 5:30, they said.

GRANDMA CARLSON *(with a sigh sits in the comfort-chair)* I suppose he's somewhere with that girl again.

MARION   Oh! If he would only let her alone! He knows what it will mean if they find it out; it's awful for him to keep us in this terrible suspense!

GRANDMA CARLSON   Do you suppose talking to her would do any good? Do you know her?

MARION   Yes, by sight; a nice enough girl all right, but then she's white and she ought to stay in her own race; she hasn't any right to be running around after our men. I know it wouldn't be of any use to talk to her; and Roy—!

GRANDMA CARLSON   Yes, dear, I know; we hardly dare to say anything to him about it; but, Marion, we've got to do something!

MARION   But, grandmother, what? I'm at my wit's end! Since they can't be married here, they're going to run away and go north someplace where they can, and *(despairingly)* I don't see anything we can do to stop them!

GRANDMA CARLSON *(sadly and preoccupied)* I suppose I'll have to tell him; well, if it will stop him—

MARION   Tell him what?

GRANDMA CARLSON *(with a start as she realizes that she said more than she intended to)* Oh, nothing, child; look again; don't you see him yet?

MARION   No. Oh! it's terrible not knowing whether he's all right or if some mob has— *(buries her face in her hands)*

GRANDMA CARLSON *(wincing)*   No,—no— don't say that!

MARION   But you know that's what will happen if it's found out before they get away!

GRANDMA CARLSON *(moaning)*   Oh, my child! I don't know which would be the hardest to bear! I'd almost rather that he should

die now than to marry a white woman, but O! Dear Lord! Not such a death as that!

(The noise of a door being unlocked is heard outside; it is opened and then shut)

MARION *(relieved)*   Here he is now; well, thank goodness, it hasn't happened yet. *(her nervous tension relaxes and her anger rises throughout the following scene)*

(LEROY enters)

LEROY *(throws cap on table)*   Hello; *(smiles sheepishly)* been giving me "Hail Columbia," I guess, haven't you?

MARION *(sarcastically)*   This is what you call 6 o'clock, I suppose, is it?

LEROY   I'm sorry, sis; I had an engagement and I couldn't make it here by then; I meant to call you and let you know, but,—well, I'm sorry.

GRANDMA CARLSON   We were just worried; you know we can't feel very easy these days, Roy, when we don't know where you are; you know the sentiment down here.

MARION *(bitterly)*   What does he care about how we feel? His family and his career too, for that matter, mean nothing to him now; and his whole heart and soul are wrapped up in his girl,—a white girl! I guess your engagement this evening was with her; I know it was!

LEROY *(trying to control his temper)*   Yes, it was; I still have the liberty of making an engagement with anyone I choose, Marion.

GRANDMA CARLSON   But you haven't the right, son, to cause us unnecessary worry and pain. You know how much your sister and I both care about you, and it wouldn't be much to just let us know where you are.

LEROY *(contritely)*   I didn't mean to worry you, Granny; I was on my way home when— her note was brought to me, and I didn't have time to call you then. You won't have to worry much longer now, anyway; we've decided to leave tomorrow night.

MARION *(shocked)*   Tomorrow night? Good Heavens, Roy! You can't go through with it! Have you lost all your manhood?

GRANDMA CARLSON *(her voice throbs with pain)*   Ah, boy, you've forgotten us! Don't you love us at all anymore since she came into your life?

LEROY   O, Granny, I hate to leave you and sis; but you know we can't stay here and marry, confound these laws! It will be better for us to go some place where we aren't known, anyway. I wish you and Marion could go with us.

MARION (*almost hysterical*)   I wouldn't go a step with you and your white woman if I was going to be killed for it! If you've lost your self-respect, I still have mine! I wouldn't spit on a woman like her! There must be something terribly wrong with her, for white women don't marry colored men when they can get anybody else! You poor fool! If it's color you want, why couldn't you stay in your own race? We have women who are as white as any white person could be! My God! What is to become of us when our own men throw us down? Even if you do love her, can't you find your backbone to conquer it for the sake of your race? I know they're as much to blame as we are, but intermarriage doesn't hurt them as much as it does us; laws would never have been passed against it if the states could have believed white women would turn Negro men down, but they knew they wouldn't; they can make fools out of them too easily, and you're too much of a dupe to see it! Well, if you marry her, may God help me never to breathe your name again! (*runs from the room sobbing*)

LEROY (*sorrowfully and pleadingly*)   Oh, Granny, you don't feel that way too, do you? Selma and I can't help it because we don't belong to the same race, and we have the right to be happy together if we love each other, haven't we?

GRANDMA CARLSON (*sadly*)   We have the right to be happy, child, only when our happiness doesn't hurt anybody else; and when a colored man marries a white woman, he hurts every member of the Negro race!

LEROY (*perplexed*)   But,—I don't understand;—how?

GRANDMA CARLSON   He adds another link to the chain that binds them; before we can gain that perfect freedom to which we have every right, we've got to prove that we're better than they! And we can't do it when our men place white women above their own!

LEROY (*imploringly*)   But, Grandmother, I love her so much! Not because she's white, but just for herself alone; I'd love her just the same if she were black! And she loves me too! Oh! I can't believe it would be wrong for us to marry!

GRANDMA CARLSON   Sometimes we best prove our love by giving up the object of it. You can't make her happy, Roy; she'll be satisfied for a while, but after that the call of her blood will be stronger than her love for you, and you'll both be miserable: she'll long for her own people; you won't be enough.

LEROY (*miserably*)   What shall I do? Oh, Lord, have mercy! Granny, I can't give her up! I couldn't live without her!

GRANDMA CARLSON (*with tears in her eyes*)   Think of the unborn children that you sin against by marrying her, baby! Oh, you can't know the misery that awaits them if you give them a white mother! Every child has a right to a mother who will love it better than life itself; and a white woman cannot mother a Negro baby!

LEROY   But, Granny—

GRANDMA CARLSON (*pathetically*)   I know, Honey! I've never told you this,—I didn't want you to know,— but your mother was a white woman, and she made your father's life miserable as long as he lived. She never could stand the sight of you and Marion; she hated you because you weren't white! I was there to care for you, but I'm getting old, Honey, and I couldn't go through it again! Boy, you can't make the same mistake your father did!

LEROY (*in repugnance*)   Oh, Granny, why didn't you tell me before? My mother, white! I've wondered why you never spoke of her! And she hated us! My God! That makes it different!

(GRANDMA CARLSON *rises and kisses him on the forehead, holding his face between her hands and looking deep into his eyes*)

GRANDMA CARLSON   I'll leave you alone with God and your conscience, and whatever you decide, I'll be satisfied. (*goes out*)

(LEROY *sits with his head bowed in his hands; presently a light tapping is heard at the window, which finally atracts his attention; he crosses to it, and seeing who is there, motions toward the door, going to open it;* SELMA *enters, almost exhausted*)

SELMA (*breathless and terrorized*)   A mob!—Hurry!—They're—coming—here—after—you.—You—must—go!—Hurry!

LEROY (*in amazement*)   A mob—after me?

SELMA   Hurry and go!—They're coming now! (*a rumble of voices is heard in the distance. Despairingly*) Oh! It's too late! (*sobs*) What shall I do? Oh, they'll—they'll—kill you!

(*The rumble grows louder as it nears the house; cries of "Lynch him!" "The dirty nigger!" "We'll show him how to fool around a white woman!" are heard.* GRANDMA CARLSON *and* MARION *enter, fearfully apprehensive*)

MARION (*seeing* SELMA)   What's the matter? What's that noise?

GRANDMA CARLSON (*as realization dawns upon her; clutches her heart*)   Oh! It can't be! (*falls on her knees and prays*) Dear God! have mercy! Oh, Father in Heaven! Do not desert us now! Hear my prayer and save my boy!

LEROY (*a light breaks over his face and he is transfigured; a gleam of holiness comes into his eyes; looking heavenward*)   Thy will be done, O Lord! (*he turns and takes* SELMA's *hands in his*) It has to be, sweetheart, and it is the better way; even though we love each other we couldn't have found happiness together. Forget me, and marry a man of your own race;

you'll be happier, and I will too, up there. Goodbye. (*he turns to* MARION) Forgive me, sis, if you can.

MARION (*sobs heartbrokenly*)   There isn't anything to forgive, Roy! It's I you should forgive! I'm sorry for everything I said! Oh, God! I can't stand this!

LEROY (*soothingly*)   Don't cry, sis; what you said was right; and I want you to know that even if this hadn't happened, I was going to give her up. (*kisses her tenderly. Picks* GRANDMA CARLSON *up from the floor and holds her close in his arms*) It's better this way, Granny; don't grieve so; just think of it as a sacrifice for UN-BORN CHILDREN!

VOICE OUTSIDE   Come out, you damned nigger, or we'll burn the house down!

MARION (*clings to him, sobbing*)   Don't go, Roy! We'll all die together!

LEROY (*puts her from him gently*)   No. (*loud and clear*) I'm coming gentlemen! (*with a last, long, loving look at the three of them he walks out to his death victorious and unafraid*)

(*Curtain*)

THE CHURCH FIGHT

1925

Ruth Ada Gaines-Shelton (1872–1938)

On April 8, 1872, in Glasgow, Missouri, Ruth Gaines-Shelton was born the daughter of the Reverend George W. and Mary Elizabeth Gaines. Her mother died when she was two, leaving her to be raised by her father, who was the minister in the African Methodist Episcopal Church. She graduated from the normal school at Wilberforce University in 1895 (she wrote the class poem "Hail and Farewell") and began teaching school in Montgomery, Missouri, where in 1898 she met and married William Obern Shelton. They had three children: George, Obern, and Mary.

Ruth Gaines-Shelton, like many of the progressive women of her day, wrote plays for her church and club groups. Her titles include *Aunt Hagar's Children*, *The Church Mouse*, *Gena, the Lost Child*, *Lord Earlington's Broken Vow*, *Mr. Church*, and *Parson Dewdrop's Bride*. *The Church Fight*, published in *The Crisis*, where it won second prize ($40) in the Amy Spingarn Contest, is the only play whose manuscript is known to be extant.

The Church Fight has the distinction of being among the first in a genre of African-American plays about "church fights," which also include James Baldwin's *Amen Corner*, Hall Johnson's *Run Little Chillun*, and Andrew Burris's *You Must Be Bo'n Again*. It also has the distinction of being a comedy not about the "race problem," but about an experience that was apparently universal enough to allow the author to use allegorical names for satrical purposes—church politics. No doubt a number of staunch church members who read the play when it was published in 1926 recognized themselves and their friends.

The Church Fight was one of the few comedies of the era to use satire to poke fun at life in the church. The employment of comedy and satire to expose and attack racial problems does not appear until mid-century with plays like Ted Shine's *Sho' Is Hot in the Cotton Patch*, Ossie Davis's *Purlie Victorious*, and C. Bernard Jackson and James V. Hatch's *Fly Blackbird*. Not until the 1980s did a satirical play appear about Black theatre itself: George C. Wolfe's *The Colored Museum*. It is interesting to speculate why comedy and satire, which were rampant in Black vaudeville and the TOBA circuits, failed to cross over into "literary" Black theatre until so late.

The Church Fight

C<small>HARACTERS</small>

ANANIAS
INVESTIGATOR
JUDAS   } the brethren
PARSON PROCRASTINATOR

SAPPHIRA
INSTIGATOR
MEDDLER   } the sisters
EXPERIENCE
TAKE-IT-BACK
TWO-FACE

(SCENE: *In the kitchen of* SISTER SAPPHIRA's *home. A small kitchen table with red table cloth on it and breakfast dishes for two; kitchen chair; cupboard with dishes in it; pans and skillets hanging up.*

TIME: *7:30 in the morning.*

BROTHER ANANIAS *and* SISTER SAPPHIRA *have just finished their breakfast.* ANANIAS *has on over-alls and jumper ready for day's work.* SAPPHIRA *is in neat house dress, gingham apron, with dust cap on)*

BROTHER ANANIAS (*lighting pipe*)   Well wife, I must go, it's 7:30 and I'll have to skip along; but I want you to remember if that committee meets here today, tell them that we ain't going to pay another cent into the Church until Parson Procrastinator leaves. Tell them Parson Shoot, from Rocky-town, says he'll come and take our Church any time.

SISTER SAPPHIRA   Don't you worry, Ananias, I ain't going to pay no more money to that man. Why he has plumb robbed the treasury. Why it's just a shame for a preacher to stay at a Church until he kills it plumb dead. Here honey, take your dinner bucket.

(ANANIAS *takes his bucket, says goodbye as he goes out the door*)

SISTER SAPPHIRA (*cleaning up table*)   I do hope they can git Brother Procrastinator moved by night. I've got so much work today it looks like I just ain't got time to fool with all them people a-coming here. But we've got to attend to God's work first. (*knock at door;*

opens door) Why, you all are here before I've got my house cleaned up; but come right in. I'm so glad you all mean business. (*Enter* SISTER INSTIGATOR *with glasses on, looking over them;* SISTER MEDDLER, *chewing gum.* SISTER EXPERIENCE *with book and pencil looking very important.* SISTER TAKE-IT-BACK, *with head down as if afraid of being discovered.* SISTER TWO-FACE, *smiling sweetly with pretty hat and veil on;* BROTHER INVESTIGATOR, *with Bible;* BROTHER JUDAS, *leaning on cane. All ladies are dressed in house dresses except* SISTER TWO-FACE, *who has a street dress on.* SISTER SAPPHIRA *shakes hands with each one calling the name as she does so)* Just sit right down and let us see what can be done. I'm just all on fire about it.

BROTHER INVESTIGATOR (*sits down at table, takes off glasses and wipes them*)   Well, Sister Sapphira, I'll tell you in the beginning, it's no easy task to move a Minister. You see, in the first place, we got to have a "charge" against him; now what charge have we against Parson Procrastinator:

SISTER INSTIGATOR   Well, Brother Investigator, we ain't got no particular charge agin him, only he's been here thirteen years and we are tired looking at him.

BROTHER INVESTIGATOR   That won't do, Sister Instigator; you must have sufficient evidence and proof that he has broken the law, or lived unrighteously.

SISTER MEDDLER   Couldn't we make up some kind of a charge agin him?

SISTER EXPERIENCE   Better not do that sisters, you'll get into trouble!

SISTER SAPPHIRA   There's no danger of that; we could just simply say that Brother Procrastinator has not walked in the straight and narrow path since he's been here.

BROTHER INVESTIGATOR   Well, Sister Sapphira, you can't say that unless you tell just *wherein* he failed to walk in the path.

BROTHER JUDAS   Well, I'll just tell you the truth, Brother Investigator; you know I know him. He and I have been arm and arm ever since he's been here. He's a pretty crooked sort of a fellow. Of course I wouldn't like for him to know I squealed on him.

SISTER TAKE-IT-BACK   Well I know one thing, and I saw this with my own eyes: I saw him hold on to Sister Holy's hand so long one night at prayer meeting until Brother Two-Face had to speak to him about it!

SISTER SAPPHIRA   There now! Do you hear that? I've been watching them two, for some time. You know Sister Holy was the one what gave him that gold pencil.

SISTER EXPERIENCE   Sisters, you all had better listen to me; you know I've been in one church fight, and I promised God that I'd never be in another. Now in the first place, no church fight can be built on a lie. It's better to let the preacher stay, than damn our souls trying to get rid of him.

BROTHER JUDAS *(singing)*   "We want no cowards in our band."

SISTER EXPERIENCE   If there's anybody here, that's afraid to come out and fight in the open, let them get out at once.

SISTER TAKE-IT BACK   Well I'm one that's not afraid; you all know me. You know what I say first, I say last; and I started out to move Brother Procrastinator and I don't expect to stop until he's gone.

BROTHER JUDAS   That's the way to win out; Sisters, you got to have that fighting spirit.

SISTER INSTIGATOR   I tell you, we just must git rid of this man. Why none of the young people will come to Church because he can't read so anybody can understand him. If he don't go, this Church is going to destruction and ruin.

BROTHER INVESTIGATOR   Now sisters and brothers, I have listened careful to every word you said and I ain't yet had sufficient evidence to ask Parson Procrastinator to go.

SISTER EXPERIENCE   Brother Investigator, I wish to drop this word of warning. When I was in the fight against Parson Hard-head, some of the sisters told so many stories that the Bishop had to turn them out of the Church for lying. Now I don't think we ought to tear the Church all to pieces just to git the Minister to go. If he ain't doing right, let the officers see that he does do right; if he ain't a good man, let the church get together and pray for God to touch his sinful heart, and convert him. For after all, we are serving God,

not man. Men may come and men may go, but God stays forever.

SISTER INSTIGATOR   I see Sister Experience ain't with us in this fight. Of course I ain't never been in a church fight before, but I am in this one heart and hand.

SISTER MEDDLER   I think we ought to find out where Brother Procrastinator got his money from to buy that $7,000 house on 6th Street.

SISTER SAPPHIRA   Oh yes! I forgot that. That does seem funny when we poor creatures can't hardly get a crust of bread to eat; now, there's a charge agin him right there.

SISTER MEDDLER   That's so, I never thought of that. That is a good charge agin him.

BROTHER INVESTIGATOR   What's that, Sister Meddler?

SISTER SAPPHIRA   Why he bought a big house on 6th Street and paid a whole lot of money spot cash for it.

BROTHER INVESTIGATOR   Well what can you do about it? That was his own affair so long as he does not infringe on ours.

SISTER INSTIGATOR   I don't know why it ain't a charge against him. It gives our church a bad name to have the parson flashing money around like he was a rich man and then agin where did he git all that money anyway? I know Morning Glory Baptist Church didn't give it to him, because we only pay him $10 a week.

SISTER MEDDLER   He don't deserve but $5 a week.

BROTHER JUDAS *(looks out window)*   Sisters, here comes Brother Procrastinator now.

BROTHER INVESTIGATOR *(goes to door)*
Come in Parson Procrastinator, I am glad you came.

(PARSON PROCRASTINATOR enters with long Prince Albert coat, stove-pipe hat and gold-headed cane; a big gold watch chain is prominent)

PARSON PROCRASTINATOR   Yes, Brother Investigator, I just got back from Conference, and heard a church fight was on agin me and that they didn't want me to come back again another year. Now I am here; what charge have you all agin me? *(silence)*

BROTHER INVESTIGATOR   I just told them, Brother Procrastinator, that they would have to have some charge agin you.

PARSON PROCRASTINATOR   That's correct; now let me see who's here. *(puts on glasses; looks around)* Why here's my old friend who will die by me I know. Ain't that so Brother Judas?

BROTHER JUDAS   Oh yes, Parson, you can always depend on me.

SISTER EXPERIENCE   Parson Procrastinator, you know I am your friend; I told them there was no charge agin you but some of them said they had a charge.

PARSON PROCRASTINATOR   Had a charge aginst me? Now who was it who said so?

SISTER TAKE-IT BACK   It wasn't me, Brother Procrastinator, I've never seen nothing wrong out of you.

SISTER SAPPHIRA   I never said it, Parson.

PARSON PROCRASTINATOR   Well, somebody *must* have said it. Look it up in the minutes, Brother Investigator.

SISTER MEDDLER   I know who said it, 'cause I was looking right in their mouth when they said it.

SISTER SAPPHIRA   I know I never had no charge agin Brother Procrastinator 'cause I don't know nothing about him only something good.

SISTER TWO-FACE   Parson Procrastinator you do look so fine since you come back from Conference, and we is all just crazy about you.

BROTHER INVESTIGATOR   *(who has been searching minutes)*   It says here in the minutes that you bought a $7,000 house on 6th Street, but I failed to put down who said it.

PARSON PROCRASTINATOR   So that's it, is it? Well, I wants the one who said it, to git right up and tell me why they call it a "charge" agin me.

SISTER EXPERIENCE   Well I never said it but know who did say it. But it's none of my business.

PARSON PROCRASTINATOR   Yes it is your business, Sister Experience, you know from your past experience what it means to have a church fight. Now I want the one what said that charge to own it.

SISTER MEDDLER   I think it was sister,—

PARSON PROCRASTINATOR   That will do, Sister Meddler. We want the sister what said it to speak for herself and if she can't say last what she said first, she is a prevaricator by the law. Now Brother Investigator since nobody will own the charge agin me, just scratch it out, and I wants all them what's for me to stand, and Brother Investigator you count 'em.

BROTHER INVESTIGATOR   All what's in the favor of Parson Procrastinator staying with us this year, stand. *(all stand except* SISTER EXPERI-ENCE*)* What's your objection Sister Experience?

SISTER EXPERIENCE   I was just sitting here counting the liars.

PARSON PROCRASTINATOR   Well that will do. That vote is carried. If it is carried by liars, just put it down, Brother Investigator; and I will meet you all at prayer meeting Friday night. *(goes out)*

SISTER TWO-FACE   Ain't he a wonderful man. I don't think we could ever get another one like him.

SISTER INSTIGATOR   Well I had intended to tell him just what I thought of him if he had stayed.

BROTHER JUDAS   Well, he's a good man, and we can't afford to let him go.

SISTER SAPPHIRA   I said that in the first place. The trouble with our people is they never stop to think.

SISTER TAKE-IT-BACK   That's just it, Sister Sapphira. Now I thank God I've never said a harmful word agin the man in my life.

SISTER MEDDLER   *(who has been standing serenely all the time with a look of disgust on her face)*   You ought all to be ashamed of yourselves after starting all this fuss and then denying it. Never mind. I'm going to tell Parson Procrastinator.

SISTER TWO-FACE   I'm glad I didn't say a word agin him. You all know I always did love Parson Procrastinator. I was the one what gave him that gold pencil, but I didn't want everybody to know it.

SISTER EXPERIENCE   Sisters, do let us go home, before we defy the law any longer.

BROTHER INVESTIGATOR   Yes, all stand please, *(with uplifted hands)* Lord, smile down in tender mercies upon those who have lied, and those who have not lied, close their lips with the seal of forgiveness, stiffen their tongues with the rod of obedience, fill their ears with the gospel of truth, and direct Parson Procrastinator's feet toward the railroad track.

BROTHER JUDAS   *(in hard voice)*   "Amen."

(All break up in confusion each saying that PARSON PROCRASTINATOR *should be moved and they weren't going to put up with him. Curtain)*

UNDERTOW

1929

Eulalie Spence (1894–1981)

Born in Nevis, British West Indies, Eulalie Spence came to the United States through Ellis Island in 1902 at the age of eight with her mother, four sisters, and father, whose livelihood as a sugar planter had been destroyed by a hurricane. The family first lived in Harlem on 135th Street and Fifth Avenue and later moved to Brooklyn, where they weathered poverty. Spence said in an interview, "One of the interesting things about our survival was that we didn't know we were poor and unfortunate. My mother insisted that we were very important people."[1] She graduated from New York City's Wadleigh High School and the New York Training School for Teachers, then received her B.A. from New York University in 1937 and her M.A. from Columbia Teachers College in 1939, where she studied playwriting with Hughes Hatcher. She was perhaps the only playwright of the Harlem Renaissance to formally attend classes in dramatic structure,

and her work shows it. Spence is easily the best craftswoman in the group of writers included here. In June 1928, she wrote in *Opportunity* magazine:

> Unfortunately, almost everyone thinks that he can write a play. Writers will grant the poet his form and the novelist his; the essayist his mould, and the writer of short story his. However, when it comes to the play, why—one merely takes one's pen in hand and presto! We have dialogue! . . . To every art its form, thank God! And to the play, the technique that belongs to it!

Eulalie Spence never married. She earned her living as a teacher of English, elocution, and dramatics at Eastern District High School in Brooklyn. There, according to Joseph Papp, one of her former students and founder/director of the New York Shakespeare Festival, Miss Spence "scrubbed his tongue" of its Brooklyn accent and made him articulate enough to act in the theatre.

Her discipline and drive for precision extended to the contents of the plays she directed, produced, and wrote.

---

1. Eulalie Spence interview, audiotape 8/22/73, Hatch-Billops Collection, New York City.

May I advise these earnest few—those seekers after light—white lights—to avoid the drama of propaganda if they would not meet with certain disaster? Many a serious aspirant for dramatic honors has fallen by the wayside because he would insist on his lynchings or his rape. The white man is cold and unresponsive to this subject, and the Negro himself is hurt and humiliated by it. We go to the theatre for entertainment, not to have old fires and hates rekindled.

Her distaste for propaganda plays set her apart from many of the African American playwrights of her time and caused her some difficulty with W.E.B. Du Bois, who favored using the stage to address the "race problem." Nonetheless, the Krigwa Players (the Crisis Guild of Writers and Artists), founded by Du Bois to create theatre, by, for, about, and near Negroes, elected to perform Spence's comedy, *Fool's Errand,* a lively one-act play about "righteous" church sisters who insist that a young man marry his girlfriend because they falsely believe she is pregnant. The Krigwa Players took the production "downtown" to the Frolic Theatre for the National Little Theatre Tournament of 1927, where it won second prize and a cash award; however, the comedy "didn't suit" Du Bois, who had preferred a "race" play with more serious subject. In addition, he claimed that the $200 prize belonged to the Krigwa Players, not to the playwright.

Spence found time to write fourteen plays, of which six were published and possibly seven produced.[2] Her first play, *Foreign Mail* won her second place in *The Crisis* playwriting contest, and she won second prize for *The Hunch* in the *Opportunity* magazine contest. In the Krigwa production of Spence's *Her,* Theophilus Lewis, drama critic for *The Messenger,* noted: "This is just the kind of actor material the Negro theater requires for chances are ten to one it will have to rest on a repertory basis. . . . Some of the acting can be applauded without reservation." Lewis goes on to praise the acting of Eulalie's sister Olga. Another sister, Doralyn, took over Rose McClendon's role in *Abraham's Bosom* at the Cherry Lane Theatre in 1927.

Spence wrote one full-length movie script, *The Whipping,* for Paramount Studios. She was paid for her work although the script was never filmed. Nearly all her plays are comedies, with the exception of *Her, La Divina Pastora* and *Undertow.* At first glance, *Undertow* seems to be about a man who failed to follow his heart and married the "wrong" woman. On closer inspection, however, we see that his wife is obsessed with the other woman's lighter color and feels that her own darkness is ugly. Although the wife is not driven mad by her blackness (as is the woman in Zora Neale Hurston's *Color Struck*), she does destroy the lives of her husband and his true love. Spence used race in her plays not for propaganda purposes but for plot motivation.

Eulalie Spence acted, she coached, she directed, she wrote theatre criticism, she wrote plays, and she taught her students to love the theatre.

---

2. Professor Kathy Perkins of the University of Illinois has located all of Spence's plays except *Foreign Mail.*

Undertow

Persons in the Play

DAN, *the man*
HATTIE, *the man's wife*
CHARLEY, *their son*
CLEM, *the other woman*
MRS. WILKES, *a lodger*

SCENE *Harlem. The dining room in* HATTIE's *private house. It is a cheerful room, never sunny, but well furnished and spotless from shining floor to snowy linen. The supper dishes have been cleared away, but the table is still set for one who did not appear. Double doors opening upon the hall are at center back. At right there is a door leading to the kitchen. At the left there are two windows facing the street.*

TIME *About 8 o'clock one winter's night.*

AT RISE HATTIE *is sitting at the head of the table frowning heavily at the place of the one who did not appear. She drums impatiently with her fingers for a few seconds then pushing her chair back with more violence than grace, rises.* HATTIE's *dark face is hard and cold. She has a disconcerting smile—a little contempt and a great deal of distrust. Her body is short and spreads freely in every direction. Her dark dress is covered by an apron which makes her look somewhat clumsy.* CHARLEY, *dressed in an overcoat and hat of the latest mode bursts noisily into the room. He is a slender fellow, about the same complexion of his mother, but possessing none of her strength of character. His good-looking face is weak, with a suggestion of stubbornness about it. His manner is arrogant and somewhat insolent)*

CHARLEY   Ah'm off, Ma.

HATTIE   So Ah see.

CHARLEY *(his glance falls on the table)*   Say, Ma—Gee whiz! Ain't Dad bin home fer supper yet?

HATTIE *(shortly)*   No.

CHARLEY *(with a low whistle)*   Dat's funny, he ain't never stayed out befo' has he?

HATTIE   Not sence Ah married him—'cept—

CHARLEY *(curiously)*   'Cept whut, Ma?

HATTIE   'Cept wunce 'fo yuh was born.

CHARLEY *(with an uproarious laugh)*   An' the old man ain't tried it sence! Reckon yuh fixed him, didn't yuh, Ma! *(he sits down beside the table and laughs once more)*

HATTIE *(sharply)*   Ah ain't trained yuh half's as well's Ah's trained yo' Dad. *(she resumes her seat)* Ah shoulda made yuh stay in school fer one thing.

CHARLEY   Yuh had mo' sense Ma! If yuh'd a bossed me lak yuh's bossed Dad, Ah'd runned away long 'fo now.

HATTIE   That ain't no danger uh Dan runnin' off. He ain't got de nerve. Sides, nobuddy'd want him.

CHARLEY   Now doan' fool yuhself, Ma! An easy simp lak Dad'd be snapped up soon 'nuff ef he ever got it intuh his head dat he could do sech a thing.

HATTIE   Dan's a fool, but he knows which side his bread's buttered on.

CHARLEY *(giving his thigh a loud slap)*   Holy smoke!

HATTIE *(irritably)*   Whut's eatin' yuh?

CHARLEY   Nuthin'.

HATTIE *(impatiently)*   Never mind lyin'! Whut's on yuh mind?

CHARLEY   Oh, nuthin'! Ah jes' thought er sumpth'n dat's all. Say, Ma—

HATTIE   Well?

CHARLEY   Ah gotta have five bucks ternight,—Need 'em bad.

HATTIE   It doan do no harm tuh need 'em. Thar's a plenty things Ah's wanted dat Ah ain't never got.

CHARLEY *(roughly)*   Where the devil do yuh think Ah kin git it, ef Ah doan ask yuh?

HATTIE   Yuh might wuk 'cassionally. Dan ain't bin home a day dese twenty-five years.

CHARLEY *(with a sneer)*   An' yuh's jes' done callin' him a fool, ain't yuh? The guys in mah crowd doan do no work see? We lives by our brains.

HATTIE   Not by exercisin' 'em, Lawd knows!

CHARLEY   How come yuh think we hits de number ev'y week! Brain work!

HATTIE   Ef yuh hits so often whut yuh allus comin' ter me 'bout money fer?

CHARLEY   Ef dat ain't lak a woman! It takes money ter make money!

HATTIE   Charley, yuh's gotta cut out dis gamblin'. Ah ain't goin' give yuh no mo' money.

CHARLEY   (*insolently*)   Yuh think Ah'm Dad, doan' yuh? Well, Ah ain't! Ah wish ter Gawd Ah knew whut yuh's got over on him. No free man would er stood yuh naggin' all dese years.

HATTIE   (*coldly*)   Dem whut can't stan' fer mah ways knows whut dey kin do.

CHARLEY   Wouldn't 'sprise me none ef Dad has walked off—

HATTIE   (*quickly*)   Whut makes yuh think so?

CHARLEY   Reckon yu'd like tuh know, wouldn't yuh?

HATTIE   'Tain't likely whut yuh could say's wurth five dollars tuh hear.

CHARLEY   Whut Ah seen wouldn't ah bin wuth nuthin' las' week, but sence Dad ain't showed up, fer supper, it's wuth a damn sight mo'. Yuh's never guess whut Ah seen him doin' one night las' week up on Lenox Avenue.

HATTIE   Well, yuh might's well say it. Yuh kin have dat five, but lemme tell yuh dat yuh'll be de loser, later, if yuh's lied tuh me.

CHARLEY   What Ah's gotta lie fer? (*he stretches his hand across the table, palm upturned*) Hand it over, Ma. (HATTIE *takes a bill, from her stocking and puts it on the table, beside her. She places her closed fist upon the money.* CHARLEY *frowns and draws his hand back*)

HATTIE   Ah ain't never refused tuh pay fer whut Ah gits.

CHARLEY   Oh, all right. Here goes. Me an' Nat Walker was strollin' up Lenox Avenue one night las' week 'bout half past six. Right ahead uh me Ah seen Dad. He was walkin' 'long, slow ez usual wid his head bent, not seein' nobuddy. All uv a sudden, a woman comin' down de Avenue, went up tuh him an' stops him. He looked up kinda dazed like an' stared at her lak he'd seen a ghost. She jes' shook him by de arm an' laughed. By dat time, we come along side an' Ah got a good look at her. She warn't young an' she warn't old. But she looked—well—As jes' doan know how she did look—all laughin' an' happy an' tears in her eyes. Ah didn't look at her much fer starin' at Dad. He looked—all shaken up— an' scared like—Not scared like neither fer Ah seen him smile at her, after a minute. He

ain't never smiled lak that befo'—not's Ah kin remember. Nat said—"Reckin yuh Dad's met an' ole gal 'er his"—But Ah only laughed— Struck me kinda funny—that! Dad meetin' an' ole gal 'er his—Ah meant tuh ask Dad 'bout her but it went clean outa mah head. (*he reaches once more for the money. This time he takes it easily, enough.* HATTIE *has forgotten it*)

HATTIE   (*after a pause*)   Was she tall?

CHARLEY   Kinda. Plenty taller'n you. (*he rises and takes his hat from the table*)

HATTIE   (*after a pause*)   Light?

CHARLEY   So—So,—lighter'n you. (*he moves toward the door*)

HATTIE   Pretty?

CHARLEY   Mebbe. She warn't no chicken— but she was good tuh look at. Tain't no use mopin', Ma. Dad ain't de fus' husban' tuh take dinner wid his girl friend. Funny, though his never doin' it befo'. Well, s'long!

(*He goes out and the door slams noisily.* HATTIE *rouses up at that and starts clearing the table. She has just left the room with the last handful of dishes when the hall door is opened quietly and* DAN *enters. He is a dark man of medium height, slender of build. He looks a little stooped. There is a beaten look about his face—a tired, patient look. He takes off his overcoat and still stands there hesitating.* HATTIE *re-enters, frowns darkly but does not speak. She places a scarf upon the table and a little silver-plated basket from the sideboard*)

DAN   (*dropping his coat and hat upon a chair*) Sorry, Ah'm late, Hattie. (*she does not answer*) Ah ain't had no supper. Reckon Ah'll get it an' eat in de kitchen.

HATTIE   (*icily*)   Reckon yuh'll hang dat coat an' hat in de hall whar dey belongs.

DAN   (*apologetically*)   Sure. Dunno how Ah come tuh ferget. (*he goes out with his clothes and returns almost immediately. He looks timidly at* HATTIE, *then passes on toward the kitchen door*)

HATTIE   (*fiercely*)   Keep outa dat kitchen!

DAN   But Ah'm hungry, Hattie. Ah ain't had nuthin' tuh eat.

HATTIE   Whar yuh bin, dat yur ain't had nuthin 'tuh eat? (DAN *doesn't answer*) Yuh kain't say, kin yuh?

DAN   Ah went tuh see a friend uh mine.

HATTIE   Half past six ain't callin' hours! (DAN *looks unhappily at the floor*) Less'n yuh's asked ter dine!

DAN   It was important! Ah had tuh go.

HATTIE   Had tuh go whar? Yuh ain't said whar yuh's bin. (DAN *does not answer*) An yuh ain't got no intention uh saying, has yuh? (DAN *does not answer. He moves once more toward the kitchen*)

HATTIE *(in a shrill voice)*   Yuh keep outa thar! Keep outa mah kitchen! Ah kep yuh supper till eight o'clock. Yuh didn' come, an Ah's throwed it out!

DAN   Ah'll fix sumpth'n else. Ah doan want much.

HATTIE   Yuh ain't goin' messin' in mah kitchen! Yuh's hidin' sumpth'n, Dan Peters, and Ah's gwine fine it out 'fo' long. Yuh ain't gonna throw no dust in mah eyes no second time—not ef Ah knows it!

DAN   All right, Ah doan' want no fuss, Hattie. Ah'll go out an' git sumpth'n.

HATTIE   Yuh kin fix de furnace 'fo' yuh go. Ah's got 'nuff tuh do runnin' a lodgin' house, 'thout fixin' fires day an' night.

DAN   Charley was home. Yuh coulda asked Charley tuh do it.

HATTIE   Charley doan' never fix no furnace. It's yo' job when yuh's home an' Ah ain't got no reason tuh wish it on Charley.

DAN   Ah'll fix it when Ah gits back. Ah'm hungry, now an' Ah's gwine tuh git sumpth'n tuh eat.

(He goes out. HATTIE *listens for the click of the iron gate, then hurries to the window and peers after him. The door is opened softly and a little brown woman sidles in. Her eyes rove constantly always seeking—seeking.* HATTIE *turns around and glares fiercely at her)*

HATTIE   What yuh want?

MRS. WILKES *(startled slightly at the grimness of the other's voice)*   Ah declare, Mis' Peters, yuh sho' does look put out! Anything de matter?

HATTIE *(shortly)*   Did yuh come down here tuh tell me dat?

MRS. WILKES *(with an uneasy laugh)*   C'ose not, Mis' Peters! . . . It's pretty cold upstairs. Ah s'pose de fire's goin' ez usual?

HATTIE   Yes.

MRS. WILKES   It's gettin' colder, Ah reckon. (HATTIE *does not answer*) It's warmer down here. As Ah always tells Mr. Wilkes, gimme a parlor floor an' basement any time. Ef thar's any heat goin' yuh's sure tuh git it—Co'se, Ah ain't complainin', Mis' Peters——

HATTIE   H'm!

MRS. WILKES   See Mr. Peters got home pretty late tuh-night, didn't he? (HATTIE *answers only with a venomous glance*) Thar's a man with reg'lar habits. Ah often tells Mr. Wilkes dat Ah wish tuh goodness he was a home lovin' man lak Mr. Peters. . . . Well, reckon Ah'll be gwine up again' seein' ez yuh's got comp'ny.

HATTIE *(with a puzzled frown)*   Comp'ny?

MRS. WILKES   Thar's a lady tuh see yuh. She's upstairs settin' in de parlor.

HATTIE   Who let her in?

MRS. WILKES   Mr. Wilkes did. He seen her on de stoop. She was jes' gwine tuh ring de bell when Mr. Wilkes come up wid his key. She ask tuh see Mis' Peters an' he told her tuh set in de parlor. Ef that's ever a stupid man it sure is mah husban'. 'Stead uh goin' down an tellin' yuh, 'er hollerin' tuh yuh, 'er sendin' her on down, he comes up-stairs an' tells *me* ter go down an' tell yuh. He'd oughta sent her down de basement do' fust place.

HATTIE   Send her down, will yuh? Some fine day, Ah 'spec we'll be cleaned out, ef yuh all's gwine let strangers in de house that 'a way.

MRS. WILKES *(with a little cough)*   Thought yuh might want tuh see her in de parlor. Ah reckon she ain't no thief, not judgin' from her looks.

HATTIE   H'h! Whut she look lak?

MRS. WILKES   She's tall—but not too tall.

HATTIE *(forcing her stiffening lips to move)* Light?

MRS. WILKES   Lighter'n yuh an' me—

HATTIE *(with a supreme effort)*   Pretty?

MRS. WILKES   Well, yuh knows her all right! She ain't never bin here befo' ez Ah knows— but yuh knows her frum de way yuh's 'scribed her. Well, 'slong! Ah'll send her down. *(she opens the hall door)* B'r! *(she shivers)* Dis hall cert'nly is cold!

(The door closes after her. For a moment HATTIE *looks bewildered. but only for a moment. With a sudden harsh laugh she rips the apron from about her waist and pushes it quickly into the side-board drawer. She goes up to the mirror over the mantle, but one look at herself is all that she can bear. As she turns sharply away the door opens and* CLEM *enters. In one glance* HATTIE'*s burning eyes take in the tall, well-dressed figure. The graying hair, the*

youthful face. If CLEM's *glance is less piercing, it is nevertheless, just as comprehensive)*

CLEM *(softly)*   It's bin a long time, Hattie. (HATTIE *opens her lips to speak, but she doesn't. She sits, rather heavily, and continues to stare at* CLEM) Ah doan' wonder yuh's 'sprised Hattie. *(She hesitates and then drawing up a chair facing* HATTIE, *she too, sits)* Ah know yuh's waitin' tuh hear whut brought me . . . It's a long story, Hattie. *(at that,* HATTIE *moves impatiently)*

HATTIE   Yuh kin start—at de end—

CLEM   At de end?

HATTIE   At de end. Whut yuh come fer? Yuh's come ter git sumpth'n—Is it—Dan?

CLEM *(leaning back in her chair with a sigh)* De same ole Hattie! De years ain't changed yuh, none.

HATTIE *(with a bitter laugh)*   An' de years ain't changed *you*, none.

CLEM   Yes. Ah reckon they has, Hattie, Ah's suffered a-plenty.

HATTIE *(with a curl of her lip)*   An' yuh think dat yuh's de only one?

CLEM   Oh no! Ah kin see yuh's not bin over happy, Hattie, an' Ah knows dat Dan ain't bin happy.

HATTIE   Whut reason yuh got ter bring up all dis talk 'bout suff'rin'? Yuh bin seein' Dan agin', ain't yuh?

CLEM   Yes. Ah met him jes' by accident one night las' week.

HATTIE   An' yuh's bin seein' him sence?

CLEM   Yes, ev'y night. Ah's bein' gwine down town ter meet him 'roun six o'clock an' Ah's ride home wid him in de "L."

HATTIE   An' tuh-night yuh had him out tuh dinner. (HATTIE's *voice has a deadly calm)*

CLEM   No. Tuh-night Ah couldn' go tuh meet him. Ah was called away on business. Ah ain't seen him tuh-night.

HATTIE   Did he know yuh was comin' here?

CLEM   No.

HATTIE   Why'nt yuh tell him, yuh was comin'.

CLEM   He wouldn' 'er let me come.

HATTIE   Well, say whut yuh's come fer, an' go. It ain't easy settin' here an' listenin' tuh yuh talkin' 'bout Dan.

CLEM *(abruptly)*   Yuh's almost driv' him crazy. An' yuh said yuh loved him. (HATTIE's *fingers clench slowly)*

HATTIE   Whar'd yuh go to? Whar you bin all dese years?

CLEM   South—Virginia, whar I come frum.

HATTIE   H'm!

CLEM   Ef Ah'd knowed yuh was gwine tuh be unkind tuh him, Ah'd never let him go! Dan ain't knowed a day's happiness sence Ah went away.

HATTIE   He—he tole yuh dat?

CLEM   Yes! Ah kin fergive yuh fer takin' him 'way frum me—an' de way yuh done it—but it ain't easy fergivin' yuh fer makin' him suffer.

HATTIE   An' dat's whut yuh's come here tuh tell me?

CLEM *(passionately)*   Dan's dyin' here, right under yo' eyes, an' yo' doan' see it. He's dyin' fer kindness—He's dyin' frum hard wuk. He's dyin' frum de want uv love. Ah could allus read him lak a book. He won't talk 'gainst yuh, Hattie, but Ah kin see it all in de way he looks—in de way he looks at me. (CLEM *dabs at her eyes with her handkerchief)*

HATTIE   Go on. *(she marvels at her own quietness)*

CLEM *(accusingly)*   He's shabby—all uv him—hat an' shoes an coat. Ef he had one suit fer ev'y five dat yuh son has, he'd be pretty well dressed.

HATTIE *(slowly)*   Yuh fergit, Charley is Dan's son ez well ez mine.

CLEM   An' yuh's set him 'gainst his dad. He sides with yuh ev'y time, doan' he?

HATTIE *(with a faint sneer)*   Did yuh read dat too, in de way Dan—looked—at yuh?

CLEM   Ef yuh had a brought Charley up dif-f'rent yuh mighta held on tuh Dan. 'Stead uh dat, yuh's brought him up tuh look down on him.

HATTIE *(she is breathing heavily, her voice comes thick and choked)*   Is yuh tru? *(rises)*

CLEM   Yuh doan' need Dan an yo' son doan' need him. Well, sence yuh ain't got no use fer him, Ah's gwine take him frum yuh, Hattie. Now yuh knows why Ah's come. *(she rises also and looks down at* HATTIE, *much to the latter's disadvantage)*

HATTIE *(forcing the words out, as though each one pains her)*   Funny—how—thoughtful yuh's got sence Ah's las' seen yuh. Yuh come inta mah house twenty years ago as a frien'—an' yuh took Dan when Ah hadn't bin married ter him a year. Yuh didn' give no 'nouncement den 'bout whut yuh was gwine ter do. Yuh jes' took him—an' me expectin' tuy be de mother uv his chile. Gawd! *(a deep shudder runs through her body)* but now—dat yuh's got mo' stylish—mo' lady-like in yuh ways yuh come tuh tell me ve'y politely, dat yuh's gwine tuh take him again. Is it mah blessin' yuh's waitin' fer? Yuh doan' need no permission.

CLEM   Yuh, yuh doan' un'erstan'—Yuh never did un'erstan' Hattie.

HATTIE   Mebbe not. Some things is hard tuh un'erstan'.

CLEM   Co'se Dan an' me could go off tergether, 'thout yuh permission Yuh knows dat well 'nuff. It's bein' done ev'y day. But we doan' want ter go lak dat.

HATTIE   Yuh mean Dan doan' want ter go that 'a-way!

CLEM   Yuh's wrong, Hattie. Dan ain't thinkin' 'er nuthin' 'er nobuddy but me. He's fer quittin' an' never sayin' a word tuh yuh but jes' goin' off, me an' him together. But Ah ain't gwine tuh go lak dat. Dis time it's gotta be diff'rent.

HATTIE   Diff'rent—how?

CLEM   Hattie, Ah wants yuh tuh free Dan. Yuh owes it tuh him. He ain't never bin free sence he's knowed yuh. Will yuh free him?

HATTIE   Free him—how?

CLEM   Give him a divo'ce.

HATTIE   A divo'ce.

HATTIE   A divo'ce—tuh marry you?

CLEM   *(pleadingly)*   Yes. 'Tain't lak yuh loved him Hattie. Ef yuh loved him Ah couldn' ask yuh. But yuh only holds onta him tru spite—Yuh hates him, mebbe—Yuh treats him lak yuh does.

HATTIE   Yuh knows Ah kain't keep him ef he wants tuh go. Reckon Ah knows it, too. Well, ef he wants tuh go he kin go.

CLEM   *(with an exclamation of relief)*   Thank Gawd! Ah didn' think yuh'd do it, Hattie.

HATTIE   Yuh coulda spared yuhself de trubble comin' here—an jes' gone off. It woulda bin more lak yuh.

CLEM   But—but—how? Yuh'd have ter know 'bout de devo'ce, Hattie.

HATTIE   Devo'ce? Ah ain't said nuthin' 'bout gettin' no devo'ce!

CLEM   But—but—yuh—Ah thought—Whut yuh mean, Hattie?

HATTIE   Yuh didn' need no devo'ce de fust time, did yuh?

CLEM   *(biting her lips to keep back the tears)* Dat—Dat was diff'rent.

HATTIE   Ah doan' see it.

CLEM   Well, it was. It's gotta be a divo'ce dis time.

HATTIE   Ah see Dan's morals has improved some sence *you* went away.

CLEM   It ain't Dan whut's holdin' out fer devo'ce—It's—it's me.

HATTIE   (HATTIE's *laugh has a bitter edge)* Den it's yo' morals dat's bin improvin'—Well, dey could stan' improvin' a-plenty. *(the fierce edge returns suddenly to her voice)* Yuh's wastin' yo' time an' mine an Dan's! 'Bout lettin' him go—He coulda gone all dese years—Ah warn't holdin' him back! He'd gone too, ef he'd knowed whar to find yuh. Ah knowed ef he ever found yuh, he'd leave me. Well, he didn' find yuh tell now. But long's Ah's got breaf tuh breathe, Ah ain't gwine say "Yes!" 'bout no divo'ce. Ef he kin git one 'thout me, let him git it! Yuh hear me? Now ef yuh's tru, yuh better get outa here. Ah ain't 'sponsible' fer whut Ah says frum now on!

CLEM   Hattie, 'fore Gawd, yuh's hard!

HATTIE   Ah was soft 'nuff, when yuh fust stepped on me. Ef Ah's hard now, 'tis yo' fault!

CLEM   Hattie—Ah ain't tole yuh de real reason why Ah wants dat di'voce—*(a note of despair has crept into her voice)*

HATTIE   No? Well, Ah ain't in'trested none.

CLEM   Still Ah wants yuh tuh hear! It's sumpthin' dat Ah ain't tole Dan. *The door is opened quietly and* DAN *enters. He starts—looks fearfully from* CLEM *to* HATTIE *and then back again to* CLEM) Come in, Dan. Ah hope yuh doan' mind ma comin' tuh see Hattie. Ah jes' had tuh come.

DAN   *(swallowing painfully)*   It won' do no good. (HATTIE *is gazing at him curiously)*

CLEM   Mebbe not, but Ah had tuh come.

DAN   Ah'm sorry, Hattie. We—we—*(he turns away as if ashamed)*

CLEM   Hattie knows ev'ything Dan. Ah's tole her. (DAN *turns toward her)*

DAN   Clem, whut was yuh sayin' when Ah come on in? Ah heard yuh—

CLEM   *(embarrassed)*   Ah didn' want tuh tell yuh—lak dis—

DAN   *(gently)*   We kain't go back now, Clem. Sence we's in de middle we's gotta git tru, somehow.

CLEM (*turning from him to* HATTIE)   Ah didn' mean tuh beg, 'less'n Ah had tuh—

HATTIE (*coldly*)   Yuh doan' have tuh—

CLEM   Ef 'twas only me—but it ain't. It's fer mah Lucy,—Dan's chile (*there is a terrible silence*) Dan's chile—Ah didn' tell yuh, Hattie, an' Ah didn' tell Dan. Whut woulda bin de use? She's a woman now an' good—an' pretty. She thinks her dad died when she was a baby an' she thinks—she thinks—Ah'm a good woman. She's proud uh me. (*as if unconscious of* HATTIE'*s presence,* DAN *grips* CLEM'*s hands. They look at each other*)

HATTIE (*as if to herself. She seems to be trying to get it all quite clear*)   She thinks yuh's a good woman! An' dat's why yuh expects me tuh give Dan a divo'ce.

CLEM (*eagerly*)   Yes, Yes! Yuh see, doan' yuh?

HATTIE   Yes, Ah see. Gawd, ef dat ain't funny! She thinks yuh's a good woman. (*she laughs loudly,—hysterically*)   Oh, my Gawd!

DAN (*sharply*)   Hattie!

HATTIE *ignoring him*   Tell me mo'—'bout dis—dis new relation, uh Dan's.

CLEM   Ah's wuked hard tuh git her de chances Ah didn' have. She's bin tuh school—she's got an' eddication. An' now she's goin' tuh git married tuh a fine feller whut'll be able tuh take care uv her. Now yuh see dat Ah kain't jes' go off wid Dan. It's got tuh be proper—a divo'ce an' all. Yuh see, doan' yuh, Hattie?

HATTIE (*nodding*)   Mother an' daughter— double weddin'.

CLEM (*anxiously*)   An yuh'll do it, Hattie? Gawd'll bless yuh, Hattie.

HATTIE (*derisively*)   How come *you's* passin' on blessins? Yuh knows a lot, doan' yuh 'bout blessins? Wonder ef yuh knows ez much 'bout curses?

CLEM   Now, Hattie—

HATTIE (*darkly*)   Yuh doan know nuthin' much 'bout curses, does yuh? Well, yuh's cursed, Clem Jackson! Cursed! Yuh's allus bin cursed sence de day yuh cast yuh eyes on Dan!

DAN (*harshly*)   Hattie, yuh, ain't got no call tuh go on lak dat.

HATTIE (*who does not seem to hear him*)   Dan was cursed when he set eyes on yuh. An' Ah was cursed when Ah took yuh fer a frien'.

CLEM (*hurriedly*)   Ah'm goin', Hattie! Ah see yuh ain't gwine give in.

HATTIE   Whut's yuh hurry? Yuh better hear whut Ah's gwine tuh say . . . Curses. Yes, we's all bin cursed, Clem. Mah Charley's cursed an' yo' Lucy—too bad.

CLEM (*angrily*)   Doan' yuh call mah Lucy's name 'long uv yours.

HATTIE (*with a sneer*)   Too bad. Wonder how she'll feel when she hears whut a good woman yuh is?

CLEM (*shrinking as if from a blow*)   Whut? Yuh—yuh wouldn'—yuh wouldn'—

HATTIE   Wouldn'—wouldn'—(*she laughs again—crazily*) Sure, Ah'll fine her! Ef it takes de rest uh mah life, Ah'll fine her. It's too good—tuh keep. How she'll stare when she knows her ma was a prostitute an' her dad—

DAN (*hoarsely*)   Damn yuh, Hattie! Doan yuh say no mo'.

HATTIE   Ah'll tell her all—all—leavin' out nuthin'.

CLEM (*pleading as if for life*)   Yuh couldn', Hattie! Yuh couldn'! Hattie—Hattie—

HATTIE   How she play me false—when Ah trusted her—an' how she lie tuh me—How she ruin' mah life—an' come on back tuh take de leavin's once more—

DAN   Doan yuh say no mo, Hattie!

HATTIE   Yuh'd shut mah mouf' wouldn' yuh? How? How—

DAN   Let's go, Clem. Let's go—

HATTIE (*shrilly*)   G'wan. Is Ah keepin' yuh? Take yuh street walker back whar she come frum. Yuh kin give Lucy mah regahds. Tell her dat a frien's gwine call on her—real soon— an' ole frien' uv her ma's.

DAN (*with a cry of rage, grips Hattie by the shoulder and shakes her*)   Yoh'll shut yo' mouf, Hattie. Promise, 'er fo' Gawd-A-Mighty.

HATTIE (*scornfully*)   How yuh's thinkin' 'er shuttin' mah mouf, Dan Peters?

DAN   Yuh'll keep 'way frum Lucy. Yuh'll promise not tuh say nuthin' 'bout Clem. (DAN *shakes her again roughly*)

HATTIE (*her speech broken with little gasping cries*)   Never! An' yuh kain't make me! Ah'll tell her 'bout dis good woman! Dis thief! Dis dirty minded whore! (*without a word,* DAN *grips her by the throat and forces her back—back against the table. Her arms claw awkwardly and then drop to her sides.* CLEM *utters a low cry and springs upon* DAN, *tearing wildly at his fingers.*)

CLEM   Dan! Leggo! Leggo, fer Gawd's sake! Dan! (*with a violent movement of disgust he thrusts* HATTIE *from him. She falls heavily from the chair, her head striking the marble base of the mantle—an ugly sound. She lies very still.* DAN *looks at her stupidly.* CLEM *throws her arms about his neck, sobbing hysterically)* Dan! Dan! Yuh come near killin' her!

DAN *(breathing heavily)*   Ah'd a done it too, ef yuh hadn't bin thar.

CLEM *(stooping over* HATTIE)   She hit her head an awful crack!

DAN   Hattie's head's harder'n mos'. Come on, Clem. We kain't stay here, now. She'll be comin' to, 'fo' long! An raisin' de roof.

CLEM *(who is still peering at* HATTIE)   Dan, thar's blood comin' out de corner uv her mouf.

DAN   She'll be waggin' it again' fo' yuh knows it.

CLEM *(going up to* DAN *and putting her hand on his shoulder)*   Dan, Ah wish yuh hadn't done it! 'Twon' do no good!

DAN   Ah couldn' stan' it no longer. Ah clean los' mah head when she call yuh—whut she did.

CLEM   Yes, Ah know. Poor Danny boy! Ah doan see how yuh's stood it all dese years.

DAN *(putting his arms about her)*   Ah was allus thinkin' uv yuh, Clem. Yuh shouldn' 'a lef' me behin'. Yuh'd oughta tole me whar tuh fine yuh. Yuh shoulda tole me 'bout Lucy.

CLEM   Yes, Ah see dat now. But yuh b'longed tuh Hattie 'n Ah thought—

DAN   Ah never b'longed tuh Hattie. *(he kisses her)* Let's go, Clem. *(she draws away from him)* Why, whut's wrong?

CLEM   Ah's gotta think uh Lucy.

DAN   Lucy?

CLEM   Yes, Lucy. She's yo' chile Dan, an' she doan' know—'bout us.

DAN   An' me—Whut 'bout me, an you—Clem—Clem—

CLEM   Ah you musn'. Then thar's Hattie. Yuh's gotta think uv Hattie—*(they both turn and look at the figure huddled there on the floor)* Dan, we'd better try'n bring her to. Get some water, Dan.

DAN   Ah won't touch her!

CLEM   It ain't human leavin' her lak dat. Help me lif' her, Dan. She'll catch her death uh cold on dat flo'! *(very unwillingly* DAN *assists. Together he and* CLEM *get* HATTIE *into a*

chair. Her head lolls persistently to one side. CLEM *rubs her hands)* Lak ice! Why, Dan, her fingers all stiff! An'—an' Dan! Feel her pulse! Dan!

(She draws back terrified. HATTIE's *body, unsupported, sags awkwardly against the table.* DAN *quickly seizes her hands, feeling her pulse. He tilts her head backward, looks into her face—feels her heart, then straightens up—his face distorted, his eyes blank.)*

CLEM *(in a whisper)*   Dan—she ain't—dead?

DAN   Dead. *(he looks down at his hands in horror)*

CLEM *(wildly)*   Dan! Whut'll we do! Whut'll we do!

DAN   Yuh'll go back tuh Lucy. She needs yuh.

CLEM   You needs me mo', Dan!

DAN   Yuh kain't help none! Ah doan stan' no chance—reckon Ah owes it tuh Lucy tuh send yuh back tuh her. Ah ain't never had de chance tuh do nuthin' fer her—but dis.

CLEM   Ah kain't go, Dan! Doan' mek me. *(her body is wracked with sobs)*

DAN *(taking her in his arms and kissing her)* We's gotta think 'bout Lucy—We're brung each other bad luck, Clem. Hattie was right.

CLEM   But Ah loved yuh Dan, an' yuh loved me.

DAN   Ah ain't never loved nobuddy else.

CLEM   Whut'll dey do tuh yuh Dan? Dey won't kill yuh? *(she clings tightly to him)* Will dey, Dan?

DAN   Co'se not, Honey! Reckon Ah'll git twenty—er fifteen years—mebbe ten—*(he buttons her coat and draws her firmly toward the door)*

CLEM   Ten years! *(she wrings her hands with a low moaning cry)*

DAN   Ah'll spend 'em all dreamin' 'bout yuh, Clem, an'—an' Lucy! Yuh musn' grieve, Honey. Go, now, fer Gawd's sake! Ah hears sombuddy comin' down! *(he pushes her out, forcibly. And then the door is shut. The outer door slams.* DAN *listens for the click of the gate. Finally he turns and looks down at* HATTIE) Ah'm sorry, Hattie! 'Fore Gawd, Ah didn' mean tuh do it!

[Curtain]

THE PURPLE FLOWER
1928

Marita Odette (Occomy) Bonner (1898–1971)

Born to Joseph Andrew and Mary Anne (Noel) Bonner, Marita Odette Bonner was raised in Boston, the youngest of three children.[1] Attending the Brookline schools, her talent for writing was recognized in high school, and by special arrangement, she was able to attend the writing classes of Charles Townsend Copeland at nearby Radcliffe College. In 1918, she enrolled at Radcliffe and participated in the English and music clubs, and also gained fluency in German, which may have been a major influence on her playwriting.

While still in college, she taught in nearby Cambridge High School; after her graduation in 1922, she moved to Washington, D.C., to teach at Armstrong High School. In *The Crisis* of December 1925, she published her prize-winning essay "On *Being Young—a Woman—and Colored,*" which revealed her to be a passionate and sensitive artist.

> "In Heaven's name, do not grow bitter. Be bigger than they are," exhort white friends who have never had to draw breath in a Jim Crow train. Who have never had petty putrid insult dragged over them—like pebbled sand on your body where the skin is tenderest.
>
> You long to explode and hurt everything white; friendly; unfriendly. But you know that you cannot live with a chip on your shoulder. . . . For chips make you bend your body to balance them. And once you bend, you lose your poise; you balance and the chip gets into you. The real you. You get hard. So—being a woman—you can wait.

Marita Bonner would write more than twenty pieces of fiction (seventeen would be published in magazines) and three plays: *The Potmaker* (1927), *The Purple Flower* (1928), and *Exit, an Illusion* (1929). In 1930, she married William Almy Occomy and bore three children. She continued to

1. Marita Bonner, easily the most original and intriguing of the Harlem Renaissance playwrights, had more or less "disappeared" from Black theatre history. Thanks to the dedicated scholarship of Professor Joyce Flynn at Harvard, we have a record of Bonner's life and collected work in *Frye Street & Environs: The Collected Works of Marita Bonner* (Boston: Beacon Press, 1987).

teach school and to write short stories, but she no longer had the time to produce the quantity of writing she had in her twenties.

Bonner's style has been called "surreal," that is, a manifestation of the writer's inner consciousness—her dreams placed upon the stage. Theatre scholar Shauna Vey has pointed out that Bonner very likely had read the German Expressionist George Kaiser's *From Morn to Midnight* in the original and may have seen the play on stage in Boston in 1917. And she might have seen O'Neill's *Emperor Jones* (1920) Off-Broadway, as well as *The Hairy Ape* and Elmer Rice's *The Adding Machine* in 1923. All this is to say that from somewhere, she developed a nonrealistic style not used by any other African American playwright except Jean Toomer, until Adrienne Kennedy's *The Funnyhouse of a Negro* in 1965.

In addition to its unique style, *The Purple Flower* calls for social and political revolution in an overt manner that other writers did not use until the militant sixties. Present-day theatre students, reading *The Purple Flower* for the first time, will be surprised both by Bonner's allegorical style and by her courage. She informs us that The Leader (Booker T. Washington in her day) was mistaken. Work won't do it! Book learning won't do it! Money won't do it! Only blood will pay for blood! Marita Bonner isn't asking, "Will there be a revolution?" but, "Is it time?" (Had she also been reading T.S. Eliot's *The Wasteland* [1922]?)

None of her three plays was ever produced in her lifetime. The plays were simply too avant-garde. But now, is it time?

The Purple Flower

(TIME   *The Middle-of-Things-as-They-are.*

[*Which means the End-of-Things for some of the characters and the Beginning-of-Things for others.*]

PLACE   *Might be here, there or anywhere—or even nowhere.*

CHARACTERS
   SUNDRY WHITE DEVILS. [*They must be artful little things with soft wide eyes such as you would expect to find in an angel. Soft hair that flops around their horns. Their horns glow red all the time—now with blood—now with eternal fire—now with deceit—now with unholy desire. They have bones tied carefully across their tails to make them seem less like tails and more like mere decorations. They are artful little things full of artful movements and artful tricks. They are artful dancers too. You are amazed at their adroitness. Their steps are intricate. You almost lose your head following them. Sometimes they dance as if they* were men—with dignity—erect. Sometimes they dance as if they were snakes. They are artful dancers on the Thin-Skin-of-Civilization.*]

THE US'S. [*They can be as white as the White Devils, as brown as the earth, as black as the center of a poppy. They may look as if they were something or nothing.*]

SETTING   *The stage is divided horizontally into two sections, upper and lower, by a thin board. The main action takes place on the upper stage. The light is never quite clear on the lower stage; but it is bright enough for you to perceive that sometimes the action that takes place on the upper stage is duplicated on the lower. Sometimes the actors on the upper stage get too vociferous—too violent—and they crack through the boards and they lie twisted and curled in mounds. There are any number of mounds there, all twisted and broken. You look at them and you are not quite sure whether you see something or nothing; but you see by a curve that there might lie a human body. There is thrust out a white hand—a yellow one—one brown—a black. The Skin-of-Civilization must be very thin. A thought can drop you through it.*

SCENE   *An open plain. It is bounded distantly on one side by Nowhere and faced by a high hill—Somewhere.*

ARGUMENT   *The* WHITE DEVILS *live on the side of the hill. Somewhere. On top of the hill grows the purple Flower-of-Life-At-Its-Fullest. This flower is as tall as a pine and stands alone on top of the hill. The* US's *live in the valley that lies between Nowhere and Somewhere and spend their time trying to devise means of getting up the hill. The* WHITE DEVILS *live all over the sides of the hill and try every trick, known and unknown, to keep the* US's *from getting to the hill. For if the* US's *get up the hill, the Flower-of-Life-at-Its-Fullest will shed some of its perfume and then and there they will be Somewhere with the* WHITE DEVILS. *The* US's *started out by merely asking permission to go up. They tilled the valley, they cultivated it and made it as beautiful as it is. They built roads and houses even for the* WHITE DEVILS. *They let them build the houses and then they were knocked back down into the valley.*

SCENE   *When the curtain rises, the evening sun is shining bravely on the valley and hillside alike.*

The US's *are having a siesta beside a brook that runs down the Middle of the valley. As usual they rest with their backs toward Nowhere and their faces toward Somewhere. The* WHITE DEVILS *are seen in the distance on the hillside. As you see them, a song is borne faintly to your ears from the hillside.*

The WHITE DEVILS *are saying:*

> You stay where you are!
> We don't want you up here!
> If you come you'll be on par
> With all we hold dear.
> So stay—stay—stay—
> Yes stay where you are!

The song rolls full across the valley)

A LITTLE RUNTY US   Hear that, don't you?

ANOTHER US *(lolling over on his back and chewing a piece of grass)*   I ain't studying 'bout them devils. When I get ready to go up that hill—I'm going! *(he rolls over on his side and exposes a slender brown body to the sun)* Right

now, I'm going to sleep. *(and he forthwith snores)*

OLD LADY *(an old dark brown lady who has been lying down rises suddenly to her knees in the foreground. She gazes toward the hillside)*   I'll never live to see the face of that flower! God knows I worked hard to get Somewhere though. I've washed the shirt off of every one of them White Devils' backs!

A YOUNG US   And you got a slap in the face for doing it.

OLD LADY   But that's what the Leader told us to do. "Work," he said. "Show them you know how." As if two hundred years of slavery had not showed them!

ANOTHER YOUNG US   Work doesn't do it. The Us who work for the White Devils get pushed in the face—down off of Somewhere every night. They don't even sleep up there.

OLD LADY   Something's got to be done though! The Us ain't got no business to sleep while the sun is shining. They'd ought to be up and working before the White Devils get to some other tricks.

YOUNG US   You just said work did not do you any good! What's the need of working if it doesn't get you anywhere? What's the use of boring around in the same hole like a worm? Making the hole bigger to stay in?

(There comes up the road a clatter of feet and four figures, a middle-aged well-browned man, a lighter-browned middle-aged woman, a medium light brown girl, beautiful as a browned peach and a slender, tall, bronzy brown youth who walks with his head high. He touches the ground with his feet as if it were a velvet rug and not sunbaked, jagged rocks)

OLD LADY *(addressing the* OLDER MAN*)* Evenin', Average. I was just saying we ain't never going to make that hill.

AVERAGE   The Us will if they get the right leaders.

THE MIDDLE-AGED WOMAN—CORNERSTONE Leaders! Leaders! They've had good ones looks like to me.

AVERAGE   But they ain't led us anywhere!

CORNERSTONE   But that is not their fault! If one of them gets up and says, "Do this," one of the Us will sneak up behind him and knock him down and stand up and holler, "Do that," and then he himself gets knocked down and we still sit in the valley and knock down and drag out!

A YOUNG US (*aside*)   Yeah! Drag Us out, but not White Devils.

OLD LADY   It's the truth Cornerstone. They say they going to meet this evening to talk about what we ought to do.

AVERAGE   What is the need of so much talking?

CORNERSTONE   Better than not talking! Somebody might say something after while.

THE YOUNG GIRL—SWEET (*who just came up*)   I want to talk too!

AVERAGE   What can you talk about?

SWEET   Things! Something, father!

THE YOUNG MAN—FINEST BLOOD   I'll speak too.

AVERAGE   Oh you all make me tired! Talk—talk—talk—talk! And the flower is still up on the hillside!

OLD LADY   Yes and the White Devils are still talking about keeping the Us away from it, too.

(*A drum begins to beat in the distance. All the* US *stand up and shake off their sleep. The drummer, a short, black, determined looking* US, *appears around the bushes beating the drum with strong, vigorous jabs that make the whole valley echo and re-echo with rhythm. Some of the* US *begin to dance in time to the music*)

AVERAGE   Look at that! Dancing!! The Us will never learn to be sensible!

CORNERSTONE   They dance well! Well!!

(*The* US *all congregate at the center front. Almost naturally, the Young* US *range on one side, the Old* US *on the other.* CORNERSTONE *sits her plump brown self comfortably in the center of the stage. An Old* US *tottering with age and blind comes toward her*)

OLD US   What's it this time, chillun? Is it day yet? Can you see the road to that flower?

AVERAGE   Oh you know we ain't going to get up there! No use worrying!

CORNERSTONE   No, it's not day! It is still dark. It is night. (*for the sun has gone and purple blackness has lain across the Valley. Somehow, though, you can see the shape of the flower on top of Somewhere. Lights twinkle on the hill*)

OLD US (*speaking as if to himself*)   I'm blind from working—building for the White Devils in the heat of the noon-day sun and I'm weary!

CORNERSTONE   Lean against me so they won't crowd you.

(*An old man rises in the back of the ranks; his beard reaches down to his knees but he springs upright. He speaks*)

OLD MAN   I want to tell you all something! The Us can't get up the road unless we work! We want to hew and dig and toil!

A YOUNG US   You had better sit down before someone knocks you down! They told us that when your beard was sprouting.

CORNERSTONE (*to YOUTH*)   Do not be so stupid! Speak as if you had respect for that beard!

ANOTHER YOUNG US   We have! But we get tired of hearing "you must work" when we know the Old Us built practically every inch of that hill and are yet Nowhere.

FIRST YOUNG US   Yes, all they got was a rush down the hill—not a chance to take a step up!

CORNERSTONE   It was not time then.

OLD MAN (*on the back row*)   Here comes a Young Us who has been reading in the books! He'll tell us what the books say about getting Somewhere.

(*A* YOUNG MAN *pushes through the crowd. As soon as he reaches the center front, he throws a bundle of books*)

YOUNG MAN   I'm through! I do not need these things! They're no good!

OLD MAN (*pushes up from the back and stands beside him*)   You're through! Ain't you been reading in the books how to get Somewhere? Why don't you tell us how to get there?

YOUNG MAN   I'm through, I tell you! There isn't anything in one of these books that tells Black Us how to get around White Devils.

OLD MAN (*softly—sadly*)   I thought the books would tell us how!

YOUNG MAN   No! The White Devils wrote the books themselves. You know they aren't going to put anything like that in there!

YET ANOTHER OLD MAN (*throwing back his head and calling into the air*)   Lord! Why don't you come by here and tell us how to get Somewhere?

A YOUNG MAN (*who had been idly chewing grass*)   Aw, you ought to know by now that isn't the way to talk to God!

OLD MAN   It ain't! It ain't! It ain't! It ain't! Ain't I been talking to God just like that for seventy years? Three score and ten years—Amen!

THE GRASS CHEWER   Yes! Three score and ten years you been telling God to tell you what to do. Telling Him! And three score and ten years you been wearing your spine double sitting on the rocks in the valley too.

OLD US   He is all powerful! He will move in his own time!

YOUNG US   Well, if he is all powerful, God does not need you to tell Him what to do.

OLD US   Well, what's the need of me talkin' to Him then?

YOUNG US   Don't talk so much to Him! Give Him a chance! He might want to talk to you but you do so much yelling in His ears that He can't tell you anything.

(There is a commotion in the back stage. SWEET *comes running to* CORNERSTONE *crying)*

SWEET   Oh—oo—!

CORNERSTONE   What is it, Sweet?

SWEET   There's a White Devil sitting in the bushes in the dark over there! There's a White Devil sitting in the bushes over in the dark! And when I walked by—he pinched me!

FINEST BLOOD *(catching a rock)*   Where is he, sister? *(he starts toward the bushes)*

CORNERSTONE *(screaming)*   Don't go after him son! They will kill you if you hurt him!

FINEST BLOOD   I don't care if they do. Let them. I'd be out of this hole then!

AVERAGE   Listen to that young fool! Better stay safe and sound where he is! At least he got somewhere to eat and somewhere to lay his head.

FINEST BLOOD   Yes I can lay my head on the rocks of Nowhere.

(Up the center of the stage toils a new figure of a square set middle-aged US. *He walks heavily for in each hand he carries a heavy bag. As soon as he reaches the center front he throws the bags down groaning as he does so)*

AN OLD MAN   'Smatter with you! Ain't them bags full of gold?

THE NEW COMER   Yes, they are full of gold!

OLD MAN   Well why ain't you smiling then? Them White Devils can't have anything no better!

THE NEW COMER   Yes they have! They have Somewhere! I tried to do what they said. I brought them money, but when I brought it to them they would not sell me even a spoonful of dirt from Somewhere! I'm through!

CORNERSTONE   Don't be through. The gold counts for something. It must!

(An OLD WOMAN *cries aloud in a quavering voice from the back)*

OLD LADY   Last night I had a dream.

A YOUNG US   Dreams? Excuse me! I know I'm going now! Dreams!!

OLD LADY   I dreamed that I saw a White Devil cut in six pieces—head there, *(pointing)* body here—one leg here—one there—an arm here—an arm there.

AN OLD MAN   Thank God! It's time then!

AVERAGE   Time for what? Time to eat? Sure ain't time to get Somewhere!

OLD MAN *(walking forward)*   It's time! It's time! Bring me an iron pot!

YOUNG US   Aw don't try any conjuring!

OLD MAN *(louder)*   Bring me a pot of iron. Get the pot from the fire in the valley.

CORNERSTONE   Give him the pot!

(Someone brings it up immediately)

OLD MAN *(walking toward pot slowly)*   Old Us! Do you hear me. Old Us that are here do you hear me?

ALL THE OLD US *(cry in chorus)*   Yes, Lord! We hear you! We hear you!

OLD MAN *(crying louder and louder)*   Old Us! Old Us!! Old Us that are gone, Old Us that are dust do you hear me? *(his voice sounds strangely through the valley. Somewhere you think you hear—as if mouthed by ten million mouths through rocks and dust—"Yes!—Lord!—We hear you! We hear you!")*

OLD MAN   And you hear me—give me a handful of dust! Give me a handful of dust! Dig down to the depths of the things you have made! The things you formed with your hands and give me a handful of dust!

(An OLD WOMAN *tottering with the weakness of old age crosses the stage and going to the pot, throws a handful of dust in. Just before she sits down again she throws back her head and shakes her cane in the air and laughs so that the entire valley echoes)*

A YOUNG US   What's the trouble? Choking on the dust?

OLD WOMAN   No child! Rejoicing!

YOUNG US   Rejoicing over a handful of dust?

OLD WOMAN   Yes. A handful of dust! Thanking God I could do something if it was nothing but make a handful of dust!

YOUNG US   Well, dust isn't much!

OLD MAN (*at the pot*)   Yes, it isn't much! You are dust yourself; but so is she. Like everything else, though, dust can be little or much, according to where it is.

(*The* YOUNG US *who spoke subsides. He subsides so completely that he crashes through the Thin-Skin-of-Civilization. Several of his group go too. They were thinking*)

OLD MAN (*at the pot*)   Bring me books! Bring me books!

YOUNG US (*who threw books down*)   Here! Take all these! I'll light the fire with them.

OLD MAN   No, put them in the pot (YOUNG US *does so*) Bring me gold!

THE MAN OF THE GOLD BAGS   Here take this! It is just as well. Stew it up and make teething rings!! (*he pours it into the pot*)

OLD MAN   Now bring me blood! Blood from the eyes, the ears, the whole body! Drain it off and bring me blood! (*No one speaks or moves*) Ah hah, hah! I knew it! Not one of you willing to pour his blood in the pot!

YOUNG US (*facetiously*)   How you going to pour your own blood in there? You got to be pretty far gone to let your blood run in there. Somebody else would have to do the pouring.

OLD MAN   I mean red blood. Not yellow blood, thank you.

FINEST BLOOD (*suddenly*)   Take my blood! (*he walks toward the pot*)

CORNERSTONE   O no! Not my boy! Take me instead!

OLD MAN   Cornerstone we cannot stand without you!

AN OLD WOMAN   What you need blood for? What you doing anyhow? You ain't told us nothing yet. What's going on in that pot?

OLD MAN   I'm doing as I was told to do.

A YOUNG US   Who told you to do anything?

OLD MAN   God. I'm His servant.

YOUNG US (*who spoke before*)   God? I haven't heard God tell you anything.

OLD MAN   You couldn't hear. He told it to me alone.

OLD WOMAN   I believe you. Don't pay any attention to that simpleton! What God told you to do?

OLD MAN   He told me take a handful of dust—dust from which all things came and put it in a hard iron pot. Put it in a hard iron pot. Things shape best in hard molds!! Put in books that Men learn by. Gold that Men live by. Blood that lets Men live.

YOUNG US   What you suppose to be shaping? A man?

OLD US   I'm the servant. I can do nothing. If I do this, God will shape a new man Himself.

YOUNG MAN   What's the things in the pot for?

OLD MAN   To show I can do what I'm told.

OLD WOMAN   Why does He want blood?

OLD MAN   You got to give blood! Blood has to be let for births, to give life.

OLD WOMAN   So the dust wasn't just nothing? Thank God!

YOUTH   Then the books were not just paper leaves? Thank God!

THE MAN OF THE GOLD BAGS   Can the gold mean something?

OLD MAN   Now I need the blood.

FINEST BLOOD   I told you you could take mine.

OLD MAN   Yours!

FINEST BLOOD   Where else could you get it? The New Man must be born. The night is already dark. We cannot stay here forever. Where else could blood come from?

OLD MAN   Think child. When God asked a faithful servant once to do sacrifice, even his only child, where did God put the real meat for sacrifice when the servant had the knife upon the son's throat?

OLD US (*in a chorus*)

In the bushes, Lord!
In the bushes, Lord!
Jehovah put the ram
In the bushes!

CORNERSTONE   I understand!

FINEST BLOOD   What do you mean?

CORNERSTONE   Where were you going a little while ago? Where were you going when your sister cried out?

FINEST BLOOD   To the bushes! You want me
to get the White Devil? *(he seizes the piece of
rock and stands to his feet)*

OLD MAN   No! No! Not that way. The
White Devils are full of tricks. You must go
differently. Bring him gifts and offer them to
him.

FINEST BLOOD   What have I to give for a
gift?

OLD MAN   There are the pipes of Pan that
every Us is born with. Play on that. Soothe
him—lure him—make him yearn for the pipe.
Even a White Devil will soften at music. He'll
come out, and he only comes to try to get the
pipe from you.

FINEST BLOOD   And when he comes out, I'm
to kill him in the dark before he sees me?
That's a White Devil trick!

OLD MAN   An Old Us will never tell you to
play White Devil's games! No! Do not kill
him in the dark. Get him out of the bushes
and say to him: "White Devil, God is using
me for His instrument. You think that it is I
who play on this pipe! You think that it is I
who play upon this pipe so that you cannot
stay in your bushes. So that you must come out
of your bushes. But it is not I who play. It is not
I, it is God who plays through me—to you.
Will you hear what He says? Will you hear? He
says it is almost day, White Devil. The night is
far gone. A New Man must be born for the
New Day. Blood is needed for birth. Blood is
needed for the birth. Come out, White Devil.
It may be your blood—it may be mine—but
blood must be taken during the night to be
given at the birth. It may be my blood—it may
be your blood—but everything has been

given. The Us toiled to give dust for the body,
books to guide the body, gold to clothe the
body. Now they need blood for birth so the
New Man can live. You have taken blood. You
must give blood. Come out! Give it." And
then fight him!

FINEST BLOOD   I'll go! And if I kill him?

OLD MAN   Blood will be given!

FINEST BLOOD   And if he kills me?

OLD MAN   Blood will be given!

FINEST BLOOD   Can there be no other way—
cannot this cup pass?

OLD MAN   No other way. It cannot pass.
They always take blood. They built up half
their land on our bones. They ripened crops of
cotton, watering them with our blood. Finest
Blood, this is God's decree: "You take blood—
you give blood. Full measure—flooding full—
over—over!"

FINEST BLOOD   I'll go. *(he goes quickly into the
shadow. Far off soon you can hear him—his voice
lifted, young, sweet, brave and strong)* White
Devil! God speaks to you through me!—Hear
Him!—Him! You have taken blood; there can
be no other way. You will have to give blood!
Blood!

(All the US *listen. All the valley listens. Nowhere
listens. All the* WHITE DEVILS *listen. Somewhere
listens.*

Let the curtain close leaving all the US, *the* WHITE
DEVILS, *Nowhere, Somewhere, listening, listening.
It is time?)*

(Curtain)

FOLK PLAYS OF THE 1920s

Willis Richardson • Jean Toomer • John Matheus
Georgia Douglas Johnson • S. Randolph Edmonds

Aconsiderable number of one-act plays written in the 1920s are subtitled "a folk tragedy," or "a folk comedy." In 1923, the Ethiopian Art Players (the first group to present a Black playwright on Broadway) subtitled themselves a "folk theatre." In the forty-page preface to his anthology, *The Book of American Negro Poetry* (1921), James Weldon Johnson wrote, "The status of the Negro in the United States is more a question of national mental attitude toward the race than the actual conditions. And nothing will do more to change that mental attitude and raise his status than a demonstration of intellectual parity by the Negro through the production of literature and art." Folk art, folk literature, folk plays were to be encouraged.

The mission to prove oneself and one's culture "worthy" was fraught with dangerous pitfalls: on the one hand, Black writers attempted to "legitimize" their ethnic culture to Europeans by "elevating" it to European forms ("we's risin'"); at the same time, they slammed the cabin door on the genuine folk culture because whites saw in it only stereotypes. W.E.B. Du Bois expressed the issue of courage-to-write-the-truth:

> The Negro today fears any attempt of the artist to paint Negroes. He is not satisfied unless everything is perfect and proper and beautiful and joyful and hopeful. He is afraid to be painted as he is, lest his human foibles and shortcomings be seized by his enemies for the purposes of the ancient and hateful propaganda.

No matter which way African Americans moved, racism's double bind laid snares. So while aspiring middle-class Blacks were warning their children against jazz (Eubie Blake refused even to utter the word), whites were desperately trying to "shake that thing." To further confuse the issues, debates in the press discussed whether they should call themselves "Colored," "Ethiopian," "Black," "Africans," "Negroes," "African Americans."

What was a "folk play?" One with a rural setting where the characters possessed little formal schooling, confronted poverty, race, and sexism, and spoke in a dialect peculiar to their region. A general feeling prevailed that the folk plays, by dignifying the people's struggles, extended a kind of egalitarian democracy to the rural people, whom Jean Toomer and Alain Locke referred to as "peasants." The folk movement in America, as in Europe, came down from the top.

W.E.B. Du Bois (Ph.D., Harvard), Alain LeRoy Locke (Ph.D., Harvard), and James Weldon Johnson (Law degree, Columbia) labeled, interpreted, and produced the literature. These African American leaders of the Negro folk theatre movement were urban, self-conscious intellectuals, and they borrowed the "elevating" folk culture from the rising nationalisms of Europe, particularly the Russians, Czechs, and the Irish. "Harlem has the same role to play for the New Negro," wrote Alain Locke in *The New Negro* (1925), "as Dublin has had for the New Ireland. . . ." In 1899, Lady Gregory and William Butler Yeats had formed a "native and poetic" theatre where the "living language of the folk" would drive the artificial stage Irishman from the boards. Tragedy need no longer be the property of kings; comedy need no longer be subject to artificiality.

The Irish folk theatre impetus entered the Negro theatre through the plays of Ridgley Torrence, a white writer. On the eve of the United States's entry into World War I, April 5, 1917, at the Old Garden Theater in New York, Emily Hapgood presented Torrence's *Three Plays for a Negro Theater*. The *New York Post* noted the importance of the event as

> the beginnings of something like a folk theater, entirely domestic if not altogether national, and of an indisputable, if as yet incalculable, racial significance. Should it persist, and thrive, it will find within its own peculiar domain many great opportunities, and before long it will be doing better work in better plays. It might even rival the achievement of the Abbey Theatre of Dublin, which had a less propitious start.

A close look at Torrence's plays, and those of other white playwrights of the twenties (Culbertson, O'Neill, Heyward, Connelly), reveals their "Negro" plays to be synthetic folk plays, seeking the exotic Negro rather than the real African Americans—whom white playwrights did not know. It remained for Black playwrights—Willis Richardson, Jean Toomer, S. Randolph Edmonds, Georgia Douglas Johnson, John Matheus—to take a fresh look at Negro life, its conflicts, its people, its idioms. It was hoped that if true Black characters could be presented on stage, the old Negro stereotypes could be driven off the boards. For another twenty years, however, a kind of Gresham's law of the theatre was to prevail: bad characterization by whites drove out valid portraits by Blacks.

African American playwrights tackled all the difficult issues of their day: racism, patriotism, poverty, lynching, birth control, religion, and miscegenation. Some plays sprang directly from the tens of thousands of southern Blacks who had migrated North for freedom and for work. John Matheus, who taught at West Virginia State College near the coal mines, wrote about the migrants in *'Cruiter* (1926), the story of a poor family leaving the old southern homestead for wartime jobs in the North. S. Randolph Edmond's *Old Man Pete* (1934) presented a similar migrant family, perhaps a few years later, living a middle-class life in Harlem, but at the expense of turning their backs on their "down home" parents. Willis Richardson in *The Deacon's Awakening* chastised male sexism; Georgia Douglas Johnson in *A Sunday Morning in the South* confronted lynching; and Jean Toomer captured the sincerity of religious conviction among the rural poor.

As the Little Theatre movement (sometimes called Art Theatre and later Folk Theatre) spread across America, amateur drama groups formed, met, produced, and disbanded. Schools, ladies' clubs, men's lodges, churches, Y's, and settlement houses provided raised platforms for stages and put on one-act plays, which seldom required more than a single set. Since experienced actors were not available for amateur productions, characters were broadly conceived and generally few in number. A production rarely boasted of more than two performances, and royalties were left unpaid because they could not be paid. The life of most theatre groups were brief. Among the most notable of these amateurs were the Ethiopian Art Players, the Harlem Experimental Theatre, the Sekondi Players, the New Negro Art Theatre, the Dunbar Players, the Gilpin Players, the Krigwa Players, and many more.

Scholars H.L. Mencken and Nathan Higgins have written that the Harlem Renaissance did not produce great art, and certainly not great theatre. Such an assessment, although caught in the double binds of race and class, raises the question: Can the creative energy of folk culture be used, but at the same time be "raised" to the level of high art (of "civilization")? The answer is to judge the art on its own terms. What did these plays set out to do? How well did they do it?

THE DEACON'S AWAKENING
1920

Willis Richardson (1889–1977)

During a career spanning thirty years in the theatre, Willis Richardson wrote forty-eight plays on subjects ranging from children's fantasies and Black historical figures to problems of family and marriage that still resonate. Perhaps his most prescient drama of conflicting views in a Black community is *The Deacon's Awakening* (1920), a crisp, convincing appeal for women's rights.

Willis Wilder and Agnes (Harper) Richardson, with their new son, Willis, Jr., moved to Washington, D.C., from Wilmington, North Carolina, in 1889, when whites were rioting against Blacks voting. Young Willis attended the M Street School (later known as Dunbar High) and studied with Mary Burrill. Carter Woodson, a teacher of Spanish, encouraged him to write and eventually published Richardson's first drama anthology. He was awarded a scholarship to Howard University in 1920, but his family could not afford to send him to college, so he studied via a correspondence school while working as a clerk at the U.S. Bureau of Printing and Engraving. In 1914, he married Mary Ellen

Jones; they raised three children, Jean Paula, Anatonelle, and Joel Justine.

Stimulated by Angelina Grimké's play *Rachel* (1916), Richardson wrote a pioneering article for *The Crisis*, "The Hope of the Negro Drama," in which he outlined the values he wanted to dramatize in his own plays: "*Rachel* is a propaganda play and a great portion of it shows the manner in which Negroes are treated by white people in the United States. Still there is another kind of play: the kind that shows the soul of the people; and the soul of this people is truly worth showing." His first adult play, *The Deacon's Awakening*, was published in *The Crisis* and produced in St. Paul, Minnesota, the following year.

With the help of E.C. Williams, his former Latin teacher at the M School, Richardson was able to get Alain Locke and Montgomery Gregory, codirectors of the Howard Players, to read his plays. When the white president of Howard forbade the group to perform Richardson's plays on the grounds that they were propaganda pieces and would hurt the school's reputation, W.E.B. Du Bois encouraged

Richardson to try Raymond O'Neil's Ethiopian Art Players in Chicago. O'Neil, who was searching for a Black folk play to produce as a companion piece to Oscar Wilde's *Salome,* produced Richardson's *The Chip Woman's Fortune* (1923), first in Chicago, then Harlem, and finally at the Frazee Theatre on Broadway, making Richardson the first African American playwright to have a nonmusical produced on the Great White Way.

Over the ensuing decade, a number of his shorter plays were performed by amateur groups. *The Broken Banjo* won the Amy Spingarn Prize in the competition conducted by *The Crisis.* One of the judges, Eugene O'Neill, commented, "I am glad to hear the judges all agreed on *The Broken Banjo* and that the play was so successfully staged; Willis Richardson should certainly continue working in his field." Richardson was again awarded *The Crisis*-sponsored prize ($100) in 1926 for *Boot Black Lover.* In 1929, he published a domestic drama, *The Idle Head,* in *The Carolina Magazine.* Seeing the need for Black children to know their history, Richardson edited two anthologies, *Plays and Pageants from the Life of the Negro* (1930), and with

May Miller, *Negro History in Thirteen Plays* (1935).

He continued to work as a clerk in the Bureau of Engraving until his retirement in 1954. Two years later, he published his collection of five children's plays, *The King's Dilemma and Other Plays for Children.* He died in 1977 in relative obscurity, but recently his role as a pioneer in African American theatre has been acknowledged.[1]

The Deacon's Awakening is a brief but powerful play in which sexism intersects with racism. A mother and daughter are determined to take advantage of the Nineteenth Amendment granting women the vote, but David, the deacon of their church, and his crony, Sol, are equally determined to prevent them. Richardson was the first dramatist to recognize the extent to which racism could breed sexism by making its victims victimize others with less power. *Pillars of the Church,*[2] is another one-act by Richardson, showing the male patriarch raging in his full arrogance against his daughters' desire for a college education. Willis Richardson was not only a thinker ahead of his time, but ahead of many to come.

---

1. Professor Christine Gray has completed a dissertation on Richardson's life and work and has republished his *Plays and Pageants* (Jackson: University Press of Mississippi, 1993).

2. James V. Hatch and Leo Hamalian, eds., *Lost Plays of the Harlem Renaissance* (Detroit: Wayne State University Press, in press).

The Deacon's Awakening

CAST

MARTHA JONES
RUTH JONES
EVA, SOL'S DAUGHTER
DAVID JONES
SOL, EVA'S FATHER

The scene is the sitting-room at the JONES' *house. In the center of the room is a table, at the right of which is a large arm-chair and at the left of which is a straight chair. At the right is a door which leads to the dining-room and kitchen. Above is a door which leads to the hall. Persons entering the hall door from the left come from the street, while those entering from the right come from other parts of the house. At the right of the hall door is a well-filled bookcase and around the walls hang a few well-chosen pictures.* MARTHA JONES *is sitting at the left of the table reading the morning paper. She is an intelligent colored woman of five and forty, wearing a house dress which makes her look as neat as her surroundings. She is different from most housewives (whose work never ends), in that she always keeps ahead of her work, and for this reason has time to read between luncheon and dinner.* MARTHA *continues to read, not raising her head until* EVA *enters from the hall.* EVA *is a brown-skinned lady of two and twenty. She is dressed to go out and is carrying a light coat on her arm.* RUTH *enters behind* EVA. *She is about* EVA'S *age but seems to be a little more determined in her manner; she is also dressed to go out.)*

MARTHA *(looking up)*   Aren't you all afraid you'll be late?

RUTH *(starting out)*   I hope not. Come on, Eva.

MARTHA *(letting the paper fall to her lap;* RUTH *stops)*   Just one minute, Ruth. There's something wrong. *(*EVA *stops in the act of pulling on her coat)*

RUTH *(her jaw dropping)*   Wrong how?

MARTHA   I believe the thing has leaked out somehow.

EVA   It can't be.

RUTH   Do you mean that someone has told, Mama?

MARTHA   It seems that way to me.

RUTH   What makes you think so?

MARTHA   Come here. *(The two move closer. She speaks in a subdued voice)*   I heard them whispering—

RUTH   Them?

MARTHA   Your father and—

EVA   And Papa?

MARTHA   Yes.

RUTH   What were they saying?

MARTHA   I heard them mention the meeting. I couldn't hear it all, but your father stayed home from work today, and I think he means to go to that meeting.

RUTH *(disappointed)*   And I had hoped to keep it a secret until after the election.

MARTHA   Of course, we won't let this stop us; but I'm sorry he decided to go on the very day you planned to make your speech.

RUTH *(in disagreement with the state of affairs)*   Just when we are at our best, too. If they would let us alone, we'd have everybody in this city ready to vote.

EVA   Will you make your speech if he comes, Ruth?

RUTH *(determined)*   Yes, I'm going to make that speech anyway.

MARTHA   That's right; we can't afford to back out now. We'd have to face it sometime in the future; so I guess it's just as well that we face it now.

RUTH   That's what I say too.

EVA   Well, I'm brave; I'll stick right beside you.

MARTHA *(after pondering a moment)*   There may be a way out of it yet.

EVA   How?

MARTHA   If I can keep Dave from going—

RUTH   But you said he was staying home for that.

MARTHA   I know, but I have a plan.

EVA *(curious)*   Tell us.

MARTHA   You see, Joe Lucas is sick; and if I can get him to go there and get Joe and Nell to keep him a while, everything will be all right. Nell and Joe are both with us.

RUTH *(pleased)*   That'll be great!

EVA   But suppose *my* father comes to the meeting? It'll be just as bad, because he'll see everything and tell.

MARTHA   Your father went to work.

EVA   That's all right, then.

MARTHA   You all run along, now, before you're too late; and I'll call Nell up and fix it with her. You'd better take a taxi. (RUTH *and* EVA *hurry out;* MARTHA *ponders a moment, then speaks through the telephone)* East 1824-W. *(a pause)* Is that you, Nell? Very well; how is Joe today? *(speaking lower)* Nell, I have a scheme I want you to help me with. Well, Dave is up in arms about the Voting Society. I don't know how he found out about it; but he is staying home today to go to the meeting. Yes, the very day they asked Ruth to speak. I want you to call him up in five minutes and try to get him to come there somehow. Tell him Joe wants to see him. Thanks! that will help us along a bit. Keep him as long as you can. Good-bye. *(she hangs up the receiver and begins to read her paper again. Presently* DAVID JONES *enters. He is a man fifty years old, of medium size and wearing large side whiskers. He has his coat off. His collar is on but is unbuttoned in front, and his shoes are both unlaced)*

DAVE *(coming to her)*   Martha, buttons this collar up for me, will you?

MARTHA *(feigning surprise)*   I didn't know you were going out. *(she rises and begins to button his collar)*

DAVE   Yes, Ah heard 'bout that suffrage meetin' they're goin' to have, and Ah'm goin' there to see what Ah can find out.

MARTHA   It's not exactly a suffrage meeting.

DAVE   What is it, then?

MARTHA   It's a meeting to urge women to vote, now that they have the right.

DAVE   It's the same thing.

MARTHA *(struggling with the collar which is too small for his neck)*   What do you want to find out?

DAVE   Ah wants to find out who's goin' to be there.

MARTHA   What good will that do?

DAVE *(facing the issue)*   Well, Ah see Ah can't get 'round tellin' you. The deacon's board appointed me to go to that meetin' and find out the names of all the women there who belong to our church so Ah can bring the names up before the deacons at the next meetin'.

MARTHA   How did they find out about the meeting?

DAVE   That's a secret.

MARTHA *(finishing her job)*   Bring the names before the board for what?

DAVE *(tying his tie)*   So we can have the women up. We don't mean to have the women in our congregation goin' to the polls to vote. Ah believe in a woman stayin' in her place and not tryin' to fill a man's shoes.

MARTHA   The women don't want to take the men's places, Dave.

DAVE *(sitting to lace his shoes)*   Yes, they do; you needn't try to take up for 'em. If Ah caught a woman Ah had anything to do with in this mess Ah'd—

MARTHA   What would you do?

DAVE   Ah—Ah don't know what Ah wouldn't do. *(the telephone rings)*

MARTHA *(answering)*   Hello—Yes. All right, he's right here. *(turning to Dave)* Dave, Nell wants to speak to you for Joe.

DAVE *(going to the telephone)*   Is he any worse?

MARTHA   She didn't say.

DAVE *(at the telephone)*   Hello—Yes. What's the matter, is he worse? Well, Ah'll hurry right over there. *(leaving the telephone)* She says Joe's a little worse. Ah'll have to run over there before Ah go to the meetin'. *(He hurries in, lacing his shoes)* Ah'm goin' to try not to be late.

MARTHA   I hope he's not bad off.

DAVE *(rising)*   Ah hope not. Where's ma coat?

MARTHA   You didn't bring it downstairs with you.

DAVE   Shucks! *(he rushes out and goes upstairs. Presently he hurries past the door, pulling on his coat.* MARTHA *smiles when she hears the door slam. She ponders a moment, then goes out through the dining room. She returns with sewing in her hand. Just as she starts to sit down,* SOL *rushes in from the street. He resembles* DAVE *save that he has a long mustache and no side whiskers. He has his hat in his hand and appears to be very much excited)*

MARTHA *(perplexed)*   What are you doing home, Sol?

SOL (*excitedly*)   Where's Dave?

MARTHA   He went around to see Joe Lucas. What's the matter?

SOL   Did you know Ruth was at that Votin' Meeting'?

MARTHA (*evasively*)   Ruth was at that meeting?

SOL   Yes, she was there. A mob of toughs broke the meetin' up and she got mussed up a little.

MARTHA (*starting and raising her hand to her cheek*)   Hurt!

SOL   No, she got off lucky—just mussed up a little. Ah reckon she'll be along in a minute. Ah'm goin' to find Dave. (*he hurries out*)

MARTHA (*to herself*)   The ruffians!

(*The telephone rings*)

MARTHA (*answering*)   Hello. You couldn't keep him? It's all right. The meeting was broken up anyway. A mob of ruffians did it. No, I'm expecting her at any minute. I understand she was handled a little roughly. I hope not, myself. Good-bye. (*as she hangs up the receiver, RUTH enters, followed by EVA. Her hair is out of shape, her dress is torn and her wrist is bound with a handkerchief*)

MARTHA (*going to her*)   I heard it happened. How was it?

EVA   The mob rushed on us.

MARTHA   Rushed on you?

EVA   Yes, they were like wild men.

MARTHA   How do you feel, Ruth?

RUTH (*grasping her wrist*)   All right, except that my wrist pains a little.

MARTHA   Had you made your speech?

RUTH   No.

EVA   The chairman was just calling the meeting to order, when the mob, mostly made up of street loafers, rushed upon the platform and pushed everybody off.

RUTH   There were some respectable looking men among them, too!

MARTHA (*angry*)   Did they put their hands on you?

RUTH   Yes; I was pushed off a chair and in trying to catch myself I hurt my wrist.

MARTHA   Your father didn't get there, did he?

RUTH   I didn't see him.

EVA   But it's just as bad; my father was there and he'll tell everything.

MARTHA   I know he was there. Did he see you?

EVA   He didn't see me, but I'm sure he saw Ruth when they were putting her in the taxi. I saw him start towards her when he first saw her; then he checked himself and rushed out of the crowd.

MARTHA   Well, if that's the case, we'll have to prepare for trouble.

RUTH (*holding her wrist*)   It had to come sometime.

MARTHA (*to RUTH*)   You'd better go up and straighten yourself out a little; your father will be here in a few minutes. I know he'll hear it before he gets here because Sol has gone to meet him.

EVA   Yes, come on, Ruth, and change your dress. I guess they'll both come in as mad as wet hens. (*they go out. The room is left vacant until DAVE and SOL enter from the street*)

SOL (*as they enter*)   Ah looked for you everywhere—Ah came here and Ah went to Joe Lucas' house, but Ah couldn't find you.

DAVE   Yes, Ah went by Joe Lucas', and when Ah got to the hall everybody was gone.

SOL   The mob broke up the meetin', that's why everybody was gone.

DAVE (*surprised*)   Mob?

SOL   Yes, mob! A mob broke up the meetin'.

DAVE (*sitting in the armchair*)   Ah heard they had trouble, but—

SOL (*standing in front of him*)   That ain't half of it.

DAVE (*looking up at him*)   What else?

SOL   Ruth was there.

DAVE (*exploding*)   Ruth?

SOL   Yes, she was there and the mob mussed her up a little, too.

DAVE (*forgetting that he is a deacon*) Mussed—what the devil was she doin' there?

SOL   That's what we've got to find out.

DAVE   Nobody said nothin' to me 'bout her goin' there.

SOL   That's what we've got to see about; what she was doin' there. All Ah know is that she was there. Ah would of doubted it, but Ah saw her with ma own eyes. Her hair was all out, her dress was torn, and she had something tied around her wrist.

DAVE   And you're sure it was Ruth?

SOL   Sure as Ah'm born.

DAVE (*rising*)   Well, Ah'll find out 'bout it.

MARTHA (*entering as he rises*)   You both back so soon?

DAVE (*facing her*)   Do you know anything 'bout Ruth bein' at that Votin' Meetin'?

MARTHA (*pleasantly*)   Yes, I believe she was there.

DAVE (*raising his voice*)   Well, what was she doin' there?

MARTHA (*resenting his tone with a cold look before speaking*)   You might ask her. I'll bring her down. (*she goes out*)

DAVE (*draws a deep breath, but seems too surprised for words; turning to* SOL)   Ah don't know what's gettin' into these women.

SOL   The devil, Ah reckon.

DAVE   Ah never saw Martha like this before.

SOL   Dave, it's this votin' business, Ah'll bet. If that gal of mine ever gets it into her head, Ah don't know what Ah'll do to her.

(MARTHA *enters, followed by* RUTH *and* EVA. *They have both changed their dresses. There is a tense silence as they enter*)

RUTH (*going to the armchair*)   Do you want to sit here, Mama?

MARTHA (*standing by* RUTH)   No, sit down, child.

RUTH (*as she sits and takes her wrist in her hand*)   You look angry, Papa; what's the matter?

DAVE (*angrily*)   Ah want to know what you were doin' at that Votin' Meeting'.

RUTH (*looking down at her wrist, then up at him*)   I went to make a speech.

(*This is a thunderbolt.* MARTHA *and* RUTH *are watching* DAVE. EVA *looks at her father to see how he takes it.* DAVE *and* SOL *are outraged*)

DAVE   What?

RUTH (*as calmly as before*)   I went to make a speech.

DAVE (*hardly able to get the words out*)   You went to make a speech?

RUTH   Yes, sir.

DAVE   How did that happen? What would you be doin' makin' a speech there?

RUTH   I'm a member of the society; and we want to have the women ready to vote when the time comes.

DAVE (*leaning forward to be sure that he catches her answer*)   You belong to that crowd?

RUTH   Yes, sir.

DAVE (*looking from* RUTH *to* MARTHA *and* EVA, *then back to* RUTH)   How long's this been goin' on?

RUTH   You mean how long have I been a member?

DAVE   Yes.

RUTH   I helped to organize the society soon after the women were given the right to vote.

DAVE   You mean to say you've been mixed up in this thing ever since it started?

RUTH   Yes sir.

DAVE   Even when Ah was at the head of the deacon's board you was workin' for this thing against me?

RUTH   I wasn't exactly against you; I was for the movement.

DAVE   It's the very same thing. (RUTH *lets this pass*)   Do you know what I'm goin' to do to you? (RUTH *looks up at him*)   Ah'm goin' to take you out of school and let you go to work. You won't go back to Howard any more. Maybe then—

SOL   That's the very thing Ah'd do with mine if she was mixed up in it.

EVA (*turning to* SOL)   I am mixed up in it, Papa.

SOL (*in surprise*)   You?

EVA   Yes sir,

SOL   You don't mean to tell me—

EVA   I was there with Ruth, and I'm a member.

SOL (*going close to her and shaking his hand in her face*)   Well, Ah won't allow it! Ah won't have it; you understand! Out of Howard you'll come. (*he says no more but glares at her*)

MARTHA (*calmly*)   Well, Ruth is not coming out of college.

DAVE   Not?

MARTHA   No, she's going to stay until she finishes.

DAVE   Are you in sympathy with her after she's disgraced us?

MARTHA   I don't consider myself disgraced.

DAVE   You don't?

MARTHA   No, not at all.

DAVE   Did you know she was mixed up in this thing?

MARTHA   Yes.

(DAVE's *mouth comes open, but he seems unable to decide what he wishes to say*)

DAVE (*finally forming some words*)   And never said anything to me about it?

MARTHA   That was because I was mixed up in it myself. We've got to get these colored women ready for the election.

DAVE (*dumbfounded*)   You're in this business too?

MARTHA   Yes, I'm a member of the society, and I give money to it—your money.

DAVE (*angrily, as he turns to go*)   Ah haven't got anything else to say.

MARTHA   Wait a minute; I've got something else to say. (*he comes back*)

DAVE   What is it?

MARTHA   We might just as well understand each other now as any other time.

DAVE   Yes, Ah reckon we had. Go on and say what you've got to say.

MARTHA   You men seem to have the wrong idea about women. You think our minds never go further than cooking and darning socks; but you're very much mistaken. We think about other things the same as you do. The time has passed when women are willing to be considered merely as parts of the house, and you men might as well get your minds right on that point.

DAVE   You don't mean to say you want to vote?

MARTHA   Yes, I do. Now that we can vote, we all want to vote.

DAVE   What do you want to vote for? You're gettin' on all right.

MARTHA   I want to vote for the same reason you want to vote, and so do the girls. When we add our voting strength to yours you'll get along better.

DAVE   You can talk all you want to, but you can't make me believe in a woman votin'.

MARTHA   I'm not trying to make you believe in it. You'll believe in it of your own accord as soon as you wake up. It's already here.

(*The two men have begun to feel that they are beaten, but are not yet willing to surrender*)

MARTHA   Come on, girls, let's get dinner.

(*She and the girls go out. The men look at each other for a moment, then* DAVE *smiles*)

DAVE   Ah reckon they got us, Sol.

SOL   That won't make me believe it's right.

(*There is a silence while* DAVE *stares in front of him and* SOL *paces the floor. Presently* MARTHA *returns*)

MARTHA   I've started the girls off with the dinner; now I want you to give me some good reason why you object to your daughters voting?

DAVE (*answering for both*)   It's too public.

SOL   Yes, it keeps 'em out too much when they ought to be home.

MARTHA   Don't you think women want to hold positions of importance sometimes?

SOL   They ought to leave that to the men.

MARTHA   That's the trouble now. We've been leaving too much to men. You cut a girl's opportunity off, then whine when a girl child is born instead of a boy.

DAVE   Who whines?

MARTHA   Both of you did and you know it. And that's the very reason. You think a girl will have to be supported, and will never be able to be anything of importance, so you object to their being born. When you tell people you have a daughter, you do it with a feeling of shame, and if they don't pity you in words, they do in their hearts.

DAVE   Don't talk foolishness, Martha.

MARTHA   You know it's the truth.

SOL   Do you think you can make us want women to vote just because men like boy children better than girls?

MARTHA   It's not a question of your wanting it. You've got to take it; it's already here. Our great trouble is to make you colored men and women aware of the fact that it is already here!

SOL (*surrendering*)   All right, have your own way about it. Ah won't have nothin' to do with it.

MARTHA   But you'll both keep nagging at us.

SOL   Ah won't; Ah never nag at anybody.

DAVE   Ah won't say another word.

MARTHA (*pleased*)   May I tell the girls?

SOL   I don't care.

MARTHA (*calling*)   Ruth! Eva!

(DAVE *and* SOL *are standing like two schoolboys who have been getting a scolding, when the girls enter with their aprons on*)

MARTHA   It's all right!

(*The girls, with cries of joy, embrace their fathers*)

[*Curtain*]

BALO

1922

Jean (Nathan Eugene) Toomer (1894–1967)

Jean Toomer was the son of a mulatto aristocrat, Nina Pinchback, and a white Georgia planter, Nathan Toomer. His father left his wife a year after his son's birth, and Eugene was raised in the home of his grandmother, whose husband had been a prominent politician during Reconstruction. Although raised with the family name of Pinchback, he later adopted his father's surname and changed his first name from Eugene to Jean. Born of a wealthy and influential family of Washington, D.C., Toomer seemed an unlikely candidate to write about folk life in rural Georgia, but in 1921, after he served for a year as a teacher of a Black school in Sparta, Georgia, not only did he discover the beauty of the "folk" but he also uncovered a part of himself. In 1922, he wrote:

> A visit to Georgia last fall was the starting point of almost everything of worth that I have done. I heard folk-songs come from the lips of Negro peasants. I saw the rich dusk beauty . . . a deep part of my nature . . . sprang suddenly to life and responded to them.

In 1922, his poetic novel, *Cane*, the result of his Georgia sojourn, exploded upon the Harlem Renaissance, lighting up its literary horizons. Toomer had rendered the "Kabnis" chapter of *Cane* in dialogue, and it is often categorized as an expressionistic play. Toomer wrote two other dramas around the same time—*Natalie Mann* and *Balo*—the latter for the Howard Players' season 1923–24. In later years, he tried his hand again with *The Sacred Factory* (1927), *The Gallonwerps* (1928), *Columbo Madras Mail* (unfinished) and *Pilgrims, Did You Say?* (unfinished).

A poet and a novelist, Toomer possessed little dramatic talent. A reading of *Balo*, which he subtitled "A Sketch of Negro Life," reveals that much of his best prose lies in the descriptions. If *Balo* is more a sketch than a play, it is also more honest than most folk drama because the characters are not burdened with plot. Instead, we meet people going about their everyday lives. We meet again the issue of whether the family should move north to better their circumstances. We meet the white farmer next door, who belies the stereotype "cracker" figure populating most folk plays. We meet the play's namesake, Balo, who is a mystic, reflecting Toomer's passionate interest in mysticism. From 1924 to 1932, Toomer had devoted himself to the philosophy of George Ivanovitch Gurdjieff, a Greek-Armenian guru who achieved popular notoriety through his Institute for the Harmonious Development of Man located in Fontainebleau, outside of Paris. Toomer devoted his life to a search for the "Great Harmony" described by Gurdjieff, in which he might lose himself. Balo, the young man of the play, searches for God and finds Jesus.

He moves toward his mystic revelation in the most humble and familiar of circumstances, akin to those of Christ's birth in a manger. No one in the family shares his vision, not even his father, who wants to be a preacher; nonetheless, all accept the boy's epiphany. Balo sees God. Like first love, his religious ecstasy is pure, overwhelming, complete—so much so that although Toomer wrote the play to be performed, it is difficult to imagine a flesh-and-blood actor achieving the sensitivity and tenderness in the theatre that Balo achieves in our imaginations. The rural "peasant" achieves that which Toomer sought and never found: union with God.

Many playwrights, white and Black, have presented the "gettin' happy" scene in a Negro church (*Porgy; Mamba's Daughters; Run, Little Chillun; Amen Corner*). These scenes can work despite the artifice imposed by the stage because of the emotion implicit in the scene and the support of music. Nevertheless, observation shows that a real person who "gets happy" (unlike a stage character) may throw her hat, gloves, and hymnal into the air, but never her purse or her spectacles—suggesting that ecstasy does not override *all* practical concerns.

Balo

CAST OF CHARACTERS

WILL LEE, *a Negro farmer*
SUSAN LEE, *his wife*
TOM, *his elder son*
BALO, *another son*
JENNINGS, *a white neighbor*
COUSIN BOB
COUSIN MAMIE, *his wife*
UNCLE NED
SAM, *Uncle Ned's companion*
CHILDREN

SCENE   *Georgia, 1924.*

TIME   *Harvest time.*

(Autumn dawn. Any week day. Outside, it is damp and dewy, and the fog, resting upon the tops of pine trees, looks like fantastic cotton bolls about to be picked by the early morning fingers of the sun. As the curtain rises, the scene is that of a Negro farmhouse interior. The single room, at all times used for sleeping and sitting, on odd occasions serves as a kitchen, this latter due to the fact that a great fireplace, with hooks for pots and kettles, occupies, together with a small family organ, the entire space of the left-hand wall. This huge hearth suggests that perhaps the place might once have been a plantation cookroom. This is indeed the case, and those who now call it home (having added two rooms to it) remember the grandmother—in her day Marsa Harris' cook—telling how she contrived to serve the dishes hot despite the fact that the big house was some hundred yards away. The old frame mansion still stands, or rather, the ghost of it, in the direct vision of the front door, its habit-*

able portion tenanted by a poor-white family who farm the land to the south of it and who would, but for the tradition of prejudice and the coercion of a rural public opinion, be on terms of a frank friendship with their colored neighbors, a friendship growing out of a similarity of occupations and consequent problems. As it is, there is an understanding and bond between them little known or suspected by northern people. The colored family farms the land to the north. The dividing line, halfway between the two homes, has no other mark save one solid stake of oak. Both farmers did well last year, resisted the temptation to invest in automobiles and player-pianos, saved their money, and so, this season, though their cotton crop failed with the rest, they have a nest egg laid away, and naturally are more conscious of their comparative thrift and prosperity than if the times were good. As was said, the curtain rises upon the general room of the Negro farmhouse. The man himself, in rough gray baggy trousers and suspenders showing white against a gray flannel shirt, is seen whittling a board for shavings and small kindling sticks to start a fire with. As he faces the audience, the half light shades his features, giving but the faint suggestion that they are of a pleasing African symmetry. Having enough kindling, he arranges it in the hearth, strikes a match, and, as the wood catches, tends and coaxes it, squatting on his hams. The flames soon throw his profile into relief. It is surprisingly like that of an Indian. And his hair (lack of hair, really), having been shaved close, completes the illusion. A quick glance around the room will now reveal a closed door (to the left) in the back wall, underneath which a narrow strip of light shows. To the right of the door, against the wall, is a heavy oak bed which has been perfectly made even at this early hour. In the right wall, by the bed, a curtained window lets in at first the gray, and then, as the mist lifts, the yellow light of morning. This side of the curtain is a magnificent oak dresser, a match for the bed, but otherwise out of place and proportion in the room. Both of these are gifts to the family (and have become heirlooms) from old Marsa. A window may be understood to be in the wall facing the audience. Likewise, in this wall, to the left, a door opens on the outside. The walls are plastered and whitewashed. They are sprinkled with calendars, one or two cheap pictures of fruit (such as are supposed to befit a dining room), and one or two inevitable deathlike family portraits. Chairs are here and there about a central table, in the middle of which, resting on a white covering, is a

wooden tray for nut picks and crackers. The floor is covered with a good quality carpet. The fire in the hearth now burns brightly, but fails to fill all but a small portion of it, and so, gives one the impression of insufficiency. While WILL LEE is still crouching down, the rear door swings open as his wife comes in. Her complexion is a none too healthy yellow, and her large, deep-set, sad and weary eyes are strangely pathetic, haunted, and almost unearthly in the flamelight. With such a slim and fragile body it is surprising how she manages to carry on her part of the contract)

SUSAN LEE (her voice is high and somewhat cracked)   Come on in. (she turns about, and reenters the kitchen. WILL, satisfied with his fire, rises and, as he follows her, speaks)

WILL   Whar's Bob an' Bettie Kate?

SUSAN (through the half-open door)   Sent them for to catch an' milk th' cows.

WILL   Whar's th' boys?

SUSAN   You-all know they was up all night a-grindin' an' a-boilin' cane. Come on in.

(WILL passes out, and soon his voice is heard in blessing)

WILL   We thanks thee, Heavenly Father, fo' yo' blessin's of th' night. Once more thou hast kept yo' children thru' th' time of Satan an' of sin. Bless us, O Lord. Thou hast brought us like th' dew thru' temptations of th' evil darkness inter th' glory of th' mornin' light. Have mercy, Lord. Keep us, an' give us strength t'do yo' will terday. An' every day. An' we asks you t' bless this yere food prepared in His dear name. Amen. Amen. (Just as WILL begins his prayer, two young fellows enter through the front door, but on hearing the blessing in progress, stop, and wait with bowed heads until it is over. Whereupon they advance, and are heard by WILL)

WILL   That you, Tom?

TOM (the larger of the two boys. A Negro farm hand with a smiling face and easy gait, distinguished at first from BALO only by his taller figure and the fact of a seedy black coat which he wears over his patched blue faded overalls)   Yassur.

WILL   How much you git?

TOM   Mighty nigh eighty gallons.

WILL   That's right. Had yo' breakfast?

TOM   Yassur.

WILL   That you thar, Balo?

BALO   Yassur, dat's me.

WILL   Reckon you had yo breakfast too?

BOTH   Yassur we done et.

WILL   *Slept any?*

BOTH   Nasur, dat we ain't.

WILL   Well, git yo' Bibles down an' read fo' fifteen minutes, then you-all jes' stretch yo'-selfs befo' th' fire an' I'll wake you up by an' by.

BOTH   Yassur.

(They get their Bibles from the organ, stretch out in front the hearth, and begin to read. BALO is nearer the audience. As he reads he mumbles his words aloud, and, by the twitching of his face and the movements of his hands, is seen to be of a curious nervous texture beneath his surface placidity. TOM soon falls asleep, and begins to breathe deeply and rhythmically. The monotony of this respiration, together with the sound of his own voice seems to excite BALO peculiarly. His strange, half-closed eyes burn with a dancing light, and his entire body becomes animated and alive. At this juncture, young voices and young feet enter the room to the rear. SUSAN has trouble in getting them seated, and WILL in blessing the food. Laughs, shouts, and admonitions, in reality, continue all during the following scene, but, as BALO does not hear them, and as the audience is absorbed in BALO, all sound from the kitchen ceases on the stage. BALO by this time has risen to his feet. Facing the audience, he continues to read, and his words become audible. He is reading St. Matthew VII, 24)

BALO

Therefore whosoever heareth these sayings of mine, and doeth them, I will liken him unto a wise man, which built his house upon a rock: And the rain descended, and the floods came, and the winds blew, and beat upon that house; and it fell not; for it was founded upon a rock. And everyone that heareth these sayings of mine, and doeth them not, shall be likened unto a foolish man, which built his house upon the sand: And the rain descended, and the floods came, and the winds blew, and beat upon that house; and it fell: and great was the fall of it.

(Here BALO's excitement is so considerable that he leaves off the Bible and chants, with additions, certain passages of it from memory)

An' th' floods came, an' th' winds blew,
An' th' floods came, an' th' winds blew,
An' th' floods came, an' th' winds blew,

O Lord, have mercy, Lord, O Lord
Have mercy on a soul what sins,
O Lord, on a darky sinner's soul.

(He repeats this two or three times and is almost beside himself when the tumult from the rear room breaks in on him. He is at first entirely bewildered, but then, with an instinctive rapidity, and before the children enter, stretches himself beside TOM on the hearth, and pretends to be asleep. Before so very long, this pretended sleep passes into the real thing. BOB and BETTIE KATE run through, take a whack at both of them, and go out the front door. WILL and SUSAN follow them into the front room, and, after they have gone, seat themselves before the fire)

WILL *(in substance, this is repeated each morning, so that SUSAN almost knows it now by heart)* Ain't much t' do this mornin', Susan. Farmin's gittin' p'oly down this way when a man what's used t' work can set afo' th' fire handlin' han's, an' it's yet a month t' Christmas. Money ain't t' be made when syrup can be bought fer what it takes t' haul th' cane, an' git it ground an' biled. An' corn at fifty cents a bushel. Cotton's th' crop fer Georgia. Weevils or no weevils. An' God will took them away when people ain't so sinful *(he indicates the boys)* when folks goes t' sleep with Bibles in their han's. Susan, whar is that there theology book? Mus' be studyin'. Can't afford t' waste no time when I's in th' service of th' Lord. Sho' can't.

TOM   It's around somewheres, Will. You-all still studyin' seriously t' be a preacher? Thought I changed you back a week ago.

WILL   That I is, sho', an' there's lots worse a heap. Sin is stompin' up an' down th' world an' Satan's drivin' with loose reins. Needs a righteous man t' grab them from him 'round this way. Wouldn't let you had that frolic here t'night but what I thought 'twould be as good a chance as any t' turn th' people t' His ways. An' that I wouldn't . . . Cousin Bob an' Mamie comin' early.

(Outside, a voice is heard calling WILL)

WILL   That you, Mr. Jennings? Come in, sir.

JENNINGS *(coming in. He is their white neighbor—a well-built man with ruddy cheeks and pointed nose, dressed like WILL but for his shirt which is of khaki)*   Nothin' ter do, eh, Will, but hold yer hands afore th' fire? Lucky last year put a few dollars in th' bank.

WILL   Yassur, lucky sho'. (*both remain standing, a little awkwardly despite the friendly greeting.* SUSAN *has kept her seat, and says nothing until directly spoken to*)

JENNINGS (*pointing to the sleeping boys*) Nothin' fer them ter do, eh, sleepin' away th' days an' it ain't yet Christmas.

WILL   Nasur. Them's been up all night tho', grindin' cane.

JENNINGS   Saw Balo there while back actin' like he was crazy. An' what do yer think he said? An' kept on repeatin' it, "White folks ain't no more'n niggers when they gets ter heaven, white folks ain't no more'n niggers when they gets ter heaven." (*laughs*) How much you get?

WILL   'Bout eighty gallons.

JENNINGS   Not bad from that little biddie piece of land, eh?

WILL   Nasur, not bad 'tall. But us has more'n we can use, an' 'twouldn't pay t' ship it at th' present price they pays fer it.

JENNINGS   Trade?

WILL   Fer what?

JENNINGS   Corn; turnips.

WILL   Nasur, got too many of them myself. Too much syrup, too. Take some along with you; don't want nothin', sir.

JENNINGS   All right, Will. Noticed yer ax handle was busted. I'll send th' boy over with a new one fer yer. An' anything else you want, just ask. Heard someone sayin' something' 'bout you goin' north ter live. I told 'em, na,—preachin' an' farmin' is th' line fer you. An' there's only one place fer them an' that's in Georgia, eh, Will?

WILL   Yassur, that's right, sho'.

JENNINGS   What you gotter say 'bout it, Susan?

SUSAN   I don't want him t' preach, Mr. Jennings. Preachin' means neglect th' farm. Up north they say there's lots of things you don't get here. An' I don't know, Mr. Jennings, but I'd like t' get somethin'.

JENNINGS   Wall, what do yer call somethin' if money in th' bank ain't somethin' when th' times are hard?

SUSAN   Yassur, money, but there's somethin' more'n life besides all th' money in th' world. I want that somethin' else; an' folks say I might could get it if I went up north.

JENNINGS   How 'bout that, Will?

WILL   Dunno, sir. Maybe so, but I knows this place, an' I don't know that. 'Specks Georgia's big enuf't hold me till I dies.

JENNINGS   Me, too, Will. Wall, mus' be goin'. I'll send a can here fer that there syrup. An' th' handle.

WILL   Don't mind th' can, Mr. Jennings, sir, jest roll a barrel over, an' roll it back when you is thru'.

JENNINGS   All right. Thanks, Will—return th' same some day. So long.

WILL (*seeing him to the door*) Yassur, good evenin', Mr. Jennings. (*he closes the door and returns to* SUSAN. *The boys are still sleeping soundly*)

WILL   Wish you'd root me out that book, Susan. (SUSAN *gets up, rummages around, and finds the book.* WILL *immediately drops into his chair, and is at once absorbed. Like* BALO, *though in not quite so pronounced a manner, he too mumbles as he reads.* SUSAN *enters the rear room. At this point the curtain descends for a moment to indicate the passing of the morning, and of the first five hours of the afternoon. When it ascends,* WILL *is seated as before, in front of the fire which now burns briskly and with a sizzling sound in thankful contrast to the dull gray light that filters through the windows. It has clouded up outside, and threatens rain. The boys have left the hearth.* WILL *has exchanged his theology book for the Bible. His eyes seem to be in a concentrated daze, focused on the glowing ashes. A voice coming from the outside arouses him.*)

VOICE   Whoo thar, you, Will?

WILL (*collecting himself*) That you, Cousin Bob? Come on in. Don't need no ceremonies t' enter this yer house. Come in. Come in. (COUSIN BOB *and his wife, Negro country folks, and six small children from twelve to two and a half years old enter through the rear door by way of the kitchen.* COUSIN MAMIE *carries a large basket covered with a spotless white napkin.*)

WILL   What's that fer on yo' arm, Cousin Mamie?

MAMIE   Supper, Cousin Will. Know'd you'd hab enuf t' share with us-all, but reckoned I'd jes' tote it wid me, 'kase dese hungry mouths don't nebber git enuf t' eat, does you, honey? (*addressing the oldest, who shakes his head bashfully in negation*) I'll jes warm 'tup over yo' fire dar when you-all goes in t' eat. (*the family all group themselves in a semicircle around the hearth, the older folks on chairs, the younger ones on the floor or standing, shifting ill at ease from foot to foot, uncomfortable in their Sunday shoes*)

COUSIN BOB   Cotton po' wid you dis year I 'specks, Will.

WILL   P'oly, Cousin Bob, p'oly. Three bales at th' outset, an' doin' good at that.

BOB   Any corn?

WILL   More'n I know what t' do with.

BOB   Pigs?

WILL   Doin' well on hogs. Cousin Bob, doin' well. (*the conversation dies out. They sit in perfect silence. Then* SUSAN *and the children come in from somewhere.* SUSAN *greets the new arrivals, kissing each child.* BOB *and* BETTIE KATE *are boisterous and demonstrative, and take delight in their more backward playmates. By the time* SUSAN'*s ritual is through with, the front door opens and a middle-aged Negro comes in, assisting an old (no one knows how old he is), gray-haired, bearded fellow who is blind. This old man has a dignity and a far-away, other-worldly expression such as might have characterized a saint of old. Indeed one immediately thinks of him as some hoary Negro prophet, who, having delivered his message, waits humbly and in darkness for his day to come. He is called* UNCLE NED, *and is so greeted by all as he enters. He returns the greeting*)

UNCLE NED   (*deep and low, and remarkably clear for one of his infirmities*)   Chillun, chillun. Blind eyes ain't supposed t' see an' ain't supposed t' cry, but, chilluns, voices allus seem t' be so sad, an' I had reckoned as if th' Lord had minded Him t' make sech reservations fer th' old. An' Uncle Ned has had his chillun since th' days befo' th' war. 'Tain't now like it used t' be—he could see 'em with his two eyes then, an' now he has t' see 'em with his heart. An' 'tain't easy any more. Hearts ain't all a-shinin' as they used t' be. (*abruptly*) God bless an' keep you all.

WILL   Th' kind Lord bless an' preserve you, Uncle Ned.

SAM   (UNCLE NED'S *companion*)   Amen. Amen. (UNCLE NED *is seated in the center, before the fire.* SUSAN *goes out; and presently calls to* WILL. WILL *beckons to* BOB *and* BETTIE KATE, *and then asks all to have a bite with him*)

WILL   Some supper, folks?

ALL   No, Will, no. Thank y' jest th' same.

MAMIE   I'll take t' feed all those that wants t' eat in here.

WILL   Reckon you will at that. (*he and the children go out.* TOM *comes in with an armful of wood, then follows* WILL. WILL *is heard blessing the food. Everyone in the front room bows his head*)

WILL   Give us this day, our daily bread, O Lord, an' hearts filled up with thanks for Him in whose dear name all food an' goodness is prepared in. Amen. Amen.

SAM   (*after* WILL)   Amen. Amen. (MAMIE *sets about warming up some sweet potatoes, meat, and corn bread. She gets a dish or two from the kitchen, and fixes one for* UNCLE NED. *The children eat from one large pan. The grown-ups talk in undertones*)

SAM   What's got inter Will he lettin' Susan have a frolic?

BOB   Dunno.

MAMIE   'Deed I dunno neither. Queer goin's on fer him sho'.

SAM   Ef I was a bettin' man I'd lay a dollar t' a cotton stalk Will'll turn this yer frolic inter a preacher's meetin' afo' he's thru'.

UNCLE NED   That's right, that's true. Will has got t' fear o' God in 'im as sho's you're born.

MAMIE   Ain't many comin' on a night like this.

SAM   That's right; niggers is sho' funny 'bout gettin' theyself wet. (BALO *comes in, but finding no seat around the fire, installs himself before the organ. His feet begin to pump, and his fingers to touch a key here and there. The sequence of notes finally arranges itself into a Negro melody. It is the one called "Steal Away." As his ear catches the tune, he begins to play in earnest. the folks all join in, at first by humming, and then they sing the words.* UNCLE NED'*s gray head swings slowly, and with his right hand he seems to be conducting.* TOM *enters from the kitchen. Likewise* WILL *and* SUSAN *and the children. They all sing. As most everyone knows, the words are:*)

[CHORUS]
Steal away, steal away, steal away to Jesus,
Steal away, steal away home,
I ain't got long to stay here.

VERSE
My Lord calls me, He calls me by the thunder,
I ain't got long to stay here.
My Lord calls me, He calls me by the lightning,
The trumpet sounds within my soul,
The trumpet sounds within my soul,
I ain't got long to stay here.

(*This is repeated several times. At each repetition the emotional excitation becomes greater. At about the third round, the ordered sequence of words is interrupted at will with such phrases as, "O Lord," "Have Mercy," yet the rhythm and the tune are maintained. Thus is achieved one of the striking, soul-stirring effects of Negro melody. The song reaches its climax, and then gradually sinks and fades away. After the singers once get well under way, BALO stops playing, except that now and then he emphasizes a passage by a full chord. He sings, and his own emotion grows greater than the rest. As the song dies out, this seems to diminish also. And when all is still, he seems more quiet than the others. But then, after a pause of some seconds, and utterly without warning, he bursts forth)*

BALO *(Rising from his seat and going to the center of the room as if in a somnambulistic trance)*

An' th' floods came, an' th' winds blew,
An' th' floods came, an' th' winds blew,
An' th' floods came, an' th' winds blew,
Have mercy, Lord, have mercy, Lord,
On me, O yes, on me, on me,
Have mercy, Lord, on me, on me.

(The folks do not seem at all surprised at this outburst. A head or two are slowly nodded while it lasts)

SAM *(as BALO finishes)*   Amen. Amen.
UNCLE NED   Have mercy, Lord, have mercy.
WILL   Amen. Amen.

(And now voices and raps on the door announce new arrivals. Two couples. They are strikingly similar both in looks and in dress. Black faces that in repose are sad and heavy, but when they break in smiles become light-hearted and gay. The men have on white shirts and collars, loose black coats, pressed dark trousers, and polished black shoes. The two women are in white shirt waists and plain dark skirts. The room, of course, is now quite crowded. The group around the fire breaks up to greet them. BALO is again left to compose himself. "Good evenin's" and "hellos" are exchanged, and by the time the wraps are disposed of on the bed, SAM has proposed a game of "kyards." They all look suspiciously, as if undecided, at WILL. He, however, turns his gaze into the fire, and by his silence gives consent. Two tables are arranged. Seated around them are the two recent couples, SAM and SUSAN, BOB and MAMIE. They begin to play, and, as they forget Will's presence, become quite lively. Some of the children watch the games. Some are still around the fire. WILL, with BALO,
TOM, *and* UNCLE NED *hug the hearth. Their conversation is audible, for the players on the stage reduce their jollity to gestures, etc., though of course in fact such is not the case)*

UNCLE NED   Cotton drapped this year as wus' as I ever seed it. An' in every weevil I see sho' th' fingers of th' Lord. Reckon you farmers better drap down on your knees an' pray, an' pray ter th' Lord fer ter free you fom yo' sins. White folks hit th' same as black this time.
WILL   They sho' is.
UNCLE NED   Boll weevils come ter tell us that it's time ter change our ways. Ain't satisfied with sinnin', but gettin' wus'. An' th' Lord looks down an' is angry, an' he says, "Stop," says he, "ken you stop now? If you ken you ken be saved. I'm a-warnin' yer. An' them what heeds my warnin' has time befo' th' Judgment ter repent their sins an' ter be born again. Ter be born again."
WILL   Amen, Unce Ned, Amen. An' true, true. Like Saul y'know, Saul of Tarsus, we is all on our way t' Damascus, an' breathin' out threatnin's an' slaughter 'gainst th' Lord. But we can be born again. We can be born again an' see th' light that Saul saw when he fell down t' th' earth, an' hear th' voice that Saul heard when he lay there kickin' on th' ground an' stirrin' up th' dust on th' road that led inter Damascus. We can be born again, that's sho'. Brother, we can be born again an' go out like Saul an' preach th' gospel of th' Lord. O Lord.

(They all, that is, all around the hearth, slip immediately and easily into humming an indefinite air derived from a melody. As this increases in volume, BALO is seen to tilt back in his chair, and his eyes roll ecstatically upward. Even more suddenly than before he jumps to his feet)

BALO

Jesus, Jesus, I've found Jesus,
Th' light that came t' Saul when he was born again,
Th' voice that spoke t' Saul when he was born again,
Jesus, Jesus, I've found Jesus,
One mo' sinner is a-comin' home.

(Here he falls to his knees, face raised in pain and exaltation, hands clasped in supplication above his head)

O Jesus, Jesus, savior of my soul,
One mo'sinner is a-comin' home,
One mo' sinner is a-comin' home.

Th' light that came t' Saul when he was born
    again,
Th' voice that spoke t' Saul when he was born
    again,
Th' light that came t' Saul when he was born
    again,
O Jesus, Jesus, savior of my soul,
Jesus, Jesus, I've found Jesus,
One mo' sinner is a-comin' home.

(BALO *stops, and gives a desperate glance around
the room. Seeing* UNCLE NED, *who has turned to
face him, he throws himself into his arms, and
breaks into a violent and spasmodic sobbing.* UN-
CLE NED *raises one arm in blessing, while with the
other he encircles him in love. The card players,
having become uneasy when* UNCLE NED *first began to talk, stopped their game entirely at* BALO's
*outburst, and now file out, heads lowered, in
sheepishness and guilt. And as the curtain descends, the others, with the exception of* UNCLE
NED *and* BALO, *are seen leaving.*

[Curtain]

A SUNDAY MORNING IN THE SOUTH

1925

Georgia Douglas Johnson (1877?–1966)

As she lay dying, a friend, fellow poet, and playwright, May Miller, who lived a few doors away on S Street in Washington, D.C., stroked Georgia Douglas Johnson's hand, repeating quietly over and over, "Poet, Georgia Douglas Johnson." Also a playwright, songwriter, and teacher, Johnson ranks high in the pantheon of Harlem Renaissance writers, with Countee Cullen, Langston Hughes, and Marita Bonner.

Born to George and Laura Jackson Camp in Atlanta, Georgia, in 1877 (some biographers say in 1886), her grandparents were English, African American, and Native American.[1] She began school in Rome, Georgia, but transferred to the public schools of Atlanta and eventually attended college at Atlanta University. To assuage her loneliness, she learned to play the violin and began to write songs. Ultimately, she transferred to Oberlin College to study music.

Returning to Atlanta to teach, in 1903 she married Henry Lincoln Johnson, a lawyer and Republican politician. In 1910, they moved to the nation's capital, where her husband became President Taft's Recorder of Deeds. The couple had two sons, Henry Lincoln, Jr., and Peter Douglas. Widowed in 1925, with one son at Dartmouth College and the other at Bowdoin College, Georgia Johnson found work in the Department of Labor as Commissioner of Conciliation. Nonetheless, she reserved some of her time to write, and over the years, her modest home in the northwest section of Washington, D.C., became the mecca for Black artists and intellectuals: Langston Hughes, May Miller, Sterling Brown, Alain Locke, Marita Bonner, Willis Richardson, Charles Sebree, Jean Toomer, and others who would assemble for her "Saturday Soirees," a literary clique that became known as the S Street Salon. Johnson nicknamed her house "Half-Way House" because "I am halfway between the people I bring together" (from the North and the South).

Known primarily for her four volumes of

---

1. Professor Winona Fletcher of Indiana University has provided excellent biographical materials in the *Dictionary of Literary Biography: Afro-American Writers from the Harlem Renaissance to 1940*, vol. 51 (Detroit: Gale Research, 1987).

poetry published between 1918 (*The Heart of a Woman*) and 1962 (*Share My World*) Johnson also wrote seven plays: a one-act comedy, *Blue Blood* (1926), about miscegenation, which was produced by the Krigwa Players in New York; *Plumes: A Folk Tragedy,* for which she won first prize in 1927 from *Opportunity* magazine and which was produced by the Harlem Experimental Theatre; *Frederick Douglass* and *William and Ellen Craft,* both history plays for children, published in *Thirteen Plays of Negro History;* and *Safe* (1929), *Blue-eyed Black Boy* (c. 1930), and *A Sunday Morning in the South,* three antilynch plays, published in the first edition of this anthology in 1974 for the first time.

As the years passed, Johnson acquired the reputation of a kindly eccentric. She continued to wear a head band, long after the 1920s fashion had passed. Around her neck she kept a tablet and a pencil to jot down ideas whenever they might come. She would stop young men on the street and lecture them on Black pride and proper public behavior and dress. Over the years, old newspapers, magazines, and discarded clothes drifted like snow into the rooms of her house, covering and filling tables, chairs, and floor. Owen Dodson, the poet, who knew Johnson in her late years, described her abode.

> She took in lame dogs, blind cats, any kind of limping animal. The animals would sleep under the rose bushes of which she was very proud—the smell of manure and roses. She took in stray people, artists who were out of money like Zora Neale Hurston for long periods. Or artists who were a little berserk. She knew how to soothe them and do for them.
>
> The house was a mess. . . . In the living room, there was a pathway through the Chicago *Defender* and the Pittsburgh *Courier;* she wrote a poem every week for the *Courier* up to a month before she died. The last one she wrote "We live too long."

A Sunday Morning in the South is not Johnson's most tightly structured drama (it was never published and probably not produced in her lifetime). The plot is predictable and the conclusion inevitable, but the play's emotional impact is, nevertheless, very powerful. Like Grimké, Johnson hoped that her play would move her audience to action.

The subject of the drama—lynching—because of the unique history of Black/white race relations in the United States, had become an American theatrical genre. Between 1882 and 1927, 3,589 Blacks, including 76 women, were lynched.[2] Hung, beaten, burned, or stabbed, the victims were commonly tortured and/or castrated before they were killed. Although groups of white men were the primary executioners or lynchers, white women and children were commonly present as onlookers, playing a supportive role in the ritual. Food was sometimes served, encouraging a picnic-like atmosphere, and participants often gathered the ears or fingers of the mutilated body as a souvenir of the outing.[3] A number of attempts in Congress to pass an antilynching law were blocked. Outraged, women's groups, inspired initially by Ida B. Wells, organized meetings and wrote articles berating the barbaric practice.

The antilynch dramas, comparable only to the passionate appeal in antislavery plays, became the second form of American protest drama. More than two dozen antilynch plays, written mostly by women, have survived.[4] Usually one acts, these folk plays were set in an African American

---

2. NAACP. *Thirty Years of Lynching in the United States* (NY: Arno Press, 1969).

3. Although the practice was concentrated in the southern states, it was a nationwide phenomenon, with only five states (Massachusetts, Vermont, New Hampshire, Rhode Island, and Connecticut) reporting no lynchings.

4. Professors Judith L. Stephens and Kathy Perkins have rescued many of these plays from oblivion.

environment, such as a home; the lynching, past or present, is described by or to women. The innocence of the victim is established, and some form of resistance or retaliation by the family or friends is planned. These dramatic innovations, pioneered by Angelina Grimké in *Rachel* (1916) and Mary P. Burrill in *Aftermath* (1919), were used and developed by Johnson.

Georgia Douglas Johnson died in 1966. Her legacy, as Ann Trapasso wrote, "included the encouragement to dream."

A Sunday Morning in the South

CHARACTERS

SUE JONES, *the grandmother, aged seventy*
TOM GRIGGS, *her grandson, aged nineteen*
BOSSIE GRIGGS, *her grandson, aged seven*
LIZA TRIGGS, *a friend, aged sixty*
MATILDA BROWN, *a friend, aged fifty*
A WHITE GIRL
FIRST OFFICER
SECOND OFFICER

PLACE   *A town in the South.*

TIME   *1924*

SCENE: *Kitchen in* SUE JONES' *two room house. A window on left, a door leading to back yard and another leading to front room. A stove against the back wall, a table near it, four chairs, an old time safe with dishes and two bottles—one clear and one dark—a wooden water bucket with shiny brass bales, and a tin dipper hanging near it on a nail.*

As the curtain rises SUE JONES *is seen putting the breakfast on the kitchen table. She wears a red bandanna handkerchief on her grey head, a big blue gingham apron tied around her waist and big wide old lady comfort shoes. She uses a stick as she has a sore leg, and moves about with a stoop and a limp as she goes back and forth from the stove to the table)*

SUE *(calling)*   Tom, Tom, you and Bossie better come on out here and git your breakfast before it gits cold; I got good hot rolls this mornin!

TOM *(from next room)*   All right grannie, we're coming.

SUE   You better ef you know whut's good for you *(opens stove door, looks at rolls, then begins humming and singing)*

Eugh . . . eu . . . eugh . . .
Jes look at the morning star
Eugh . . . eu . . . eugh . . .
We'll all git home bye and bye . . .

(as she finishes the song TOM *and* BOSSIE *come hurrying into the kitchen placing their chairs at the table; there is one already at the table for* SUE. SUE *takes rolls out of stove with her apron and brings them to the table)*   It's as hard to git yawll out of the bed on Sunday morning as it is to pull hen's teeth.

TOM *(eating. The Church bell next door is heard ringing)*   Eugh—there's the church bell. I sho meant to git out to meeting this morning but my back still hurts me. Remember I told you last night how I sprained it lifting them heavy boxes for Mr. John?

SUE *(giving* BOSSIE *a roll and a piece of sausage)*   You hadn't oughter done it; you oughter ast him to let somebody hep you—you ain't no hoss!

TOM   I reckin I oughter had but I didn't know how heavy they was till I started and then he was gone.

SUE   You oughter had some of my snake oil linament on it last night, that's whut?

TOM   I wish I hader but I was so dead tired I got outer my clothes and went straight to bed. I muster been sleep by nine er clock I reckin.

SUE   Nine er clock! You is crazy! Twant no moren eight when I called you to go to the store and git me a east cake fur my light rolls and you was sleeping like a log of wood; I had to send Bossie fur it.

BOSSIE   Yes, and you snored so loud I thought you would a choked. *(holding out his plate and licking his lips with his tongue)* Grannie kin I have some more?

SUE   Whut? Where is all thot I jest give you?

BOSSIE   (*rubbing his stomach with his other hand and smiling broadly*)   It's gone down the red lane struttin'.

SUE   Well this is all you gointer git this mornin. (*helping him to more rolls and sausage*) When you git big and work like Tom you kin stuff all you wants to.

BOSSIE   I aint never gointer break my back like Tom working hard—I'm a gointer be a—a preacher that's whut and . . .

SUE   (*catching sight of someone passing the window as she approached the back door*)   I bleve that's Liza Twiggs must be on her way to church and smelled these light rolls and coffee. (*a knock is heard at the back door*) Let her in, Bossie!

(BOSSIE *jumps up from the table, hurries to the door and opens it*)

LIZA   (*enters sniffling*)   Mawning yawll.

SUE   Morning Liza—on your way to church?

LIZA   Yes the first bell just rung and I thought I'd drop in a minute. (*whiffs again*) Coffee sho smells good!

SUE   Tastes better'n it smells—Pull up a cheer and swaller a cupful with one of these light rolls.

LIZA   (*drawing up a chair*)   Don't keer if I do. (*she is helped to coffee and rolls while* BOSSIE *looks at her disapprovingly. To* SUE) How is your leg gitting on?

SUE   Well as I kin expect. I won't never walk on it good no mo. It eats and eats. She is lucky I'm right here next door to church (*to* TOM) Open that winder Tom so I kin hear the singing. (TOM *opens window. To* LIZA) Folks don't like to set next to me in church no mo. Tinks its ketching—a cancer or somethin'. (*then brightly*) Whut you know good?

(*From the church next door is heard the hymn, drifting through the window:* "Amazing grace how sweet the sound / That saves a wretch like me . . .")

LIZA   (*listening*)   They done started "Amazing grace." (*music continues as a background for their talk*) (*still eating*) That music she is sweet but I got to finish eatin first, then I'll go . . .

SUE   I ast you whut you know good.

LIZA   Well, I don't know nothin tall good, but I did hear as how the police is all over now trying to run down some po Nigger they say that's tacked a white woman last night right up here near the Pine Street market. They says as how the white folks is shonuff mad too, and if they ketch him they gointer make short work of him.

SUE   (*still drinking coffee*)   Eugh, eugh, eugh, you don't say. I don't hold wid no rascality and I bleves in meeting out punishment to the guilty but they fust ought to fine out who done it tho and then let the law hanel 'em. that's what I says.

LIZA   Me too. I thinks the law oughter hanel 'em too, but you know a sight of times they gits the wrong man and goes and strings him up and don't fin out who done it till it's too late!

SUE   That's so. And sometimes the white uns been knowed to blackin they faces and make you bleve some po Nigger done it.

TOM   They lynch you bout anything too, not jest women. They say Zeb Brooks was strung up because he and his boss had er argiment.

LIZA   Sho did. I says the law's the law and it ought er be er ark uv safty to pertect the weak and not some little old flimsy shack that a puff of wind can blow down.

TOM   I been thinking a whole lot about these things and I mean to go to night school and git a little book learning so as I can do something to help—help change the laws . . . make em strong . . . I sometimes get right upset and wonder whut would I do if they ever tried to put something on me . . .

LIZA   Pshaw . . . everybody knows you . . . nobody would bother you . . .

SUE   No sonnie, you won't never hafter worry bout sich like that but you kin hep to save them po devels that they do git after.

(*Singing comes from the church next door:*)

> Shine on me, shine on me.
> Let the light from the lighthouse shine on me,
> Shine on me, shine on me,
> Let the light from the lighthouse shine on me.

TOM   It takes a sight of learning to understand the law and I'm a gointer . . . (*a quick rap is heard at the door and it is almost immediately pushed open and an* OFFICER *enters as the four at table look up at him in open mouthed amazement*)

FIRST OFFICER   Tom Griggs live here?

SUE (*starting up excitedly*)   Yes Sir (*stammering*)

FIRST OFFICER (*looking at* TOM)   You Tom Griggs?

TOM (*puzzled*)   Yes sir.

FIRST OFFICER (roughly)   Where were you last night at ten o'clock?

SUE (*answering quickly for* TOM)   Right here sir, he was right here at home. Whut you want to know fer?

FIRST OFFICER (*to* SUE)   You keep quiet, old woman. (*to* TOM) Say, you answer up. Can't you talk? Where were you last night at ten o'clock.

TOM (*uneasily*)   Gramma told you. I was right here at home—in bed at eight o'clock.

FIRST OFFICER   That sounds fishy to me—in bed at eight o'clock! And who else knows you were here?

SUE   Say Mr. Officer, whut you trying to do to my granson. Shore as God Amighty is up in them heabens he was right here in bed. I seed him and his little brother Bossie there saw him, didn't you Bossie?

BOSSIE (*in a frightened whisper*)   Yessum, I seed him and I heered him!

FIRST OFFICER (*to* BOSSIE)   Shut up. Your word's nothing. (*looking at* SUE) Not yours either. Both of you'd lie for him. (*steps to back door and makes a sign to someone outside, then comes back into the room taking a piece of paper from his vest pocket and reads slowly, looking at* TOM *critically as he checks each item*) Age around twenty, five feet five or six, brown skin . . . (*he folds up the paper and puts it back into his vest*) Yep! fits like a glove. (SUE, LIZA *and* TOM *look from one to the other with growing amazement and terror as* SECOND OFFICER *pushes open the door and stands there supporting a young white girl on his arm*)

SECOND OFFICER (*to girl*)   Is this the man?

WHITE GIRL (*hesitatingly*)   I—I'm not sure . . . but . . . but he looks something like him . . . (*holding back*)

FIRST OFFICER (*encouragingly*)   Take a good look, Miss. He fits your description perfect. Color, size, age, everything. Pine Street Market ain't no where from here, and he surely did pass that tway last night. He was there all right, all right! We got it figgered all out. (*to* GIRL, *who looks down at her feet*) You say he looks like him?

WHITE GIRL (*looking at him again quickly*)   Y-e-s (*slowly and undecidedly*) I think so. I . . . I . . . (*then she covers her face with her arm and turns quickly and moves away from the door, supported by* SECOND OFFICER. FIRST OFFICER *makes a step toward* TOM *and slips handcuffs on him before any one is aware what is happening*)

SUE (*holding on to her chair and shaking her cane at the* OFFICER, *while* BOSSIE *comes up close to her and snivels in her apron*)   Whut you doing? What you doing? You can't rest my granson—he ain't done nothing—you can't rest him!

FIRST OFFICER   Be quiet, old woman. I'm just going to take him along to the sheriff to question him, and if he's telling the truth he'll be right back here in no time.

SUE   But you can't rest him; he don't know no mo bout that po little white chile than I do—You can't take him!

TOM (*utterly bewildered*)   Granma, don't take on so. I'll go long with him to the sheriff. I'll splain to him how I couldn't a done it when I was here sleep all the time—I never laid eyes on that white lady before in all my life.

SUE (*to* TOM)   Course you ain't. (*to* OFFICER) Mr. Officer, that white chile ain't never seed my granson before—All Niggers looks alike to her; she so upset she don't know whut she's saying.

FIRST OFFICER (*to* SUE *as he pulls* TOM *along*)   You just keep cool Grannie, he'll be right back—if he's innocent. (*to* TOM) And the quieter you comes along the better it will be for you.

TOM (*looking back at his grandma from the doorway with terror in his eyes*)   I'll be right back Granny—don't cry—don't cry—Jest as soon as I see—(*the* OFFICER *pulls him out of the doorway*)

LIZA (*standing with her hands clasped together, her head bowed and swaying from side to side with emotion. She prays*)   Sweet Jesus, do come down and hep us this mornin. You knows our hearts and you knows this po boy ain't done nothing wrong. You said you would hep the fatherless and the motherless; do Jesus bring this po orphan back to his ole cripple grannie safe and sound, do Jesus!

BOSSIE (*crying and pulling at his grandma's apron*)   Grannie, Grannie, whut they gointer do to my brother? Whut they gointer do to him?

SUE (*brokenly*)   The good Jesus only knows,
but I'm a talking to the Lord now asting Him
to . . . (*a rap is heard at the door; it is almost immediately pushed open and* MATILDA BROWN *enters hurriedly and excitedly*)

MATILDA (*breathlessly*)   Miss Liza, as I was
coming long I seed Tom wid the police and
there was some white mens wid guns a trying
to take him away from the police—said he'd
done been dentified and they want gointer be
cheated outen they Nigger this time. I, I flew
on down here to tell you, you better do somethin'.

sue (*shaking nervously from side to side as she
leans on her cane for support*)   Oh my God,
whut kin I do?

LIZA (*alertly*)   You got to git word to some of
your good white folks, that's whut and git em
to save him.

SUE   Yes . . . That's whut . . . Lemme see . . .
(*she stands tense thinking a moment*) I got it . . .
Miss Vilet . . . I got to git to Miss Vilet . . . I
nused her when she was a baby and she'll do
it . . . Her pa's the Jedge.

LIZA   That's right! I'll go. You can't go quick.

MATILDA   No. Lemme go; I kin move in a
hurry, lemme go!

SUE   All right Tildy. Tell Miss Vilet her ole
nuse Sue is callin on her and don't fail me; tell
her they done took Tom and he is perfect in-
nercent, and they gointer take him away from
the police, and ax her to ax her pa the Jedge
to go git Tom and save him fur God's sake.
Now hurry, Tildy, fly!

BOSSIE (*to* SUE)   Lemme go long; I knows
how to git there quick cutting through the ole
field.

LIZA   Yes they knows Bossie and he kin hep
tell.

SUE   Yes Bossie, gone, yawll hurry, hurry!
(MATILDA *and* BOSSIE *hurry out of the back door
and* SUE *sinks down into a chair exhausted while*
LIZA *comes over to her and pats her on the back*)

LIZA   Now, now evrythin's gointer be all
right . . . Miss Vilet 'll fix it . . . she ain't gointer let her ole mammy call on her for
nothing . . . she'll make her pa save him.

SUE   Yes, she's a good chile . . . I knows
she'll save him.

(SUE *moves her lips in prayer. From the church
next door comes the sound of singing; the two
women listen to the words with emotion*

Alas and did my savior bleed
And did my sovereign die
Would he devote his sacred head
For such a worm as I.

Must Jesus bear the cross alone
And all the world go free,
No, there's a cross for every one
And there's a cross for me.

SUE *rocks back and forth in chair, head buried in
her apron.* LIZA *walks up and down the floor,
throws her hands up imploringly now and then*)

LIZA   Oh Lord, hep us to bear our cross!
Hep us!

SUE (*drooping*)   Liza I'm feeling sorter fainty
lack; git me my bottle of camphor out of the
safe yonder.

LIZA (*going to safe*)   Yes chile, I'll git it. You
done gone through a whole lot this morning,
God knows. (*takes up a bottle and holds it up for*
SUE *to see*) This it?

SUE (*shaking her head*)   Eugh eugh, that's
my sweet oil. It's the yuther one in the black
bottle . . . see it?

LIZA (*taking out bottle and smelling it*)   Yes
here it is. Strong too. It'll do you good. I has
them sinking spells too sometimes (*comes
over to* SUE *with stopper out of bottle and holds it
to her nose*) There draw a deep bref of it; feel
better?

SUE   I'll feel better tereckly. My old heart is
gittin weak.

LIZA   Set back comfortable in your cheer
and listen to the singin; they all sho talkin to
the Lord fur you in that church this mornin.
Listen!

(*The church is singing*):

I must tell Jesus, I cannot bear my burdens alone
In my distress he surely will help me
I cannot bear my burdens alone.

I must tell Jesus, I cannot bear my burdens alone
Jesus my Lord he surely will help me
Jesus will help me, Jesus alone

LIZA   That's all, that's all we kin do jes tell
Jesus! Jesus! Jesus please bow down your ear!
(*walks up and down mumbling a soft prayer as
the singing continues mournfully*)

SUE   I reckin Tildy's bout on her way back
now. I knows Miss Vilet done got her pa by
now, don't you reckin, Liza.

LIZA *(sympathetically)*   Course; I spects Tom'll be coming back too any minit now. Everybody knows he ain't done no harm.

SUE *(listening to running feet at the door and sitting up straight in chair)*   Who dat coming? *(MATILDA pushes open the door and comes in all excited and panting while BOSSIE follows her crying)* Whut's the matter? Didn't you find Miss Vilet?

MATILDA *(reluctantly)*   It want no use.

SUE   No use?

LIZA   Whut you mean?

MATILDA   I mean—I mean—

LIZA   For God's sake Tildy, whut's happened?

MATILDA   They—They done lynched him.

SUE *(screams)*   Jesus! *(gasps and falls limp in her chair. Singing from church begins. BOSSIE runs to her, crying afresh. LIZA puts the camphor bottle to her nose again as MATILDA feels her heart; they work over her a few minutes, shake their heads and with drooping shoulders, wring their hands. While this action takes place the words of this song pour forth from church:*

Lord have mercy.
Lord have mercy,
Lord have mercy over me.

(Sung first time with words and repeated in a low hum as curtain slowly falls)

'CRUITER

1926

John F. Matheus (1887–1983)

John Matheus was born in Keyser, West Virginia, on September 10, 1887. His father, John William, served as a bank messenger and a tanner, and his mother, Mary Susan Brown Matheus, instilled in him a love of literature. When he was still a boy, his family moved to Steubenville, Ohio, where he graduated high school in 1905. He then enrolled in Western Reserve University to study Latin, Greek, German, and the Romance languages. After graduating *cum laude* in 1910, he married Maud Roberts (she died in 1915) and began teaching Latin and modern foreign languages at Florida A & M. He received his M.A. in Romance Languages and Education from Columbia University in 1921.

Matheus traveled and lived for periods in Cuba, Haiti, England, Holland, Germany, Sierra Leone, Liberia, Mexico, and Paris, where he took classes at the Sorbonne. The settings for his plays reflect his travels. *Black Damp* (1929) concerns West Virginia miners who forget their racial differences when they are trapped in an explosion underground. *Ti Yette* (1930), set in New Orleans, is the story of a jealous mu-

latto who kills his Creole sister rather than let her marry a white man. In *Tambour* (1929), a Haitian peasant, who has a passion for his drum, wins a victory over the chief of the army and gains a beautiful woman. *Ouanga* (1941), an opera with music by Clarence Cameron White, is based on the life of the Haitian hero Jean Jacques Dessalines. It was produced at the Metropolitan Opera House in New York in 1956.

Matheus also wrote twenty-four stories, many based in the coal towns of West Virginia, Ohio, and Pennsylvania where he had grown up. He wrote, "Through all this section of our nation, even as the black coal seams run under hills, mountains and deep into the ground, so runs that other black seam of race and color." That seam is apparent in his best play, *'Cruiter* (dialect for "recruiter"), one family's story of the first Great Migration. In the years 1915–1918, upward of 750,000 southern Blacks migrated north. (The second Great Migration in the 1930s and 1940s would bring six million out of the South.) These population shifts, though accelerated by industrial demand for labor, were not sud-

238

den ones, but rather part of a continuous migration that began in 1877, when the withdrawal of federal troops from the South allowed the reinstitution of slavery conditions—disenfranchisement, forced labor, and complete social segregation.

World War I, the Great War to save democracy, created a labor shortage that sent northern industry recruiters south. White southerners, fearing that their cheap labor would take a permanent "Day of Absence," tried to prevent Blacks from leaving. In one instance, a hundred African Americans, taken from a train in Savannah, were arrested and detained for "loitering." The Jacksonville City Council required agents to buy a $1,000 permit for recruiting labor to be sent outside the state. Macon, Georgia, raised the fee to $25,000.

Professor Matheus first heard these stories while teaching at Florida A & M and found that "from Chicago, Detroit, the recruiters of Black labor would surreptitiously appear in the rural areas to take scores of farm hands in trucks to Northern centers. I know about this from talking to country folk. 'Cruiter is the result."

Matheus took great care to transcribe regional speech, including the actual sounds of words ("We mought a sont auah chickens tuh Sis Ca'line") and the idioms from Middle English that have been pre-served by the folk culture ("Ah jest as leef die a fightin'"). After the play had won a prize in *Opportunity* magazine, it was published by Alain Locke in his seminal anthology *Plays of Negro Life* and was subsequently reprinted in V.F. Calverton's *Anthology of Negro American Literature* (1929).

Popular in schools for a number of years, this one-act is truly a folk play in its setting, its language, and its characters and their problems. Randolph Edmonds's *Old Man Pete* (1934) should be read in conjunction with Matheus's *'Cruiter* because it presents a similar migrant family, perhaps a few years later, living a middle-class life in Harlem, but at the expense of turning their backs on their "down home" parents, characters like Granny, who retained traditional values.

'Cruiter exposes the impact of the migration in a touching and dramatic fashion, but at the curtain the story had not run out. It will be picked up in Chicago by Richard Wright (*Native Son*) and Ted Ward (*Big White Fog*), and in Pittsburgh by August Wilson (*Fences*).

In 1973, at the age of eighty-five, Matheus married Ellen Turner Gordon, and four years later, West Virginia State College awarded him an honorary Doctor of Letters.

'Cruiter

CHARACTERS

GRANNY *aged seventy-seven, a typical Negro
"Mammy"*
SONNY, *her grandson, aged twenty-three*
SISSY, *his wife, aged twenty*
A WHITE MAN, *a recruiting agent for a Northern
munitions factory*

SCENE   *A farm cottage in lower Georgia.*

TIME   *Just after the entry of the United States into
the World War.*

*(Early morning and Spring, 1918, in lower Geor-
gia. The rising of the curtain reveals the large room
of a Negro cabin. The walls are the reverse of the
outside weatherboarding. A kerosene lamp is on a
shelf. At the end of the room looking toward the
audience is a door leading to a bedroom, where the
starchy whiteness of a well-made bed is visible. In
front of the spectators, at the rear of the room, is a
window without glass, half-closed by a heavy
wooden shutter. Four feet from the window is a
door, wide open, leading to a garden. Rows of col-
lards are seen, an old hoe, and in the background a
path to the big road.*

*On the right is a wide, old-fashioned fireplace, where
a big pine log makes a smoldering blaze. GRANNY,
her head swathed in a blue bandanna, is bending
over the fire, stirring the contents of a huge iron
kettle. In the center of the room is a rough table. A
hunk of salt pork is on the table and a rusty knife.
Under the window is another table supporting a
fifteen quart galvanized iron bucket. A gourd dipper is hanging on the wall between the window and
the door. Under the gourd a tin washpan is suspended. Below the basin a box in which oranges
have been crated. A backless chair is under the
center table. A mongrel dog is curled under it.)*

Scene One

GRANNY *with her profile to the audience, stirring
the kettle and singing)*

> Nobody knows de trouble Ah've seen,
> Nobody knows but Jesus;
> Nobody knows de trouble Ah've seen—

(stopping abruptly)—Ah mus' put some mo'
watah to dese plague-taked grits. *(walks to the
water bucket, takes down the gourd dipper and
fills it with water. Returning to the kettle she
slowly pours in the water, stirring as she pours
and singing)* "Nobody knows de trouble Ah've
seen"—dah now! *(hobbles to the open door and
looks across the big road toward the east)* 'Pears
like Sonny and Sissy ought to be hyar. It is
(squinting at the sun) it's mighty nigh onto six
o'clock. *(a rooster crows lustily beyond the door.
She claps her hands and stamps her feet)*—Skat!
Skat, sir. Yo' honery rascal—bringin' me company so early in the mornin'. Ah ain't wantin'
to see nobody wid all Ah got tuh do. *(a mocking bird sings)* Jes' listen tuh dat bird. Hallelujah! Praise de Lam'. *(sings)*

> Oh, when de world's on fiah,
> Ah wants God's bosom
> Fo' mah piller.

*(goes to the table in the center of the room and be-
gins to slice the bacon)* "Fo' mah piller." *(voice is
heard outside)*

SONNY   Whoa, mule, whoa, Ah say.
GRANNY *(putting the bacon in a large iron spi-
der)*   Ah knowed dey'd be a-gwine fum de
field. *(sound of two pairs of shoes is heard; the
heavy tread of SONNY, the lighter tread of SISSY)*
SONNY *(wearing brogans and overalls)*
Mo'in', Granny. Dat bacon sho' smells good.
SISSY *(enters, wearing a blue calico wrapper)*
How yo' feelin', Granny?
GRANNY   Ah ain't feelin' so peart dis mo'in'.
Mus' be needin' some spring tonic.
SONNY *(taking down the washpan and dipping
water from the bucket into the pan)*   Well, us
done planted a haf'n acre co'n. *(washing his
face vigorously)* Ah don't know whut Ah'm
goin' to do 'bout de cotton dis yeah, ef Ah
don't go tuh wah.
SISSY *(dropping down in the doorsil)*   Phew!
Mah back is sho' breakin'—stoopin' an'
stoopin', drappin' dat co'n.

GRANNY   Well, yo' know yo' po' pappy allus
use tuh put in de cotton tuh pay Mistah Bob
fo' he's rations fum de Commissary.

SONNY   But dere warn't nary a pesky ole
weevil then neither. 'Sides Mistah Bob done
tol' me de guv'ment wanted somethin' t'eat.
Say dat de Germans ah goin' to sta've us out
an' we mus' plant co'n an' 'taters an' sich. He
lows, too, Ah got tuh gi' 'em all us maks dis
yeah, 'scusin' ouh keep, tuh he'p him fo' not
sendin' me to camp.

GRANNY   How come? He ain't no sheriff.

SONNY   Don't kere, he somethin' t'other wif
dis here Draftin' Bo'd. Yo know dey done sent
off Aunt Ca'line's crazy Jim?

GRANNY   Mah Jesus! Mah Jesus! Yo'se all
Ah's lef', Sonny. Gi' it tuh him. Yo' sho'll git
kilt ef yo' has to go off fightin'; like yo' gran'-
pappy bruder, Samuel, was kilt, when he jined
de Yankee Army.

SONNY   But 'tain't his'n an' Ah jest as leef
die a fightin' dan stay heah an' tek his sass an'
'uptiness an' gi' him all Ah mak, lak Ah was
on de chain gang.

SISSY   (coming in from the doorsill and throwing
out the dirty water in the basin)   Sonny, Sonny,
don't yo' know dese hyar whi' fo'ks?

SONNY   (wiping his hands on his overalls)
Don't Ah know 'em? Co'se Ah knows 'em.
When Ah was in town Sat'day didn't Ah see
Mistah Bob 'sputin' wif ol' Judge Wiley. Didn't
Ah heah him say dis wah was raisin' hell wid
his business, takin' all de niggahs fum de plan-
tations?

GRANNY   Ah knowed dis here disturbance
was comin', 'cause Ah seed a light in de sky
eb'ry night dis week.

SISSY   (washing her hands and wiping them on
her dress)   Where's dey takin' 'em to, Sonny?
Do yo' think dey goin' to take yo'?

SONNY   How does Ah know? Whatevah
whi' fo'ks wants o' we-all, we-all jes' nacherly
got tuh do, Ah spose, but Ah ain't ter gwine
tuh give Mistah Bob all my wuk an' Sissy's fo'
tuh keep me out a wah. Ah ain't skeered.

GRANNY   Boy, yo' don't know whut yo'
talkin' 'bout. Ah done seed one wah. Men kilt,
heads shot off—all de whi' fo'ks in dey big
houses, de wimmins, cryin' dey eyes out an' ol'
Gen'ral Sherman shootin' an' sottin' on fiah
evahthing waht 'ud bu'n. (mechanically takes
the spider off the fire, then the kettle of grits, dish-
ing up both on a large, heavy crockery platter)

SISSY   (looking at GRANNY with tenderness. She
and SONNY exchange glances, showing appreciation of her)   Heah, Granny, lemme he'p yo' fix
breakfas'.

GRANNY   Go 'way chile. Yo' got a heap to do
he'pin' Sonny all day in de field.

SISSY   Oh, that ain't nothin'. (pulling out the
backless chair, then bringing up the orange box
and turning it lengthwise so that she and SONNY
can sit upon it)

SONNY   (patting SISSY's hand)   Po' chile, Ah
ain't gwine to have yo' wukin' dis er-way.
'Tain't right.

SISSY   Hush, chile, Granny's askin' de
blessin'.

GRANNY   (bowing her head)   Bress dis food
we'se 'bout tuh receive fo' Christ's sake.
Amen. (she serves their plates generously of the
bacon and grits and some gravy made with the
bacon)

SONNY   (eating with his knife)   Er, ah,
Granny—

GRANNY   Sonny, de co'n meal's 'bout gone.
Dere's enough fo' co'npone to-day.

SONNY   (laying down his knife)   Sissy, don't
lemme fergit to take some co'n meal when Ah
goes tuh town to-morrow, Sat'day, ef us is heah.

SISSY   Ef us is heah? Whut yo' mean,
Sonny?

GRANNY   He mean ef de Lawd's willin'.
How come, chile yo' don't tek Him into yo'
plannin'?

SONNY   (absent-mindedly)   No, Granny, Ah
means jes' whut Ah say, ef all o' us is heah.

SISSY AND GRANNY   (looking at SONNY in
amazement)   Wha' we gwine tuh be?

SONNY   (hangin' his head)   Ah don't know
how to tell yo' 'bout it. Ah been a-thinkin' an'
a-plannin' an' skeered to let on.

SISSY   (impatiently)   Whut's yo' talkin' 'bout?

SONNY   (doggedly)   Ah'm talkin' 'bout leavin'
heah.

GRANNY   How we goin' tuh leave? Wha' to?
Hit teks heaps o' money to git away.

SONNY   Yo' don't hae tuh have no money,
no nuthin'. Jes' git away.

SISSY   (incredulous)   How?

GRANNY   What's ailin' yo' boy?

SONNY   When Ah was in town las' Sat'day a
whi' man done tol' me he was lookin' fo' wukers.

GRANNY   Whut whi' man?

SONNY   He said he was a 'cruiter. Lots a
fo'ks ah talkin' 'bout him. Yo' all out heah in

de country, yo' don't know nothin' 'bout whut's goin' on. Ah'm tellin' yo'. He sez tuh me ez Ah was standin' in de Gen'ral Sto', kin' o' whisperin' lak: "Do yo' wan' tuh mek some money?"

GRANNY   Be keerful o' dese heady fo'ks. Dey ain't out fuh no good.

SONNY   But, Granny, he talked hones'.

GRANNY   Ah know dey ain't no mo' wuk roun' heah dan whut we all is doin'.

SONNY   But dis ain' 'round heah.

SISSY   Wha' is ut, Sonny?

SONNY   Up No'th.

SISSY   (lighting up) Up No'th!

GRANNY   (with scorn) UP NO'TH!

SONNY   (bubbling with enthusiasm)   Yes. Up No'th—wha' we kin be treated lak fo'ks. He told me he would tek us all, tek us an' put us on de train at River Station below town, 'cause a deputy sheriff done 'rested a pa'cel o' niggahs, whut was tryin' tuh follow some other 'cruiter.

SISSY   Wha' he now? When could he come?

SONNY   He say he was comin' tuh see 'bout ut Friday, today (with hesitation) Dat's why Ah had to tell yo' all.

GRANNY   Up No'th? Sonny, dey tell me it's too col' up No'th.

SONNY   No, Granny, de 'cruiter say us kin live ez wa'm ez down heah—houses all het by steam. An' Sissy won't have to wuk in no fields neither, ner yo'.

GRANNY   But Ah done been down heah seventy-seven yeahs.

SONNY   (triumphantly)   But, Granny, Ah won't have tuh leave yo' tuh fight de wa' 'gin dem Germans.

GRANNY   Who say so?

SONNY   De 'cruiter.

GRANNY   How he know?

SONNY   Oh—Ah jes' knows he knows. He sounds lak it when he talks.

SISSY   Sonny, why wouldn't yo' have to go tuh wa'?

SONNY   He say somethin' Ah don't quite git de meanin' ob, but Ah 'membahs dis. He say Ah could wuk in some kin' o' a—a 'nition fac- tory, wha' dey meks guns an' things, tuh fight de Germans. Dat's why Ah wouldn't have to go.

GRANNY   (looking off into space and tapping her foot slowly)   But yo' can't believe dese whi' fo'ks. Dey're sich liars.

SONNY   But he's tellin' de troof.

SISSY   Ah hope he's tellin' de troof.

SONNY   (emphatically)   He is. He's talkin' sense.

GRANNY   Eat yo' breakfus', chillun. Hit's git- tin' col'. 'Spec yo'll nebbah heah any mo' fum dat 'cruiter. (they begin to eat. GRANNY gets up to get some hot grits, carrying the pot around and replenishing each plate)

SONNY   (his mouth full)   We wuk—wuk— wuk. Whut does us git fo' ut? Ouah victuals an' keep. De mules git dat. We ain't no bettern de mules down heah.

GRANNY   Yo' ain't seen no slavery days, Sonny.

SONNY   Why, slavery days ah right heah now.

GRANNY   Dey can't sell yo'.

SONNY   But dey kin buy us. Ole Mistah Bob thinks he's done bought us. Dey put blood- hounds on some po' niggah who was tryin' tuh leave ol' man Popperil's plantation. Whut's dat but slavery?

SISSY   But, Sonny, Lincum done sot us free. Didn't he, Granny?

GRANNY   'Course he did. Sonny know dat.

SONNY   He ain't sot me free. (an automobile horn is heard at a distance)

SONNY   (jumping from the orange crate and speaking joyfully)   Dere now. Whut did Ah say? Ah bet dat's him, de 'cruiter.

GRANNY   Comin' on Friday. No day to mek new business on Friday. Bad luck's bound to follow yo'.

SISSY   'Pears lak tuh me bad luck's been fol- lering us. (the horn sounds near. They all go to the door to look) There 'tis, comin' down de road lickity-split.

SONNY   Sho' nuf! Sissy, da hit is, an' hit sho' looks lak de 'cruiter's cah.

GRANNY   Looks say nuthin'.

SONNY   See. He's stoppin' right by ouah place.

SISSY   Sho' is. (a brisk voice is heard) Hey there!—

(Steps sound. THE WHITE MAN is seen coming down the path. He stops in front of the open door, hat on and wearing gloves. He talks rapidly and with finality)

THE WHITE MAN   This woman your wife?

SONNY   Yas, this is her, Mr. 'Cruiter, an' hyah is mah Granny. (GRANNY nods her head coldly)

THE WHITE MAN   Well, everything is ready. I came through the country early this morning to avoid other cars on the road. If you say the word I will be back here after you about eleven o'clock to-night. Don't miss this opportunity, folks.

GRANNY   Yo' don't know whut yo're axin', Mistah 'Cruiter.

THE WHITE MAN   Why, Missus, I am giving this boy a chance to get out, to be a man, like anybody else, make plenty of money and have time to enjoy it. (*turning to* SISSY) What do you say? Don't you want to live like a lady and wear fine clothes?

SISSY   (*grinning bashfully*)   Yas, sir.

SONNY   'Course, Mr. 'Cruiter, Ah sho' wants tuh go.

THE WHITE MAN   You know there are many jumping at the chance.

GRANNY   Honey, yo' can't tell him now. Whut yo' gwine tuh do wif yo' things?

SONNY   Us ain't got nothin' nohow, Granny.

THE WHITE MAN   (*looking at his watch*)   Well, I must hurry. Tell you what I'll do. I have to come down the road to-night anyway as far as the adjoining plantation.

SISSY   (*turning to* GRANNY)   Mistah Popperil's place.

THE WHITE MAN   I'll blow the horn three times. If you want to come I'll take you. Don't miss this chance of your lifetime. Good wages, transportation to Detroit straight, a good job waiting for you and freedom. (*he leaves hastily*)

GRANNY   (*sinks down on the steps*)   Huh!

(SISSY *looks at* SONNY *expectantly.* SONNY *stands undecided, scratching his head. The automobile is heard leaving in the distance, down the big road*)

GRANNY   (*singing*)

Nobody knows de trouble Ah've seen,
Nobody knows but Jesus.

(SISSY *and* SONNY *stand looking on the ground*)
'Twon't be right fo' tuh run dat er-way—without tellin' nobody. 'Tain't Christian, Sonny.

SONNY   Ah ain't stud'in' 'bout Christian.

GRANNY   Yo' talk lak a po' sinnah, boy.

SISSY   Well, Granny, let us try it. Come on.

GRANNY   Ef we leave dis place dis a-way, we dasn't come back, even ef yo' didn't lak it.

SONNY   Ah wish Ah knowed whut tuh do.

GRANNY   Yo' ain't got no faith, son. Yo' ought tuh trust God, lak us did way back dar in slavery days. An' He heard ouah prayahs.

SISSY   Sonny prays, Granny.

SONNY   But Ah neveh gits no answer.

SISSY   Mebbe dis is an answer.

SONNY   (*looking at the heavens*)   De sun's risin'. Even ef we go we got tuh keep on wukin' to-day, 'cause ol' Mistah Bob's liable to come heah any time.

GRANNY   Sonny, Sissy, Ah can't leave dis place. Why, bress me, my mammy's died heah, ol' Missus is buried heah, yo' gran'daddy crossed ovah Jordan in dis ve'y house, yo' own po' mammy, atter yo' worthless pappy was kilt in de cotton mill, died heah too. Ah'm too puny to leave heah now, too far gone mahself.

SONNY   Granny, ain't Ah allus wuked and he'p to tek kere o' yo' evah since Ah been big enough to hoe a row?

GRANNY   Yo' has been a mighty dutiful chile, Sonny. Ah ain't sayin' nutin' 'gin yo' honey. Ah ain't wantin' tuh stan' in yo' light. But Ah can't he'p ut. Ah can't beah tuh leave heah, wha all ma fo'ks ah a-layin' an' go 'way 'mongst heathen people.

SISSY   But, Granny, you'd be happy wif us, won't yo'?

GRANNY   Yas, chile, Ah'd be happy all right, but Ah'm lak Ephraim Ah reckon, wedded to mah idols. (*forcing the words*) Yo'-all go' long an' lemme stay heah.

SONNY   (*fiercely*)   But, Granny, yo' know how Mistah Bob's gwine tuh tek it, when he fin's us done gone. Ah nevah 'd feel safe leavin' yo' behin'.

GRANNY   Dat's a'right. Ain't Ah wuked fo' he's pappy?

SONNY   He ain't keerin' fo' 'at. He's liable to th'ow yo' out wif nuttin'.

GRANNY   Ain't dis mah cabin? (*looks around tenderly*) Ain't Ah lived heah fo' fifty yeahs?

SONNY   But it's on Mistah Bob's lan'.

GRANNY   Yo' kin sen' me some money an' excusin' de asthma an' de misery in mah head Ah kin keep a youngah 'oman dan me pantin', when it come tuh wuk.

SISSY   Granny, yo' *mus'* come wid us.

SONNY   Ah can't think o' leavin' yo' behin'.

GRANNY   (*getting up from the steps and walking wearily into the kitchen*)   Don't pester me now. Mebbe—mebbe—Ah knowed trouble was comin', seein' dem lights in de elements.

SISSY   (*whispers to* SONNY)   She say "Mebbe."

SONNY   (*whispering*)   Ah wished Ah knowed what tu do.

GRANNY (*looking up and seeing them whispering*)   Go long, chillun, yo' needn't be keepin' secrets fum yo' ol' Granny. Mebbe yo're right; mebbe Ah'm right. Dis is a cu'ios worl' anyhow. But dat whi' man ain't come back yit. Dey ain't tekin' niggahs on steam cahs fo' nuttin'. Whi' fo'ks *is* whi' fo'ks.

SONNY   Well, Granny, we'll see.

GRANNY   Ah'll fix yo'-all's dinner an' bring it down yander to de bottom tree.

SONNY (*to* SISSY)   Come on, Sissy, us'll put in one day more anyhow. (*they leave. As the sound of their footsteps ceases the rooster is heard to crow again*)

GRANNY (*going to the door*)   Plague tek yo' honery self. (*picks up a spoon and throws in direction of the sound*) Cl'ar out a heah—crowin' up company. Ah don't need no 'cruiters. (*she becomes silent and then sings*)

> Down in de Valley—couldn't heah mah Jesus,
> Couldn't heah nobody pray, O Lord!—

(*Curtain*)

Scene Two

(*Same place 10:45 that night. The faint glow of the kerosene lamp accentuates the desolate shadows.* GRANNY *is sitting on the backless chair, her hands folded.* SISSY *is packing clothes in an old dress suitcase. A big bag with a string tied around it rests beside* GRANNY. SONNY, *dressed in overalls and a gray coat, walks back and forth as he talks*)

GRANNY   He ain't comin'.

SONNY   'Tain't time yit. (*looking at his dollar watch*) It's only a quarter tuh 'leven.

GRANNY   He ain't comin', Ah say.

SONNY   Don't put a bad mouf on us, Granny.

SISSY (*to* SONNY)   Come heah, he'p me shet dis thing. (SONNY *helps her close the stuffed suitcase*)

GRANNY   Bad mouf, chile, Ah's been sittin' heah prayin' fo' yo'-all. We ain't nuttin', but wif de ol' Marster we ah pow'ful strong.

SISSY (*holding her head*)   Mah head's turnin' 'round all in a whirl.

SONNY   Ah yo' ready, Granny?

GRANNY   Reckon so.

SISSY   Do yo' think he's comin'?

SONNY   Sho'.

GRANNY (*shaking her head*)   Can't keep fum thinkin' 'bout yo' mammy, how she wouldn't wan' yo' tuh leab heah dis a-way.

SONNY   Ah believe she'd wan' us tuh go.

SISSY   Whut yo' all talkin' 'bout sich fo'? Yo' mak me skeert.

GRANNY   'Tain't no use bein' skeert. Yo' got tuh face de ol' Marster some o' dese times.

SISSY   Oh, Ah ain't skeert o' no ol' Marster, but yo' mek me think o' ghos'es.

SONNY   Ah'm skeert o' de clutches o' ol' Mistah Bob. He don't mean us no good. Ah jes' know ef mammy an' pappy could speak dey'd shoo us on.

GRANNY   How yo' know so much?

SONNY   Ain't Ah done seed de way he looked at niggahs—wicked lak he could swallow 'em whole?

GRANNY (*sighs*)   —Lordy! Lordy!

SISSY   Whut time is it, Sonny?

SONNY (*lookin at his watch*)   —Ten tuh 'leven.

GRANNY (*singing*)   "—O Lordy, Lordy, won't yo' ketch mah groan."

SONNY   Us ain't goin' tuh no funeral, Granny. Ah feels lak it's a picnic—a 'Mancipation Celebration picnic.

SISSY   Ah'm rarin' tuh go, too, 'specially sence yo' tol' me 'bout de schools up yander. Ouah chillun kin go tuh whi' fo'ks school.

GRANNY   Whi' fo'ks ain't goin' treat niggahs wif book learnin' any bettern we-all.

SONNY   We kin treat each othah bettah den. Ah kin treat mahself bettah. An' so kin mah chillun.

GRANNY   Yo' young niggahs ah sho' uppity, but Ah hope yo' ain't got no wool ovah yo' eyes.

GRANNY   We mought a sont ouah chickens tuh Sis Ca'line.

SISSY   She mought a tol' somebody, too, an' dere we'd be.

GRANNY   Yo' got dat box fixed for Berry?

SONNY   He's already in ut. He ain't used tuh bein' shut up lak dat, de lazy varmint.

GRANNY (*walks to the door and looks out*) The stars ah shinin'. (*comes back and gets a drink from the bucket*)

SISSY (*excitedly*)   SAKES ALIVE! Ah see de lights a-comin', 'mobile lights.

SONNY (*running to the door*)   She is. We goin' fum heah.

GRANNY (*moodily silent. The glare from the headlights of the automobile lights up the room, shining in through the open door.* GRANNY *looks in wonder at the light*) Ah, chillun, de Lawd is wif us. (*sings*) "Shine on me. Let de light fum de lighthouse, shine on me." (*the chug of the engine is heard and the grinding of the brakes, as the car pulls up. The horn blows three times.* THE WHITE MAN *runs down the walk*)

THE WHITE MAN   Are you ready? We have no time to lose.

SONNY   We's waitin'. (*gathers up bag, suitcase and hat and starts towards the door*)

SISSY   Don't forgit Berry.

THE WHITE MAN   Who's Berry?

SISSY   De dog.

THE WHITE MAN   What do you mean? We can't take dogs on this trip.

GRANNY   Whut's de mattah wif yo', man? Think we're goin' tuh leave Berry?

THE WHITE MAN   See here. It is impossible to take any dog. He'll make too much noise and besides I can't be bothered looking out for him.

SONNY   Well, Berry 'll have tuh stay heah, dat's all.

GRANNY   Den Ah stays too.

SONNY   Whut yo' say?

GRANNY (*stubbornly*) Ah ain't goin' tuh leave Berry.

THE WHITE MAN   Ah, come on—cut the argument. We got to make that train.

SISSY (*worried*) He kin fend fo' hisself.

GRANNY   Go on yo' chillun, go on. Ah don't wan' tuh go nowhow. Ah jes' been a-pretendin' tuh git yo' started. Ah kin git along. Ain't Ah got along wif whi' fo'ks fo' seventy yeahs an' mo'?

SONNY (*angrily*) Whut yo' wan' tuh act dis a-way fo'?

THE WHITE MAN   Well, come on or stay, people. Time's passing.

SONNY   Ah'm goin', Granny. Don't yo' see Ah can't stay heah? Ef Ah stay Ah'm goin' tuh git kilt fo' sassin' dese whi' fo'ks; ef Ah go tuh wa', Ah hastuh leave yo' jes' de same an' mebbe git kilt. Ef Ah go No'th and die, Ah'll be a dead free man. (*he puts down bundles and embraces* GRANNY) Mah po' ol' Granny. Ah'm goin' tuh send yo' plenty a money an' Ah'll be back, come Christmas, mebbe to tek yo' atter we gits settled.

GRANNY (*frightened*) Don't, don't come back, not heah. Promise me dat, chile. Yo' know Mistah Bob. He git yo'.

SONNY   No, he won't, Ah'll show him.

THE WHITE MAN (*impatiently*) We must be going.

SISSY   Fo' God, Granny, come on.

GRANNY (*firmly*) Ah done said mah say.

SONNY   Den, good-bye, Granny. (*gives her money*) Ah send yo' plenty mo' fust pay day an' Ah'm goin' tuh have a payday ebery week.

SISSY (*kissing* GRANNY) Good-bye.

GRANNY (*her arms around them both*) Mah po' chillun. Mah po' chillun. (*they tear themselves from her embrace.* THE WHITE MAN *leads the way to the car.* SONNY *takes up the suitcase, but leaves the bag.* SISSY *follows. The sound of the three pairs of footsteps dies away*)

SONNY *and* SISSY (*calling from the car*) Granny?

GRANNY (*standing in the doorway*) Chillun.

SISSY   Pray fo' us, Granny. (*the car is heard lurching ahead. The light disappears. The sounds die away.* GRANNY *stands for a minute in the deep silence, looking in the direction of the vanished car. A whining is heard. She looks out in the darkness*)

GRANNY   Bress mah soul! Berry! (*she pulls in a crated box, containing the cur. She gets a poker and pries the box open. The dog is wild with appreciation*) Come heah, Berry. (*pulls up the backless chair by the table and sits down, patting the dog*) Berry, you'se all Ah got lef' now. (*rests her elbow on the table, shuts her eyes*) Lordy, Ah'm so tiahed, so tiahed. (*she sits up suddenly, listening attentively*) Who dat knockin' at mah do'? (*she gets up slowly and looks out. Nothing. Shuts the door and bolts it. Sits down again and buries her face in her hands. Again she raises up and listens*) Who dat, knockin' agin? (*once more she gets up more painfully, unbolts and opens the door. Nothing. Closing it she totters feebly to the chair*) Berry, Ah'm tuckered out. (*croons*) "Somebody knockin' at mah do'!" (*stops. Listens*) Come in. (*falls back in chair, her head rests on the table, her arms limp. She mumbles*) Come in, 'Cruiter. Reckon Ah'm all ready.

(*Curtain*)

OLD MAN PETE

1934

S. Randolph Edmonds (1900–1983)

The man who would deservedly come to be known as "The Dean of the Black Academic Theatre" was born in Lawrenceville, Virginia, to a family of sharecroppers. In his early twenties, S. Randolph Edmonds launched his career in writing for the theatre with a one-act play called *Job Hunting*. He completed his undergraduate education at Oberlin College (B.A. in English, 1926), where he organized the Dunbar Forum, a cultural organization for Black students, which produced several of his early plays.

In 1931, he was directing the dramatics program at Morgan College in Baltimore, where he brought national attention to the local Krigwa Group headed by Gough McDonnell, with a production of three Black plays: Georgia Douglas Johnson's *Blue Blood* (1927), Willis Richardson's *Flight of the Natives* (1927), and May Miller's *Riding the Goat* (1929). The success of these performances demonstrated that audiences wanted to see serious plays about African American life and history. But Urban League president Edward Shakespeare Lewis wanted Krigwa to broaden its selection of plays and to integrate its productions.

When the issue was forced, Edmonds resigned and formed his own group, the Monumental Theatre. After it folded, he went to New York to study for his master's degree at Columbia University, and in that same year (1934), his play about Nat Turner, the Black insurrectionist, won Edmonds a scholarship to the Yale School of Drama.

Except for a stint in the armed forces as an officer assigned to develop shows for Black troops (1943–44) at Fort Hauchuca, Arizona, Edmonds, over the course of the next forty years, devoted himself to teaching and completing forty-six plays, many of them about Black historical figures. Sixteen of them were brought together in three anthologies: *Shades and Shadows* (1930), *Six Plays for the Negro Theatre* (1934), and *The Land of Cotton and Other Plays* (1943). His full-length play about the problems of southern leadership, *Earth and Stars* (1946), has been produced over one hundred times by schools and colleges. He also published nearly forty articles concerning African American theatre.

At Dillard University in New Orleans,

while directing the Dillard Players' Guild (1935–1947), he called together nineteen Negro colleges and formed the Southern Association of Dramatic and Speech Arts (SADSA). In 1948, he was invited to take the chair of the drama department at Florida A & M, where he would meet his future wife, Irene Colbert, who specialized in writing and producing plays for children's theatre. He served as chair of the department for twenty years, while also directing the Florida A & M Playmakers Guild. In 1969, the year after Irene died, he retired and returned to Lawrenceville, where he lived with his second wife, Ara Manson Turner, until his death. While retired, he wrote a history of the Black theatre, which appears in *The American Theatre: A Sum of Its Parts.*[1] His daughter Henrietta carried on the Edmonds tradition by writing children's plays, one of which achieved great popularity after it was performed at Howard University.

Old Man Pete is a revised and retitled version of Edmonds's prize-winning play, *Peter Stith* (1926). The action unfolds on the edge of Harlem during the flapper era. The Lewis children (perhaps a son and daughter-in-law similar to the pair in *'Cruiter*) have assembled to decide what to do with their elderly parents, who interfere with their nocturnal pleasures. It is soon apparent that the two generations have clashed: the old traditional values of the southern rural Blacks have no place in the new values of the urban Blacks of the North. However, the play also demonstrates Edmonds's belief that the attractions of Harlem were not for everyone—a conviction he would reiterate in *One Side of Harlem* (1928) and *Gangsters Over Harlem* (1939). On the one hand, he was fascinated by the living, creative force of Harlem, and on the other, repelled by what he saw as its coldness, artificiality, and materialism. Like others of his day, Edmonds was ambivalent toward the urban heart of African American culture.

Old Man Pete

1. *The American Theatre: A Sum of Its Parts* (New York: Samuel French, 1971).

CAST

"PETE" COLLIER, *an old man.*
MANDY COLLIER, *his wife.*
SAM COLLIER, *their oldest son.*
MARIA LEWIS, *their daughter.*
WILMUR LEWIS, *her husband.*
JOHN COLLIER, *their youngest son.*
VIVIAN COLLIER, *his wife.*
A POLICEMAN, GUESTS, *etc.*

SCENE 1. *John's apartment in Harlem.*
SCENE 2. *A section in Central Park.*

SCENE 1

(*The living-room of a cozy little flat in Harlem. It is a place furnished and arranged in good taste. There are two doors—the one to the left leads from outside, and the one to the right leads to the kitchen and other rooms in the house. There are two large windows near the back.*

The furniture, while not the most expensive kind, shows that the inhabitants are living well. There is a small baby grand piano on the left, a settee stretching along the wall under the two windows, and a bookcase filled with volumes on the right. Lamps and chairs are placed conveniently about. Everywhere there are feminine, artistic touches, which give a genuine atmosphere of comfort to the modern Harlem apartment.

At the opening of the curtain MARIA LEWIS *and her husband,* WILMUR, *are seated. They are well dressed in the latest conservative styles. When* JOHN *comes in he is dressed in a work suit which needs pressing and an overcoat on his arm.* MARIA *and her husband are around forty and* JOHN *is about thirty-five. It is about eight o'clock on a winter evening)*

JOHN (*tossing a newspaper to* WILMUR, *and getting his overcoat)*   I'll be back in a minute. I've got to beat it down to the laundry and get my shirt before that Chinaman at the corner closes up his shop. By that time Sam ought to be here. Vivian will be in later.

MARIA   All right, John. But put on your overcoat. It is freezing weather outside.

(JOHN *goes out)*

WILMUR (*lighting a cigarette and blowing out a cloud of smoke)*   What is this family conclave about to-night?

MARIA   I'm sure I don't know. John said he wanted to see all of the members of the family together here to-night.

WILMUR (*rising and moving about as if slightly agitated)*   Well, it wouldn't take a prophet to foretell what the meeting is called for.

MARIA   What do you mean?

WILMUR   You know exactly what I mean. You know as well as you know your name that John called us here to-night to decide what is to be done about your mother and your old man. He wants to get rid of them.

MARIA (*evasively)*   He didn't say what he wanted.

WILMUR   You all ought to have left the old people down in Virginia where they were born. I always thought it was a dumb idea bringing them up here. You ought to have known they wouldn't fit in. No, all of you had to be so generous.

MARIA   It isn't a crime to want to do something nice for your mother and father, Wilmur.

WILMUR   I know it isn't; but why bring them to New York? With all due respects to them, they will never adapt themselves to Harlem. Where are they now?

MARIA   John said something about their going out to an early service in the church.

WILMUR   Yeah, I know. They've gone around to that sanctified dump on 133rd Street again. I wish they would go around there and stay.

MARIA (*resenting his remarks)*   That's unkind of you, Wilmur, to talk about my father and mother like that.

WILMUR   Well, if you must know the truth, I am tired of being made the laughing stock of Harlem. Everywhere I go somebody asks me, "Where is your pa?" "Where is your ma?" "Did they get happy at the meeting last night?" and a whole lot of other silly things until it's just gotten on my nerves, that's all. I don't see which one of you ever thought of bringing them up here in the first place.

MARIA   Oh, Wilmur, that can't really be you talking like that.

WILMUR (*vehemently)*   Oh, yes, it is too! I'm filled up, I tell you. I've got enough. I try to have a decent home where my friends can come and enjoy themselves; but I can't do it as long as your mother and father act like they do. I—

MARIA   Don't talk like that, Wilmur.

WILMUR   I wouldn't mind so much if they acted like human beings. Sam gave the old man two suits. Why can't he put them on? Why do they have to wear those antique rags of the South? One day Slim came around to see me before he left the city. Your father sat around and entertained him in his undershirt about farming and driving railroad spikes. When Charles and Betty came one day, he entertained them with his plantation dialect. (*exasperated)* I'm filled up, I tell you.

MARIA   What can I do about it, Wilmur? I have told them about it time and time again. I can't hurt their feelings.

WILMUR   You've got to do something. When they discuss the matter to-night, you let them stay here with John or send them back to Sam. I don't care what you do as long as you don't take them back in our house.

MARIA   Somebody has got to take care of them.

WILMUR (*putting on his coat, and speaking with an air of finality)*   I am going on home to let you three discuss the matter without any embarrassment. You can take your choice, however; if they come to our house, I will leave. That's all. (*starts to leave;* MARIA *tries to stop him)*

MARIA   Oh, Wilmur! Wilmur!

(WILMUR *pays no attention to her, but rushes on out of the door. She looks after him for a second, then bursts into tears. She dries her tears quickly, however, and powders her face as she hears the key in the lock.* JOHN *and* SAM *come in.* SAM *is about forty-five and is dressed in a conservative business suit. They take off their overcoats. They rub their hands and ears from the cold*)

JOHN   I met Sam just as I was entering the building on my way back.

SAM   I thought he would walk right over me, too.

JOHN (*looking around*)   Where is Wilmur?

MARIA   He was expecting someone to call to-night on business; so he went on home. Didn't you meet him in the hall? He just stepped out.

SAM   No, we didn't. We come up on the elevator. Maybe he went down the stairs.

JOHN   I'll put this laundry in the bedroom. I'll be right back. (*he exits*)

SAM   Do you know what John wants?

MARIA   I don't know; but I think it is about Father and Mother.

SAM   I guess you are right.

MARIA   What are we going to do?

(*Before he can answer* JOHN *comes back into the room*)

JOHN   I had to have a clean shirt. The gang is going to drop by here to-night and have a cocktail or two before going on a cabaret party.

MARIA   It's too cold for me to think of cabarets. Where are you going?

JOHN   It is cold, but the gang will go anyway. We'll start out at The Bamboo Inn. I don't know where we will end up.

SAM   You'd better take it easy. Too many cabarets will wreck you, you know.

JOHN   Don't worry. We don't go out often enough for that. (*abruptly changing the subject*) I asked you to come over to-night because I wanted to see which of you will take Father and Mother. You know they have been here two weeks now.

SAM   I figured that was about what you wanted when I got your message. Maybe Maria will take them. I've got to go out of town next week on business.

MARIA   Maybe you could keep them for another week, John. They could go to Sam's when he comes home.

SAM   I'd like to have a little time to get straight when I get back. Why can't you take them, Maria?

MARIA (*confused*)   Well, Wilmur will be so busy next week, perhaps the next two or three weeks working overtime. I'd like to be without anybody until he can be home more.

JOHN   Come on now. You are not playing fair. I'm busy, too. I've got to go out of town next week for a few days myself, and Vivian and I would like to be alone for a while, too. You remember they have been here two weeks.

MARIA   You know we kept them about two weeks and a half.

JOHN (*annoyed*)   Neither of you seems to want them. Well, it's a cinch that Vivian and I can't keep them all the time.

SAM   I'm thinking we ought to have left them at home in Virginia.

MARIA   I think so, too.

JOHN (*impatiently*)   But we're not dealing with suppositions and oughts. We are dealing with a problem right here and now. Maria was the first to suggest bringing them up here; and now she is the main one wanting to get out of keeping them.

MARIA   Now don't put it all on me. You and Sam were just as anxious as I was.

JOHN   But that isn't solving the problem. What are we going to do with them? I know Vivian and I can't take care of them all the time.

MARIA   You take them again, Sam. Then maybe I'll take them again; and then it will be John's turn once more. I just can't take them now.

SAM (*meditating*)   Maybe we ought to get a little two-room apartment for them. Each of us would have to chip in to pay the expenses.

MARIA   I'll have to see what Wilmur says about that.

SAM   Maybe we'll be able to get them into a home in a few months.

JOHN   We've got to do something.

SAM   I tell you what, John, you keep them another week. By that time we can settle what to do.

JOHN   I suppose I can persuade Vivian to keep them. She had counted on one of you taking them to-morrow.

MARIA   That is the best thing to do, John. We can then work out what we ought to do. We certainly can't give them the impression of not wanting them. I think it would break their hearts.

SAM (*putting on his overcoat*)   Are you going on home now, Maria?

MARIA (*putting on her coat*)   I guess I might as well.

SAM   Come on, then.

(MARIA *puts on her coat, and they prepare to leave*)

JOHN   Remember now, we keep them for another week. After that somebody else will have to look after them. We positively can't keep them any longer.

(*There is a rattle of the key in the lock.* VIVIAN *comes in. She is a typical flapper. Her hair is cut in the latest bob, and she has a lot of rouge and paint on her face*)

VIVIAN   My God it's cold outside! I thought I would freeze before I got here.

JOHN   It is cold outside.

VIVIAN   How are you, Maria? And you, Sam?

SAM   How are you, Vivian?

(VIVIAN *and* MARIA *kiss each other*)

VIVIAN   You aren't going so soon? You needn't hurry.

SAM   I can't stay. I've got to get right on back home. Maybe Maria will stay.

MARIA   No. I've got my things on, so I might as well run along. We'll be over some-time this week.

VIVIAN   All right, then, if you must go. But come around any old time. You must bring your wife to see us soon, Sam.

SAM   I will, Vivian.

(*They say good-bye and go out*)

VIVIAN   Well, what's the verdict?

JOHN   They asked me to keep them another week. Neither one could take them just now.

VIVIAN   And what about after the week?

JOHN   Sam said something about making some arrangements for a small apartment or seeing about getting them in a home.

VIVIAN   And we are to keep them until all these arrangements are made. You are a fine one to let them pull that stuff over on you.

JOHN   Somebody's got to look out for them until all arrangements are made.

VIVIAN   But why should it be us? I wouldn't mind it, but they are such nuisances. I hope I'm not like that when I get old.

JOHN   Remember, dear, they are my father and mother.

VIVIAN   You know they are nuisances as well as I do, only you don't want to say so.

JOHN   Vivian!

VIVIAN   You know I always say just what I think, John. It is too late for me to change now. Sam and Maria dumped them on us because they found out that it is true they're nuisances.

JOHN   Well, let's not discuss it.

VIVIAN   Very well; but I just want you to know that I'm tired of having them in the way, too. They've been here for two weeks now and Sam and Maria should take them.

JOHN   Don't talk like that, Vivian.

VIVIAN   Talking like that won't settle matters, and you know it.

JOHN   I can't ask them to leave.

VIVIAN   Well, that's your red wagon. I just want you to know that I am tired, that's all.

JOHN   They won't bother us to-night anyway.

VIVIAN   I do hope they show at least that much common sense.

JOHN   You're unsympathetic, Vivian.

VIVIAN   Call it what you will, my patience is at an end.

JOHN   We can tough it out another week. So let's forget it. I've got everything for the cocktails.

VIVIAN (*looking at her wrist watch*)   Let's go in and get dressed and have everything ready. The gang will be by here in a few minutes. You know the bunch plans to stop at several houses before winding up at the cabaret.

JOHN (*following her into the room to the right*) I know. Billy told me all about the plans.

(*As they go out, a key rattles in the lock.* PETE *and* MANDY *come into the room unbuttoning their win-*

ter coats. They take them off and throw them on chairs. PETE *is old and grey-headed, and walks with a stick. He is wiry and tough, however. He is dressed in a pair of close-fitting grey breeches and a wide-swinging black coat. His whiskers are long and unshapely.* MANDY *is elderly with grey hair and is dressed in a long sweeping calico dress. When she takes off her coat and old-fashioned hat, she leaves a red shawl around her shoulders)*

PETE   Hit's cold out dere, Mandy. De air is raw. Winter is sho heah.

MANDY   And dey tells me dat snow stays on de ground de yeah 'round, too.

PETE   We don't hab tuh wurry 'bout no winter up heah. Yuh don't hab tuh chop wood fuh dese houses. Dey is heated wid steam.

MANDY   Ah'll miss hit, dough, setting by de chimley and lookin' at de open fire.

PETE   *(seating himself)*   Let's set down a few minutes in heah befo' goin' tuh our room. 'Tain't nobody using hit.

MANDY   Yeah, we mought ez well set awhile. *(seating herself)* Didn't yuh lak dat sermon tunight, Pete?

PETE   I sho' did. Dat's de best sermon we is heard since we been heah.

MANDY   Hit's de best all right. I couldn't keep from shouting tuh save ma life, and a sermon sho' has tuh be good tuh make Mandy Collier shout.

PETE   We's been tuh many dese fine buildings since we been heah; but hit all go tuh prove dat fine buildings don't make fine churches 'less de sperit is dere.

MANDY   Dat's de gospel truf. Ah didn't heah a single "Amen" in all dem fine churches.

PETE   Well, Mandy, we's been heah 'bout six weeks now. How does yuh lak New Yawk?

MANDY   Ah can't say Ah's crazy 'bout hit, Pete. Does yuh lak hit up heah?

PETE   Sho' Ah does. Whut make yuh don't lak hit, Mandy?

MANDY   Well, everybody is in sich a hurry. Ef yuh don't git outen dere way, dey will walk right over yuh. Den everything is so crowded heah. People is cooped up lak chickens. De room we sleep in ain't big as a closet. Den yuh hab tuh climb so many steps 'cause de elevator is broke mos' de time. Ah ain't used tuh climbin' a thousand pair steps tuh sleep in a hen coop.

PETE   Yuh'll git used tuh hit by and by. Why, Ah's almos' a born New Yawker by now.

MANDY   *(sighing)*   Ah'd ruther live in Fuginia any day.

PETE   Come on, Mandy, git over dem blues.

MANDY   Ah hates tuh set 'round all day and do nothing. Ah ain't used tuh hit. At home Ah always had somethin' tuh do. Ef hit wa'n't cleaning, Ah was feedin' de pigs, milkin', churnin' er somethin'. Heah Ah ain't gut nuthin' tuh do.

PETE   Ah don't min' settin' 'round. Ah's wurked hard all ma life. Ah needs a res' now.

MANDY   Yuh mean yuh is lazy.

PETE   Wal, we's gut our chilluns anyway. Ah'll always keep dis letter dat Sam writ us when we was home.

MANDY   Read hit ag'in, Pete. Let me heah how hit sounds once mo'.

PETE   *(getting out his glasses and reading)* "Dear Mother and Father: John, Maria and myself thought the farm was too much for you to attend to in your old age; so we would like for you to sell the farm and come up and live with us in New York. Sell out as soon as possible and send us a telegram when you start. You took care of us in childhood and the three of us certainly ought to be able to take care of you in your old age. We are anxiously awaiting your coming. Your affectionate son, Sam." Dat boy really show his eddication, don't he, Mandy? Dat's whut Ah calls a real eddicated letter. Folks thought we was fools when we sent our chilluns tuh school. In fact, old Doot Williams told me so hisse'f. But yuh ought tuh seen de 'spression on his face when Ah showed him dis letter from Sam.

MANDY   Maggie Yates told me de same thing when Ah told huh 'bout dat letter. She said, "Yuh won't never git 'long in dat big city. Yuh is too old-fashioned. Yo' chilluns will git 'shamed o' yuh."

PETE   Ah guess old Maggie is still waggin' huh mouf. As ef we could ever git too old-fashioned fuh our chilluns! Dat is a good one.

MANDY   Sometimes Ah thinks Maggie Yates is right.

PETE   Yuh ain't gittin' cold feet, is yuh, Mandy?

MANDY   No, Pete. Hit ain't dat; but yuh never can tell.

PETE   Yuh certainly is gut a lot o' faith, Mandy. Won't Ah hab a good time tellin' de chilluns how yuh doubted 'em.

MANDY   Ah, don't mean tuh doubt dem, Pete. Ah s'pose hit's jes' bein' in a strange place.

PETE   Dat's hit, Mandy. We's gut a chance tuh see somethin' in dis strange place. Why up heah we's gut trains under de groun' and trains in de air. Plenty dese buildings up heah is eight times ez high ez de fust national building at home. Jes' think of hit, eight times ez high! And yuh remember de buildin' wid de rollin' steps whar yuh git right on and dey carry yuh right up tuh de top. Dere is always somethin' tuh see dat's new heah.

MANDY   Yeah, Ah jes' hopes hit las', dough.

PETE   Cose hit's gwine tuh las'. How come yuh think hit ain't?

(The bell rings. JOHN *comes into the room and pushes the buzzer. He has changed his clothes)*

JOHN   How are you, Mother? How are you, Father?

PETE   We's up and 'bout, Son. We jes' come in frum de church. De air is raw outside.

JOHN   It is cold. The papers say to-night will be the coldest we have had in twenty years.

MANDY   Ah'm glad we don't hab tuh git up early.

JOHN   *(diplomatically)*   We are having some company for a little while. They won't be here long. If you and Mother will stay in your room, we won't bother you at all.

PETE   Sho, sho. We'll go right in. We don't want tuh be in yo' way.

MANDY   Come on, Pete. *(they get their coats and go out)*

*(*VIVIAN *comes in in a beautiful gown in the latest fashion. She seems far more the flapper type since she has dressed up)*

VIVIAN   Everything ready?
JOHN   Yes, I think so.

*(*PETE *comes in with his shirt tails out and in his socks. He searches around the room, then bellows)*

PETE   Mandy! Whar did yuh say ma chawin' 'backer is at?

VIVIAN   *(very much annoyed)*   What are you looking for? Here, get into your room before

those people get up here. The idea of your coming out here like that!

PETE   'Scuse me, daughter. 'Scuse me.

(He hurriedly disappears. There is a ring on the bell. JOHN *opens the door. Several couples come in. They greet* VIVIAN *warmly. She kisses one or two women.* JOHN *shakes hands with the men)*

A GIRL   Give me a shot of something, Vivian. I am freezing to death.

A MAN   It is ten below zero now, and the papers said it is going to get colder.

A GIRL   It is beginning to snow outside.

A MAN   Aw, can't you think of something else to talk about except the weather?

ANOTHER MAN   Here is something else to think about anyway. Let's drink. *(he indicates the tray of glasses that* JOHN *has brought in)*

JOHN   Here you are, folks. This is just a starter off for the night. *(he passes the glasses; all take one and drink)*

VIVIAN   Here is a table. Would some of you like to play a game of contract before we go?

A GIRL   I will, kid. Come on, somebody.

(Two couples sit at the table and begin playing)

VIVIAN   Have a cigarette? *(she passes the cigarettes and the men and women take them and begin smoking)*

ONE MAN   Say, John, how is your pa?

(A snicker goes around the crowd)

JOHN   He's all right, thank you. I fail to see the joke, however.

VIVIAN   Never mind. It wasn't meant for you to see, dear.

ONE GIRL   Play a piece, Jack.

*(*JACK *goes to the piano and begins to play a low, mournful blues)*

A GIRL *(to one of the men)*   Come dance with me, papa. I can't stand it no longer.

(Several couples dance for a short time. Then JACK *stops playing for a second)*

A GIRL   Give me another drink, somebody.

ANOTHER GIRL   I hope I don't get drunk to-night. I got high as a kite the last time we had a cabaret party.

(After the piano player gulps down a drink that is given him, he starts another fast number)

A GIRL   How about a dance, Vivian?

(*She gets out in the center of the floor and does the dance. The others clap their hands and shout various things at her. She stops amid a burst of applause*)

ONE GIRL   Well, it's time for the party to be breaking up, if we want to go by Alice's.

ANOTHER GIRL   Yes, let's get going. By the time we stay there awhile, the cabaret will be in full swing when we get there.

VIVIAN   You don't have to hurry.

JOHN   No. Stay as long as you like.

A GIRL   I guess we'd better go on.

ANOTHER GIRL   I'll have another shot before I go

A MAN   Let's all have another shot.

(*The glasses are filled once more. Everybody drinks.* JOHN *and* VIVIAN *help them with their coats. As all are about to leave*)

VIVIAN   John and I will join you at Alice's in a few minutes—just as soon as we get the room a little straight.

A GIRL   We'll look for you, kid.

(*They all go out*)

JOHN   That's a dizzy bunch.

VIVIAN   Yes, but they're heaps of fun, though. Come on, let's hurry and get things straightened up so we can join them. (VIVIAN *lights a cigarette. They commence to get the chairs straight*)

(PETE *comes in with his night cap on and his breeches. He also has on a red flannel undershirt with his suspenders hanging behind him*)

PETE   'Scuse me.

VIVIAN (*irritated*)   What do you want?

PETE   Daughter, Ah mus' hab a chaw o' 'backer befo' Ah can sleep.

VIVIAN (*half to herself*)   You and your old tobacco make me sick.

JOHN   Vivian!

VIVIAN (*so irritated she doesn't care what she says*)   Yes, they make me sick.

(*Before anybody can say anything further* MANDY *comes in dressed in an old-fashioned nightgown covered by an old robe*)

MANDY   Yuh is de fugittenist man in de wurl, Pete. Ah knows Ah saw dat 'backer

'round heah somewhar. (*she looks around and finds it on the bookcase*) Heah 'tis right on de bookcase in front yo' eyes.

PETE   Thank yuh, Mandy. Ah don't know whut Ah'd 'a' done without a chaw.

(*He takes a chew*)

MANDY (*to* VIVIAN)   Yuh shouldn't smoke cigarettes, honey. Hit don't look nice. Good gals don't smoke.

VIVIAN (*bursting out*)   What have you got to do with it? What do you mean by meddling in my business?

JOHN   Vivian! Vivian, please, dear.

MANDY   Ah didn't mean no harm, honey. Ah didn't mean no harm.

VIVIAN (*sarcastically*)   No. You never mean any harm. You are always doing something dumb that you don't mean. I know what you want. You just want to start your usual sermon about wild parties and drinking whiskey. I know what you're going to say, and I don't want to hear it!

PETE (*getting angry*)   John, is yuh gwine stand dere and let dat gal talk tuh yo' mammy lak dat?

JOHN   What can I do, Father?

VIVIAN   Why don't you do something about it, you grey-headed old fool.

JOHN   Come on, Vivian. Let's go to Alice's.

PETE   Yeah. Take huh away befo' Ah lose ma temper. She's too brazen. A gal lak dat ought tuh be horse whupped. She ain't got no manners.

VIVIAN (*very angry*)   You ought to learn some manners yourself. You act like somebody half civilized. The idea of your talking about whipping somebody! (*crying*) You get out of my house, the both of you! Get out!

JOHN (*catching her by the hand*)   Come on, Vivian!

PETE   We'll git out, all right. We'll go tuh Maria's in de mawning.

MANDY   Calm yo'se'f, Pete.

VIVIAN (*jerking her hand out of* JOHN'S)   Turn me loose. (*to* PETE) It ain't no use of your going to Maria's, nor Sam's neither. They were here this evening, and neither one would take you. You'd better go back to the sticks where you came from.

MANDY (*getting a little angry herself*)   Yuh is a liar, gal. Sam and Maria never done nothin' lak dat.

VIVIAN   Well, go on to them, then. Go anywhere, just so you get out of my house.

JOHN   Don't, Vivian. It's not necessary to have a quarrel.

VIVIAN   It ain't no use for you to try to smooth things over. You think just as I do, but you're not man enough to say so.

pete   Dat gal is spiled. A good fannin' would straighten huh out.

VIVIAN (*very angrily to* JOHN)   You standing there talking and looking, and letting them say anything to me. You're no man, that's what. If you don't make them go, I'll go myself. I'll never put my foot in this house as long as they're here.

JOHN   Vivian! Vivian!

(VIVIAN *darts into the other room and gets her coat and goes out with a grim determination. She slams the door after her*)

PETE   A gal dat ain't gut no manners is better off gone.

JOHN   I don't thank you a bit for coming here and causing trouble between my wife and me.

PETE (*surprised*)   What! You uphold dat gal in huh sassiness?

JOHN   She is my wife.

PETE   Wife or no wife, she ain't gut no business talkin' tuh old folks lak dat. She is a hussy, dat's whut.

JOHN   Father, don't say another thing about my wife. I'm going out to get her now, and I don't expect you to give her any more trouble.

(JOHN *gets his coat and goes. As he shuts the door,* PETE *shakes his fist at the door, and shouts*)

PETE   Follow yo' wanton strumpet! Fugit de ones dat bawned yuh! Turn yo' back on de ones dat nursed yuh! Git out o' ma sight, plague take yo' ungrateful hide, git out o' ma sight!

MANDY (*trying to console him*)   Don't git wurked up so, Pete. Calm yo'se'f.

PETE (*meditating for a moment*)   Mandy, dat gal is right. We is no longer wanted. We's gwine.

MANDY   Gwine whar, Pete?

PETE   Back tuh Fuginia.

MANDY   But we ain't gut de money, Pete.

PETE   Ah, yes we is. Ah always kept de fare back home. Ah didn't trust to no chances, al-dough Ah never thought we would come tuh dis.

MANDY (*wiping her eyes*)   But hit's too cole outside. Listen tuh dat wind.

PETE   Don't let's argue, Mandy. Ah said we is gwine, and we is gwine tuh do hit. Ah wouldn't stay in dis house another instant—no siree, not another instant. Let's git dressed and leave dis place behind us.

MANDY   But we can't go back home and tell de folks dat our chilluns don't want us. Ah can heah Maggie Yates' mouf now. Dat's too hard fuh us to do, Pete. (*she starts to cry*)

PETE   Life is hard, Mandy, hard as pig iron! Don't cry, Mandy, we's done no mo' dan others. We jes' bawned chilluns tuh turn on us lak spiders. Whut do we care whut Maggie Yates say, or anybody else say 'long ez we's gut each other. Fuh nearly fifty yeahs now yuh is leaned on de strong arm ob Old Man Pete Collier. He is de one who is gwine tuh stick till de end. Come on, let's pack up, Mandy. We'll leave dese ungrateful chilluns in de hands ob a just God. (*he takes her by the hand and leads her into the next room*)

[*Curtain*]

Scene 2

A section of Central Park. The trees and ground are draped with snow. The wind is blowing, and the snow is still falling. A park bench is stretched along the walk. PETE *and* MANDY *are bundled up with heavy coats.* PETE *has an old rusty suitcase in his hand, and* MANDY *has a red shawl tied around her head*

MANDY (*showing great weariness*)   Ah wonder how much futher de station is frum heah.

PETE   Hit ain't fur. De man said ef we went right thru heah, we wouldn't be fur away from a car dat would take us right dere.

MANDY   Ah's tired, Pete. Le's res' heah a bit.

PETE   Jes' a minute, den. Hit's too cold tuh stop long.

MANDY   Look at de snow fall and listen at de wind.

PETE   Don't mind de elements. Do lak me. (*shaking his fist in the air*) Wind, blow yo' darndest gale. Heavens, pile yo' snow in drifts ez high ez de tallest building; an' we'll wade thru dem somehow tuh git away from dem ungrateful chilluns.

MANDY   Don't take on so, Pete. Ah's been thinkin' since we left de house. Maybe hit ain't de chilluns' fault; maybe hit is us who is tuh blame. Maybe we is jes' done got old and outgrowed our chilluns. Le's go back tuh de house.

PETE   Ah'd ruther go to hell and burn in torment fire a thousand yeahs befo' Ah'd go back tuh dat ungrateful house.

MANDY   Don't say dat, Pete.

PETE   Chilluns ain't got no business outgrowing dere parents, or dere parents outgrowing dem. De way we slaved tuh send dem all tuh school—no siree, yuh can't let dem off dat easy.

MANDY   Ah s'pects yuh is right. (*silence for a second*) Ain't yuh feelin' cold, Pete?

PETE   Naw. Never felt hotter in ma life.

MANDY   Ah ain't so cold. Ah's jes' tired. We's walked a long ways.

PETE   Le's push on, Mandy. De night is raw out heah. Hit'll be better in de fine railroad station.

MANDY   Ah can't, Pete. Ah's gut tuh res'. (*she props her head up with her hands*)

PETE   Wal, res' a bit, Mandy. Ah'll walk 'round tuh keep warm. Yuh was right—back dere in de house. 'Tain't gwine tuh be easy tuh live down de 'sults ob de people at home; but somehow we's gut tuh do hit. We's faced things tugether fuh many a yeah, dough, and always come out de big end ob de hawn. (*shakes her*) Wake up, Mandy, dis is a cold night. Hit's too cold tuh stay out heah long. Wake up!

MANDY   Don't bother me, Pete. Let me sleep jes' a little longer. Ah feels so nice and warm.

PETE   All right, jes' a little longer den. (*walking around and hitting himself to keep warm*) Ah's sho hit's de bes' tuh go back home and live our las' yeahs among fr'en's dan in dis Gawd fusaken city whar nobody cares whether yuh lives er dies. (*stops and shakes her*) Wake up, Mandy. Le's go. 'Tis cold out heah. Wake up, Mandy! She is fast asleep all right. (*he pulls off his coat and puts it around her*) Ah can keep warm walkin' 'bout. (*after awhile*) Wake up, Mandy. Dis is a raw night, and we mus' move on. (*drops beside her on the bench and puts his arm around her*) Ah don't blame yuh much. Ah is tired mase'f. Ah is sort o' sleepy, too. (*he rests his head on her shoulder for awhile Then he sleepily shakes her*) Wake up, Mandy! Wake up, Mandy! (*silence*) Wake up, Mandy! Ah heah de cows low'ring; but hit's dark and cold out heah. Only de snow makes hit light. (*brokenly*) De sky is dark, Mandy; but down in Fuginia de sun is shining. Le's git in de sun. (*a brief silence, then he feebly continues*) Wake up, Mandy! Ah heahs de horses neighing and de pigs is squealing. Dey is hongry, Mandy. Le's go feed de pigs.

(*Silence for awhile. Day breaks. A* POLICEMAN *enters*)

POLICEMAN (*hitting on the seat with his club*) Move on, folks! It is twenty below zero. It is the coldest wave that ever struck New York, and here you are sitting in the park. You'll freeze here. (*hitting the seat again*) Move on, I tell you. (*pushes them*) Gosh, them fools are frozen stiff. (*he looks sorrowfully at them*)

[*Curtain*]

FROM THE DEPRESSION

H.F.V. Edward · Langston Hughes · Theodore Ward

The advances made by African American artists in professional theatre during the 1920s were curtailed by the Great Depression. The number of Broadway shows by or about Blacks steadily dwindled. Even the Black musicals that had showered Broadway in the 1920s—*Runnin' Wild, Shuffle Along, Keep Shufflin', From Dixie to Broadway, Rang Tang, Chocolate Dandies, The Black-birds*—virtually disappeared in the 1930s. Three thousand Black performers, writers, and others associated with the theatre in New York were unemployed in 1931. The prospect for work in the arts, like most fields, was dismal. Fear, anger, and despair permeated the country as social, economic, and political problems continued to mount. The theatre reflected these issues in plays like *Waiting for Lefty, One-Third of a Nation*, and H.F.V. Edward's play, *Job Hunters*, which records what he observed daily in the unemployment office where he worked. Hollywood circumvented the serious issues with movies like Busby Berkeley's *Gold Diggers* series, while popular songs were simply escapist ("We're in the Money," "With Plenty of Money and You").

White depictions of exotic Negroes—*Green Pastures, Savage Rhythm, Scarlet Sister Mary, Brass Ankle, Mamba's Daughters, Porgy and Bess*—were produced frequently. Black playwrights, on the other hand, found their opportunities severely limited. Langston Hughes was elated by the prospect of his poetic tragedy, *Mulatto*, being presented on Broadway, only to become disillusioned when the white producer sexed it up for commercial appeal.

In 1935, the Federal Theatre Project (under the government Works Progress Administration) was officially launched with four companies in New York City. Two of them, the Federal Negro Theatre and the Negro Youth Theatre, were housed in Harlem's Lafayette Theatre. The following year an African dance troupe and a vaudeville division were added. These companies provided employment for nearly one thousand African American artists. Theatre personnel outside New

York could find work in some of the Negro companies scattered about the country, the most prominent ones being in Seattle and Chicago.

One of the most valuable services of the Federal Theatre Project was the apprenticeship and encouragement it provided Black playwrights. It sponsored a number of plays by Black authors that would not have been produced otherwise due to the content's lack of appeal to white audiences. In 1941, Arthur Davis, Sterling Brown, and Ulysses Lee praised the Federal Theatre Project for presenting "the largest number of serious, ambitious plays by Negro authors ever to be presented on the professional stage, and for giving the best productions that Negro playwrights have ever been afforded."[1] Among the writers whose plays were supported by the Project were Hughes Allison, Rudolph Fisher, J.A. Smith, Theodore Browne, and Theodore Ward.

Several independent Black theatre groups formed in the 1930s: the Harlem Suitcase Theatre, the Negro People's Theatre, and the Rose McClendon Players, followed in 1940 by the American Negro Theatre and the Negro Playwrights Company. But it would be nearly thirty years before some of the plays that these groups premiered would be published.

The three plays in this section were all written during the Depression. *Job Hunters* shows the suffering and privation of the unemployed. *Don't You Want To Be Free?* and *Big White Fog* are political plays that offer solutions based on the Black and white working class. All the plays breathe the despair of a society gone wrong. And all offer hope.

---

[1]Sterling Brown, Arthur Davis, and Ulysses Lee, *The Negro Caravan* (New York: Citadel Press, 1941), p. 504.

JOB HUNTERS
1931

H.F.V. *Edward* (1898–1973)

A play might develop from an idea or theme that the writer wishes to explore; it might grow around a character or set of characters; or it might evolve from a story, a newspaper article, or a personal experience or observation. *Job Hunters* was based on H.F.V. Edward's experience as a temporary interviewer for the New York State Employment Service during the Great Depression. A portion of his time was spent in the field trying to locate job vacancies, a task he found discouraging since few jobs were available. More depressing, however, was his work in the "dingy Harlem office on Lenox Avenue and 132nd Street" where the wretched of the community desperately sought employment. At the time, according to Edward, the unemployment rate was 27 percent for all Americans, and approximately 40 percent for Blacks.

In 1933, one-half of Harlem's 350,000 residents were on relief. This statistic can be understood only in light of other statistics: (1) the average monthly wage of an African American working man had been $89.60, compared to $110.00 for whites in Harlem; (2) 60 percent of African American married women worked, compared to 15 percent of married white women; (3) the average population density of Harlem was 233 person per acre, compared to 133 for the rest of Manhattan; (4) African American families paid 40 to 50 percent of their income for rent, compared to 25 percent for whites; (5) the mortality rate of Harlem Hospital was more than twice that of the predominantly white Bellevue or Coney Island hospitals.[1]

After six months with the Employment Service, Edward was hired by *The Crisis* as bookkeeper and advertising manager. For a number of years, the magazine had sponsored playwriting contests and encouraged the writing and production of African

---

[1] Roi Ottley and William J. Weatherby (eds.), *The Negro in New York: An Informal Social History, 1626–1940* (New York: Praeger Publishers, 1969), pp. 265–280.

American plays. Edward found the atmosphere at *The Crisis* exhilarating, especially the presence of W.E.B. Du Bois and the popular young writers of the day who visited the office from time to time. This creative environment motivated Edward to try his hand at playwriting, and the result was *Job Hunters.*

The play ends with a prophetic warning about the Chicago riots. His predictions came true on March 19, 1935. By the next day, 200 stores had been smashed, with an estimated $2 million in damages. Three

Blacks were dead and hundreds of others were wounded and arrested.

H.F.V. Edward was a man of superior attainments: a West Indian intellect and former British sprinting champion who participated in the pre-Olympic games of the Wilco Athletic Association at Yankee Stadium during the 1920s. From 1935 to 1939, he was an administrator of the Negro branch of the Federal Theatre Project at the Lafayette Theatre in Harlem, where his duties included supervision of personnel and promotion.

Job Hunters

CAST OF CHARACTERS

WILLIAM JOHNSON, *official of Public Employment Office*
WARREN THOMAS, *a student of sociology and volunteer worker*
CLARENCE WHITE,
GEORGE WASHINGTON,
FRANCIS TAYLOR,   } *unemployed*
A CHAUFFEUR,
A MECHANIC,
FIRST UNEMPLOYED
SECOND UNEMPLOYED
THIRD UNEMPLOYED
FOURTH UNEMPLOYED
FIFTH UNEMPLOYED
REPRESENTATIVE OF THE "HEAVENLY MESSENGER"
DISTRIBUTOR OF THE "WORKMEN'S DAILY"
A WOMAN SPEAKER OF THE WORKERS' LEAGUE
A GROUP OF UNEMPLOYED

SCENE   *the office of a public employment office in Harlem.*

TIME   *July, 1931.*

OFFICIAL (*as he dusts desks and opens blinds. Line of men can be seen standing outside window*) It is three minutes to eight. I must hurry; government employment offices must be punctual and Harlem's Office must keep its good reputation. No C.P.T. here! (*pause*) Another day when I must listen to people's troubles and moanings. Yes, (*recites*) The fever and the fret, here is where men sit and hear each other groan. (*knock at the door. Shouts*) Be patient, two more minutes. (*more knocks at door. Louder*) Stop knocking! (*looks at his watch*) It isn't eight o'clock yet. (*continued knocking and rattling. Angry*) What's the matter with that impatient bunch! (*goes to the door, unlocks and opens it*)

STUDENT VISITOR (*entering*)   Good morning, Mr. Johnson. My name is Thomas, Warren Thomas. The director of public employment offices asked me to report to you.

OFFICIAL   Oh yes, Mr. Brady phoned me about you. You are a student working as a volunteer, aren't you? (*relocks door*)

STUDENT VISITOR (*talkative and enthusiastic*) Yes, I am studying sociology at the University of Pennsylvania. I am tremendously interested in government employment service, old age pension, unemployment insurance and such social legislation. You see, I am a socialist. I believe public employment offices are essential. It is the duty of the community to see that men get work and if they cannot find it, they should get unemployment insurance benefits, . . .

OFFICIAL (*interrupting*)　Well, you can sit here near my desk, (*moving a chair to his desk*) and watch our system of registrations and placements. You'll learn a lot about life's problems here.

STUDENT VISITOR　I didn't see a single white man in the line outside. Does the law here demand segregation?

OFFICIAL　Oh no, but the law is one thing and the prejudices of the officials enforcing it,—that's another.

STUDENT VISITOR　Have a cigar?

OFFICIAL (*smiling*)　Well, we don't permit smoking in this office, but—I'll be glad to smoke it at home tonight after I have had supper. (*puts cigar carefully into his pocket—looks at his watch*) It's eight now, I must open the door. (*goes across stage, opens door, men enter and sit down on benches, official returns to his desk. A chauffeur walks to the gate, stands there with a letter in his hand looking at the official*)

CHAUFFEUR　Mr. Johnson, you sent me a letter, said you had a job for me?

OFFICIAL　Come in, let me see the letter— (*looks at the letter*) Oh yes, take a seat, please? (*motions him to sit on chair in front of desk*) We have a job here for a hackman, must be experienced and have licenses. Now, I know you have driven a taxi here for five years. This job pays 40 per cent of the earnings. What do you think of it?

CHAUFFEUR (*evidently disappointed*)　Oh,— why yes, I was in the taxi business for some time, but nowadays, mister, there ain't no money in it. And (*hesitating*) well, to tell you the truth, when I was in the taxi business, I got in with the sportin' crowd. You know how it is. Then with drinkin' and gamblin' I didn't bring any money home.—(*pause*) No,—I guess I don't take it. I promised the missus to quit the taxi game. Gee, I'd like to have sump'n steady, anything like chauffeurin' or truckin'.

OFFICIAL　I am sorry, that's all I have in the chauffeuring line today. Stay around or call again tomorrow, will you?

(CHAUFFEUR *leaves desk, but stays in the office for a while*)

OFFICIAL (*picks up slip of paper from desk, stands up, walks toward gate while reading*)　Just a minute of quiet! (*reads*) I want an experienced car-washer, eight hours shift, nightwork, $25 per week, no Sunday night work. (*four men rush up through the gate*) Are you experienced with high pressure hose? (*all nod affirmatively*) I am sorry I have only one job, I have to pick one from among you. Let me have your names. (*men gives names to official, who writes them down and then looks up their cards*)

FIRST UNEMPLOYED (*sitting on front bench reading newspaper*)　Here one banker says prosperity is just around the corner.

SECOND UNEMPLOYED　Yea, but he didn't say what street.

THIRD UNEMPLOYED　Sure ain't in Harlem.

OFFICIAL　Mr. Jackson, your experience seems to fit best into that job. Here is your card, good luck. (*addressing the others*) I am sorry, men. (*they walk back to the waiting room dejectedly*)

OFFICIAL (*again addressing men*)　I have another job here, if it can be called a job. Bell Hop wanted, small hotel, no wages, tips only, must bring own uniform.

(*Group of unemployed are amused, laugh*)

SECOND UNEMPLOYED　Now, aint that sump'n.

THIRD UNEMPLOYED　Got to take your sandwich to work too?

OFFICIAL　Is there anybody here, who wants to register? Anyone here who has not registered?

(CLARENCE WHITE *and* GEORGE WASHINGTON *come through gate and are seated, official motions* CLARENCE WHITE *to take seat near desk*)

OFFICIAL　What is your name? (*writing particulars on card*)

CLARENCE WHITE　Clarence White.

OFFICIAL　Address?

(FOURTH UNEMPLOYED *snores loudly. The others look at him*)

OFFICIAL (*to* CLARENCE WHITE)　Education?

(FOURTH UNEMPLOYED *snores again, unemployed laugh*)

OFFICIAL (*looks up*)　Please wake that man up.

(FOURTH UNEMPLOYED *after much shaking by other unemployed awakens, looks drowsy*)

OFFICIAL (*to* FOURTH UNEMPLOYED)　Are you registered here?

FOURTH UNEMPLOYED   No Sir.

OFFICIAL   Will you come in here and be seated.

(FOURTH UNEMPLOYED *stretches, walks slowly, takes a bite of chewing tobacco, group of unemployed is amused. He slumps down on chair inside gate*)

OFFICIAL   A little less noise please! (*addressing* CLARENCE WHITE) Why did you leave the job you held for three years after being graduated from high school?

CLARENCE WHITE (*doubting, hesitating, faltering*)   Well, I guess I can tell you. (*drawing closer to official*) You see, I had some trouble with the boss about my wages. You know, always overtime and no extra pay. Well, I got sore and took it out in goods and—I was caught.

OFFICIAL   I am glad you told me about that. Now when I am asked about references I shall be informed about the situation. Call here every day, will you? Something will turn up that will suit you. (CLARENCE WHITE *gets up and joins the waiting unemployed*) Next please!

GEORGE WASHINGTON (*taking seat at desk*) Good mornin', how are yo'?

OFFICIAL   Good morning.

GEORGE WASHINGTON   Very well, thank yo suh.

OFFICIAL   What's your name and address?

GEORGE WASHINGTON   George Washington, 56 West 137th Street. Apartment 33.

OFFICIAL   In what state were you born?

GEORGE WASHINGTON   Georgia, Suh, Gordon County.

OFFICIAL   How old are you?

GEORGE WASHINGTON   Sixty-nine, comin' seventy on de 25th of next month, if de Lord spares me.

OFFICIAL   How far did you go in school—what grade?

GEORGE WASHINGTON   We ain't had much schoolin' in dem days in Georgia, no suh—jes about a year.

OFFICIAL   What kind of work did you do then—farming?

GEORGE WASHINGTON   Sho, farmin', den I went to Miami, Florida, worked on construction. Yo know, jes after dat big fire dey had dere about forty years ago.

OFFICIAL (*amused*)   Listen, Grandpop, I am not as old as all that.

GEORGE WASHINGTON (*laughing heartily*) Sho, yo ain't—sho, yo ain't.

OFFICIAL (*after having laughed heartily*)   How long have you been in New York?

GEORGE WASHINGTON   Goin' on thirty-five years.

OFFICIAL   What was your last steady job?

GEORGE WASHINGTON   Longshoreman wid de Ward line. Worked dere ten years till last August. De boss came 'long and said: George, he said, listen, yo better take a rest. Yo gettin' too old for de job. Dat's what he said. Ain't worked since, steady. 'Couse, I'd saved a few dollars. So, I helped de missus wid de washin'. She's my second wife, a good woman, yes, suh. She's been doin' de washin' for Mrs. Epstein for years. Mrs. Epstein, she live on Jerome Avenue, corner of 170th Street.—I always take de wash up to her. So, about October ob last years she said to me: George, when things don't go so good, come and see me. Well, things got kind-a-tight. So, I went to see Mrs. Epstein. She's a fine lady, always talk good to me. She gave me a letter to some society down town and den I got de three-days-a-week job. But yo know, dat's finished now.

OFFICIAL   Have you ever registered for Old Age Pension?

GEORGE WASHINGTON   What is dat?

OFFICIAL   Don't you know that the State pays people over seventy about $30 per month?

GEORGE WASHINGTON   No, Suh.

OFFICIAL (*writing on slip*)   You go to this office, tell them, that I sent you,—here is my card—and register for Old Age Pension.

GEORGE WASHINGTON (*overwhelmed*)   Oh, yo sure do me good, thank yo suh, thank yo suh, goodby suh, thank yo. (*leaves office bowing out*)

STUDENT VISITOR   Social legislation is certainly a blessing.

OFFICIAL   Yes, but what can those men do, who are too young for Old Age Pension and too old for industry?

REPRESENTATIVE OF THE "HEAVENLY MESSENGER" (*enters, jovial*)   Good morning, good morning, Mr. Johnson, may I leave some copies of the *Heavenly Messenger* here?

OFFICIAL   Go ahead, you know where the rack is!

SECOND UNEMPLOYED   Better give us sump'n to eat.

REPRESENTATIVE   But you need a strong spirit to face adversity.

OFFICIAL   Hey, don't let us have any sermons and arguments.

(REPRESENTATIVE *leaves copies in the rack and goes out, some men pick up copies*)

STUDENT VISITOR   How can we have Christan fellowship in this world as long as we have to fight one another for jobs, for bread?

OFFICIAL   Yes, you are right. (*pause*)   Well, (*to* FOURTH UNEMPLOYED) you are next. Why were you so sleepy?

FOURTH UNEMPLOYED   I've been hikin' all the way from North Carolina. Came to see my married brother here, day befo' yisteday. But mah brother lost his job, an' his wife don't want to keep 'm no longer. So they bust up house-keepin'. I've been lookin' round two days, but couldn't catch nuthin'. Ah got no place to sleep an' that piece of apple 'bacci is all keeps me from starvin'.

OFFICIAL (*to* THIRD UNEMPLOYED)   Say, Joe, come here a moment! (*comes over to desk*) You know what church is giving out food today? Take this man over and see that he gets something to eat and a place to sleep, will you?

THIRD UNEMPLOYED   Sure, come along, brother. Today it is the Saint Peter, they don't feed you so good no,—tomorrow, let me see, it's Mother Nazareth, you sure get a good square meal there . . . (*as they go walking out*)

DISTRIBUTOR OF "WORKMAN'S DAILY" (*enters, carrying copies*)   Anybody here want the *Workman's Daily*, the fighter for the working classes?

OFFICIAL   Please, this is no market place or public thoroughfare, besides, the men want food and jobs and not newspapers.

DISTRIBUTOR   If the men read this paper they will know how to get food and jobs.

OFFICIAL   Please, no selling in here, I say.

DISTRIBUTOR   All right, boss. (*leaves*)

MECHANIC (*leaving group of unemployed and walking to gate*)   Have you anything for me, sir? I have been looking everywhere, can't find a thing to do. Rent is behind, the landlord is getting nasty, the grocer's bill is overdue.

OFFICIAL   I am sorry, I have no inquiry for a mechanic.

MECHANIC   Anything will do, haven't you got anything?

OFFICIAL   Hang around a bit, I may have something soon.

MECHANIC   I cannot sit around quiet. I must have something soon. (*leaves apparently greatly troubled*)

OFFICIAL (*to* STUDENT VISITOR)   This man is an expert auto mechanic. Had his own shop for fifteen years in a small town in Alabama. Somehow, he got into a fight with a white man, his life was threatened and he came up here with his family, leaving all his property behind.

STUDENT VISITOR   Probably escaped a lynching—shocking.

(*Telephone rings, unemployed's attention centers on* OFFICIAL)

OFFICIAL (*answering telephone*)   Public Employment Office.—What is the name? Yes, I have it. What are the hours? Six days a week. How much? $70 per month and room. What is your telephone number? Sure, I'll have a man there in about an hour. Yes, thank you, sir. (*writes out order. To the men*) I want a porter, a light colored porter for an apartment house, experienced, work from 7 to 7, six days a week, $70 per month and room.

(FIFTH UNEMPLOYED *walks up*)

OFFICIAL   Are you single?

FIFTH UNEMPLOYED   Yes Sir.

OFFICIAL   Have you done porter work?

FIFTH UNEMPLOYED   Sure.

OFFICIAL   What is your name? (*conversation continues*)

FIRST UNEMPLOYED (*reading newspaper*) Here is a white man, a broker, shoot his'self 'cause he's broke.

SECOND UNEMPLOYED (*stretches himself,—with an air of a philosopher*)   I tell you, some white folks can't stand bein' po'. Guess, we don't feel it 'cause we've always been po'. Shoot his'-self,—crazy, who ever heard of a cullud man shoot his'self, 'cause he's po'?

OFFICIAL (*to* FIFTY UNEMPLOYED)   Here is the card. See the address? Go there right away. Got no fare? Here take this nickel. (*exit* FIFTH UNEMPLOYED)

(FRANCIS TAYLOR *walks up to the gate*)

OFFICIAL   What can I do for you?

FRANCIS TAYLOR   I'd like to have a job, sir.

OFFICIAL   Have you registered here?

FRANCIS TAYLOR   No, sir.

OFFICIAL   Take a seat. What is your name?

FRANCIS TAYLOR   Francis Taylor.

OFFICIAL   Address?

FRANCIS TAYLOR   26 West 99th Street.

OFFICIAL   How old are you?

FRANCIS TAYLOR   Thirty-three years.

OFFICIAL   How many children?

FRANCIS TAYLOR   Eight.

OFFICIAL   Eight?—Did you get any work under the scheme of the Prosser Committee?

FRANCIS TAYLOR   Yes, I did. Fifteen dollars a week for three days work.

OFFICIAL   Were you able to live on $15 with a family of a wife and eight children?

FRANCIS TAYLOR   Well, we had to.

OFFICIAL (*reflecting*)   How old is your wife?

FRANCIS TAYLOR   Thirty years old.

OFFICIAL   Is she in good heath?

FRANCIS TAYLOR   She has trouble with her heart, she goes to the hospital. I go there too, have lumbago pretty bad.

OFFICIAL   Have you ever heard of a Birth Control Clinic?

FRANCIS TAYLOR (*startled at turn of conversation, sulkily*)   Yes, the A. I. C. P. told me to go there with the wife.

OFFICIAL   Did you go?

FRANCIS TAYLOR   No, I don't believe in that.

OFFICIAL   In what?

FRANCIS TAYLOR   They say it's so you won't have no more babies.

OFFICIAL   Do you want to have more?

FRANCIS TAYLOR   No, we ain't going to have no more, but I don't believe in going to a hospital for that. Hospitals is for when you get sick.

OFFICIAL (*aroused*)   So it's all-right when you are sick but you don't believe in preventing sickness. Who pays the hospital bills for you and your wife? Somebody does. If your children are underfed and become sick, charity must provide help. Somebody must pay. Why? Because you are obstinate and refuse to keep your wife in the best health possible. (SPEAKER OF WORKERS' LEAGUE *enters and distributes handbills*) Here is the address of the clinic, go there and find out what it is all about. Then act for yourself. (FRANCIS TAYLOR *reads the slip, rises slowly and disgruntled, joins the crowd.* OFFICIAL *notices tumult*) What's going on there. Here, lady, what are you do-ing? Do you hear me? (*gets up and advances towards her*) Stop giving out handbills. This is a public employment office.

SPEAKER   Why don't you give these men work? By the way, who do you think I am?

OFFICIAL   Why, you are the Communist speaker from the street corner.

SPEAKER   I am speaking for the Workers' League, we are working for the emancipation of the working classes. . . .

OFFICIAL (*interrupting*)   All right, make your speeches on the street. I cannot permit you to hold your meetings in here. This is a public employment office.

SPEAKER (*jeering*)   Employment Office, yes, (*imitating*) sorry, I haven't anything men, come back tomorrow.

OFFICIAL   Please, go now. (*takes her gently by the arm*)

SPEAKER   Take your hand off my arm, you're forgetting yourself! I thought you were a gentleman. (OFFICIAL, *defeated, rushes to his desk, takes telephone in hand,—hesitates*) Here boys, take these handbills! (*to official, taunting*) I suppose you want to call the police. Tell'm you need protection from a little woman. They'll come and do their best to keep ideas out of the workers' head—with nightsticks. Ha, ha. . . . (*exit*)

OFFICIAL (*tense with excitement to student visitor*)   Nothing would please her more than to have the police here, so she can get free publicity for her propaganda. (*to men talking and reading handbills*) That's all for this morning. We open again at one o'clock. (*a few leave, others rush suddenly to the window. Through right window, men can be seen running*) What's the matter now?

MEN AT WINDOW   Another poor devil is being dispossessed. Putt'n out another family.

MECHANIC (*after having passed the windows enters excitedly*)   My furniture is out on the street. I have been out all morning lookin' for work—just got home—found sheriffs putt'n out my furniture—wife and kids are on the street too—what can I do, Mr. Johnson?

OFFICIAL   Be calm, just sit down. I will call up the Mayor's Emergency Committee. (*picks up the telephone*) Courtland 2340. Pardon me, Courtland 7-2340. Is this the Mayor's Emergency Committee on Unemployment? This is the Public Employment Office, Harlem. I have a very sad eviction case here, an eviction case.

What? You do not handle any more eviction cases? Not since May 31st. Who is now taking care of . . . Nobody? What is going to happen to those poor families? Oh, you only take in children of broken homes and refer them to institutions. Call up the A.I.C.P.? The Association for the Improvement of the Conditions of the Poor is over-burdened with work. I know that. So, you can't do anything? All right, thank you. (*hangs up, dejected, troubled*)

STUDENT VISITOR   Now, if we had Unemployment Insurance . . .

OFFICIAL   Yes, but we haven't.

STUDENT VISITOR   Isn't there a group of interested professional people to whom . . .

OFFICIAL (*interrupting*)   The professional people have their problems. But they are not vitally interested in the problems of the laboring Negroes.

STUDENT VISITOR   Maybe the political leaders . . .

OFFICIAL   They are too busy with politics.

STUDENT VISITOR   Isn't there a community organization . . .

OFFICIAL   No, there is no civic organization representing the broad interests of the community. (*to himself*) No Prosser Committee now. A.I.C.P. over-burdened. No relief from the Red Cross, this is no Act of God. (*to ME-CHANIC*) Listen, go to the police station, tell them about your troubles. Let's see what they will do. Come back here at once. I will do my best in the meantime to help you. (*shakes hands*)

(MECHANIC *leaves hurriedly, a group of unemployed, who had stood at the door, follow. Sad silence between* OFFICIAL *and* STUDENT VISITOR. *The voice of a newspaper boy can be heard behind the scene.*)

NEWSBOY   The *Harlem News*—All about the Chicago Riot—Three dead in the Chicago Riot—the *Harlem News*.

OFFICIAL (*to* STUDENT VISITOR)   Here is a nickel, please get me a paper.

(STUDENT VISITOR *runs out*)

OFFICIAL (*to himself*)   I feel so helpless. Here is white society holding down the Negro to small jobs and small pay. Business becomes slack, the laborers are dumped on the street. But they must live! (*shakes head*) Real leadership is lacking. Oh, what is the way out of this misery?

STUDENT VISITOR (*returning with paper, reading*)   Chicago Negroes stop eviction. Three Negroes killed. Court suspends all eviction orders.

OFFICIAL   Blood, more blood. Force, the claws and fangs of the beast, is it the only way out of this brutal civilization?

[Curtain]

DON'T YOU WANT TO BE FREE?

1937

Langston Hughes (1902–1967)

Many young Black playwrights of the 1930s took a somber view of Broadway's condescending depiction of African American life. The liberal policy of the Federal Theatre Project allowed these playwrights for the first time to portray their society with verisimilitude. Richard Wright, who was associated with the Chicago Negro Theatre unit for a time, envisioned an African American theatre that would break away from the colorful stories and stereotypes perpetuated by Broadway. Langston Hughes, along with Theodore Ward in Chicago and Theodore Browne in Seattle, helped inaugurate just such a theatre.

When Hughes returned from his assignment as a war correspondent in Spain, he rejected the commercialism of his previous plays and decided to establish his own theatre—a people's theatre. Louise Patterson suggested the hall of the International Workers Order on New York's 125th Street. This was the first home of the Harlem Suitcase Theatre in 1937. It had minimal lighting, no scenery or properties, and was intimate enough to allow the audience to be drawn into the action. Hughes believed that

For a true black theater, music and dance must be integral to the action; the music must be blues and spirituals, and not, as in most musicals involving Negroes, sentimental or risqué travesties of black style.[1]

The Suitcase Theatre relied on amateur actors, charged thirty-five cents, and played to audiences that were 75 percent Black. The program was usually two or three short pieces: *The Slave* or *The Man Who Died at Twelve O'Clock*, or several skits written by Hughes lampooning white caricatures of Blacks: *Em-Fuehrer Jones*, *Limitations of Life*, and *Little Eva's End*. The pièce de résistance was always *Don't You Want To Be Free?*, which was written expressly for this theatre.

Don't You Want To Be Free? marks Hughes's departure from conventional play structure. His style became

loose-limbed and improvisational in effect, montage-like rather than static and monumental, always strongly lyrical and rhythmic

---

1. Arnold Rampersad, *The Life of Langston Hughes*, vol. 1 (New York: Oxford University Press, 1986), p. 357.

in a linking of intense moments of Langston's own poetry, and with music—black music—blended into its tissue as an essential element. Its major criteria . . . came not from the white stage but from Hughes's sense of the distinguishing features of modern, urban black culture and his own poetic gifts.[2]

This style is evident many years later in Hughes's gospel musical plays.

Although the Suitcase Theatre lasted only two years (it did not survive its transplant to the library basement on 135th Street), the idea of a Negro people's theatre spread to other cities. In March 1939, Hughes founded the New Negro Theatre in Los Angeles.

Don't You Want To Be Free?, which opened in February 1937 and ran for 135 performances, was the longest-running play in Harlem during Hughes's life. It was highly successful by any standard, not only because of the simplicity and beauty of the poetry and songs, but also because of its direct appeal to the problems of the audience (most businesses in Harlem were owned by whites and only one in six employees of these businesses was Black).

The play's appeal to unite poor Blacks and whites against exploitation by the rich remains powerful although, in retrospect, it is difficult to believe this was ever a real possibility.

Langston Hughes lived a nomadic and lonely life. His mother, Carrie Hughes, left him in the care of her mother, Mary Langston, for long periods of time in Lawrence, Kansas. His father, Jim Hughes, divorced from Carrie, settled in Mexico and became a rather prosperous businessman. Young Langston's interest in theatre was due in part to his mother, who longed for a career in show business. She cast him in dramatic programs at her church in Kansas City and took him to see plays when he visited her there. His first play, *The Gold Piece*, written for children, was published in 1921. During his lifetime he wrote fifty-nine plays, operas, and musicals, and did seven collaborative works with three other authors. Hughes is perhaps best known as a poet and was honored with the title "Poet Laureate of Harlem"—his home and the inspiration for much of his work.

Don't You Want To Be Free?

Production Notes

by Langston Hughes

(Provided by Dorothy and Reuben Silver [formerly] of the Karamu Theatre in Cleveland)

Don't You Want To Be Free? is an impressionistic play endeavoring to capture within the space of an hour the entire scope of Negro history from Africa to America. It should move swiftly from one scene to another with no waits other than those indicated by the action. It should be presented in a modern manner with no curtains or stage effects other than a lynch rope which hangs at the back, center, throughout the entire performance, and serves as a symbol of Negro oppression. This rope is used actively only in the lynching scene when the Young Man puts his head into the noose on the words, "All you crackers got me." He takes his head from the noose on the words, "Not I." Symbolic of the eternal resurrection of an oppressed people.

---

2. Ibid., p. 359.

This play may be produced on any sort of stage or platform.* In cases where the stage or platform has no backstage exits, the entire cast may be seated on the front rows of the auditorium just before the performance and make their entrance into the scene from there. Audience-space should still be employed for much of the action. Since the idea behind this type of production is to cause the audience to feel that they, as well as the actors, are participating in the drama. For instance, the Young Man should begin the play by entering without any previous signal, with the house lights on, down the center aisle of the auditorium, delivering his first speech from the floor in front of the stage, very simply, as though he were making an announcement. He then steps upon the stage for the beginning of the play—the poem, "I am a Negro."

GROUPS TO BE CONTACTED FOR PROMOTION: This play should appeal especially to Negro History groups, labor unions, social workers, and liberal and progressive organizations of all types, as well as Negro and fraternal groups. It is suggested that the play be performed in a small auditorium, perhaps two performances a week over a period of several weeks, rather than performing the play just once in a large auditorium—since this is the type of play which catches on by word of mouth advertising, so people should be given a change to hear about it. Also, a small hall packed to the doors is much more encouraging to actors than a large hall partially filled. Then, too, several performances of the same play help greatly in perfecting the acting technique of the group.

From Slavery
Through the Blues
To Now—and then some!

With Singing, Music, and Dancing

CHARACTERS

A YOUNG MAN
A BOY
A GIRL
A WOMAN
A MAN
AN OLD WOMAN
AN OLD MAN
AN OVERSEER
A MULATTO GIRL
A WIFE
A HUSBAND
A LAUNDRY WORKER
A MEMBER OF THE AUDIENCE
TWO NEWSBOYS
VOICES
A CHORUS

(SETTING: *a bare stage, except for a lynch rope and an auction block. No scenery and very few props.*

---

*This paragraph is an abridged version of the original.

No special lighting. Only actors needed—and an audience. There is no curtain, so a YOUNG MAN *simply comes forward and begins to speak)*

YOUNG MAN   Listen, folks! I'm one of the members of this group, and I want to tell you about our theater. This is it right here! We haven't got any scenery, or painted curtains, because we haven't got any money to buy them. But we've got something you can't buy with money, anyway. We've got faith in ourselves. And in you. So we're going to put on a show. Maybe you'll like it because it's about you, and about us. This show is for you. And you can act in it, too, if you want to. This is your show, as well as ours. Now I'll tell you what this show is about. It's about me, except that it's not just about me now standing here talking to you—but it's about me yesterday, and about me tomorrow. I'm colored! I guess you can see that. Well, this show is about what it means to be colored in America. Listen: (*crash of cymbals*)

I am a Negro:
    Black as the night is black,
    Black like the depths of my Africa.

I've been a slave:
    Caesar told me to keep his door-steps clean.
    I brushed the boots of Washington.

I've been a worker:
    Under my hand the pyramids arose.
    I made mortar for the Woolworth Building.

I've been a singer:
    All the way from Africa to Georgia
    I carried my sorrow songs.
    I made ragtime.

I've been a victim:
    The Belgians cut off my hands in the
      Congo.
    They lynch me now in Texas.

I am a Negro:
    Black as the night is black,
    Black like the depths of my Africa.

(*Tom-toms. From either side come an African* BOY, *left, and* GIRL, *right, dressed in clothes of bright colors. The* GIRL *begins to dance in the African manner, whirling slowly to the beating of the drums*)

BOY

The low beating of the tom-toms,
The slow beating of the tom-toms,
    Low . . . slow
    Slow . . . low—
    Stirs your blood.
      Dance!
A night-veiled girl
    Whirls softly into a
    Circle of light
    Whirls softly . . . slowly,
Like a wisp of smoke around the fire—
    And the tom-toms beat,
    And the tom-toms beat,
And the low beating of the tom-toms
    Stirs your blood

(*Cool music like rippling water. Lifting her arms to the sun, the* GIRL *speaks*)

GIRL

To fling my arms wide
In some place of the sun,
To whirl and to dance
Till the white day is done.
Then rest at cool evening
Beneath a tall tree
While night comes on gently,
    Dark like me—

That is my dream!

To fling my arms wide
In the face of the sun,
Dance! whirl! whirl!
Till the quick day is done.
Rest at pale evening . . .
A tall slim tree,
Night coming tenderly
    Dark like me.

(*The* BOY *has drawn near the* GIRL *and stands before her. She looks at him, takes his hands, and they gaze into each other's eyes*)

YOUNG MAN   I guess I was like that boy a long time ago, when we lived in Africa, and the sun was our friend. I guess I was crazy about that girl that I met at night in the moonlight under the palm trees.

(*Roll of drums, like thunder! The* BOY *and* GIRL *run away, right. The* YOUNG MAN *speaks to the audience*)

I was Africa then
But the white men came.
I was in my own land, then.
But the white men came.

They drove me out of the forest
They took me away from the jungles.
I lost my trees.
I lost my silver moons.

Now they've caged me
In their circus of civilization.
Now I'm in a cage
In their circus of civilization.

In 1619 the first slaves came to Jamestown, brought in chains in sailing vessels to America.

(*Enter right four slaves:* GIRL, BOY, OLD MAN, *and* WIFE *chained by the wrists together. They walk in a straight line, moaning musically across the stage. The* YOUNG MAN *joins them. They are followed by an* OVERSEER *with a whip. All exit left except the* GIRL *and the* OVERSEER. *The* GIRL *mounts the slave-block, wild-eyed and frightened*)

OVERSEER   Get along now! Get on! Step along there! (*approaching auction block*) Folks, look here what I got! A nice healthy Black gal, folks. Wild! Ain't trained, but a little of this will break her in. (*holds up his whip*) Congo women can't be beat for working, and she's a Congo woman. Good for house or fields. Look at them legs, wiry and strong. (*feels her legs*) Look at them hands. Long fingers, just right for pickin' cotton. (*to the* GIRL) Open your mouth, gal! (*punches her with the whipstock*) Open your mouth. (GIRL *opens her mouth*) See! Healthy! Nice white teeth! (*with a leer*) This girl's all right for most anything. What am I offered for her, gentlemen? Speak up! Make your bids. What am I offered for her?

VOICE   One hundred dollars.

OVERSEER   Heh? One hundred dollars! What? That ain't a starter! What am I offered for this gal, gentlemen? I got a hundred.

VOICE   One hundred fifty!

OVERSEER   One hundred fifty! Hundred fifty! Good for cooking, washing, hoeing, anything you want.

VOICE   Two hundred!

OVERSEER   That's more like it! Two hundred! Two . . .

VOICE   Two hundred ten.

VOICE   Two hundred twenty.

VOICE   Two hundred fifty.

OVERSEER   Two hundred fifty! Two hundred fifty . . .

VOICE   Three hundred!

OVERSEER   Three hundred! Do I hear another? What? Three hundred dollars worth of black gal! Going! Going! Gone! (*strikes the floor with his whip. There is a loud scream from the* GIRL) Gone for three hundred dollars! Here, take her. Make her work now. (*he pushes the* GIRL *off the block and she goes aside sobbing, right. Dark voices are heard chanting*)

VOICES

Cook them white folks dinner,
Wash them white folks clothes,
Be them white folks slave-gal,
That is all she knows.
Be them white folks slave-gal,
That is all she knows.

(OLD MAN *enters left in the overalls and ragged shirt of a slave. He mounts the block*)

VOICE   Kinder old folks, but still got plenty in him. Nothing like an old work-horse. He's well broke in. Something of a preacher, too. Helps keep the other slaves out o' mischief o' Sundays. What am I offered? Fifty? . . . Hundred? . . . Hundred fifty. Going, going, gone! For a hundred and fifty! Get off the block, you

old ape! Get off the block, and lemme get somebody up here I can make money off of. (*he pushes the* OLD MAN *away. He goes aside, muttering*)

VOICES

Whip done broke his spirit,
Plow done broke his back.
All they wants a slave, that's all,
When a man is Black.
Nothin' but a slave, that's all,
If a man is Black.

OLD MAN   No, no! No, no!

(*The* YOUNG MAN *enters left. The* OVERSEER'S *face glows. He rubs his hands*)

OVERSEER
Ah! Here's a nice fine Black buck!
Strong's you'd want to see
Boy, get up on that block
And make some dough for me!

YOUNG MAN
No!

OVERSEER
What? No!
Who're you talkin' to?

YOUNG MAN
You!

OVERSEER
You must've gone crazy
Talking like that to me.
Get up on that block!

YOUNG MAN
No! I want to be free! (*kicks block off stage*)

OVERSEER
Free?

YOUNG MAN
Yes, free!
Not sold like a slave.
Before I'll be sold again
I'll go down to my grave.

(*The* OVERSEER *strikes him with his whip*)

GIRL   Oh!

YOUNG MAN   No! no! no! (*as he backs away and falls before the blows of the* OVERSEER'S *whip*)

OVERSEER   I'll teach you to want to be free! To talk back to me! (*lashing him.* YOUNG MAN *falls*)

GIRL   Oh! . . . Oh! . . . Oh!

OLD MAN (BEGINS TO SING)
Go down, Moses,
Way down in Egypt land,
And tell ole Pharoah
CHORUS
To let my people go.

OVERSEER (*turns to* OLD MAN *and strikes him with his whip*)   Shut up, you dog!

(*As the* OLD MAN *falls, the* GIRL *takes up the song*)

GIRL
Go down, Moses,
Way down in Egypt land,
And tell ole Pharoah

CHORUS
To let my people go!

OVERSEER (*in wild confusion, rushes to the* GIRL *and strikes her*)   Shut up, you god-damned dogs! Shut up!

(*But then the* YOUNG MAN *rises and takes up the song*)

YOUNG MAN
Go down, Moses,
Way down in Egypt land,
And tell ole Pharoah
To let my people go.
CHORUS
And tell ole Pharoah
To let my people go.

(*A great wave of revolt rises disguised as a song. The* OVERSEER *is powerless against it. He calls for troops, for arms. He pulls a gun*)

OVERSEER   Send soldiers! Get out the militia! Shoot these dogs!

(*Shots are heard. The* OLD MAN *falls prone. The* GIRL *falls. An* OLD WOMAN *enters right and kneels over the dead*)

OVERSEER (*as he shoots*)   Shut up! Shut up! Shut up! (*he exits left*)

YOUNG MAN (*coming forward toward the audience*)   But we didn't shut up! We were never wholly quiet! Some of us always carried on our fight and kept alive the seeds of revolt. Nat Turner was one. Denmark Vesey was another who tried to lead the slaves to freedom. Harriet Tubman was another who sought roads to escape. Sojourner Truth another. Some they beat to death. Some they killed. But some of us always kept on, even though the way looked dark.

OLD WOMAN   So dark! So dark! (*sings over the bodies of her dead*)

Oh, nobody knows
The trouble I've seen!
Nobody knows but Jesus.
Nobody knows
The trouble I've seen.
Glory, Hallelujah!

Sometimes I'm up,
Sometimes I'm down.
Oh, yes, Lawd!
Sometimes I'm almost
To the ground.
Oh, yes, Lawd!

CHORUS
Oh, nobody knows
The trouble I've seen . . .

OLD WOMAN (*as the* CHORUS *hums*)   Children scattered. Home gone. Sons and daughters sold away. I don't know where they are. (*rises*) But I look at the stars and they look at the stars. And somehow I feels better. And now I walks the world lookin' for truth. I'se a so-journer lookin' for truth.

YOUNG MAN   Sojourner Truth!

OLD WOMAN   Yes, son.

YOUNG MAN   Is we ever gonna be free?

OLD WOMAN   Son, we gonna be free. Ain't you heard them names?

YOUNG MAN   What names?

OLD WOMAN   Black names and white names in the air. Listen! (*flag rises*)

VOICES   Douglass! Douglass! Frederick Douglass! William Lloyd Garrison! Emerson! . . . Whittier! . . . Lowell! . . . Douglass! John Brown! Lincoln! John Brown! Abraham Lincoln. (*roll of drums. Bugle calls*)

OLD WOMAN   The Civil War! And freedom!

YOUNG MAN (*takes flag*)   White soldiers and Black soldiers fighting for our freedom.

OLD MAN (*rising*)   Slaves rising from the dead for freedom.

GIRL *(rising)*   Women lifting up their heads for freedom.

CHORUS
Glory! Glory! Hallelujah!
Glory! Glory! Hallelujah!
Glory! Glory! Hallelujah!

YOUNG MAN   Everybody sing! *(he starts the verse)*

CHORUS
John Brown's body
Lies a-mouldering in his grave . . .
    (Repeat Chorus)

(As they sing, all exit right. Enter the MAN and the WOMAN in old clothes, left, cross right. They begin to hoe in a field)

WOMAN   John, this ain't no freedom.
MAN   Free, to work and get no pay. Lucy, how come we's

Just a herd of Negroes
Driven to the field,
Plowing, planting, hoeing,
To make the cotton yield.

When the cotton's picked
And the work is done
Boss man takes the money
And we get none.

Leave us hungry, ragged
As we were before.
Year by year goes by
And we are nothing more

Than a herd of Negroes
Driven to the field—
Plowing life away
To make the cotton yield.

WOMAN   Yes, honey, all you say is true, 'cause

There stands the white man,
Boss of the fields—
Lord of the land
And all that it yields.

And here bend the black folks,
Hands to the soil—
Bosses of nothing,
Not even our toil.

MAN   The South! Honey, the South's so pretty, magnolia trees and cotton, but sometimes it's bad, too. So evil and bad!

(Enter OVERSEER bringing chair)

WOMAN   The white folks won't pay us nothing, that's the trouble. Besides the Jim Crow cars, and the Jim Crow schools, and the lynchings—when you work, they don't pay you nothing.
MAN   That's what happened to Wilbur, to our boy! All over a little mite o' money.
WOMAN   Yes, that's what happened to Wilbur. He went to ask the man for his money—and they killed him.

(On the left, the OVERSEER sits in a chair tilted back, smoking a big cigar. Enter the YOUNG MAN, right, crosses left)

YOUNG MAN   Mr. Mallory, the crops all sold, ain't it? Can you gimme my part now?
OVERSEER   Your part? What you mean, your part, George?
YOUNG MAN   I mean my money that you owe me.
OVERSEER   You better be careful how you use that word *owe*, boy. I don't owe you nothing.
YOUNG MAN *(trying to restrain himself)*   But I raised nine bales, Mr. Mallory, And my contract calls . . .
OVERSEER   Your contract? Hell! What about my bills? What about the commissary store? What about that sow belly and corn meal I been advancing you all the year for you and your lazy old woman, and them kids of yours that you thinks too good to work in the cotton fields. Trying to send pickaninnies to school! Huh! You're an uppity Black boy, anyhow. Talkin' about what I owe you! Why even after the nine bales was sold, you owed me more'n a hundred dollars. Why, you ungrateful scoundrel. Get on back there in that field and start plowin' for next year's crop.
YOUNG MAN   Mr. Mallory, I ain't goin'. Not till I see the figures.
OVERSEER   You ain't going? What you mean, you ain't going? Don't talk back to me!
YOUNG MAN   I ain't going. I'm tired o' workin' for nothing.

OVERSEER (*rising*)   Are you trying to say I don't pay my field hands? Get out o' here. You impudent Black cuss, you! Get out o' here!

YOUNG MAN   No, sir, Mr. Mallory, not without my money.

OVERSEER   You impudent dog! Get out o' here before I beat the hell out of you.

YOUNG MAN   No!

(*The* OVERSEER *walks up to the* YOUNG MAN *and hits him in the mouth. The* YOUNG MAN *stands as if in a daze, then he suddenly deals the* OVERSEER *a blow that sends him reeling unconscious to the floor. There is a crash of cymbals. Whistles. The far-off cry of a mob. The* MOTHER *and* FATHER *are terror-stricken. The* YOUNG MAN *looks for a place to hide. There is no hiding place*)

MAN   Hurry, son, hurry! They gonna kill you!

WOMAN   Run, Wilbur! Oh, honey, run! Go the swamp way, so's the dogs can't smell no tracks. Run!

MAN   Hurry! Hurry! Hurry! Son, hurry!

YOUNG MAN (*darting wildly about*)   There ain't no place to run. I hit the white man. I done hit the boss! And there ain't no place to run. Nobody helps me. Nobody to protect me. (*he approaches the lynch rope that dangles from the sky and puts his head into the noose*) I know it! You got me! All you crackers got me. Dead! I'm dead!

(*His body slumps as if dead.* NEWSBOYS *enter selling papers*)

NEWSBOYS   Negro lynched in Alabama! Big Lynching Near Selma! Read all about it! Read about the lynching! Negro accused of rape! Big lynching!

WOMAN (*standing before the hanging youth*) My boy is dead!

MAN (*bitterly*)   Damn the ones what kilt him! Damn their souls to hell!

WOMAN   John, my boy is dead, I'm all alone—and my boy is dead! (*begins to sing*)

I couldn't hear nobody pray.
Oh, Lawdy! Couldn't hear nobody pray.
Way down yonder by myself,
I couldn't hear nobody pray!

(*Enter a young* MULATTO GIRL, *who sits down beside the hanging body, center, and begins to recite*)

MULATTO GIRL

Way down South in Dixie,
(Break the heart of me!)
They hung my dark young lover
To a cross road's tree.

Way down South in Dixie,
(Bruised body high in air)
I asked the white Lord Jesus
What was the use of prayer.

Way down South in Dixie
(Break the heart of me)
Love is a naked shadow
On a gnarled and naked tree.

OVERSEER (*left—rising and shouting*)

Pull at the rope! O!
Pull it high!
Let the white folks live
And the Black man die.

MAN

Yes, pull it, then,
With a bloody cry!
Let the Black boy swing
But the *white folks* die.

OVERSEER

The white folks die?
What do you mean—
The white folks die?

MAN

That Black boy's
Still body says:

YOUNG MAN

Not I!

MAN

Not I!

VOICES

Not I! Not I! Not I!

(*The* OVERSEER *sneaks away*)

YOUNG MAN   They killed Christ, didn't they, when he tried to change the world?

WOMAN   But did he die?

EVERYBODY   No!

YOUNG MAN   They killed John Brown, did-n't they, when he tried to free the slaves?

WOMAN   But did he die?

VOICES   No!

YOUNG MAN   What did Angelo Herndon say when they had him in prison for trying to help the poor? What did Herndon say?

VOICE   Let them kill Herndon, if they will, but a million more will rise to take my place.

YOUNG MAN   You can't kill the working class, he said. And when we rise . . .

WOMAN (*begins to sing*)

> In that great gettin' up mornin'
> Fare you well! Fare you well!
> (*repeat*)
>
> CHORUS
> There's a better day a-comin'!
> (*etc.*)

(*The old spiritual rises triumphally as the* YOUNG MAN *takes his head from lynch rope. He comes with tramp's bundle on stick and stands before the* MULATTO GIRL. *The* MAN *and* WOMAN *exit right as the singing dies down*)

YOUNG MAN   So many things is wrong in this world, honey, but the wrongest thing of all is poverty. Being poor. You're the girl I loved once, now look at you! All painted and pow-dered, and wrong. But I know what happened. I don't blame you for it. You was young and beautiful once, and golden like the sunshine that warmed your body. But because you was colored, honey, this town had no place for you, nothing for you to do.

MULATTO GIRL   So one day, sitting on old Mrs. Latham's back porch polishing the silver, working for two dollars a week, I asked myself two questions. They ran something like this: What can a colored girl do on the money from a white woman's kitchen?

VOICE   Two dollars a week.

MULATTO GIRL   And ain't there any joy in this town?

VOICE   Two dollars a week.

YOUNG MAN   Now the streets down by the river are your streets. (*turning away*) And the sinister shuttered houses of the bottoms hold a yellow girl seeking an answer to her questions.

VOICE (*softly*)   Two dollars a week.

MULATTO GIRL   The good church folks won't even mention my name any more.

YOUNG MAN   But the white men who visit those houses . . .

MULATTO GIRL (*triumphantly*)   Pay more money to me now than they ever did before when I worked in their kitchens. (*distant laughter*)

YOUNG MAN (*bitterly*)   I'm going away. I got to go away.

MULATTO GIRL   Goodbye, Wilbur.

YOUNG MAN (*without looking back*)   I'm go-ing up North. (*as he walks left*) I'm going far away.

MULATTO GIRL   Goodbye, Wilbur! (*she pow-ders her face and begins to recite*)

> My old man's a white old man!
> My old mother's Black!
> But if ever I cursed my white old man
> I take my curses back.
>
> If ever I cursed my Black old mother
> And wished she were in hell,
> I'm sorry for that evil wish
> And now I wish her well.
>
> My old man died in a fine big house.
> My ma died in a shack.
> I wonder where I'm gonna die,
> Being neither white nor Black?

(*As she walks away, a piano begins to play the blues, the sad old Negro blues. She exits right. The* YOUNG MAN *sings as he picks up his pick and be-gins to trudge the road*)

> YOUNG MAN
>
> Goin' down de road, Lawd,
> Goin' down de road,
> Down de road, Lawd,
> Way, way down de road.
> Got to find somebody
> To help me carry dis load.
>
> Sun's a-settin',
> This is what I'm gonna sing.
> Sun's a-settin'
> This is what I'm gonna sing:
> I feel de blues a-comin'
> Wonder what de blues 'll bring?
>
> Road, Road, Road, O!
> Road, road . . . road . . . road, road!

Road, road, road, O!
On de No'thern road.
These Mississippi towns ain't
Fit fer a hoppin' toad.

(*The* YOUNG MAN *sits down beside the road. Enter* WIFE, *right, and* BOY, *left*) Gee, but I got the blues. (*the piano sings with the sad weary notes of the blues*) Do you—all know what the blues is?

WIFE

The blues ain't nothin'
But the dog-goned heart's disease.
I say, blues ain't nothin' but
The dog-gone heart's disease.
When you got the blues, you
Sho can't find no ease.

(*sighs*) I got the blues. Reckon I'll run down the street a minute, see can I walk 'em off! (*she dresses and powders to exit later from her dreary flat. At left, undressing in a dark hall bedroom, the* BOY *answers, too*)
BOY   I got the blues. Guess I'll go to bed. Maybe I can sleep 'em off.
YOUNG MAN   The blues is songs folks make up when their heart hurts. That's what the blues is. Sad funny songs. Too sad to be funny, and too funny to be sad. (*exit* WOMAN) Colored folks made up the blues! Listen!

(*Loudly, the piano player beats out his blues*)

BOY

I got the Weary Blues
And I can't be satisfied.
Got the Weary Blues
And can't be satisfied—
I ain't happy no mo'
And I wish that I had died.

(*But the player keeps on playing softly in the night*)

YOUNG MAN   You see, that's the blues. (*at right, a* HUSBAND *comes home from work and throws his hat and dinner pail on the table*) Sometimes there's the family blues.
HUSBAND   God-dog it!

I works all day
Wid a pick an' a shovel
Comes home at night,—
It ain't nothin' but a hovel.

I calls for ma woman
When I opens de door.
She's out in de street,—
Ain't no good no more.

I does her swell
An' I treats her fine,
But she don't gimme no lovin'
Cause she ain't de right kind.

I'm a hard workin' man—
But I sho pays double.
I tries to be good but
Gets nothin' but trouble.

(*He sits down at the table and begins to sing*)

Trouble, trouble, I has 'em all my days.
Trouble, trouble, has 'em all my days.
Seems like trouble's gonna drive me to my grave.

(*He snatches up his hat and leaves*) I'm gonna get drunk.

YOUNG MAN   And sometimes there's the loveless blues—when all you got left is a picture of the one you care for.

(*At left, the* BOY *who has been looking at his girl's picture begins to sing*)

BOY

All I want is your picture,
Must be in a frame.
All I want is your picture,
Must be in a frame—
So when you're gone
I can see you just the same!

(*He stops and begins to talk to the picture*)

Cause you don't love me, baby,
Is awful awful hard.
Gypsy done showed me
My bad luck card.

There ain't no good left
In this world for me.
Gypsy done tole me,—
Unlucky as can be.

(*Throws down picture*)

I don't know what
Po' weary me can do.
Gypsy says I'd kill ma self
If I was you.

(*The* BOY *gets up, puts on his coat, and begins to sing*)

> I'm goin' down to the railroad
> And lay my head on the track,
> Goin' down to the railroad,
> Lay my head on the track,
> If I see the train a comin',
> I'm gonna jerk it back.

(*He exits, left. At right,* WOMAN *enters, looks around anxiously and begins to cry*)

YOUNG MAN   And then there is them left-lonesome blues.

WIFE   Oh, Lawd! Looks like Jackson done left me. And I wasn't gone nowhere but to put my numbers in. Jackson, you done broke my heart this evenin'.

> I ain't got no heart no mo'
> Next time a man comes near me
> Gonna shut and lock my door,
> Cause they treats me mean—
> The ones I love.
> They always treats me mean.

(*She begins to sing*)

> Oh, you mens treats women
> Just like a old pair o' shoes.
> You mens treats women
> Just like a old pair o' shoes.
> You kicks 'em round and
> Does 'em like you choose.

(*She goes and stands beside the piano on the opposite side from the* HUSBAND)

YOUNG MAN   And then there is those morning after blues.

HUSBAND   It's the next day now (*begins to sing*)

> I was so sick last night I
> Didn't hardly know my mind.
> So sick last night I
> Didn't know my mind.
> I drunk some bad licker that
> Almost made me blind.

> Had a dream last night I
> Thought I was in hell.
> I drempt last night I
> Thought I was in hell.
> Woke up and looked around me—
> Babe, your mouth was open like a well.

> I said, Baby, baby,
> Please don't snore so loud.
> Baby! Please don't snore so loud.
> You jest a little bit o' woman but you
> Sound like a great big crowd.

WIFE (*replies in song*)

> Now, listen, Mr. Jackson,
> Don't say that to me.
> Listen, Mr. Jackson,
> Don't say that to me,
> Cause if you do,
> We is bound to disagree.

HUSBAND   Baby, you ain't gonna leave me, is you? You's all I got.

WIFE   Yes, I'm gonna leave you. You all I got, too, but I sure can get along without you. So, goodbye!

ALL (*singing*)

> Blues, blues, blues!
> Blues, blues . . . blues, blues, blues!
> Blue is what's the matter
> When you loses all you got to lose.

(*Exit* HUSBAND *right,* WIFE *left*)

YOUNG MAN   Colored folks made the blues! Now everybody sings 'em. We made 'em out of being poor and lonely. And homes busted up, and desperate and broke. (*rises*) But me, I haven't got any blues! I got a little job, not much. (*leans against wall*) Got a little time to stand on the corner at night and watch the girls go by! Boy, these Harlem girls'ye sure got it! Looky yonder! (*enter, right, the* GIRL, *beautiful in a red dress. As she passes, he recites*)

> Man alive! When Susanna Jones wears red
> Her face is like an ancient cameo
> Turned brown by the ages.

VOICE

> Come with a blast of trumpets,
> Jesus!

YOUNG MAN

> When Susanna Jones wears red
> A queen from some time-dead Egyptian night
> Walks once again.

VOICE

> Blow trumpets, Jesus!

YOUNG MAN

And the beauty of Susanna Jones in red
Burns in my heart a love-fire sharp like pain.

VOICE

Sweet silver trumpets,
 Jesus!

(*The* GIRL *exits left and the* YOUNG MAN *takes off his coat and starts polishing a brass spitoon. As he works he talks to himself*)

YOUNG MAN   Gee, if I just had a little money, I think I'd get married. But I kinder hate to start out with nothing. Suppose we had a kid? Well, I'd want my kid to have a decent break, that's what. At least a chance to go to high school. I didn't even have that. Had to start to work soon as I was big enough. My folks never did get ahead. There ain't many decent jobs a colored boy can get nohow. Here I am polishing spitoons in a hotel. But I've travelled around plenty, been all over America mighty near. And most towns, there just ain't nothin' much for a colored boy to do. Lots of factories won't even hire colored men. Lots of places I can't join unions. Anyhow this old spitoon looks right good. (*he holds up the shining spitoon proudly*) When a thing's clean, it always looks better, no matter what. But, gee! Have *I* always got to do the cleaning? Always the dirty work? Me! Always? (*he recites as he polishes*)

Clean the spitoons, boy.
  Detroit,
  Chicago,
  Atlantic City,
  Palm Beach.
Clean the spitoons.
The steam in hotel kitchens,
And the smoke in hotel lobbies,
And the slime in hotel spitoons:
Part of my life.
  Hey, boy!
  A nickel,
  A dime,
  A dollar,
Two dollars a day.
  Hey, boy!
  A nickel,
  A dime,
  A dollar,

Two dollars
Buy smokes, shoes,
A ticket to the movies.
House rent to pay,
Gin on Saturday,
Church on Sunday.
  My God!
Movies and church
and women and Sunday
all mixed up with dimes and
dollars and clean spitoons
and house rent to pay.
  Hey, boy!
A bright bowl of brass is beautiful to the Lord.
Bright polished brass like the cymbals
Of King David's dancers,
Like the wine cups of Solomon.
  Hey, boy!
A clean spitoon on the altar of the Lord.
A clean bright spitoon all newly polished,—
At least I can offer that.

(*The* BOSS *enters, left, crosses right*)

OVERSEER   Com'mere, Boy!
YOUNG MAN   Yes, sir.
OVERSEER   Listen, George.
YOUNG MAN   Wilbur's my name.
OVERSEER   Well, whatever your name is, listen. I'm the boss and I got to cut down expenses. You know, that bank crash—folks ain't spending money. I'm gonna let the bellboys do the house man's work from now on. You can get your check and go.
YOUNG MAN (*stunned*)   Yes, sir, Mister Mallory, but . . .

(*The* OVERSEER *walks to the other side, and seats himself for a shine. He calls to the* OLD MAN *who enters, right*)

OVERSEER   Hey, George!
OLD MAN   Yes, sir! Yes, sir!
OVERSEER   Gimme a shine!

(*As he shines his shoes,* WOMAN *enters left and begins to dust*)

OLD MAN   Yes, sir! Yes, sir!

I must say yes, sir.
To *you* all the time.
Yes, sir! Yes, sir!
All my days
Climbing up a great big mountain
Of yes, sirs.

Rich old white man
Owns the world.

Gimme your shoes
To shine.
Yes, sir, boss,
Yes, sir!

YOUNG MAN (*pointing at the* OLD MAN)   That
was my grandfather. (*on the left, the* WOMAN *in
a maid's apron is working*) And my mother, out
working for the white folks. When I was a kid,
never nobody home to take care of me. I don't
want my kids to grow up that away. Look at
my mother.

WOMAN

All day, subdued, polite—
Thoughtful to the faces that are white.

OLD MAN

Oh, tribal dance!
Oh, drums!
Oh, veldt at night!

YOUNG MAN

Forgotten watch-fires on a hill somewhere!

OLD MAN

Oh, songs that do not care!

WOMAN

At six o'clock, or seven, or eight, you're through
You've worked all day,
Then Harlem waits for you.
The el, the sub, a taxi through the park.

YOUNG MAN

Oh, drums of life in Harlem after dark.

WOMAN

Oh, dreams! Oh, songs!

OLD MAN

A little rest at night.

WOMAN

Oh, sweet relief from faces that are white!

(*Takes off her apron, puts on her coat and hat, and
goes home, crossing right, to her son, the* YOUNG
MAN)

OVERSEER   Say, George! Be careful of my
corns!
OLD MAN   Yes, sir, Mr. Mallory, yes, sir!
OVERSEER   And polish those shoes good
now! I want to see my face in 'em when you
get through. (*the* OLD MAN *bends over his task*)
WOMAN   Good evening, son!
YOUNG MAN   Mom, I lost my job!
WOMAN   You lost your job?
YOUNG MAN   Yes! they laid me off tonight.
WOMAN   Well, honey, you'll find another
one. Maybe.
YOUNG MAN   I don't know, Mom. Things is
so tight, I done lost heart! Look how long I
been a man now, and ain't never had a job
that amounted to nothing. I've been all over,
and everywhere just the same. The dirty work
for colored folks, the cheap work, underpaid
work! I'm tired, Mom. Soon as I come here to
be with you a while and we get this little flat,
first thing I do is lose my job. And the landlord's just sent us a notice about raising the
rent, too. Mom, I'm about ready to give up. I
swear I am!
WOMAN   Son, you ain't gonna give up no
such a thing. Listen! You gonna keep right on
just like I been keeping on. Did you ever stop
to think about it, honey, about your mother,
and all the rest of us colored women—what
we been up against all through history, son. Sit
down and lemme tell you, for (*piano music*)

I'm standing here today
Like a living story of that long dark way
That I had to climb, that I had to know
In order that our race might live and grow.
Look at my face, boy, dark as the night,
Yet shining like the sun with hope and light.
I'm the child they stole from the sand
Three hundred years ago in Africa's land.
I'm the dark girl who crossed the wide sea
Carrying in my body the seed of the Free.
I'm the woman who worked in the field,
Bringing the cotton and corn to yield.
I'm the one who labored as a slave,
Beaten and mistreated for the work that I gave—
Children sold away from me, husband sold, too.
No safety, no love, no respect was I due.
Three hundred years in the deepest South,
But love put a song and a prayer in my mouth.
Love put a dream like steel in my soul.
Now through my children, we're reaching the goal.

I couldn't read then. I couldn't write.
I had nothing back there in the night.
Sometimes the valley was filled with tears,
But I kept trudging on through the lonely years.
Sometimes the road was hot with sun.
But I had to keep on till my work was done.
I *had* to keep on! No stopping for me—
I was the seed of the coming Free.
I nourished our dream that nothing could
    smother
Deep in my breast—the Negro Mother.
I had only hope then, but now through you,
Dark child of today, my dreams must come true.
All you dark children in the world out there,
Remember my sweat, my pain, my despair.
Remember my years heavy with sorrow—
And make of those years a torch for tomorrow,
Make of my past a road to the light,
Out of the darkness, the ignorance, the night.
Lift high my banner out of the dust.
Stand like free men supporting my trust.
Believe in the right, let none push you back.
Remember the whip and the slaver's track.
Remember how the strong in struggle and strife
Still bar you the way, and deny you life—
But march ever forward, breaking down bars.
Look ever upward at the sun and the stars.
Oh, my dark children, may my dreams and my
    prayers
Impel you forever up the great stairs—
For I will be with you till no white brother
Dares keep down the children of the Negro
    Mother.

OVERSEER (*who is now a Landlord, coming to knock at their door, right*)   Madam, did you get my notice about raising your rent, ten dollars a month more?
WOMAN   Yes, sir, I got the notice, but I am tired of that. I ain't gonna pay no more. We're paying enough.
OVERSEER   You'll pay it or move, and no smart talk about it, neither.
YOUNG MAN (*rising*)   Say, listen here! Who're you to speak to my mother like that?
OVERSEER   I'm the landlord. If you don't like it, get out of my place.
YOUNG MAN   Lemme see you get instead!
OVERSEER   What? This is my house!
YOUNG MAN   Yes, but you don't live in it! We live here! (*he towers above the Landlord*) This is Harlem.

(*The* OVERSEER *backs away and puts on a waiter's apron.* WOMAN *begins to peel potatoes,* YOUNG MAN *to study. At the left a* BOY *holding a menu calls*)

BOY   Say, waiter! Where is that waiter? . . . Hey, waiter! Give me an order of spaghetti and a bottle of beer, please.
OVERSEER   Sorry! We don't serve colored here.
BOY   What? You mean on 125th Street, and don't serve colored?
OVERSEER   Sure, this is a white place.
BOY (*rising*)   And you don't serve colored people?
OVERSEER   You heard me, big boy.
BOY   I might of heard you, but this is Harlem speaking now. Get me that spaghetti. I'm tired of this stuff! Talking about you don't serve colored people. Ain't I an American?

(OVERSEER *backs away.* OLD WOMAN *enters left as a picket carrying a sign that reads*

DON'T BUY HERE!
THIS STORE DOES NOT
EMPLOY NEGRO CLERKS

Slowly she walks back and forth in front of a store bearing the sign: MEAT MARKET. *The* OVERSEER *rushes out in the white apron of a Butcher*)

OVERSEER   What you doing in front of my store? What I done to you? What for you walking up and down with that sign, destructing my business? Long as you trade with me, what is this?
OLD WOMAN   You know what it is, Mr. Schultz! You know how long I been trading with you, don't you?
OVERSEER   More'n ten years, Mrs. Brown.
OLD WOMAN   And all that time, I ain't never seen a colored clerk in this store, not one. My boy growed up and went through high school, and to college, and got more education than you ever had, but when one of your clerks died, and my boy come here to ask you for a job, you said: "No, you might give him a little janitor's job, but you got to have a *white* clerk." (*loudly*) That's why I'm picketing out here, Mr. Schultz. Harlem is tired! No work! No money! I tell you, Harlem's tired!

(OLD WOMAN *brandishes her sign and the* BUTCHER *flees, to take off his apron and put on a coat and a pair of pince-nez glasses with a flowing black ribbon. He is the editor of a daily paper and carries a handful of proofs. The* YOUNG MAN *enters*)

YOUNG MAN   You're the editor of the *Daily Scribe?*

OVERSEER   I am.

YOUNG MAN   I wrote a letter to your paper more'n two weeks ago about the hard times we colored folks've been having, and you didn't print it. I wish you'd tell me how come?

OVERSEER   Ah yes! I remember that letter. I'll tell you, boy, why we didn't print it. That letter would stir up trouble. I know times are hard, but you colored people have always been good citizens, peaceful and nice. Why get excited now? Just wait. Times'll be better—the Republicans will be in again soon. Believe in God, boy, in the good old stars and stripes, and be loyal to your country.

YOUNG MAN

But, Mr. Editor,
I've been loyal to my country
A long time, don't you see?
Now how about my country
Being loyal to me?

I fought in 1812 and 1863,
San Juan Hill in Cuba,
And for Democracy—
And fighting's not the only thing
I've done for liberty:
I've worked and worked a plenty,
Slave and free.

So when I pledge allegiance
To our flag so fair,
I keep looking at the stars and stripes
A-waving there,
And I'm wishing every star
Would *really* be a star for me,
And not just half a star
Like Jim Crow Tennessee—
And no false convict's stripes such as
Scottsboro's put on me.

I want that red and white and blue,
Mr. Editor,
To mean the same thing to me

As it does to you—
For I've been just as loyal
To my country as you have,
Don't you see?

Now, how about my country
Being loyal to me?

OVERSEER   Why—er—uh—you're a radical!

(*Enter a* WHITE WORKER)

WHITE WORKER   I don't think so!

OVERSEER   Who're you?

WHITE WORKER   A white worker. You don't have to be colored to know what hard times are. Or to want a square deal. I can tell you that!

OVERSEER   Well, what do you want?

WHITE WORKER   A world where there won't be no hard times. And no color line—labor with a white skin'll never be free as long as labor with a black skin's enslaved.

OVERSEER   By God, you're a radical, too!

(WHITE WORKER *and* YOUNG MAN *shake hands*)

YOUNG MAN   Friend, you understand.

WHITE WORKER   I understand!

OVERSEER   Radicals! Radicals! Lock 'em up! Lock 'em up! Radicals! Lock 'em up! Radicals! Radicals! (*exits, yelling loudly*)

YOUNG MAN   Quiet, please—'cause Harlem is tired!

WHITE WORKER (*as he leaves with* YOUNG MAN)   We're all tired!

(WIFE *enters left, broom in hand*)

WIFE   Yes, we're tired! Tired as we can be! (WIFE *sweeps.* OVERSEER *removes glasses, puts on dark hat, carries a brief case, and is now an insurance man: goes to* WIFE *and knocks*) Yes?

OVERSEER (*cockily*)   Insurance man! Got your book ready?

WIFE   You want me to pay you?

OVERSEER   Of course. It's due, isn't it?

WIFE   Um-hum! You from the Cosmopolitan Company, ain't you?

OVERSEER   I am.

WIFE   And you don't hire no colored folks in your office, do you?

OVERSEER   Not so far as I know. Why?

WIFE   You won't give colored people certain kinds of policies you carries, neither, will you?

OVERSEER   Well, you see, in some cases your people are bad risks.

WIFE   But my money's *good* money, ain't it?

OVERSEER   Of course it is.

WIFE   And you want my money, don't you?

OVERSEER   Why, yes. Of course, I do.

WIFE   Well, you ain't gonna get it! (*fiercely*) A company that won't hire none of my people, what won't half insure us, and then sends a man to Harlem to collect from me that keeps his hat on in the house! (OVERSEER, *frightened, snatches off his hat*) Well, you ain't gonna get nary a penny of mine! Get out of here. Go on back downtown to your Jim Crow office. Tell 'em Harlem is tired. (*she shows him out*) I'm gonna join a colored insurance company myself.

(*The* OVERSEER *flees. Panting, he sits down in a chair right and is now a laundry boss. He begins to pay out money, while several girls pass before him*)

MULATTO GIRL   Chile, you better wrap up good. It's kinder chilly out there.

LAUNDRY WORKER   Catch your death o' pneumonia, working all day in this steaming oven.

GIRL   You told that right.

MULATTO GIRL   I sure am glad it's pay day. Let's get in line here and get our money.

OVERSEER   Here, Dorothy Mae! Here's your wages. Now don't get drunk tonight! . . . Here, Miss Lizzie, something for your preacher tomorrow. Now, behave yourself in church! Here! (*as a good looking* LAUNDRY WORKER *approaches him for her wages*) Say, Toots, uh, listen . . .

LAUNDRY WORKER   Toots who?

OVERSEER   Why, er . . .

LAUNDRY WORKER   Is this six dollars all you're giving me for a whole week's work in your laundry?

OVERSEER   That's all you earned, girlie.

LAUNDRY WORKER   Sixty hours in this steaming hole, and that's all I've earned? You must be crazy. I've ironed six hundred shirts this week, at least.

OVERSEER   Well, six dollars is your salary.

LAUNDRY WORKER   Then you take that salary and stick it on back in your drawer, from now on, 'cause I am tired of working for nothing. Harlem is tired. You're living in a big house up in White Plains, and me slaving all day for nothing in your laundry. You making all your money off of colored folks, and taking every dollar of it out of Harlem to spend. I'm tired.

OVERSEER   (*jumping up*) You must belong to the union. You move on before I call the police. You're an agitator!

LAUNDRY WORKER   What police? Some of these days *you're* going to have to move on, because Harlem is tired. Fact is, I think you ought to move now.

WIFE   Yes, you ought to move!

BOY   Get going!

(OVERSEER *clutches his money and rushes away. But he is surrounded by people, threatening him and crying in anger. The Harlem riots of March 19, 1935 begin*)

WOMAN   Gouging me for rent!

BOY   You won't serve colored people!

YOUNG MAN   Won't gimme a job!

LAUNDRY WORKER   Working us like slaves!

OLD MAN   Living on Harlem!

WOMAN   Getting rich off of black people.

YOUNG MAN   Jim Crow landlord!

WOMAN   Won't rent us a house downtown.

OLD MAN   Starving my children!

LAUNDRY WORKER   Get out of Harlem!

WIFE   Yes, get out of Harlem!

OVERSEER   (*trying to escape*) Help! Help me! Help! What have I done? Help me! (*blows police whistle*) Help! Help! Help! Help!

NEWSBOYS   (*from all directions, enter* NEWSBOYS *shouting*) Riot in Harlem! Negroes running riot! Riot! Read all about it! Riot! Riot! Riot! MARCH 19th RIOT IN HARLEM! RIOT IN HARLEM. Read all about it. HARLEM IS TIRED! Harlem's tired!

WOMAN   (*as the siren dies down. Quietly*) Harlem is tired.

BOY   Yes, Harlem is tired.

LAUNDRY WORKER   Harlem is tired!

YOUNG MAN   You understand, folks? Harlem's tired.

MEMBER OF AUDIENCE   (*rising*) But say?

YOUNG MAN   Yes?

MEMBER OF AUDIENCE   Riots won't solve anything, will they, brother?

YOUNG MAN   No, riots won't solve anything.

MEMBER OF AUDIENCE   Then what must we do?

YOUNG MAN   Organize.

MEMBER OF AUDIENCE   With who?

YOUNG MAN   With the others who suffer like me and you.

LAUNDRY WORKER   Organize with the laundry workers, then.

WOMAN   Organize with the tenants' leagues.

BOY   Organize with the students' unions.

YOUNG MAN   Colored and white unions to lift us all up together.

MEMBER OF AUDIENCE   You mean organize with white folks, too?

YOUNG MAN   That's what I mean! We're all in the same boat! This is America, isn't it? It's not all colored. Not all white. It's both.

MEMBER OF AUDIENCE   You mean organize with that white waiter who won't serve you? Organize with him?

YOUNG MAN   Yes, I mean with that waiter, too. His problem's the same as ours—if he only knew it.

MEMBER OF AUDIENCE   Well, they ought to hurry up and find out then! Some of 'em won't even let us in their unions. Yet we're all workers! Let the white workers learn to stop discriminating against us, if they want us with 'em.

YOUNG MAN   Right! They've got to learn. And we must teach them. But when they do learn, and black and white really get together, what power in the world can stop us from getting what we want?

BOY   Nothing!

WOMAN   That's right!

WIFE   You tell 'em!

YOUNG MAN   Right! They've got to learn— but there are some who know already, and they've organized unions that are strong and growing.

MEMBER OF AUDIENCE   Who are they?

YOUNG MAN   The Auto Workers of Detroit. (*enter a Negro and a white,* AUTO WORKERS) The Sharecroppers of the South. (*enter a white and black,* SHARECROPPERS) The Miners of Birmingham. (*enter two* MINERS, *one white and one colored*) The Stevedores of the West Coast. (*enter a black* STEVEDORE *and a white* STEVEDORE) And others, too. I know—not yet enough, but they are learning. And when we

do learn, and black and white really get together, what power in the world can stop us from getting what we want?

BOY   Nothing!

WOMAN   That's right!

WIFE   You tell 'em.

YOUNG MAN   Tomorrow belongs to the workers, and I'm a worker!

WOMAN   I am, too!

OLD MAN   And me!

LAUNDRY WORKER   Me, too!

MEMBER OF AUDIENCE   And me! I get your point. (*sits down*)

YOUNG MAN   Good! We're Negro workers! Listen! This is what we're going to say to all other workers, just this: I, a Negro, offer you my hand. I offer you my strength and power. Together, we can make America a land where all of us are free from poverty and oppression and where no man or woman need ever be hungry, cold, or kept down again. White worker, here is my hand. Today we're man to man.

MAN   White worker, here's my hand.

BOY   Here's my hand.

LAUNDRY WORKER (*speaking*)

Who wants to come and join hands with me?
Who wants to make one great unity?
Who wants to say no more black or white?
Then let's get together, folks,
And fight, fight, fight!

ENTIRE CAST (*singing*)

Who wants to come and join hands with me?
Who wants to make one great unity?
Who wants to say no more black or white?
Then let's get together folks,
And fight, fight, fight!

Who wants to make America a land
Where opportunity is free to every man?
Who wants to test the power of the worker's
     might?
Then let's get together, folks,
And fight, fight, fight!

Who wants to make Harlem great and fine?
Make New York City a guiding light to shine?
Who wants to lead the workers toward the light?
Then let's get together, folks,
And fight, fight, fight!

(*As they sing the audience joins with them, and various members of the audience, workers, doctors, nurses, professional men, teachers, white and black, come forward to link hands with the characters in the play until the players and the audience are one*)

Oh, who wants to come and join hands with me?
Who wants to make one great unity?
Who wants to say, no more black or white?
Then let's get together, folks,
And fight, fight, fight!

BIG WHITE FOG
1938

Theodore Ward (1902–1983)

Play selection was one of the major concerns of the Federal Theatre Project. They were under the constant scrutiny of Congress, which suspected that participants were either communists or communist sympathizers, and that the plays promoted socialist ideology. Some top level administrators encouraged Black playwrights to produce plays that explored urban, social, and racial problems, as well as contemporary issues. Hallie Flanagan, the Project director, believed that the Negro units could make the public aware of injustice by dramatizing them. Other administrators took a more cautious stance, not wanting to offend Congress lest funding for the Project be cut.

In Chicago *Big White Fog* opened at the Great Northern Theatre on April 7, 1938, running for thirty-seven performances before a mixed audience.

It premiered in New York on October 22, 1940, at the Lincoln Theatre, on 135th Street and Lenox Avenue, under the auspices of the newly formed Negro Playwrights Company. It ran sixty-four performances. The cast included Canada Lee, Hilda Offley, Frank Silvera, and Lionel Monagas (who had played the lead in Garland Anderson's *Appearances* in 1925). Perry Watkins was set designer, and Powell Lindsay directed.

The major newspaper reviewers predictably praised the performers and the seriousness of the Negro Playwrights Company, but they condemned the play. It remained for Black critic Ralph Ellison writing in 1940, to see the value of the play:

> In its three-act attempt to probe the most vital problems of Negro experience, *Big White Fog* is like no other Negro play. The author takes a movement which has been passed off as a ludicrous effort by Negroes to ape British royalty and reveals in it that dignity of human groping which is characteristic of all oppressed peoples.[3]

The movement in question is Marcus Garvey's Universal Negro Improvement Asso-

---

3. Ralph Ellison, "Big White Fog," *New Masses*, Vol. 37 (November 12, 1940), p. 22.

ciation. The play begins in 1922, at the height of its appeal, and relies on two specific incidents from the Garvey saga: the failure of the Black Star Steamship Line and Garvey's imprisonment.

In the five years from 1916 (when Marcus Garvey arrived in America from Jamaica) to 1921, Garvey built the UNIA into the largest Black organization America had ever seen—2 million dues-paying members and 6 million worldwide followers. A combination of reasons contributed to his success. First was the appeal of his four-point program, which called for Black solidarity and autonomy and for establishing Africa as a global economic power.

Garvey's own messianic personality and his genius for public relations also helped. As provisional president of Africa, Mr. Garvey created the Court of Ethiopia, in which only "100 per cent Negroid" people could hold office. Classes were held for children in Negro history, etiquette, military tactics, and race pride. Brown and Black dolls were manufactured. Christ was declared the "Black Man of Sorrows," and the Virgin Mary a Black woman.

Theodore Ward uses Garvey's work as a vehicle to represent the success and the failure of Black nationalism. Against nationalism he sets Dan, the brother-in-law, a Black capitalist. Ward demonstrates that both philosophies fail the Negro in a crisis and recommends a third approach: socialism/communism as the correct path.

Ward joined the Federal Theatre Project in Chicago where he wrote plays and acted. He was appearing in their production of *The Swing Mikado* in New York when the FTP ended. Ward remained in New York and in 1940 became one of the founders of the Negro Playwrights Company. The Theatre Guild production of his play *Our Lan'* opened at the Royale Theatre in September 1947 under the direction of Eddie Dowling and ran for five weeks.

During the 1950s, Ward returned to Chicago, working at the South Side Center of the Performing Arts and continued to write and conduct writing seminars.

It is a tribute to Ward that the Guthrie Theater included *Big White Fog* in its 1995–1996 repertory season.

Big White Fog

CHARACTERS

VICTOR MASON, *a Garveyite leader*
ELLA, *his wife*
LESTER ⎱
WANDA ⎰
CAROLINE ⎰ *their children*
PHILLIP ⎰
DANIEL ROGERS, *their brother-in-law*
JUANITA, *Ella's sister, his wife*
MARTHA BROOKS, *mother of Ella and Juanita*

PERCY MASON, *brother of Victor*
CLAUDINE, *friend of Wanda's*
NATHAN PISZER, *a Jewish student*
MARX, *a Jewish used-furniture man*
COUNT STRAWDER ⎱
COUNT COTTON ⎰ *Garveyites*
BROTHER HARPER ⎰
BLACK CROSS NURSES
BAILIFFS, POLICEMEN, WHITE AND NEGRO WORKERS, AMBULANCE ATTENDANTS

ACT ONE

Scene One

(*Living-room of the* MASONS, *in Dearborn Street, Chicago.*

TIME: *an afternoon in August, 1922.*

It is a large, congenial room, bearing the tell-marks of use polished by care, and indicating that people of means once lived there.

On the left, a large window with stained glass above and a window seat below. Beyond it, in the corner, is a hall-tree, and next to the latter, the front door with a transom of stained glass of the same pattern.

Against the rear wall, a flight of stairs leading to the upper floor. Downstage right, a door leads into the kitchen and dining room.

There is a couch in the center with an over-stuffed chair to the left of it, and behind it is an oblong table, against the stairway. A typewriter is on the table with a small chair at the left end of it.

A Victrola is against the right wall. Downstage left is another easy-chair, and beyond it, near the window, is a rocking chair, commanding a view of Fifty-first Street as it intersects Dearborn Street.

A Postman's whistle sounds, and ELLA *appears from the rear, going to the door where she retrieves a letter from the mail-box outside. As she reenters, she stands fingering the letter and immersed in thought—a buxom mulatto, aged about 38, and wearing a cool housedress which accentuates her general air of renunciation*)

JUANITA (*entering, unceremoniously behind her*) Hello, Ella.

ELLA (*startled*) Oh! Juanita—You liked to scared me to death—What storm blew you to Dearborn Street?

JUANITA (*a good looking mulatto, slender and smartly dressed—she has a decided verve of manner and vigor of speech*) Oh, I just thought I'd drop by to see how you all were—(*she turns to the mirror of the hall-tree in the corner behind her*) What's that you got there, a notice from your landlord?

ELLA (*tossing letter on table beneath stairway*) No. It's for Les. Must be the answer about his scholarship.

JUANITA (*coming down*) No! (*happily*) You know. I'd almost forgotten about him winning that scholarship!

ELLA (*going into rear*) Well, you wouldn've if you lived around here.

JUANITA (*sitting on arm of couch and looking off right*) I suppose not—But I hope it's good news.

ELLA (*returning with pan of green peas, which she takes to couch and begins to shell*) They've kept him in suspense long enough—Did you bring Mama's pattern?

JUANITA Lord no! I knew there was something I was forgetting—Where is she?

ELLA Gone to the park. She took the children out for a breath of air.

JUANITA If you had any sense you'd make Vic take a flat near the park.

ELLA You know we can't afford the rent, Juanita.

JUANITA You could if you made Vic go into partnership with Dan.

ELLA (*wearily*) It's no use starting that talk again. Vic's made up his mind he's going to Africa, and there's nothing short of the voice of God likely to change him.

JUANITA (*sarcastically*) Ha! Ten years from today he'll still be in Chicago, carrying his hod.

ELLA They've got over four million paid-up members!

JUANITA (*searching for ash-tray*) That's a lot of bunk! Nothing but bunk to catch more suckers like Vic.

ELLA Vic's in the know, and he wouldn't lie to me. They've just made him a captain in the African Legionnaires.

JUANITA (*with an outburst of laughter*) Captain in the African Legionaires—That's a good one!

ELLA Stop your silly laughing. Vic's nobody's fool.

JUANITA No? He's being taken for a ride just like the rest.

ELLA That's all you know about it.

JUANITA (*pointedly*) You don't see any of our really big people falling for Marcus Garvey's jive, do you?

ELLA (*loyally*) They're too jealous of his power! They don't like it because the masses are with him.

JUANITA You mean they've got too much sense to let a monkey-chasing mountebank like him come over here and jive them out of their cold cash!

ELLA   You make me sick—You can't see anything but money.

JUANITA   No. You're quite right, my dear. But I don't make any pretense about it.

ELLA   Is that an insinuation?

JUANITA   Ella, you know damn well, if Vic was in the money, neither of you would give a damn about Africa.

ELLA   I haven't lived with Vic nineteen years for nothing. He's interested in the race.

JUANITA   Yeah. Then he ought to be trying to do something for it here—like going in with Dan and opening that Kitchenette—our people are crying for decent places to live, and they'll pay good money for the privilege.

ELLA   Vic's planning to buy shares in the Black Star Line—

JUANITA   (*laughing*)   The Black Star Line—Why that's the biggest joke Marcus Garvey ever thought of—Where're they going to get men to run it?

ELLA   From the West Indies—

JUANITA   (*groaning*)   Oh, my God . . . (*the door opens, and* CAROLINE, *seeing her aunt, dashes down*)

CAROLINE   Aunt Juanita! I didn't know you was here!

JUANITA   *Was?*

(PHILIP *enters—He is a little black boy of 10*)

CAROLINE   Were—(*she is a child of 12, with long braids and copper-colored skin*)

JUANITA   (*to* PHILLIP)   Why haven't you been to see Aunt Juanita lately?

PHILLIP   (*bouncing his ball*)   We was over there last Wednesday, but you wasn't home—

JUANITA   Aunt Juanita is a pretty busy woman, Honey—You should call me up and let me know when you're coming—(*Seeing her mother, as Phillip's ball gets away from him and he dashes behind couch to retrieve it*) Hello, Mama—

BROOKS   (*coming down, brusquely*)   Move Caroline! Lemme get off these feet! (*a somewhat wizened mulatto, aged about 60, she is much spryer than she pretends*)

JUANITA   (*as her mother takes chair center*) How're you feeling?

BROOKS   Them chillun jes 'bout wore me out, and what with the walk back from the park, I'm jes 'bout dead, I 'spect.

PHILLIP   (*joining his mother on couch*) Grandma's been playing ball.

ELLA   Playing ball?

PHILLIP   Yes'm.—We had a lot of fun, didn't we, Grandma?

JUANITA   Are you trying to kill yourself, Mama?

BROOKS   Now you all jes let me 'lone—(*sharply*). And you get out of here, Phillip, with your big mouth.

ELLA   You'll be laid up for a week—Why didn't you take the street car back, like I told you?

BROOKS   (*to* JUANITA, *ignoring other*)   Did you bring me mah pattern back?

JUANITA   I forgot it, Mama. But I'll get Les to bring it tomorrow.

BROOKS   Jes like I figgered. You so busy runnin' round with your bobbed-hair, and playin' cards, you can't remember nothin'. I told you I needed that pattern so I could make Wanda's waist 'fore school opens!

JUANITA   Oh, calm yourself, Mama. You'll get it.

CAROLINE   Mama, may I have a slice of bread and butter?

PHILLIP   (*springing up*)   Me, too, Mama?

ELLA   It's pretty near time for your dinner. But I reckon so—(*as they run out rear*) And don't take but one apiece neither!

JUANITA   (*playfully*)   What's this, Mama, I hear about you planning to go to Africa?

BROOKS   (*disgustedly*)   Don't you mention no Africa to me, I'm sick o' hearin' it!

ELLA   Yes, for God's sake, Juanita; don't get her started.

JUANITA   Didn't you just tell me, Vic's made up his mind to go?

BROOKS   (*vigorously*))   And I reckon you think 'cause I'm poor and can't help myself I got to go, hanh? Well, don't fool yourself. I ain't no Affikan; I'm a Dupree! I was born in this country and I'm goin' die in it, Vic or no Vic!

ELLA   (*exasperatedly*)   Mama, nobody's trying to make you go anywhere!

BROOKS   No, and they better not be. I done let that black crank root me up once with his fool talk 'bout we goin' find freedom up here in the North. But he ain't goin' 'suade me again. I'se too old for another transplantin'.

ELLA   I guess you'd both rather be in Mississippi picking cotton—?

JUANITA   Chicago's one thing but Africa's another.

BROOKS   Yes, Lawd!

JUANITA   Vic'd forget that stuff too, Mama—If it wasn't for her encouraging him, like a fool!

BROOKS (*sighing*)   She ain't got mah blood in her veins—No Dupree would-er thought 'bout marryin' sich a *black* crank in the first place.

ELLA (*angrily*)   You and your Dupree blood! You make me sick.—Furthermore, I've warned you. I'm sick of your flaunting Vic's color in my face—And especially when Phillip may hear you! And I'm not going to tell you again—

JUANITA (*seeing* LES *through window*)   Drop it, Ella—Here comes Les.

ELLA   Never mind. I mean what I say. If Vic's good enough to live on, you'll respect him—

LES (*entering, he sees his aunt as he tosses his baseball glove on table*)   Hello, Aunt Juanita! (*he is light brown, about 20, in a white shirt and corduroy slacks*)

JUANITA   Hi, Les!

ELLA (*excitedly*)   Your letter's here!

LES   My letter—Where? (*he dives for table*)

BROOKS   What letter?

JUANITA   From his scholarship.

LES (*nervously, fingering letter*)   This is it! This is it, all right—Lawd, I wonder if the stuff is here . . .

JUANITA   You'll never know, silly, unless you read it.

BROOKS   No, he won't.

LES   Jesus—You don't suppose—

ELLA   Open it, Les.

LES   All right. I'm going to—(*he opens letter*)

JUANITA   What does it say?

ELLA   Yes. Read it aloud so we all can hear—

LES (*dancing a gig*)   Hot dog! Hot ziggedy damn! (*hugging his aunt*)   Oh, boy, oh boy!

ELLA   If you don't stop your foolishness and read that letter, Lester Mason, I'll pick up something and brain you!

LES   Wait, Mama. Just listen to this: (*reading excitedly*) "Jason Scholarship Fund . . . Copeland Technical Institute—"

ELLA (*impatiently*)   Oh, skip all that!

LES (*going on*)   "My dear Mr. Mason . . . I have just returned from abroad to find your application for appointment as a Jason Scholar of Chemistry in the Copeland Technical Institute, and likewise the letter of Principal Horace Judson, confirming your record and recommending you for the award—"

JUANITA   Does that mean you get it?

LES   He says it's up to the Board—But listen: (*reading*) "This, however, is of little consequence, since we shall be meeting again in a day or so, when considering the high quality of your performance in chemistry, I am convinced favorable action will be taken; so that you can be with us this Fall . . . Yours truly, Rothmore C. Galen, Chairman, The Jason Scholarship Fund."

JUANITA   Well, that is something!

ELLA   I'm so glad, Les. (*her eyes brim and she wipes away a tear of joy*)

BROOKS   Don't seem to say a thing to me.

JUANITA   It means he's certain to go to college, Mama.

BROOKS   Seems like a mighty poor way of saying it.

LES (*hugging her*)   That's just the way big men write, Grandma. (*she shakes him off*)

JUANITA   And you say it's for four years, Les?

LES   If my marks are good.

ELLA   Your father will be tickled to death.

JUANITA   Who wouldn't be. (*pointedly*) It should make him see this country in a better light.

LES   Oh, Papa's all right. I won't be the first Negro to receive a scholarship—(*catching sight of* WANDA—*his very pretty mulatto sister—he joins her*) What d'you think, Wanda? I just got an answer from my application!

WANDA   You mean about your scholarship?

LES   Yah. Looks like I'm Copeland bound.

ELLA (*as* WANDA *goes to table to examine mail, her attitude belying the happiness of the others as well as the fact she's only seventeen*)   Well, can't you say anything?

WANDA (*turning, embarrassed*)   I was just thinking, Mama—(*quickly*) But I'm glad you got it, Les. I knew you would—When do you leave?

LES (*bringing her to chair*)   I don't know yet.

Everything's not really settled. Here——(*gives her letter*) Read it for yourself.

JUANITA (*as* WANDA *reads*) If it's for four years, Les——(*impishly*) your father'll have to leave you here, won't he?

LES (*puzzled*) What d' you mean, Aunt?

JUANITA (*laughing*) He's going to Africa, isn't he?

ELLA Oh, stop teasing him, Juanita——And, Les, it's time for you to be getting out on your route.

LES Lord, Mama. I had completely forgotten my papers! (*going*) See you all later. (*suddenly turning back to* WANDA) Give me that——(*to all*) And don't you all say anything to Papa, will you? I want to surprise him. (*exit running*)

ELLA All right. We won't.

BROOKS He sure is tickled pink.

JUANITA With a fine break like that, he'll be a big man someday.

BROOKS (*sourly*) Yeah. If he don't turn out like his Pa.

ELLA (*to* WANDA) Perhaps, you'll win one this year.

JUANITA There's no reason why she shouldn't with the brain she's got.

WANDA (*drily*) Thanks, Aunt. But I'm not interested in any scholarship.

ELLA What do you mean?

WANDA (*rising and going*) Oh, nothing.

ELLA (*arresting her*) Don't tell me. You did mean something?

JUANITA Yes, she did. (*to* WANDA) Surely, you aren't jealous of your own brother?

WANDA (*sarcastically*) Jealous! Don't kid me, Aunt Juanita. Les is perfectly welcome to the scholarship.

ELLA You don't act like it.

JUANITA She certainly doesn't. I've been watching her ever since she came in.

WANDA What am I supposed to do, shed tears over it?

JUANITA You ought to be proud to see him get such a break.

WANDA It's a fine break all right——Marvelous——Splendid! (*bitterly*) When he gets out of school, maybe they'll give him a job on the dining-car figuring out how many calories there are in the average bowl of soup!

ELLA Wanda!

JUANITA Well, did you ever!

WANDA You needn't pretend to be so astonished, either of you——

JUANITA (*sharply*) Why you're crazy. The field of chemistry is wide open to our people—— Look at Doctor Carver!

WANDA Yeah, Doctor Carver! One out of a million! But what about Papa? Tuskeegee graduate, carrying a hod! And Uncle Dan, Butler's Black Pride, wearing a Kappa Key on a pullman car! I've heard him say himself, they must've given it to him to open the berths with!

ELLA (*feebly*) Your father was educated to be a farmer.

WANDA That's it. He's a farmer, but where's his farm?

JUANITA (*hesitantly*) But. But your Uncle Dan's working for a point.

WANDA They're both just kidding themselves. (*going*) But I'm not going to (*turning to* ELLA) and you might as well know it right now, Mama. I'm not going back to school!

ELLA (*indignantly*) Is that so? Since when did you get big enough to tell me to my face what you're not going to do?

BROOKS She needs slapping down!

WANDA I'm no longer a child, Grandma!

BROOKS You hear that, Ella! (*outraged*) Oh, if you was only mine. I'd take you down a button hole lower.

WANDA But I happen not to be yours, Grandma!

BROOKS Ella, are you goin' stand there and let her sassy me like this?

ELLA (*jerking* WANDA *around*) Stop your impudence and answer me!

WANDA (*belligerently*) Well, you had to know sooner or later. I'm sick of school, and there's no use in your trying to send me back.

ELLA (*nonplussed*) Well!

JUANITA But, Wanda. If you quit school, you won't even be able to make a decent marriage.

WANDA I'm not interested in marriage. I'm going to work.

JUANITA And what kind of job do you suppose you're going to find?

WANDA I already got one.

ELLA Doing what?

WANDA Claudine's going to get me on with her . . . as soon as the other girl goes back to school.

ELLA (*incredulously*)   In the drugstore?

WANDA   Yes. The boss has already told me I'll do. I'm the type.

JUANITA (*contemptuously, in outrage*)   Jerking soda! My own niece meeting every tramp who takes a notion to buy a bottle of pop!

BROOKS   I warned you, Ella. I told you 'bout lettin' her run round with that fast Claudine!

JUANITA   Can't you see if you go on, you could at least teach school?

WANDA   Teach school! Aunt, you make me laugh!

ELLA   What's wrong with that?

WANDA   It's Jim Crow, that's what—even if you ever do get an appointment.

JUANITA   But a drugstore?—Why, why it's ridiculous, positively ridiculous!

WANDA   I don't care. I've as much right to nice things as anyone else. If I go to work I can get them.

ELLA   So you think you've been neglected, hunh? I'd like to know who you think around here looks any better than you do?

BROOKS   Nobody. There ain't a girl on this street looks any better.

WANDA   Yeah. I'm right on Dearborn Street. But alongside the girls over East I look like mud.

JUANITA   But I always try to help you, don't I?

WANDA   Yes. And I thank you, Aunt Juanita. But I'm tired of wearing your castoff things.

JUANITA (*shocked*)   Well . . . !

WANDA   I meant no offense, Aunt. But in two months I'll be full grown woman, and I'm going to live!

BROOKS   What do you mean you "goin' live?"

WANDA (*going*)   Oh, you wouldn't understand, Grandma.

BROOKS (*cutting her off, boiling*)   No. I'm too old, you little hussey. I ain't got sense enough to understand. But it might surprise you to know, you pigheaded little wench, I said them same words to mah Mammy fore yours was born!

WANDA (*going*)   Then I don't see why you asked.

ELLA (*arresting her as she starts out*)   Maybe Mother's just a back number, too, Darling. But she'd like to know?

WANDA (*animatedly*)   Get some joy out of life, Mama! Have clothes and be able to go places and do things, like Uncle Percy!

BROOKS (*disgustedly*)   The drunken bum. Your Uncle Percy's a disgrace to the family— Do you think just because he wears good clothes and sleeps in the cabarets, he's livin'?

WANDA   At least he's not kidding himself like the rest of the family. He knows there's nothing for us in this country—And the white folks proved it, too; when they ripped his uniform off his back when he came home from France!

JUANITA   You can't hold all the white people guilty for the act of a few hoodlums! And it's no excuse for his throwing himself away!

WANDA   That's your idea. But Uncle Percy's living so when he gets old, he won't have anything to regret.

ELLA   Nothing to regret, hunh?—You just wait till your father hears of this.

WANDA   Let him. There's nothing in this country for a Negro girl to look forward to, and you know it as well as I. I'm going to make it for myself, and you and Papa might as well get used to the idea. Because whether you like it or not, I'm going to live my own life—(*she goes as* MASON *enters front door*) even if I have to leave here! (*she runs out*)

VIC (*a tall, very black man, dressed in an old suit, his hands stained with mortar—but his dignified bearing and keen eyes show him to be a man of considerable intelligence and character. He turns to* ELLA)   What's the matter with her?

ELLA   Nothing, Vic.

JUANITA (*grimly*)   It's no use procrastinating, Ella. You might as well settle it right now.

VIC (*curious*)   Wanda's not in trouble, is she?

BROOKS   No. But if you don't watch out she's goin' be!

VIC   Ella, what is this?

ELLA   Wanda's going to quit school.

VIC   Is that so?

ELLA   Yes. She tried her best to lay me out. Says she's tired of wearing other people's castoff things, and is going to work so she can *live!*

VIC (*going to hall-tree to hang hat*)   Well, I don't see anything to get excited about. Let her quit.

ELLA (*shocked*)   Let her quit! You mean that?

VIC   Sure. What difference does it make? They're only filling her head with a stack of white folks' lies anyway.

JUANITA   White folks' lies!

VIC   Yes, white folks' lies. There isn't a word of truth about the Black man in all her books put together!

BROOKS   If that don't prove you's cranky-headed, I donno what will.

ELLA (*to him*)   Have you lost your reason?

VIC   Ella, I see exactly what I'm talking about.

ELLA   Oh, you do? (*seeing* CAROLINE *and* PHILLIP *entering*) Go get ready for your dinner—(*as the children ascend stairs, she continues bitterly*) Well, you just go right ahead. Let her quit. She's yours. Let her ruin herself. Let her slide down to hell!

JUANITA   Now you're talking, Ella—Any father in his right mind—

VIC (*sharply*)   Now, wait a minute, both of you. Give me a moment to explain—and I promise you—

ELLA (*furious*)   I don't want to hear any explanations, or promises either—I've had enough of them.—"A stack of lies"—the whole world's a stack of lies! You brought me out of the South with one—You and your fine talk about freedom and giving the children a chance to be somebody!

VIC (*injuredly*)   I'm sorry you feel that way about it, Ella. I know I haven't done all I promised. But you could at least give me credit for my effort—

ELLA   I'll get a lot of comfort out of that!

VIC   But, I'm still trying, Ella. What do you think I'm carrying a hod by day and wrestling in the movement all night for? Wanda's just reached the point where she sees what we're up against in this country. (*turning to the stairs*) Be patient a little longer. (*halting as he starts up*) We'll soon be out of this rut and on our way to Africa. I can see her now, like a mother weeping for her long lost children, calling to us, "Come home." Soon, and it won't be long now. You're going to see the Black man come out of the darkness of failure into the light of achievement with the cloak of human greatness about his shoulders . . . Yes, Lord! And our enemies shall tremble when he stretches forth his mighty hand to gather in his share of the God-given stars of glory! (*leaving them spellbound, he disappears with dignity above*)

ELLA (*helplessly*)   What can you do with a man like that?

(*Curtain*)

Scene Two

TIME: *afternoon, a week later.*

LES *is observed seated in the window, reading a book. In a moment* PERCY *descends wearing a gaudy silk dressing gown*)

PERCY (*a handsome brown man, he stretches like a panther as he reaches the floor, and comes out of it with a grunt*)   Phumph! Reading again, hunh?

LES   Yep.

PERCY   That's all you ever do . . . (*going out rear*) You're getting to be a regular sissy. (*returning shortly with glass of water*) Where's everybody?

LES   Out I guess—Except Wanda. Mama and Grandma went shopping.

PERCY (*takes pint of gin from pocket of robe and places it on end table of couch*)   I gotta have some ginger ale.

LES   Caroline and Phillip are out there playing.

PERCY (*crosses to window to call*)   Phillip! . . . Come here a minute, will you? (*takes coin from pocket and sits on couch*)

PHILLIP (*entering*)   Watchu want, Uncle Percy?

PERCY (*giving him coin*)   Here. Run get me a bottle of ginger ale. And hurry now—(PHILLIP *runs out*) Lawd, my head feels like a keg of nails. (*he pours drink then goes to table to search through papers*) Umph. No mail! (*goes back to couch to drink liquor and chase it with water*) What kind of a book did you say that was?

LES   I didn't say.

PERCY (*sharply*)   Well, what kind is it, then—love story?

LES   No. It's a book Papa gave me.

PERCY   Yeah—What's the name of it?

LES   *Looking Backward* by Edward Bellamy.

PERCY   Never heard of it.

LES   No. It isn't likely.

PERCY   Now just what did you mean by that crack?

LES   Nothing, Uncle Percy—Only it's not exactly a novel.

PERCY   (*rising and going to window*)   Oh, What kind is it, then?

LES   It's a book on socialism.

PERCY   What?

LES   (*smiling*)   Surprised?

PERCY   (*disgustedly*)   Socialism! You're going to keep on till your Daddy makes a nut out of you yet. (*going back to couch*) Have you heard anymore from the school?

LES   Not yet. But I ought to get a letter any day now.

PERCY   Do you think you'll get it?

LES   You mean the letter or the scholarship?

PERCY   The scholarship!

LES   I don't see any reason why I shouldn't. I got an "A" out of the course.

PERCY   (*pouring another drink*)   I don't know what good it'll do you, from what I've seen of the rest of the educated bigshots in the family. But I guess you'll need clothes. You can have that pin-striped grey suit of mine and the brown you say you like so well.

LES   (*unbelievingly*)   Awh, you're kidding me, Uncle Percy!

PERCY   You got to tog down if you want to go places—

LES   Hot pajamas!

PERCY   You got to make appearances—If I have any luck at the hotel this week, I'll set you up to a new one. With the three you ought to be sharp as a tack when you hit that campus.

LES   (*overjoyed*)   Lord, Lord, are you telling me!

(*PHILLIP enters with ginger ale*)

PERCY   You sure took your time.

PHILLIP   They was busy. (*he offers change*)

PERCY   (*magnanimously waving change away*) That's all right.

PHILLIP   (*gleefully, running out*)   Thank you, Uncle Percy!

CLAUDINE   (*entering, encountering boy*)   Hey! Look out! (*exit PHILLIP*)

LES   Oh, hello, Claudine!

CLAUDINE   Hi! (*she is a very pretty mulatto of 18 wearing a summer frock*) Wanda home?

LES   Yes—I'll call her. (*he runs upstairs, as she saunters in, suddenly determined to try her wiles on the older man*)

CLAUDINE   What're you doing, Uncle Percy—having a ball all by yourself?

PERCY   Just trying to give my aching head a break—Have a . . . er some ginger ale?

CLAUDINE   (*laughing slyly*)   Don't play me cheap, Big Boy. I've been around!

PERCY   (*amused*)   Oh, you have!

CLAUDINE   I saw you in the Dreamland last week—and were you *high!*

PERCY   (*surprised*)   You in the Dreamland—?

CLAUDINE   Sure—Only—

PERCY   Only what?

CLAUDINE   Oh, the kids I run with only go for the notoriety—Three highballs and they pass out.

PERCY   (*slyly probing*)   Sure 'nough! Can't Wanda take it either?

CLAUDINE   Wanda's too scared to go anywhere—but why don't you take me sometime?

PERCY   Me take you cabereting?

CLAUDINE   What's the matter—(*laughing petulantly*) Ain't I hot enough for you? (*suddenly whirling like a model*)

PERCY   Oh, sure.

CLAUDINE   You don't act like it.

PERCY   You're too young for me, Kid. I'm a tough Papa.

CLAUDINE   (*resting her knee on chair center*) I'm nineteen, almost— And don't think I can't take care of myself!

PERCY   You're a keen little chick, all right. But you'd better give Les a break.

CLAUDINE   I can't be bothered with the cradle—(*laughing as she sees WANDA descending*) Hi, kiddo! Are you ready?

(*VIC enters in his good suit*)

WANDA   Yes. (*greeting father*) Hello, Papa.

VIC   Well, you're certainly looking cool, Claudine—How's your folks?

CLAUDINE   Quite well, thank you.

WANDA   Papa, Claudine and I are going to Thirty-fifth Street.

VIC   Well, be sure you're back in time for dinner.

WANDA   (*going*)   OK, Papa.

CLAUDINE   (*saucily*)   Don't forget what I told you, Uncle Percy. (*exit with WANDA*)

WANDA   (*as they disappear*)   What's this between you and my Uncle?

VIC (*indicating gin*)   At it again, hunh?

PERCY   Take it easy, Captain—

(*Outside,* DAN *is heard exchanging greetings with girls*)

DAN (*appearing in front door*)   Well, how's everybody?

VIC   Just fine, Dan. And how're you?

DAN (*coming downstage, a stocky brown man aged about 37, immaculately groomed*)   Never felt better nor had less in my life. (*seeing* LES *descending*) I hear you're fixing to leave us, Les.

LES   Not for sure, Uncle Dan. I haven't received the final word yet.

DAN   You'll get it. The thing for you to do now is get yourself in the right frame of mind to make the best of your chance.

PERCY   You needn't worry about him— (*offering drink*) Have a little snort?

DAN (*taking chair*)   No, thanks. I haven't time for that stuff these days. Furthermore, it's too hot.

PERCY   You're getting to be as big a heel as Vic—How's the road?

DAN   Things are picking up right along. I had eight sections all the way from Los Angeles—How's tricks on the bellstand?

PERCY   They ain't walking no more.

DAN   No?—And you, Vic?

VIC   Still the same. My hod ain't getting no lighter. But the movement's swinging along.

DAN   I hear you're planning a World Conference!

VIC   How did you know?

DAN   I picked up one of your Big Moguls in Denver, on his way to the Coast—(*laughing*) Called himself the Duke of the Niger!

VIC (*unamused*)   Yeah.

DAN   Yeah. And you talk about a spade. He sure was one for you. He kept the car in an uproar all the way to Los Angeles.

PERCY   Clowning for the Pecks, hunh?

DAN (*emphatically*)   And how!

PERCY (*acrimoniously*)   I could drown one of that kind in a tub of carbolic acid!

VIC (*to* DAN)   And you say he was a Garveyite?

DAN   That's what he claimed.

LES   What did he say, Uncle Dan?

DAN   What didn't he say, the fool! "Jerusalem for the Jew!" he kept preaching, with the white folks egging him on; "Ireland for the Irish, and Africa for the Africans!"—It was disgusting. But I doubt if it ever occurred to him he was playing right into the white man's hands.

VIC   How's that?

DAN (*warmly*)   By telling them just what they want to hear, that's what—advocating segregation!

VIC (*defensively*)   You don't understand the new spirit, Dan. We're out to wrest our heritage from the enemy.

DAN (*challengingly*)   What *our*? My heritage is right here in America!

VIC (*quietly*)   What? A lynchrope?

PERCY   You said a mouthful, Captain.

DAN   Like hell. If those chumps down South haven't got sense enough to get out from under Mr. George, they ought to be strung up.

VIC   You talk like an imbecile, Dan—Have you forgotten East St. Louis, Tulsa, and Washington? And what about what they did to Percy there when he came back from France?

DAN (*irritatedly*)   I haven't forgotten anything. But all this agitation doesn't mean a thing. You can't do anything for people who don't care anything about themselves. You only stir up strife. Let them alone, I say, and try to get something out of them for yourself. There's chance enough for anybody in this country if he's got get-up enough to take it.

PERCY   Yea. A chance to be door mats for the white folks' feet!

DAN   Doormats, my eye. Adjust yourself, I say. Outwit the white man. Get something in your pocket and stop expecting the millennium!

VIC (*grimly*)   You know what, Dan. It just strikes me what's wrong with educated Negroes like you.

DAN   Oh, yeah! Give me the benefit of your great wisdom?

VIC   Your education is like a pair of knee pads, which enables you to crawl through the slime of white prejudice without the least sense of pain or dishonor!

DAN (*stung*)   If I didn't know you so well, I'd take that as an insult. But you're radical. You can't see that the only difference between your feelings and mine is simply a matter of control.

VIC   Of course, with the help of your education.

DAN   You bet. I've got too much sense to let prejudice blind me to the thing that counts in this world. Get your share of the *mazuma*, I say, and all else will be added unto you!

VIC   We're all the same to the white man, rich or poor—But what I want is freedom here and now!

DAN   So do I. But I say first get the cash.

PERCY   By crawling on your belly?

DAN   Tommyrot! A man can do business with his own people—Take this proposition of mine now, Vic. Everywhere our folks are looking for a place to live—It's the chance of a lifetime—

VIC   You're still just thinking about yourself. But I'm not. If I was, I'd pack out of here for some foreign country before sunrise.

DAN   (*earnestly*)   Even so, Man. You're not going to Africa tomorrow. And you can't deny you'll need money when you do go. Come in with me. To open this kitchenette will make us both public benefactors.

VIC   You mean private beneficiaries!

DAN   What?

LES   How's that, Papa?

VIC   Never mind.

PERCY   I don't know about that, Captain. As long as we've got to be bled by somebody, I'd rather it be a Black man.

DAN   Now you're talking sense, Percy. If the race gave Negro business half a chance, we'd soon get somewhere.

VIC   (*hotly*)   Bunk. Mixed up with the white man as we are, Africa is the only solution.

DAN   All right. But what about temporarily—just to help me get started—?

VIC   I'm backing the Garvey Movement, Dan. Right this minute I'm expecting the committee to bring me some stock—the shares I'm taking in the Black Star Line. I feel it's my duty to put what little money I can behind it.

DAN   Shucks, Vic. In six months we'll be sitting so pretty, you'll be able to purchase all the stock you want and then some.

VIC   Sure—So you say!

DAN   I've figured it all out, I tell you. We can lease a six-flat building for $400 a month. We'll cut it up into forty apartments that'll rent for twenty bucks apiece. That's an income of $800 a month—or $200 apiece after the rent is paid—Where're you going to beat that?

PERCY   That's a lot of dough.

BROOKS   (*entering front door and heading for her favorite rocker*)   Make room you all and lemme git off these feet!

ELLA   (*entering behind her, her arms full of parcels*)   Here, Les, make yourself useful.

LES   (*joining her and taking parcels*)   Did you bring the paper?

ELLA   (*tossing Negro Newspaper on table*)   Yes—there it is.

(*Exit* LES *into rear*)

DAN   Looks like you're planning to open a grocery store.

ELLA   (*following* LES *out back*)   We need one to feed this family. (*exit*)

DAN   (*affably*)   You're sure looking well, Mama.

BROOKS   (*pleased at being noticed*)   I'm doing pretty fair, thank you, Dan—though I'm tired out right now.

DAN   Juanita said "hello." (*turning back to* VIC) But as I was saying. If we put $1500 apiece in the business, we can furnish the building from top to bottom and soon be on easy street—

VIC   But $1500—

DAN   We've got to avoid credit, and start off with a clean slate—

VIC   But $1500. That's just about every single cent I own—!

(LES *enters to pick up newspaper, crosses to window seat and begins reading*)

DAN   What difference does it make? You'll have your principal back in eight months!

VIC   (*going*)   I'll have to think about it.

DAN   Where're you going?

VIC   I've got to get into my uniform before the committee comes. (*he ascends stairs*)

DAN   It's the chance of a lifetime. Don't forget that, and you can always pull out anytime you say.

VIC   So you say! (*exit above*)

PERCY   (*to* DAN, *chuckling*)   He's sure salty, ain't he?

DAN   As a pickled herring.

LES   (*springing up, excitedly*)   For crying out loud! (*coming forward*) Listen to this—Where's Papa?

DAN   Upstairs. What is it?

LES   (*reading*)   "Black Star Liner Halted at Pier!"

PERCY   Halted? What for?

DAN   No! (*joining* LES) Lemme see!

LES (*as other takes paper*)   Lord, Lord—I wonder what Papa's going to say!

BROOKS (*anxiously*)   What is it, Les?

LES   They've stopped the *Republic* from sailing.

BROOKS   To Affiki—How come?

PERCY   Read it out, Dan.

DAN (*laughing*)   This is a scream—(*he strides to foot of stairs to shout*) Vic! Oh, Vic! Come on down here! Wait till he gets an earful of this—Black Star Line, eh? If he ain't a lucky man, the Sante Fe's a bus line!

ELLA (*reentering*)   What's going on here?

DAN   They've stopped that piece of junk of Marcus Garvey's from sailing.

ELLA   My God! Who stopped it?

DAN   The government, that's who.

VIC (*appearing above*)   What's the trouble?

DAN (*going up to foot of stairs*)   Come on down here and take a look at this. (*as* VIC *descends, buttoning the jacket of his Garvey Uniform*) I told you a man'd be a fool to trust that Monkeychaser—(*handing him paper*) Read this—(*as* VIC *pauses to read, he himself rejoins others*) A hell of a movement. The only time they know what's going on is when they see it in the newspapers!

STRAWDER (*apparently having knocked, he appears in doorway, a heavyset black man of 40, with several others behind him—All dressed in the regalia of the Garveyites—black uniforms trimmed with red and white plummed helmets*) Good evening, Folks!

ELLA (*turning*)   Oh, good evening, Mr. Strawder—Come in, won't you?

VIC (*oblivious of all*)   It's a lie! A dirty rotten lie!

ELLA   Vic!

VIC (*noticing guests*)   Excuse me, Gentlemen. I didn't see you come in.

STRAWDER   Is anything wrong, Captain Mason?

VIC (*leading* STRAWDER *down to couch*)   Wait until you hear this—Here, Les, read this for me, Son—And you all sit down.

LES (*as* STRAWDER *gingerly eases himself into seat on couch, and others gather behind it*) "Black Star Liner Halted at Pier—"

COTTON   What's that?

LES (*reading*)   "New York—As the Black Star Line Steamship, *Republic*, prepared to sail

on its maiden voyage today, passengers aboard and spectators upon the crowded Hudson River pier were thrown into panic, culminating in near riot, when Maritime Inspector Davis O'Rouke declared the boat unseaworthy and issued orders forbidding the Captain from clearing port—"

STRAWDER (*stunned*)   Great God A'mighty!

VIC   Sit down, Count Strawder. You haven't heard the worst yet—Read on, Les.

LES (*reading*)   "Inspection of the *Republic* came as a result of widespread rumors which recently began circulating in Harlem to the effect that leaders of the co-operative enterprise, which sought to establish the line, had been buncoed, when they purchased the giant craft at a cost of approximately a million dollars, despite the fact that the antiquated ship had not been in commission since the World War—"

DAN (*laughing derisively*)   Wouldn't that squeeze you! (*a glance from* VIC *quells him*)

LES (*continuing*)   "It was reported that Marcus Garvey, Provisional President of the proposed Black Republic of Africa, and leader of the movement, had taken flight to Canada!"

COTTON (*with a cry of pain*)   Oh, no! . . .

STRAWDER (*with an air of despair*)   Well suh!

HARPER   What you make of it, Captain Mason?

VIC   It's a lie, Brother Harper—a dirty trick!

DAN   A trick—?

BROOKS (*derisively*)   It's a trick all right. That Marcus Garvey's done tricked the folks out o' their money—Talkin' bout a *Black* land for the *Black* man! A *Black* land for the *Black* man!

VIC   Hush, Mama! You don't understand.

BROOKS   Don't tell me I don't understand. I told you he wasn't no good, and when I tell a pusson sometin' they can take it for granted. If I tell you a chicken dip snuff, jes look under her wing and you'll find the box! (DAN *explodes with irrepressible laughter*)

VIC (*angrily*)   What do you think this is, a circus? This is no laughing matter. This is a dirty white frame-up on the whole race if ever there was one!

STRAWDER   How you mean, Captain Mason?

VIC   It's plain as the nose on your face, Count. They think if they discredit our leader they'll bust up the movement!

DAN (*staggered*)   Well, I'll be a—Are you crazy, Vic? That inspector was a Government man!

VIC   That's just what I know.

COTTON (*incredulously*)   And you think Uncle Sam had a hand in it?

VIC   Open your eyes, Count. The big men run this country, don't they? Haven't they got everything to gain by destroying the confidence of our members?

DAN   Tommyrot! Tommyrot! If it wasn't for the big white folks, they'd have kicked us out and imported enough Hunkies to take our place long ago.

STRAWDER   There's something to that, Captain!

VIC (*bitterly*)   The Negro's nothing to the white man but a good thing! As workers and consumers who can't get anywhere, we're sweeter than sugar cane!

STRAWDER   I think I get what you mean, Captain. Now that I remember, I mentioned our movement to the boss, no longer'n a week ago, and he blew right up in the air about it. He say—

(*Sound of Postman's whistle*)

LES (*heading for door*)   The mailman! . . . Lord, I hope it's for me! (*meeting* WANDA *entering with letter*) Who's it for?

WANDA (*handing him letter*)   You.

LES (*going downstage left*)   This is it! It's here, Papa!

PERCY   From the scholarship, eh?

WANDA   Yes.

ELLA   I'm so glad, Les. (*she watches his countenance as he reads*)

VIC (*explanatorily to others*)   My boy won a scholarship to college, and that's the letter about it.

ELLA (*seeing pain on boy's face*)   What s the matter . . . ? Is . . . ?

LES (*biting his lip*)   Well, I guess . . . It's all off!

VIC (*rising in consternation*)   What?

ELLA   Oh, God!

WANDA (*her eyes swimming*)   Oh, Les . . . you don't mean . . . (*she joins him to take letter*)

LES   I happen to be a little too Black, I guess.

ELLA (*unbelievingly*)   There must be some mistake—

DAN (*taking letter from* WANDA)   Let me see! (PERCY *joins him as he takes step toward couch, to read aloud*) "My dear Mr. Mason. I have been instructed to inform you that on the basis of information received from one in your community, stating that you are a Negro . . ."

PERCY (*reading over his shoulder*)   "the board has no other alternative than to deny your application, since under the provisions of the late Mr. Jason's will, the executors are expressly constrained from making any monies from the Fund available to members of your race—" The dirty bastards!

WANDA (*going to* LES)   I'm so sorry, Les!

ELLA   It isn't fair! God, you know it isn't fair!

PERCY (*going upstage left, angrily*)   The only fair thing about a white man is the color of his skin!

VIC (*nodding his head slowly*)   Nobody else could be guilty of such a cheap, petty piece of business—(*hoarsely to* LES) But it's all right, boy!

DAN (*darkly*)   I wish I could put my hands on the one who told them he was colored!

BROOKS   I bet it was somebody round here.

STRAWDER   You can bet on it. Somebody did that out of jealousy.

COTTON (*woefully*)   Yeah. One of our own people, too!

VIC   They would've found out anyway, soon's he arrived—(*resolutely*) But this settles it! (*to* STRAWDER) Got your subscription list handy, Count?

ELLA   What're you fixing to do?

VIC (*searching for his breastpocket, forgetful that he's wearing uniform*)   Answer my son's letter—Are you with me?

ELLA (*with a tinge of dismay*)   You know I am. But what're you—

VIC   Wanda, run upstairs and get me my check book.

DAN (*as she runs up*)   But, Vic!—

VIC   Get out your list, Count!

DAN   Ella! (*she is silent, and he turns back to* VIC, *sensing the futility of his action*) Oh, I know how you feel, Vic. But you can't afford to let this thing drive you to do anything so rash.

STRAWDER (*at end table, with pen and papers*)   How many shares you going to take, Captain?

VIC (*firmly*)   Fifteen hundred! (*the* GARVEYITES *crowd behind couch to watch the desperate transaction*)

DAN (*desperately*)   But, Vic. It's worthless, Man!

VIC (*quietly*)   To you, perhaps.

DAN   This is madness! . . . Wait, Vic. Wait until you feel better. Let it go until tomorrow at least!

VIC (*exasperatedly*)   You and your tomorrow. Will you never stop talking about tomorrow? What does it take to make you see there's none for us in the God forsaken country? (WANDA *returns to hand him check book*) Thanks. (*he makes out check*)

DAN (*to* ELLA)   Are you going to be a fool, too? Can't you see what he's doing? Speak to him!

PERCY (*exploding, bitterly*)   Speak to him! Speak to him! What do you want her to say? Tell him to drop everything and stay here and let these dirty, damn hypocrits tear the hearts out of the rest of the children? (*exit above*)

ELLA (*in tears*)   I'd rather choke first.

DAN (*surrendering*)   All right. All right. If you're going to let bitterness get the best of you, it's your funeral—But don't say I didn't warn you. (*going*) With that damn steamship nothing but junk, that stock isn't worth the paper it's printed on! (*exit to street*)

VIC (*handing check to* STRAWDER)   Here you are, Count.

STRAWDER (*rising*)   I made out three certificates for $500 each.

BROOKS (*in despair*)   Lawd! Lawd! Lawd!

VIC (*taking shares*)   Thanks.

STRAWDER (*deeply moved, and extending his hand*)   Don't thank me, Captain Mason. I don't deserve it. You're one out of a thousand. And I'm going to write to our leader and tell him how you're sticking by him in this hour of need.

VIC (*his eyes on his star*)   It's a mighty poor man that needs to be thanked for following the star of his people's destiny, Count. I'm looking East!

STRAWDER (*going, he dons his helmet*) Well—Gooday! (*he stalks with dignity toward door, as others offer their hands to Vic and follow him out*)

VIC (*as the last of the plumed figures disappear, and* ELLA *sinks onto couch in silent tears*)   Don't cry, Ella! (*for a moment his hand rests upon her shoulder*)

LES (*bewildered, he stares upon the world with an inward eye*)   Seems like the world ain't nothing but a big white fog, and we can't see no light nowhere!

(ELLA *sobs*)

VIC (*fervidly and with a sense of compassion for his wounded son*)   Look to the East, Son, and keep on looking! Beyond the darkness and mist that surrounds us here, Africa the Sun of our hope is rising!

(*All is disconsolation, as the Curtain falls slowly*)

ACT TWO

Scene One

TIME: *August, a year later.*

Everything is as we saw it last, except that now WANDA *is seated at the oblong table, typing as her father dictates from a batch of notes.*

MRS. BROOKS *occupies the rocker, watching the doings on the street through the window;* ELLA *is sewing, as she mends the jacket of* VIC's *uniform.*

There is a steady rhythm of WANDA's *typing for a moment following the rise of the curtain, then she looks up at her father inquiringly*)

VIC (*dictating in response to her glance*) "Therefore, we must of necessity conclude that by relying upon the Nine tried and proven principles of the English Producers-and-Consumers-Cooperatives"—comma— "we shall eventually be able to build an agrarian cooperative economy—

WANDA   How do you spell agrarian?

VIC   A-g-r-a-r-i-a-n—Get it? (*she nods*) "cooperative economy of lasting benefit to the Republic"—Period. Paragraph.

ELLA (*preoccupiedly*)   How long do you think the strike will last, Vic?

VIC (*casually*)   A month or so, maybe— (*dictating*) Unfortunately—

ELLA (*anxiously*)   That long—? What makes you think so?

VIC (*annoyed*)   Never mind, Ella. Let the strike drop. I've got to get this paper done.

ELLA   I was only thinking how Les is going to feel if you leave him behind.

WANDA   That's right, Papa. He's bound to

be disappointed after the way he's been boasting of going with you and seeing New York and Harlem!

VIC   I can't help that. This is a general walkout—painters, bricklayers, plasterers and all—In fact, I wouldn't think of making the trip if I hadn't promised this paper—(*to* WANDA) Where were we?

WANDA   "Unfortunately."

BROOKS (*looking out window*)   Here's Les now.

VIC (*going on*)   "Unfortunately, the hostile nature of the Negro's environment in the agricultural South does not permit of experimentation there." Period. "Otherwise—"

LES (*entering upstage left, excitedly*)   You know what, Papa. Uncle Dan is just as dirty as he can be. He just put one of his tenants out this afternoon and she hasn't any place to stay!

VIC   Is that so?

LES   He set her right out on the sidewalk because her rent was three weeks overdue, and Mrs. Davis was a nice woman too.

ELLA   Three weeks—? That all?

LES   You don't know Uncle Dan, Mama. He's hard as they make 'em. Anybody get behind in their rent, he usually puts a plug in their doorlock the next day.

WANDA   So he called himself giving her a break, huh?

LES   Yeah. I guess so—Maybe because she has a baby and her husband ran off with another woman.

ELLA   Poor thing!

VIC   Dan has no more conscience than a bedbug.

LES   For two cents I wouldn't go back to work for him—You ought to have seen her sitting on the sidewalk crying.

ELLA   There ought to be a law against such things!—Poor soul, I wonder what she's going to do. . . . Was she a young woman?

LES   About twenty-five I guess.

BROOKS (*emphatically*)   I reckon she'll make it then.

VIC (*indignantly*)   And he wanted me to be his partner!

WANDA   Was Aunt Juanita there?

LES   No. But it wouldn't've made any difference; the way she lays on everybody about their rent—

BROOKS (*strangely excited*)   Here they come, now, driving a brand new car!

WANDA (*springing up from chair and crossing to join her*)   A new car? (ELLA *follows suit*)

LES   I forgot to tell you.

WANDA (*excitedly*)   Come see, Papa.

ELLA (*Looking out*)   My but it's beautiful! What kind of a car is it, Les?

LES   A Cadillac.

BROOKS   Lawd, a Cadillac!

VIC (*crossing to look*)   Phumph! (*turning back, displeased*) A fortune on wheels!—But I guess it's no mystery how he got it.

JUANITA (*entering, breezily*)   Well, are the travelers ready!

ELLA (*going back to seat*)   Not quite. Come on in, you all.

DAN (*entering, proudly*)   See my new boat, Vic?

VIC   Yeah. And from the looks of it, you don't have to tell me your kitchenette's making money.

DAN (*grandly*)   Just thought I'd make Juanita a little present. But it's costing me plenty. Thirty-eight hundred bucks is a lot of money, take it from Daniel.

BROOKS   Thirty-eight hund'd dollars—Lawdy!

JUANITA (*laughing*)   How do you like it, Mama?

BROOKS   Lawd, chile; it's out of this world.

WANDA   You must be tickled to death, Aunt.

JUANITA (*going to window seat*)   Oh, I'm not shedding any tears, dear!

DAN (*sitting*)   I reckon not.—But say, Vic. Aren't you making a mistake taking Les to New York? I really need him, and you know yourself he'll need every cent he can earn if he's going to enter the U this fall?

VIC (*with a tinge of bitterness*)   Well, you can ease your mind on that score—(*As* LES *rises*) I'm sorry, Les. I was just going to tell you. . . . You see, they called a strike on the job—

DAN   A strike!

VIC   Yes. The contractors are defiant—! And you see, Les. Well, I don't know just how long I may be out of work—

LES (*crestfallen*)   So you can't spare the money!

VIC   I hope you don't feel too bad about it. I wouldn't go myself if I didn't have part on the program.

LES   If you can't afford a thing, you can't.

DAN (*encouragingly*)   At a boy, Les! In a few years you'll be able to take a trip around the world—Once you get your education.

ELLA   Hadn't you better finish your paper, Vic.

VIC (*gratefully*)   Yes, yes. Of course. (*to* JUANITA *and* DAN) Excuse me, will you—I've only got a paragraph or two more.

DAN   Les was telling me about—What's the subject?

VIC   The Outlook for Cooperative Farming in Africa.

DAN   Sounds interesting.

VIC   Read the last sentence back to me, Wanda.

WANDA (*at machine*)   "Unfortunately, the hostile nature of the Negro's environment in the agricultural South does not permit of experimentation there. Otherwise—"

VIC (*dictating*)   Oh, yeah. "Otherwise it would be distinctly advantageous to try out the plan here," comma, "as it might easily prove the solution of the race problem in this country." Period. "For should the Negro successfully wrest his economic independence from his white oppressors," comma, "their attitude of superiority would inevitably disappear, since it would then no longer possess any basis in reality." Period. Paragraph. "But this is, of course, merely to indulge in fortuitous wishing"; Semi-colon "so that in passing, I am constrained to give you: The Agrarian Cooperative Economy of the Provisional Republic of Africa, the hope and destined fulfillment of the Negro's dream. For just as the gigantic Pyramids of Egypt (*he is being moved by his own eloquence*) stand in eternal witness of the strength of our Black forefather's hands, so shall the New Africa, which we shall have built through this means, stand before the generations of tomorrow in final testimony of the Black man's wisdom." That's all.

LES   Gee, Papa. That's good!

DAN (*admiringly*)   It's too bad, Vic, you can't see anything but Garvey!

JUANITA   I'll say so. You'll bring the house down.

VIC   I'm glad you like it.—Get it together, Wanda—(*he joins her to lay aside his notes*) Where're the children, Ella?

ELLA (*going to the door*)   Outside, somewhere.

DAN   There's only one thing, Vic—the doubtfullness of your ever establishing the Republic aside—especially since Garvey's conviction—There's only one thing I can see that's wrong with your conclusion.

ELLA (*in door, calling*)   Caroline!

VIC (*to* DAN)   Yeah—

ELLA (*to children*)   Come, you and Phillip—Papa's going!

VIC (*to* DAN)   What's that?

DAN   You make the mistake of thinking the white man's idea of his superiority is something more than a delusion.

VIC   I was speaking about the effect of him having everything in the palm of his hand.

DAN   But that's temporary.

ELLA (*apprehensively*)   Vic, you haven't got time to argue! (*she holds his jacket*)

VIC (*starting to don it, but only succeeding in getting in one arm*)   All I'm saying is the white man's on top and he knows it, and as long as he stays on top all the books in the world won't change him.

DAN   There's more ways than one to skin a cat—

VIC   Yeah. Like what?

DAN   Use the white man's method, that's what—the process of individual achievement.

ELLA (*desperately, still trying to get him into his jacket*)   It's pretty near train time, Vic.

BROOKS   They're goin' keep on till they'll be hot at each other again!

VIC   Try offering your white man's method to the millions we got down South, (*shaking his finger*) living on corn bread and molasses and dying like flies from hook-worm and pellagra!

DAN (*sharply*)   Let them come North!

JUANITA   Oh, why don't you cut it out, Dan. Vic's got to—

DAN (*angrily*)   You shut up! (*to* VIC) Why can't they come North, like we did—There's plenty of room up here for everybody!

VIC   Bunk. But even if there was, I'd still be against it.

DAN (*acridly*)   Of course. Because you know it would put you race saviors out of business!

VIC (*losing his temper*)   Yeah—Well, there's one thing you can't deny: I'm against cutting my own brother's throat to get somewhere!

ELLA   For God's sake, Vic, stop it!

(PHILLIP *and* CAROLINE *enter*)

DAN   The weak and shiftless always find some idea to blame for not having anything!

VIC   You're sitting pretty, ain't you?

DAN   I don't have to want for anything!

VIC   No you don't—living like a leach on the blood of your own people!

DAN   That's a lie!

JUANITA   Dan!

VIC   If it's a lie, how is it in a year you've been able to pay $4,000 for that automobile out there?

DAN (*sneeringly*)   What's the matter, getting jealous?

VIC (*blazing*)   For two cents I'd tell you what to do with that car!

DAN   Oh, yeah!

VIC   You're damn right! (*to* LES) Go, call me a taxi! (LES *starts to obey, but is stopped by glance from* ELLA)

BROOKS   I knowed it! I knowed it!

DAN (*angrily*)   Suits me! (*going*) Come on, Juanita. To hell with him!

JUANITA (*arresting him*)   No, Dan! This is all uncalled for.

DAN   Like hell it is. Do you think I'm going to stand here and swallow his rotten insinuations?

ELLA   You're both acting like children— Why don't you forget it—

VIC (*peremptorily to* LES)   Didn't I tell you to call me a taxi!

(*Exit* LES, *running*)

JUANITA   You ought to be ashamed of yourself, Victor Mason. Here you are two brother-in-*laws* arguing like cats and dogs. It's a shame!

VIC (*with finality*)   You're wasting your breath!

JUANITA (*joining* DAN, *angrily*)   Well, if that's the way you feel, *Goodbye!* (*exit, with* DAN)

BROOKS (*seeing* PHILLIP *with her work basket*) Phillip, you let that basket alone! (ELLA *dons hat at hall-tree*)

VIC (*to* PHILLIP)   Can't you keep out of mischief, boy!

PHILLIP (*pouting*)   Papa, I wasn't doing nothing with her old basket!

LES (*in door*)   Here's your cab, Papa. (*he gets father's bags*)

VIC (*kissing* CAROLINE)   Be a good girl, you hear. (*turning to* PHILLIP) Don't let your Ma have to give me any bad reports about you. (*patting his shoulder*) I'm going to try to bring you both something when I get back. (*to* WANDA) Did you get it together? (*she nods and hands him manuscript*) You've been a big help to me—(*kisses her forehead. Exit* LES) Take care of yourself. (*following* LES *out*) Goodbye, Mama! (ELLA *goes out behind him*)

CAROLINE (*following mother*)   Mama, may I go to the station with you? (*exit* CAROLINE)

PHILLIP (*on her heels*)   Me, too, Mama? (*exit* PHILLIP)

(BROOKS *turns to the window, as the Curtain falls*)

Scene Two

(TIME: *the following January.*

From the window the light of a dreary winter dusk shrouds the figure of MRS. BROOKS, *who stands there, gazing into the street.*

This atmosphere of bleakness, in fact, pervades the whole house and tends to emphasize the mood of the family which is one of apprehension and misgiving)

ELLA *enters from above, her descent slow, her aspect full of weariness and dejection*)

ELLA (*halting on stair*)   Is it still snowing?

BROOKS (*immobile*)   No. It's stopped

ELLA (*strangely annoyed*)   It would! (*she descends*)

BROOKS   Some life—dependin' on the elements!

ELLA   We have to be thankful, Mama; things aren't worse.

BROOKS (*turning, gruffly*)   If you'd-er made Vic keep that money, he wouldn't have to be shovelin' no snow—How is she?

ELLA (*turning to table to inspect punch bowl and cups there*)   About the same. She drank the tea, but she's complaining about a headache.

BROOKS (*apprehensively*)   You better call the doctor, then. She may be comin' down with the flu!

ELLA (*wearily*)   I just spent the last nickle I had for the stuff to make the eggnog.

BROOKS (*sharply*)   Lawd, lawd! I don't know which one of you all is the worst, you or Vic— You know that chile's sick, and you ain't hardly got bread to eat, yet you spend your last cent for eggnog!

ELLA   Oh, for heaven's sake, Mama! I can't have the leaders coming here to honor my own husband and not serve anything, can I?

BROOKS (*acridly*)   If it was left to me, I'd serve em some water and give em a piece of my mind!

ELLA (*starting to kitchen*)   If she isn't better by morning, I'll see Juanita—(*halting and turning*) Where's Phillip?

BROOKS   Outside.

ELLA (*astounded*)   Outside—! (*upbraidingly*) Why didn't you make him stay in here?

BROOKS (*coldly*)   I told him. But he's jest like his Pappy!

ELLA (*crossing up to front door*)   Lord, have mercy! (*opening door to call*) Phillip! . . . You Phillip!

PHILLIP (*in street*)   Yes'm!

ELLA (*angrily*)   You come in this house! (*shuts door and comes down*) I don't know what I'm going to do with that boy.

BROOKS   Let him keep on runnin' round in the snow with them shoes he got on and he'll be up there with Caroline, if you don't have to bury him!

PHILLIP (*entering*)   Yes'm—(*he wipes his nose with the back of his sleeve*)

ELLA (*outdone*)   Nose running! (*shaking him*) Didn't Mama tell you to stay in this house?

PHILLIP   Mama, I wasn't doing nothin' but trying out Mac's new sled!

ELLA   I should try your back-side! (*pushing him into chair*) Let me see those over-shoes? (*pulls off shoe and exhibits it*) Just look at that hole!

BROOKS   I could-er told you their feet was on the ground a week ago. But I thought I better hold my tongue.

ELLA (*to* PHILLIP)   Go upstairs and get in bed—(*as he obeys*) And don't disturb Caroline . . . I'll bring you some hot eggnog in a little while. (*on stairs the boy sneezes*)

BROOKS   Phumph! You hear that? (ELLA *is silent, as she goes up to deposit shoes under hall-tree*) I don't blame you for not answerin'. You could-er took that money you spent for eggnog and bought em both a pair—'stid o'

puttin' on the dog for that black crank you call your husband.

ELLA (*glancing out of window*)   It's snowing again, Thank God! (BROOKS *grunts—and she, herself, crosses to switch on lights*) I reckon we'd better have a little light.

BROOKS (*seeing boy from window*)   Here's Les, n' Wanda. (*turning to greet him, as he enters with sister, feeling his ears*) Gittin' colder, hunh?

(ELLA *turns anxiously toward* WANDA *and becomes hesitant*)

LES (*doffing overcoat, as* WANDA *removes over-shoes*)   I don't think so, Grandma—(*seeing punch bowl*) Punch bowl out!

(ELLA *remains preoccupied*)

BROOKS (*feigning surprise*)   Oh, ain't you all heard? We's havin' a lil celebration this evenin'—Your Pappy's goin' be decorated!

WANDA   Decorated by whom? For what?

BROOKS   Ask your Mammy—She know's all about it.

LES   What is it, Mama?

ELLA   I don't know myself—(*cheerfully*) Only, Mr. Strawder called up and said to keep your father home, as they were coming over to bestow some kind of honor on him.——But, Wanda—

LES (*admiringly, as he enters kitchen*)   Good old Papa! He's sure forging right ahead! (*exit*)

BROOKS   He's forgin' ahead all right—Right straight to the poor house!

WANDA (*turning to stairs*)   Mama, when's it coming off?

ELLA   I don't know. Mr. Strawder said they'd be here early.

WANDA (*going*)   Well, I hope they come before I have to go.

ELLA (*intercepting her, hesitantly*)   Wanda—

WANDA (*halting on stair*)   Yes—

ELLA   Have you—Could you spare me a little money—a few dollars?

WANDA (*exploding wildly*)   Money! Money! Can't you find anything else to speak to me about except money? Where'd I get money from this time of week—I just gave you all I had payday!

ELLA (*hurt*)   Well, you needn't shout at me.

WANDA   I'm sorry, Mama. But you know I've no money.

ELLA   I wouldn't've asked you. But you know your father's still on strike—and Caroline's sick—

LES (*re-entering*)   Caroline!

WANDA   What's the matter with her?

ELLA   She got her feet wet and the teacher sent her home.

BROOKS (*volunteering*)   For being ill-clad and needin' a doctor.

LES   No! (*crossing to stairs*) Where is she—in bed?

ELLA   Yes. (*as he runs up stairs*) I'm not worrying about the doctor so much. But she and Phillip both need overshoes.

BROOKS   It's a shame 'fore Heaven.

WANDA   I'm already in a hole, Mama. (*going*) But I'll see if I can get the boss to let me have a few dollars tonight.

ELLA   Nevermind. Maybe your father'll get hold of a dollar or two today. (*exit WANDA*)

BROOKS (*warningly*)   She goin' get tired of his money business pretty soon. You see how she flew off the handle, don't you?

ELLA   Yes. But maybe it'll be a little easier for her after this. Vic said this morning he was going to ask Les for help.

BROOKS (*surprised*)   Ask Les? (*sharply*) How in the world's Les goin' do anything, and him goin' to college?

ELLA (*going toward rear*)   I reckon his father's going to make him drop out.

BROOKS   Lawdy! It's goin' break his heart!

ELLA (*in door*)   If he comes down, keep him here. Tell him Vic wants to see him.

BROOKS (*arresting her, as she hears stomping on porch*)   I 'spect that's Vic now.

ELLA (*seeing VIC enter, she measures him for a moment in silence*)   Well, what'd you do today?

VIC (*he sets shovel in corner and joins her, taking out change*)   Made Six-bits!

ELLA (*takes change to weigh it in palm*) Phumph! Six-bits!—How long do you think we can keep this up?

VIC (*turning back to remove wraps*)   I'm doing the best I can, Ella. (*she goes out rear in silence*)

BROOKS (*shortly, watching him*)   Do you know Caroline and Phillip's sick!

VIC (*shocked*)   What's the matter with them?

BROOKS   They got the flu, I 'spect.

VIC (*crossing and calling*)   Ella! What's this about the children being sick?

ELLA (*off-stage*)   Take a look at their leaky shoes out there and you'll know for yourself.

VIC (*turning*)   Their leaky shoes—?

LES (*descending and catching sight of him*) Hello, Papa—I hear you're going to be decorated tonight.

VIC   What nonsense is this?

LES (*indicating table*)   See the punch bowl!

VIC (*going up to table*)   Now I wonder what this can mean?

LES (*getting coat*)   I've got to go by the kitchenette. But if they come, hold everything for me.

VIC (*as he starts out*)   Wait a minute, Son. There's something I wanted to ask you to do for me. (*regretfully*) I've been hoping to avoid asking you. But I reckon I needn't go into details. You see the hole I'm in—

LES   Yes . . . But what is it?

VIC   I guess there's no hope of my getting back to work before spring. So I thought I might ask you if you'd mind trying to help with the house until times get better?

LES (*staggered*)   But, Papa—How?

VIC   Dan's paying you $10 a week, isn't he?

LES   Yes. But I need every cent for school—(*suddenly understanding*) You don't mean you want me to drop out—?

VIC   I hate mighty bad to ask it, son—.

LES (*regretfully*)   I see.

VIC   You'd only be out this Quarter—By spring I'm sure I'll be back on the job—?

LES (*going*)   OK. Papa. I'll do it.

VIC (*gratefully*)   Thank you, Son. You'll never regret it. (*exit LES*)

PERCY (*entering from street, as LES passes him hurriedly*)   Well! What's the matter with him?

VIC   Nothing.—How's things with you?

PERCY   Oh, I guess I'm still kicking—How're you, Mrs. Brooks. (*he turns to hall-tree to doff wraps*)

BROOKS   Pretty fair, I reckon.

VIC (*rejoining him*)   Look, Percy. Do me a favor. It looks like Caroline's got the flu, and Phillip's trying to come down with it—Let me have a little money—About a hundred dollars.

PERCY (*staggered*)   A hundred dollars! Captain, I ain't got the first quarter. Business at the hotel is shot to hell, and that Chippy I'm tied up with is bleeding me to death——(ELLA *enters and he nods to her*)

VIC (*sighing*)   Well, I guess that settles that. (*pause*) I just thought I might be able to let Les stay in school.

PERCY   Is it that bad?

VIC   Couldn't be worse.

PERCY (*cynically*)   I thought Wanda was doing all right!

ELLA (*catching note in his voice*)   What do you mean?

PERCY (*darkly*)   Where is she?

ELLA (*eying him*)   In her room, I guess.

PERCY   Where'd she get that fur coat?

ELLA   What fur coat?

PERCY   She's got a fur coat, hasn't she?

ELLA   No. She's got a cloth coat.

PERCY   Just like I thought.

VIC   What do you mean, Percy?

PERCY   I suppose you've got trouble enough. But for her sake, I guess I might as well tell you——

VIC   Do you mean Wanda's been in some kind of trouble?

PERCY   I don't know. But I saw her in the Dreamland with a *Nogooder*, wearing a sealskin coat.

BROOKS (*incredulously*)   A sealskin coat . . .

PERCY   Yep——

ELLA   You can't mean it!

PERCY   And if it didn't cost $500, it didn't cost a dime!

ELLA (*stunned*)   Lord have mercy!

PERCY (*grimly*)   I knew she was supposed to be taking care of the house. So . . . I figured it couldn't mean but one thing.

BROOKS (*outraged*)   I been 'spectin' somethin' like this——(*to* ELLA) I told you! I warned you!

ELLA (*striding to foot of stairs, calling*) Wanda!

WANDA (*above, timorously*)   Yes! What is it?

ELLA (*imperatively*)   Come down here!

VIC (*hanging on to straw*)   Maybe she borrowed it from somebody!

PERCY (*cynically*)   Where're you going to find anybody dumb enough to take that kind of risk?

WANDA (*appearing above, a note of fear in her voice, sensing the impending storm*)   What is it, Mama? (*slowly, she descends*)

ELLA (*abruptly, as she reaches floor*)   Where's that sealskin coat you been wearing?

WANDA   What sealskin coat?

PERCY (*coldly*)   The one you had on last night, that's what!

WANDA (*speechless*)   Last night? (*she glances desperately around, trapped*)

VIC   You did have on one, didn't you?

ELLA   And don't try to lie either, because Percy saw you!

WANDA (*cornered*)   But, Mama—Uncle Percy doesn't know what he's talking about— I . . . I . . .

VIC (*sharply*)   Answer my question! Didn't you have on such a coat?

WANDA (*after a moment*)   Yes. I did.

ELLA   Where'd you get it?

WANDA (*suddenly fighting*)   I bought it.

ELLA   You bought it? When? Where'd you get $500 to pay for it.

WANDA   It isn't paid for . . . I just got it out Christmas.

VIC   Well, where is it?

WANDA (*smoldering*)   Claudine's.

BROOKS (*sharply*)   Sounds mighty fishy to me!

ELLA   What's it doing at Claudine's if you bought it?

WANDA   I've been leaving it there because I knew you'd kick about my having it.

ELLA   You're lying. You're lying as fast as you can open your mouth!

WANDA   I'm not lying. It's the truth!

ELLA   And I suppose you're going to try to tell me you've got receipts to show for it?

WANDA   Yes, I have.

VIC   Get them!

WANDA (*embarrassed*)   I can't right now. They're over at Claudine's.

BROOKS (*grunting wisely*)   Ugh Phumn!

WANDA (*desperately*)   Oh, I know what you're thinking. But it's true. I did buy that coat, and I've got the receipts to prove it!

ELLA   Well, you just get out of here and get them. And don't come back till you bring them, either. (WANDA *runs upstairs*)

BROOKS (*coldly*)   Well, I reckon you'd better tell her goodbye, then!

VIC (*loyally*)   I believe she's telling the truth.

BROOKS (*angrily*)   If I was you, I wouldn't open mah mouth—You and Percy neither!

PERCY (*angrily*)   Now what the hell did I have to do with it?

BROOKS (*accusingly*)   She took after you, didn't she? If it hadn't been for you round here setting' her sich a bad example, she never would-er started this "goin' live" business—(*sharply*) And, Ella, if I was you, I'd bless him out, and Vic, too, right this minute—(*she pauses, as* WANDA *descends and goes out in silence, and a wave of loving regret flows over her and breaks in a note of sad prophecy*) That gal's goin' make your heartache one of these days, sure's you're born! (*silence*)

VIC (*turning to stairs, after a moment*)   I'm going up and get into my uniform before the committee comes—(*seeing the door opening, he halts and* DAN *enters*)

DAN (*pouncing upon him*)   Say, Vic. What do you mean by taking that boy out of school?

VIC (*annoyed*)   Now hold your horses. Lester Mason happens to be my son!

DAN   So what? I'm responsible for him being in school.

VIC   I grant you that. But you can be civil about it—

DAN   You've got a nerve!

VIC   Nevermind. In the first place, it's only temporary. I just asked him to sacrifice going back this quarter.

DAN   What right've you got to demand such a sacrifice?

VIC   I'd rather not discuss that.

DAN   Oh, you wouldn't, eh? Well, let me tell you this: I'm not paying Les to support you. Not by a damn sight!

PERCY   I wouldn't take that attitude, Dan. Put yourself in his place. The children are upstairs sick in bed, and you know how far the little money goes Wanda's been making.

DAN (*joining him, accusingly*)   Yeah. You can think of that now. But when I saw this coming and tried to warn him, you were the first to jump up and claim I was wrong.

PERCY   That's history now!

VIC   Nevermind, Percy. Let him go on. He's been waiting for a chance to try to rub it in.

DAN (*surprised*)   I'm not trying to rub anything—

VIC   Actions speak louder than words. You know I'm up against it. You know I've been up against it for months. But you've got your first time to offer me a dime.

DAN   I'm not offering my money to anyone who's too proud to ask for it.

VIC   So you wanted me to come crawling to you, eh?

PERCY   Yeah, So he could Lord it over you!

DAN   Lord, hell! You're both just jealous of my success.—But just to show you there's nothing cheap about me, I tell you what I'll do. I'll let you have enough money to see you through—

PERCY (*surprised*)   No!

DAN   That is, if you're willing to give up this foolish Garvey business and act like you've got some sense?

VIC   What exactly do you mean?

DAN   I'll let you have two or three hundred dollars, if you'll turn over that Black Star Line Stock.

ELLA   Dan, you don't mean it?

VIC   As collateral?

DAN   Collateral hell! What kind of a business man do you think I am?

VIC   You'd sell it, then?

DAN   What do you care, as long as I'm sucker enough to take it off your hands—

VIC   Phumph! Big hearted Dan—But forget it. I can't do it.

DAN   No. You'd rather frustrate the life of your son, while you hang on to your silly dream!

VIC   Call it what you like. At my age a man can't start looking forward to carrying a hod for the rest of his life.

DAN   At your age a man should be thinking about the future of his children.

VIC   That's just it. Things haven't changed for us in this country, have they? Aren't we still in the hands of the enemy, brow-beaten, stigmatized—(*wearily*) But what's the use—If you want to lend me a little money, all right. I'll appreciate it and pay you back, if it takes me till my dying day. But don't ask me to part with my stock.

(LES *enters*)

DAN   Business is business—Ella, you see my point, don't you?

ELLA   Yes, I do—Vic, give it to him. Take the money. It can't hurt Garvey. It will only be a matter of it changing hands—

VIC   Ella, that stock's worth $1500, have you forgotten that?

ELLA   It won't be worth a dime if Caroline needs a doctor!

PERCY (*supporting her*)   A smart flea, Captain, knows when to hop!

VIC (*firmly*)   I've had my say.

ELLA   Yes, you have. But I haven't had mine. I'm getting sick to death of this scrimping and worrying and waiting from day to day for something that never comes—(*furiously*) Do you know the rent hasn't been paid? That we hardly got bread to eat in this house? And the children need shoes?

VIC   It's no use getting hot, Ella. I know all that. But good sense should tell you; it's a mighty poor slave that'll give up trying to break his chains just because there's a nick in the hammer!

DAN (*going*)   OK. Captain. If you're going to remain a fool, hang on to your stock. I'm not going to argue with you all night. I'm going. But get this through your head; you needn't expect a dime from me as long as you do. (*exit*)

ELLA   Wait, Dan—(*desperately*) Call him back, Vic. Call him back!

VIC   It's no use, Ella—(*going*) The stock is all we've got. (*he ascends stairs. Exit*)

LES   What's it all about, Mama—(*she turns in silence, and crosses swiftly to go out back, to* PERCY) Is this because Papa's taking me out of school?

PERCY   Not exactly—(*there is a knock at the front door*)

BROOKS (*hearing it*)   Answer the door, Les—Don't you hear somebody knocking?

LES (*opens door to admit* PISZER, *a young Jewish student, wearing a mackinaw and tam to match*) Piszer! This is a surprise! Come in!

PISZER (*warmly in response to the other's friendliness*)   Hello, Mason. I was on my way downtown, and I just thought I'd drop by to see if you'd care to go along?

LES   On a night like this! You're kidding. But come, I want you to meet my folks—

ELLA (*reentering*)   Who is it, Les?

LES   Mom, this is Nathan Piszer, my classmate—Piszer, my mother.

ELLA (*graciously*)   I'm very pleased to welcome you into our home.

PISZER (*shaking hands*)   You're very cordial, Mrs. Mason. Thank you.

LES   My Grandmother, Mrs. Brooks—

BROOKS (*courtseying*)   I'm pleased to meet you.

LES   And my uncle, Mr. Mason.

PERCY (*shaking hands*)   How do you do?

LES   Give me your coat and sit down.

ELLA   Yes, do, Mr. Piszer. You're no stranger here. Les has talked so much about you, we all feel we know you.

PISZER   Thank you, Mrs. Mason. But seriously, I can't stay. (*turning to* LES) I'm on my way down to Orchestra Hall, and I thought perhaps you might like to go along—Some Van Gorham is lecturing on Russia, and they say he's a pretty keen observer—?

LES   Gee, I'd like to. But I m afraid I can't tonight. You see, we're holding a little celebration for my Dad—and—

PISZER   Is that so? Then I'm probably intruding—

LES   No, no! Not at all. We'd like you to stay, wouldn't we, Mama?

ELLA   Yes, you must, Mr. Piszer.

LES (*pressing him*)   Then, I want you to meet my Dad—

PISZER (*intrigued*)   I'd like to—

LES   Good—Give me your coat—

PISZER (*doffing coat*)   But why're you honoring him?

LES (*laughing*)   You've got me there! But you see he's one of the local leaders of the Garvey Movement, and I guess it's a sort of surprise. (*he takes coat*)

PISZER (*following him*)   You say the Garvey Movement—? Gospell discussed it in class the other day—But I'd no idea your folks were connected with it.

LES (*joining him and going to couch*)   What'd Gospell have to say?

ELLA (*going*)   You must excuse me, Mr. Piszer. But I must get into the kitchen—Come, Mama, and fix Phillip's eggnog.

BROOKS (*all a-flutter*)   I'm so sorry to leave you, Mr. Piszer. Your conversation is so interesting. (*exit with* ELLA)

LES (*offering Piszer chair*)   Go on, Piszer. What'd Gospell have to say?

PISZER   Well, frankly, he thought the movement visionary.

LES   He did, hunh? But I guess he'd say the same about the Back-To-Palestine idea of your people. But there's nothing impractical about it. There's no hope for my race in this country, and any program that offers escape is all right with me—How about you, Uncle Percy?

PERCY   Of course, Les. But you can't expect him to see it like we do.

PISZER   I don't know, Mr. Mason. Gospell seemed to think neither of them would hold water—As he pointed out, there may be another solution.

LES   Did he say that?

PISZER   Yes. He thinks the only lasting solution for the problem of minority groups today is unity with the majority on a common ground.

LES *(laughing)*   That's rich! Unity with the majority on a common ground!

PISZER   You're skeptical—?

PERCY   As a Jew, can *you* blame him?

PISZER   In a way—yes.

LES *(convinced)*   Nothing could be more visionary?

PISZER   It may sound remote. But what's there to prevent all the underprivileged from getting together on problems in which they have a common interest?

LES   You want me to tell you?

PISZER   Sure—Go ahead.

LES *(bitterly)*   The same thing that makes them call you "Sheeny" and me "Nigger!"

PISZER   Oh, no doubt most of my people would say the same. But I'm beginning to wonder if it isn't a matter of simply being just distrustful.

LES   We'd be fools not to be.

PERCY   Right, Kid. All this inter-racial concilliation is nothing but a trap to catch the Negro in!

PISZER   But what about Socialism?

LES *(laughing)*   What?—Don't tell me you've gone Bolshevik?

PISZER   Have you read Lenin?

LES *(subsiding)*   No—Have you?

PISZER   A fellow loaned me a copy of his "State and Revolution" yesterday, and it kept me awake all night.

LES *(glancing at PERCY)*   Yeah—

PISZER   Yeah. Perhaps, you'd like to see it—?

BROOKS *(crossing with eggnog)*   'Scuse passin, Les. I got to get upstairs to mah Sick.

(There is a loud knocking and stomping out front)

LES *(springing up, and going to door)*   Sounds like a mob! *(admitting group)* Oh, hello, Mr. Strawder—Come on in, you all! *(calling)* Mama! Here's Mr. Strawder and them!

(STRAWDER and the others pile in, doffing their overcoats to reveal the splendor of their regalia—the men, wearing colored sashes above their black, red-striped uniforms—the women, in white with black crosses on their sleeves, the insignia of the Black Cross Nurses of the Movement. All, in high spirits and good cheer)

COTTON *(as they pile in, excitedly)*   Where's Brother Mason—Where's the Captain what ain't no Captain no more!—*(one of the NURSES claps her hands across his mouth, and STRAWDER glares at him angrily)*

ELLA *(entering with pot of steaming eggnog)*   I'm afraid we've only got standing room. But I've made some eggnog to warm you up!

HARPER *(leading cheering, as BLACK CROSS NURSES assist ELLA in serving)*   Hurray, for Sister Mason!

COTTON   Now that's right. It's just what we need on a night like this—*(seeing VIC descending with MRS. BROOKS behind him)* Make way for the Lord of Agriculture!—*(one of the NURSES snatches his arm, and he, recognizing his error, claps the palm of his hand across his mouth and creeps into corner, as STRAWDER glares at him angrily. BROOKS comes down to aid in serving)*

STRAWDER *(commanding)*   Silence! *(addressing VIC, as the latter halts on stairs)* Brother Mason, it is my great privilege and honor to greet you on this occasion, and to convey to you the sentiments of our great president. *(he pauses dramatically)* For your great paper on the Future of Cooperative Farming in Africa, what you read at the Negro World Conference, our great leader has commanded me to greet you with the title of Lord of Agriculture of the Provisional Republic of Africa—*(the crowd cheers)* Quiet, everybody. Let me finish before you start celebrating. *(PHILLIP and CAROLINE creep down on stairs to peep through bannister. To VIC)* Step down, my Lord—*(as VIC descends, he turns)* Sister Gabrella! *(SISTER GABRELLA and another NURSE step forward with long red sash, which they place on VIC)*

PISZER *(to LES, aside)*   Lord of Agriculture? I don't get it!

LES *(aside)*   It means head of the Department of Agriculture.

PISZER   Why not "Secretary?"

LES   It's more striking, I guess.

PISZER   Yeah. But less democratic, eh?

STRAWDER (*as the* NURSES *step back from* VIC)
And now, my Lord, I bestow upon you this
emblem of your high and mighty rank! (*the
group cheers, as he pins on medallion*)

PHILLIP   Look at Papa!

ELLA   Children—Get back to bed! (*they
scamper off above*)

HARPER (*lifting glass*)   I want to make a
toast. . . . Friends and Brothers of the UNIA,
let us drink to the man who has put us on the
map and set our banner flying before the eyes
of our Black brothers all over the world, Victor
Mason, Lord of Agriculture of the Republic of
Africa, the glory of our local chapter today—

COTTON   Speech! Speech!

VIC (*lifting his hand for silence, as others go on
crying*)   Brothers and Sisters, I thank you for
this great display of affection. (*suddenly
solemn*) But I cannot respond to your toast as
something extended to me personally. I appreciate the great honor which our leader has
conferred upon me. But I feel I ought to call
your attention to the way I think about what
I've done . . . I only prepared and read a
paper . . . It may be good as some say. Yet it's
only a paper, and none of the things it deals
with have been accomplished. We're still in
the hands of the enemy, with our children cut
off from opportunity, and the lynch-rope and
faggot lying ready for any Black man who
dares to raise his head. (*grievously*) We have
yet, my friends, to acquire a single inch of the
soil of Africa we can call our own. And while
we celebrate, our great leader stands within
the shadow of the penitentiary, branded as a
common criminal . . . These are dark and terrible truths, my friends, and as I face them, I
feel—well, the only proper response I can
make to your toast, is to ask you to drink a
pledge with me. (*lifting cup, which is handed
him*) Brothers and Sisters and members of my
family, let us pledge our hearts and minds and
the last ounce of our strength to carry on—to
carry on without ceasing, until our cause is
won, and the Black man has achieved his
place in the Godgiven sun: A free man, honored and respected in the eyes of the nations
of the world!

(*The silence is eloquent, as they all drink*)

STRAWDER (*moved*)   My Lord, that was a
speech to be proud of! (*his tone is like a bene-*

diction, *and* VIC *is seen aloof, his eye fixed on his
dark star, as the curtain descends*)

Scene Three

(TIME: *early evening, a month later.*

*The atmosphere remains the same, a dreariness
hanging over all like a pall and seeming to pene-
trate through the window from the sooty snow-
laden street, as* PHILLIP *sits there looking out.*
CAROLINE *is lying on the couch beneath a quilt,
with her grandmother beside her, whom she is
watching as she dresses a black doll*)

CAROLINE (*petulantly, after a moment*)
That's not right, Grandma!

BROOKS (*tossing the doll in the other's lap with
an impatient thrust, then rising*)   Here, you
take this black thing! I don't want no more to
do with it! (PHILLIP *darts a glance at her, and simultaneously kicks the rocker in an automatic, vicious reflex*) Are you trying to break that chair?
What's the matter with you? (*guiltily*) You act
like you crazy. (PHILLIP *rises abruptly and crosses
to Victrola, where he sulks, as she goes on, com-
plainingly*) I never seen sich chillun—for gittin'
on a person's nerves!

CAROLINE   Awh, Grandma, I was just telling
you, you got her skirt on backwards.

BROOKS (*annoyed at herself*)   I reckon I
ought to know which is the front, when I
made it.

CAROLINE (*to her doll*)   Poor lil Black Judy.
Grandma treats that honey-child like an orphan, don't she?

(*There is a sound of stomping on the porch*)

LES (*entering, as they all turn to look*)   Phew!
(*closing the door behind him, he blows his breath
into his fists, then, flapping his arms, goes on to*
PHILLIP) You're lucky you didn't have to go to
school today!

BROOKS   How cold is it now?

LES (*hanging his coat up*)   About 10 below, I
guess. (*he goes up stairs*)

ELLA (*appearing from rear*)   Was that Les?

CAROLINE   Yes'm.

ELLA (*seeing* PHILLIP *in corner*)   What're you
doing sulking over there?

PHILLIP (*dully*)   Nothing. (*she eyes him questioningly*)

BROOKS (*seeing* VIC *descending*)   Dinner
'bout ready?

ELLA   Just about.

VIC   Anybody seen the paper?

ELLA (*turning to go*)   There isn't any paper.

VIC (*annoyed, going to window*)   There isn't?—
I'm going to have to write in about that boy
yet!

ELLA   You'd do better paying his bill!

VIC (*turning in surprise*)   You haven't paid
him?

ELLA   What was I going to pay him with?

VIC (*coming over*)   But it ain't but fifteen
cents a week! (*in huff*) I can't see why in God's
world you can't manage that!

ELLA (*going, angrily*)   Is that so? Well, hereafter you see that he gets it! (*exit rear*)

VIC (*sick*)   Phumph! (*the entrance of* WANDA
*from the street is like a shock to him, for she is in
tears and shivering*) Now what's the matter
with you? And where's your coat?

(LES *descends*)

WANDA (*sobbing*)   They took it!

BROOKS   Who took it?

LES (*excitedly*)   Stickup men?

WANDA   No . . . The Sheriff.

BROOKS (*excitedly*)   The Sheriff! (*shouting*)
Ella!

VIC (*amazed*)   But how?

WANDA (*extending paper*)   He just took it
with this.

VIC (*joining her*)   What is it—a lien?

ELLA (*entering*)   What's the matter?

BROOKS (*dramatically*)   The Sheriff's done
had-er hold of Wanda. Done took that sealskin coat off her!

VIC (*to* WANDA)   How many payments do
you owe?

WANDA   Only seven.

VIC   Seven—That's $35—(*shaking his head,
helplessly*) Lord, Lord!—But there's nothing I
can do.

ELLA   More good money burnt up! (WANDA
bursts into tears anew, and runs upstairs)

LES   But Papa. She practically owns the
coat!

VIC   What does the law care!

BROOKS   She had no business buyin it!

(*There is silence, and* DAN, *swaddled in an expensive grey ulster, enters—a vulturous smirk on his
lips*)

VIC   What brings you here on a night like
this?

DAN (*swaggering down*)   Then you haven't
heard—?

VIC   Heard what?

DAN   The news about Garvey.

VIC   No. What about him?

DAN (*triumphantly*)   They took him to Atlanta today, that's what!

LES   Oh, no!

VIC (*staggered*)   Are you sure?

DAN   You bet! I told you that monkeychaser
was no good!

VIC   But the Supreme Court—?

DAN   Denied his appeal, and they took him
into custody this morning.

VIC (*sitting with an air of defeat*)   Well, sir!

ELLA (*sympathetically*)   Don't take it so hard,
Vic. It's no more than you expected.

VIC   I guess you're right, Ella. He never had
a chance. But what makes it hard—the thing
that really hurts so is the part our folks had in
the whole frame up.

LES   How do you mean, Papa?

VIC   I'm talking about our so-called leaders,
Son. They're the ones who sicced the white
folks on him. In their jealousy and fear of his
power they turned informers—The assassins!
Assassins!

BROOKS   Les, I thought you told me Marcus
Garvey confessed 'bout that money?

LES (*hesitantly*)   Well, he did, Grandma. But
not for stealing himself. It was the ones he
trusted.

DAN   Bah! They were all in cahoots together. It came out at the trial—(*turning to*
VIC) But you can't stand the truth. Instead of
admitting you were wrong, you've got to try to
stigmatize your own people. I told you all
along—

ELLA (*ominously*)   Now just a minute, Dan.
If you've come here to crow over us, you can
get out!

DAN   Hold on, Ella. Don't misunderstand
me. I feel as bad over this thing as you do. But
there's such a thing as reason—First he tried
to put the blame on the white folks for wanting to break up the movement. Now it's our
own leaders—What kind of sense is that?—
Hell, the truth is the truth!

VIC (*rising*)   Yeah. But if it was big as the
Woolworth Building you wouldn't see it. (*goes
to telephone*) Victory 11780.

ELLA   Who're you calling?

VIC   Strawder. (*as his call is answered*) That

you, Count? This is Mason. Have you heard about Garvey? . . . (*after a moment*) Well, you needn't do that. We should call a meeting right away, in my judgment. Show the white folks we can't be fooled by their trickery. Explain to the members . . . How about Sunday? . . . Yes, yes, exactly. You get out the cards. What?—I'll see that you get the keys right away. Goodbye—(*hanging up*) We'll show them—Les, get your coat, and take these keys to the hall to Count Strawder.

LES (*taking keys*)   Yes, Sir. (*he goes to get coat*)

DAN   For Christ's sake, Vic. Why in the hell don't you wake up? Your movement's dead as a mackrel!

VIC (*angrily*)   Why do you persist in meddling in my affairs?

DAN (*backing away*)   OK, OK, Big shot. (*going. Prophetically*) But you mark my word: With Garvey in jail, your $1500 is burnt up, and from now on, your movement's going to peter out like a pail full of water with a hole in the bottom. (*exit*)

ELLA   You'd better come and get your dinner, Vic. (*to* PHILLIP) Go set the table. (*exit* PHILLIP)

VIC   No, Ella. You all go ahead. I'm going up and lie down for a while.

LES (*as father turns to go*)   I'm sorry, Papa.

VIC   It's a mighty blow, Son. But no man is indispensable to a good cause. We'll carry on.

ELLA (*arresting him*)   If you don't mind, Vic. Take Caroline up to bed. She's been down here too long already—(*to* LES) And you'd better go get that dinner before you go out of here.

LES   But the keys—?

ELLA   They can wait. You need something in your stomach. (*to* CAROLINE, *as* VIC *bears her away*) I'll bring you some soup in a little while. (*exit* LES *to kitchen*)

VIC (*carrying* CAROLINE *above*)   How do you feel?

CAROLINE   All right. (*exit* VIC *and* CAROLINE)

ELLA (*seeing her mother trying to thread needle*) Give it to me, Mama.

BROOKS (*as* ELLA *threads it*)   Well, Ella. It looks like Dan was right after all—

ELLA   Mama, I'm in no mood to stand your criticism this evening!

BROOKS   No, I reckon not. After the food we'll leave. (*she rummages through work basket*) Now, where's my sizzers? (*angrily*) Ain't no-

body teched them sizzers but Phillip. (*rising to call*) Phillip!

PHILLIP (*in rear*)   Yes'm!

BROOKS (*crossing*)   Where's my sizzers?

PHILLIP (*in rear*)   I don't know, Grandma. I ain't seen em!

BROOKS (*rushing out*)   You ain't hunh? . . . You stinkin' rascal! (*there is an outburst from* PHILLIP) Didn't I tell you not to bother my sizzers!

ELLA (*crossing, her voice rising above the shouts of the child*)   Turn him loose, Mama! Turn him loose! (*the cries of the child subside, and* BROOKS *enters in a huff, out of breath*) Lord, Mama, I don't know what I'm going to do about you. I told you if you want any of the children whipped to call me or Vic to do it for you. You see how it wears you out. You can't be wrestling with that boy! The first thing you know you'll fall and knock your head against something! (PHILLIP *enters, meanwhile, sulking as he glares at* GRANDMOTHER)

BROOKS (*angrily*)   You don't have to beat 'round the stump! (*shaking her finger at* PHILLIP) If you don't want me to put mah hands on that Black scamp, why don't you say so?

ELLA (*angrily*)   Mama, I've asked you not to call that boy Black where he can hear you!

BROOKS   Yes he's Black. Black like his cranky Daddy!

ELLA   Don't mind her, Phillip—Go upstairs and sit with Caroline till I call you. (PHILLIP *ascends stairs and slowly disappears*)

BROOKS   But I know when my bread is brown. (*going out rear*) I'm goin' git my few rags and git out-er here. That's what I'm goin' do! (*exit rear*)

ELLA (*crossing to door there*)   Oh, yeah? And where do you think you're going to find a place to stay—Juanita's?

BROOKS (*offstage*)   Yes, Juanita's! She'll give me a place to lay mah weary head.

ELLA   She will, hunh? You just wait. You'll see!

BROOKS (*entering with armful of clothing*) Don't you fool yourself. Don't you do it. Juanita's got Dupree blood in her veins! (*she dumps garments on couch*)

ELLA   You and your Dupree blood!—But I know what's the matter with you. You want to get over to Dan's where you think you won't suffer—!

BROOKS   That's a lie!

ELLA *(furiously)*   For ten years this house has been good enough for you. But now you think we're in the bread line. So you want to save your own skin. You want to get over there where you think you'll be safe!

BROOKS   That's another lie! Tain't no sich! *(VIC appears above, buttoning jacket. But she doesn't see him)* You's jes making that up out-er jealousy, like that evil, Black, good-for-nothin' fool you call your husband!

VIC *(woundedly)*   So!

ELLA *(glancing up, frightened)*   Vic!

(BROOKS, realizing she has committed the unpardonable sin in inner-racial relations, backs up)

VIC *(coming down, his voice cold and hostile)* So I'm a evil, Black, good-for-nothing nigger!

ELLA *(joining him, anxiously)*   For God's sake, Vic. Overlook it!

VIC *(to BROOKS, as she stands at bay)* What've I ever done to make you say such a harsh thing about me?

ELLA *(soothingly)*   Nothing, Vic. And she knows it.

BROOKS *(in belligerent fear)*   Don't you put no words in mah mouth! I ain't scared of him and nobody like him.

ELLA *(striding toward her)*   Will you shut up!

BROOKS   Don't you tell me to shut up! Don't you do it!

ELLA *(turning to VIC)*   Don't pay her no mind, Vic. She's just upset. Excited—because I got after her about whipping Phillip!

VIC   You needn't try to cover up for her, Ella. I've stumbled into something and you know it!

ELLA   But she's just imagining things—

VIC   Like calling me the dirtiest thing she can think of, eh?

ELLA   Don't get off on the wrong track, Vic. What she said she said out of anger with me. And if you hadn't come down here so quietly, you never would've heard her.

VIC *(angrily)*   What am I supposed to do, blow a trumpet everytime I move in my own house?

ELLA   No, Vic. Of course not. I only meant—

VIC *(to BROOKS, coldly)*   I'm too Black for your Dupree blood, isn't that it?

BROOKS *(venomously)*   The cap must fit you or you wouldn't be wearing it!

ELLA *(pained)*   Oh, Mama!

VIC   You miserable old hypocrite.

BROOKS   Well, there's one thing. I ain't never been no hypocrite with you!

ELLA   Lord, Mama. You ought to be ashamed of yourself!

BROOKS   Shame nothin'. I ain't got nothing to be shamed of!

VIC *(coldly)*   No. But you let this sink into your twisted soul. You don't hate me. You envy me. You envy my Black skin because in your heart, you know yours is nothing but a badge of shame!

ELLA *(hurt)*   Oh, Vic!

BROOKS   Ella, you goin' stand there and let him insult me like that?

ELLA *(to VIC)*   Could she help it if she was born out of wedlock?

VIC *(sharply)*   No. What I resent is her vicious attitude. She's got nothing against me, and she knows it. But she's like the rest of her kind, who let the color of their skin drive them to think Black people are some kind of dirt beneath their feet, when nothing could be more idiotic than the pride they take in the blood of their raping ancestors!

BROOKS   You hear that, Ella! *(crying in outrage, as she gathers clothing)* To think the day would ever come when anybody'd say sich things bout me! But I'll git you. I'll git even with you, you Black viper, if it's the last thing I do! *(going to door and turning with parting shot)* You'll see if I don't! *(exit)*

ELLA *(stunned)*   If anybody had told me you could be so petty, I'd've spit on them!

VIC *(quietly)*   The truth always seem ugly when it's hard to look at. But a man can't stand everything.

ELLA *(preoccupiedly)*   It serves me right. I should've listened years ago.

VIC   Just what do you mean by that?

ELLA   Don't ask me what I mean. Don't ask me anything.

VIC   But, Ella—

ELLA *(venemously)*   I despise you!

VIC   Ella, for God's sake—

(LES appears in door right)

ELLA   Yes, I despise you. You hear me. I despise you! And I think you're everything Mama said and then some. You ain't nothing but an evil, Black fool!

LES (*plunging forward*)   For Christ's sake, Mama! What're you saying?

ELLA   Get back in that kitchen and finish your supper, and stay out of my business!

LES   But, Mama—You can't mean what you said—Not you!

VIC   Do as you're told, and get back in your place!

LES   No, Papa. I heard everything, and it isn't fair!

VIC   Shut up! Your Ma's just upset—though God knows I had no intention of hurting her feelings.—(*distraught*) I guess the news about Garvey, then this, just about floored me—(*to* ELLA) But you must know I meant no offense to you.

ELLA (*bitterly*)   You can keep your apologies. I don't want them. For twenty years I've let you treat me like a doormat, and run things to suit yourself. (*furiously*) And now you've got the nerve to insult Mama right before my face. Who do you think you are, King Jesus!

VIC (*quietly*)   I've always considered you, Ella.

ELLA   You let Wanda quit school against my wishes! Who else but you and your fool ideas started her on the road to hell? And this Garvey business: Where's all the money I helped you save? (*in sudden tears*) Whose fault is it I can't stop a bread wagon to feed my children?

VIC (*shouting*)   So you blame me for the world!

LES   Oh, Please—! Both of you—calm yourselves—

ELLA (*ignoring him*)   I've been a woman and a wife to you. But I'm through with you! (*she starts out*)

LES   Oh, Mama, no! Wait a minute—

ELLA (*turning to shout*)   You hear me. I'm through with you!

VIC (*joining her*)   You can't mean that, Ella. You wouldn't leave me?

ELLA   No. But I can make you wish I would!—If it wasn't for Caroline and the rest, I'd follow Mama out of this house and never put my feet back in it again!

VIC (*sadly*)   I'll get out if you want me to.

ELLA (*going*)   Suit yourself. Get out or stay! Or better still, go on to Africa. Maybe you'll find the company of your own kind in the jungle! (*exit above*)

VIC (*wounded grievously, and crying aloud, he, staggers down to bang the back of the chair beside couch*)   Prejudice! Prejudice! Everywhere you turn, nothing but prejudice! A Black man can't even get away from it in his own house! (*overwhelmed by the irony, he emits a prolonged grunt*) Phummmmmnnnnh! Phummmmmnnnh! Phummmmmnnnnh! (*impelled by the onslaught of pain, as he recognizes the very essence of his oppression, his voice reverberates with agony*) And like a fool I dreamed of getting away from it in Africa! (*slowly, he sinks into the chair, and* LES *is seen drawing near to place his hand on his shoulder in sympathy and understanding, as the curtain falls*)

ACT THREE

Scene One

(TIME: *1932, or ten years later.*

The living-room is the same, except that now everywhere is manifest some sign of the family's desperate impoverishment, as it continues its struggle in the midst of the general breakdown of the nation's economy, or the great depression.

Present are ELLA, *wearing a frayed apron and the aspect of care;* WANDA, *in a good skirt and sweater of light material—indicative of her continued capacity to earn a living; and* MARKS, *a Used-Furniture dealer, in a disreputable old suit and fedora*)

MARKS (*a man of fifty-odd years with eloquent gestures, seemingly at the end of his wits in the effort to strike a bargain*)   Sell! Sell! Efery-body vants to sell. But nobody vants to buy.—Can I help it if effery-body vants to sell, Mrs. Mason, and nobody vants to buy?—Maybe you didn't hear there's a depression—?

ELLA (*stubbornly*)   But, Mr. Marks, you can give me more than $3 for that couch. I paid $79 for it!

MARKS (*with a quick, snapping glance at couch*) You should pay $79 for such a couch—Oh, moi, oh, moi—$79 for such a couch!—Come, I'll make it $3.50.

WANDA (*outraged*) $3.50!

MARKS (*confidingly*)   To anybody else I wouldn't pay half so much.

ELLA   I wouldn't think of it.

MARKS (*appealingly*)   Maybe I should keep it a whole year and couldn't sell it to nobody!

WANDA   Oh, yeah!

ELLA *(indicating machine)*   Well, what'll you give me for that Victrola?

MARKS *(throwing up his hands)*   The Victrola you couldn't giff me!

WANDA   Oh, no—?

MARKS *(annoyed by her sarcasm)*   Listen, Lady. Business is bad—You know that? Nobody vants to buy a Victrola. Nobody wants to buy anything. *(to ELLA)* Vell, vat you say?

ELLA *(indicating chair center)*   What about that chair—?

MARKS *(examining chair, slowly)*   The chair—it isn't so good. But . . . maybe vit the chair and couch together I could giff you $5.

WANDA *(angrily)*   Tell him to go to hell, Mama!

MARKS   Vat's the matter vit you? I offer Mrs. Mason the top price, and you tell me to go to hell!—You think I ain't got no feelings?—I'm a man vit a family. You vant I should ruin myself?

WANDA   Swell chance, you've got to ruin yourself!

MARKS *(turning to ELLA)*   Vell, vat you say? You vant to sell?

ELLA *(dejectedly)*   No. Nevermind. I just thought I could raise a few dollars to help me get another place. But the little you offer won't do us any good.

MARKS *(sympathetically)*   Times are bad, Mrs. Mason.—But you vant find anybody'll giff you more, even if you should search the city over.

ELLA *(bitterly)*   I'd rather put them in the stove! *(she wipes her eyes)*

WANDA   Don't, Mama.

MARKS   Come, I'll giff you $6?

WANDA   Big hearted Mr. Marks!

ELLA *(desperately)*   Make it $10 and you can have them.

WANDA   No, Mama. No!

MARKS   I should make it $10? Vy I could buy a finer couch and chair for $5—*(he starts out)* You don't vant to do business, Mrs. Mason.

ELLA   Take them for $8.

MARKS *(with finality)*   I'll giff you $6.50 and no more!

ELLA *(breaking)*   I'll chop them to pieces first!

WANDA *(furiously)*   You get out of here— You—you—you're a disgrace to your race!

MARKS *(backing out)*   All right! All right! Don't get sore!

CLAUDINE *(as he bumps into her as she enters)* Hey! Why don't you look where you're going—What're you a crab or something?

MARKS *(disappearing)*   Escuse me—*(exit MARKS)*

WANDA *(half-heartedly greeting the newcomer—in a summer frock, quite chic)*   Hello, Claudine.

CLAUDINE *(noticing ELLA, as she comes down)* What's the matter—?

WANDA *(embarrassed)*   Don't cry, Mama. Everything's going to be all right. You go upstairs and lie down for a while and quiet your nerves.

CLAUDINE *(sympathetically)*   Is there anything I can do for you, Mrs. Mason?

ELLA   No, Claudine. I guess I'll just have to let them set us out, and make the best of it. *(she climbs stairs in tears)*

CLAUDINE *(sitting on arm of couch)*   You all going to be evicted, too, hunh?

WANDA   I guess so. Papa's gone to Court now.

CLAUDINE   Well, that's too bad!

WANDA *(crossing to window seat)*   Mama tried to raise a little money on the furniture. But I wish you could've seen how he tried to take advantage of her—

CLAUDINE   Well, it's all your own fault!

WANDA   Where do you get that stuff; it's my fault?

CLAUDINE   If you had any sense you wouldn't be in this trouble.

WANDA   Oh, yeah?

CLAUDINE   You're damn right. *(nervously, she lights cigarette)* I wish I could get a break with an old chump like Hogan. I'd show you something. I'd take his sugar so quick, he'd think I was a gangster!

WANDA   I've told you, I don't go for *that!*

CLAUDINE   No. You're too dumb.—Here you are with your Mama about to be set out in the street, and all you've got to do is ask that old sucker in order to save her.

WANDA   I know. I know. But I just can't bring myself round to it.

CLAUDINE   Balooney! Crazy as Hogan is about you, all you have to do is ask him for the dough.

WANDA   I know. In fact, I already have.

CLAUDINE *(surprised)*   You have?—Then you've got more sense than I gave you credit for!

WANDA   I just thought I'd ask him last night to see what he'd say.

CLAUDINE   Sweet patootie' And he shelled right out—

WANDA   No. There's a catch in it. He wanted me to promise to be nice to him—I can't stomach that!

CLAUDINE   Don't talk foolish, Wanda. There won't be nothing to it.—Hogan's not so bad. He's just old—Anyway . . . (*going to table for ash tray*) you're no virgin, you know!

WANDA (*sharply*)   No. But I'm no whore!

CLAUDINE (*snuffing cigarette*)   You're a fool, if you ask me. But she's your mother, Kiddo. If you don't care whether she's set out in disgrace before all the neighbors, it's your lookout. But I'll tell you one thing: You'd never catch me turning my mother down for the sake of such a flimsy idea. (*going*) But I've got to get home. You'd better think it over like you got some sense. (*exit*)

WANDA (*contemplatively*)   Think it over— (*she shudders*) God! (*she buries her face in the palm of her hands and is lost until she hears* ELLA *descending*) I thought you were going to lie down for a while?

ELLA   My pillow's like a bag of rocks— Claudine gone?

WANDA   Yes.

ELLA   Isn't it time for you to be going to work?

WANDA   What time is it?

ELLA   My clock said 5:30. But I wouldn't trust it.

WANDA (*preoccupiedly, still sitting*)   I guess I'd better get ready.

ELLA   I guess you'd better.

DAN (*appearing, seedily dressed and bereft of his former cocksuredness—accompanied by* LES) Well, what'd they do? (*he sits*)

ELLA   I don't know. Vic's still downtown.

LES (*in sweatshirt and trousers, he notices his mother's eyes*)   You've been crying.

WANDA   Marks upset her.

LES   Marks? What Marks?

WANDA   The used-furniture man—You should've heard what he offered her for that couch and chair—$6.50! (*she goes above*)

DAN   Can you beat it?—But it's no more than you can expect from a Jew!

LES   That's prejudice, Uncle Dan. (*he gets magazine from table*)

DAN   Call it what you like. But I'm sick of them—They're all alike!

LES   The white man says the same thing about us. But the Jews are no different from any other people. If *anything,* they've contributed a damn sight more.

DAN   Oh, yeah—Another of your Communistic ideas, eh?

LES   It didn't take the Communists to find that out. (*he sits*) The whole world's been aware of it ever since the coming of Christ— And look at Marx and Einstein, and Freud and Spinoza!

(CAROLINE *enters*)

ELLA (*coldly*)   For God's sake, let the Jews rest! (*seeing* CAROLINE) I thought you went to Juanita's?

CAROLINE (*pretending to search for mail on table—A fine looking girl of twenty, neatly dressed*)   I just left her.

ELLA (*suspiciously*)   You didn't stay long.

CAROLINE (*glancing at* DAN, *who squirms*)   I can't understand her anymore, Mama. She acts so funny.

ELLA   What do you mean, she acts funny?

CAROLINE (*glancing at* LES, *who is smiling, apparently enjoying* DAN's *predicament*)   Oh, I don't know, Mama—Did Papa get back?

ELLA (*persisting*)   It's mighty strange you can't explain what you mean—

CAROLINE (*studiously avoiding* DAN, *who has inched toward the edge of his chair, she goes to couch*)   I just don't know what to think, Mama. But everytime I go there lately, she watches me and Grandma like a hawk.

DAN (*uneasily*)   That's just your imagination.

CAROLINE   Maybe so. But she made me feel so much like I was in the way, I just told her goodbye and came home. (*she reads*)

DAN (*defensively*)   Juanita's just worried like everybody else over these hard times.

ELLA (*after a moment*)   I wish your father would come on!

LES   The courts are packed, Mama. They're evicting right and left.

DAN (*relieved at turn of conversation*)   They have to protect people's property.

LES   Yeah. Protect the property and to hell with the people!

ELLA   For fifteen years Cochran never missed a month getting his rent on this house.

DAN   Sure. But what can you expect when nine out of ten tenants are nothing but dead beats.

LES   That's a lot of hooey—Anyway, if the big dogs can't give us work, they've no right to expect any rent. Furthermore, a just Government would make them bear their part of the responsibility.

DAN *(bitterly)*   Yeah. I bore my part and you see what it got me!

LES   It serves you right for kidding yourself.

DAN   Oh, yeah?

LES   You doggone tooting! You've never been anything but a *Negro striver*, trying to go big. Now, even though you've been wiped out, you still can't see what hit you!

DAN *(angrily)*   You rattle-brained, young snipe! If you weren't my own nephew——!

ELLA   Dan, is that necessary?

LES   Don't mind us, Mama.

ELLA   We've all made mistakes—

DAN   Mistake nothing. Suppose I'd-er kept my money in the bank, would I have it?

LES   That's just another contradiction in the present rotten order. And you and Papa were both wrong—You for putting faith in it. Papa for thinking the Garvey Movement anything more than an impractical, chauvinistic dream.

DAN   You wise punk! You're just like your Daddy: You think you see everything! Nobody can't—

ELLA *(exploding)*   Oh, stop it! I'm sick of listening to nothing but talk, talk! For twenty years that's all we've had in this house—And ain't nobody done nothing yet!

DAN *(rising)*   I guess you're right, Ella. *(joining LES)* Gimme a cigarette.

LES   I can't afford them.

DAN *(going)*   I guess not. But maybe you Reds'll include them in the rations when you get in power.

LES *(smiling)*   At least, you can bet everybody'll be able to smoke them!

DAN *(ironically)*   Oh, absolutely! *(turning to ELLA)* I'll be back, Ella. I'm just going to the corner. *(exit front door)*

ELLA *(going)*   I guess I'll go put the little we got on the stove. *(exit into rear)*

CAROLINE   I think you're foolish to argue with him, Les. You'll never recruit him in a thousand years. *(WANDA descends with purse)*

LES *(rising, his eyes on WANDA)*   Yeah. I may not. But the times will.—*(to WANDA)* I've been waiting for a chance to see you.

WANDA *(going to front door)*   Yeah. Well, you'll have to do it later.

LES *(intercepting her)*   Oh, no you don't. I said I wanted to talk to you, and I don't mean tomorrow—*(to other)* Excuse us will you, Caroline.

CAROLINE *(going)*   Of course . . . *(she starts above)*

WANDA   But I tell you, I've got to get to the drugstore.

LES   I can't help that—*(seeing CAROLINE has halted on stairs in curiosity, he casts a commanding glance on her, and she hurries out of sight)* Sit down.

WANDA   I won't sit down. You can't bully me.

LES *(ominously)*   Mama's in the kitchen. Perhaps, you'd rather I spoke to her?

WANDA *(frightened)*   What do you mean?

LES   You know what I mean.

WANDA   You haven't got anything on me!

LES   No? But let's not be melodramatic. Sit down and keep your voice low.

WANDA *(she hesitates, measuring him for a moment, then sits)*   All right. *(he turns away in silence, and takes a stride or two apparently gathering his thoughts)* Well, why don't you say what you're going to say?

LES *(joining her)*   I don't suppose you realize it, Wanda. But it's been pretty painful to Papa and me, sitting round here day after day, allowing you to bear the burden of the house—

WANDA   When have you heard me complaining?

LES   Never. But it's begun to look as if it's about to get you down, isn't that so?

WANDA *(rising—excited)*   No. Who said it was?

LES   Nobody. But the facts seem to indicate it.

WANDA *(rising)*   Come to the point!

LES   All right. I will. I saw you get out of that car around the corner last night.

WANDA *(flushing)*   You what—

LES *(accusingly)*   You're slipping!

WANDA *(desperately)*   But it was nothing like that, Les. Honest. He was just an old drug salesman who always comes into the store.

LES   Then why didn't you let him bring you to the door?

WANDA (*truthfully*) Because I knew you or some of the rest would misunderstand—that's why!

LES (*quietly*) Don't lie, Wanda. You're a grown woman, and you don't have to tell me anything. But you know damn well, (*his voice fills with bitter irony*) when a white man begins to take a "nigger girl" riding, it can't mean but one thing!

WANDA (*grieved*) But you're wrong!

LES (*with deadly conviction*) I'm not. You're trifling with him.—(*with a wave of moral indignation, he presses*) Aren't you?

WANDA (*cowering*) No! No!

LES (*twisting her wrist*) I say you are!

WANDA (*outraged, but surrendering*) All right. Have it your way.

LES You little bum!

WANDA (*hurt and angry*) You lie! Hogan never touched me!

LES Oh, no. And I suppose he didn't even try—That he had nothing but a wish to assist the poor little "nigger gal" home?

WANDA (*bitterly*) Am I responsible for what a man thinks?

LES That's a convenient little subterfuge!

WANDA I've got as much right to use it as any other woman.

LES (*sharply*) Oh, you have? Well, what was the purpose of it here, may I ask?

WANDA (*coldly*) You know as well as I do what we're up against!

LES (*darkly*) Umph phumn! Just as I thought. (*he turns away*)

WANDA (*following him, pleadingly*) We've got to have some place to stay, haven't we? Can't you see, Les? I only thought I might be able to borrow a few dollars from him!

LES (*whirling*) And you got them, I suppose?

WANDA (*suddenly resenting the implication*) That's my business!

LES You dirty little Chippy!

WANDA (*quailing*) Les!

LES (*furious*) You're not as good as a Chippy!—Any girl that'd stoop to such a thing and call herself decent—

WANDA (*growing hysterical*) That's right! Wipe your feet on me! Drag me in the dirt!

LES (*suddenly recalling their situation*) Sh! Mama'll hear!

WANDA (*wildly*) Let her. I don't care! I don't care about nothing! (*she starts for front door*)

LES (*catching her*) Hush, I tell you!

WANDA (*twisting away from him—ravingly*) I won't. You can tell the whole damn world for all I care. You think I'm nothing but a whore, why shouldn't she!

ELLA (*appearing from rear*) For God's sake, what's going on here?

LES Nothing, Mama.

WANDA (*coming down*) Oh, yes there is. Come on in. You'll get the thrill of your life. Les's got a little story to tell you—(*turning to him, and going*) Go on, Les. Tell her. Tell it to Mama. Give her your spicy little tale—(*she runs into the street*)

ELLA What in the world is it?

LES Nothing, I tell you.

ELLA Don't lie to me. What is it?

LES She's just hysterical.

ELLA (*insistently*) Hysterical? Hysterical about what?

LES The house, I guess. She's worried about the notice.

ELLA (*sharply*) You're lying. Tell me the truth!

LES I am, Mama.—She's worried about getting money for another place.

ELLA (*sitting, partly satisfied*) Yes—Go on.

LES There isn't anything else to say.

ELLA Don't tell me.—What about this spicy tale business?

LES Nothing you'd be interested in.—(*suddenly seeing a way out*) She came up with a wild scheme to raise money to get a place.

ELLA What sort of wild scheme?

LES (*joining her—easily*) It's unimportant, Mama. I've already put my foot down. Anyway, I intended to tell you when I came in. I think we're going to get relief in another week or so.

ELLA (*puzzled*) What do you mean—"relief?"

LES Help, Mam—Food, rent, maybe even employment—We're moving in on Governor Emerson tomorrow.

ELLA Who's "we"?

LES Oh, justa bunch of folks like me, who're sick of waiting for "prosperity to turn the corner," while their folks starve and their sisters creep down into the gutter. (DAN *reenters*)

ELLA And you're going with them?

LES You bet!

DAN (*coming down*) Going where?

LES   To Springfield—to see the Governor about conditions.

ELLA   Have you said anything to your father?

LES   No. Not yet.

DAN   I guess not. (*suddenly sharp*) You haven't forgotten what the police did to that mob in Ohio the other day, have you?

LES   I m not worrying about that.

DAN   No. You and that bunch of riff-raff I see you with don't give a damn about nothing— But I warn you, you're headed for trouble!

LES   I'm already in trouble. And so's the rest of us. But you can't understand that.

DAN   I can't, eh? Well, there's one thing I do understand, and so will you Reds before long!

LES   (*laughing*)   Yeah. What's that?

DAN   (*pounding*)   You can't beat the Government!

LES   You and your blind pessimism—You make me sick!

DAN   You'll learn when the rifles begin to talk!

LES   Let them. The quicker the better.

ELLA   Lester!

DAN   The young fool!

LES   (*immature and recklessly*)   The disinherited will never come to power without bloodshed!

ELLA   Les, don't say such things!

DAN   Let him rave on. He'll wake up one of these days.

LES   (*seriously*)   It's you who're asleep, not me. Your world has crashed. But you're so full of capitalist dope, you don't even know we're building a new one. (*he starts upstairs*)

DAN   (*angrily, seeming to pin him against the stairway*)   You're building a wall to be put up against and shot!

LES   (*going above*)   I'd rather look forward to that than a pauper's grave! (*exit above*)

ELLA   (*helplessly*)   I don't know what in the world's come over him!

DAN   (*darkly*)   That's what you get for letting him raise himself!

ELLA   Don't blame me. I've done the best I could by him.

DAN   Like hell!—For ten years all you and Vic've done is sit around here like a pair of petrified mummies and let him go straight to the dogs!

PERCY   (*on porch, singing, drunkenly*)   "Is there anybody here want to buy a lil dog. Buy a lil dog—(*appearing, he sways in doorway*) Is there anybody here want to buy a lil dog—I got one for to sell him . . . !" (LES *appears above*)

DAN   (*gauging* PERCY, *disgustedly*)   Just look at that!

LES   (*descending quickly*)   Lay off him, Uncle Dan. (*taking the drunk man*) Come on in, Uncle Percy, and sit down before you fall.

DAN   A regular bum!

PERCY   (*staggering, he pulls away from* LES, *and halts swaying*)   What you mean, I'm a bum? Whatcha mean?

DAN   You'd better sit down and try to sober up!

PERCY   (*fumbling in back pocket*)   Sober up? Do I look like I'm drunk to you? Do I, hunh?

ELLA   You'd better take him in the back, Les, and put him in Mama's room. He may get sick here.

LES   Come on, Uncle Percy. I'll put you to bed.

(VIC *appears in doorway*)

DAN   (*seeing* PERCY *pull flask, he joins them to try and take it away*)   Gimme that!

PERCY   (*hugging flask*)   Oh, no you don't, Big Shot. No you don't. This is my *moon*.

DAN   I say give it to me!

VIC   Let him alone, Dan.

DAN   (*angrily*)   Can't you see he's drunk?

VIC   (*coming in, his face grim with care—he is wearing his old Garvey uniform, which is now faded and bedraggled*)   What difference does it make! (PHILLIP *follows him in*)

PERCY   (*Triumphantly*)   That a boy, Vic, old man. Get him told!

VIC   (*To* LES—*quietly*)   Take him somewhere and put him to bed—Go on, now, Percy. Let him put you to bed.

PERCY   (*obediently*)   Awh right, Vic. Anything you say, old man. (*he allows* LES *to escort him across to door leading to rear, where he halts*) I know you wouldn't tell me nothing wrong— And if you say I'm drunk and ought to go to bed—Well, well, I'm drunk and ought to go to bed—(*going with* LES—*a ragged, broken, pathetic figure with one foot in the grave*) I know I must be drunk if you say so—(*exit*)

DAN   He's going to keep on fighting that stuff until it kills him.

VIC (*gloomily*)   Maybe he'll be better off dead.

DAN (*alertly*)   I judge you didn't come out so well . . . ?

VIC (*avoiding any direct contact with* ELLA, *with whom there has been no reconciliation and to whom he never speaks directly*)   No. I didn't.

DAN (*sympathetically*)   How much time did the judge give you?

(LES *reenters*)

VIC (*hollowly*)   Twenty days.

ELLA (*gasping*)   Twenty days!

DAN (*astounded*)   That all—?

PHILLIP (*behind couch*)   I guess Papa was lucky to get that—(*indicating father's clothing*) after the Judge noticed that uniform.

VIC (*sharply*)   Will you never learn to hold your tongue?

PHILLIP   I didn't mean no harm, Papa—I just—

VIC   Dry up! You never do.

DAN   There's no use hiding anything, Vic. We're all in the family.

VIC   I've nothing to hide. He just got tough when I admitted I used to be a Garveyite.

LES   What did he say, Papa?

VIC (*quoting bitterly*)   "Oh, so you're one of the niggers who think this country isn't good enough for you, eh? Well, well, and you've got the nerve to appeal to this Court for leniency?"—As if that wasn't enough, he went on to rub it in by telling me how thankful we ought to be because his people brought us out of savagery—But I couldn't say anything.

DAN (*thoughtlessly*)   You had no business wearing that uniform down there.

VIC (*sharply*)   What was I going in, my ragged drawers?

DAN (*quietly*)   I'm sorry, Vic. I wasn't thinking. (*after a moment, amid the general air of dejection*) Have you any idea what you're going to do?

VIC (*bitterly*)   Move to Hooverville—I guess.

DAN   Don't be sardonic, Vic.

VIC (*sharply*)   If you think I don't mean it, find me a truck!

LES (*easily*)   Forget it, Papa. We're not going anywhere.

VIC   Eh?

LES   I said we're not going to move a step!

VIC (*puzzled*)   What're you talking about—(*he stiffens, hearing* MRS. BROOKS)

BROOKS (*on porch calling*)   Les! . . . Where Les—

LES (*going to door—surprised*)   It's Grandma! (*the others sit amazed*)

BROOKS (*entering in a huff with a bundle of clothing under her arm*)   Les—Les, I want you to go yonder to Juanita's and bring me the rest of mah things. Cause I ain't fixin' to stay there another blessed night! (*wearily, she drops into chair, center*)

ELLA   For God's sake, Mama—What's happened?

BROOKS (*indignantly*)   That hussey done come up here and forgot her raisin', that's what! But if she thinks I'm goin' live in sich dirt, she never was so wrong in her life! Mah garment's clean and spotless fore the Savior, and she and nobody else ain't goin' change it!

ELLA (*to* DAN)   What in the world's she talking about?

DAN (*evasively*)   You can search me. But it sounds like she's losing her mind.

BROOKS (*angrily*)   Don't you try to call me crazy, you sneakin' blackguard! Don't you dare try it! If you don't want me to lay you out, don't you open your mouth!

DAN (*placatingly*)   Awh, go on, Mama—Whatever it is forget it! (*cunningly*) Ella and Vic don't want to hear that stuff. They've got trouble enough of their own—Here they are about to be evicted, kicked out in the street—

ELLA (*suspicious of him*)   Nevermind, Dan—There must be something wrong, or she wouldn't be here—Go on, Mama. What is it?

BROOKS   You bet your bottom dollar there is! (*to* DAN) And you needn't think you can shut me up, neither! Cause—

DAN (*joining her, angrily*)   Shut you up! Why should I want to shut you up? (*turning to others and quickly crossing to window*) If you all want to listen to her crazy tales, let her go ahead. It doesn't make a damn bit of difference to me what she says!

ELLA   Go on, Mama. What happened!

BROOKS   I got after her 'bout rentin' rooms and havin' all kinds of lowdown good-for-nothin' tramps layin' up in her house—(*glancing around at* DAN) while some folks I ain't mentionin' keep duckin' in and out and makin' out they can't see what's goin' on—(*going on to others*) So she says: "Mama, do you know how you're livin? Do you know who's takin' care of you? Do you know nobody's givin me a dime to look after this house? Where you think I'm goin' git rent to keep a roof ovuh your head?" Like as if I never kept a roof ovuh bofe of you all's heads for twenty years without spottin mah garment—But ask me if I didn't bless her out? I bet you she'll remember what I told her to her dyin' day!—After that, I just got mah things together and come on to you, cause I know you'd give me a clean place to lay mah weary head, even if we did fall out bout the chillun and Vic and me had a word or two—Cause I know he ain't goin' hold no more malice against me for what I said 'bout him, than I hold against him for what he said 'bout me—(*turning to son-in-law*) Now ain't that right, Vic?

VIC (*smiling, admiring her shrewdness*)   Of course, Mama—(*his smile fading*) though I'm sorry to say, things ain't like they used to be here. We're just about to be kicked into the street, and if something don't happen in the next twenty days, we will be. But you're welcome to stay if you want to.

BROOKS (*trapped*)   Twenty days!

ELLA   Twenty days!

BROOKS   Lawd, lawd, Lawd! (*she catches sight of* DAN *smiling gloatingly*) But I'd heap rather sleep in the street with you all than spot mah garment in the wallow they got ovah there.

LES (*hugging her with smile*)   Don't worry, Grandma. A lot of things can happen in twenty days!

(*Curtain*)

Scene Two

(TIME: *three weeks later.*

The light of a small lamp is burning, revealing the room in upheaval. There are packing cases and barrels about, showing that the family is preparing to vacate the premises, or to be evicted.

Though it is near 3:30 a.m., BROOKS, *in an old robe, is seen alone, peering out into the night from the window. In a moment, she turns toward door, expectantly)*

BROOKS *as* LES *enters, her voice hushed but excited)*   Les, has you seen anything of Wanda?

LES (*arrested*)   Wanda!—No. Why do you ask?

BROOKS (*sotto voce*)   Do you know she ain't come in this house yet—And it's after three o'clock?

LES (*placing batch of leaflets on table*) Wanda's a grown woman, Grandma.

BROOKS   Grown or not grown, she's got no business out in the streets this time o' night—I'm worried about her.

LES   You'd better go back to bed and try to get some sleep—(*laughing, as he turns to climb stairs*) You may not get another chance after tonight, you know!

BROOKS (*arresting him*)   I ain't worried 'bout that. But somethin' must-er happened to Wanda!

LES (*joining her to give her a pat*)   You're just imagining things, Grandma. Go on back to bed.

BROOKS (*tightening her robe*)   I can't sleep— How Ella can, beats me. After the way she cried round here these last few days—'specially this afternoon 'fore Wanda come. Then she got calm as a picture of a Saint—(*probingly*) You reckon Wanda could-er told her somethin'?

LES   Now, Grandma, what do you suppose she could've told her?

BROOKS   I donno. Neither one of them don't talk to me like they used to—(*going back to window*) You'd think I was some stranger round here.

LES   Oh, they're just worried—just as you are—(*going*) But I'm going to bed. Goodnight!

BROOKS (*peering out of window*)   Wait, Les! (*waving to him, excitedly*) Come here a minute and see if that ain't Claudine yonder!

LES (*joining her*)   Claudine! . . . (*he sees figure*) Now what do you know about that?—It's her all right—(*he goes to door to open it and call in a whispered voice*) Claudine! Come here!

BROOKS (*ominously*)   I told you there was somethin' wrong. I knowed it. My mind don't fool me!

LES (*as girl approaches*)   Claudine, what in the world are you doing out in the street this time of night?

CLAUDINE (*appearing, anxiously*)   Wanda here? (*she is wearing a gown with a lace stole around her shoulders*)

LES (*closing door behind her*)   No.

CLAUDINE   She ain't come home?

LES   No, not yet—Why? There isn't anything wrong, is there?

CLAUDINE *(nervously)*   No. I just wanted to see her.

BROOKS   It's mighty funny you got to be watchin' for her in the street, instid of coming to this house!

LES   Yes, it is! Claudine, you're hiding something—

BROOKS *(seeing CLAUDINE signalling him to be silent)*   Ugh hunh! So it is somethin!

CLAUDINE   No, no, Mrs. Brooks—I was just feeling a little faint.

BROOKS   You needn't tell that lie. You wouldn't be here this time o' night—You don't want me to hear!

CLAUDINE *(rapidly)*   No, really, Mrs. Brooks —Wanda's all right—*(going)* You'll see if she isn't—I was just—

BROOKS *(intercepting her)*   You hold on! You ain't goin' leave me like this—I'll call Ella first!

LES *(anxiously)*   No, Grandma! For God's sake! Leave it to me.

BROOKS   How come I can't be trusted?

LES *(helplessly)*   It isn't that, Grandma—You wait here *(he starts out with CLAUDINE)*

BROOKS *(striding to stairs)*   Maybe she'll talk to Ella!

LES *(whirling to grab her)*   No, Grandma! *(seeing CLAUDINE escaping)* Wait, Claudine! Wait! *(desperately)* She'll get away. I've got to catch her—But for God's sake, keep your mouth shut until I get back.

(He runs out, leaving the door open, in his haste to catch the fleeing girl. BROOKS rushes to the window to remain there in her frustration, staring into the darkened street. Blackout)

Scene Three

(TIME: the following morning.

ELLA *is seen, packing blankets into a case)*

ELLA *(calling into kitchen)*   Caroline, haven't you finished with those dishes yet?

CAROLINE *(off-stage, exasperatedly)*   Oh, give me time, Mama. I'll be through in a minute!

ELLA   You've been at them long enough to have them washed and packed—Lord, if I don't lose my mind this morning, I never will!

CAROLINE *(entering with armful of plates)* Well, it's not doing you any good to worry—

Wanda and Les're both probably together somewhere. *(she goes to barrel where she begins packing dishes)*

ELLA   It's mighty funny neither your Father nor Phillip's been able to find them.

CAROLINE   You'd do better worrying about what we're going to do when the Bailiffs come.

ELLA   We ain't going to do nothing but let them set us out. Then I'm going to thank them for doing us the favor.

CAROLINE *(struck by her unconcern)*   You sound mighty calloused— like you've never seen the homeless in Washington Park.

ELLA *(turning with a smile)*   I've got the money, Caroline, to get a place!

CAROLINE   You have?

ELLA   Yes. Wanda gave me $50 yesterday!

CAROLINE   Mama, you're joking?

ELLA *(pulling roll of bills from her bosom and waving them triumphantly)*   What do you call this?

CAROLINE *(incredulously)*   But, Mama, where'd she get all that money?

ELLA *(laughing with joy)*   Her boss. He loaned it to her.

VIC *(appearing in open door)*   Well, did she get back?

CAROLINE   No. Didn't you find her?

VIC *(coming in wearily)*   No. Nobody's seen hide nor hair of her. And she hasn't been near the drugstore since early last night.

CAROLINE   What about Les—Was there no trace of him?

VIC *(shaking his head negatively)*   I went to the Reds and saw Piszer. But he said Les left the park about 2:30 this morning—on his way here.

CAROLINE   Well, he never showed up. His bed hasn't been slept in.

ELLA *(worried)*   Lord, I wish that telephone wasn't disconnected!

VIC *(volunteering the remark for her benefit)*   I called the police, and every hospital in town.

BROOKS *(entering with old suitcase, and seeing VIC)*   Where's she?

VIC   I've had no luck.

CAROLINE *(seeing WANDA and LES in door)* Here they are!

VIC *(whirling)*   Thank God!

ELLA *(pouncing on WANDA)*   Where've you been?

WANDA *(lying)*   I'm sorry, Mama. But I was in an accident. Claudine and I went for a ride to Gary with some fellows last night, and the car broke down.

BROOKS (*sharply*)   Of all the audacity!—Claudine and you! Then what was she doing here lookin' for you at three o'clock this mornin'?

ELLA (*surprised*)   Three o'clock this morning!

LES (*covering for* WANDA)   You don't understand, Grandma. The car Wanda was in broke down, and Claudine and them, not knowing, came on. But when they got here and the rest didn't show up, naturally, Claudine was afraid something might've happened to her.

BROOKS (*sighing*)   Oh, then tell me somethin'.

WANDA (*relieved*)   I thought several times we were going to have to walk back.

ELLA (*relieved, but mother-like*)   It would've served you right! Worrying everybody to death!—I can't see to save my life why you haven't got more sense than to be going off in the rattle-trap of every Tom, Dick, and Harry you meet!

WANDA (*going*)   I'm sorry, Mama. But it couldn't be helped. I'm going up and wash up. (*exit above*)

VIC   Well, this sure is a relief—(*taking seat*) Now if only the Bailiffs weren't due, I'd feel like celebrating.

CAROLINE   Shucks, Papa. Who cares about the Bailiffs?—They're welcome to set us out, aren't they, Mama?

ELLA (*proudly, as she continues packing*)   I reckon they can come if they want to.

VIC (*to* CAROLINE)   What're you talking about?

CAROLINE   Oh, wake up, Papa. Mama's got the money to rent us a new place!

BROOKS (*surprised*)   What's that?

CAROLINE (*happily*)   Wanda borrowed it from her boss yesterday!

VIC   God be praised!

LES (*darkly*)   Forget it, Papa. This is no matter for rejoicing.

VIC   Why not?—Do you think it's not a relief, knowing we don't have to sleep in Washington Park?

LES   You can't afford to take this way out. (ELLA *whirls, puzzled, her heart skipping a beat*)

VIC (*dreading to question him*)   I don't think I understand you, Les.

BROOKS   Sounds like he's crazy.

LES (*ignoring her*)   You've a duty to others, Papa.

VIC   What duty?

PISZER (*entering open door*)   Good morning, Folks!

LES (*going on*)   Your duty to yourself and the thousands who're facing eviction this morning—(*ironically*) with no daughter lucky enough to borrow from her boss!

VIC   You mean refuse to get out?

LES   It's the only way to stop the landlords, Papa. We've got to resist them.

VIC   You're asking me to turn the family into guinea pigs, Son.

LES   I am asking you to help us set an example for the rest, like any honest leader.

VIC   Things can't go on this way, Les. I'd be a fool to jeopardize the family, knowing it.

LES   I've always given you credit for seeing clean through this rotten society, Papa. But you talk like a blind man now. After preaching freedom and happiness all these years, you ought to know our only hope is in resistance—You saw what good it did us to try to appeal to the Governor, didn't you? Why didn't they even let us see him?

PISZER (*sophomorically, but earnest*)   The State is only a reflection of the ruling class. It's impossible for it to be concerned about the poor, who have to struggle for every concession.

VIC (*impatiently*)   I know all that, Son. But I can't blind myself to the facts. A poor Negro like me can only get it in the neck if he bucks the law—And anything may happen in another month.

LES (*desperate, knowing he cannot use the knowledge he possesses without disloyalty to* WANDA)   In another month you'll be right back where you started from!—Suppose you take the money Mama's got and rent another place. Can Wanda keep up the rent, or do you think her boss is going to play the sweet Angel again?

PISZER   You won't be alone, Mr. Mason. We set ten families back in their homes this week. We can do the same for you. Say the word and in ten minutes we'll have a thousand Comrades at your door—

JUANITA (*rushing in with* DAN *at her heels*)   Has she come yet, Ella?

ELLA   Yes. She's upstairs. She and Claudine drove off to Gary with some young men and the car broke down. But they got back all right.

JUANITA (*relieved*) Well, I'm sure glad to hear that. I was worried to death.

DAN Me too! (*jovially to* VIC) Well, old man, I see you're still here.

VIC (*gloomily*) Yeah. But my time ain't long.

DAN Well, don't let it worry you. You all can come over to my house, though I can't promise you how long it'll be before they kick us all out together.

VIC Thanks very much, Dan.—But (*he glances uneasily at* LES) we've got the money for a place.

JUANITA (*happily*) You have—?

CAROLINE Yes. Wanda borrowed it from her boss yester—(*she halts, hearing running footsteps on porch*)

PHILLIP (*bursting in to blurt*) Papa, you know what? (LES *tries to intervene*) Wanda's in jail!

VIC (*laughing*) In jail! Why you're crazy—

(*The others join in the laughter, believing it's a good joke*)

PHILLIP (*defensively*) Well, Claudine said so!

BROOKS (*suddenly struck, and grunting as in a flash she suspects they'd been taken in*) Ugh phumn!

ELLA (*stunned*) She did?

PHILLIP Yes, she did! She told me—

LES (*nudges him, and interposes*) Awh, you don't know what you're talking about. Wanda and Claudine both spent the night in Gary— She's upstairs now!

PHILLIP She is?

LES Sure.

PHILLIP That's funny—(LES *nudges him again, but he's too carried away by his own feelings and embarrassment*) I wonder what Claudine wanted to go telling me that stuff for—?

ELLA (*still suspicious*) What did she say?

LES (*interposing, as he glares at* PHILLIP) Don't pay any attention to him, Mama. Claudine's just been pulling his leg.

PHILLIP (*heatedly*) Pulling nothing!—How you know she wasn't in jail? How you know she didn't just get out on bond, like Claudine said she was going to?

ELLA Claudine said that?

LES But, Mama, I tell you—

ELLA (*sharply*) You shut up! And let me hear the rest of this. Go on, Phillip, what did she say?

PHILLIP (*aware at last that something is wrong, but unable to restrain himself*) She said Wanda got caught in a raid last night—

JUANITA A raid?

PHILLIP (*going on*) with some white man named Hogan. But for us not to worry because the woman who runs the place was going to get her out on bond this morning. (*the family is stunned*)

BROOKS (*outraged—scandalized*) Caught in a raid with a white man! I knowed it! I knowed it!—I warned you, Ella. I told you—

LES Hush, Grandma, for God's sakes—

BROOKS Don't you tell me to hush—Claudine never would-er been hidin' out there three o'clock in the mornin' if there wasn't somethin' to this—

LES Awh, that's ridiculous, Grandma. If the police had caught them, don't you see Claudine couldn't've been here!

PHILLIP (*blurting*) Claudine said they would've caught her too, if she hadn't jumped out of the window!

ELLA (*striding to foot of stairs, and calling, imperiously*) Wanda! You come down here to me!

VIC (*loyally, though dreadingly*) I can't believe Wanda's mixed up in anything like this.

ELLA (*as* WANDA *appears above*) Come down here!

JUANITA (*as* WANDA *creeps down*) Give her a chance, Ella! (*in silence they watch as girl comes down*)

ELLA (*coldly*) Where were you last night?

WANDA (*frightened*) I—I just told you—Me and Claudine—

ELLA (*sharply*) I want the truth!

WANDA (*glancing around, like a cornered animal*) I'm telling you, Mama!

ELLA Didn't you just get out of jail?

WANDA (*desperately*) No, no—Who said that? (*to* LES, *accusingly*) Les, did you—(*she catches herself*)

ELLA (*shooting in the dark*) Oh, so you were!

WANDA (*striding to* LES, *she strikes him across the mouth*) Take that, Mr. Big-mouth! (LES *turns away and all are silent in their pain*)

JUANITA Lord, have mercy, Wanda. He didn't do it. It was Phillip.

WANDA Phillip?

JUANITA Yes.

WANDA (*quietly*) I'm sorry, Les.

LES Forget it.

ELLA (*woundedly*)   Is it true, too, you were laying up with a white man?

WANDA (*on the verge of tears*)   You had to have the money, Mama—(*pathetically, her eyes search their faces for a sign of understanding, and she utters with a sob*) What else could I do? (*unable to face their stony silence, she lingers for a moment, then runs above to hide her shame*)

BROOKS (*dumfounded, as* ELLA *turns to the window with bowed head*)   Lawd, Lawd, Lawd!

LES (*to* PHILLIP)   I guess you're satisfied. (PHILLIP, *quailing, turns away*)

VIC (*rousing himself*)   Well, I reckon this changes the face of everything.

LES   How do you mean?

VIC (*ready at last to fight*)   Suppose you can still get help?

LES   All you want, Papa.

DAN (*excited*)   Not the Reds?

VIC (*firmly*)   Get them. The Bailiffs'll be along any minute.

LES (*going*)   Come on, Piszer! (*they exit running*)

JUANITA (*gravely*)   You're making an awful mistake, Vic!

VIC   I've got to stand my ground!

DAN   But there'll be trouble, Man!

VIC (*bitterly*)   I got a taste for trouble now!

JUANITA   Oh, Vic, why be a fool?

VIC (*angrily*)   I suppose you think I should use that tainted money! (ELLA *whirls*)

JUANITA   I thought she borrowed it!

VIC   We were all fools enough to think so— the little tramp!

ELLA (*outraged, her old animosity surging up to condemn him, she extracts roll of money and hurls it into his face*) Here!   You take this! It belongs to you!

DAN   Ella!

JUANITA (*stepping between them, admonishingly*)   Oh, Ella—For Heaven's sake!

ELLA (*as* VIC *stands bewildered*)   Get out of my way, and don't tell me nothing!

CAROLINE   Mama, Mama, please!

(PERCY *enters, half drunk and unshaven*)

ELLA (*raging*)   Calling somebody a tramp! Who made her a tramp?

JUANITA   Don't, Ella!

ELLA (*storming*)   Who started her on the road to hell?—You! You!

DAN   No, Ella. It was just fate!

ELLA (*seizing the idea*)   It was fate all right. Fate from the day she was born—With something less than a Black fool for a father she was booked for the gutter!

VIC (*bowed beneath the impact as one before a fatal blow*)   Yeah! . . .

(PERCY *sobers*)

JUANITA (*catching his pain*)   Oh, Ella. How can you say such a cruel thing?

ELLA   You ask me how? I'll tell you how. Because I'm sick to death of him, that's how! I thought I had enough when he talked like he did about Mama. But now that I've lived to see my child ruined on account of his stupidity, there's nothing I'd like better than to see him dead!

PERCY (*angrily to* VIC)   You going to stand there and let her talk to you like that?

VIC (*groaning*)   That's all right, Ella. It's all right—

BAILIFF (*appearing in door with men behind him*)   Does Victor Mason live here?

DAN   Yes. What is it? (*he indicates* VIC)

BAILIFF (*entering, followed by his men*)   I've got a court order to evict you. (*to his men*) Go on, Boys. Set them out! (*without ado, the men begin removing furnishings*)

VIC (*ominously*)   You can save yourselves a lot of trouble, if you let that stuff alone!

BAILIFF (*as men pause*)   What'd you mean?

VIC (*sharply*)   I'm not going to stand no eviction!

BAILIFF   Are you looking for trouble?

VIC (*angrily*)   Call it what you like—(*he halts, hearing voices*)

VOICES (*singing as they approach in the distance*)   "Mine eyes have seen the glory . . ."

PHILLIP (*at window, above the sound of the Battle Hymn*)   It's Les and them. A whole army of them!

BAILIFF   The Reds, eh? (*excitedly, to* VIC) Well, you'd better call them off! They won't get away with *this* case!

(*Police sirens roar in the distance, prophetically*)

DAN (*frightened*)   Vic, my offer still stands!

VIC   And what're you going to do when they set you out?

DAN   There'll be time enough to think of that later.

(*The sirens cease, as brakes are heard screeching*)

BAILIFF (*to his men*)   Go on, Boys. Set 'em out! (*as men carry out pieces, he turns to* VIC, *warningly*) You'd better be reasonable! The cops have their orders! We're not going to stand for anymore of this Red interference!

VIC (*strides to door.* PHILLIP *attempts to follow him*)   Go back!

BAILIFF (*following to door, as* VIC *disappears outside*)   All right. You're asking for it!

BROOKS (*in terror*)   Have mercy, Jesus!

(*The sound of the singing increases, then is suddenly drowned out by the screech of another siren, and silence reigns*)

VOICE (*commandingly, outside*)   All right, Comrades. Let's go!

CAROLINE (*at window*)   They're bringing the things back!

OFFICER (*ominously, outside*)   Halt! In the name of the law I command you not to interfere!

VOICE (*raising song again*)   "Glory, Glory, Hallelujah!"

OFFICER   Halt! Halt! I command you to halt!

BROOKS   Help us, Sweet Jesus!

(VIC *is seen on porch at head-end of piece of furniture*)

CAROLINE (*screaming*)   The police've got guns out, Mama. They've got guns out! (*suddenly screaming*) Look out, Papa! (*there is the sudden roar of gunfire, and* VIC *is seen clutching the door jam*)

VIC (*groaning*)   Ahhhhhah! (*he clings to the door jam, where shortly he is caught by* LES. DAN *runs to join them*)

LES   Help me get him on the couch— (CAROLINE *attempts to assist*) Move, Caroline!

WANDA (*appearing above, appalled by the sight of her father*)   Oh, God! (*she runs below, as* LES *and* DAN *succeed in placing* VIC *on couch*)

PERCY (*suddenly enraged, he rushes to doorway to shake his fist in a futile gesture of defiance*)   You God damn murdering bastards! You dirty killers! (DAN *runs up to grab him and pull him inside*) Turn me loose, Dan. Turn me aloose!

DAN (*wrestling him into chair*)   No, Percy! No!

PERCY (*in tears, his stupor gone*)   Them bastards shot my brother!

WANDA (*joining him*)   You can't help him, Uncle Percy! (*he subsides in tears, and she joins* LES)

LES (*woundedly*)   Shot in the back, like a dog!

LIEUTENANT (*appearing with* PATROLMAN, *he turns to cast over his shoulder*)   Yeah. There's one in here! (*coming down*) Who told you to move that man?

PERCY (*springing up*)   Get the hell out of here! (DAN *grabs him*) Don't hold me, Dan. Let em wash me! God damn em! Let em wash me!

WANDA (*joining them*)   Please, Uncle Percy. There's no use getting yourself hurt. Calm down. You're disturbing Papa. (PERCY *subsides*)

LIEUTENANT (*to* LES)   I asked you who gave you orders to move that man?

LES (*bitterly*)   What were we supposed to do, let him lie there like a dog?

LIEUTENANT (*looking around*)   You shouldn't 've moved him! (*he starts toward telephone*)

LES   That telephone is disconnected.

LIEUTENANT (*to* PATROLMAN)   Get an ambulance.

PATROLMAN   Mockleson's already sent in the call.

LES   How do you feel, Papa?

VIC   Just kind of numb! (LES *casts an appealing glance to his mother, but she turns to the window*)

LIEUTENANT (*noticing* BAILIFFS *re-entering, but that the doorways fills at once by grim-faced white and Black men, acting in concert to prevent any further removal of furnishings*)   Get back! Clear out of here! (*the workers are immobile, and he pulls his gun*) I said clear out of here!

PISZER (*defiantly*)   Go on with your butchering. We're not budging an inch!

PATROLMAN (*after a moment*)   I think we'd better call in, Lieutenant. These bastards 're crazy.

LIEUTENANT (*to* BAILIFFS)   You fellows had better drop this until we get further orders. (*going*) Let us by! (*the men in the doorway, accepting the victory, fall back, and the* OFFICERS *exit, the* BAILIFFS *following*)

VIC (*weakly*)   Where's Ella? (WANDA *draws behind couch*)

LES (*he glances toward her, but she doesn't turn, and he lies*)   She went in the back for a minute, Papa.

VIC   Don't lie, Son. (*shortly*) Lift my head up.

CAROLINE (*dropping beside him*)   Oh, Papa! (LES *raises pillow, and turns toward his mother*)

LES   Mama . . . ! Won't you please—?

VIC   Don't make it hard for her, Son. I reckon she's got cause enough to hate me . . . beyond the grave. (*he pauses to gather his strength*) Anyway, it's no more than life's taught me a Black man's got to expect. (*he caresses* CAROLINE's *hair*) I want you all to try to be true to yourselves and one another. I want you to stick by each other and never let nothing come between you—(*turning to* WANDA *above him*) And that goes for you, too, Wanda. (*she bows her head in silence*) I spoke a little hard about you . . . But I didn't mean it . . . because I understand. (*after a moment*) You'll all find it pretty hard . . . for like Les said . . . "This world ain't . . . nothing but . . . a big white fog, and nobody can't see . . . no light anywhere!"

LES (*quietly*)   I was mistaken, Papa.

VIC (*weakly, after a moment*)   You think so?

LES   I know I was, Papa. But you be quiet now, and don't tax your strength.

VIC   I've got to talk, Son. I'm done for.

WANDA (*turning away*)   Oh, God!

CAROLINE   No, Papa—

VIC   Hush, Caroline, if I've got to go, I've simply got to go, and your tears can't help me none—(*with difficulty*) But what did you mean, Les?

LES   Only, that I was looking in the wrong direction then, Papa.

VIC   Yes.

LES   There is a light.

VIC   What light?

LES (*he searches within for the means to express his truth. Then, turns to the door with its crowded faces*)   Look in the door, there, Papa.

VIC (*straining upward*)   What is it? . . . I can't seem to see.

LES (*swallowing*)   It's my Comrades, Papa.

VIC   Your Comrades—?

LES   Yes. You remember them, don't you?

VIC   Oh, yes. Of course—I owe them a much bigger thanks than—

LES   It's not that, Papa. I wanted you to see they're Black and white.

VIC (*weakly*)   Tell them to come closer. (*the men draw near, and he feels for them with outstretched arms*) Where are they?

PISZER (*quietly*)   Here we are, Comrade Mason!

VIC   I guess my sight is gone. (*he sinks back*)

CAROLINE   Papa! Papa!

LES (*examining him*)   I guess he's gone! (*he turns away, broken*—ELLA, *hearing his verdict, turns from the window*)

ELLA (*relenting, she creeps toward the dead man, her voice filled with grief, though scarcely audible*)   Vic! . . . Vic!

(*In the distance an ambulance siren is heard, and slowly the curtain descends*)

LEGEND AND HISTORY

Zora Neale Hurston • May Miller • Theodore Browne

Charles Fuller • Abram Hill • John D. Silvera

The African American community is rich with individuals whose actions have elevated them to the status of legend. These are often men and women whose names never appear in newspapers and whose faces are never seen on television, but whose actions are widely known and talked about in their communities. Their fame may be based on superhuman deeds, such as those of John Henry (as in Theodore Browne's *Natural Man*), or the wicked, corrupt behavior of characters like Stackalee or the notorious Frankie and Johnny. Legends and tall tales were used as entertainment for antebellum Blacks and is part of an oral tradition that continues today in barbershops, taverns, in the workplace or wherever small groups of African Americans assemble to shuck and jive. Among the more popular legends were these based on the actual careers of bad men such as Billy Bob Russell, Snow James, Roscoe Bill, Bad Lee Brown and Toledo Slim. These men had no redeeming qualities, but were ruthless, destructive, selfish, and asocial. They became folk heroes because they were bold enough to exert power in a society designed to subdue and deprive Black Americans. Bad is not always used in a derogatory manner, but is sometimes used in praise or admiration for legendary figures such as John Henry, Jack Johnson, or Joe Louis—men who confronted and defeated white society on its territory and by its rules.

In 1926, Carter G. Woodson established Negro History Week in order to instill pride in African Americans about their heritage and the contributions their forefathers made toward the development of the United States. He also wanted to make white Americans aware of these accomplishments, which historians had all but ignored. Public attention paid to African Americans was meager and often demeaning. They were characterized as inferior, slovenly, or ludicrous. This image was perpetuated by the American theatre through racial stereotypes such as Raccoon in Andrew Barton's *The Disappointment; or The Force of Credulity* (1767), and Sambo in Robert Murdock's *The Triumph of Love* (1795). Films, radio, and television continued this practice with stereotypes like Amos and Andy, Beulah, and Buckwheat. Since African American students could not learn about themselves from history texts, concerned artists such as May Miller, Randolph Edmonds, and Willis Richardson decided that plays could be an entertaining and effective tool of enlightenment. In 1935, Richardson and Miller edited *Negro History in Thirteen Plays,* a collection that Dr. Woodson hailed as being another step toward freeing the mind from the imposed concept of inferiority. Since the 1920s, the NAACP and the Urban League had also taken steps in this direction by encouraging playwrights and promoting the production of their plays. African American colleges organized drama clubs and produced a series of plays during the school year, including new works published in *The Crisis* and *Opportunity.* History plays and pageants were presented in public schools and churches, along with religious history plays such as *Simon the Cyrenian* (1917) and May Miller's *Graven Images* (1929).

What, then, is the function of Black authors in writing history plays? The major purpose is to liberate the Black audience from an oppressive past, to present a history that provides continuity, hope, and glory. Zora Neale Hurston's *The First One* (1927) is a reinterpretation of the father/son relationship between Noah and his darker son, Ham. *Liberty Deferred,* although never produced, was a bold step in telling the truth of African American history. The impact of plays such as these have positive survival value for the race.

The author of history plays has dramatic license to create an aura of time and place rather than give strict adherence to historical fact. These plays should be judged by their verisimilitude to the Black experience and by their art—keeping in mind how well the wedding of form and content has been celebrated. "No playwright," according to Samuel A. Hay in his book, *African American Theatre: An Historical and Critical Analysis,* ". . . so completely mastered the dramatization of real and imagined historical events as did Charles Fuller." Thus, his Pulitzer Prize–winning play, although written a half century after the other plays in this section, is included as a proper culmination to the Black tradition of legend and history.

THE FIRST ONE
1927

Zora Neale Hurston (1901–1960)

In 1977, Robert Hemenway's biography, *Zora Neale Hurston: A Literary Biography,* sparked a renewed interest in one of the Harlem Renaissance's most talented and eccentric figures. Laurence Holder produced a one-act play , *Zora* (1978). George C. Wolfe adapted three of Hurston's stories and produced them at the New York Public Theatre under the title *Spunk* (1989), and finally George Houston Bass was instrumental in persuading Michael Schultz to direct Zora Hurston's and Langston Hughes's folk play *Mule Bone* (1991) on Broadway. Nonetheless, most people thought of Hurston as a novelist (*Their Eyes Were Watching God,* 1937) and an anthropologist (*Mules and Men,* 1935). Few people knew that Hurston had also written other plays, including *Color Struck* (1925) and the one published here, *The First One.*

Hurston tells the story of how Ham, the son of Noah, came to be Black. As a folklorist, Hurston knew the Black biblical tradition, and she was well aware that African Americans had a long practice of humanizing their gods—a tradition plagiarized and corrupted by Marc Connelly for *Green Pas-*

tures (1930). Hurston's play begins after the flood, when Noah and his family decide to thank God for preserving them. Ham, instead of bringing a material gift, brings his creative gifts—dance, song, joy, and abandon. Noah, having drunk too much, is tricked by Shem's and Japheth's wives into cursing Ham, a curse he can never take back. Hurston's reworking of the Bible is similar to that of May Miller in *Graven Images* in that the audience is allowed to review familiar events from a new perspective.

Hurston, born on January 7, 1901, in Eatonville, Florida, had grown up in the midst of Black folklore. She received her early education in Eatonville. After attending Morgan Academy in Baltimore, she enrolled in Howard University. A scholarship helped her to transfer to Barnard College in New York where she earned her B.A. in 1928. After graduation, she worked for a time as secretary to novelist Fanny Hurst, who encouraged her to write. Aided by a Rosenwald Fellowship, a Guggenheim grant, and funds from Mrs. R. Osgood Mason, she studied anthropology and folklore for four years at Columbia University with Dr. Franz Boas. In this capacity, she was able to travel and study in Haiti and the British West Indies.

Her restless spirit led her to various ventures—producing a program of Negro spirituals and work songs at the John Golden Theatre in New York, writing film scripts for Hollywood, teaching drama at North Carolina College for Negroes. During this time, and long before, she wrote articles, stories, and her plays. Her novel, *Their Eyes Were Watching God*, is considered her masterpiece, although her research into southern folklore is treasured, too, for its anecdotal tales and her accurate transcription of speech patterns and dialect.

In the latter years of her life, she returned to Florida, stopped publishing, and dropped out from the literary scene where she had played a major role. In her last years, apparently she worked as a housekeeper and maid, and at her death, she had so little money that she was buried in an unmarked grave. Alice Walker, the author of *The Color Purple*, located Hurston's grave and provided one of America's most original literary voices with a monument.

The First One
A Play in One Act

CAST OF CHARACTERS

NOAH
MRS. NOAH
SHEM
MRS. SHEM
HAM
MRS. HAM
JAPHETH
MRS. JAPHETH
EVE
SONS
OTHERS

TIME   *Three years after the Flood*

PLACE   *Valley of Ararat [in historic Armenia].*

PERSONS   *Noah, his wife, their sons: Shem, Japheth, Ham; Eve, Ham's wife; the sons, wives and children (6 or 7).*

Morning in the Valley of Ararat. The Mountain is in the near distance. Its lower slopes grassy with grazing herds. The very blue sky beyond that. These together form the background. On the left downstage is a brown tent. A few shrubs are scattered here and there over the stage indicating the temporary camp. A rude altar is built center stage. A shepherd's crook, a goat skin water bottle, a staff and other evidences of nomadic life lie about the entrance to the tent. To the right stretches a plain clad with bright flowers. Several sheep or goat skins are spread about on the ground upon which the people kneel or sit whenever necessary.

(Curtain rises on an empty stage. It is dawn. A great stillness, but immediately NOAH enters from the tent and ties back the flap. He is clad in loose fitting dingy robe tied about the waist with a strip of goat hide. Stooped shoulders, flowing beard. He gazes about him. His gaze takes in the entire stage)

NOAH *(fervently)*   Thou hast restored the Earth, Jehovah; it is good. *(turns to the tent)* My sons! Come, deck the altar for the sacrifices to Jehovah. It is the third year of our coming to this valley to give thanks offering to Jehovah that he spared us.

(Enter JAPHETH bearing a haunch of meat and SHEM with another. The wife of NOAH and those of SHEM and JAPHETH follow laying on sheaves of grain and fruit, dates and figs. They are all middle-aged and clad in dingy garments)

NOAH   And where is Ham—son of my old age? Why does he not come with his wife and son to the sacrifice?

MRS. NOAH   He arose before the light and went. (*she shades her eyes with one hand and points toward the plain with the other*) His wife, as ever, went with him.

SHEM (*impatiently*)   This is the third year that we have come here to this Valley to commemorate our delivery from the flood. Ham knows the sacrifice is made always at sunrise. See! (*he points to rising sun*) He should be here.

NOAH (*lifts his hand in a gesture of reproval*) We shall wait. The sweet singer, the child of my loins after old age had come upon me, is warm to my heart—let us wait.

(*There is offstage, right, the twanging of a rude stringed instrument and laughter. HAM, his wife and son come dancing on downstage right. He is in his early twenties. He is dressed in a very white goat skin with a wreath of shiny green leaves about his head. He has the rude instrument in his hands and strikes it. His wife is clad in a short blue garment with a girdle of shells. She has a wreath of scarlet flowers about her head. She has black hair, is small, young and lithe. She wears anklets and wristlets of the same red flowers. Their son about three years old wears nothing but a broad band of leaves and flowers about his middle. They caper and prance to the altar. HAM's wife and son bear flowers. A bird is perched on HAM's shoulder.*)

NOAH (*extends his arms in greeting*)   My son thou art late. But the sunlight comes with thee.

(HAM *gives bird to* MRS. NOAH, *then embraces* NOAH)

HAM (*rests his head for a moment on* NOAH'S *shoulders*)   We arose early and went out on the plain to make ready for the burnt offering before Jehovah.

MRS. SHEM (*tersely*)   But you bring nothing.

HAM   See thou! We bring flowers and music to offer up. I shall dance before Jehovah and sing joyfully upon the harp that I made of the thews of rams. (*he proudly displays the instrument and strums once or twice*)

MRS. SHEM (*clapping her hands to her ears*) Oh, Peace! Have we not enough of thy bawling and prancing all during the year? Shem and Japheth work always in the fields and vineyards, while you do naught but tend the flock and sing!

MRS. JAPHETH (*looks contemptuously at both* HAM *and* NOAH)   Still thou art beloved of thy father . . . he gives thee all his vineyards for thy singing, but Japheth must work hard for his fields.

MRS. SHEM   And Shem—

NOAH (*angrily*)   Peace! Peace! Are lust and strife *again* loose upon the Earth? Jehovah might have destroyed us all. Am I not Lord of the world? May I not bestow where I will? Besides, the world is great. Did I not give food, and plenty to the thousands upon thousands that the waters licked up? Surely there is abundance for us and our seed forever. Peace! Let us to the sacrifice. (NOAH *goes to the heaped up altar.* HAM *exits to the tent hurriedly and returns with a torch and hands it to* NOAH *who applies it to the altar. He kneels at the altar and the others kneel in a semi-circle behind him at a little distance.* NOAH *makes certain ritualistic gestures and chants*) O Mighty Jehovah, who created the Heaven and the firaments thereof, the Sun and Moon, the stars, the Earth and all else besides—

OTHERS
I am here
I am here, O, Jehovah
I am here
This is thy Kingdom, and I am here.

(*a deep silence falls for a moment*)

NOAH   Jehovah, who saw evil in the hearts of men, who opened upon them the windows of Heaven and loosed the rain upon them— And the fountains of the great deep were broken up—

OTHERS (REPEAT CHANT)

NOAH   Jehovah who dried up the floods and drove the waters of the sea again to the deeps—who met Noah in the Vale of Ararat and made covenant with Noah, His servant, that no more would he smite the Earth—And Seed time and Harvest, Cold and Heat, Summer and Winter, day and night shall not cease forever, and set His rainbow as a sign.

NOAH AND OTHERS
We are here O Jehovah
We are here
We are here
This Is Thy Kingdom
And we are here.

(NOAH *arises, makes obeisance to the smoking altar, then turns and blesses the others*)

NOAH   Noah alone, whom the Lord found worthy; Noah whom He made lord of the Earth, blesses you and your seed forever. (*at a gesture from him all arise. The women take the meat from the altar and carry it into the tent*) Eat, drink and make a joyful noise before Him. For He destroyed the Earth, but spared us. (*women reenter with bits of roast meat—all take some and eat. All are seated on the skins*)

MRS. NOAH (*feelingly*)   Yes, three years ago, all was water, *water*, WATER! The deeps howled as one beast to another. (*she shudders*) In my sleep, even now, I am in that Ark again being borne here, there on the great bosom.

MRS. HAM (*wide-eyed*)   And the dead! Floating, floating all about us—We were one little speck of life in a world of death! (*the bone slips from her hand*) And there, close beside the Ark, close with her face upturned as if begging for shelter—my *mother*! (*she weeps, HAM comforts her*)

MRS. SHEM (*eating vigorously*)   She would not repent. Thou art as thy mother was—a seeker after beauty of raiment and laughter. God is just. She would not repent.

MRS. HAM   But the unrepentant are no less loved. And why must Jehovah hate beauty?

NOAH   Speak no more of the waters. Oh, the strength of the waters! The voices and the death of it! Let us have the juice of the grape to make us forget. Where once was death in this Valley there is now life abundant of beast and herbs. (*he waves toward the scenery*) Jehovah meets us here. Dance! Be glad! Bring wine! Ham smite thy harp of ram's thews and sing!

(MRS. NOAH *gathers all the children and exits to the tent.* SHEM, JAPHETH, *their wives and children eat vigorously.* MRS. HAM *exits, left.* HAM *plays on his harp and capers about singing.* MRS. HAM *reenters with goat skin of wine and a bone cup. She crosses to where* NOAH *reclines on a large skin. She kneels and offers it to him. He takes the cup—she pours for him.* HAM *sings*)

HAM
I am as a young ram in the Spring
Or a young male goat.
The hills are beneath my feet
And the young grass.

Love rises in me like the flood
And ewes gather round me for food.

(*His wife joins in the dancing.* NOAH *cries "Pour" and* MRS. HAM *hurries to fill his cup again.* HAM *joins others on the skins. The others have horns suspended from their girdles.* MRS. HAM *fills them all.* NOAH *cries "pour" again and she returns to him. She turns to fill the others' cups*)

NOAH (*rising drunkenly*)   Pour again, Eve, and Ham sing on and dance and drink— drown out the waters of the flood if you can. (*his tongue grows thick.* EVE *fills his cup again. He reels drunkenly toward the tent door, slopping the liquor out of the cup as he walks.*) Drink wine, forget water—It means death, *death*! And bodies floating, face up! (*he stares horrified about himself and creeps stealthily into the tent, but sprawls just inside the door so that his feet are visible. There is silence for a moment, the others are still eating. They snatch tidbits from each other*)

JAPHETH (*shoves his wife*)   Fruit and herbs, woman! (*he thrusts her impatiently forward with his foot. She exits left*)

SHEM (*to his wife*)   More wine!

MRS. SHEM (*irritated*)   See you not that there is plenty still in the bottle! (*he seizes it and pours.* HAM *snatches it away and pours.* SHEM *tries to get it back but* HAM *prevents him. Reenter* MRS. JAPHETH *with figs and apples. Everybody grabs.* HAM *and* SHEM *grab for the same one,* HAM *gets it*)

MRS. SHEM (*significantly*)   Thus he seizes all else that he desires. Noah would make him lord of the Earth because he sings and capers. (HAM *is laughing drunkenly and pelting* MRS. SHEM *with fruit skins and withered flowers that litter the ground. This infuriates her*)

NOAH (*calls from inside the tent*)   Eve, wine, quickly! I'm sinking down in the WATER! Come drown the WATER with wine.

(EVE *exits to him with the bottle.* HAM *arises drunkenly and starts toward the tent door*)

HAM (*thickly*)   I go to pull our father out of the water, or to drown with him in it. (HAM *is trying to sing and dance*) "I am as a young goat In the sp-sp-sp-. (*he exits to the tent laughing.* SHEM *and* JAPHETH *sprawl out in the skins. The wives are showing signs of surfeit.* HAM *is heard laughing raucously inside the tent. He reenters still laughing*)

HAM (*in the tent door*)   Our Father has stripped himself, showing all his wrinkles. Ha! Ha! He's as no young goat in the spring. Ha! Ha! (*still laughing, he reels over to the altar and sinks down behind it*) The old Ram, Ha! Ha! Ha! He has had no spring for years! Ha! Ha! (*he subsides into slumber.* MRS. SHEM *looks about her exultantly*)

MRS. SHEM   Ha! The young goat has fallen into a pit! (*she shakes her husband*) Shem! Shem! Rise up and become owner of Noah's vineyards as well as his flocks! (SHEM *kicks weakly at her*) Shem! Fool! Arise! Thou art thy father's first born. (*she pulls him protesting to his feet*) Do stand up and regain thy birthright from (*she points to the altar*) that dancer who plays on his harp of ram thews, and decks his brow with bay leaves. Come!

SHEM (*brightens*)   How?

HIS WIFE   Did he not go into the tent and come away laughing at thy father's nakedness? Oh (*she beats her breast*) that I should live to see a father so mocked and shamed by his son to whom he has given all his vineyards! (*she seizes a large skin from the ground*) Take this and cover him and tell him of the wickedness of thy brother.

MRS. JAPHETH (*arising takes hold of the skin also*)   No, my husband shall also help to cover Noah, our father. Did I not also hear? Think your Shem and his seed shall possess both flocks and vineyard while Japheth and his seed have only the fields? (*she arouses* JAPHETH, *he stands.*)

SHEM   He shall share—

MRS. SHEM (*impatiently*)   Then go in (*the women release the skin to the men*) quickly, lest he wake sober, then will he not believe one word against Ham who needs only to smile to please him.

(*The men lay the skin across their shoulders and back over to the tent and cover* NOAH. *They motion to leave him*)

MRS. SHEM   Go back, fools, and wake him. You have done but half.

(*They turn and enter the tent and both shake* NOAH. *He sits up and rubs his eyes.* MRS. SHEM *and* MRS. JAPHETH *commence to weep ostentatiously*)

NOAH (*peevishly*)   Why do you disturb me, and why do the women weep? I thought all sorrow and all cause for weeping was washed away by the flood. (*he is about to lie down again but the men hold him up*)

SHEM   Hear, father, thy age has been scoffed, and thy nakedness made a thing of shame here in the midst of the feasting where all might know—thou the Lord of all under Heaven, hast been mocked.

MRS. SHEM   And we weep in shame, that thou our father should have thy nakedness uncovered before us.

NOAH (*struggling drunkenly to his feet*)   Who, who has done this thing?

MRS. SHEM (*timidly crosses and kneels before* NOAH)   We fear to tell thee, lord, lest thy love for the doer of this iniquity should be so much greater than the shame, that thou should slay us for telling thee.

NOAH (*swaying drunkenly*)   Say it, woman, shall the lord of the Earth be mocked? Shall his nakedness be uncovered and he be shamed before his family?

SHEM   Shall the one who has done this thing hold part of thy goods after thee? How wilt thou deal with them? Thou hast been wickedly shamed.

NOAH   No, he shall have no part in my goods—his goods shall be parcelled out among the others.

MRS. SHEM   Thou art wise, father, thou art just!

NOAH   He shall be accursed. His skin shall be black! Black as the nights, when the waters brooded over the Earth!

(*Enter* MRS. NOAH *from tent, pauses by* NOAH)

MRS. NOAH (*catches him by the arm*)   Cease! Whom dost thou curse?

NOAH (*shaking his arm free. The others also look awed and terrified and also move to stop him. All rush to him.* MRS. NOAH *attempts to stop his mouth with her hand. He shakes his head to free his lips and goes in a drunken fury*)   Black! He and his seed forever. He shall serve his brothers and they shall rule over him—Ah—Ah—. (*he sinks again to the ground. There is a loud burst of drunken laughter from behind the altar*)

HAM   Ha! Ha! I am as a young ram—Ha! Ha!

MRS. NOAH (*to* MRS. SHEM)   Who cursed Noah?

MRS. SHEM   Ham—Ham mocked his age. Ham uncovered his nakedness, and Noah grew wrathful and cursed him. Black! He could not mean *black*. It is enough that he should lose his vineyards. (*there is absolute silence for a while then realization comes to all.* MRS. NOAH *rushes in the tent to her husband, shaking him violently*)

MRS. NOAH (*voice from out of the tent*) Noah! Arise! Thou art no lord of the Earth, but a drunkard. Thou hast cursed my son. Oh water, Shem! Japheth! Cold water to drive out the wine. Noah! (*she sobs*) Thou must awake and unsay thy curse. Thou must! (*she is sobbing and rousing him.* SHEM *and* JAPHETH *seize a skin bottle from the ground by the skin door and dash off right.* MRS. NOAH *wails and the other women join in. They beat their breasts. Enter* EVE *through the tent. She looks puzzled*)

MRS. HAM Why do you wail? Are all not happy today?

MRS. NOAH (*pityingly*) Come, Eve. Thou art but a child, a heavy load awaits thee. (EVE *turns and squats beside her mother-in-law*)

EVE (*caressing* MRS. NOAH) Perhaps the wine is too new. Why do you shake our father?

MRS. NOAH Not the wine of grapes, but the wine of sorrow bestirs me thus. Turn thy comely face to the wall, Eve. Noah has cursed thy husband and his seed forever to be black, and to serve his brothers and they shall rule over him. (*Reenter the men with the water bottle, running.* MRS. NOAH *seizes it and pours it in his face. He stirs*) See, I must awaken him that he may unspeak the curse before it be too late.

EVE But Noah is drunk—surely Jehovah hears not a drunken curse. Noah would not curse Ham if he knew. Jehovah knows Noah loves Ham more than all. (*She rushes upon* NOAH *and shakes him violently.*) Oh, awake thou (*she shrieks*) and uncurse thy curse. (*All are trying to rouse* NOAH. *He sits, opens his eyes wide and looks about him.* MRS. NOAH *caresses him.*)

MRS. NOAH Awake, my lord, and unsay thy curse.

NOAH I am awake, but I know of no curse. Whom did I curse?

MRS. NOAH AND EVE Ham, lord of the Earth. (*He rises quickly to his feet and looks bewildered about*)

JAPHETH (*falls at his feet*) Our father, and lord of all under Heaven, you cursed away his vineyards, but we do not desire them. You cursed him to be black—he and his seed forever, and that his seed shall be our servants

forever, but we desire not their service. Unsay it all.

NOAH (*rushes downstage to the footlights, center. He beats his breast and bows his head to the ground*) Oh, that I had come alive out of my mother's loins! Why did not the waters of the flood bear me back to the deeps! Oh Ham, my son!

EVE (*rushing down to him*) Unspeak the Curse! Unspeak the Curse!

NOAH (*in prayerful attitude*) Jehovah, by our covenant in this Valley, record not my curses on my beloved Ham. Show me once again the sign of covenant—the rainbow over the Vale of Ararat.

SHEM (*strikes his wife*) It was thou, covetous woman, that has brought this upon us.

MRS. SHEM (*weeping*) Yes, I wanted the vineyards for thee, Shem, because at night as thou slept on my breast I heard thee sob for them. I heard thee murmur "Vineyards" in thy dreams.

NOAH Shem's wife is but a woman.

MRS. NOAH How rash thou art, to curse unknowing in thy cups the son of thy loins.

NOAH Did not Jehovah repent after he had destroyed the world? Did He not make all flesh? Their evils as well as their good? Why did He not with His flood of waters wash out the evil from men s hearts, and spare the creatures He had made, or else destroy us all, *all*? For in sparing one, He has preserved all the wickedness that He creates abundantly, but punishes terribly. No, He destroyed them because vile as they were it was His handiwork, and it shamed and reproached Him night and day. He could not bear to look upon the thing He had done, so He destroyed them.

MRS. NOAH Thou canst not question.

NOAH (*weeping*) Where is my son?

SHEM (*pointing*) Asleep behind the altar.

NOAH If Jehovah keeps not the covenant this time, if He spare not my weakness, then I pray that Hams heart remains asleep forever.

MRS. SHEM (*beseeching*) O Lord of the Earth, let his punishment be mine. We coveted his vineyards, but the curse is too awful for him. He is drunk like you— save him, Father Noah.

NOAH (*exultantly*) Ah, the rainbow! The promise! Jehovah will meet me! He will set

His sign in the Heavens! Shem hold thou my right hand and Japheth bear up my left arm. (NOAH *approaches the altar and kneels. The two men raise his hands aloft.*) Our Jehovah who carried us into the ark—

SONS   Victory, O Jehovah! The Sign.

OTHERS (*beating their breasts*)   This is Thy Kingdom and we are here.

NOAH   Who saved us from the Man of the Waters.

SONS   Victory, O Jehovah! The Sign.

OTHERS   We belong to Thee, Jehovah, we belong to Thee.

(*There is a sudden, loud raucous laugh from behind the altar.* HAM *sings brokenly,* "I am a young ram in the Spring.")

NOAH (*hopefully*)   Look! Look! To the mountain—do ye see colors appear?

MRS. NOAH   None but what our hearts paint for us—ah, false hope.

NOAH   Does the sign appear, I seem to see a faint color just above the mountain. (*another laugh from* HAM)

EVE   None, none yet. (*beats her breast violently, speaks rapidly*) Jehovah, we belong to Thee, we belong to *Thee.*

MRS. NOAH AND EVE   Great Jehovah! Hear us. We are here in Thy Valley. We who belong to Thee!

(HAM *slowly rises. He stands and walks around the altar to join the others, and they see that he is Black. They shrink back terrified. He is laughing happily.* EVE *approaches him timidly as he advances around the end of the altar. She touches his hand, then his face. She begins kissing him*)

HAM   Why do you all pray and weep?

EVE   Look at thy hands, thy feet. Thou art cursed black by thy Father. (*she exits weeping left*)

HAM (*gazing horrified at his hands*)   Black! (*he appears stupefied. All shrink away from him as if they feared his touch. He approaches each in turn. He is amazed. He lays his hand upon* SHEM)

SHEM (*shrinking*)   Away! Touch me not!

HAM (*approaches his mother. She does not repel him, but averts her face*)   Why does my mother turn away?

MRS. NOAH   So that my baby may not see the flood that hath broken the windows of my soul and loosed the fountains of my heart.

(*There is a great clamor offstage and* EVE *reenters left with her boy in her arms weeping and all the other children in pursuit jeering and pelting him with things. The child is also Black.* HAM *looks at his child and falls at* NOAH's *feet*)

HAM (*beseeching in agony*)   Why Noah, my father and lord of the Earth, why?

NOAH (*sternly*)   Arise, Ham. Thou art Black. Arise and go out from among us that we may see thy face no more, lest by lingering the curse of thy Blackness come upon all my seed forever.

HAM (*grasps his father's knees.* NOAH *repels him sternly, pointing away right.* EVE *steps up to* HAM *and raises him with her hand. She displays both anger and scorn*)

EVE   Ham, my husband, Noah is right. Let us go before you awake and learn to despise your father and your God. Come away Ham, beloved, come with me, where thou canst never see these faces again, where never thy soft eyes can harden by looking too oft upon the fruit of their error, where never thy happy voice can learn to weep. Come with me to where the sun shines forever, to the end of the Earth, beloved the sunlight of all my years. (*she kisses his mouth and forehead. She crosses to door of tent and picks up a water bottle.* HAM *looks dazedly about him. His eyes light on the harp and he smilingly picks it up and takes his place beside* EVE)

HAM (*lightly cynical to all*)   Oh, remain with your flocks and fields and vineyards, to covet, to sweat, to die and know no peace. I go to the sun. (*he exits right across the plain with his wife and child trudging beside him. After he is offstage comes the strumming of the harp and* HAM's *voice happily singing:* "I am as a young ram in the Spring." *It grows fainter and fainter until it is heard no more. The sun is low in the west.* NOAH *sits looking tragically stern. All are ghastly calm.* MRS. NOAH *kneels upon the altar facing the mountain and she sobs continually.*

We belong to Thee, O Jehovah
We belong to Thee.

She keeps repeating this to a slow curtain)

(*Curtain*)

GRAVEN IMAGES
1929

May Miller (1899–1995)

Since ancient times the people of Africa have celebrated life and death in theatre ritual. Much of this was oral drama, passed on by tradition but never written down. In the Western tradition, Black people were spoken about in the Roman plays—an Ethiopian slave girl appears in *The Eunuch* by Terence. Moors abound in Spanish plays from the twelfth century onward. The Black man makes his first entry onto the English stage in the Christmas liturgical plays; he enters as a king, one of the three Magi who come to offer gifts to the baby Jesus.

Graven Images is inspired by an Old Testament verse: "And Miriam and Aaron spake against Moses because of the Ethiopian woman he had married." (Numbers 12:1). The play, written around 1929 for eighth grade children, may be the first in which a "snow white devil" is struck down through divine justice. It aims to show how Black man is woven into the fabric of the universe. "We belong," this play exclaims; "we have always been, and we will always be."

May Miller (Sullivan) was a descendent of those African Americans who, after the Emancipation, realized that education was of primary importance if Blacks were to survive and prosper. Her mother, Annie Mae Butler, taught at the Baltimore Normal School, and her father, Kelly Miller, was a distinguished professor of sociology and Dean of Arts and Sciences at Howard University. Miller received her B.A. from Howard, continued her study at American and Columbia universities, and like her parents, became a teacher. She taught speech and drama at Frederick Douglass High School in Baltimore for twenty years. Her teacher, Mary Burrill, who taught English and speech at Dunbar High School in Washington, D.C., encouraged her to write plays. During the 1920s and 1930s she wrote nearly twenty one-act plays, conceived with the intent of instilling pride in her students and providing them with insight into African American history and culture. She was an active member of Georgia Douglas Johnson's literary salon, along with Zora Neale Hurston, Mary Burrill, Angelina Grimke, Marita

Bonner and Eulalie Spence. Her home on S Street in Washington was open to writers and poets—Frank Horne, Owen Dodson, Gwendolyn Brooks, Charles Sebree, and Toni Morrison. With Willis Richardson, she edited a volume of plays for children: Among the many plays that she has written, are *Sojourner Truth*, *Christophe's Daughters*, *Nails and Thorns*, and *Riding the Goat*. In her middle years she gave up playwriting, devoting her attention to writing poetry. Her poems have been published in *Phylon*, *Alan Swallow's P.S.*, *Common*

Ground, *The New York Times*, *Poetry*, *The Antioch Review*, *The Crisis*, *The Nation*, and many other leading magazines and anthologies. May Miller has published seven volumes of poetry: *Into the Clearing* (1959), *Poems* (1962), *Not That Far* (1973), *The Clearing and Beyond* (1974), *Dust of Uncertain Journey* (1975), *Halfway to the Sun* (1981), and *The Ransomed Wait* (1983). Her poetry, unlike her plays, avoided racial issues; she believed that "poetry should not serve as a lecture platform."

Graven Images

"And Miriam and Aaron spake against Moses because of the Ethiopian woman he had married."
Numbers 12:1

PERSONS OF THE PLAY

MOSES
AARON, *the brother of Moses*
MIRIAM, the sister of Moses
ZIPPORAH, *the wife of Moses*
JETHRO, *the father-in-law of Moses*
ITHAMAR, *youngest son of Aaron*
ELIEZER, *the second son of Moses*
PLAYMATES OF ITHAMAR
ATTENDANTS AND MAIDENS BEARING INCENSE, OINTMENT, CANDLESTICKS AND THE HOLY VESSELS INTO THE TABERNACLE

TIME   *1490* B.C.

PLACE   *Hazeroth, Egypt*

(SCENE: *The arena before the tabernacle. Back stage a flight of steps leads to the tabernacle. On both sides of the steps the columns rise. At the base of the columns basins of incense are burning. To the left front stage an abandoned idol is half hidden by a tree. To the right a few trees are left standing and a stump shows plainly that the temple has been erected in a clearing. It is high noon. The scene is enveloped in a bright golden light.*

ITHAMAR, *a stout lad of twelve clad in a short tunic, runs hurriedly on the stage. He looks toward the tabernacle and then slowly around him. He spies the golden bull)*

ITHAMAR   Oh! Oh! Uh-huh! Uh-huh! (*he smiles in satisfaction at having discovered the idol. He cautiously runs toward the tabernacle and up the steps. He peers in and listens. Nodding, he runs down the steps and to the side stage)* Lo, lads! Lo, lads! (*a troupe of boys of about* ITHAMAR's *age run boisterously in)*

FIRST BOY   What is it, Ithamar?

ITHAMAR   They took it away and we knew not where they hid it, but I have found it. Here it is.

SECOND BOY (*in amazement)*   The golden bull that our sires cast out of the tabernacle!

FIRST BOY   The golden bull!

BOYS (*in chorus)*   The golden bull!

FIRST BOY   What fun!

SECOND BOY   Now that we have found it, what shall we do?

FIRST BOY   It shall be a target, of course, and we shall hurl stones. A prize to the one who hits the bull's eye!

BOYS (*in a chorus, as they rush to pick up stones)*   The bull's eye! The bull's eye! (*amid much confusion they start hurling stones)*

ITHAMAR   Stay! Stay! (*the noise subsides*) We shall try by turn.

SECOND BOY   If our elders come, they will punish us by turn, too, for it is said they wish to keep the bull unscarred.

ITHAMAR   But our elders will not come here. The tabernacle is empty.

SECOND BOY   The noise might lead them here.

ITHAMAR   Then we can't play target.

BOYS (*throwing down their stones*)   Bah!

FIRST BOY   Come, Ithamar, what can we play?

ITHAMAR   We could play worship.

FIRST BOY   Maybe, but it is not so pleasant as stoning.

ITHAMAR   We can bow down before the bull even as our sires did before they built the tabernacle to God Jehovah.

SECOND BOY   But our sires will punish us for that, too.

ITHAMAR   We shall be quiet and our sires will not know.

SECOND BOY   Some one might tell.

ITHAMAR   You are the only some one I know, coward.

FIRST BOY   Come, Ithamar, let the scared one alone. Let us start the worship.

ITHAMAR   Who will begin?

FIRST BOY   You, Ithamar, you shall start the worship. Every one will follow you in turn. Come, make high praise to the golden bull! (*the boys form a circle around the golden bull*)

BOYS (*in chorus*)   Ithamar! Ithamar!

ITHAMAR (*stepping forward and kneeling before the bull*)   O! most sacred bull, it is Ithamar, the son of Aaron, the first high priest of Israel, who kneels before you. He offers you this golden armlet worth two shekels of silver. Be kind to me and my playmates. (*he places the armlet on the bull's ears*)

BOYS (*clapping their hands and shouting lustily*) Well done, Ithamar! Well done! Next! Next!

ITHAMAR (*grasping the first boy*)   You go next.

BOYS (*lustily*)   Talba next! Talba!

FIRST BOY (*stepping forward and kneeling*)   O! most sacred bull, I, Talba, am only a poor lad. My father is no high priest of Israel and I have no armlet to offer. This ragged girdle is all I have, but you may have it. (*he hangs the girdle from his tunic over the back of the bull*)

BOYS (*clapping and shouting lustily*)   Next! Next!

ITHAMAR (*approaching the second boy*) Scared one, you shall make worship next, for then we shall know you will not tell.

SECOND BOY   But I know not what to say and I have nothing to offer.

FIRST BOY   I had nothing.

SECOND BOY   I have not even a ragged girdle.

ITHAMAR   Come, you cannot escape so easily.

BOYS (*pressing closer and pushing their frighened comrade forward*)   No, come! Come!

SECOND BOY   How shall I begin?

ITHAMAR   Begin as I began—O most sacred bull!

BOYS (*echoing*)   O most sacred bull!

SECOND BOY (*timidly kneeling before the idol*) O most sacred bull, I have nothing to give you—not even a girdle like Talba's. But, sacred bull, if you will promise not to hurt me, I shall let Ithamar chop off a curl and give it to you for your bald head.

FIRST BOY   Bravo! come, Ithamar, chop off the curl.

ITHAMAR   A golden curl for a golden bull! (ITHAMAR *picks up a sharp stone and the boys grasp the timid child and lay his head on a stump for* ITHAMAR *to chop off a curl. The child struggles*)

FIRST BOY   Keep still; he does not want your head, fool.

SECOND BOY (*struggling*)   Pray let me up. There's a curl at home I'd rather give, and it will not hurt so much.

BOYS   No, no, a golden curl for a golden bull! (*while the boys have been busily engaged a group of little girls has entered*)

FIRST GIRL   Pray don't cut off his curl if it hurts so badly. Take one of mine; I have so many more.

FIRST BOY   You are a girl, you would cry.

FIRST GIRL   Indeed, I would not. (ITHAMAR, *looking up, stops the cutting of hair. The* SECOND BOY, *thus released, retreats to the edge of the crowd where he may escape readily*)

ITHAMAR   Besides, the golden bull does not want a girl's curl.

BOYS (*in chorus*)   A girl's curl! Bah!

SECOND GIRL   If you will not take the curl, may we play?

ITHAMAR   We are worshiping the golden bull and he does not like girl children.

SECOND GIRL   Let him close his eyes; he will not know the difference.

ITHAMAR   Oh, no, no, that would never do. We must not deceive when we worship.

FIRST GIRL   Then you cannot let us play?

ITHAMAR   Let me see, what are little girls good for? (*the boys look doubtfully at the girls*)

FIRST BOY   Ithamar, I will tell you—let them dance their worship as the virgins of our sires.

ITHAMAR   Maybe the golden bull would not mind that, but I am sure he does not want women to speak.

FIRST BOY   All right, little girls, we may let you dance.

BOYS (*in chorus*)   Yes, yes, a dance!

FIRST GIRL   And will you, at the end of the dance, bow when we bow? Then we shall all worship together.

ITHAMAR   But remember you must bow lower than we, for you are girls.

GIRLS (*eagerly*)   All right.

ITHAMAR   On with the dance, then.

FIRST BOY (*pushing the boys back*)   The dance!

BOYS   The dance! The dance!

(*The girls dance and at the end prostrate themselves before the golden bull. The boys follow their example, kneeling before the idol. While the dance has been going on a little brown boy of about ten years has quietly entered. Unobserved he has watched and as they bow he bursts into loud laughter*)

ELIEZER   Ha! Ha! So in Hazeroth little boys and girls dance and worship idols while their parents worship Jehovah.

FIRST BOY   Well, who are you to laugh and whence do you come?

ELIEZER   I am Eliezer, but recently come from the household of Jethro, my grandsire, in the land of Midian.

ITHAMAR   Oh, so you are my cousin of whom my sire, Father Aaron, spoke.

ELIEZER (*nodding anxiously*)   Uh—huh.

ITHAMAR   I am Ithamar, your cousin, son of Aaron, your uncle; and these, my friends and playmates. Welcome!

ELIEZER (*bowing*)   I give thanks to you for the welcome.

FIRST BOY   You may join us, if it pleases you.

ELIEZER   But it pleases me not. In Midian we are never permitted to play with idols.

ITHAMAR   You mean that you do not want to worship our idol.

FIRST GIRL   Do not ask him again, Ithamar; we do not like foreign boys.

SECOND GIRL   And I know not why, but the sight of him is strange.

FIRST GIRL   He is Ithamar's cousin.

SECOND GIRL   But they are so different.

ITHAMAR (*boastfully*)   I am not a coward.

ELIEZER   Neither am I.

ITHAMAR (*pushing* ELIEZER *toward second boy*) You two scared ones play together. Come, boys, back to our sport and leave them.

ELIEZER   Yes, and when our elders come, they shall be punished for their sport.

SECOND BOY (*in fear*)   Our elders are coming here?

ELIEZER   Of course, our elders are coming. Moses is already gathering the worshipers that Jethro may carry back to Midian news of the great tabernacle.

FIRST BOY (*overhearing*)   What do you know of our great Moses?

ELIEZER   Your Moses, indeed! My Moses! Did you not know that I am the son of Moses and Zipporah?

FIRST BOY   Bah! Bah! and who believes that?

SECOND BOY   Are you truly the son of Moses?

BOYS   Bah! Bah!

ELIEZER   Tell them, Ithamar, am I not?

ITHAMAR   Yes, he is; but my Aunt Miriam says that his mother is a black woman and that he and his brother, Gershom, are no true children of Israel.

SECOND GIRL   I knew the sight of him was strange.

ELIEZER   Yes, and I overheard my elders say that your two brothers, Nadab and Alihu, were struck dead for offering strange fire to God.

BOYS (*shrinking from* ITHAMAR)   Oh! Oh!

ITHAMAR   Yes, but they are dead and you are living and I shall not play with you. The others may do as they please.

FIRST BOY (*to* ELIEZER)   Can you show any reason why we should play with you, son of a Black woman?

SECOND BOY   But he isn't Black; he's only golden.

FIRST BOY   And pray, what does he know that we should play with him?

SECOND BOY   He knows more than Ithamar. He knew our sires were coming and Ithamar did not.

FIRST BOY (*to* ELIEZER)   If we do play with you, what sport can you offer?

ELIEZER   We can still play worship.

SECOND BOY   How can we play worship without an idol?

ELIEZER   I shall be your idol.

ITHAMAR   Bah! such an idol!

ELIEZER   Indeed, and why not? I shall make a far better idol than this (*he springs lightly to the platform in front of the idol*) Look, this idol is gold. (*he strips his tunic off to the waist*) Am I not gold? (*the boys press forward murmuring their assent*) Come feel your idol. It is cold but I am warm. Warm gold. (*the boys press closer*) And see! see! You worship this thing that does not so much as nod his thanks. It's still, but I move, I move.

SECOND BOY   He might make a very good idol.

FIRST BOY   We shall not listen to Ithamar. He is a better idol—warm, moving gold.

BOYS   Aye! Aye!

SECOND BOY   Well, let's begin playing before our sires come.

FIRST BOY   Come, boys! (*boys surround* ELIEZER, *crying their assent*)

FIRST GIRL   And you will let us play, too?

ELIEZER   Yes, you may worship me too.

SECOND BOY   When our sires come and ask, "What worship you?" . . .

FIRST GIRL   We shall answer, "A little boy."

FIRST BOY   No, silly, we shall say, "Great sires, we worship a child whom God hath created in his own image." Then, our sires will be pleased and they will reply, "Verily, verily, peace be with ye," and pass into the tabernacle.

ITHAMAR (*going off stage*)   They will, indeed, eh? We shall see.

FIRST BOY   Pay no attention to him. Come, let's play.

ELIEZER   Let the girls dance again for me.

(*The girls have just formed a circle and are about to dance when a solemn chant is heard in the distance. The girls stop*)

FIRST BOY   Our sires are coming to the tabernacle.

SECOND BOY   I knew it; and now we can't play.

(*The strains of the chant grow louder as the procession files in. The prophets lead the line.* MOSES *and* JETHRO *are ahead of all others. As* MOSES *enters the children bow their heads*)

CHILDREN   Father Moses!

MOSES   Peace be with ye!

(*The worshipers enter the tabernacle and a long line of youths and maidens bearing incense, candlesticks and sacred vessels follows. When the last worshiper has entered, the chant dies away to an echo. The children who had joined the chant now return to their sport.* MIRIAM, *a plump handsome woman of forty, is led on the stage by* ITHAMAR)

ITHAMAR   Now, you see, Aunt Miriam, that which I told you is true. He makes himself an idol and the children worship him.

MIRIAM   No, no, this must not be. (*to the children*) What is this that you do, little ones? (*the children fall back in consternation*)

FIRST GIRL   We worship a child whom God hath created in his own image.

MIRIAM   In his own image, indeed! Pray did Father Moses tell you God was an Ethiop?

CHILDREN   No, no.

MIRIAM   This child is no image of God. Jehovah. He is Black like his mother.

CHILDREN (*retreating from* ELIEZER)   Oh! Oh!

SECOND GIRL (*to first girl*)   I told you the sight of him was strange.

MIRIAM (*grasping* ELIEZER *and dragging him from platform*)   Black one, you had best hide your shame from the followers of your father and not place your complexion where all may see. (*to the children*) Now away with you! No more foolish sport of this kind; mind you.

SECOND BOY   I knew our elders would scold.

ITHAMAR (*to the children as they go off stage*)   I told you not to listen to him, didn't I?

(ELIEZER *sobbing has retreated to the back of the platform behind the golden bull where he hides from dreaded blows from* MIRIAM. *A faint refrain of the chant is heard in the tabernacle.* MIRIAM *approaches and listens. She starts up the steps, then*

as if changing her mind, turns and starts off stage.
AARON *comes out of the tabernacle and stands at the top of the steps)*

AARON   Why do you delay? The worship has started and the maidens eagerly await you.

MIRIAM   Why do they await me? Surely the black Jethro has seen our great tabernacle 'ere this.

AARON   Yes, but they now patiently await the word of God concerning our going from Hazeroth. You must lead the worship of the maidens.

MIRIAM   I shall be with them. I delayed only to stop the children's foolish sport.

AARON   What sport?

MIRIAM   Eliezer, the young son of Moses, has been making of himself an idol.

AARON   And what matters that?

MIRIAM   Only it is not wise that the followers of Moses should be constantly reminded of his black wife and brown children.

AARON   And if they are, what?

MIRIAM   Surely they will say, "He is no true prophet of the God of Abraham, of Isaac and of Jacob, for he has married an Ethiop and his children are Ethiopian."—However, that may end happily, for the people may call for a new leader.

AARON   Sh! God will punish you for such talk.

MIRIAM   God may punish me, but the people will select a new leader.

AARON   Who will that be?

MIRIAM   You, of course. Are you not the first high priest of the children of Israel?

AARON   Oh, no, that could not be!

MIRIAM   Why not? Has the Lord spoken only to Moses? Has he not spoken to us also? Why should we, who are also the children of Amram, the Levite, follow that son who has forgotten so far as to marry an Ethiop?

AARON   That which you speak is sinful. 'Tis God's will that Moses lead us and God Jehovah will punish you for speaking against him and me for listening.

MIRIAM   Coward! What I have said is sweet to your ears, too. *(going up the tabernacle steps)* What you fear to say your sister, Miriam, dares!

AARON   I fear only God.

MIRIAM   Has God said that only Moses knows His will?

AARON   So Moses has said.

MIRIAM   Why should Moses not speak thus, as long as by so speaking he assures for himself the place of leader? And we cringe and follow.

AARON   But who am I to lead Israel?

MIRIAM   You are the first born of Amram and by far more ready of tongue than the brother you now follow.

AARON   But that brother is the chosen leader of Israel.

MIRIAM   He should lead Israel who is truly an Israelite, one uncontaminated by Ethiopian blood.

AARON   O! to lead my people.

MIRIAM   You can.

AARON   *(as if dreaming)*   And we should go out from Hazeroth and pitch tents in the wilderness and the people would cry out, "O! Father Aaron, where does Israel move now?" They would look to me for answer.

MIRIAM   They would harken to your word and with one voice call, "Father Aaron! Father Aaron, the true leader of Israel! Moses is no more."

ELIEZER *(jumping hastily from the platform and coming forth to face MIRIAM)*   You lie, you lie. My sire, Moses, lives. He is in the tabernacle praying for us.

MIRIAM *(grasping ELIEZER)*   So you are eavesdropper, too, listening to words intended for other ears. *(she slaps his face)* Eavesdroppers are always thus rewarded for their pains.

AARON *(freeing the child from MIRIAM's grasp)* He is only a child, Miriam.

MIRIAM   Yes, child of an Ethiop!

AARON   God shall surely punish you.

MIRIAM   Indeed *(she turns and laughs, then starts toward the tabernacle)*

AARON *(grasping MIRIAM's arm)*   Hold! where do you go?

MIRIAM   Into the tabernacle to speak against Moses, our brother. The evil is done. The child has heard; he will prate to his elders.

AARON   Hold! Hold!

MIRIAM *(freeing her arm and grasping his)* Come, your sister, Miriam, dares.

AARON   And may the God of our fathers have mercy upon us!

(MIRIAM *enters the tabernacle and* AARON *reluctantly follows. The second boy peeps slyly on the stage. Discovering* ELIEZER *hidden behind the idol, he approaches*)

SECOND BOY   Have our elders truly gone?

ELIEZER   Yes, every one.

SECOND BOY   And are you sure the wicked Miriam will not return?

ELIEZER   She will not return soon. I heard Aaron, my uncle, tell Miriam that they were awaiting God's word of our going out from Hazeroth.

SECOND BOY   Is Miriam really your aunt?

ELIEZER   Yes, the sister of my father, Moses. Why?

SECOND BOY   She doesn't like you much; does she?

ELIEZER   I guess she does love Ithamar more; but you do not believe that which she said—do you?

SECOND BOY   What—what did she say?

ELIEZER   You remember well that she said I was not made in the image of God.

SECOND BOY   Well, are you?

ELIEZER   Of course, and God will punish anyone who says I am not.

SECOND BOY   And how do you know that?

ELIEZER   Aaron, the brother of my sire, said so. He told Miriam so, too.

SECOND BOY   And what did she say?

ELIEZER   She didn't believe it, for she laughed and went into the tabernacle.

SECOND BOY   I laugh, too, for I don't believe that you are either.

(*As the children talk, a great uproar is heard in the tabernacle. The crowd surges to the door and down the steps with* MIRIAM *running ahead. The children hide behind the idol*)

WORSHIPPERS   Unclean! Unclean! (MIRIAM *runs down the steps and collapses at the foot.* AARON *starts to lift her but looks in her face and draws back in fear*) Unclean! Unclean!

AARON   O! God of Abraham, of Isaac and of Jacob, have mercy on her and forgive me, a sinner who spoke against thy servant.

(MOSES *stands in the doorway of the tabernacle; and* MIRIAM, *looking up, sees him*)

MIRIAM (*stretching her hands to* MOSES)   Oh, my brother, Moses, I have sinned against God

and you, but I beseech you to pray God to take away this leprosy. See, my arms are as white as snow. My flesh is half consumed. Let me not be as one dead.

WORSHIPPERS   Unclean! Unclean!

(MOSES *lifts his arms in prayer and silence falls*)

MOSES   God of my father, and of Abraham, Isaac and Jacob, heal her now, O God, I beseech thee!

MIRIAM (*looking hopefully to* MOSES *and at her arms*)   Am I healed now?

MOSES (*shaking his head*)   No, my sister.

MIRIAM   Shall I be condemned to live on dead as I am?

MOSES   For seven days thou shalt be ashamed and for seven days must thou be shut out from camp. 'Tis God's will.

WORSHIPPERS (*repeating in awe*)   God's will. (MIRIAM *rises and staggers off stage, the mob following at a distance shouting "Unclean"*)

MOSES (*stretching forth his hands*)   Verily, verily, I say unto ye, my people, let not the camp be moved until she return to us after seven days. Then shall we journey and pitch camp in the wilderness of Param. Peace be with ye!

(*The psalm singers issue from the tabernacle and follow* MOSES, *chanting. When the last singer has gone, the boys come from behind the idol*)

ELIEZER   So you laughed with Miriam, did you? Maybe you want to go with her into the wilderness.

SECOND BOY   Oh! no, truly not. I will play worship again, truly I will, if you ask your God not to punish me.

ELIEZER   Will you bring back your playfellows?

SECOND BOY   Yes, yes, and you shall be our idol.

ELIEZER   And when our elders come, what will you say?

SECOND BOY   When my elders come and ask, "What is this that you do, little one?" I shall answer. . . .

ELIEZER (*impatiently*)   Yes! Yes!

SECOND BOY   I shall answer, "I worship a child."

ELIEZER (*prompting*)   Whom God hath created. . . .

SECOND BOY   Yes, I know. Let me say all of it. "I worship a child whom God hath created in his own image." Now, will you ask your God to forgive me?

ELIEZER   All right, but be gone and call your play-fellows.

SECOND BOY *(going off stage)*   Lo, lads! Lo, lads!

(ELIEZER *springs to the platform and sits hugging his knees in delight in anticipation of the coming sport as the curtain falls)*

NATURAL MAN

1937

Theodore Browne (1910–1979)

Natural Man was first produced as a folk opera on January 28, 1937, in Seattle by the Negro unit of the Federal Theatre Project. It was staged four years later by the American Negro Theatre in Harlem with most of the music omitted. Theodore Browne based his script on the John Henry legends, unverifiable stories passed along by tradition. It was probable that such a man existed, although the legends and ballads may be a composite of several Black steel-driving men. These men—convicts who were forced to labor for no wages—built the southern railways. John Henry's most notable characteristic is his physical strength. He is an outgrowth of the stereotypical "brute Negro"—an imposing figure, cut from the same physical cloth as Crown in Dorothy and DuBose Heywood's *Porgy,* but there the similarity ends. In Browne's hands, the "brute Negro" has been transformed into a Black revolutionary hero. This John Henry is aware of the racism around him and angered by it. He speaks out, fights back. He is a symbol of unyielding pride and the African American's determination to survive when the odds are against him.

The play is set in the 1880s, years after the emancipation, but the yoke of bondage continues to exist. John's life is permeated with racial enmity both in his past with the Jailbirds and the Guards, and in his current relationship with the railway boss, Captain Walters, who regards his Black workers as less than machines—to be used and discarded at will. John Henry resents this condescending attitude and paternalistic manner. He will not become submissive. He is a man—a king—and if being his own man means death, so be it.

Theodore Browne treats the John Henry legend realistically rather than as fantasy. He refuses to view John Henry as a "quaint" stereotype, creating him, instead, as a multifaceted character. This allows Browne to examine the emotional and psychological effects of racism on his protagonist. The play was a success with both Black and white audiences. Black audiences easily identified with John Henry, since the humiliating acts of prejudice inflicted upon him were identical to those that they endured. They understood his seething anger and his decision to die a man rather than accept the indignities of white men. He became their hero, not for laying railroad tracks but for standing up to "the man." White audiences and critics, on the other hand, interpreted the play as a conflict between the natural man and mechanization, whereas Browne had in fact created a conflict between a Black militant and a white hierarchy. This failure to understand Browne's message was understandable because Black drama and characters were not thought of as "revolutionary" at that time.

Natural Man is the kind of play that Browne envisioned for an African American theatre. Such a theatre would celebrate the heroic aspects of the Black experience by focusing on the accomplishments of those individuals who helped create this nation: Black men and women whose lives could inspire and motivate audiences.

Browne was the assistant director and resident playwright of the Negro unit of the Federal Theatre Project in Seattle, where he not only wrote original plays but also adapted classical drama for Black performers. In 1940, along with Owen Dodson, Powell Lindsay, Langston Hughes, Theodore Ward, and George Norford, he organized the Negro Playwrights Company in Harlem. Its purpose was to present the realities of African American life and to provide a working theatre for Black artists. The American Negro Theatre, also founded in 1940, produced *Natural Man*, without music, on May 7, 1941, in Harlem.

Natural Man

A Play In Eight Episodes based on the Legend of John Henry.

CAST OF CHARACTERS

JOHN HENRY, *a steel driving man*
CHARLEY, *a steel driver*
BIG'N ME, *a steel driver*
LUTHER, *a steel driver*
JIM, *a steel driver*
HARD TACK, *a steel driver*
BRITT, *a steel driver*
POLLY ANN, *John Henry's woman*
CAPTAIN TOMMY WALTERS, *white railway boss*
THE CREEPER, *a black troubadour*
SALESMAN OF STEEL DRILLS
SPECTATORS
WOMAN, *a street walker*
BARTENDER
SWEETMAN, *a pimp*
BUSTER, *a bouncer*
JESS, *a bouncer*
PICKPOCKET

WHITE POLICEMAN
WHITE JAILBIRDS
SHERIFF
FIVE CONVICTS
BOY
GUARD
CONGREGATION
PREACHER
OLD WOMAN
FOUR HOBOES

First Episode

(TIME   *noon. The early eighties, on the day preceding the great contest between John Henry and the steam drill.*

SETTING   *before the entrance to the Big Ben Tunnel in West Virginia. The setting is stylized. A framework of logs that form a crudely shaped rectangle and supports the earth above the dugout. A raised landing, both ends of which slope down to the stage flooring. The entire action of the various episodes take place outside this entrance, except, at intervals, when we see the silhouetted figure of* JOHN HENRY *wielding his hammer directly inside the tunnel.*

The whole stage is dark, except for a dullish spray of light falling upon the landing. From inside the tunnel comes the voice of JOHN HENRY, *singing a "Hammer Song," each line of which he under-scores with a hammer beat. As he sings, a motley crew of Negro steeldrivers issue, one after the other, from the blackness of the tunnel and into the shaft of the light on the landing. They sprawl about the landing and open up their dinner pails and commence to eat, silently, as* JOHN HENRY, *out of sight, sings and hammers)*

JOHN HENRY   This old hammer—huh!
        Rings like silver—huh!
        This old hammer—huh!
        Rings like silver—huh!
        This old hammer—huh!
        Rings like silver—huh!
        Shines like gold, boys—huh!
        Shines like gold—huh!

        Ain't no hammer—huh!
        In these mountains—huh!
        Ain't no hammer—huh!
        In these mountains—huh!
        Rings like mine, boys—huh!
        Rings like mine—huh!

CHARLEY   Say, Big'n Me, what your old lady put in that pail?

BIG'N ME   Never you mind what my old lady put in this pail!

LUTHER   Tell by the way he's eating and sopping his lips, sure must taste good!

JIM   Charley Boy's treening that there dinner pail just like some cat treening fish-heads!

HARD TACK   Won t do him a speck of good either! What you say, Big'n Me?

BIG'N ME   Chirp it, Brother! My mouth's full and I can't talk!

JIM   Why the name of God you don't get yourself an old lady, Charley Boy?

CHARLEY   Too much the loser!

HARD TACK   Know a certain old gal whose palms' just itching to handle your money!

BRITT   Who? That little re-headed yaller gal from New Orleans?

HARD TACK   She's soft as hell on Charley Boy, too!

CHARLEY   She ain't no damn good! Got a hand full of gimmies and a mouth full of much-oblige.

BRITT   Love 'em and leave 'em. That's my policy.

CHARLEY *(looks in* BIG'N ME's *pail)*   Spare-ribs and sweet-potatoes! Lord, today!

BIG'N ME   Tennessee you may see, yet, but not a damn rib of these here spare-ribs will you get!

CHARLEY   Big'n Me's old lady sure must be powerful sweet on him!

BIG'N ME   Don't you let my woman's sweet-ness worry you none!

HARD TACK   May wake up one these morn-ings and find himself dead!

JIM   Charley Boy, you can't make it off cheese and crackers!

LUTHER   You need a mess of pork chops to drive that steel!

BIG'N ME   Something to stick to your stom-ach. Something greasy!

VOICES OF MALE CHORUS *(off stage)*
        Never mind that fancy dish, Babe,
        Never mind that silver knife and fork.
        Just dump my vittles in a dinner-pail,
        And, when I eat, don't talk!

        Celery, lettuce—that's rabbit food
        Bring me some sow-belly and beans.
        Them's what's going stick by you, Babe,
        And help you blow up steam!

(Roars of belly-laughter from the Steeldrivers)

CHARLEY   Say, Hard Tack, where the hell was you last night?

HARD TACK   I went in town to raise some righteous hell.

LUTHER   There was hell-raising a-plenty right here in camp.

BRITT   Tell him about that fancy city-slicker with them trained dice!

BIG'N ME   Man, old Candy sure put his trade-mark on that Dude!

CHARLEY   Never see such razor-slashing in all my born days!

HARD TACK   Everywhere you go in town folks talking about the big contest to-morrow.

JIM   John Henry and that steam drill! Like some world championship bout!

BRITT   Who they saying'll win, Hard Tack?

CHARLEY   They doing any betting? What's the odds?

HARD TACK   Five to one on John Henry. White folks doing most the betting. Saw a white guy pull out a roll of yaller money, man, big enough to choke a mule, and he laid every God's bit of it on John Henry! Say he bet on John Henry any day when it comes to driving steel!

BIG'N ME   White folks got to hand it to old John Henry! Boy, don't he make 'em all sit up and take notice?

BRITT   That fool sure can swing a wicked hammer!

LUTHER   That's the living truth! All his brains is in his muscles!

CHARLEY   Arms like steel and head like solid rock!

HARD TACK   Any you-all ground-hogs like to bet? My five bucks says John Henry'll beat that old steel drill.

CHARLEY   Five bucks? That wouldn't buy my gal a pair of shoes!

HARD TACK   Hell you say! That slew-footed wench ain't never wore a pair of shoes cost that much!

LUTHER   How's any meat-man going whip something run by steam?

HARD TACK   All right, you put your money where your mouth is!

LUTHER   White man smart. He sits up all night long figuring out a way to put us all right back in slavery.

BIG'N ME   Steam may be all right, but she'll never take the place of a natural man. Nossir!

BRITT   Them science guys so smart, though, they can invent most nigh anything.

HARD TACK   You can take your brains and your deep books I'll take mother-wit.

JIM   Tell that fool something! Mother-wit! Now you talking!

CHARLEY   Mother-wit and arms of steel! A solid, natural man!

HARD TACK (*as* POLLY ANN *appears*)   Well, look who's here, boys! Polly Ann!

JIM   Hot dog! I sure likes the way that gal walks!

BRITT   Rears back her head and struts just like a maltese cat!

CHARLEY   I'd dump my week's pay in her lap any day!

LUTHER   Ah, do it, Pretty Mama, do it!

HARD TACK (*clowns with her as the others watch approvingly*)   Well, I ain't no lover,
No lover's son,
But, Baby, I can do your loving
Till your lover come!

LUTHER   Look! She all dressed up in her Sunday-go-to-meeting!

CHARLEY   Polly Ann sure do look like ready money and careless love!

HARD TACK   New shoes! New dress! All she need now is a brand-new sugar-daddy!

POLLY ANN   Don't get excited, Hot Papa! My shopping days is over!

HARD TACK (*cavorting*)   Now, who bought you
    those pretty little shoes?
Who bought you the dress you wear so fine?
And who kissed your red rosy checks?
And who's going to be your man?

POLLY ANN   John Henry bought these pretty little shoes.
John Henry bought the dress I wear so fine.
John Henry kissed my red rosy cheeks.
Doggone it! You know I don't need no man!

HARD TACK   You know them pretty shoes she's
    dogging out?
Dress she wear so fine? Well I tell you.
Them shoes she got from a railroad man.
That dress she got from a driver in the mine!

(*The men all roar with laughter, as* POLLY ANN *rolls her eyes prettily*)

John Henry he had a little woman,
Just as pretty as she could be.
They's only one objection I has to her—

POLLY ANN   What?—

HARD TACK   She wants every man she see!

POLLY ANN   That's a pop-eyed lie, and you knows it! John Henry never had a gal been truer to him.

CHARLEY   If you weren't so true, I done had you for my woman long time ago. From the day I laid eyes on you!

POLLY ANN   Say, tell me where is my steel-driving daddy?

BIG'N ME   He never quit work yet.

JIM   He claim he figuring out a new way how to swing that hammer tomorrow.

POLLY ANN   Well, what's wrong with the way he been swinging it?

JIM   That's what I'd like to know. Never could figure how he swing from both hips.

LUTHER (*suddenly*) Lord! Lord! Just listen to that man drive steel!

BRITT Listen to that hammer ring! Like a hollow-ground razor blade!

JOHN HENRY (*from inside, sings*) Come here, my
  pretty little mama—huh!
  Come and sit on your daddy's knee—huh!
  You have been the death of many a man—huh!
  But you won't be the death of me!—huh!
POLLY ANN (*she sings back to him*) You might
  be bigger than me, Hot Papa—huh!
  You might be the biggest man alive—huh!
  But you try any two-timing with this gal—huh!
  She'll cut you down to her size!

CHARLEY She sure talks like a natural woman!

POLLY ANN (*impatiently*) John Henry, you come on out here! Your somnteat's getting cold.

JOHN HENRY Just one more swing will get it! (*hammers, then he appears, smiling*)

BRITT Boy, you sure make that hammer talk!

POLLY ANN Way you swinging that hammer, won't be no rocks left for you to drill tomorrow!

JOHN HENRY Just thought I needed to sort of exercise a little more. Work up an appetite.

POLLY ANN I hopes you gets your fill of steel-driving!

JOHN HENRY Baby, a steel-driving champ's like a prizefighter. Always got to keep in condition.

POLLY ANN You ain't afraid you'll forget how to swing that hammer? (*rhapsodic*) Lord, when I come out the house, the earth rocked under my feet!

JOHN HENRY That was just my hammer falling down!

POLLY ANN And, when I get here to the tunnel, feel like the whole tunnel caving in!

JOHN HENRY Go way from here, gal! You only hear the echo of that hammer ring!

STEELDRIVERS She only hear the echo of that hammer ring!

JOHN HENRY There was once a mountain
  And the mountain was so tall, that
  They sent word for me to come
  Blow that mountain small!
STEELDRIVERS Blow that mountain small, Boy!
  Blow that mountain small!

JOHN HENRY (*with boyish exuberance*) Man, I can hardly wait! Tomorrow seem so far-off like. Can hardly wait. Studying about how I'm going beat that old steam drill down, figuring out this kind of stroke, and figuring out some other, till my brains whirl like a spinning-top. All I can think of the whole week long. A brand-new ten-pound hammer and a brand-new drill, carved from solid steel. Buddy-boys, when I do commence to drive that steel, all of you going hear music such as you never hear before! Natural music. When you hears that hammer ring, it'll sound like the silver chimes in Glory and a band of snow-white angels singing! Sparks of fire will jump from them rocks like the Devil a-spitting thru his teeth. Ain't no hammer in this whole land going out-ring mine, Boys, going outring mine!

HARD TACK You tell'em, John Henry!
BIG'N ME You tell'em!
CHARLEY Boy, I ain't got the heart to tell'em!

JOHN HENRY Take all the rocks I done busted from here to Macon. Take all the spikes I done drove in railroad ties. The great large mountains I done hollow out, so to make a hole for trains to run through. Laying steel tracks for trains to fly over. Busting rocks to make smooth gravel roads. I done all that! Done the work of a natural man. Me and my hammer, Boy, building railroad tracks and gravel roads. Now, who comes first? Me or this man-made steam drill? Who fixed it so a locomotive engine can have a track to run on? Who? Well, it was me, that's who! I come first. Bring on your fancy, new-fangled steam drills, line'em up six in a row and start'em all drilling at the same time as me, and I'll bet you any kind of money that I beat every damn one of them put together!

(CAPTAIN TOMMY, *a middle-aged white man enters*)

CAPTAIN TOMMY What's this I hear you saying, John Henry?

STEELDRIVERS Captain Tommy! Howdy, Captain!

CAPTAIN TOMMY Howdy, Boys!

JOHN HENRY (*modestly*) Nothing much, Captain. Just letting these boys know how I feels about this steam drill.

CAPTAIN TOMMY Well, you think you man enough to beat that steam drill?

JOHN HENRY   If I don't beat it, Captain, you can run me till I'm lean!

BIG'N ME   He'll beat it sure, Captain.

BRITT   Fastest steeldriver in the whole United States!

LUTHER   Sure is! A steel-driving fool!

JIM   A natural-born steeldriver!

BRITT   That boy born with a hammer in his hand!

CHARLEY   He drives steel out of this world!

HARD TACK   He'll whip that old steam drill so, she'll moan and sigh!

CAPTAIN TOMMY   All right! Tomorrow will tell the tale. May the best man win! Oh, yes— and speaking about tomorrow, I guess you boys may as well take the rest of the day off.

STEELDRIVERS   Thank you, Captain Tommy! Thank you, Boss!

CAPTAIN TOMMY   Sort of figured you boys would like to celebrate on the night before the great contest.

STEELDRIVERS   Yessir, Captain, we sure do! Yessirree!

CAPTAIN TOMMY (*chuckles, then with affected sternness*)   And see to it you behave yourselves. Don't get mixed up in no shooting or cutting scrapes. If you get in jail, might as well make up your mind to stay there until after the contest.

HARD TACK   Boss, that jailhouse couldn't hold me whilst that contest was going on!

CHARLEY   I'd carry on so that the jailer would throw me the key and let me unlock the cell door myself!

CAPTAIN TOMMY   By the way, John Henry— I'm counting on you to win.

JOHN HENRY   Well, you sure counting right, Captain Tommy!

CAPTAIN TOMMY   Tomorrow, after the contest, I'll drive you and Polly Ann to town, and you can pick out the best suit of clothes in any tailor shop. I don't give a continental how much it costs either. The best! As good as anything I wear myself. On top of that, I'm making you a present of fifty brand-new silver dollars.

BRITT   Fifty brand-new silver cogwheels!

LUTHER   Natural-made money!

JIM   Money that rings like steel!

BIG'N ME   Now, I knows he going win!

POLLY ANN   You hear that, Honey Man? Fifty brand-new silver dollars to jingle in the pockets of your brand-new suit!

JOHN HENRY   Thank you, Captain!—Say, you ain't now going to town?

CAPTAIN TOMMY   I'm on my way there right now.

JOHN HENRY   Well, bring me back a ten-pound hammer. I'm going drive that steel on down! (CAPTAIN TOMMY *exits.* JOHN HENRY *is exultant*)

Tomorrow at sunrise,
Like a natural man
Tomorrow at sunrise,
Like a natural man
Going take that hammer, drive that
Steel the fastest in the land!

STEELDRIVERS

Going take that hammer, Drive that
Steel the fastest in the land!

(*A small, nondescript Negro literally creeps into the scene. The steeldrivers and* POLLY ANN *are facing* JOHN HENRY *and do not see the stranger when he enters and stands in back of them. In his shirtsleeves and hatless,* THE CREEPER, *as he is called, is dressed in mismatched garish attire. A black troubadour, he carries a cheap-looking canvas-covered guitar case. [He is to be a one-man Chorus to underscore the legend-in-the-making charisma of* JOHN HENRY.] THE CREEPER *stands looking up at* JOHN HENRY, *grinning broadly.* JOHN HENRY *recognizes him instantly, a look of consternation comes into his face*)

JOHN HENRY   Creeper! (*the others all turn around to behold the* CREEPER, *grinning like a spreading adder*)

CREEPER (*in a soft-spoken, "clabber-mouth" voice*)   Nobody diffent! Yessuh, folks, I the old Creeper himself! Ain't nothing to me. John Henry knows me of old. (*to* JOHN HENRY) How is you, Boy?

JOHN HENRY (*vehemently*)   Creeper, I've tried every which way I knows how to lose sight and sound of you, but somehow you always catch up with me You and that tarnashun guitar-box. And you like a buzzard waiting 'round for something to heave its last breath!

STEELDRIVERS (*in unison*)   Where this dude come from?
What th'hell you doing 'round here, Bo?
Let's we drive him to hell outta this camp!
He's a jinx!
Come on, you half-pint runt, travel!—

JOHN HENRY   No, take your hands off him! Leave him 'lone Leave him be. He ain't bother nobody. You-all don't know him like I do. He ain't the kind you shake off easy.—You hear me now, Creeper, I want you to git this straight, you hear me? I got myself a job to do. Biggest I ever yit tackle. I'm going beat that steam drill they bringing in here tomorrow, else lay down and die. Now, you and nothing you say going stop me!

CREEPER   You knows I'm with you, John Henry. Yessuh, be with you to the end.

JOHN HENRY   Come on, Polly Ann.

POLLY ANN   John Henry, what is the meaning of this? (*as she follows him*) Who this Creeper dude, and why come he follow you like a bloodhound dog?—

BRITT   Never seen John Henry worked up like this before.

HARD TACK   Something's on his mind. Memories, I guess. This dude here bring up memories.

CHARLEY   Say, Creeping Man, open her up and play something!

LUTHER   Beat out some low-down blues on that guitar!

CREEPER (*grins, withdrawing*)   I be round tomorrow. Play something for you. Something special. Song I make up bout John Henry. I has a heap of songs, and they's all bout John Henry, too. (*he ambles off*)

LUTHER   I be a sonavagun!

HARD TACK   Peoples!

CHARLEY   Man, he walks like lice dropping off him!

BRITT   Outta this world and in the next! (*Fade out*)

Second Episode

TIME: *sunrise, the following day.*

SETTING: *same as the first episode*

CAPTAIN TOMMY WALTERS *and another white man, the* SALESMAN, *are discovered on the landing. They speak with rapid, stacatto precision, their voices hollow and metallic. They are like two competing auctioneers. They are heard above the murmur of the crowd of spectators below)*

SALESMAN   All right, all right, if that's the way you want it.

CAPTAIN TOMMY   My boy against your steam drill.

SALESMAN   Right, sir!

CAPTAIN TOMMY   Hell, it's a cinch my boy'll win!

SALESMAN   I'm game enough to wager he hasn't got a chance.

CAPTAIN TOMMY   We'll see about that. Fourteen-hour stretch. Let's see—(*he looks at his watch*) Pretty near to starting time. From four o'clock sharp to six in the evening.

SALESMAN   You're putting him under an awful strain, Mister Walters.

CAPTAIN TOMMY   I know what he can do.

SALESMAN   Sunrise to sunset.

CAPTAIN TOMMY   Yep, sunrise to sunset. You're going to see some genuine first-class steel-driving. Just wait. McCurdy, I've been in this business over twenty-five years. I reckon I know a good steeldriver when I see one. Most of my boys are hand-picked. I do the hiring and firing around here. I get most of them off the chain gang. Pay their fines, then give them a chance to work it off. Some of them boys were up for life. I buy their freedom and give them a new start.

SALESMAN   That's downright charitable, Mister Walters.

CAPTAIN TOMMY   Take that boy John Henry. Yep, John Henry. Most valuable hand I got. Wanted in Georgia for killing a white man. Was on the chain gang. He ups and kills one of the guards, then made a get-away. I could send him back today or tomorrow, but I'd be a damn fool if I did!

SALESMAN   This steam drill's been tested. She's capable of doing the work of four men.

CAPTAIN TOMMY   What th' hell do you Yankee carpetbaggers know about steel-driving? If this boy of mine don't beat your steam drill, I'll double that damn order!

SALESMAN   Now, you're talking!

CAPTAIN TOMMY   Two minutes to four. Better get your men ready to start that steam drill.

SPECTATORS (*cheering loudly, as they appear with* JOHN HENRY *and* POLLY ANN)   John Henry, himself!
Steel-driving champ!
Here he is, folks!
John Henry! John Henry!
There's Polly Ann with him!
Gangway for the hammer-king!

CAPTAIN TOMMY (*to* SALESMAN)   . . . and be ready to start the minute the gun fires! (SALESMAN *exits*. JOHN HENRY *mounts the landing*) Well, Boy, how do you feel?

JOHN HENRY   Like the victory done in my hand!

CAPTAIN TOMMY   That's the spirit!

POLLY ANN   Sure is a heap of folks out there to see you beat that steam drill!

JOHN HENRY   They expecting me to win, too.

CAPTAIN TOMMY   That's right. You can't let them down.

JOHN HENRY   Nossir, Captain, and I won't neither.

POLLY ANN   Of course, you won't! I'm going be right by, shouting my lungs out for you to win. Look—a whole hamper basket full of fried chicken and clabber biscuits for your dinner!

CAPTAIN TOMMY (*over the cheering crowd*) All right, it's time to start!

POLLY ANN   Go to it, Hot Papa! Show the whole wide world what a natural man can do!

CAPTAIN TOMMY (*to* JOHN HENRY)   Be ready to start the minute the gun fires. (*as* JOHN HENRY *turns to enter the tunnel*) Oh, say—the warden of the Jasper County State Prison sent me your record the other day.

JOHN HENRY (*unnerved*)   Jasper County? Is they going to take me back there?

CAPTAIN TOMMY (*cruelly, menacing*)   You got a pretty bad record, John Henry. You're an escaped convict, don't forget.

JOHN HENRY   I go back, it means a lifetime on that chain gang.

CAPTAIN TOMMY   They won't be that easy on you.

JOHN HENRY   What you mean by that, Captain Tommy?

CAPTAIN TOMMY   You know damn, plague-take-it well what I mean! You killed a white man.

JOHN HENRY   I wasn't aiming to, Captain. I done it in self-defense. He was going shoot my guts out over nothing. I never caused no trouble before. I always done the work of four men every day. I must have lost my head or something. I didn't aim to kill. I just couldn't stand there and—

CAPTAIN TOMMY   Never mind, I know all about it. I'm a personal friend of the governor. Helped him get elected, in fact. Listen, Boy—I want you to win, do you understand? Do you hear me?

JOHN HENRY   I'll win sure as my name is John Henry!

CAPTAIN TOMMY   If you don't—well—I won't be needing you around here anymore.

JOHN HENRY (*grimly*)   I understand, Boss . . . I'll win. I've got to now.

(*He goes inside the tunnel, as the crowd cheers. The lights dim out on the landing. During the loud cheering, the report of a revolver rents the air.* JOHN HENRY *starts hammering, the chugging noise of the steam drill is heard. We see only the silhouetted figure of* JOHN HENRY *inside the tunnel, wielding his hammer. He is assisted by a shaker who holds the steel drill in position*)

VOICES OF SPECTATORS (*in unison*)
John Henry'll beat that steam drill down!
Look at that hammer fall!
No man-made steam drill will whip him!
He's making that hammer talk!
Lord, Lord! Glory be!
He's the best in the land!
That man's a mighty man!

(CAPTAIN TOMMY *and the* SALESMAN *are downstage at right*)

CAPTAIN TOMMY   Cost more to run that machine than it does to pay a driller.

SALESMAN   But she does the work of four men.

CAPTAIN TOMMY   Well, I'm from Missouri. You got to show me!

SALESMAN   You'll only need to hire about one-fourth of the men you have now.

CAPTAIN TOMMY   I'm thinking about what will happen when this job closes up. Suppose I don't get another contract?

SALESMAN   You don't have to worry about that.

CAPTAIN TOMMY   The hell I don't!

SALESMAN   Your excavation company is one of the biggest in the South.

CAPTAIN TOMMY   Don't forget I got plenty competition, too. Other companies cutting my throat, under-bidding me and using convict labor. I'll be in one devil of a fix with steam drills on my hand and nothing to drill. With hand labor you play safe. You work'em as long as you need them Speed'em up when it's necessary. Hire as many as you like when times are good. When things get bad, you let as many go as you like, and nothing's lost. Play safe is my motto. I'll take cheap Black labor any day!

(*A swell of cheering from the crowd. The stage is completely dark now. The cheering gives way to the mass chant of the spectators*)

VOICES OF SPECTATORS   John Henry, if you don't win, well, I won't be needing you around here anymore. You are an escaped convict. You killed a white man. You know what they do with a Black man who kills a white man? They burn him alive. They string him up and burn him alive!

POLLY ANN (*highlighted: she is hysterical*) Captain Tommy, you can't let them take my man from me! He's all I got in the world. He's all I want to have. I love him, and I been true to him. Don't take him away, please! They'll kill him, and that'll be the death of me. They'll kill him! They'll kill him!

(*The lights fade out on* POLLY ANN *and come up on* THE CREEPER. *He is downstage, extreme left, well outside the playing arena, which is now entirely blacked out and being readied for the sequence to follow.* THE CREEPER, *guitar in hand, strikes a detonating ominous chord, signal for the black-out on* POLLY ANN *and an instant shift to him, commanding the attention of the audience*)

CREEPER (*with authority*)   No man born of woman can beat a steam drill down! (*plays and sings mournfully*)

Say, a man's been round,
Took John Henry's name.
Say, a man's been round,
Took John Henry's name.
Say, "John Henry, your Maker calls you.
Please, answer to your name."

Polly Ann, your man's in trouble,
Can't ease his worried mind.
Polly Ann, your man's in trouble,
Cain't ease his worried mind.
Win or lose with that steam drill,
He still got his worried mind.

(*speaking*) Poor boy! Poor boy! You on trial for your life. Ol' Creeper knows what's going on inside that mind of yours whilst you down in that Big Ben Tunnel pounding, pounding your life away, oh, Lord, ha'mercy!—seeing it all

pass in one big procession before you: Beale Street, the Jailhouse, Chain Gang, Hobo Jungle . . . Remember that Dive on Beale Street? Lord! Lord!—(*sings*)

Let him go to Beale Street,
Where life is gay.
I say, let him go to Beale Street,
Where life is gay.
What he's looking for on Beale Street
Won't drive his blues away!

(*Lights dim out on the* CREEPER *and come up on the Beale Street scene*)

Third Episode

SETTING: *a dive on Beale Street in Memphis. Two opposing floods of lights, very soft, running diagonally left to right, leaving a semi-darkened area in between, form two lighted circles. One reveals a bar, the other a table and two chairs. A tall, thin man is attending bar. During the scene, men and women are discovered at intervals drinking there. At the table are seated* JOHN HENRY *and a street walker. Her make-up is exaggerated and her dress decorative, in keeping with her profession. The other patrons, all characters out of the Negro underworld, are seen in outline, shadowy, seated at other tables about the place.*

Throughout this episode, the speech, the action and everything have the slow, lethargic rhythm of the blues)

JOHN HENRY (*groggy from hard drinking*)   One more drink, Baby, just one more drink . . .
WOMAN (*bored*)   Your hand just glued to that bottle!
JOHN HENRY   Likker never killed nobody. Say, come on have one with me. Ain't no fun drinking alone.
WOMAN   Well, you'll drink this one alone, cause I ain't drinking, see.
JOHN HENRY   What's the matter you ain't drinking? You my company, ain't you?
WOMAN   I ain't drinking. Had enough.
JOHN HENRY   Well, my likker's particular who drinks it!
WOMAN   The undertaker won't have to mess burying you. Just pour you back in a bottle!
JOHN HENRY   Having a little fun, Pretty Mama. Just out to enjoy life. (*he turns the bottle up to his head*)

WOMAN   Say, that ain't no way to be drinking out in public! Use the glass. What you figger it was—a finger bowl?

JOHN HENRY   I drinks like I suppose to drink. Like a natural man. That's way we drink where I come from. Likker never be my master, understand? Cause why? I ain't got no master! Shucks! Nobody make me take low. Never! Cause I'm natural born. President in the White House, Congress—nobody! All the same to me. I been everywhere. I seen everything. Makes no difference who they is, nor where they come from. Never take low, no time. That's me! President of the United States, Congress . . . Hell! Put a ten-pound hammer in his hand, wouldn't know what to do with it! Know that there road—the railroad what runs all the way from Atlanta to Shreeport? Well, I lay them rails, them pretty, sweet rails! That gravel road going into Macon? I built that road. Busted every damn rock of it!

WOMAN   I listened to you say that once, I listened to you say it fifty times!

JOHN HENRY   Lord, Lord, if there was no more rocks to bust, no more spikes to drive, I'd lay down and die! I went to Glory and I don't find none there, I'd up and leave and walk and walk till I find myself a brand new world, where there nothing but rocks and steel and ten-pound hammers! . . . Life! Hell, they ain't no life here. You call all this life? Well, you listen here to me, Babe. I tell you what life is, see. Life is a ten-pound hammer, a steel drill, and a great big solid rock! (*he rises, animated*) Where's my hammer? Steady that drill, Boy, cause here I come—Huh! Great day in the morning! Listen to that hammer ring—Huh!

WOMAN   (*disgusted. She tries without success to yank him back down to his seat, but he brushes her aside*)   You pike down! Where you think you is? (*sits back down*)

JOHN HENRY   (*transfixed with joy*)   Thirty miles to north of Macon! Throw some cool water on this hammer, Boy! She burning up. Every time this hammer falls, the ground just shakes under my feet. All I do is steady her, she hammers herself! Got to bust this rock all the way to Macon. Must make it there by dark. Sweet woman got fried chicken on the table waiting for me. Boy, steady that drill! This hammer sure means business. Crazy this hammer is, she liable to mistake your head for that drill! (*sings*)

Steel-driving man—huh!
Natural-born.
Steel-driving man—huh!
Natural-born.
Got arms like steel, Babe,
A heart like solid stone.

WOMAN   Here, take it easy, Hot Papa! You ain't on nobody's rock pile!

JOHN HENRY   I'm going find me some steel to drive.

WOMAN   For the time being, you better sit down.

JOHN HENRY   (*sits*)   Say, I like you. Damn fi' don't! You talks way I likes to hear a woman talk. No fancy, high-English words. Natural, Baby, natural. How'd you like to be my woman? Travel and follow me every-which-a-where—all over this country—from coast to coast, Babe.

WOMAN   What you offering me—a start in life? Listen, here, Brother Low-down—excuse me, Mister Steel-driving man—I left Yamicraw, Georgia for better or worse. So, I'll take the worse, and stay right here!

JOHN HENRY   Here—buy some more likker.

WOMAN   I thought you done spent out?

JOHN HENRY   Here's the rest of it. Hell, money don't mean nothing to me. Today in my pocket, tomorrow in somebody else's. When this goes, I goes. Me and my old hammer, starting all over again!

WOMAN   (*more friendly*)   What kind this time will it be? Bourbon or rot-gut?

JOHN HENRY   What kind I been drinking?

WOMAN   Rot-gut.

JOHN HENRY   All taste the same.

WOMAN   Don't start that old wringing-and-twisting. I'm drinking Bourbon!

JOHN HENRY   Bourbon? Name sounds too funny. I likes the sound of rot-gut.

WOMAN   I still say I'm drinking Bourbon. (*snaps her fingers for the Bartender*) Say, Charleston, a drink of Bourbon and a shorty of rot-gut. (*to* JOHN HENRY) I don't see how a man can drink so much rot-gut whiskey and live!

JOHN HENRY   Cain't nothing kill me. Not even a bolt of lightning. Not even a forty-five pistol. Only thing can kill me is a hammer—a ten-pound hammer and a steel drill. Got to bust me same as you bust a rock!

WOMAN (*as* BARTENDER *waits*) Ain't you going pay the man?

JOHN HENRY Won't this pay him? Take what you want, Buddy!

WOMAN (*to* BARTENDER) Oh, no, you don't! (*hands him a coin*) Here!

BARTENDER Double-crosser! I'll fix you!

WOMAN This is my trick, Skipper! (*to* JOHN HENRY) Come on, Big Daddy, drink up!

JOHN HENRY Gonna be long-gone, Brown Sugar, Long-gone from Memphis. Beale Street. Solid gone. These old bear claws of mine just itching for a grip-hold that hammer!

WOMAN (*laughing*) You the first man I see want to talk bout nothing but work!

JOHN HENRY That's all I know, Fair Brown. That's all I ever wonts to know! The rest don't count. Hammer. Steel. Rocks. Them's my friends. My bosom-friends. They's me! Don't even have to talk to them. Just sing, and they commence to sing right back at me. Like some echo from off the hills. Music. Great, natural music. Righteous music right out of Glory! . . . Memphis! Beale Street! Great mind to get my hammer and set fire to every blamed cobblestone! Despise this place! Ain't no good, nossir. Just ain't no good. And making a fool out'n me! Spending my hard-earned money—

WOMAN (*frightened*) Here, you need another. Steady yourself.

JOHN HENRY Rot-gut! (*raises bottle, breaking out in peals of bitter laughter*) You ain't no good, Rot-gut! Ruination of many a poor man! Creeping up on a man. Trying to make him forget . . . White folks . . . A man ain't nothing but a man!—(*he rises to his feet, decisively*) Can't stay here! Got to catch me a freight train, and ride! Ride over them steel rails I laid! Great day in the morning! Ride them rods! Travel! There still a heap of rocks in the world, and a heap of steel. I going out of here, gonna put my nose to the ground, scent steel and rocks like a bloodhound dog! (*he sings with abandon, determination*)

> I'm a long-gone papa,
> Ain't got no time to lose.
> I'm a long-gone papa,
> Ain't got no time to lose.
> If I stay here, Pretty Mama,
> 'Fraid I'll get them low-down blues.
> (CHORUS)—them low-down blues.

> Woke up late this morning,
> Blue as a man can be.
> Woke up late this morning,
> Blue as a man can be.
> Looked into the mirror,
> Saw what Memphis done to me.
> —Memphis done to me.

> Good Book tell you,
> Man reap what he sow.
> Good Book tell you,
> Man reap what he sow.
> Going where I can reap
> The biggest rocks that grow.
> —biggest rocks that grow.

> Long-gone from here, Fair Brown.
> Don't you weep or sigh.
> Long-gone from here, Fair Brown.
> Don't you weep or sigh.
> When you hear a freight train passing,
> You know I'm passing by.
> —know I'm passing by.

CHORUS (*harsh and mocking*) Ha! Ha! Ha! Ha!

JOHN HENRY (*angrily*) What you-all Ha-hawing bout? Crazy?

CHORUS Ha! Ha! Ha! Ha!

(JOHN HENRY, *overcome by the whiskey, flops down in the chair, lays his head upon the table in a drunken sleep. A trio of sweetmen, loudly dressed and dandified, appear on the landing and "strut their stuff"*)

SWEETMEN

> How he can hate Beale Street,
> I don't understand.
> How he can hate Beale Street,
> I don't understand.
> Rather be a lamp-post on Beale Street
> Than a pick-and-shovel man.
> —pick-and-shovel man.

> You know a man's a fool to work,
> When women are so free.
> You know a man's a fool to work,
> When women are so free.
> Gonna always have a sweet mama
> Doing my work for me.
> —doing my work for me.

(*The trio of sweetmen are blacked-out. The Chorus hums and moans the blues strains. The*

Woman, assuring herself that JOHN HENRY *is now asleep, picks up the money from the table and starts out. On reaching the bar, she is waylaid by her lover or* SWEETMAN)

SWEETMAN   Come on, Sister, dig! Need some dough. Feel my gambling luck rising.

WOMAN   Didn't make but two dollars off that guy.

SWEETMAN   Stop lying! You wouldn't fool with him long as you did.

WOMAN   I'm telling the honest truth, Daddy.

SWEETMAN   Charleston put me wise to your tricks.

JOHN HENRY (*wakens, angry*)   Beale Street. Damn it! Woman took my money and gone! Let her have it! Satisfied now. Broke. Somebody go bring me my hammer!

SWEETMAN   Come across, you lying—

WOMAN   Don't hit me, Sweet man!

SWEETMAN   Get on in there! (*he shoves her into the darkness, follows*)

(*Trio of streetwalkers appear on the landing. They are painted and gaudily garbed*)

STREETWALKERS   Love for sale on Beale Street.
Man can pick and choose.
Love for sale on Beale Street.
Man can pick and choose.
Woman take way all your
   money,
Drink up all your booze.
   —all your rot-gut booze.

If my style of love don't please
   you,
Aint nothing I can do.
If my style of love don't please
   you,
Ain't nothing I can do.
If you looking for the real thing,
Beale Street's no place for you.
   —no place for you.

(*They are blacked-out.* JOHN HENRY *gets up, staggers over to the bar*)

JOHN HENRY   No place for me! No doggone place for me! (*to* BARTENDER) Say, Buddy, how bout one more rot-gut? On the house this time, Buddy. Ain't got no money left. Lowdown strumpet run way with every penny to my name!

BARTENDER   Ain't giving way nothing but air, Brother, and that's hot!

JOHN HENRY   I been a steady customer—

BARTENDER   No free drinks. Get the hell outta here!

JOHN HENRY   No man allowed to talk that way to me! Come from behind that counter. Come on out, you thieving hound! You messing with a man now—a natural-born man, hear me?

BARTENDER   Hey, Buster! Jess! Throw this bum outta here!

BUSTER   All right, Tickle Britches, let's travel!

JOHN HENRY   I can walk out by myself.

JESS   So you wonts to start a fight?

BARTENDER   Bad for business, hanging round.

JOHN HENRY (*brushes bouncers aside*)   'Way from me! I didn't need no help coming in and I don't need no help going out!

(BUSTER *and* JESS *retreat. A pickpocket rushes in from the street, looks about nervously. One of the women in the place comes downstage and joins him*)

PICKPOCKET   Here, Woman—(*grabs hold of her hand*) Get rid of this stuff. It's hot.

HOSTESS   Police see you come in here?

PICKPOCKET   Dunno, but they's after this ice.

(*A white policeman enters. The woman quits the pickpocket, goes up to* JOHN HENRY)

HOSTESS   Big and handsome let's dance. (*she snuggles up to him, in full view of the audience she plants the jewelry on him*)

JOHN HENRY (*pushes her away*)   Go way from me, Woman! Through being made a fool of. I'm using my head, see. Gonna be smart as the next one. Git it up, Bartender! How bout that drink? Do I git it, or must I destroy this place like a earthquake?

BARTENDER (*acquiesces*)   Keep your shirt on. I hope it poisons you!

POLICEMAN (*to pickpocket*)   Come on! What you do with it?

PICKPOCKET   I swear, Officer!

POLICEMAN   You'll hit the rock-pile for this!

HOSTESS   Officer, he ain't took nothing. Yonder's the one.

POLICEMAN   You sure? You better be!

HOSTESS   You search him and see.

POLICEMAN (*crosses to* JOHN HENRY; *jabs him with billy*)   All right, you—where is it?

JOHN HENRY   Don't know what you talking bout, Policeman.

HOSTESS   Feels in his left-hand pocket.

JOHN HENRY   What you-all talking about?

HOSTESS   That's where he got it.

POLICEMAN   Don't try anything.

JOHN HENRY (*feels his pocket, discovers*)   How this get in my pocket? I don't understand . . .

POLICEMAN   You gonna have all the time in the world, Big Boy, to figger that out! (*applies hand-cuffs*)

JOHN HENRY (*bitterly*)   Memphis! Beale Street! I great mind to—

POLICEMAN   Move on, move on!

CROWD   Ha! Ha! Ha! Ha!

If you looking for the real thing,
Beale Street's no place for you!

(*As the lights dim out*)

Fourth Episode

(SETTING: *Jail.* JOHN HENRY *is visible in a soft blue light, seated on a stool before the iron bars of his cell. To one side of him crouches the dwarfed figure of the* CREEPER. *The off-stage voices throughout this scene are the voices of* WHITE JAILBIRDS)

A WHITE JAILBIRD   Hey, Sambo?

JOHN HENRY   My name ain't Sambo.

OTHER WHITE JAILBIRDS   Say, what they nab you for, Colored Brother?
Yeah, how th'hell you get in here?
He asked the jailer for a night's lodging! (*laughter*)
What you do—get in a scrape?

JOHN HENRY   No, I was minding my own business.

JAILBIRDS   You hear that, Fellows? He was minding his own business! (*laughter*)
How deep did you cut that guy?
He didn't aim to cut him. His razor slipped!

CREEPER (*pacifying*)   Now, cool down. Leave them smart guys talk. Say nothing, they shut up.

JAILBIRDS   Did you leave your trade-mark on him, Bo?
What he do—Pull some loaded dice on you?
Maybe he caught him in bed with his gal! (*loud, side-splitting laughter*)

JOHN HENRY   Go ahead, Mister White Folks, laugh! Laugh all you wonts to. Laugh till your bellies ache! Go head, make fun of me! You got everything. Got the world in a jug and the stopper in your hand!

JAILBIRDS   Listen to that possum-eater! Say, Dark Boy, how bout a song?
Yeah, sing that one about way down yonder in the corn field.
"Who stole the lock on the chicken-house door?"

CREEPER (*restraining* JOHN HENRY)   Cain't you see they just trying to get your goat? Use your head!

JAILBIRD   Come on, Rufus-Rastus, be a good sport, and sing us a good old coon-song!

JOHN HENRY   I say I don't know no songs to sing.

JAILBIRD   Bet he jest left the plantation, too!

CREEPER (*being a natural-born diplomat, obliges and plays his guitar and sings*)   My old Missy promise me
—Raise rukus tonight!
When she die, she set me free
—Raise rukus tonight!
Well, she live so long, her head got bald
—Raise rukus tonight!
Thought I never get free at all
—Raise rukus tonight!

CHORUS
Oh, come along, Children, come along,
Whilst the moon is shining bright,
Get on board, down that river flow,
Us gonna raise rukus tonight!

JOHN HENRY (*over the music*)   White man's country. White man's world. Big Mister Great-I-Am! Make all the high and mighty laws and rulings. Change everything to suit himself. Black man got to bow and scrape to him, like he was God Almighty Himself. Black man got to go to him with his hat in his hand and ask for the right to live and breathe, sleep and eat, sweat and slave! Got to go to Almighty White Boss for every little thing. Even down when it comes to thinking. Black man got to go to him for that, too. Nothing he say or do what the white man ain't got something to say bout it! (*the* CREEPER *has stopped playing*)

JAILBIRDS   What do you want, Black Boy—a seat in the White House? He wants a government of the Blacks, for the Blacks, and by the Blacks! (*peals of mocking laughter*)

Say, George Washington, what would you-all
do they made you the President of the United
States?

He'd have white slaves to wait on the Black
aristocracy!

Congress and the Senate full of greasy, potbel-
lied Nigras!

Eating hush-puppies, smoking big cheroots,
feet propped on the desks!

Sign outside the White House door read:
"Check your knives and razors at the door!"

Why, everybody in the army and the navy
would be a general or an admiral!

Wonder how it feels to be a nigger?

A nigger? Never given it a thought.

Who wants to be one anyway?

Tell us, Sambo, how it feels to be like you?

JOHN HENRY (*stands before the bars, facing audience*)   You want to know how I feel?

JAILBIRD   Sure, tell us.

JOHN HENRY   Like a giant in a strait jacket!

JAILBIRD   Giant in a strait jacket? That must
be a helluva feeling! (*the men all roar with
laughter*)

JOHN HENRY   Like a natural man mongst a
heap of muscle-bound sissies!

JAILBIRD   How do you get that way, you?

JOHN HENRY   Like a great king without a
throne to sit on!

JAILBIRDS   Ha! Ha! Ha! Ha! King without a
throne! Ha! Ha! Ha! Ha!

JOHN HENRY   You damned right, a king!
Every inch, White Folks, every inch! That's
me. King without a throne, but king right on.
You may be sitting on the throne, but that
don't make you king cause you sit there.
Nossir! I built that throne. I built that stone
palace you live in. Yes, even down built the
roads so you could travel from place to place.
And I ain't asking you-all to thank me for
what I do. I ain't asking you to be my friend.
Ain't wishing to eat at the same table with
you. Ain't wanting you to put yourself out of
the way for me at all, understand? All I ask is
that you let me *be*. You can have the swell
palace and the golden throne, but don't mess
up with my crown! I'm going strut the earth
with that crown on my head, till Old Gabriel
sounds his trumpet for me to go on up to
Glory! And I'm going walk right smack into
the Glory Kingdom with that crown still on
my head!

JAILBIRDS   Give my regards to Saint Peter!

Boys, how about giving the Black king a grand
send-off?

Sure, why not? The old razzberries! For the
king!—

(*The* JAILBIRDS *boo and hiss, until a Police Guard
yells to them:* "Hey, you mugs, pike down!")

We're giving the Black king a grand send-off!
The king is croaked! Long live the king! (*more
laughter, booing and hissing*)

JOHN HENRY (*towers above it all*)   All right,
you punks! Thanks for the send-off! But,
that's where you wrong. The king ain't
croaked yet. He's still walking the earth,
and Old Death ain't laid his cold hands on
him yet. He's still walking the earth like a
natural man. When they do shove dirt in his
face, his spirit's going rise up from the lonesome grave, and walk the earth for him. His
spirit's going walk the earth like a natural
man. Going walk and walk, till the whole
earth is destroyed by fire, like the Good Book
say it will on the Day of Judgment. And all
your goddamned laws and man-made steam
engines and gadgets'll be melted like wax!
Then the spirit's going take on his natural
flesh again, and wait till the earth cools off.
The Almighty's going put a ten-pound hammer in his hand. Tell him, go on back to
earth and see what he can do. Start all over
again. Hammer out a new earthly kingdom,
all his own. Yes, Lord, a solid, natural kingdom
that'll last forever! And once more, the
natural man's going take his rightful seat on
the throne, and rule the earth like a mighty
king!

(*Boos, hisses, bedlam. The* JAILER *comes on stage,
followed by another white man, the* SHERIFF)

JAILER   All right, all right! Damn it, quiet!
Raised enough hell for one night! (*the bedlam
gradually subsides*)

SHERIFF   Open her up, and let's have a look
at him.

JAILER   O.K., Sheriff . . . (*unlocks cell. To
JOHN HENRY*) Step out . . . I reckon he oughta
do, Sheriff.

SHERIFF (*after a cursory appraisal*)   Trouble-
maker, ain't he? Uppity? Sassy? Got a heap of
spirit?

JAILER   I reckon you got a remedy for that,
Sheriff.

SHERIFF   Yeah. I reckon I has. I like spirit. Gimme something to work on!

JAILER   Gonna take him back with you?

SHERIFF   Uh, huh.

JAILER   Oh, Phil—? (*voice answers*) One to go. Ball-and-chain!

(*The lights dim out*)

Fifth Episode

(SETTING: *a rock quarry. Five convicts are discovered just below the landing in a faint haze of light. Stripped to the waist, their torsos gleam with perspiration, as they go through the animated motion of pounding rocks with their hammers. The "hammer song" is led by a* LEADER *off-stage. The* CONVICTS *supply the "huh," striking the rocks at the same time*)

VOICE OF THE LEADER   Swing that hammer—huh
Like a natural man.
Swing that hammer—huh
Like a natural man.
Guard behind you,
Rifle in his hand.

Ball and chain
Won't let me be.
Ball and chain
Won't let me be.
This chain gang, Babe,
Be the death of me.

Daybreak to sundown
My hammer ring.
Daybreak to sundown
My hammer ring.
Body so weary
Can hardly sing.

If this hammer kill me,
And I dies,
If this hammer kill me,
And I dies,
I'll hant that white boss
Scratch out his eyes.

White folks got no right
Treat me so cruel.
White folks got no right
Treat me so cruel.
Working me same like
They works a mule.

FIRST CONVICT   Not so plague-take-it fast, John Henry!

SECOND   The faster you swing that hammer, longer they going keep you here!

THIRD   Way you work, warden throw that calendar way!

FIRST   That old guard ain't watching nohow.

THIRD   He over behind that bush.

FIRST   I hope he strains himself!

SECOND   I hope he sits on a diamond-back rattler!

THIRD   Working a body to death, hot as it is!

FIRST   Got nary a drop of human feeling in his veins!

JOHN HENRY   Lordy! I didn't have this hammer, I go crazy thinking. Don't do for me to start thinking. Man, I fills up inside like I'm going bust wide open!—Larry, how you feels now, Boy? Is you feel any better?

BOY   No, I sick. Right down sick. I feels worse now I ever was.

JOHN HENRY   I wishes there was something I could do for you, Larry Boy. Gits my goat to stand by and see you in misery and nothing I can do to help.

BOY   Hopes I be all right soon. I can only hold out. I was home, my ma 'ud care for me.

SECOND   They ought to get that boy to a hospital.

THIRD   He ain't been right since they keep him in that sweat-box.

FIRST   Three whole days, feed him only bread and water.

JOHN HENRY   Rebbish bastards!

SECOND   You mark my words. Some day God Almighty going send a cyclone throughout this land!

JOHN HENRY   Will he spare us colored folks?

SECOND   I ain't talking bout the colored folks.

JOHN HENRY   Cain t wait for God!

FIRST   I just wish I could organize a whole army!

THIRD   White folks git through with you, wouldn't be a Black man left!

FIRST   Hell! I ain't got but one life nohow. A man ain't nothing but a man!

JOHN HENRY   Buddy, you said something! That's my kind of preaching. A man ain't nothing but a man. Ain't they more of us put together then they is guards holding we-all here in slavery, flailing hell out of us when we don't move fast enough to suit them, feeding us swill even down a hog wouldn't want to eat, and driving we-all in the broiling sun, from daybreak to sundown, like we was some dumb ox? A handful of them holding us slaves!

THIRD They has guns and us ain't.

JOHN HENRY Is you afraid to die? Well, I ain't! I be blown to hell before I stays here the rest of my life. You going die anyhow, you stay here. And it won't be dying like a natural man suppose to die.

THIRD Better keep your trap shut, John Henry!

SECOND That old guard hear you, kill you sure!

FIRST Sure break your heart to die and not take a white man with you!

JOHN HENRY Brother, you looking at a man. Lord don't deal me out but one life to live. He give every man just one life. He didn't say or 'tend for you to be a slave. He didn't say for some to rule and the rest be slaves. He meant for every man to be a king. King in his own rights. I got my job to do. The white man got hisn'. And I don't give a damn what the white man do. Long as he don't interfere with me, I'm satisfied .

FIRST Me and you both! Just let me be!

JOHN HENRY Black man's easy to get along with, long as folks treat him human. He do his work and never squawk. It's meddling with and mistreating what makes him mean. Cause he talk back and stand up for his rights, Mister Charlie don't like that. You a bad so-and-so when you ask for your rights. Work your fool head off to please him, try to be his friend, Mister Charlie ain't going let you. I'm this way: I ain't going be no door-mat for Mister Charlie to wipe his feet on. Nossir! I prize myself. I ask no favor. I does my work the best I knows how. All I ask is that he treat me honest. Don't cheat me. Don't mess up with my hard-earned money. Just pay me off and lemme go bout my business. Ain't that way you-all think?

FIRST That's what I think!

SECOND Nothing diffunt!

THIRD I don't ask to 'sociate with Mister Charlie.

SECOND Him and his business don't worry me none.

JOHN HENRY And you mean to tell me you willing to stay here and be treated like we is? Sweat blood? Only thanks you receive is a kick in the behind and a rawhide lash across your naked back!

FIRST Nossir, I ain't wishing to stay here!

SECOND Got a wife and youngun waiting for me.

THIRD Damn! I sure like to see old Beale Street!

FIRST Quick! Snap it up! Here come that guard!

VOICE OF LEADER Ball and chain—huh
Won't let me be.
Ball and chain—huh
Won't let me be.
This old chain-gang
Be the death of me.

BOY (delirious) Oh, Lord! I can't! Lordy! Can't hammer no more!

GUARD (off-stage. As CONVICTS pause) Hey, up there! You-all git a move on! Swing them hammers!

VOICE OF LEADER Daybreak to sundown—huh
My hammer ring.
Daybreak to sundown—huh
My hammer—

BOY (gasping) Mama! Lord, have mercy! Mama!—(he falls in a dead faint)

FIRST Oh, my Jesus!

SECOND What happen?

THIRD He fainted!

FIRST Boy ain't well nohow.

SECOND Ain't eat a mouthful in three days.

THIRD Food won't stay on his stomach.

FIRST He spit up blood.

SECOND He got the consumption.

JOHN HENRY (ministering to the BOY) Larry Boy—? Where at that water bucket? Wait a second . . . No use now. His heart done stop beating . . . He ain't breathing.

CONVICTS Dead as a door-knob! Kicked the bucket! Long gone from here!

JOHN HENRY Lord Jesus, have mercy on him!

GUARD (from the landing) What's wrong with him?

JOHN HENRY Boy took sick and died.

GUARD   You're a damned liar! He's stalling. Come on, you there! Get on your feet!

JOHN HENRY   I tells you the boy's dead.

GUARD   See for myself how dead he is! (*he comes down with lash in one hand, his rifle in the other*)

JOHN HENRY   You can't do that!

GUARD   You tell me what I can't do?

JOHN HENRY   You flog a man what's dead?

GUARD   Stand back!

JOHN HENRY   It ain't human. I ain't going let you!

GUARD   Stand back! Goddam you!

JOHN HENRY   I respects the dead.

GUARD (*throws down his lash, raises his rifle*) So help me, I'll blow your soul to hell!

(JOHN HENRY *wrests the rifle from the* GUARD, *knocking him down, pounds his head with the butt. The lights dim, as he takes the keys from the* GUARD's *belt and frees himself of the ball and chain*)

CONVICTS   You kill him!
Stone dead!
Split his head wide open!
Hurry, John Henry! Get way fast as you can!
Hurry! Them other guards is coming this way!
No time to waste. They catch you, they kill you sure!

(*Total darkness. The weird, prolonged blowing of a freight train whistle is heard and the chugging of the locomotive*)

FIRST   Head straight for that freight train, Boy!

JOHN HENRY   I'm long-gone from here!

(*Train noise mounts, a succession of rifle shots rend the air*)

Sixth Episode

(SETTING: *a camp-meeting. A small band of Negro worshippers are seated on benches facing a crude, make-shift pulpit, from which a portly preacher exhorts them to worship. There are two rows of benches with a narrow aisle between them. The meeting is well under way, as the lights come up, and there is a mood of unrestrained religious fervor as the Congregation, led by the* PREACHER, *sing* "Shine On Me")

CONGREGATION   "Shine on me, Lord, shine on me.
I want the light from the lighthouse
To shine on me. . . ."

(*Incidental murmurs and cries of "Praise be the Lord!" "Have mercy, Lord!" "Blessed Savior!" etc., as the old hymn is being sung. Some of the members stand and sway to the rhythm, clapping their hands or patting their feet. As the Congregation relaxes softly into humming, the* PREACHER *speaks out over this, giving to his deliverance a sort of mournful, heart-felt quality*)

PREACHER   Open up your troubled hearts to Jesus. Don't wait too long, Sisters and Brothers. Don't wait till you sick and afflicted on your dying-bed to call to Him. For we know not the hour, the time of day, and the night. We knoweth not when Old Death gwine snatch us way. Sometimes he creeps up on the sinner man, and the sinner man ain't expecting him. Overtakes the weary traveler a long ways from home. You working in the field. Whilst you sleep in your bed, lost in slumber. Old Death's a mighty reaper!

CONGREGATION   Amen! Do, Jesus! Glory Halleluyuh!

PREACHER   And he got no shame. Walks the troubled waters of the sea and the ocean. He visits with the rich and the poor alike. Stretches out his arms and spreads his pestilence and his destruction throughout the land! Amen!

CONGREGATION   Amen! Yes, he do! Death's a mighty man!

PREACHER   Onliest somebody is gonna hope you is Jesus! Praise His Name! I'm talking about Jesus! Through all your trials and tribulations, through the Valley of the Shadow of Death—

CONGREGATION   Yes, Jesus! Walk with me! (*an* OLD WOMAN *rises and starts to sing, the whole Congregation joining in, swaying and intoning*)

I want Jesus to walk with me.
I want Jesus to walk with me.
Whilst I'm on my pilgrim's journey,
I want Jesus to walk with me.

PREACHER   Don't you want Jesus to *talk* with you?

CONGREGATION   Oh, do, Jesus! (*a young girl rises, filled with religious fervor, and shouts as she walks up and down the aisle, "Save my soul, Jesus! Don't let me sin no more!" She kneels before the pulpit, her face buried in her hands, and weeps*)

CONGREGATION   I want Jesus to talk with me.
 I want Jesus to talk with me.
 Whilst I'm on my pilgrim's journey,
 I want Jesus to talk with me.

PREACHER   Don't you want Jesus to *comfort* you?

CONGREGATION   I want Jesus to comfort me.
 I want Jesus to comfort me.
 Whilst I'm on my pilgrim's journey,
 I want Jesus to comfort me.

OLD WOMAN *(her voice cracked and full of grief, she gives her "testimony")*   Jesus, have mercy on my boy, wherever he is tonight. I wants you to talk with him, Jesus. He left home, his heart troubled and hurt. Ain't there something you can do to help him, Jesus? Thank you, Jesus. I'm a lone old woman, and all my days is numbered and short. I knows I wont be here long, Lord. May be I wont never see my boy's face again in this life, Lord, but, wherever he is tonight, wont you go to him and wont you tell him that his old mammy's praying for him? Tell him that his old mammy forgives all he's ever did. Take the grief out of his heart, Jesus. Tell him 'tain't right and Christian to gamble and drink and keep bad company. Tell him that the sinner life ain't the life his old mammy wonts him to lead. Thanks be to the Lord! *(she sits down, her head bowed)*
PREACHER *(over the humming of the Congregation)*   Bless your heart, Sister Jones. Bless the hearts of mothers everywhere who got sons that strayed a long ways from home.
CONGREGATION   Amen! Amen!
PREACHER   That's fallen by the wayside.
CONGREGATION   Wayside, Lord!
PREACHER   Mothers whose boys is weary travelers long the dark and stormy highways, in the alleys, in the shameful houses of the red-light districts, and, and taking up with scarlet women of the evening!
CONGREGATION   Ain't it so? Yea, yea!
PREACHER   Bless them lonely sinners whose hearts may be racked with grief or sorrow. And guide them, O Heavenly Father, into the paths of righteousness!

(Suddenly, there is a flash of lightning, followed by a terrifying clap of thunder. [The thunder and lightning will continue throughout the remainder of this scene, growing in intensity.] The PREACHER, to abate the fears of the group, immediately leads them in singing, "Amazing Grace, How Sweet The Sound." The ragged, mud-begrimed figure of JOHN HENRY appears at the rear. His appearance bespeaks of days of hardships encountered while hiding in the swamp, after his escape from the chain-gang. As he walks slowly, strangely up the aisle, the singing ceases abruptly and the faces of the worshippers are taut with dread and wonderment)*

PREACHER *(bravely)*   Come forward, Brother. Is your heart troubled?
JOHN HENRY   Yes, Preacher, my heart is troubled, a heap troubled. I been standing outside listening to your sermon and to what the old lady here say bout her son. So, I made up my mind to come inside. I wasn't aiming to at first. I figgered, maybe, you-all church people wouldn't want me round.
PREACHER   You in the house of the Lord, Brother. I don't know as whether I remembers seeing you round here before.
JOHN HENRY   No, you ain't never seen me before.
PREACHER   My name is Reverend D. K. Valley—Elder Valley, as most folks calls me. *(he shakes hands with JOHN HENRY, who carries in the other hand the gun he took from the guard)* . . . Glad to have you, Brother—Sorry, you didn't tell me your name?
JOHN HENRY   Just call me "Brother," cause who I is ain't nobody's business. *(he addresses his remarks partly to the PREACHER and partly to the Congregation)*—I ain't saying I'm a true Christian, and I ain't saying I'm no true sinnerman either. I only know that I'm natural born. I had a mother that birthed me, but, long time ago, fore I gits in trouble, my mother she was laid to rest in the lonesome graveyard, neath the oak trees and the sleeping willows. She's gone on up to Glory. And I been walking the earth all by myself ever since. Ain't no man living or dead I ever mistreated. But I gits in a mess of trouble and they shackled my feet with a ball and chain and took my rights away. But I done my work, till the white guard on the chain gang started messing up with me, and make me mad, then I—I killed him stone dead and upped and run way.
PREACHER *(recoils in terror)*   You ain't oughta come here, Brother!
JOHN HENRY   Where else could I come to?
PREACHER   You liable to git us all in trouble.

CONGREGATION   Us cain't help no convict! We's God-fearing people! We all be killed! They burn down our church!

JOHN HENRY   Preacher, you understand? I had to come to somebody. I ain't got no friend in the world. Six weeks all by myself in the dismal swamp and not a living soul to talk to nearbout drive me stracted! Cain't you tell me what to do? Cain't any you-all God-fearing Christians tell me what to do?

PREACHER (*regains his composure, benignly*) Hear me, Brother, hear me. They is two kinds of laws. They's the law of man, and they's the law of God. (*his remarks are punctuated by murmurs of "Amen" from the Congregation*)—Now, we mortal folks is jedged by both them laws. Go on back, I say, go long back to the chain gang and surrender yourself and be jedged by the law of man. Render unto Caesar! And after you done that, you render yourself unto God.

CONGREGATION   Preacher right!

JOHN HENRY (*scornfully*) When Caesar git through with me, it be too late for God!

PREACHER   The world, my Brother, ain't made for the natural man. God ain't round to protect you no more. God's turnt his back on this sinful world. Washed his hands clean of this abomination. I say, woe unto the natural man! Woe unto the proud and the high-and-mighty! For you is hemmed in by four walls of solid earth and, oh, my Brother, you cain't break through them! Harken unto the Word of the Lamb! Turn the other cheek! Yea! Yea! Praise God. Git humble. Pray. Git meek. Meek as the Lamb. For the Lord say, Blessed is the meek, for they shall inherit the earth and the Kingdom-Come! (*the PREACHER is now carried away by his own eloquence, as the Congregation shout "Amens"*)—Pray, Brother! Git down low . . . low in the dirt . . . Repent ye, saith the Lord!

(*Simultaneously, with a flash of lightning and the clap of thunder, JOHN HENRY drops to his knees, as if smitten by an unseen power. Confused, fear-ridden, he makes an effort to pray, shaking his head. The members have gathered round him, singing with great animation. Suddenly, JOHN HENRY rises to full height and cries out*)

JOHN HENRY   You cain't move me! Let the lightning strike me dead! Oh, Lord, I ain't got nothing ginst your mighty laws and rulings, but I ain't going allow no man-made laws to rule over me!

A WORSHIPPER   Man, you stay here, you bring trouble to all us colored folks!

JOHN HENRY   I'm leaving.

OLD WOMAN   Wait, Son. Where at is you aiming to go?

JOHN HENRY (*with bravado*) I cain't say. All I knows is I'm heading for the crossing and I'm catching the first freight train that comes along. She'll slow down at the crossing and I'll hop her. And I'm going where I can make some hard-earned money and spend it as I please. Enjoy life. That's what I'm going do. Have me some good times. Maybe, I run cross that son of yours where I'm going. I do, I tell him all you say—to pray and walk with Jesus. (*he laughs out loud, a hollow, denigrating laugh*) Why don't you just have me tell him that his old mammy loves the ground he walks on and she ain't caring what he do. Maybe, he ain't bad like way you think. Maybe he's just natural-born like me. Cain't live like you and the preacher want him to. Maybe he cain't bow his head and walk humble . . . You has to let him be. (*to the PREACHER*)—Well, Reverend, before I go, I want to leave you something for the church. This all I got—this here shot-gun. I won't be needing it no more.

(*Freight train whistle blows. JOHN HENRY gives the PREACHER and the Congregation a knowing look, departs. While the PREACHER contemplates the gun, suddenly, someone jumps to his feet, catalyzes the rest to join him in singing*)

CONGREGATION   "This train is bound for Glory, this train! This train is bound for Glory, this train! . . . etc."

(*Black out*)

Seventh Episode

(SETTING: *a hoboes' camp near the railroad yard. It is close by a railroad siding. JOHN HENRY and several hoboes are discovered, gathered around a dying fire*)

FIRST HOBO   Four days and we'll be blowing into Key West.

SECOND   Going where that chilly wind don't blow!

THIRD   That old Cannon Ball sure can fly!

FOURTH   Awful cold at night through them mountains!

SECOND   Hope we get one them empty banana cars that got a heap of straw inside.

FIRST   Saw a great big flock of black birds this morning heading south.

FOURTH   And here's one more going do the same!

FIRST   South for me in winter. North won't see me till she thaws out.

THIRD   Say, Partner—which way you heading?

JOHN HENRY   Can't say yet. Don't know where I liable to go.

THIRD   You better string along with we-all.

SECOND   Go where there's summer whole year round!

JOHN HENRY   I'm all twisted and turned round. Cain't seem to make up my mind which way to turn. I been on the move for six months, and still ain't got nowhere.

FIRST   Them first six months always the hardest.

SECOND   Yeah, you wait till you been at it eight long years!

THIRD   This all I done since I left home.

FOURTH   They say a freight train whistle scared my mammy whilst she carrying me!

JOHN HENRY   All I done for the past six months or so, sleeping in box-cars, riding them rods. Onliest sound I hear is freight train whistle. Gimme the jim-jams listening to that lonesome whistle. Every time she blow, I feels like I ain't got a friend in the world!

FIRST   That old whistle used to give me the lonesome blues too.

SECOND   Now she sounds like pipe-organ music!

JOHN HENRY   Listen, Buddy, your ears ain't heard no real, honest-to-God music, like when you hit the head of a piece of steel with a ten-pound hammer. Ain't no sound in the world carry so much sweetness!

THIRD   I never hear tell of a hammer sounding like that!

SECOND   Man, you crazy! Ain't never was no music in no hammer!

FIRST   I tried steel-driving once—just once, and, boy, she near-bout ruint me!

THIRD   I got a fair dose of it on the chain gang in South Carolina.

SECOND   Hammer music, shucks! Freight train whistle sounds all right to me.

FOURTH   Freight train any day! That what you say, Peg Leg?

THIRD   Old Peg Leg here just a natural-born rambler!

SECOND   Even down knows how to talk to a freight train!

FOURTH   Come on, Peg Leg, show him way you talk to that Cannon Ball when she come round that mountain!

(The men make the sound of a train engine puffing out steam, a slow chug, then increasing as the train gathers momentum. PEG LEG cups his hands to his mouth to produce the mournful wailing of the train whistle far away. He proceeds to make all sorts of variations upon train whistle sounds to the sheer admiration of the others, who break in with "All aboard for Birmingham!" "We near that crossing just before to get to Atlanta!" "Blowing for that trestle outside Dallas!")

JOHN HENRY *(jittery, jumps to his feet)*   Stop it, you guys! Cut it out, you hear me? What you trying to do, drive me stracted? Six months of hearing nothing but that damn noise. Hear them wheels rolling, them box-cars rattling, brakes a-squeaking so to make your flesh crawl. Hearing nothing but them mammy-less noises day and night. In my sleep even. I'm sick and tired of it!—*(JOHN HENRY has been withdrawing towards the tunnel entrance, backing away from the bewildered hoboes, until he is up on the landing)*—I can't stand it no longer! Goddam, I can't stand it!

(Suddenly, the mouth of the tunnel begins to glow like an open furnace, coloring the entire background a fiery red, as though the mountain were ablaze; concurrently, the foreground darkens, the hoboes vanish. JOHN HENRY stalks into the tunnel and out of sight)

Eighth Episode

(The action is continuous. The Spectators mill excitedly about the entrance to the tunnel)

FIRST SPECTATOR   The mountain going burn to ashes!

CAPTAIN TOMMY *(addressing the Crowd from the landing)*   Stand aside! Let'em through!

(Several workmen, buckets hoisted above their heads, are pressing through the crowd)

SECOND SPECTATOR   John Henry done hammer till he set the rocks on fire!

CAPTAIN TOMMY   Hurry, you-all, with them water buckets. Quick! Get in there!

MEN WITH BUCKETS   Yassuh, we's hurrying! Lemme through here! Gimme room!

SALESMAN *(wringing his hands)*   What? This all you can do? Jumping Jehoshaphat! That steam drill cost me a fortune! My life's savings!

CAPTAIN TOMMY   Go on, go on, you boys! Get in there and put that fire out! *(the men hurry into the glowing pit and out of sight)*

SALESMAN   This contest was all your idea to begin with. Why th'hell you threaten him? He's a human being, same as you and me. And a mighty damn fine human specimen, you ask me!

CAPTAIN TOMMY   Well, Dadblabbit, I ain't asking you! You blabbering carpetbagger!

SALESMAN   God, what a man! You think you can break his spirit?

CAPTAIN TOMMY   Think? I did break his spirit. He was cringing. He pleaded and begged. I twisted him round my little finger, because I'm his master. That's why he beat that steam drill! You've got to make them fear you!

POLLY ANN *(confronts CAPTAIN TOMMY)* Hate you! I hate you, Captain Tommy! I'm here to tell you, you the meanest man that ever live!

CAPTAIN TOMMY   You dar talk to me—

POLLY ANN   You sick that steam drill on John Henry, done drove him clear out his mind. You even down make him spite the Almighty. You turn him ginst the mountain. You done gone and make him so mad he hammer the rocks till he set them on fire, destroy himself and everything! *(she breaks down and weeps)*

SALESMAN   Walters, you've got to get him out of there! I'm warning you, so help me God! If my machine is destroyed, I'll sue you for every damn cent it cost me!

CAPTAIN TOMMY   Hard Tack, Britt, Charley, all you boys, get hell in that tunnel and bring John Henry out of there!

HARD TACK   Cap'n, we cain't do a thing!

BRITT   John Henry too powerful.

CHARLEY   And he's angry. John Henry ain't no man to mess with when he's angry.

CAPTAIN TOMMY   Talk back to me, you onery rascals! Go in and get him—or I'll ship every rotten one of you back to the chain gang!

CHARLEY   Lord, Cap'n, don't you know John Henry stronger than six of we-all put together?

HARD TACK   He like that mountain, them rocks and the steel!

CAPTAIN TOMMY   Stop him, do you hear? He's destroying my mountain, he's destroying your jobs, you swine!

(JOHN HENRY emerges from the tunnel all by himself, worn, haggard, his hammer in his hand. He pauses on the landing, steadying himself, looking down upon the crowd of spectators)

SPECTATORS   Look—there he is! John Henry! There John Henry!

POLLY ANN *(she is downstage center)*   John Henry—

JOHN HENRY   I comes out peaceful.

POLLY ANN   You hurt, Honey? Is you powerful hurt?

SALESMAN   You boys give me a hand and we'll get him to a doctor. This man's hurt bad.

JOHN HENRY   You cain't help me none. Too late. Too late now for me.

SALESMAN   We want to help you, John Henry. It isn't too late. There is something we can do for you. Whatever it be, we want to do it. Believe me . . .

JOHN HENRY   Brother, you just cain't help a dying man. I seen the handwriting on the wall. My whole life done passed before me in that tunnel. Then I knowed the cold hand of Death was upon me. I gits crying mad and I hammer till I sets them rocks afire. Then I comes to my senses. I gits still and quiet and very peaceful inside. I don't mind a thing, no, not a solitary thing in this world! *(his voice rising lyrical and eloquent)* I'm as free now as the Blueridge Mountain, the Mississippi River, the Tall Lonesome Pine! *(while he is speaking, the stage darkens, until there is only the solitary shaft of light upon the landing where JOHN HENRY stands. As he looks out over the heads of the audience, another light frames the face of the*

CREEPER, *who is downstage, extreme right. The* CREEPER, *his back to* JOHN HENRY, *is also looking out over the heads of the audience)* They say they got mountains and rocks up there.

 CREEPER It's all mountain and rock country.

 JOHN HENRY And they building great tunnels right and left.

 CREEPER Even under the river-beds!

 JOHN HENRY And, say——If any the other boys should ask for me, just tell them the last thing you see of him was his coat-tail flapping in the wind! Tell'em, say, he long-gone from here to drive hell out of steel!

(The CREEPER *launches into his song, as* JOHN HENRY, *hammer across his shoulder, symbolically sets out for parts unknown)*

CREEPER *(alone)* O' come along, Boys, and line up the track,
 A man ain't nothing but a man.
 John Henry, Lord, ain't never coming back.
 He died with his hammer in his hand.
 He died with his hammer in his hand.
 John Henry, Lord, ain't never coming back.
 He died with his hammer in his hand!

(Curtain)

A SOLDIER'S PLAY
1981

Charles Fuller (1939–   )

A *Soldier's Play* gives us a glimpse of what it was like for African American soldiers serving in a segregated army during the Second World War. At best, they were tolerated by their white officers and openly resented by whites in those southern states where they were trained. Many whites believed Blacks were incapable of battle, although in fact they fought valiantly in every war from the Revolution forward.

Although African Americans opposed Nazism and its Aryan doctrine, they entered World War II with some apprehension. They had fought in World War I hoping that their willingness to die for their country would prove their loyalty and secure their right to full citizenship. Yet when they returned victorious from the battlefields in Europe following World War I, they were subjected to the same inequities that had plagued them in the past. Racial hatred flared, erupting in riots and lynchings and an atmosphere of intolerance where prominent citizens and government officials could openly flaunt their membership in the Ku Klux Klan. Now

America was entering a war to preserve freedom and democracy, a freedom that one-tenth of its population was not allowed to share. Black leaders petitioned President Roosevelt, calling for equality in training for servicemen and demanding that officers be accepted on ability rather than race; that medical and other specialized personnel be integrated; and that discrimination in the air force and navy be discontinued. The War Department replied that the army would accept Negroes in proportion to their population in the country, and that they would be placed in separate units. White officers commanding Negro units would not be replaced, and the only Negro officers assigned to these units would be chaplains and medical personnel.

Blacks were outraged by this response and launched a vigorous and steady protest not only for equality in the armed forces, but in the defense industry and other government apprentice programs. In spite of this, African American regiments remained basically service units doing menial work that white personnel did not want to do. Life in the service for these men was a microcosm of their lives as citizens. Even so, they served with the same conviction that Sergeant Waters expresses: "The First War, . . . didn't change much . . . but this one—it's gonna change a lot of things."

Fuller's drama is skillfully constructed and boasts extraordinary characters. Sergeant Waters, whose values and aspirations are those that have been instilled in him by white society, is the most complex character. Filled with self-hatred, he strives to rise above the oppression that he is subjected to by becoming what he believes the white man is willing to accept. In his pursuit of white acceptance, however, he resorts to their tactics—he is insensitive, degrading, and hostile; he becomes a bigot and a racist. His resentment of illiterate, inarticulate, southern Blacks like C.J., whom he feels hinder the progress of the race, allows him to become as cruel and evil as the Louisiana Klansmen or the Nazis who were willing to annihilate an entire race. Fuller offers us an interesting opportunity to examine the role that racism plays in shaping the personalities of his characters, particularly Waters, C.J., Peterson, and Davenport.

Charles Fuller served in the U.S. Army from 1959 to 1962, then returned to Philadelphia, his home, where he became the founding manager of the Afro-American Art Theatre. His first play produced in New York was *The Perfect Party*, which ran for twenty-one performances Off Broadway in 1969. In 1976, his play *In the Deepest Part of Sleep*, became the first in a series of his works produced by the Negro Ensemble Company. It was followed by *The Brownsville Raid* (1976), *Zooman and the Sign*, which won a 1981 Obie Award in playwriting, and *A Soldier's Play*, for which he won the Pulitzer Prize in 1982. (An acclaimed movie version of the play was released as *A Soldier's Story*.) His most recent works are *Sally* (1988), *Prince* (1989), *Jonquil* (1989), and *Burner's Frolick* (1990).

A Soldier's Play

CAST OF CHARACTERS

Tech/Sergeant VERNON C. WATERS
Captain CHARLES TAYLOR
Corporal BERNARD COBB
Private First Class MELVIN PETERSON
Corporal ELLIS
Private LOUIS HENSON
Private JAMES WILKIE
Private TONY SMALLS
Captain RICHARD DAVENPORT
Private C.J. MEMPHIS
Lieutenant BYRD
Captain WILCOX

ACT ONE

TIME   *1944*

PLACE   *Fort Neal, Louisiana*

(SCENE: *The inner shell of the stage is black. On the stage, in a horseshoe-like half circle, are several platforms at varying levels.*

On the left side of this horseshoe is a military office arrangement with a small desk (a nameplate on the desk reads: CAPTAIN CHARLES TAYLOR*), two office-type chairs, one straightbacked, a regimental and an American flag. A picture of F.D.R. is on the wall.*

On the right side of the horseshoe, and curved toward the rear, is a barracks arrangement, with three bunk beds and footlockers set in typical military fashion. The exit to this barracks is a free-standing doorway on the far right. (This barracks should be changeable—these bunks with little movement can look like a different place.) On the edge of this barracks is a poster, semi-blown-up, of Joe Louis in an army uniform, helmet, rifle, and bayonet. It reads: PVT. JOE LOUIS says, "We're going to do our part—and we'll win because we're on God's side."

On the rear of the horseshoe, upstage center, is a bare platform, raised several feet above everything else. It can be anything we want it to be—a limbo if you will.

The entire set should resemble a courtroom. The sets, barracks and office, will both be elevated, so that from anywhere on the horseshoe one may look down onto a space at center stage that is on the stage floor. The levels should have easy access by either stairs or ramps, and the entire set should be raked ever so slightly so that one does not perceive much difference between floor and set, and the bottom edges of the horseshoe. There must also be enough area on both sides of the horseshoe to see exits and entrances.

Lighting will play an integral part in the realization of the play. It should therefore be sharp, so that areas are clearly defined, with as little spill into other areas as possible. Lights must also be capable of suggesting mood, time, and place.

As the play opens, the stage is black. In the background, rising in volume, we hear the song "Don't Sit Under the Apple Tree," sung by the Andrews Sisters. Quite suddenly, in a sharp though narrow beam of light, in limbo, TECH/SERGEANT VERNON C. WATERS, a well-built light-brown-skinned man in a World War II, winter army uniform, is seen down on all fours. He is stinking drunk, trying to stand and mumbling to himself)

WATERS *(repeating)*   They'll still hate you! They still hate you . . . They still hate you!

(WATERS is laughing as suddenly someone steps into the light. [We never see this person.] He is holding a .45-caliber pistol. He lifts it swiftly and ominously toward Waters' head and fires. Waters is knocked over backward. He is dead. The music has stopped and there is a strong silence onstage)

VOICE   Le's go!

(The man with the gun takes a step, then stops. He points the gun at WATERS again and fires a second time. There is another silence as limbo is plunged into darkness, and the barracks is just as quickly lit.

We are in the barracks of Company B, 221st Chemical Smoke Generating Company, at Fort Neal. Five black enlisted men stand at "parade rest" with their hands above their heads and submit to a search. They are CORPORAL BERNARD COBB, a man in his mid to late twenties, dressed in a T-shirt, dog tags, fatigues, and slippers. PRIVATE JAMES WILKIE, a man in his early forties, a career soldier, he is dressed in fatigues from which his stripes have been removed, a baseball cap, and is smoking a cigar. PRIVATE LOUIS HENSON, thin in his late twenties, early thirties, he is wearing a baseball T-shirt that reads "Fort Neal" on the front, and "4" on the back, fatigues, and boots. PRIVATE FIRST CLASS MELVIN PETERSON, a man in his late twenties, he wears glasses, looks angelic. His shirt is opened but he does not look sloppy; of all the men, his stripe is the most visible, his boots the most highly polished. PRIVATE TONY SMALLS, a man in his late thirties, a career man, he is as small as his name feels. All five men are being searched by CORPORAL ELLIS, a soldier who is simply always "spit and polish." ELLIS is also black and moves from man to man patting them down in a police-like search. CAPTAIN CHARLES TAYLOR, a young white man in his mid to late thirties, looks on a bit disturbed. All the men's uniforms are from World War II)

TAYLOR   I'm afraid this kind of thing can't be helped, men—you can put your arms down when Ellis finishes. *(several men drop their arms.* ELLIS *is searching* PVT. HENSON) We don't want anyone from Fort Neal going into Tynin looking for red-necks.

COBB   May I speak, Sir? *(TAYLOR nods)* Why do this, Captain? They got M.P.'s surrounding us, and hell, the Colonel must know nobody colored killed the man!

TAYLOR   This is a precaution, Cobb. We can't have revenge killings, so we search for weapons.

PETERSON   Where'd they find the Sarge, Sir?

TAYLOR   In the woods out by the Junction—and so we don't have any rumors. Sergeant Waters was shot twice—we don't know that he was lynched! *(pause)* Twice.

Once in the chest, and a bullet in the head. (ELLIS *finishes with the last man*) You finished the footlockers?

ELLIS   Yes, Sir! There aren't any weapons.

TAYLOR   (*relaxes*)   I didn't think there would be. At ease, men! (*the men relax*) Tech/ Sergeant Waters, in my opinion, served the 221st and this platoon in particular with distinction, and I for one shall miss the man. (*slight pause*) But no matter what we think of the Sergeant's death, we will not allow this incident to make us forget our responsibility to this uniform. We are soldiers, and our war is with the Nazis and Japs, not the civilians in Tynin. Any enlisted man found with unauthorized weapons will be immediately subject to Summary Court Martial. (*softens*) Sergeant Waters' replacement won't be assigned for several weeks. Until that time you will all report to Sergeant Dorsey of C Company. Corporal Cobb will be barracks N.C.O.—any questions?

PETERSON   Who do you think did it, Sir?

TAYLOR   At this time there are no suspects.

HENSON   You know the Klan did it, Sir.

TAYLOR   Were you an eyewitness, Soldier?

HENSON   Who else goes around killin' Negroes in the South?—They lynched Jefferson the week I got here, Sir! And that Signal Corps guy, Daniels, two months later!

TAYLOR   Henson, unless you saw it, keep your opinions to yourself! Is that clear? (HENSON *nods*) And that's an order! It also applies to everybody else!

ALL   (*almost simultaneously*)   Yes, Sir!

TAYLOR   You men who have details this afternoon, report to the Orderly room for your assignments. The rest of you are assigned to the Colonel's quarters—clean-up detail. Cobb, I want to see you in my office at 1350 hours.

COBB   Yes, Sir.

TAYLOR   As of 0600 hours this morning, the town of Tynin was placed off-limits to all military personnel. (*slight groan from the men*) The Friday night dance has also been canceled— (*all the men moan,* TAYLOR *is sympathetic*) O.K., O.K.! Some of the officers are going to the Colonel—I can't promise anything. Right now, it's canceled.

ELLIS   Ten-hutt!

(*The men snap to. The* CAPTAIN *salutes. Only* COBB *salutes him back. The* CAPTAIN *starts out*)

TAYLOR   As you were!

(*The* CAPTAIN *and* ELLIS *exit the barracks. The men move to their bunks or footlockers.* WILKIE *goes to the rear of the bunks and looks out*)

COBB   They still out there, Wilkie?

WILKIE   Yeah. Got the whole place surrounded.

HENSON   I don't know what the hell they thought we'd go into that town with—mops and dishrags?

WILKIE   Y'all "recruits" know what Colonel's clean-up detail is, don't you? Shovelin' horseshit in his stables—

COBB   Ain't no different from what we been doin'. (*he lies down and begins scratching around his groin area*)

PETERSON   (*to* COBB)   Made you the barracks Commander-in-Chief, huh? (COBB *nods*) Don't git like ole Stone-ass— What are you doin'?

COBB   Scratchin'!

HENSON   (*overlapping*)   Taylor knows the Klan did it—I hope y'all know that!

SMALLS   (*sudden*)   Then why are the M.P.'s outside with rifles? Why hold us prisoner?

PETERSON   They scared we may kill a couple "peckerwoods," Smalls. Calm down, man!

WILKIE   (*quickly*)   Smalls, you wanna play some Coon-can?

(SMALLS *shakes his head "no." He is quiet, staring*)

COBB   (*examining himself*)   Peterson, you know I think Eva gave me the "crabs."

HENSON   Cobb, the kinda' women you find, it's a wonda' your nuts ain't fell off—crabs? You probably got lice, ticks, bedbugs, fleas— tapeworms—

COBB   Shut up, Henson! Pete—I ain't foolin', Man! (*he starts to open his pants*)

PETERSON   Get some powder from the PX.

WILKIE   (*almost simultaneously*)   Which one of y'all feels like playin' me some cards? (*he looks at* HENSON)

HENSON   Me and Peterson's goin' down the mess hall—you still goin', Pete?

PETERSON   (*nods*)   Wilkie? I thought all you could do was play "Go-fer"?

HENSON   (*slyly*)   Yeah, Wilkie—who's ass can you kiss, now that your number one ass is dead?

COBB   (*laughing*)   That sounds like something C.J. would sing! (*looks at himself again*) Ain't this a bitch? (*picks at himself*)

WILKIE (*overlapping to* HENSON)   You know what you can do for me, Henson—you too, Peterson!

PETERSON   Naughty, naughty!

(WILKIE *moves to his bunk, justifying*)

WILKIE   I'm the one lost three stripes—and I'm the only man in here with kids, so when the man said, jump, I jumped!

HENSON (*derisively*)   Don't put your wife and kids between you and Waters' ass, man!

WILKIE   I wanted my stripes back!

COBB   I'm goin' to sick-call after chow.

WILKIE (*continuing*)   Y'all ain't neva' had nothin', that's why you can't understand a man like me! There was a time I was a Sergeant Major, you know!

(HENSON *waves disdainfully at him, turning his attention to* COBB)

HENSON   Ole' V-girl slipped Cobb the crabs! How you gonna' explain that to the girl back home, Corporal? How will that fine, big-thighed Moma feel, when the only ribbon you bring home from this war is the Purple Heart for crab bites? (HENSON *laughs as* SMALLS *stands suddenly*)

SMALLS   Don't any of you guys give a damn?

PETERSON   What's the matta', Smalls?

SMALLS   The man's dead! We saw him alive last night!

COBB (*quickly*)   I saw him too. At least I know he died good and drunk!

SMALLS (*loud*)   What's the matter with y'all?

HENSON   The man got hisself lynched! We're in the South, and we can't do a god-damn thing about it—you heard the Captain! But don't start actin' like we guilty of some-thin'. (*Softens*) I just hope we get lucky enough to get shipped outta' this hell hole to the War! (*to himself*) Besides, whoever did it, didn't kill much anyway.

SMALLS   He deserved better than that!

COBB   Look, everybody feels rotten, Smalls. But it won't bring the man back, so let's forget about it!

(PETERSON *moves to pat* SMALLS *on the back*)

PETERSON   Why don't you walk it off, man?

(SMALLS *moves away to his bunk.* PETERSON *shrugs*)

HENSON   Yeah—or go turn on a smoke machine, let the fog make you think you in London!

(SMALLS *sits down on his bunk and looks at them for a moment then lays down, his face in the pillow*)

WILKIE (*overlapping*)   Let Cobb bring his Eva over, she'll take his mind off Waters plus give him a bonus of crabs!

(*The men laugh, but* SMALLS *doesn't move as the lights begin to slowly fade out*)

HENSON (*counting*)   —an' blue-balls. Clap. Syphilis. Pimples! (COBB *throws a pillow at* HENSON) Piles! Fever blisters. Cockeyes. Cooties!

(*The men are laughing as the lights go out. As they do, a rather wiry black officer wearing glasses,* CAPTAIN RICHARD DAVENPORT, *dressed sharply in an M.P. uniform, his hat cocked to the side and "strapped" down the way the airmen wear theirs. He is carrying a briefcase, and as he walks across the stage from the wings, we are aware of a man who is very confident and self-assured. He is smiling as he faces the audience, cleaning his glasses as he begins to speak*)

DAVENPORT   Call me Davenport—Captain, United States Army, attached to the 343rd Military Police Corps Unit, Fort Neal, Louisiana. I'm a lawyer the segregated Armed Services couldn't find a place for. My job in this war? Policing colored troops. (*slight pause*) One morning, during mid-April, 1944, a colored Tech/Sergeant, Vernon C. Waters, assigned to the 221st Chemical Smoke Generating Company, stationed here, before transfer to Europe, was brutally shot to death in a wooded section off the New Post Road and the junction of Highway 51—just two hundred yards from the colored N.C.O. Club, by a person or persons unknown. (*Pauses a little*) Naturally, the unofficial consensus was the local Ku Klux Klan, and for that reason, I was told at the time, Colonel Barton Nivens ordered the Military Police to surround the enlisted men's quarters—then instructed all his Company Commanders to initiate a thorough search of all personal property for unauthorized knives, guns—weapons of any kind. (*slight pause*) You see, ninety percent of the Colonel's command—all of the enlisted men stationed here are Negroes, and the Colonel felt—and I suppose justly, that once word of the Sergeant's death spread among his troops, there might be some retaliation against the white citizens of Tynin. (*shrugs*) What he did worked—there was no retaliation, and no racial incidents. (*pause*) The week after the killing took place, several correspondents from the Negro press wrote lead articles about it. But the headlines faded— (*smiles*) The NAACP got me involved in this. Rumor has it, Thurgood Marshall ordered an immediate investigation of the killing, and the army, pressured by Secretary of War Stimson, rather randomly ordered Colonel Nivens to initiate a preliminary inquiry into the Sergeant's death. Now, the Colonel didn't want to rehash the murder, but he complied with the army's order by instructing the Provost Marshal, my C.O., Major Hines, to conduct a *few* question-and-answer sessions among the men of Sergeant Waters' platoon and file a report. The matter was to be given the lowest priority. (*Pause*) The case was mine, five minutes later. It was four to five weeks after his death—the month of May. (*he pauses as the light builds in* CAPTAIN TAYLOR's *office.* TAYLOR *is facing* DAVENPORT, *expressionless.* DAVENPORT *is a bit puzzled*) Captain?

TAYLOR   Forgive me for occasionally staring, Davenport, you're the first colored officer I've ever met. I'd heard you had arrived a month ago—you're a bit startling. (*Quickly*) I mean you no offense. (*Starts back to his desk and sits on the edge of it, as* DAVENPORT *starts into the office a bit cautiously*) We'll be getting some of you as replacements, but we don't expect them until next month. Sit down, Davenport. (DAVENPORT *sits*) You came out of Fort Benning in 'forty-three?

DAVENPORT   Yes.

TAYLOR   And they assigned a lawyer to the Military Police? I'm Infantry and I've been with the Engineers, Field Artillery, and Signal Corps—this is some army. Where'd you graduate law school?

DAVENPORT   Howard University.

TAYLOR   Your daddy a rich minister or something? (DAVENPORT *shakes his head no*) I graduated the Point— (*pause*) We didn't have any Negroes at the Point. I never saw a Negro

until I was twelve or thirteen. (*pause*) You like the army I suppose, huh?

DAVENPORT   Captain, did you see my orders?

TAYLOR   (*bristling, slightly*)   I saw them right after Colonel Nivens sent them to Major Hines. I sent my orderly to the barracks and told him to have the men waiting for you.

DAVENPORT   Thank you.

TAYLOR   I didn't know at the time that Major Hines was assigning a Negro, Davenport. (DAVENPORT *stiffens*) My preparations were made in the belief that you'd be a white man. I think it only fair to tell you, that had I known what Hines intended I would have requested the immediate suspension of the investigation— May I speak freely?

DAVENPORT   You haven't stopped yet, Captain.

TAYLOR   Look—how far could you get even if you succeed? These local people aren't going to charge a white man in this parish on the strength of an investigation conducted by a Negro!—and Nivens and Hines know that! The Colonel doesn't give a damn about finding the men responsible for this thing! And they're making a fool of you—can't you see that?—and—take off those sunglasses!

DAVENPORT   I intend to carry out my orders—and I like these glasses—they're like MacArthur's.

TAYLOR   You go near that sheriff's office in Tynin in your uniform—carrying a briefcase, looking and sounding white and charging local people and you'll be found just as dead as Sergeant Waters! People around here don't respect the colored!

DAVENPORT   I know that.

TAYLOR   (*annoyed*)   You know how many times I've asked Nivens to look into this killing? Every day, since it happened, Davenport. Major Hines didn't tell you that!

DAVENPORT   Do you suspect someone, Captain?

TAYLOR   Don't play cat-and-mouse with me, Soldier!

DAVENPORT   (*Calmly*)   Captain, like it or not, I'm all you've got. I've been ordered to look into Sergeant Waters' death, and I intend to do exactly that.

(*There is a long pause*)

TAYLOR   Can I tell you a little story? (DAVENPORT *nods*) Before you were assigned here? Nivens got us together after dinner one night, and all we did was discuss Negroes in the officer ranks. We all commanded Negro troops, but nobody had ever come face to face with colored officers—there were a lot of questions that night—for example, your quarters—had to be equal to ours, but we had none—no mess hall for you! (*slight pause*) Anyway, Jed Harris was the only officer who defended it—my own feelings were mixed. The only Negroes I've ever known were subordinates—My father hired the first Negro I ever saw—man named Colfax—to help him fix the shed one summer. Nice man—worked hard—did a good job too. (*remembering; smiles thoughtfully*) But I never met a Negro with any education until I graduated the Point—hardly an officer of equal rank. So I frankly wasn't sure how I'd feel—until right now—and— (*struggles*) I don't want to offend you, but I just cannot get used to it—the bars, the uniform—being in charge just doesn't look right on Negroes!

DAVENPORT (*rises*)   Captain, are you through?

TAYLOR   You could ask Hines for another assignment—this case is not for you! By the time you overcome the obstacles to your race this case would be dead!

DAVENPORT (*sharply*)   I got it. And I *am* in charge! All your orders instruct you to do is cooperate!

(*There is a moment of silence*)

TAYLOR   I won't be made a fool of, Davenport. (*straightens*) Ellis! You're right, there's no need to discuss this any further.

(ELLIS *appears on the edge of the office*)

ELLIS   Yes, Sir!

TAYLOR   Captain Davenport will need assistance with the men—I can't prevent that, Davenport, but I intend to do all I can to have this so-called investigation stopped.

DAVENPORT   Do what you like. If there's nothing else, you'll excuse me won't you, Captain?

TAYLOR (*sardonically*)   Glad I met you, Captain.

(DAVENPORT *salutes and* TAYLOR *returns it. For an instant the two men trade cold stares, then*

DAVENPORT *gestures to* ELLIS, *and the two of them start out of the office by way of the stage.* DAVENPORT *follows* ELLIS *out. Behind them,* TAYLOR *stares after them as the lights in his office fade out.* DAVENPORT *removes his glasses*)

ELLIS   We heard it was you, Sir—you know how the grapevine is. Sad thing—what happened to the Sarge.

DAVENPORT   What's on the grapevine about the killing?

(*The two men stop as slowly, almost imperceptibly, on the right the barracks area is lit. In it a small table and two chairs have been set up.* ELLIS *shrugs*)

ELLIS   We figure the Klan. They ain't crazy about us tan yanks in this part of the country.

DAVENPORT   Is there anything on the grapevine about trouble in the town before Sergeant Waters was killed?

ELLIS   None that I know of before—after, there were rumors around the post—couple of our guys from the Tank Corps wanted to drive them Shermans into Tynin—then I guess you heard that somebody said two officers did it—I figure that's why the Colonel surrounded our barracks.

DAVENPORT   Was the rumor confirmed—I didn't hear that! Did anything ever come of it?

ELLIS   Not that I know of, Sir.

DAVENPORT   Thanks, Ellis—I'd better start seeing the men. (*they start into the barracks from the stage door*) Did you set this up? (ELLIS *nods*) Good— (*he sets his briefcase on the table*) Are they ready?

ELLIS   The Captain instructed everybody in the Sarge's platoon to be here, Sir. He told them you'd be starting this morning.

(DAVENPORT *smiles*)

DAVENPORT (*to himself*)   Before he found out, huh?

ELLIS (*puzzled*)   Sir?

DAVENPORT   Nothing. Call the first man in, Corporal—and stay loose, I might need you.

ELLIS   Yes, Sir! Sir, may I say something? (DAVENPORT *nods*) It sure is good to see one of us wearin' them Captain's bars, Sir.

DAVENPORT   Thank you.

(ELLIS *salutes, does a sharp about-face, and starts out*)

ELLIS (*loud*)   Private Wilkie!

WILKIE (*offstage*)   Yes, Sir! (*almost immediately* WILKIE *appears in the doorway. He is dressed in proper uniform of fatigues, boots, and cap*)

ELLIS   Cap'n wants to see you!

WILKIE   Yes indeedy! (*moves quickly to the table, where he comes to attention and salutes*) Private James Wilkie reporting as ordered, Sir.

DAVENPORT   At ease, Private. Have a seat. (*to* ELLIS *as* WILKIE *sits*) That will be all, Corporal.

ELLIS   Yes, Sir.

(ELLIS *salutes and exits.* DAVENPORT *waits until he leaves before speaking*)

DAVENPORT   Private Wilkie, I am Captain Davenport—

WILKIE (*interjecting*)   Everybody knows that, Sir. You all we got down here. (*smiles broadly*) I was on that first detail got your quarters togetha', Sir.

(DAVENPORT *nods*)

DAVENPORT (*coldly*)   I'm conducting an investigation into the events surrounding Sergeant Waters' death. Everything you say to me will go in my report, but that report is confidential.

WILKIE   I understand, Sir.

(DAVENPORT *removes pad and pencil from the briefcase*)

DAVENPORT   How long did you know Sergeant Waters?

WILKIE   'Bout a year, Sir. I met him last March—March fifth—I remember the date. I had been a Staff Sergeant exactly two years the day he was assigned. This company was basically a baseball team then, Sir. See, most of the boys had played for the Negro League, so naturally the Army put us all together. (*chuckles at the memory*) We'd be assigned to different companies—Motor Pool—Dump Truck all week long—made us do the dirty work on the Post—garbage, clean-up—but on Saturdays we were whippin' the hell out of 'em on the baseball diamond! I was hittin' .352 myself! And we had a boy, C.J. Memphis! He coulda' hit a ball from Fort Neal to Berlin, Germany—or Tokyo—if he was battin' right-handed. (*pauses, catches* DAVENPORT'S *impatience*) Well, the army sent Waters to manage

the team. He had been in Field Artillery—Gunnery Sergeant. Had a Croix de Guerre from the First War, too.

DAVENPORT   What kind of man was he?

WILKIE   All spit and polish, Sir.

(*At that moment in limbo a spotlight hits* SERGEANT WATERS. *He is dressed in a well-creased uniform, wearing a helmet-liner and standing at parade-rest facing the audience. The light around him, however, is strange—it is blue-gray like the past. The light around* DAVENPORT *and* WILKIE *abates somewhat. Dialogue is continuous*)

DAVENPORT   Tell me about him.

WILKIE   He took my stripes! (*Smiles*) But I was in the wrong, Sir!

(WATERS *stands at ease. His voice is crisp and sharp. His movements minimal. He is the typical hard-nosed N.C.O.—strict, soldierly*)

WATERS   Sergeant Wilkie! You are a non-commissioned officer in the army of a country at war—the penalty for being drunk on duty is severe in peace-time, so don't bring me no po'-colored-folks-can't-do-nothin'-unless-they-drunk shit as an excuse! You are supposed to be an example to your men—so, I'm gonna' send you to jail for ten days *and* take them goddamn stripes. Teach you a lesson—You in the army! (*derisively*) Colored folks always runnin' off at the mouth 'bout what y'all gonna do, if the white man gives you a chance—and you get it, and what do you do with it? You wind up drunk on guard duty—I don't blame the white man—why the hell should he put colored and white together in this war? You can't even be trusted to guard your own quarters—no wonder they treat us like dogs— Get outta' my sight, *Private!*

(*Light fades at once on* WATERS)

DAVENPORT   What about the other men?

WILKIE   Sometimes the Southern guys caught a little hell—Sarge always said he was from up North somewhere. He was a good soldier, Sir. I'm from Detroit myself—born and raised there. Joe Louis started in Detroit—did you know that, Sir?

DAVENPORT   What about the Southerners?

WILKIE   Sarge wasn't exactly crazy 'bout 'em—'cept for C.J. Now C.J. was from the South, but with him Sarge was different—

probably because C.J. was the best ball player we had. He could sing too! (*slight pause*) Sarge never got too close to nobody—maybe me—but he didn' mess with C.J., you know what I mean? Not like he did with everybody else.

(*In limbo, the spotlight illuminates* C.J. MEMPHIS, *a young, handsome black man. He is in a soldier's uniform, cap on the side. He is strumming a guitar.* WATERS *is watching him, smiling. Their light is the strange light of the past.* C.J. *begins to sing, his voice deep, melodious, and bluesy*)

C.J.   It's a low / it's a low, low / lowdown dirty shame! Yeah, it's a low / it's a low, low / lowdown dirty shame!
WILKIE (*before* C.J. *finishes*)   Big, Mississippi boy!

(WILKIE *and* C.J. *simultaneously sing*)

C.J. AND WILKIE   They say we fightin' Hitler! But they won't let us in the game!

(C.J. *strums and hums as* WATERS *looks on*)

WILKIE   Worked harder and faster than everybody—wasn' a man on the team didn't like him. Sarge took to him the first time he saw him. "Wilkie," he says.
WILKIE AND WATERS (*simultaneously*)   What have we got here?
WATERS   A guitar-playin' man! Boy, you eva' heard of Blind Willie Reynolds? Son House? Henry Sims?

(C.J. *nods to everything*)

C.J.   You heard them play, Sarge?
WATERS   Everyone of 'em. I was stationed in Mississippi couple years ago—you from down that way, ain't you?
C.J.   Yes, Sah!
WATERS   Well, they use ta play over at the Bandana Club outside Camp J.J. Reilly.
C.J.   I played there once!
WATERS (*smiles*)   Ain't that somethin'? I'd go over there from time to time— People use ta come from everywhere! (*to* WILKIE) Place was always dark, Wilkie—smoky. Folks would be dancin'—sweatin'—guitar pickers be strummin', shoutin'—it would be wild in there sometimes. Reminded me of a place I use ta go in France durin' the First War—the women, the whiskey—place called the Café Napoléon.

C.J.   You really like the Blues, huh?
WATERS   No other kind of music—where'd you learn to play so good? I come by here yesterday and heard this "pickin'"—one of the men tol' me it was you.
C.J.   My Daddy taught me, Sarge.
WATERS   You play pretty good, boy. Wilkie, wasn' that good?
WILKIE   Yes indeed, Sarge.
WILKIE (*to* DAVENPORT)   I mostly agreed with the Sarge, Sir. He was a good man. Good to his men. Talked about his wife and kids all the time— (WATERS *starts down from the limbo area, as the lights around* C.J. *fade out.* WATERS *pulls a pipe from his pocket, lights it as he moves to the edge of the* CAPTAIN's *office and sits on the edge of the platform supporting it. He puffs a few times.* WILKIE's *talk is continuous*) Use ta write home every day. I don't see why nobody would want to kill the Sarge, Sir.

(WATERS *smiles*)

WATERS   Wilkie? (WILKIE *rises and walks into the blue-gray light and the scene with* WATERS. DAVENPORT *will watch*) You know what I'ma get that boy of mine for his birthday? One of them Schwinn bikes. He'll be twelve—time flies don't it? Let me show you something?
WILKIE (*to* DAVENPORT)   He was always pullin' out snapshots, Sir.

(WATERS *hands him a snapshot*)

WATERS   My wife let a neighbor take this a couple of weeks ago—ain't he growin' fast?
WILKIE   He's over your wife's shoulder!
(*hands it back.* WATERS *looks at the photo*)
WATERS   I hope this kid never has to be a soldier.
WILKIE   It was good enough for you.
WATERS   I couldn't do no better—and this army was the closest I figured the white man would let me get to any kind of authority. No, the army ain't for this boy. When this war's over, things are going to change, Wilkie—and I want him to be ready for it—my daughter too! I'm sendin' both of 'em to some big white college—let 'em rub elbows with whites, learn the white man's language—how he does things. Otherwise we'll be left behind—you can see it in the army. White man runnin' rings around us.

WILKIE   A lot of us didn't get the chance or the schoolin' the white folks got.

WATERS   That ain't no excuse, Wilkie. Most niggahs just don't care—tomorrow don't mean nothin' to 'em. My Daddy shoveled coal from the back of a wagon all his life. He couldn't read or write, but he saw to it we did! Not havin' ain't no excuse for not gettin'.

WILKIE   Can't get pee from a rock, Sarge.

(WATERS *rises abruptly*)

WATERS   You just like the rest of 'em, Wilkie—I thought bustin' you would teach you something—we got to challenge this man in his arena—use his weapons, don't you know that? We need lawyers, doctors—generals—senators! Stop thinkin' like a niggah!

WILKIE   All I said—

WATERS   Is the equipment ready for tomorrow's game?

WILKIE   Yeah.

WATERS   Good. You can go now, Wilkie. (WILKIE *is stunned*) That's an order!

(WILKIE *turns toward* DAVENPORT, *as the light around* WATERS *fades out*)

WILKIE   He could be two people sometimes, Sir. Warm one minute—ice the next.

DAVENPORT   How did you feel about him?

WILKIE   Overall—I guess he was all right. You could always borrow a ten-spot off him if you needed it.

DAVENPORT   Did you see the Sergeant anytime immediately preceding his death?

WILKIE   I don't know how much before it was, but a couple of us had been over the N.C.O. Club that night and Sarge had been juicin' pretty heavy.

DAVENPORT   Did Waters drink a lot?

WILKIE   No more than most— (*pause*) Could I ask you a question, Sir? (DAVENPORT *nods*) Is it true, when they found Sarge all his stripes and insignia were still on his uniform?

DAVENPORT   I don't recall it being mentioned in my preliminary report. Why?

WILKIE   If that's the way they found him, something's wrong ain't it, Sir? Them Klan boys don't like to see us in these uniforms. They usually take the stripes and stuff off, before they lynch us.

(DAVENPORT *is quiet, thoughtful for a moment*)

DAVENPORT   Thank you, Private—I might want to call you again, but for now, you're excused.

(WILKIE *rises*)

WILKIE   Yes, Sir! (*sudden mood swing, hesitant*) Sir?

DAVENPORT   Yes?

WILKIE   Can you do anything about allotment checks? My wife didn' get hers last month.

DAVENPORT   There's nothing I can do directly—did you see the finance officer? (WILKIE *nods*) Well—I'll—I'll mention it to Captain Taylor.

WILKIE   Thank you, Sir. You want me to send the next man in?

(DAVENPORT *nods*. WILKIE *salutes, does an about-face, and exits*. DAVENPORT *returns the salute, then leans back in his chair thoughtfully. The next man,* P.F.C. MELVIN PETERSON *enters. Dressed in fatigues, he is the model soldier. He walks quickly to the table, stands at attention, and salutes*)

PETERSON   Private First Class Melvin Peterson reporting as ordered, Sir!

DAVENPORT   Sit down, Private. (PETERSON *sits*) Do you know why I'm here?

PETERSON   Yes, Sir.

DAVENPORT   Fine. Now, everything you tell me is confidential, so I want you to speak as freely as possible. (PETERSON *nods*) Where are you from?

PETERSON   Hollywood, California—by way of Alabama, Sir. I enlisted in 'forty-two—thought we'd get a chance to fight.

DAVENPORT   (*ignores the comment*)   Did you know Sergeant Waters well?

PETERSON   No, Sir. He was already with the Company when I got assigned here. And us common G.I.'s don't mix well with N.C.O.'s.

DAVENPORT   Were you on the baseball team?

PETERSON   Yes, Sir—I played shortstop.

DAVENPORT   Did you like the Sergeant?

PETERSON   No, Sir.

(*Before* DAVENPORT *can speak,* ELLIS *enters*)

ELLIS   Beg your pardon, Sir. Captain Taylor would like to see you in his office at once.

DAVENPORT   Did he say why?

ELLIS   No, Sir—just that you should report to him immediately.

DAVENPORT (*annoyed*)   Tell the men to stick around. When I finish with the Captain I'll be back.

ELLIS   Yes, Sir!

(ELLIS *exits*)

DAVENPORT (*to* PETERSON)   Feel like walking, Private? We can continue this on the way. (*begins to put things in his briefcase*) Why didn't you like the Sergeant?

(DAVENPORT *and* PETERSON *start out as the light begins to fade in the barracks. They go through doorway, exit and reenter the stage in full view*)

PETERSON   It goes back to the team, Sir. I got here in—baseball season had started so it had to be June—June of last year. The team had won maybe nine—ten games in a row. There was a rumor that they would even get a chance to play the Yankees in exhibition. So when I got assigned to a team like that, Sir—I mean, I felt good. Anyway, ole' Stone-ass—

DAVENPORT   Stone-ass?

PETERSON   I'm the only one called him that—Sergeant Waters, Sir.

(*As the two of them pass in front of the barracks area, the light begins to rise very slowly, but it is the blue-gray light of the past. The chairs and table are gone, and the room looks different*)

DAVENPORT   Respect his rank, with me, Private.

PETERSON   I didn't mean no offense, Sir. (*slight pause*) Well, the Sergeant and that brown-nosin' Wilkie? They ran the team—and like it was a chain gang, Sir. A chain gang!

(*The two men exit the stage. As they do,* C.J. MEMPHIS, HENSON, COBB, *and* SMALLS *enter in their baseball uniforms. T-shirts with "Fort Neal" stamped on the fronts and numbers on the back, and baseball caps. They are carrying equipment—bats, gloves.* C.J. *is carrying his guitar. Smalls enters tossing a baseball into the air and catching it. They almost all enter at once, with the exuberance of young men. Their talk is locker-room loud, and filled with bursts of laughter*)

HENSON   You see the look on that umpire's face when C.J. hit that home run? I thought he was gonna die on the spot, he turned so pale!

(*They move to their respective bunks*)

SMALLS   Serves the fat bastard right! Some of them pitches he called strikes were well ova' my head!

(C.J. *strums his guitar,* COBB *begins to brush off his boots*)

COBB   C.J.? Who was that fine, river-hip thing you was talkin' to, "Homey"?

(C.J. *shrugs and smiles*)

HENSON   Speakin' of women, I got to write my Lady a letter. (*he begins to dig for his writing things*)

COBB   She looked mighty good to me, C.J.

SMALLS (*overlapping*)   Y'all hear Henson? Henson, you ain't had a woman since a woman had you!

(HENSON *makes an obscene gesture*)

C.J. (*overlapping* SMALLS)   Now, all she did was ask me for my autograph.

COBB   Look like she was askin' you fo' mor'n that. (*to* SMALLS) You see him, Smalls? Leanin' against the fence, all in the woman's face, breathin' heavy—

HENSON   If Smalls couldn't see enough to catch a ground ball right in his glove, how the hell could he see C.J. ova' by the fence?

SMALLS   That ball got caught in the sun!

HENSON   On the ground?

COBB (*at once*)   We beat 'em nine to one! Y'all be quiet, I'm askin' this man 'bout a woman he was with had tits like two helmets!

C.J.   If I had a give that gal what she asked fo'—she'da give me somethin' I didn't want! Them V-gals git you a bad case a' clap. 'Sides, she wasn't but sixteen.

SMALLS   You shoulda' introduced her to Henson—sixteen's about his speed.

(HENSON *makes a farting sound in retaliation*)

C.J.   Aroun' home? There's a fella folks use ta call, Lil Jimmy One Leg—on account of his thing was so big? Two years ago—ole young pretty laid clap on Jimmy so bad, he los' the one good leg he had! Now, folks jes' call him little!

(*Laughter*)

C.J.   That young thing talkin' to me ain' look so clean.

HENSON   Dirty or clean, she had them white boys lookin'.

COBB   Eyes poppin' out they sockets, wasn' they? Remind me of that pitcher las' week! The one from 35th Ordnance? The one every-body claimed was so good? Afta' twelve straight hits, he looked the same way!

(PETERSON *enters carrying two baseball bats*)

SMALLS   It might be funny ta y'all, but when me and Pete had duty in the Ordnance mess hall, that same white pitcher was the first one started the name callin'—

HENSON   Forget them Dudes in Ord-nance—lissen to this! (HENSON *begins to read from a short letter*) "Dear, Louis"—y'all hear that? The name is Louis—

COBB   Read the damn letter!

HENSON   (*makes obscene gesture*) "Dear Louis. You and the boys keep up the good work. All of us here at home are praying for you and inspired in this great cause by you. We know the Nazis and Japs can't be stopped unless we all work together, so tell your bud-dies to press forward and win this war. All our hopes for the future go with you, Louis, Love Mattie." I think I'm in love with the Sepia Winston Churchill—what kinda' letter do you write a nut like this?

COBB   Send her a round of ammunition and a bayonet, *Louis!*

(HENSON *waves disdainfully*)

PETERSON   Y'all oughta listen to what Smalls said. Every time we beat them at base-ball, they get back at us every way they can.

COBB   It's worth it to me just to wipe those superior smiles off they faces.

PETERSON   I don't know—seems like it makes it that much harder for us.

C.J.   They tell me, coupla' them big-time Negroes is on the verge a' gittin' all of us to-getha'—colored and white—say they want one army.

PETERSON   Forget that, C.J.! White folks'll neva' integrate no army!

C.J.   (*strums*)   If they do—I'ma be ready for 'em! (*sings*) Well, I got me a bright red zoot-suit / And a pair a' patent leatha' shoes / And my woman she sittin' waitin' / Fo' the day we

hea' the news! Lawd, lawd, lawd, lawd, / Lawd, lawd, lawd, lawd!

(SERGEANT WATERS, *followed by* WILKIE, *enters, immediately crossing to the center of the barracks, his strident voice cutting off* C.J.*'s singing and play-ing abruptly*)

WATERS   Listen up! (*To* C.J.) We don't need that guitar playin'-sittin'-round-the-shack mu-sic today, C.J.! (*Smiles*) I want all you men out of those baseball uniforms and into work clothes! You will all report to me at 1300 hours in front of the Officers Club. We've got a work detail. We're painting the lobby of the Club.

(*Collective groan*)

SMALLS   The officers can't paint their own club?

COBB   Hell, no, Smalls! Let the great-colored-clean-up company do it! Our motto is: Anything you don't want to do, the colored troops will do for you!

HENSON   (*like a cheer*)   Anything you don't want to do, the colored troops will do for you! (*he starts to lead the others*)

OTHERS   Anything you don't—

WATERS   That's enough!

(*The men are instantly silent*)

HENSON   When do we get a rest? We just played nine innings of baseball, Sarge!

SMALLS   We can't go in the place, why the hell should we paint it?

COBB   Amen, brother!

(*There is a moment of quiet before* WATERS *speaks*)

WATERS   Let me tell you fancy-assed ball-playin' Negroes somethin'! The *reasons* for any orders given by a superior officer is none of y'all's business! You obey them! This country is at war, and you niggahs are soldiers—nothin' else! So baseball teams—win or lose—get no special privileges! They need to work some of you niggahs till your legs fall off! (*In-tense*) And something else—from now on, when I tell you to do something, I want it done—is that clear? (*the men are quiet*) Now, Wilkie's gonna' take all them funky shirts you got on over to the laundry. I could smell you suckers before I hit the field!

PETERSON   What kinda' colored man are you?

WATERS   I'm a soldier, Peterson! First, last, and always! I'm the kinda' colored man that don't like lazy, shiftless Negroes!

PETERSON   You ain't got to come in here and call us names!

WATERS   The Nazis call you schvatza! You gonna tell them they hurt your little feelings?

C.J.   Don't look like to me we could do too much to them Nazis wit' paint brushes, Sarge.

(The men laugh. The moment is gone, and though WATERS *is angry, his tone becomes overly solicitous, smiling)*

WATERS   You tryin' to mock me, C.J.?

C.J.   No, Sah', Sarge.

WATERS   Good, because whatever an ignorant, low-class geechy like you has to say, isn't worth paying attention to, is it? *(pause)* Is it?

C.J.   I reckon not, Sarge.

PETERSON   You' a creep, Waters!

WATERS   Boy, you are something—ain't been in the company a month, Wilkie, and already everybody's champion!

C.J. *(interjecting)*   Sarge was just jokin', Pete—he don't mean no harm!

PETERSON   He does! We take enough from the white boys!

WATERS   Yes you do—and if it wasn' for you Southern niggahs, yessahin', bowin' and scrapin', scratchin' your heads, white folks wouldn' think we were all fools!

PETERSON   Where you from, England?

(Men snicker)

HENSON *(at once)*   Peterson!

WATERS *(immediately)*   You got somethin' to say, Henson?

HENSON   Nothin', Sarge.

(HENSON shakes his head as WATERS turns back to PETERSON)

WATERS   Peterson, you got a real comic streak in you. Wilkie, looks like we got us a wise-ass Alabama boy here! *(he moves toward* PETERSON*)* Yes, Sir— *(he snatches PETERSON in the collar)* Don't get smart, Niggah!

(PETERSON yanks away)

PETERSON   Get your fuckin' hands off me!

(WATERS smiles, leans forward)

WATERS   You wanna' hit ole Sergeant Waters, boy? *(whispers)* Come on! Please! Come on, Niggah!

(CAPTAIN TAYLOR enters the barracks quite suddenly, unaware of what is going on)

HENSON   Tenn-hut!

(All the men snap to)

TAYLOR   At ease! *(he moves toward* WATERS *feeling the tension)* What's going on here, Sergeant?

WATERS   Nothin', Sir—I was going over the *Manual of Arms*— Is there something in particular you wanted, Sir? Something I can do?

TAYLOR *(relaxed somewhat)*   Nothing— *(to the men)* Men, I congratulate you on the game you won today. We've only got seven more to play, and if we win them, we'll be the first team in Fort Neal history to play the Yanks in exhibition. Everyone in the regiment is counting on you. In times like these, morale is important—and winning can help a lot of things. *(pause)* Sergeant, as far as I'm concerned, they've got the rest of the day off.

(The men are pleased)

WATERS   Begging your pardon, Sir, but these men need all the work they can get. They don't need time off—our fellas aren't getting time off in North Africa—besides, we've got orders to report to the Officers Club for a paint detail at 1300 hours.

TAYLOR   Who issued that order?

WATERS   Major Harris, Sir.

TAYLOR   I'll speak to the Major.

WATERS   Sir, I don't think it's such a good idea to get a colored N.C.O. mixed up in the middle of you officers, Sir.

TAYLOR   I said, I'd speak to him, Sergeant.

WATERS   Yes, Sir!

TAYLOR   I respect the men's duty to service, but they need time off.

WATERS   Yes, Sir.

(Pause)

TAYLOR   You men played a great game of baseball out there today—that catch you made in centerfield, Memphis—how the hell'd you get up so high?

C.J. *(shrugs, smiles)*   They say I got "Bird" in mah blood, Sir.

(TAYLOR *is startled by the statement, his smile is an uncomfortable one.* WATERS *is standing on "eggs"*)

TAYLOR   American eagle, I hope. (*laughs a little*)

C.J.   No, Sah', Crow— (WATERS *starts to move but* C.J. *stops him by continuing. Several of the men are beginning to get uncomfortable*) Man tol' my Daddy the day I was born, the shadow of a crow's wings—

TAYLOR (*cutting him off*)   Fine— Men, I'll say it again—you played superbly. (*turns to* WATERS) Sergeant. (*he starts out abruptly*)

WATERS   Tenn-hut!

(WATERS *salutes as the men snap to*)

TAYLOR (*exiting*)   As you were.

(TAYLOR *salutes as he goes. There is an instant of quiet, the men relax a little, but their focus is* C.J.)

WATERS (*laughing*)   Ain't these geechies somethin'? How long a story was you gonna' tell the man, C.J.? My God! (*the men join him, but as he turns toward* PETERSON *he stiffens*) Peterson! Oh, I didn't forget you, boy. (*the room quiets*) It's time to teach you a lesson!

PETERSON   Why don't you drop dead, Sarge?

WATERS   Nooo! I'ma drop you, boy! Out behind the barracks—Wilkie, you go out and make sure it's all set up.

WILKIE   You want all the N.C.O.'s?

(WATERS *nods.* WILKIE *goes out smiling*)

WATERS   I'm going outside and wait for you, geechy! And when you come out, I'm gonna' whip your black Southern ass—let the whole company watch it too! (*points*) You need to learn respect, boy—how to talk to your betters. (*starts toward the door*) Fight hard, hea'? I'ma try to bust your fuckin' head open—the rest of you get those goddamn shirts off like I said!

(*He exits. The barracks is quiet for a moment*)

COBB   You gonna' fight him?

HENSON (*overlapping*)   I tried to warn you!

PETERSON   You ain't do nothin'!

SMALLS   He'll fight you dirty, Pete—don't do it!

(PETERSON *goes to his bunk and throws his cap off angrily*)

COBB   You don't want to do it?

PETERSON   You wanna' fight in my place, Cobb? (*he sits*) Shit!

(*Slight pause.* HENSON *pulls off his shirt*)

C.J.   I got some Farmers Dust—jes' a pinch'll make you strong as a bull—they say it comes from the city of Zar. (*Removes a pouch from his neck*) I seen a man use this stuff and pull a full-grown mule outta' a sinkhole by hisself!

PETERSON   Get the hell outta' here, with that backwater, crap—can't you speak up for yourself—let that bastard treat you like a dog!

C.J.   'Long as his han's ain't on me—he ain't done me no harm, Pete. Callin' names ain't nothin', I know what I is. (*Softens*) Sarge ain't so bad—been good to me.

PETERSON   The man despises you!

C.J.   Sarge? You wrong, Pete—plus I feel kinda' sorry for him myself. Any man ain't sure where he belongs, must be in a whole lotta' pain.

PETERSON   Don't y'all care?

HENSON   Don't nobody like it, Pete—but when you here a little longer—I mean, what can you do? This hea's the Army and Sarge got all the stripes.

(PETERSON *rises, disgusted, and starts out.* SMALLS *moves at once*)

SMALLS   Peterson, look, if you want me to, I'll get the Captain. You don't have to go out there and get your head beat in!

PETERSON   Somebody's got to fight him.

(*He exits. There is quiet as* SMALLS *walks back to his bunk*)

C.J. (*singing*)   It's a low / it's a low, low / lowdown dirty shame! It's a low / it's a low, low / lowdown dirty shame! Been playin' in this hea' army / an ain't even learned the game! Lawd, lawd, lawd, lawd—

(C.J. *begins to hum as the lights slowly fade out over the barracks. As they do, the lights come up simultaneously in the* CAPTAIN's *office. It is empty.* PETERSON [*in proper uniform*] *and* DAVENPORT *enter from offstage. They stop outside the* CAPTAIN's *office*)

PETERSON   He beat me pretty bad that day, Sir. The man was crazy!

DAVENPORT   Was the incident ever reported?

PETERSON   I never reported it, Sir—I know
I should have, but he left me alone after that.
(*shrugs*) I just played ball.

DAVENPORT   Did you see Waters the night
he died?

PETERSON   No, Sir—me and Smalls had
guard duty.

DAVENPORT   Thank you, Private. That'll be
all for now. (PETERSON *comes to attention*) By the
way, did the team ever get to play the Yankees?

PETERSON   No, sir. We lost the last game to
a Sanitation Company.

(*He salutes.* DAVENPORT *returns it.* PETERSON
does a crisp about-face and exits. Slowly DAVEN-
PORT *starts into the* CAPTAIN's *office surprised that
no one is about*)

DAVENPORT   Captain? (*there is no response.
For a moment or two* DAVENPORT *looks around.
He is somewhat annoyed*) Captain?

(*He starts out.* TAYLOR *enters. He crosses the room
to his desk where he sits*)

TAYLOR   I asked you back here because I
wanted you to see the request I've sent to
Colonel Nivens to have your investigation ter-
minated. (*he picks up several sheets of paper on
his desk and hands them to* DAVENPORT, *who ignores them*)

DAVENPORT   What?

TAYLOR   I wanted you to see that my reasons have nothing to do with you personally—
my request will not hurt your army record in
any way!—(*pause*)—there are other things to
consider in this case!

DAVENPORT   Only the color of my skin,
Captain.

TAYLOR (*sharply*)   I want the people responsible for killing one of my men found and
jailed, Davenport!

DAVENPORT   So do I!

TAYLOR   Then give this up! (*rises*) Whites
down here won't see their duty—or justice.
They'll see *you!* And once they do, the law—
due process—it all goes! And what is the
point of continuing an investigation that can't
possibly get at the truth?

DAVENPORT   Captain, my orders are very
specific, so unless you want charges brought
against you for interfering in a criminal in-

quiry, stay the hell out of my way and leave
me and my investigation alone!

TAYLOR (*almost sneering*)   Don't take yourself
too seriously, Davenport. You couldn't find an
officer within five hundred miles who would
convey charges to a court-martial board against
me for something like that, and you know it!

DAVENPORT   Maybe not, but I'd—I'd see to
it that your name, rank, and duty station got
into the Negro press! Yeah, let a few colored
newspapers call you a Negro-hater! Make you
an embarrassment to the United States Army,
Captain—like Major Albright at Fort Jefferson—and you'd never command troops
again—or wear more than those Captain's
bars on that uniform, Mr. West Point!

TAYLOR   I'll never be more than a Captain,
Davenport, because I won't let them get away
with dismissing things like Waters' death. I've
been the commanding officer of three outfits!
I raised hell in all of them, so threatening me
won't change my request. Let the Negro press
print that I don't like being made a fool of
with phony investigations!

DAVENPORT (*studies* TAYLOR *for a moment*)
There are two white officers involved in this,
Captain—aren't there?

TAYLOR   I want them in jail—out of the
army! And there is no way *you* can get them
charged, or court-martialed or put away! The
white officers on this post won't let you—they
won't let me!

DAVENPORT   Why wasn't there any mention
of them in your preliminary report? I checked
my own summary on the way over here, Captain—nothing! You think I'ma let you get
away with this? (*there is a long silence.* TAYLOR
walks back to his desk as DAVENPORT *watches
him.* TAYLOR *sits*) Why?

TAYLOR   I couldn't prove the men in question had anything to do with it.

DAVENPORT   Why didn't you report it?

TAYLOR   I was ordered not to. (*pause*)
Nivens and Hines. The doctors took two .45-
caliber bullets out of Waters—army issue. But
remember what it was like that morning? If
these men had thought a white officer killed
Waters, there would have been a slaughter!
(*pause*) Cobb reported the incident innocently
the night before—then suddenly it was all
over the Fort.

DAVENPORT   Who were they, Captain? I
want their names!

TAYLOR   Byrd and Wilcox. Byrd's in Ord-
nance—Wilcox's with the 12th Hospital
Group. I was Captain of the Guard the night
Waters was killed. About 2100 hours, Cobb
came into my office and told me he'd just seen
Waters and two white officers fighting outside
the colored N.C.O. Club. I called your office,
and when I couldn't get two M.P.'s, I started
over myself to break it up. When I got there—
no Waters, no officers. I checked the officers'
billet and found Byrd and Wilcox in bed. Several officers verified they'd come in around
2130. I then told Cobb to go back to the barracks and forget it.

DAVENPORT   What made you do that?

TAYLOR   At the time there was no reason to
believe anything was wrong! Waters wasn't
found until the following morning. I told the
Colonel what had happened the previous
night, and about the doctor's report, and I was
told, since the situation at the Fort was poten-
tially dangerous, to keep my mouth shut until
it blew over. He agreed to let me question
Byrd and Wilcox, but I've asked him for a
follow-up investigation every day since it happened. (*slight pause*) When I saw you, I exploded—it was like he was laughing at me.

DAVENPORT   Then you never believed the
Klan was involved?

TAYLOR   No. Now can you see why this
thing needs—someone else?

DAVENPORT   What did they tell you, Captain? Byrd and Wilcox?

TAYLOR   They're not going to let you charge
those two men!

DAVENPORT (*snaps*)   Tell me what they told
you!

(TAYLOR *is quiet for a moment. At this time, on
center stage in limbo,* SERGEANT WATERS *is staggering. He is dressed as we first saw him. Behind
him a blinking light reads:* 221st N.C.O. Club. *As
he staggers toward the stairs leading to center stage
two white officers,* LIEUTENANT BYRD, *a spit-and-
polish soldier in his twenties, and* CAPTAIN WILCOX,
*a medical officer, walk Onstage. Both are in full
combat gear—rifles, pistol belts, packs—and both
are tired.* TAYLOR *looks out as if he can see them*)

TAYLOR   They were coming off bivouac.

(*The two men see* WATERS)

TAYLOR   They saw him outside the Club.

(*He rises, as* WATERS *sees* BYRD *and* WILCOX, *and
smiles*)

WATERS   Well, if it ain't the white boys!

(WATERS *straightens and begins to march in a
mock circle and then down in their direction. He is
mumbling, barely audibly:* "One, two, three, four!
Hup, hup, three, four! Hup, hup, three four!"
BYRD's *speech overlaps* WATERS')

BYRD   And it wasn't like we were looking
for trouble, Captain—were we, Wilcox?

(WILCOX *shakes his head no, but he is astonished
by* WATERS' *behavior and stares at him disbelieving*)

WATERS   White boys! All starched and stiff!
Wanted everybody to learn all that symphony
shit! That's what you were saying in France—
and you know, I listened to you? Am I right
now? Am I?

BYRD   Boy, you'd better straighten up and
salute when you see an officer or you'll find
yourself without those stripes! (*to* WILCOX *as*
WATERS *nears them smiling the "coon" smile and
doing a "Juba"*) Will you look at this niggah?
(*loud*) Come to attention, Sergeant! That's an
order!

WATERS   No, Sah'! I ain't straightenin' up
for ya'll no more! I ain't doin' nothin' white
folks say do, no more! (*Sudden change of mood,
smiles, sings*) No more, no more / no more, no
more, noooo! No more, no more / no more,
no more, nooooooo!

(BYRD *faces* TAYLOR *as* WATERS *continues to sing*)

BYRD (*overlapping*)   Sir, I thought the man
was crazy!

TAYLOR   And what did you think, Wilcox?

(BYRD *moves toward* WATERS, *and* WATERS, *still
singing low, drunk and staggering, moves back and
begins to circle* BYRD, *stalk him, shaking his head
no as he sings.* WILCOX *watches apprehensively*)

WILCOX (*at once*)   He did appear to be intoxicated, Sir—out of his mind almost! (*he
turns to* BYRD) Byrd, listen—

(BYRD *ignores him*)

DAVENPORT (*suddenly*)   Did they see anyone
else in the area?

TAYLOR   No. (*to* BYRD) I asked them what
they did next.

BYRD   I told that niggah to shut up!

WATERS (*sharply*)   No! (*change of mood*) Followin' behind y'all? Look what it's done to me! —I hate myself!

BYRD   Don't blame us, boy! God made you black, not me!

WATERS (*smiles*)   My Daddy use ta say—

WILCOX   Sergeant, get hold of yourself!

WATERS (*points*)   Listen!

(BYRD *steps toward him and shoves him in the face*)

BYRD   I gave you an order, niggah!

(WILCOX *grabs* BYRD, *and stops him from advancing, as* WATERS *begins to cry*)

WATERS   My Daddy said, "Don't talk like dis'—talk like that!" "Don't live hea'—live there!" (*To them*) I've killed for you! (*to himself; incredulous*) And nothin' changed!

(BYRD *pulls free of* WILCOX *and charges* WATERS)

BYRD   He needs to be taught a lesson!

(*He shoves* WATERS *onto the ground where he begins to beat and kick the man, until he is forcibly restrained by* WILCOX. WATERS *moans*)

WILCOX   Let him be! You'll kill the man! He's sick—leave him alone!

(BYRD *pulls away, he is flushed.* WATERS *tries to get up*)

WATERS   Nothin' changed—See? And I've tried everything! Everything!

BYRD   I'm gonna' bust his black ass to Buck Private! —I should blow his coward's head off! (*shouts*) There are good men killing for you, niggah! Gettin' their guts all blown to hell for you!

(WILCOX *pulls him away. He pulls* BYRD *offstage as the light around* WATERS *and that section of the stage begins to fade out.* WATERS *is on his knees groveling as the lights go out around him*)

DAVENPORT   Did they shove Waters again?

TAYLOR   No. But Byrd's got a history of scrapes with Negroes. They told me they left Waters at 2110—and everyone in the officers' billet verifies they were both in by 2130. And neither man left—Byrd had duty the next morning, and Wilcox was scheduled at the hospital 0500 hours—both men reported for duty.

DAVENPORT   I don't believe it.

TAYLOR   I couldn't shake their stories—

DAVENPORT   That's nothing more than officers lying to protect two of their own and you know it! I'm going to arrest and charge both of them, Captain—and you may consider yourself confined to your quarters pending my charges against *you!*

TAYLOR   What charges?

DAVENPORT   It was *your* duty to go over Nivens' head if you had to!

TAYLOR   Will you arrest Colonel Nivens too, Davenport? Because he's part of their alibi—he was there when they came in—played poker—from 2100 to 0330 hours the following morning, the Colonel—your Major Hines, "Shack" Callahan—Major Callahan, and Jed Harris—and Jed wouldn't lie for either of them!

DAVENPORT   They're all lying!

TAYLOR   Prove it, hotshot—I told you all I know, now you go out and prove it!

DAVENPORT   I will, Captain! You can bet your sweet ass on that! I will!

(DAVENPORT *starts out as the lights begin to fade and* TAYLOR *looks after him and shakes his head. In the background, the sound of "Don't Sit Under the Apple Tree" comes up again and continues to play as the lights fade to black*)

ACT TWO

(SCENE: *As before.*

Light rises slowly over limbo. We hear a snippet of "Don't Sit Under the Apple Tree," as DAVENPORT, *seated on the edge of a bunk, finishes dressing. He is putting on a shirt, tie, bars, etc., and addresses the audience as he does so*)

DAVENPORT   During May of 'forty-four, the Allies were making final preparations for the invasion of Europe. Invasion! Even the sound of it made Negroes think we'd be in it—be swept into Europe in the waves of men and equipment—I know I felt it. (*thoughtfully*) We hadn't seen a lot of action except in North Africa—Sicily. But the rumor in orderly rooms that spring was, pretty soon most of us would be in combat—somebody said Ike wanted to find out if the colored boys could fight—shiiit, we'd been fighting all along—right here, in these small Southern towns— (*intense*) I don't have the authority to arrest a white *private* without a white officer present! (*slight pause*) Then I get a case like this? There was no way I wouldn't see this through to its end. (*smiles*) And after my first twenty-four hours, I wasn't doing too badly. I had two prime suspects—a motive, and opportunity! (*pause*) I went to Colonel Nivens and convinced him that word of Byrd and Wilcox's involvement couldn't be kept a secret any longer. However, before anyone in the Press could accuse him of complicity—I would silence all suspicions by pursuing the investigation openly—on his orders— (*mimics himself*) "Yes, Sir, Colonel, you can even send along a white officer—not Captain Taylor though—I think he's a little too close to the case, Sir." Colonel Nivens gave me permission to question Byrd and Wilcox and having succeeded sooo easily, I decided to spend some time finding out more about Waters and Memphis. Somehow the real drama seemed to be there, and my curiosity wouldn't allow me to ignore it.

(DAVENPORT *is dressed and ready to go as a spotlight in the barracks area opens on* PRIVATE HENSON. *He is seated on a footlocker. He rises as* DAVENPORT *descends to the stage. He will not enter the barracks, but will almost handle this like a courtroom interrogation. He returns* HENSON's *salute*)

DAVENPORT   Sit down, Private. Your name is Louis Henson, is that right?
HENSON   Yes, sir.

(HENSON *sits, as* DAVENPORT *paces*)

DAVENPORT   Tell me what you know about Sergeant Waters and C.J. Memphis. (HENSON *looks at him strangely*) Is there something wrong?
HENSON   No, Sir—I was just surprised you knew about it.
DAVENPORT   Why?
HENSON   You're an officer.
DAVENPORT (*quickly*)   And?
HENSON (*hesitantly*)   Well—officers are up here, Sir—and us enlisted men—down here. (*Slight pause*) C.J. and Waters—that was just between enlisted men, Sir. But I guess ain't

nothin' a secret around colored folks—not that it was a secret. (*Shrugs*) There ain't that much to tell—Sir. Sarge ain't like C.J. When I got to the company in May of las' year, the first person I saw Sarge chew out was C.J.! (*he is quiet*)
DAVENPORT   Go on.

(HENSON's *expression is pained*)

HENSON   Is that an order, Sir?
DAVENPORT   Does it have to be?
HENSON   I don't like tattle-talin', Sir—an' I don't mean no offense, but I ain't crazy 'bout talkin' to officers—colored or white.
DAVENPORT   It's an order, Henson!

(HENSON *nods*)

HENSON   C.J. wasn' movin' fast enough for him. Said C.J. didn' have enough *fire-under-his-behind* out on the field.
DAVENPORT   You were on the team?
HENSON   Pitcher. (*pause.* DAVENPORT *urges with a look*) He jus' stayed on C.J. all the time—every little thing, it seemed like to me—then the shootin' went down, and C.J. caught all the hell.
DAVENPORT   What shooting?
HENSON   The shootin' at Williams' Golden Palace, Sir—Happened last year—way before you got here. Toward the end of baseball season. (DAVENPORT *nods his recognition*) The night it happened, a whole lotta' gunshots went off near the barracks. I had gotten drunk over at the Enlisted Men's Club, so when I got to the barracks I just sat down in a stupor!

(*Suddenly shots are heard in the distance and grow ever closer as the eerie blue-gray light rises in the barracks over the sleeping figures of men in their bunks.* HENSON *is seated staring at the ground. He looks up once as the gunshots go off, and as he does, someone—we cannot be sure who—sneaks into the barracks as the men begin to shift and awaken. This person puts something under C.J.'s bed and rushes out.* HENSON *watches—surprised at first, rising, then disbelieving. He shakes his head, then sits back down as several men wake up.* DAVENPORT *recedes to one side of the barracks watching*)

COBB   What the hell's goin' on? Don't they know a man needs his sleep? (*he is quickly back to sleep*)

SMALLS (*simultaneously*)   Huh? Who is it?
(*looks around, then falls back to sleep*)
DAVENPORT   Are you sure you saw someone?
HENSON   Well—I saw something, Sir.
DAVENPORT   What did you do?

(*The shooting suddenly stops and the men settle down*)

HENSON   I sat, Sir—I was juiced—(*shrugs*)
The gunshots weren't any of my business—
plus I wasn't sure what I had seen in the first
place. Then out of nowhere, Sergeant Waters,
he came in.

(WATERS *enters the barracks suddenly, followed by*
WILKIE. HENSON *stands immediately, staggering a
bit*)

WATERS   All right, all right! Everybody up!
Wake them, Wilkie!

(WILKIE *moves around the bunks shaking the men*)

WILKIE   Let's go! Up! Let's go, you guys!

(COBB *shoves* WILKIE's *hand aside angrily as the
others awaken slowly*)

WATERS   Un-ass them bunks! Tenn-hut!
(*most of the men snap to.* SMALLS *is the last one,
and* WATERS *moves menacingly toward him*)
There's been a shooting! One of ours bucked
the line at Williams' pay-phone and three soldiers are dead! Two colored and one white
M.P. (*paces*) Now the man who bucked the
line, he killed the M.P., and the white boys
started shootin' everybody—that's how our
two got shot. And this lowdown niggah we
lookin' for, got chased down here—and was
almost caught, 'til somebody in these barracks
started shootin' at the men chasin' him. So,
we got us a vicious, murderin' piece of black
trash in here somewhere—and a few people
who helped him. If any of you are in this, I
want you to step forward. (*no one moves*) All
you baseball niggahs are innocent, huh?
Wilkie, make the search. (PETERSON *turns
around as* WILKIE *begins*) Eyes front!
PETERSON   I don't want that creep in my
stuff!
WATERS   You don't talk at attention!

(WILKIE *will search three bunks, top and bottom,
along with footlockers. Under* C.J.'s *bed he will find
what he is looking for*)

WATERS   I almost hope it is some of you
geechies—get rid of you Southern niggahs! (*to*
WILKIE) Anything yet?
WILKIE   Nawwww!
WATERS   Memphis, are you in this?
C.J.   No, Sah', Sarge.
WATERS   How many of you were out
tonight?
SMALLS   I was over at Williams around
seven—got me some Lucky Strikes—I didn't
try to call home, though.
COBB   I was there, this mornin'!
WATERS   Didn't I say *tonight*—uncle?
WILKIE   Got somethin'!

(WILKIE *is holding up a .45-caliber automatic pistol, army issue. Everyone's attention focuses on it.
The men are surprised, puzzled*)

WATERS   Where'd you find it?

(WILKIE *points to* C.J., *who recoils at the idea*)

C.J.   Naaaawww, man!
WATERS   C.J.? This yours?
C.J.   You know it ain't mine, Sarge!
WATERS   It's still warm—how come it's un-
der your bunk?
C.J.   Anybody coulda' put it thea', Sarge!
WATERS   Who? Or maybe this .45 crawled
in through an open window—looked around
the whole room—passed Cobb's bunk, and
decided to snuggle up under yours? Must be
voodoo, right, boy? Or some of that Farmers
Dust round that neck of yours, huh?
C.J.   That pistol ain't mine!
WATERS   Liar!
C.J.   No, Sarge—I hate guns! Makes me feel
bad jes' to see a gun!
WATERS   You're under arrest—Wilkie, es-
cort this man to the stockade!

(PETERSON *steps forward*)

PETERSON   C.J. couldn't hurt a fly, Waters,
you know that!
WATERS   I found a gun, soldier—now get
out of the way!
PETERSON   Goddammit, Waters, you know
it ain't him!
WATERS   How do I know?
HENSON   Right before you came in, I
thought I saw somebody sneak in.
WATERS   You were drunk when you left the
Club—I saw you myself!

WILKIE   Besides, how you know it wasn't C.J.?

COBB   I was here all night. C.J. didn't go out.

(WATERS *looks at them, intense*)

WATERS   We got the right man. (*points at* C.J., *impassioned*) You think he's innocent, don't you? C.J. Memphis playin', cotton-picker, singin' the Blues, bowin' and scrapin'—smilin' in everybody's face—this man undermined us! You and me! The description of the man who did the shooting fits C.J.! (*to* HENSON) You saw C.J. sneak in here! (*points*) Don't be fooled—that yassah boss is hidin' somethin'—Niggahs ain't like that today! This is 1943—He shot that white boy!

(C.J. *is stunned, then suddenly the enormity of his predicament hits him and he breaks free of* WILKIE, *and hits* WATERS *in the chest. The blow knocks him down, and* C.J. *is immediately grabbed by the other men in the barracks.* COBB *goes to* WATERS *and helps him up slowly. The blow hurt* WATERS, *but he forces a smile at* C.J., *who has suddenly gone immobile, surprised by what he has done*)

WATERS   What did you go and do now, boy? Hit a noncommissioned officer.

COBB   Sarge, he didn't mean it!

WATERS   Shut up! (*straightens*) Take him out, Wilkie.

(WILKIE *grabs* C.J. *by the arm and leads him out.* C.J. *goes calmly, almost passively.* WATERS *looks at all the men quietly for a moment, then walks out without saying a word. There is a momentary silence in the barracks*)

SMALLS   Niggah like that can't have a mother.

HENSON   I know I saw something!

PETERSON   C.J. was sleepin' when I came in! It's Waters—can't y'all see that? I've seen him before—we had 'em in Alabama! White man gives them a little ass job as a servant—close to the big house, and when the boss ain't lookin', old copycat niggahs act like they the new owner! They take to soundin' like the boss—shoutin', orderin' people aroun'—and when it comes to you and me—they sell us to continue favor. They think the high-jailers like that. Arrestin' C.J.—that'll get Waters another stripe! Next it'll be you—or you—he can't look good unless he's standin' on you!

Cobb tol' him C.J. was in all evening—Waters didn' even listen! Turning somebody in. (*mimics*) "Look what I done, Captain-Boss!" They let him in the army 'cause they know he'll do anything they tell him to—I've seen his kind of fool before. Someone's going to kill him.

SMALLS   I heard they killed a Sergeant at Fort Robinson—recruit did it—

COBB   It'll just be our luck, Sarge'll come through the whole war without a scratch.

PETERSON   Maybe—but I'm goin' over to the stockade—tell the M.P.'s what I know—C.J. was here all evening! (*he starts dressing*)

SMALLS   I'll go with you!

COBB   Me too, I guess.

(*They all begin to dress as the light fades slowly in the barracks area.* HENSON *rises and starts toward* DAVENPORT)

DAVENPORT   Could the person you thought you saw have stayed in the barracks—did you actually see someone go out?

HENSON   Yes, Sir!

DAVENPORT   Was Wilkie the only man out of his bunk that night?

HENSON   Guess so—he came in with Sarge.

DAVENPORT   And Peterson—he did most of the talking?

HENSON   As I recall. It's been awhile ago—an' I was juiced!

(DAVENPORT *rises*)

DAVENPORT   Ellis!

(ELLIS *appears at the door*)

ELLIS   Sir!

DAVENPORT   I want Private Wilkie and P.F.C. Peterson to report to me at once.

ELLIS   They're probably on work detail, Sir.

DAVENPORT   Find them.

ELLIS   Yes, Sir!

(ELLIS *exits quickly and* DAVENPORT *lapses into a quiet thoughtfulness*)

HENSON   Is there anything else? —Sir?

DAVENPORT (*vexed*)   No! That'll be all—send in the next man.

(HENSON *comes to attention and salutes.* DAVENPORT *returns it as* HENSON *exits through the barracks. There is a silence,* DAVENPORT *rises, mumbling something inaudible to himself.* COBB

appears suddenly at the doorway. He watches
DAVENPORT *for a moment)*

COBB   Sir? (DAVENPORT *faces him)* Corporal
Cobb reporting as ordered, Sir. (*he salutes*)
DAVENPORT   Have a seat, Corporal. (COBB
crosses the room and sits) And let's get something straight from the beginning—I don't
care whether you like officers or not—is that
clear?

(COBB *looks at him strangely)*

COBB   Sir?

(*Pause,* DAVENPORT *calms somewhat)*

DAVENPORT   I'm sorry—Did you know
Sergeant Waters well?
COBB   As well as the next man, Sir—I was
already with the team when he took over. Me
and C.J., we made the team the same time.
DAVENPORT   Were you close to C.J.?
COBB   Me and him were "homeys," Sir!
both came from Mississippi. C.J. from
Carmella—me, I'm from up 'roun' Jutlerville,
what they call snake county. Plus we both
played for the Negro League before the war.
DAVENPORT   How did you feel about his
arrest?
COBB   Terrible—C.J. didn't kill nobody, Sir.
DAVENPORT   He struck Sergeant Waters—
COBB   Waters made him, Sir! He called that
boy things he had never heard of before—C.J.,
he was so confused he didn't know what else
to do—(*pause)* An' when they put him in the
stockade, he jus' seemed to go to pieces. See,
we both lived on farms—and even though
C.J.'s daddy played music, C.J., he liked the
wide open spaces. (*shakes his head)* That cell?
It started closin' in on him right away. (*blue-
gray light rises in limbo where* C.J. *is sitting on the
edge of a bunk, a shadow of bars cuts across the
space. His guitar is on the bunk beside him)* I
went to see him, the second day he was in
there. He looked pale and ashy, Sir—like
something dead.

(C.J. *faces* COBB)

C.J.   It's hard to breathe in these little
spaces, Cobb—man wasn' made for this
hea'—nothin' was! I don't think I'll eva' see a'
animal in a cage agin' and not feel sorry for it.
(*to himself)* I'd rather be on the chain gang.

(COBB *looks up at him)*

COBB   Come on, Homey! (*he rises, moves
toward* C.J.)
C.J.   I don't think I'm comin' outta' here,
Cobb—feels like I'm goin' crazy. Can't walk in
hea'—can't see the sun! I tried singin', Cobb,
but nothin' won't come out. I sure don't
wanna' die in this jail!
COBB (*moving closer)*   Ain't nobody gonna'
die, C.J.!
C.J.   Yesterday I broke a guitar string—lost
my Dust! I got no protection—nothin' to keep
the dog from tearin' at my bones!
COBB   Stop talkin' crazy!

(C.J. *is quiet for a moment. He stares forward.
Slowly in center stage,* WATERS *emerges. He faces
the audience)*

C.J.   You know, he come up hea' las' night?
Sergeant Waters?

(WATERS *smiles, pulls out his pipe, lights it)*

WATERS (*calmly)*   You should learn never to
hit sergeants, boy—man can get in a lot of
trouble doin' that kinda' thing durin' war
time—they talkin' 'bout givin' you five years—
they call what you did, mutiny in the navy.
Mutiny, boy.
C.J.   That gun ain't mine!
WATERS   Oh, we know that, C.J.! (C.J. *is surprised)* That gun belonged to the niggah did
the shootin' over at Williams' place—me and
Wilkie caught him hidin' in the Motor Pool,
and he confessed his head off. You're in here
for striking a superior officer, boy. And I got a
whole barracks full of your friends to prove it!
(*smiles broadly, as* C.J. *shakes his head)*
DAVENPORT (*to* COBB *at once)*   Memphis
wasn't charged with the shooting?
COBB   No, Sir—
WATERS   Don't feel too bad, boy. It's not
your fault entirely—it has to be this way. The
First War, it didn't change much for us, boy—
but this one—it's gonna' change a lot of
things. Them Nazis ain't all crazy—a whole lot
of people just can't fit into where things seem
to be goin'—like you, C.J. The black race can't
afford you no more. There use ta be a time
when we'd see somebody like you, singin',
clownin'—yas-sah-bossin'—and we wouldn't
do anything. (*smiles)* Folks liked that—you

were good—homey kinda' niggah—they
needed somebody to mistreat—call a name,
they paraded you, reminded them of the old
days—cornbread bakin', greens and ham
cookin'—Daddy out pickin' cotton, Grand-
mammy sittin' on the front porch smokin' a
pipe. (*slight pause*) Not no more. The day of
the geechy is gone, boy—the only thing that
can move the race is power. It's all the whites
respect—and people like you just make us
seem like fools. And we can't let nobody go on
believin' we all like you! You bring us down—
make people think the whole race is unfit!
(*quietly pleased*) I waited a long time for you,
boy, but I gotcha! And I try to git rid of you
wherever I go. I put two geechies in jail at
Fort Campbell, Kentucky—three at Fort
Huachuca. How I got you—one less fool for
the race to be ashamed of! (*points*) And I'ma
git that ole boy Cobb next! (*light begins to fade
around* WATERS)

DAVENPORT (*at once*)   You?

COBB   Yes, Sir. (*slight pause*)

DAVENPORT   Go on.

C.J.   You imagin' anybody sayin' that? I
know I'm not gittin' outta' hea', Cobb! (*quiets*)
You remember I tol' you 'bout a place I use ta
go outside Carmella? When I was a little ole
tiny thing? Place out behind O'Connell's
Farm? Place would be stinkin' of plums, Cobb.
Shaded—that ripe smell be weavin' through
the cotton fields and clear on in ta town on a
warm day. First time I had Evelyn? I had her
unda' them plum trees. I wrote a song for
her— (*talks, sings*) My ginger-colored
Moma—she had thighs the size of hams!
(*chuckles*) And when you spread them Mo-
maaaa! / (*talks*) You let me have my jelly roll
and jam! (*pause, mood swing*) O'Connell, he
had a dog—meanes' dog I eva' did see! An'
the only way you could enjoy them plum trees
was to outsmart that dog. Waters is like that
ole dog, Cobb—you hadta' run circles roun'
ole Windy—that was his name. They say he
tore a man's arm oft once, and got to likin' it.
So, you had to cheat that dog outta' bitin' you
every time. Every time. (*slowly the light begins
to fade around* C.J.)

COBB   He didn't make sense, Sir. I tried
talkin' about the team—the War—ain't
nothin' work—seem like he jes' got worse.

DAVENPORT   What happened to him?

(COBB *looks at him incredulously*)

COBB   The next day—afta' the day I saw
him? C.J., he hung hisself, Sir. Suicide—jes'
couldn't stand it. M.P.'s found him hung from
the bars.

DAVENPORT *is silent for a moment*)

DAVENPORT   What happened after that?

COBB   We lost our last game—we jes'
"threw" it—we did it for C.J.—Captain he was
mad 'cause we ain't git ta play the Yankees.
Peterson was right on that one—somebody
needed to protest that man!

DAVENPORT   What did Waters do?

COBB   Well afta' we lost, the commanding
officer, he broke up the team, and we all got
reassigned to this Smoke Company. Waters,
he started actin' funny, Sir—stayed drunk—
talked to hisself all the time.

DAVENPORT   Did you think you were next?

COBB   I ain't sure I eva' believed Waters said
that, Sir—C.J. had to be outta' his head or he
wouldna' killed hisself—Sarge, he neva' came
near me afta' C.J. died.

DAVENPORT   What time did you get back
the night Waters was killed?

COBB   I'd say between 2120 and 9:30.

DAVENPORT   And you didn't go out again?

COBB   No, Sir—me and Henson sat and listened to the radio 'til Abbott and Lou
Costello went off, then I played checkers with
Wilkie for 'notha' hour, then everybody went
to bed. What C.J. said about Waters? It ain't
botha' me, Sir.

(DAVENPORT *is silent*)

DAVENPORT   Who were the last ones in that
night?

COBB   Smalls and Peterson—they had
Guard Duty.

(TAYLOR *enters the barracks area and stops just inside the door when he sees* DAVENPORT *isn't quite
finished*)

DAVENPORT   Thank you, Corporal.

(COBB *rises at attention and salutes.* DAVENPORT
returns it and COBB *starts out. He nods to* TAYLOR,
who advances toward DAVENPORT)

TAYLOR (*smiling*)   You surprise me, Davenport—I just left Colonel Nivens. He's given
you permission to question Byrd and Wilcox?

(DAVENPORT *nods*) How'd you manage that? You threatened him with an article in the Chicago *Defender,* I suppose.

DAVENPORT   I convinced the Colonel it was in his best interests to allow it.

TAYLOR   Really? Did he tell you I would assist you?

DAVENPORT   I told him I especially didn't want you.

TAYLOR   That's precisely why he sent me—he didn't want you to think you could get your way entirely—not with him. Then neither Byrd or Wilcox would submit to it without a white officer present. That's how it is. (*there is a rather long silence*) But there's something else, Davenport. The Colonel began talking about the affidavits he and the others signed—and the discrepancies in their statements that night. (*Mimics*) He wants me with you because he doesn't want Byrd and Wilcox giving you the wrong impression—he never elaborated on what he meant by the wrong impression. I want to be there!

DAVENPORT   So you're not on *that* side anymore—you're on *my* side now, right?

TAYLOR   (*bristles*)   I want whoever killed my Sergeant, Davenport!

DAVENPORT   Bullshit! Yesterday you were daring me to try! And today we're allies? Besides, you don't give that much of a damn about your men! I've been around you a full day and you haven't uttered a word that would tell me you had any more than a minor acquaintance with Waters! He managed your baseball team—was an N.C.O. in your company, and you haven't offered *any* opinion of the man as a soldier—sergeant—platoon leader! Who the hell was he?

TAYLOR   He was one of my men! On my roster—a man these bars make me responsible for! And no, I don't know a helluva lot about him—or a lot of their names or where they come from, but I'm still their commanding officer and in a little while I may have to trust them with my life! And I want them to know they can trust me with theirs—here and now! (*pause*) I have Byrd and Wilcox in my office. (DAVENPORT *stares at him for a long moment, then rises and starts out toward center stage*) Why didn't you tell Nivens that you'd placed me under arrest?

(DAVENPORT *stops*)

DAVENPORT   I didn't find it necessary.

(*They stare at one another.* TAYLOR *is noticeably strained*)

DAVENPORT (*starts away*)   What do you know about C.J. Memphis?

(TAYLOR *follows*)

TAYLOR (*shrugs*)   He was a big man as I recall—more a boy than a man, though. Played the guitar sometimes at the Officers Club—there was something embarrassing about him. Committed suicide in the stockade. Pretty good centerfielder—

(DAVENPORT *stops*)

DAVENPORT   Did you investigate his arrest—the charges against him?

TAYLOR   He was charged with assaulting a noncommissioned officer—I questioned him—he didn't say much. He admitted he struck Waters—I started questioning several of the men in the platoon and he killed himself before I could finish—open-and-shut case.

DAVENPORT   I think Waters tricked C.J. into assaulting him.

TAYLOR   Waters wasn't that kind of a man! He admitted he might have provoked the boy—he accused him of that Golden Palace shooting—

(*Behind them the* CAPTAIN's *office is lit. In two chairs facing Taylor's desk are* LIEUTENANT BYRD *and* CAPTAIN WILCOX, *both in dress uniform*)

TAYLOR   Listen, Waters didn't have a fifth-grade education—he wasn't a schemer! And colored soldiers aren't devious like that.

DAVENPORT   What do you mean we aren't devious?

TAYLOR (*sharply*)   You're not as devious as—! (DAVENPORT *stares as* TAYLOR *waves disdainfully and starts into the office*) Anyway, what has that to do with this? (*he is distracted by* BYRD *and* WILCOX *before* DAVENPORT *can answer.* TAYLOR *speaks as he moves to his desk*) This is *Captain* Davenport—you've both been briefed by Colonel Nivens to give the Captain your full cooperation.

(DAVENPORT *puts on his glasses.* TAYLOR *notices and almost smiles*)

BYRD (*to* DAVENPORT)   They tell me you a lawyer, huh?

DAVENPORT   I am not here to answer your questions, Lieutenant. And I am Captain Davenport, is that clear?

BYRD (*to* TAYLOR)   Captain, is he crazy?

TAYLOR   You got your orders.

BYRD   Sir, I vigorously protest as an officer—

TAYLOR (*cuts him off*)   You answer him the way he wants you to, Byrd, or I'll have your ass in a sling so tight, you won't be able to pee, soldier!

(BYRD *backs off slightly*)

DAVENPORT   When did you last see Sergeant Waters?

BYRD   The night he was killed, but I didn' kill him—I should have blown his head off, the way he spoke to me and Captain Wilcox here.

DAVENPORT   How did he speak to you, Captain?

WILCOX   Well, he was very drunk—and he said a lot of things he shouldn't have. I told the Lieutenant here not to make the situation worse and he agreed, and we left the Sergeant on his knees wallowing in self-pity. (*shrugs*)

DAVENPORT   What exactly did he say?

WILCOX   Some pretty stupid things about us—I mean white people, Sir.

(BYRD *reacts to the term* "Sir")

DAVENPORT   What kind of things?

BYRD (*annoyed*)   He said he wasn't going to obey no white man's orders! And that me and Wilcox here were to blame for him being black, and not able to sleep or keep his food down! And I didn't even know the man! Never even spoke to him before that night!

DAVENPORT   Anything else?

WILCOX   Well—he said he'd killed somebody.

DAVENPORT   Did he call a name—or say who?

WILCOX   Not that I recall, Sir.

(DAVENPORT *looks at* BYRD)

BYRD   No— (*sudden and sharp*) Look— the goddamn Negro was disrespectful! He wouldn't salute! Wouldn't come to attention! And where I come from, colored don't talk the way he spoke to us—not to white people they don't!

DAVENPORT   Is that the reason you killed him?

BYRD   I killed nobody! I said, "where I come from!" didn't I? You'd be dead yourself, where I come from! But I didn't kill the—the *Negro*!

DAVENPORT   But you hit him, didn't you?

BYRD   I knocked him down!

DAVENPORT (*quickens pace*)   And when you went to look at him he was dead, wasn't he?

BYRD   He was alive when we left!

DAVENPORT   You're a liar! You beat Waters up—you went back and you shot him!

BYRD   No! (*rises*) But you better get outta' my face before I kill you!

(DAVENPORT *stands firm*)

DAVENPORT   Like you killed Waters?

BYRD   No! (*he almost raises a hand to* DAVEN-PORT)

TAYLOR (*at once*)   Soldier!

BYRD   He's trying to put it on me!

TAYLOR   Answer his questions, Lieutenant.

DAVENPORT   You were both coming off bivouac, right?

WILCOX   Yes.

DAVENPORT   So you both had weapons?

BYRD   So what? We didn't fire them!

DAVENPORT   Were the weapons turned in immediately?

WILCOX   Yes, Sir—Colonel Nivens took our .45's to Major Hines. It was all kept quiet because the Colonel didn't want the colored boys to know that anyone white from the Fort was involved in any way—ballistics cleared them.

DAVENPORT   We can check.

BYRD   Go ahead.

TAYLOR   I don't believe it—why wasn't I told?

WILCOX   The weapons had cleared—and the Colonel felt if he involved you further, you'd take the matter to Washington and there'd be a scandal about colored and white soldiers—as it turned out, he thinks you went to Washington anyway. (*to* DAVENPORT) I'd like to say, Captain, that neither Lieutenant Byrd or myself had anything whatsoever to do with Sergeant Waters' death—I swear that as an officer and a gentleman. He was on the ground when we left him, but very much alive.

TAYLOR   Consider yourselves under arrest, *Gentlemen!*

BYRD   On what charge?

TAYLOR   Murder! You think I believe that crap—

DAVENPORT   Let them go, Captain.

TAYLOR   You've got motive—a witness to their being at the scene—

DAVENPORT   Let them go! This is still my investigation—you two are dismissed!

(BYRD *rises quickly*, WILCOX *follows his lead*)

WILCOX   Are we being charged, Sir?

DAVENPORT   Not by me.

WILCOX   Thank you.

(WILCOX *comes to attention, joined by a reluctant* BYRD. *They both salute*. DAVENPORT *returns it*)

BYRD   I expected more from a white man, Captain.

TAYLOR   Get out of here, before I have you cashiered out of the army, Byrd!

(*Both men exit quietly, and for a moment,* TAYLOR *and* DAVENPORT *are quiet*)

TAYLOR   What the hell is the matter with you? You could have charged both of them—Byrd for insubordination—Wilcox—tampering with evidence.

DAVENPORT   Neither charge is murder—you think Wilcox would tell a story like that if he didn't have Hines and Nivens to back it up? (*slightly tired*) They've got a report.

TAYLOR   So what do you do now?

DAVENPORT   Finish the investigation.

TAYLOR   They're lying, dammit! So is the Colonel! You were ordered to investigate and charge the people responsible—charge them! I'll back you up!

DAVENPORT   I'm not satisfied yet, Captain.

TAYLOR   I am! Dammit!—I wish they'd sent somebody else! I do—you—you're afraid! You thought you'd accuse the Klan, didn't you?—and that would be the end of it, right? Another story of midnight riders for your Negro press! And now it's officers—white men in the army. It's too much for you—what will happen when Captain Davenport comes up for promotion to major if he accuses white officers, right?

DAVENPORT   I'm not afraid of white men, Captain.

TAYLOR   Then why the hell won't you arrest them?

DAVENPORT   Because I do what the facts tell me, Captain—not you!

TAYLOR   You don't know what a fact is, Davenport!

(ELLIS *enters suddenly and salutes*)

ELLIS   Begging your pardon, Sir.

TAYLOR   What is it, Corporal?

ELLIS   Ah—it's for Captain Davenport— (*To* DAVENPORT) We found Private Wilkie, Sir. We haven't located P.F.C. Peterson yet. Seems him and Private Smalls went out on detail together, and neither one of 'em showed up—but I got a few men from the company lookin' for 'em around the N.C.O. Club and in the PX, Sir.

DAVENPORT   Where's Wilkie?

ELLIS   He's waiting for you in the barracks, Captain.

(DAVENPORT *nods, and* ELLIS *goes out after saluting. The lights come up around* WILKIE, *who is seated in a chair in the barracks reading a Negro newspaper.* DAVENPORT *is thoughtful for a moment*)

TAYLOR   Didn't you question Wilkie and Peterson yesterday? (DAVENPORT *starts out*) Davenport? (DAVENPORT *does not answer*) Don't you ignore me!

DAVENPORT   Get off my back! What I do—how I do it—who I interrogate is my business, Captain! This investigation is mine! (*holds out the back of his hand, showing* TAYLOR *the color of his skin*) Mine!

TAYLOR   Don't treat me with that kind of contempt—I'm not some red-neck cracker!

DAVENPORT   And I'm not your yessirin' colored boy either!

TAYLOR   I asked you a question!

DAVENPORT   I don't have to answer it!

(*There is a long silence, the two men glare at one another—*TAYLOR *in another time, disturbed*)

TAYLOR   Indeed you don't—*Captain.*

(*Pause*)

DAVENPORT   Now, *Captain*—what if Byrd and Wilcox are telling the truth?

TAYLOR   Neither one of us believes that.

DAVENPORT   What if they are?

TAYLOR   Then who killed the goddamn man?

DAVENPORT   I don't know yet. (*slight pause*) Is there anything else?

(TAYLOR *shakes his head no as* DAVENPORT *starts toward center stage headed toward* WILKIE)

TAYLOR   No, hotshot. Nothing.

(DAVENPORT *enters the barracks area,* WILKIE *quickly puts his paper aside and snaps to attention and salutes.* DAVENPORT *returns it but remains silent, going right to the desk and removing his pad and pencil. The light around the office fades out*)

DAVENPORT (*snapping at* WILKIE)   When did you lose your stripes? (*he is standing over* WILKIE)

WILKIE   Couple months before they broke up the team—right after Sergeant Waters got assigned to us, Sir.

DAVENPORT   Nervous, Wilkie?

WILKIE (*smiles haltingly*)   I couldn't figure out why you called me back, Sir? (*laughs nervously*)

DAVENPORT   You lost your stripes for being drunk on duty, is that correct?

WILKIE   Yes, Sir.

DAVENPORT   You said Waters busted you, didn't you?

WILKIE   He got me busted—he's the one reported me to the Captain.

DAVENPORT   How did you feel? Must have been awful— (DAVENPORT *paces*) Weren't you and the Sergeant good friends? Didn't you tell me he was all right? A nice guy?

WILKIE   Yes, Sir.

DAVENPORT   Would a nice guy have gotten a friend busted?

WILKIE   No, Sir.

DAVENPORT   So you lied when you said he was a nice guy, right?

WILKIE   No, Sir—I mean—

DAVENPORT   Speak up! Speak up! Was the Sergeant a nice guy or not?

WILKIE   No, Sir.

DAVENPORT   Why not? Answer me!

WILKIE   Well, you wouldn't turn somebody in over something like that!

DAVENPORT   Not a good friend, right?

WILKIE   Right, Sir—I mean a friend would give you extra duty—I would have—or even call you a whole buncha' names—you'd expect that, Sir—but damn! Three stripes? They took ten years to get in this army, Sir!

Ten years! I started out with the 24th Infantry—I—

DAVENPORT   Made you mad, didn't it?

WILKIE   Yeah, it made me mad—all the things I did for him!

DAVENPORT (*quickly*)   That's right! You were his assistant, weren't you? Took care of the team— (WILKIE *nods*) Ran all his errands, looked at his family snapshots, (WILKIE *nods again*) policed his quarters, put the gun under C.J.'s bed—

(WILKIE *looks up suddenly*)

WILKIE   No!

DAVENPORT (*quickly*)   It was you Henson saw, wasn't it, Wilkie?

WILKIE   No, Sir!

DAVENPORT   Liar! You lied about Waters, and you're lying now! You were the only person out of the barracks that night, and the only one who knew the layout well enough to go straight to C.J.'s bunk! Not even Waters knew the place that well! Henson didn't see who it was, but he saw what the person did— he was positive about that—only you knew the barracks in the dark!

WILKIE (*pleadingly*)   It was the Sarge, Captain—he ordered me to do it—he said I'd get my stripes back—he wanted to scare that boy C.J.! Let him stew in jail! Then C.J. hit him— and he had the boy right where he wanted him— (*confused*) But it backfired—C.J. killed hisself—Sarge didn't figure on that.

DAVENPORT   Why did he pick Memphis?

WILKIE   He despised him, Captain—he'd hide it, 'cause everybody in the company liked that boy so much. But underneath— It was a crazy hate, Sir—he'd go cold when he talked about C.J. You could feel it.

(*In limbo the blue-gray light rises on* C.J. *and* WA-TERS. C.J. *is humming a blues song and* WATERS *is standing smiling, smoking a pipe as he was in Act One.* WATERS *turns away from* C.J. *His speech takes place over* C.J.'s *humming*)

WATERS   He's the kinda' boy seems innocent, Wilkie. Got everybody around the post thinking he's a strong, black buck! Hits home runs—white boys envy his strength—his speed, the power in his swing. Then this colored champion lets those same white boys call him "Shine"—or "Sambo" at the Officers

Club. They laugh at his blues songs, and he just smiles—can't talk, barely read or write his own name—and don't care! He'll tell you they like him—or that colored folks ain't supposed to have but so much sense. (*intense*) Do you know the damage one ignorant *Negro* can do? (*remembering*) We were in France during the First War, Wilkie. We had won decorations, but the white boys had told all the French gals we had tails. And they found this ignorant colored soldier. Paid him to tie a tail to his ass and parade around naked making monkey sounds. (*shakes his head*) They sat him on a big, round table in the Café Napoléon, put a reed in his hand, a crown on his head, a blanket on his shoulders, and made him eat bananas in front of them Frenchies. And ohhh, the white boys danced that night—passed out leaflets with that boy's picture on them—called him "Moonshine, King of the Monkeys." And when we slit his throat, you know that fool asked us, what he had done wrong? (*pause*) My Daddy told me, we got to turn our backs on his kind, Wilkie. Close our ranks to the chittlin's, the collard greens—the cornbread style. We are men—soldiers—and I don't intend to have our race cheated out of its place of honor and respect in *this* war because of fools like C.J.! You watch everything he *does*—Everything!

(*Light fades slowly around* WATERS *and* C.J., *and as it does*, C.J. *stops humming*)

WILKIE   And I watched him, Sir—but Waters—he couldn't wait! He wouldn' talk about nothin' else—it was C.J., this—C.J. all the time!

DAVENPORT (*troubled*)   Why didn't he pick Peterson—they fought—

WILKIE   They fought all the time, Sir—but the Sarge, he liked Peterson. (*nods*) Peterson fought back, and Waters admired that. He promoted Pete! Imagine that—he thought Peterson would make a "fine" soldier!

DAVENPORT   What was Peterson's reaction—when C.J. died?

WILKIE   Like everybody else, he was sad—he put together that protest that broke up the team but afta' that he didn' say much. And he usually runs off at the mouth. Kept to himself—or with Smalls.

(*Slight pause*)

DAVENPORT   The night Waters was killed, what time did you get in?

WILKIE   Around nine forty-five—couple of us came from the Club and listened to the radio awhile—I played some checkers, then I went to bed. Sir? I didn't mean to do what I did—it wasn't my fault—he promised me my stripes!

(*Suddenly out of nowhere in the near distance is the sound of gunfire, a bugle blaring, something like a cannon going off. The noise is continuous through scene.* DAVENPORT *rises, startled*)

DAVENPORT   I'm placing you under arrest, Private!

(ELLIS *bursts into the room*)

ELLIS   Did you hear, Sir? (DAVENPORT *surprised shakes his head no*) Our orders! They came down from Washington, Captain! We're shippin' out! They finally gonna let us Negroes fight!

(DAVENPORT *is immediately elated, and almost forgets* WILKIE *as he shakes* ELLIS's *hand*)

DAVENPORT   Axis ain't got a chance!

ELLIS   Surrre—we'll win this mother in six months now! Afta' what Jesse Owens did to them people? Joe Louis?

(HENSON *bursts in*)

HENSON   Did y'all hear it? Forty-eight-hour stand-by alert! We goin' into combat! (*loud*) Look out, Hitler, the niggahs is comin' to git your ass through the fog!

ELLIS   With real rifles—it's really O.K., you know?

HENSON   They tell me them girls in England—woooow!

(DAVENPORT *faces* WILKIE *as* COBB *enters yelling*)

COBB   They gonna let us git in! We may lay so much smoke the Germans may never get to see what a colored soldier looks like 'til the war's over! (*to* HENSON) I wrote my woman jes' the otha' day that we'd be goin' soon!

ELLIS   Go on!

HENSON (*overlapping*)   Man, you ain't write nothin'!

(DAVENPORT *begins to move* WILKIE *toward* ELLIS)

HENSON   If the army said we was all discharged, you'd claim you wrote that! (*he quiets watching* DAVENPORT)

COBB   (*quickly*)   You hea' this fool, Sir?

HENSON   Shhhhh!

DAVENPORT   (*to* ELLIS)   Corporal, escort Private Wilkie to the stockade.

ELLIS   (*surprised*)   Yes, Sir!

(ELLIS *starts* WILKIE *out, even though he is bewildered by it. They exit*)

HENSON   Wilkie's under arrest, Sir? (DAVENPORT *nodes*) How come? I apologize, Sir—I didn't mean that.

DAVENPORT   Do either of you know where Smalls and Peterson can be located?

(HENSON *shrugs*)

COBB   Your men got Smalls in the stockade, Sir!

DAVENPORT   When?

COBB   I saw two colored M.P.'s takin' him through the main gate. Jes' awhile ago—I was on my way ova' hea'!

(DAVENPORT *goes to the desk and picks up his things and starts out*)

COBB   Tenn-hut!

(DAVENPORT *stops and salutes*)

DAVENPORT   As you were—by the way—congratulations!

(DAVENPORT *exits the barracks through the doorway*)

HENSON   Look out, Hitler!

COBB   The niggahs is coming, to get yo' ass.

HENSON AND COBB   Through the fog.

(*The lights in the barracks go down at once. Simultaneously, they rise in limbo, where* SMALLS *is pacing back and forth. He is smoking a cigarette. There is a bunk, and the shadow of a screen over his cell. In the background the sounds of celebration continue.* DAVENPORT *emerges from the right, and begins to speak immediately as the noises of celebration fade*)

DAVENPORT   Why'd you go AWOL, soldier?

(SMALLS *faces him, unable to see* DAVENPORT *at first. When he sees him, he snaps to attention and salutes*)

SMALLS   Private Anthony Smalls, Sir!

DAVENPORT   At ease—answer my question!

SMALLS   I didn't go AWOL, Sir—I—I got drunk in Tynin and fell asleep in the bus depot—it was the only public place I could find to sleep it off.

DAVENPORT   Where'd you get drunk? Where in Tynin?

SMALLS   Jake's—Jake's and Lilly's Golden Slipper—on Melville Street—

DAVENPORT   Weren't you and Peterson supposed to be on detail? (SMALLS *nods*) Where was Peterson? Speak up!

SMALLS   I don't know, Sir!

DAVENPORT   You're lying! You just walked off your detail and Peterson did nothing?

SMALLS   No, Sir—he warned me, Sir—"Listen, Smalls!" he said—

DAVENPORT   (*cutting him off*)   You trying to make a fool of me, Smalls? Huh? (*loud*) Are you?

SMALLS   No, Sir!

DAVENPORT   The two of you went A-W-O-L together, didn't you? (SMALLS *is quiet*) Answer me!

SMALLS   Yes!

DAVENPORT   You left together because Peterson knew I would find out the two of you killed Waters, didn' you? (SMALLS *suddenly bursts into quiet tears, shaking his head*) What? I can't hear you! (SMALLS *is sobbing*) You killed Waters didn't you? I want an answer!

SMALLS   I can't sleep—I can't sleep!

DAVENPORT   Did you kill Sergeant Waters?

SMALLS   It was Peterson, Sir! (*as if he can see it*) I watched! It wasn't me!

(*The blue-gray light builds in center stage. As it does,* SERGEANT WATERS *staggers forward and falls on his knees. He can't get up he is so drunk. He has been beaten, and looks the way we saw him in the opening of Act One*)

SMALLS   We were changing the guard.

WATERS   Can't be trusted—no matter what we do, there are no guarantees—and your mind won't let you forget it. (*shakes his head repeatedly*) No, no, no!

SMALLS   (*overlapping*)   On our way back to the Captain's office—and Sarge, he was on the road. We just walked into him! He was ranting, and acting crazy, Sir!

(PETERSON *emerges from the right. He is dressed in a long coat, pistol belt and pistol, rifle, helmet, his pants bloused over his boots. He sees* WATERS *and smiles.* WATERS *continues to babble*)

PETERSON   Smalls, look who's drunk on his ass, boy! (*he begins to circle* WATERS)

SMALLS (*to* DAVENPORT)   I told him to forget Waters!

PETERSON   Noooo! I'm gonna' enjoy this, Smalls—big, bad Sergeant Waters down on his knees? No, sah—I'm gonna' love this! (*leans over* WATERS) Hey, Sarge—need some help? (WATERS *looks up; almost smiles. He reaches for* PETERSON, *who pushes him back down*) That's the kinda' help I'll give yah, boy! Let me help you again—all right? (*kicks* WATERS) Like that, Sarge? Huh? Like that, dog?

SMALLS (*shouts*)   Peterson!

PETERSON   No! (*almost pleading*) Smalls— some people, man— If this was a German would you kill it? If it was Hitler—or that fuckin' Tojo? Would you kill him? (*Kicks* WATERS *again*)

WATERS (*mumbling throughout*)   There's a trick to it, Peterson—it's the only way you can win—C.J. could never make it—he was a clown! (*grabs at* PETERSON) A clown in black-face! A niggah!

(PETERSON *steps out of reach. He is suddenly expressionless as he easily removes his pistol from his holster*)

WATERS   You got to be like them! And I was! I was—but the rules are fixed. (*whispers*) Shhhh! Listen. It's C.J.— (*laughs*) I made him do it, but it doesn't make any difference! They still hate you! (*looks at* PETERSON, *who has moved closer to him*) They still hate you! (WATERS *laughs*)

PETERSON (*to* SMALLS)   Justice, Smalls. (*he raises the pistol*)

DAVENPORT (*suddenly, harshly*)   That isn't Justice!

(SMALLS *almost recoils*)

PETERSON (*simultaneously, continuing*)   For C.J.! Everybody!

(PETERSON *fires the gun at* WATERS's *chest, and the shot stops everything. The celebration noise stops. Even* DAVENPORT *in his way seems to hear it.* PETERSON *fires again. There is a moment of*

quiet onstage. DAVENPORT *is angered and troubled*)

DAVENPORT   You call that Justice?

SMALLS   No, Sir.

DAVENPORT (*enraged*)   Then why the fuck didn't you do something?

SMALLS   I'm scared of Peterson—just scared of him!

(PETERSON *has been looking at* WATERS's *body throughout. He now begins to lift* WATERS *as best he can, and pull him offstage. It is done with some difficulty*)

SMALLS   I tried to get him to go, Sir, but he wanted to drag the Sergeant's body back into the woods—

(*Light fades quickly around* PETERSON, *as* DAVENPORT *paces*)

SMALLS   Said everybody would think white people did it.

DAVENPORT (*somewhat drained*)   Then what happened?

SMALLS   I got sick, Sir—and Peterson when he got done, he helped me back to the barracks and told me to keep quiet. (*slight pause*) I'm sorry, Sir.

(*There is a long pause, during which* DAVENPORT *stares at* SMALLS *with disgust, then abruptly starts out without saluting. He almost flees.* SMALLS *rises quickly*)

SMALLS   Sir?

(DAVENPORT *turns around.* SMALLS *comes to attention and salutes.* DAVENPORT *returns it and starts out of the cell and down toward center stage. He is thoughtful as the light fades around* SMALLS. DAVENPORT *removes his glasses and begins to clean them as he speaks*)

DAVENPORT   Peterson was apprehended a week later in Alabama. Colonel Nivens called it, "Just another black mess of cuttin', slashin', and shootin'!" He was delighted there were no white officers mixed up in it, and his report to Washington characterized the events surrounding Waters' murder as, ". . . the usual, common violence any commander faces in Negro Military Units." It was the kind of "mess" that turns up on page three in the colored papers—the Cain and Abel story of the week—the headline we Negroes can't quite read in comfort. (*shakes head and paces*) For me? Two colored soldiers are dead—two on their way to prison. Four less men to fight with—and none of their reasons—nothing anyone *said,* or *did* would have been worth a life to men with larger hearts—men less split by the madness of race in America. (*pause*) The case got little attention. The details were filed in my report and I was quickly and rather unceremoniously ordered back to my M.P. unit. (*smiles*) A style of guitar-pickin' and a dance called the "C.J." caught on for a while in Tynin saloons during 1945. (*slight pause*) In northern New Jersey, through a military foul-up, Sergeant Waters' family was informed that he had been killed in action. The Sergeant was, therefore, thought and unofficially rumored to have been the first colored casualty of the war from that county and under the circumstances was declared a hero. Nothing could be done officially, but his picture was hung on a "Wall of Honor" in the Dorie Miller VFW Post #978. (*pause*) The men of the 221st Chemical Smoke Generating Company? The entire outfit—officers and enlisted men—wiped out in the Ruhr Valley during a German advance. (*he turns toward* TAYLOR, *who enters quietly*) Captain?

TAYLOR   Davenport—I see you got your man.

DAVENPORT   I got him—what is it, Captain?

TAYLOR   Will you accept my saying, you did a splendid job?

DAVENPORT   I'll take the praise—but how did I manage it?

TAYLOR   Dammit, Davenport—I didn't come here to be made fun of— (*slight pause*) The men—the regiment—we all ship out for Europe tomorrow.

DAVENPORT   You came to say goodbye to *me,* Captain?

TAYLOR (*hesitates*)   I was wrong, Davenport—about the bars—the uniform—about Negroes being in charge. (*slight pause*) I guess I'll *have* to get used to it.

DAVENPORT   Oh, you'll get used to it—you can bet your ass on that, Captain—you will get used to it.

(*Lights begin to fade slowly as the music "Don't Sit Under the Apple Tree" begins to rise in the background, and the house goes to black*)

THE END

LIBERTY DEFERRED
1938

John D. Silvera (1915–   )
Abram Hill (1911–1986)

Liberty Deferred is a "found" play. It was stored for years in an old airplane hanger in Baltimore, along with other manuscripts, records, and memorabilia from the lost archives of the Federal Theatre Project. In 1974, these materials were discovered by Professors Lorraine Brown and John O'Connor and transferred to George Mason University. The play is a carefully researched history of the African American experience from the advent of slavery through Reconstruction and the problems of racial discrimination and social, economic, and political injustice. The major incidents and dialogue are drawn directly from historical sources.

The play was written as a Living Newspaper, a form suggested by Hallie Flanagan, head of the Federal Theatre Project, to put as many actors to work in productions as possible. Rather than performing leading roles, actors were required to perform small parts throughout these plays. (There are more than thirty-five scenes, with more than seventy speaking characters plus extras, including singers and dancers in the first half, and numerous new characters are introduced in the second half.)

The Living Newspaper developed as a theatrical form that could disseminate news, information, and propaganda effectively in Russia following the Bolshevik Revolution in 1917. During the 1930s in America, it became a more precise and detailed form of investigative theatre.[1] A Narrator-Voice functioned very much in the manner of the Greek chorus, interrupting and commenting on the action, and siding with certain characters. Many Brechtian devices such as projections, films, maps, puppets, trolleys, symbolic area and space staging, and journalistic commentary were used.

The Living Newspaper was the ideal form for the expansive history that Hill and Silvera intended to dramatize. The frame for the story, a white couple's visit to Harlem, immediately sets up the precon-

---

[1]Lorraine Brown, ed., *Liberty Deferred and Other Living Newspapers of the 1930s* (Fairfax, VA: George Mason University Press, 1989), p. ix.

ceived images that whites have of African Americans—the grinning, shuffling, dancing, singing, happy-go-lucky, carefree, contented darky. Ted and Linda, a Black couple, are offended by these stereotypes and set out to destroy them by allowing us to witness the factual history of Blacks in America. Stereotypes are now replaced by intelligent, discontented, defiant Black characters who desire freedom, justice, and equality.

This early draft of the play has been edited, and only Part I appears here. It is concerned with the origin of slavery and takes us through the emancipation; it is complete within itself. Fact after fact explain the reasons for slavery and the country's reluctance to abolish it. Historical figures appear: Thomas Jefferson, Eli Whitney, Denmark Vesey, Dred Scott, Harriet Tubman, and others, presenting the pros and cons of bondage, or refuting the argument that slaves were ignorant and content with their lot.

Part II continues the story from Reconstruction to the late 1930s, allowing the authors to examine such problems as voting, lynching, education, housing, and employment. One of the most effective scenes is called Lynchotopia. This fantasy sequence is set in heaven, where lynched victims describe the horrors of their deaths. It is a powerful and gruesome way of protesting the nation's tolerance of lynching. (The Federal Theatre never produced *Liberty Deferred* because some of the administrators believed that its content might be offensive to congressmen from the South.)

Liberty Deferred

Cast of Characters

MARY LOU DIXON
JIMMY NORTH
TED
LINDA
FIRST MERCHANT
SECOND MERCHANT
THIRD MERCHANT
FIRST PLANTER
SECOND PLANTER
SERVANT
TOBACCONIST
CAPTAIN
MASTER
DENMARK VESEY
NORTHERN
IMMIGRANT
QUAKER
THOMAS JEFFERSON
MILL OWNER
PLANTATION OWNER
OVERSEER

ELI WHITNEY
SLAVE DEALER
BENJAMIN FRANKLIN
SENATOR EARLY
JOHN WHEATLEY
PHILLIS WHEATLEY
LOUDSPEAKER
SPOKESMAN
MISSOURIES
SECOND CONGRESSMAN
CALHOUN
DRED SCOTT
HARRIET TUBMAN
WILLIAM LLOYD GARRISON
ISSAC KNAPP
REV. PLUMMER
REV. J. C. POSTELL
BISHOP MEADE
ASCOTT
TANEY
FREDERICK DOUGLASS
JEFFERSON DAVIS
ABRAHAM LINCOLN

A NEGRO WOMAN
A WHITE SOLDIER
A RED CAP
UNCLE TOM
THE (TWO) BLACK CROWS
CRAP SHOOTERS
COTTON PICKERS
JUDGE
THE UNEMPLOYED OF LONDON
TOBACCO CUSTOMERS
TWENTY BLACK NATIVES
SINGERS
DANCERS
BENJAMIN BANNEKER
CHORUS
SLAVES
ABOLITIONIST
WESTERNERS
SOUTHERNERS
A WHITE SENATOR

PROLOGUE

(MUSIC—*A rhapsodic arrangement of Negro spirituals, American Revolutionary and Civil War airs—climaxing to modern blues treatment. After this reaches fulfillment, it segues to sound of typical dance music coming over radio.*

SPOT *comes up downstage right.* JIMMY NORTH *and* MARY LOU DIXON, *two well-dressed white people are seen seated on tall stools at an imaginary cocktail bar. They pantomime the business of drinking—the sounds of the cocktail shaker, clink of glasses, etc., coming over loudspeaker. They tap an appreciative toe to the lively rhythm being broadcast.* MARY LOU *is gabbing away, in a thick Southern drawl*)

MARY LOU   I do declare Jimmy, this is *living!*
JIMMY   Oh, we get around. We know how to live.
MARY LOU   It ain't a bit like Hometown—everything is mighty different down home. So easygoin'—so—well, shucks, it's dead compared to New York.
JIMMY   There's always something doing here.
MARY LOU   I've never had such excitement in all my poor little life!
JIMMY (*to invisible bartender*)   Let's have another, Eddie. Two of the same!
MARY LOU (*tipsily*)   Whe-e-e!

(*They reach for imaginary glasses, lift them as in a toast and drink in pantomime*)

MARY LOU   What's next, Jimmy-boy? What's next for the poor little girl from the South? Make it a wow! I've got to go back to li'l sleepy old Hometown with fond memories of this here visit.
JIMMY   There's a great view from the Empire State—there's the boardwalk down at Coney—there's Greenwich Village—there's a ride on a Fifth Avenue bus—there's Grant's Tomb—but you wouldn't want to see that, I guess—
MARY LOU (*slightly pained*)   Reckon not, honey-lamb.
JIMMY (*cocks an ear to music, now hot*) Listen! Hear that down-beat! Hear that swing! Hear them rock it! I've got it!
MARY LOU   Got it, Jimmy? What'll we do?
JIMMY   Harlem, honey. Uptown, where they rock! Listen, hear that—? Well, that's a funeral dirge next to what you'll hear uptown—up in Harlem!
MARY LOU (*a trifle vaguely*)   Harlem? Why, isn't that where—
JIMMY   Yeah, man! That's where they truck on down. Lay it to rest. Swing it high. Right out of the world. Come on, uptown, baby—and let your hair down!
MARY LOU   But, isn't that where the—?
JIMMY   That's where the blues were born! That's where there's hi-de-ho, and tyah tyah. Come on uptown and you'll see why Abe Lincoln wrote the Emancipation Proclamation!

(*He starts to snap his fingers and sway as if "out of this world."* MARY LOU *says the following in the manner of an aside*)

MARY LOU   Harlem? That's darktown. 'Tain't fit for a white girl in my position to be traipsing about places like that. I know Jimmy means well and all that—but—mixin' with niggers. But, after all, I mean, the folks in Hometown needn't know . . . (*then aloud to* JIMMY) Harlem, Honey? I'd just adore that.
JIMMY   Good! Let's go. I'll show you how our darkies live!

(*The music comes up full in a captivating synthesis of everything that spells jazz. The couple climb down off their stools, and with a spot following them, they truck across to stage left and seat them-*

selves at a small table of the nightclub sort. They pick up noisemakers and use them. JIMMY takes some confetti and streamers from his pocket and tosses them in the air, festively)

JIMMY   You gotta know these blacks, gotta understand their ways. Come the Harlem moon and their day's begun—gin, swing, trucking and sin. That's all they ask . . . they like their fun straight . . . just a happy-go-lucky, devil-may-care bunch of God's chillun. I know these people . . . I know 'em.

(With this, the music surges to a really throbbing beat—yet taking the form of an overture, the aim of which is to contain all the characteristic—in terms of music—of the Negro people. It may be platitudinous music with all the clichés one might expect—snatches of banjos twanging, raucous trombones, occasional fragments of torch-singing voices, wailing saxophones, spirituals—in other words, it is a sound background for the visual scenes which will be as follows:

Flash One: *A team of Big Apple dancers, stage center, going through all the wild movements of the routine. An overhead device discloses them in varicolored, spectacular beams of light.

Flash Two: From the wings well downstage and in the beam of an offstage spot, a Red Cap, laden down to capacity with all manner of luggage and golf-bags, staggers into view, places his load on the floor, and, in the idealized manner of the railroad advertisements, smiles broadly, bowing and scraping as he accepts an imaginary tip. This is all done with emphasis on subservience—as the whites are accustomed to see him.

Flash Three: A group of "cotton pickers"—that is, the musical-comedy version of them—in pastel-shaded sateen overalls, pretty straw hats, gay bandanas about their necks. They go through pretty motions of "pickin cotton," and their lips move in unison as if in song. They are all grins and contentment—the popular Hollywood version of the plantation worker singing at his work.

---

*Note: These are some representative flashes which should all be done in an elaborate, saytrical manner—the object of which is to portray the Negro as he is too often shown on the screen, stage, and over the air; in fact, as he is seen through the eyes of JIMMY and MARY LOU, who represent White Supremacy, as they sit at their night club table at left.

Flash Four: A group of loudly, vulgarly dressed Negroes playing at craps, going through all the rituals of the game—the Hollywood version of the Negro at his "favorite past-time."

Flash Five: The Black Crows, the traditional vaudeville act, of which even many Negroes permit themselves enjoyment. There should be a touch of Steppin' Fetchit in the business—exaggerated lips painted white, all the lackadaisical, comic, and buffoonish traits played up—the classic conception of the "darky." The two Black Crows go through a fragment of this routine, moving their lips as if going through their uproarious lines.

Flash Six: An old Uncle Tom Negro—lugubrious, stereotypical—standing before a stylized Magistrates' Bench, the Judge looking down from his Olympian or Heavenly Authority. They pantomime some conversation briefly, also in pantomime. The Negro delivers some remark, upon which the Judge roars with laughter. This should aim at a reenactment of the thousand-versioned classic about what the old darky said to the Judge.

With the last of these flashes, and with the stage a vivid canvas, or rather, caricature, of the Negro as most whites insist upon seeing him, the music loses some of its fever-heat and subsides to a slow, moody dance beat, to which, into the midst of all this, TED and LINDA slowly dance until they are at stage center. When they reach this position, every one of the characters, hitherto playing his part as the whites expect him to, suddenly stops in his tracks and stares, almost accusingly, at JIMMY and MARY LOU. It is almost as if each one had dropped his clownish mask in self-disgust.

TED and LINDA, now standing stage center, are silent, almost somber. Mutely he proffers a cigaret and as silently she accepts. They light up and enjoy a few satisfying drags. Along with this, lights dim to dark on all the other Negro characters leaving TED and LINDA in a single small shaft of light. There remain now the two couples, white and black, in their respective places)

LINDA (her voice heavy)   Oh, Ted. Ted.
TED   I know, Linda—what can we do? You see what the odds are.
LINDA   Don't they see anything else?
TED   Nope. They have blinders attached to their eyes—made out of stuff which is a combination of newsprint, movie film, and essence-of-microphone, with just a dash of

greasepaint. You can buy those blinders any day in the week.

LINDA   Aren't we to blame, also?

TED   You know better than that. Just take yourself, for example.

LINDA   Myself?

TED   You turned your back on the path of least resistance. You worked—slaving, studying—to become a nurse. You wanted to heal the sick. O.K. You showed them you could qualify. Have you got that appointment yet? Are you earning a living at your profession?

LINDA   My name is on the waiting list, Ted.

TED *(he emits an explosive laugh)*   Ha! And I wish you and I had a buck for every name that's above it!

LINDA   You're becoming too bitter, Ted.

TED   Did my bitterness lessen my value as a research worker? Did *I* make the decision to take the name of Ted Smith off the payroll and leave the white chap's name on—even though I had two years priority? When the axe had to fall, it had to fall on the black man's neck.

LINDA   A man with your training and ability is sure to get a job—soon, too.

(Suddenly, JIMMY is heard to exclaim, enthusiastically, as he peers toward the spot where the Big Apple dancers were performing)

JIMMY   Truck on down! Yeah, man! Look at that, Mary Lou! Ain't that something!

MARY LOU *(temporarily without the Bourbon attitude)*   Out of this world! T-yah. T-yah.

TED *(his speech, rather than his expression, indicates his awareness of this)*   Maybe if I trained as a hoofer I'd get a job. *(sardonically)* What do you say, Linda. Let's get up an act.

LINDA *(a trifle hurt)*   Please, Ted—

TED   The colored man has only two commodities to sell in this scheme of things—his muscle or his subservience. The sweat of the brow or scrape and bow!

LINDA   Ted, you've changed. You used to fill me with such hope.

TED *(more softly—takes her in his arms)*   Remember four years ago—you, standing there in your cap and gown.

(Swift dim to dark. Loudspeaker, over which is enunciated the closing phrases of a valedictory speech in solemn intonations by school headmaster, ending with the usual references to opportunity, the American principles, equality, regardless of race or creed, and so forth. As the speech gets under way, LINDA is seen standing with a group, mostly white, in caps and gowns—diplomas in hand—a look of youthful hope on their faces. The lights dim on this just before the close of this traditional speech, and with the last words of it, we see LINDA and TED again as before. She hasn't the cap and gown on, but she holds the diploma)

TED *(mockingly)*   Opportunity and Equality, regardless of race or creed—Hi-de-ho!

JIMMY *(raucously picking up this phrase)*   Hi-de-ho! Can *they* dance! Can *they* dance!

MARY LOU   I must admit it. They can dance!

TED *(again, his speech, rather than his expression, connects this with the last)*   Dancing on the levee. Dancin' on the end of a rope!

(This speech is topped by a single phrase from the spiritual, sung by a Negro chorus offstage)

CHORUS   LET MY PEOPLE GO!

JIMMY   Completely abandoned. Free as the air!

TED   Free! They think this is our people—singing, grinning, dancing from the cradle to the coffin. Free!

(The Negro spiritual again, as before)

CHORUS   LET MY PEOPLE GO!

LINDA   We've been freed, Ted. We've had a measure of freedom given to us.

TED   Have we, Linda? "Let my people go!" That cry rings out today, and it's been ringing out for over three hundred years!

(Blackout. When dark, a commotion is heard—confused moving about—in the downstage area. Blue foots come up disclosing the unemployed of London—ill-dressed, hungry-looking, and so forth)

LOUDSPEAKER   LONDON, ENGLAND—IN THE MIDST OF AN ECONOMIC CRISIS, OVER THREE HUNDRED YEARS AGO . . .

(The crowd ad-libs up full—)

CROWD   Jobs! Give us work! Bread for our families! Work! etc.

(Entering from wings right and taking a dominant position on stage right extension, a group of lavishly

dressed, wealthy MERCHANTS, *after a moment, quell the disorder and gain an audience with the men)*

FIRST MERCHANT   Commerce is at a standstill.

SECOND MERCHANT   There are no jobs in London.

THIRD MERCHANT   But we have a plan, my good men . . .

SECOND MERCHANT   How would you like to go to a land where gold and silver is more plentiful then copper is with us—where the sands of the shores are lined with precious jewels?

THIRD MERCHANT   Where the mountains shine with precious stones, where there is work and opportunity for all?

CROWD   Yes! Yes! Work! Work! Jobs!

FIRST MERCHANT   You'll get work, my good men—in America!

(Blackout)

LOUDSPEAKER   AMERICA. THE BEGINNING OF THE SEVENTEENTH CENTURY. OPPORTUNITIES FOR WORK . . .

(Slow dim to dark. When stage is dark, a chart, in the olden style showing simply and graphically the British Isles, the Atlantic, and the coast of America, is projected on downstage scrim. Full projection at first, then a pin-spot travels from England, across the Atlantic to America: Virginia. Together with this westward movement of the pin-spot are various sound effects. They suggest the travail of the difficult journey, music that suggests storm at sea and so forth. This is topped by a shrill piercing Indian war-cry, when pin-spot reaches Virginia.

At stage left spots come up and we see a wooden hogs-head marked "Tobacco." Beside this stands the colonial counterpart of the British Merchant Adventurer—the Southern Bourbon—richly dressed, well-fed, and conscious of his power as a PLANTER. *An indentured servant stands next to him, in his hands some farming implement.)*

PLANTER   You're idle, man. This tobacco needs looking after. *(explosively)* There's work to be done!

SERVANT   Sire, how long is it that I've been in Virginia?

PLANTER   Why, you lazy, good-for-nothing dolt, you've been here long enough to know better. What's that? What have you got there?

(The worker has meantime taken a piece of paper from his pocket and is glancing at it)

SERVANT   A handbill that was given to me when I was walking about London looking for work. *(reading freely)* Says, m'lord, that in America a man would find prosperity and a future. There was much land to be had and work for all and no starvation.

PLANTER   Damn, man, what are you complaining about?

SERVANT *(unruffled)*   And all we had to do, to pay our passage over here, was to work out the debt so incurred by donating our labor until such a debt was paid. We were told what this system was called—er—what is it again, sire?

PLANTER   Indenture! And it is the law of Virginia, man. You didn't have the money to pay for your passage on the boat and so I paid it for you. And so you became indentured to me according to the law and you're paying me back with your labor.

SERVANT   I have *paid* you back, sire. You see, my term of indenture was five years. Today, that five years is over and my debt is paid.

PLANTER   You mean you are not going to work any longer?

SERVANT   Of course, I'll be working, sire. That is if you pay me the proper wages.

(The PLANTER *groans as . . . blackout. As soon as the spot blacks out on* PLANTER, *the only remaining element on stage is the projected chart, as before. This sustains while)*

LOUDSPEAKER   THE LONDON COMPANY'S ENTERPRISE IN THE NEW CONTINENT FAILED TO PRODUCE ANYTHING AS ROMANTIC AS JEWELS, PRECIOUS STONES, GOLD AND SILVER. BUT THERE WERE OTHER TREASURES.

(Lights come up behind that portion of scrim showing England, disclosing a tobacconist's shop. In a stylized fashion, we see several men go through the procedure of approaching the counter, making a purchase, filling their pipes, taking a deep, satisfying pull, exhaling the smoke, and walking away. At first the transactions are at regular intervals, but soon the pace is so brisk that the merchant can't

calmly take care of his trade. The effect should succeed in establishing a general condition and not a specific shop. When the men come in the greatest numbers and it becomes obvious that the TOBACCONIST *is falling short of the demand, he raises his hands in despair and, looking down toward stage left, in front of scrim, he shouts and brings into view the same* PLANTER. *Their juxtaposition now is: the* PLANTER, *stage left, in front of chart, and the English* TOBACCONIST, *at stage right, discernible behind the map of England)*

TOBACCONIST   Send more tobacco!

PLANTER   You're receiving as much tobacco as we can raise, but there are problems—labor, for instance.

TOBACCONIST *(snorting)*   Fiddlesticks, man. England is sending you men by the boatload.

PLANTER   And what men! Some of them voluntary servants—the independent upstarts! But most of them here against their wishes—criminals, public debtors, dragging down the public morals.

SECOND PLANTER   And by the time they learn the routine, they're free to become *our* competitors!

(As they grumble, a man joins them, apparently coming from nowhere. He is a swashbuckling, sea-faring man, of the same period)

CAPTAIN   Gentlemen, stop crying about your high labor costs and all the bother of indentured servants! What I mean to say is— my ship is anchored down by the dock—and, gentlemen—it has an interesting cargo.

(Music and the sound of the African drums. Then overhead spot comes up, stage center, disclosing the deck of the Dutch ship; on level the inside view of the ships rail, or bulwark, with perhaps a suggestion of rigging—all flat settings—the trio step into the lighted area)

CAPTAIN   Spice from India. Hemp from Malay. Wine from Spain. And another kind of cargo, gentlemen—gold—from Africa!

THE PLANTERS *(avidly)*   Gold?

CAPTAIN   Black gold, gentlemen, from the Dark Continent. *(he spits contemptuously)* Why pay a man wages? They'll grow your rice, indigo, and tobacco—they'll grow it from one season to another, from sunup to sundown!

(As he says all this, there is heard shuffling of naked feet, clanking of shackles, and the coarse swearing of the bo's'n and his men, punctuated by occasional cracking of whip—and soon twenty black natives, chained and shackled in irons, naked almost, and in great suffering, are herded into the company of the CAPTAIN *and the awe-struck* PLANTERS)*

FIRST PLANTER   Savages!

SECOND PLANTER   Black men, from Africa!

CAPTAIN   —willing, obedient servants—*(as he speaks, one of the natives, the target for one of the bo's'n's vicious blows, drops to the deck. The* CAPTAIN *strides over to the fallen native, grabs him by his hair, as if he were just so much livestock, looks into his face, and flings the native back on deck)* They die off like pigs! But them as can make it—by Gott, they're good!

FIRST PLANTER *(after brief, spellbound pause, whispers)*   Slaves!

CAPTAIN *(shrugs shoulders)*   Must we put it that way?

SECOND PLANTER *(steps forward, puts hand on native's arm)*   By God, sir, if he's as willing as he is strong . . .

FIRST PLANTER *(coming to decision)*   What is your price, Captain?

CAPTAIN   Fifty pounds per head—and they're yours—body and soul!

FIRST PLANTER *(taking out purse)*   Done!

SECOND PLANTER *(likewise)*   And I'll take the other ten!

(They make the transaction and leave while the slaves are led off amid the same cursing and brutality. The dead Black lies prone beneath the ship's rail, and the CAPTAIN, *stepping on him, leans over it peering down at the departing planters, now offstage. He laughs into the darkness and shouts after them)*

CAPTAIN   Hey there! *(answering call from deck, below)* There's one more thing which I include in the bargain, gentlemen. *(he reaches down and then holds aloft an enormous black-snake whip)* You'll find it very useful!

(He tosses it to the gentlemen on the dock, and fondling the bags of gold, laughs, as lights dim to dark. All this behind downstage scrim. The stage is dark. Suddenly the black silence is shattered by a series of intermittent, loud reports. Blue floods come up on cyc, and on a huge cotton bale stands

the Southern Bourbon lashing out with an enormous black-snake whip, the same as that thrown to
him by the CAPTAIN. His face is lighted weirdly by
an overhead pin-spot

Cracks of whip. The scene will unfold itself with
first the sound of the cracking whip, then the blue
cyc with the slave driving Bourbon silhouetted
against it; then the toiling Negroes coming up into
view over the second level and massing before it;
then the spot up on the counting desk of the Bourbon at stage left; and then the movement of all the
goods, symbolizing export, off right, into dark. Also
the occasional appearance of the figures coming in
from wings on trucks.

Building up with this visual effect, slowly, then full
blast, is an off-stage chorus of Negro voices singing
an arrangement that should be a blend of spiritual
and song-of-protest)*

CHORUS   LET MY PEOPLE GO!
LOUDSPEAKER

> 1619: Virginia exports twenty thousand pounds
> of tobacco!
> 1664: Virginia and Maryland export twenty-five
> million pounds of tobacco!
> 1649: Three hundred slaves in Virginia!
> 1683: Three thousand slaves in Virginia!
> 1689: Five thousand slaves in Virginia!
> 1715: Twenty-three thousand slaves in Virginia!
> At the time of the American Revolution, there
> are two hundred and six thousand slaves in
> both Virginia and Maryland!
> In 1765 there are ninety-thousand slaves and
> South Carolina produces thirty-two thou
> sand tons of rice

(Dim out whole scene, but we still hear the cracking of the whip. Spot up stage left where, on truck,
we see a QUAKER at his pulpit)

QUAKER   Upon the Bible it must appear to
every honest, unpredjudiced man, that the
Negroes are equally entitled to the common
privileges of mankind with the Whites; that
they have the same rational powers, the same
natural affections, and are as susceptible to

---

*Note: As to the spoken part of this scene, it will consist of
such as the following utterances; incomplete now, but fuller
upon more extensive research. The disposition of the speeches,
by loudspeaker or actors, yet to be determined.

pain and grief as they; that, therefore, bringing
and keeping them in bondage is an instance of
oppression and injustice of a most grievous
nature, such as is scarcely to be paralleled by
any example in the present or former ages.

(Blackout and QUAKER off)

LOUDSPEAKER   IN 1776 SOUTH CAR
OLINA PRODUCES FIFTY-FIVE THOU
SAND TONS OF RICE FOR EXPORT!

(Dim on everything except the upstage Bourbon
cracking whip. There are offstage musket and cannon shots and on downstage scrim projection of
Liberty Bell, followed by superimposed projection
of facsimile of Declaration of Independence. Spot
comes up on apron, stage left on figure who might
be Thomas Jefferson)

JEFFERSON   . . . We hold these truths to be
self-evident, that all men are created equal,
that they are endowed by their creator with
certain unalienable rights, that among these
are life liberty and the pursuit of happiness.

(Blackout on Jefferson. The sound of machinery)

MILL OWNERS   Raw Materials! The mills
must be kept spinning! Sell us cotton! Name
your price! More cotton!

(Another man rushes toward them, also from far
side of stage. He carries the same kind of bag, and
he anticipates their wants. Without speaking, he
extends a handful of cotton.

SPOKESMAN (examines the stuff, picks at it,
passes it around to his associates. They shake
their heads negatively)   Those black seeds.
They stick like the very devil.

(Blackout on the Mill-Owner section of the stage.
Spot up stage right. A group of feverishly working
Negro women. Among them, the OVERSEER and
the PLANTATION OWNER)

PLANTATION OWNER (to overseer)   I'm paying
you to get some work out of these black devils.
Now get that cotton cleaned!

(The slaves sense what is coming and pluck away
faster and faster at the white balls, attempting to
separate the seeds)

OVERSEER (in ugly tones)   Goddam black
heathens! Do I have to lay this whip on your

filthy hides? Or are you going to be nice and get that cotton cleaned for your master! *(The* OVERSEER *secretly senses the impossibility of getting them to work any faster, but behind the same brutal expression he mutters in disgust. The* PLANTATION OWNER *comes on again, and in answer to his inquiring look)* It's no use, Boss. These Blacks are getting the seeds out as fast as it can be done. The best female in the gang can't get moren' a pound of cotton cleaned in an hour!

(Blackout)

(As the overseer's last remark is made, a spot dims up slowly on apron left, disclosing a young man, about thirty. Also, lights come up downstage area and a group, the prototypes of the Southern Planters, is observed. Then spot is up full, the young man walks toward them—directly to a large object that is covered with a tarpaulin. With his approach—)

LOUDSPEAKER   1793 YANKEE INVENTIVENESS STEPS INTO THE BREACH. A YOUNG NORTHERNER ELI WHITNEY . . .

(Whitney steps up to the object, dramatically removes the tarpaulin, and we see the cotton gin)

ELI WHITNEY   Gentlemen, I give you the cotton gin!

(Note: if it is at all possible to get a replica of the gin, it would be effective to present an actual demonstration of the process)

(Blackout. Spot up further to stage right, into which the same group of Southern Planters move, conversing excitedly)

SECOND PLANTER   That machine cleaned a thousand pounds of raw cotton where only ten pounds were cleaned before!

THIRD PLANTER   And it cleans cotton a hundred times faster than by hand!

FOURTH PLANTER   I won't be able to grow enough cotton to keep up with the demand!

FIFTH PLANTER   I'm going to need more land!

FIRST PLANTER   And more men to plant it!

SECOND PLANTER   More acres!

THIRD PLANTER   More darkies!

FOURTH PLANTER   Cotton is King!

LOUDSPEAKER   AT THE TIME OF THE COTTON GIN'S INVENTION, THE SOUTH EXPORTED . . .

FIRST PLANTER   One hundred and thirty-two thousand pounds!

LOUDSPEAKER   IN 1804 . . . COTTON PRODUCTION—

SECOND PLANTER   Thirty-eight million, one hundred eighteen thousand pounds for export!

ALL THE PLANTERS   Cotton is King!

(Blackout. As soon as the last scene dims to dark behind scrim, facsimilies of contemporary advertisements of slave auctions and sales are projected upon scrim. A truck slides in from the wings, set for auctioneers stay. When lights come up—with the projected facsimiles for background—a group of planters are standing about looking over the merchandise for sale—Negroes: young, old, male, and female)

SLAVE DEALER *(over hubbub, bangs gavel)* Sold! To Mr. Richards for the sum of four hundred and fifty dollars! Take a look at this fine specimen.

ANOTHER PLANTER   Seven hundred and fifty dollars!

SLAVE DEALER   Seven hundred and fifty bid! Seven hundred and fifty! Do I hear—?

ANOTHER PLANTER   Eight hundred dollars!

SLAVE DEALER   Eight hundred dollars! Eight hundred dollars—once! Eight hundred dollars—twice! Eight hundred—*(he bangs the gavel)* Sold to the gentlemen from Piedmond County! *(the slave is led off)*

(Spot up, apron right. During the following, the slave trading goes on in pantomime. In the spot we see Benjamin Franklin.)

LOUDSPEAKER   BENJAMIN FRANKLIN, REPRESENTING THE PENNSYLVANIA ABOLITION SOCIETY, PETITIONS CONGRESS . . .

FRANKLIN *(speaks to audience)*   . . . (we) earnestly entreat your attention to the subject of slavery; that you will be pleased to countenance the restoration to liberty of . . . this distressed race and that you will step to the very verge of the power vested in you for discouraging every species of traffic in the *persons of our followmen.*

(*Blackout on* FRANKLIN. *Spot comes up stage left, in vicinity of the pantomimed slave market scene, still being played against projected facsimiles.* SENATOR EARLY *speaks*)

LOUDSPEAKER   SENATOR EARLY OF GEORGIA REPLIES . . .

EARLY   Wherever people of color are found in a state of freedom in considerable numbers, they are considered as the instruments of murder, theft, and conflagration. We are told it is cruel and disgraceful to keep them in slavery. . . . But would it not be more cruel to place them in a situation where we must, in self-defense—understand me, gentlemen—get rid of them in some way? We must either get rid of them or they of us.

(*Spot out on* EARLY. *The pantomiming ceases— they all look up, as*)

LOUDSPEAKER   . . . BE IT ENACTED BY THE SENATE AND THE HOUSE OF REPRESENTATIVES OF THE UNITED STATES OF AMERICA, IN CONGRESS ASSEMBLED: THAT FROM AND AFTER THE THIRTY-FIRST DAY OF DECEMBER, ONE THOUSAND EIGHT HUNDRED AND SEVEN, IT SHALL NOT BE LAWFUL TO IMPORT AND BRING INTO THE UNITED STATES OR THE TERRITORIES THEREOF, ANY NEGRO, MULATTO, OR OTHER PERSON OF COLOR, AS A SLAVE.

(*At the end of this statement, the traders, who have been frozen in a listening attitude, now exchange smirking glances—some of them snapping their fingers in contempt or thumbing their noses.* JIM *and* MARY LOU, *as before. They are indignant—half out of their seats—looking as if for someone in authority*)

JIMMY (*apologetically*)   It's probably a gag, honey. It's probably just a new routine.

MARY LOU   Poor slaves. Ain't one of them blacks worth a pinch of snuff. Ain't one of them—not a single of them—ever did a thing for civilization.

(*Spot up suddenly on* TED *standing same position as before*)

TED   There were plenty that were good, al-right . . . plenty that had what it takes . . . all they needed was a chance for recognition, which here and there they got.

(*The spot rises on* PHILLIS. *She is seen sitting on a stool, knitting.* JOHN WHEATLEY *enters with a letter.*)

JOHN (*giving her the letter*)   A letter for you, Phillis.

PHILLIS (*opening the letter, she glances at it and leaps into the air*)   It's from General Washington. (*reads*) "Cambridge, February 28, 1776. Miss Phillis: Your favor of the 26th of October did not reach my hands till the middle of December. Time enough you will say, to have given an answer ere this. Granted. But a variety of important occurrences continually interposing to distract the mind and withdraw the attention I hope, will apologize for the delay and plead my excuse for the seeming but not real neglect. I thank you most sincerely for your polite notice of me in the elegant lines you enclosed, and however undeserving I may be of such, encomium and panegryic, the style and manner exhibit a striking proof of your poetic talent; in honor of which, and as a tribute justly due you, I would have published the poem had I not been apprehensive that, while I only meant to give the world this new instance of your genius. I might have incurred the imputation of vanity. This, and nothing else, determined me not to give it place in the public prints. If you should ever come to Cambridge, or near headquarters, I shall be happy to see a person so favored by the muses, and to whom Nature has been so literal and beneficient in her dispensation.

I am with great respect
Your obedient humble servant
George Washington.

(*Blackout. The spot rises on* PRESIDENT THOMAS JEFFERSON, *sitting at his desk writing. A* SERVANT *enters and bows*)

SERVANT   Mr. President. There is a gentleman to see you . . . a mister Benjamin Banneker.

JEFFERSON   A commission is being appointed to survey and make plans for the new Washington, D.C. We will make our Capital the most beautiful in all the world. I can think of no wiser choice than to appoint you a member of that commission.

(Spot up on both TED *and* MARY LOU*)*

TED   Capable—? The only thing they weren't capable of was throwing off their own shackles.

MARY LOU   Look here, boy. You're living in the twentieth century. Times were different when my forefathers owned big plantations.

TED   But there was no difference in a man's capacity to feel pain and misery.

MARY LOU   They were a damn sight better off than in the African jungle.

TED   Did they ask to be taken from the jungle?

MARY LOU   Well, my grand-dad wasn't responsible for that. But I sure enough hate to hear that stuff about pain and misery. Slaves they were and slaves they were content to be.

(Blackout)

LOUDSPEAKER   ON A SOUTHERN PLAN-TATION

(The spot rises on a group of slaves. They have dropped their working implements and straining over one another to get a glimpse of a book one of the slaves is reading. They are unaware of the master, who has quietly stepped upon the scene. He watches them and then walks over as the slaves jump up)

MASTER   What in the hell are you blacks a doing? *(the slaves tremble)* Gimmie that . . .

(He reaches for the book and snatches it from one of the slaves. Examines it and denounces the slaves)

Teach a Negro to read and you spoil a good field hand. Ah, what's this? "Walker's Appeal Addressed to Colored Citizens of the World." Who wrote this damn thing?

(Pause)

WALKER, A NEGRO   Don't you know this confounded book is poison? Telling you to revolt, eh? Well let me tell you what happened to that wild buck Nat Turner up there at Dismal Swamp. He tried to revolt; went on a rampage and killed more than fifty whites. It lasted for two weeks, but the whites ran him and his crowd of bucks down after eight weeks.

Burned him with hot irons, his face was mutilated; his body stuck with forks. They cut off his head and spiked it on whipping posts.

(The slaves stand humble and frightened.)

Well that's what some hero is gonna get. Which one of you reads?

(The slaves point out the slave who was reading the book.)

Take this and burn it, then bring me my whip. I'm going to lash your hide. Git to work there all of you! Git to work!

Blackout

LOUDSPEAKER   DENMARK VESEY

(The spot rises on a group of slaves.)

DENMARK   Curse the massa! Curse his gold! Damn him suffering. Come we fight—we have but one time to die. Let's die fighting like men. Fight! Fight! Fight!

(The SLAVES *are worked up into a spirit of revolt. At the word fight, they join into the spirit of rhythm . . . stamping their feet . . . singing . . .)*

SLAVES   Come we set the black man free . . . free . . . free . . .

Blackout

SETTING: *The spot rises on a large map of the United States as of 1855. Map may be transparent so that groups representing toiling slaves may be seen during the action. Several men representing the following are grouped about the map, Planters, Northerns, Industrialist, Westerns, Quakers,* ABO-LITIONERS *and Free Negroes.*

PLANTERS   And I say that the cotton growers of the South demand that slavery be extended through any territory.

(One of the planters goes up to the map and makes a sweeping indication of the whole map)

NORTHERNERS   Such a policy is absurd. There must be no more slave states.

NORTHERN   With your enslavement of the blacks you have cheapened the white man's labor.

IMMIGRANT *(in foreign accent)*   You tell us in Europe, come to America, we come over

4,000,000,000. Where can we work? How can we feed our family? You pay the Blacks nothing and want to pay us nothing.

ABOLITIONISTS   Free the blacks.

SPOKESMAN *(One man who has stepped out from the group attempts to bring the argument to a conclusion)*   Why can't we settle this matter amicable—we'll compromise. *(He goes up to the map and draws an imaginary line from east to west)*—suppose we draw a line from here to here. Now have your slaves here and no slavery will be permitted north of 36 degrees 30 minutes.

MISSOURIES   No, no, we must have slavery in Missouri.

OTHER BOSSES   No, we want Missouri a free State.

SPOKESMAN   All right! All right! We will make this one concession, with the exception of Missouri, slavery shall never be established in any State in the territory North of line 36 degrees 30 minutes.

2ND CONGRESSMAN   I am in agreement with Mr. Henry Clay that we have "five bleeding wounds." California should be admitted as free, Utah and New Mexico, when ready for statehood, will determine by their Constitution whether or not they desire slavery . . . Establish a boundary line between Texas and New Mexico . . . Prohibit the barter of slaves in the District of Columbia . . . And without the consent of Maryland . . . Enact a new "Fugitive Slave Law" . . . These are the "Five bleeding wounds," and I say that's the way to satisfy the North and the South.

CALHOUN *(excitedly)*   We have "debated this matter in Congress for ten months . . . I declare this plan to be unconstitutional . . . Congress has no power to keep slavery out of any territory or state . . ." *(Up to the map.)* . . . I want slavery to go anywhere a master sees fit to carry it. . . .

CALHOUN *(Resignedly)*   "If you of the North will not do this, then let our Southern States separate and depart in peace. I propose that the Constitution be amended to provide for two Presidents, one for the North and one for the South, and each having the veto power."

(The CONGRESSMEN are struck with awe. They rise slowly and stand motionless)

(Blackout)

(Setting: The spot rises on the levels. The signs of Missouri-Illinois and Minnesota are present again. Enter DRED SCOTT and HARRIET. They have just met.)

HARRIET   You seem troubled . . . Can I help you . . .

DRED   No one can help me . . . I have been in two free states, yet I am a slave.

HARRIET   I am a slave too . . . Perhaps we can help each other. What's your name?

DRED   Dred Scott . . . Yours?

HARRIET   Harriet . . . You know the abolitionists are working so we can be free.

DRED   If we had someone to fight for us.

HARRIET   They are fighting . . . Look . . .

(She looks around and takes out a newspaper. HARRIET and DRED watch the paper. The lights dim out on them and up on WILLIAM LLOYD GARRISON and ISSAC KNAPP and their printing press in a garret room.)

LOUDSPEAKER   WILLIAM LLOYD GARRISON

GARRISON *(Reads)*   . . . The Liberator, January 1, 1831 . . . Motto . . . "Our country men are all mankind."

(Projection comes down and shows picture of national capital with a flag inscribed . . . "LIBERTY" flying down from the dome. In the foreground is a SLAVE market with a SLAVE being flogged at the whipping post. Projection goes up)

GARRISON   "I shall contend strenuously for the immediate enfranchisement of our slave population. I will be as harsh as the truth and as uncompromising as justice. I will not retreat a single inch and I will be heard. We have the meeting of the Anti-slavery Society on Sunday. We must have a preacher to make the opening address.

(Fadeout)

LOUDSPEAKER   WHAT DOES THE CLERGY THINK OF SLAVERY?

(Spot up on KNAPP and REV. PLUMMER)

REV. PLUMMER   This is the most meddlesome, impudent, reckless, fierce and wicked excitement I ever saw. If abolitionists will get the country in a blaze it is but fair that they should receive the first warning at the fire. Get out . . . get out infidel . . . !

(Lights go out on them.)

LOUDSPEAKER   REV. J.C. POSTELL

REV. POSTELL *(Spot up)*   "It is not a moral evil. The fact that slavery is of Divine appointment would be proof enough with the Christians that it could not be a moral evil. I subscribe myself the friend of the Bible and the opposor of Abolitionists."

(Blackout)

LOUDSPEAKER   THE RIGHT REV. MEADE, BISHOP OF THE ANGLICAN CHURCH.

(The organ music of an ecclesiastical instrument swells)

BISHOP MEADE *(To a slave)*   "Blessings on you, my child. Almighty God hath been pleased to make you a slave here, and to you nothing but labor and poverty in this world which you are obliged to submit to. He will reward you for it in heaven and the punishment you suffer unjustly here shall turn to your exceeding great glory thereafter.

LOUDSPEAKER   BUT BISHOP . . . WHAT ABOUT THE LAW? THE ENGLISH LAW, BISHOP . . . THE ENGLISH COURTS STATE THAT UPON BAPTISM A SLAVE COULD RIGHTFULLY CLAIM HIS FREEDOM.

BISHOP MEADE *(Stuttering)*   Well . . . er . . . er . . . Well in that instance we cannot obey the law . . . Christian ministers are commanded to exhort servants to be obedient to their own masters and to please them in all things.

(Blackout)

LOUDSPEAKER   DRED SCOTT APPEALS TO THE SUPREME COURT AT WASHINGTON.

(The spot goes up on DRED SCOTT, *who is standing on the Missouri level.* CHIEF JUSTICE TANEY *is seated behind a high dias in the back. A group of people enter. They break up into groups and talk quietly among themselves. They are the* MISSOURIANS . . . *the* WESTERNERS . . . *and the* SOUTHERNERS. *No attempt is made here at personalities, but just representative attitudes)*

SCOTT   According to Congress the Missouri Compromise, I am a free man by going into Illinois . . . and according to the Northwestern Ordinance I am a free man by going into Minnesota . . .

SOUTHERNERS   Once a slave always a slave . . .

WESTERNERS   We Westerners won't tolerate Negroes . . . We have no place for them free or otherwise.

MISSOURIANS   England has freed her slaves . . . Spain has freed hers. France hers . . . America wipe out your shame.

SCOTT   Free me . . . free . . . My old master cannot make me a slave again . . .

TANEY   The three distinct provisions making you a free man are in conflict with the Constitution, which provides for the protection of property. You are property which belongs to Mr. Stanton . . . You are not a citizen and have no standing in a federal court. . . .

LOUDSPEAKER   BY 1850 FIFTY THOUSAND SLAVES HAD ESCAPED TO THE NORTH AND TO CANADA. FREDERICK DOUGLASS AT ROCHESTER, N.Y. JULY 4, 1852.

DOUGLASS *(Spot up)*   "What to the American slave, is your fourth of July? I answer: a day that reveals to him, more than all other days in the years, the gross injustice and cruelty to which he is the constant victim. To him your celebration is a sham, your boasted liberty, an unholy license; your national greatness, swelling vanity; your sounds of rejoicing are empty and heartless, your denunciation of tyrants, brass-fronted impudence; your shouts of liberty and equality, hollow mockery; your prayers and hymns, your sermons and thanksgivings, with all your religious parade and solemnity, are, to him, more bombast, fraud, deception, impiety and hypocrisy—a thin veil to cover up crimes which would disgrace a nation of savages. . . ."

(Applause)

(Blackout)

LOUDSPEAKER   JEFFERSON DAVIS.

JEFFERSON DAVIS   "The North is impairing the security of property and slaves and reducing those states which hold slaves to a condition of inferiority . . . the new Constitution of the Confederacy has put at rest forever all the agitating questions relating to our peculiar institutions. African slavery as it exists among us . . . the proper status of the Negro in our form of civilization."

(Blackout)

(The sound of election trumpets are heard)

VOICES: Lincoln is elected! Lincoln is elected!

SOUTHERNER *(Spot up)* "We separate, because of the hostility of Lincoln to our institutions . . . If he were inaugurated without our consent there would be slave insurrections in the south.

(Spot comes up on Abe Lincoln seated at executive desk, dictating to secretary.)

LINCOLN Take this letter to Mr. Horace Greeley, please. Dear Mr. Greeley—if there be those who would not save the union unless they could at the same time save slavery, I do not agree with them. My paramount object in this struggle is to save the union, and it is not either to save or to destroy slavery. If I could save the union without freeing any slaves I would do it. If I could do it by freeing all the slaves I would also do that. What I do about slavery and the colored race, I do because I believe it would help save the union.

(They are interrupted in this matter by the sound of distant explosion and cannon fire. Both look up silently, questioningly.

The crackle and click of a telegraph key is heard—and over this—)

PROJECTION

HARPERS FERRY
 BOONEVILLE
  WILSON'S CREEK
   BATTLE OF RICHMOND MOUNTAIN
    ARMY OF THE POTOMAC
     MANASSAS
      FORT HENRY
       FORT DONALDSON
        PEAK RIDGE
         SHILOH
          ISLAND NUMBER TEN
           MONITOR AND MERRIMAC

LOUDSPEAKER SOUTH......CAROLINA......MILITARY......FIRES......ON......FORT......SUMTER.

LINCOLN *(with gravity)* I call for 75,000 militia to serve for three months in suppressing the opposition and reclaiming the seized properties of the United States.*

(Lights dim on LINCOLN but do not black out. Spots up at end of stage disclose group of Confederate Officers—blue uniforms. On hearing Proclamation they belligerently draw their sabers. Entire scene......)

DIMS TO DARK

Spot comes up stage left where JIMMY *and* MARY LOU *were before. They, the white spectators are still there, but now she is dressed in the crinolines of the period . . . he remains in modern dress. On their night-club table between them a gleaming sword is buried, quivering. The spot has come up just as she turns away from him and almost hisses—)*

MARY LOU Damn Yankee!!

(JIMMY freezes for an instant, then silently exits. MARY LOU stares transfixed at what now unfolds before her on the general stage.)

(The scrim has been lowered, meantime. Cannon and rifle fire sustain while upon the scrim there is projected a series of legends that suggest the most well-known highlights of the Civil War; battles and incidents. These might be projected in the manner of movie-montago, with the legends looming in from a distant perspective.)

---

*This is a digest—get Proclamation of April 13, 1861 or 2.)

BALL'S BLUFF
SEVEN PINES
FAIR OAKS
SEVEN DAY'S BATTLE
FREDERICKSBURG
MALVERN HILL ASSAULT
RICHMOND
RAPPAHANOCK
CEDAR MOUNTAIN
VICKSBURG
GETTYSBURG
CHATTANOOGA
LOOKOUT MOUNTAIN
SEIGE OF KNOXVILLE
CHICAMAUGA
MISSIONARY RIDGE
SHENANDOAH VALLEY
BATTLE OF WINCHESTER
BATTLE OF COLD HARBOR
BATTLE OF CEDAR CREEK
KENNESAW MOUNTAIN
MARCH TO THE SEA
HAMPTON ROADS CONFERENCE
FORT STEDMAN
ENCOUNTER AT FIVE FORKS
APPOMATTOX

(Spot up, to the right)

A NEGRO WOMAN   "The grandest successes of the war are not the victories gained but the advance of the cause of freedom. If the war had been closed without crushing slavery, our victories would have been defeats and our struggles would have been worse than useless. . . . Place yourselves in the condition of the freedman. . . . yesterday a slave . . . today your chains are snapped asunder . . . The signing of the Declaration of Independence was the shining epoch in your history; but the Anti-Slavery Amendment forms the commencement of a grander era!"

BLACKOUT

(Spot up, to the left)

A WHITE SENATOR   I thank God that slavery is dead and buried! And I want to say to you to remember and carry it your neighbor, and let it go from neighbor to neighbor across the continent that the freedmen of the United States shall be protected in their rights!

BLACKOUT

BIBLIOGRAPHIES

Selected Bibliography of Books on Black Drama and Its Theatre Artists

Carter, Steven R. *Hansberry's Drama: Commitment amid Complexity.* Urbana: University of Illinois Press, 1991.

Coleman, Gregory D. *We're Heaven Bound: Portrait of a Black Sacred Drama.* Athens: University of Georgia Press, 1994.

Cooper, Ralph. *Amateur Night at the Apollo.* New York: HarperCollins, 1990.

Dictionary of Literary Biography. Vols. 5, 33, 38, 50, 51, 76. Detroit: Gale Research, 1980s.

Fabre, Geneviève, Michel Fabre, William French, and Amritjit Singh. *Afro-American Poetry and Drama, 1760–1975: A Reference Guide.* Detroit: Gale Research, 1979.

Fletcher, Tom. *100 Years of the Negro in Show Business!* New York: Burdge & Co., 1954. Reprint, New York: Da Capo Press, 1984.

Fraden, Rena. *Blueprints for a Black Federal Theatre 1935–1939.* New York: Cambridge University Press, 1994.

Gray, John, ed. *Black Theatre and Performance: A Pan-African Bibliography.* Westport, CT: Greenwood Press, 1990.

Grupenhoff, Richard. *The Black Valentino: The Stage and Screen Career of Lorenzo Tucker.* Metuchen, NJ: Scarecrow Press, 1988.

Haskins, James. *Black Theater in America.* New York: Thomas Y. Crowell, 1982.

Hatch, James V. *Sorrow Is the Only Faithful One: The Life of Owen Dodson,* Urbana: University of Illinois Press, 1993.

Hay, Samuel A. *African American Theatre: An Historical and Critical Analysis.* New York: Cambridge University Press, 1994.

Heath, Gordon. *Deep Are the Roots: Memoirs of a Black Expatriate.* Amherst, MA: University of Massachusetts Press, 1992.

Hill, Errol. *Shakespeare in Sable: A History of Black Shakespearean Actors.* Amherst, MA: University of Massachusetts Press, 1984.

———. *The Theatre of Black Americans.* New York: Applause Theatre Book Publishers, 1987.

Hughes, Langston, and Milton Meltzer. *Black Magic.* Englewood Cliffs, NJ: Prentice-Hall, 1968.

Kellner, Bruce, ed. *The Harlem Renaissance: A Historical Dictionary for the Era.* Westport, CT: Greenwood Press, 1984.

Klotman, Phyllis Rauch. *Frame by Frame: A Black Filmography.* Bloomington: Indiana University Press, 1979.

Lester, Neal A. *Ntozake Shange: A Critical Study of the Plays.* New York: Garland Publishing, 1995.

Mapp, Edward. *Directory of Blacks in the Performing Acts,* 2d ed. Metuchen, NJ: Scarecrow Press, 1978.

Molette, Carlton W., and Barbara J. *Black Theatre: Premise and Presentation,* 2d ed. Bristol, IN: Wyndham Hall Press, 1992.

Neal, Larry. *Visions of a Liberated Future: Black Arts Movement Writings.* New York: Thunder's Mouth Press, 1989.

Newman, Richard. *Black Access: A Bibliography of Afro-American Bibliographies.* Westport, CT: Greenwood Press, 1984.

Ortolani, Benito, ed. *International Bibliography of Theatre:* New York: Theatre Research Data Center, 1982. Also volumes published in 1983, 1984, 1985, 1986, 1987, 1988–89, 1990–91, 92–93.

Peterson, Jr., Bernard L., *Contemporary Black American Playwrights and Their Plays.* Westport, CT: Greenwood Press, 1988.

———. *Early Black American Playwrights and Dramatic Writers*. Westport, CT: Greenwood Press, 1990.

———. *A Century of Musicals in Black and White: An Encyclopedia of Musical Stage Works By, About, or Involving African Americans*. Westport, CT: Greenwood Press, 1993.

Riis, Thomas L. *Just before Jazz: Black Musical Theater in New York 1890–1915*. Washington, DC: Smithsonian Institute Press, 1989.

Rush, Theressa G., Carol F. Myers, and Esther S. Arata. *Black American Writers, Past and Present: A Biographical and Bibliographical Dictionary*, 2 vols. Metuchen, NJ: Scarecrow Press, 1975.

Sampson, Henry T. *Blacks in Blackface: A Source Book on Early Black Musical Shows*. Metuchen, NJ: Scarecrow Press, 1980.

———. *The Ghost Walks: A Chronological History of Blacks in Show Business, 1865–1910*. Metuchen, NJ: Scarecrow Press, 1988.

Schiffman, Jack. *Uptown: The Story of Harlem's Apollo Theatre*. New York: Cowles Book Company, 1971.

Southern, Eileen. *Biographical Dictionary of Afro-American and African Musicians*. Westport, CT: Greenwood Press, 1983.

———, ed. *African American Theater: Out of Bondage* (1876) and *Peculiar Sam; or, The Underground Railroad* (1879). New York: Garland Publishing, 1994.

Southern, Eileen, and Josephine Wright. Compiled by *African-American Traditions in Song, Sermon, Tale, and Dance, 1600s–1920: An Annotated Bibliography of Literature, Collections, and Artworks*. Westport, CT: Greenwood Press, 1990.

Szwed, John, and Roger D. Abrahams. *Afro-American Folk Culture: An Annotated Bibliography of Materials from North, Central, and South America and the West Indies*, 2 vols. Philadelphia: Institute for the Study of Human Issues, 1978.

Tanner, Jo A. *Dusky Maidens: The Odyssey of the Early Black Dramatic Actress*. Westwood, CT: Greenwood Press, 1992.

Toll, Robert C. *Blacking Up: The Minstrel Show in Nineteenth-Century America*. New York: Oxford University Press, 1974.

Watkins, Mel. *On the Real Side: Laughing, Lying, and Signifying: The Underground Tradition of African American Humor that Transformed American Culture, from Slavery to Richard Pryor*. New York: Simon & Schuster, 1994.

Williams, Mance. *Black Theatre in the 1960s and 1970s: A Historical-Critical Analysis of the Movement*. Westport, CT: Greenwood Press, 1985.

Woll, Allen. *Dictionary of the Black Theatre*. Westport, CT: Greenwood Press, 1983.

———. *Black Musical Theatre From Coontown to Dreamgirls*. Baton Rouge: Louisiana State University Press, 1989.

Selected Bibliography of Anthologies Containing Scripts by Black Playwrights

Baraka, Amiri. *Four Black Revolutionary Plays*. Indianapolis, IN: Bobbs-Merrill, 1969.

———. *The Motion of History and Other Plays*. New York: Morrow, 1977.

Branch, William, ed. *Black Thunder*. New York: Mentor, 1992.

Brasmer, William, and Dominick Consolo, eds. *Black Drama: An Anthology*. Columbus, OH: Merrill, 1970.

Brown-Guillory, Elizabeth, ed. *Wines in the Wilderness*. Westport, CT: Greenwood Press, 1990.

Bullins, Ed. *Five Plays by Ed Bullins*. Indianapolis, IN: Bobbs-Merrill, 1968.

———. *Four Dynamite Plays*. New York: William Morrow, 1971.

———. *The Theme Is Blackness*. New York: William Morrow, 1973.

Carter, Steve. *Plays by Steve Carter*. New York: Broadway Play Publishing, 1986.

Dean, Phillip Hayes. *The Sty of the Blind Pig and Other Plays*. Indianapolis, IN: Bobbs-Merrill, 1973.

Edmonds, Randolph. *The Land of Cotton and Other Plays*. Washington, DC: Associated Publishers, 1942.

Flynn, Joyce, and Joyce Occomy Stricklin, eds. *Frye Street & Environs: The Collected Works of Marita Bonner*. Boston: Beacon Press, 1987.

Hamalian, Leo, and James V. Hatch, eds. *Roots of African American Drama*. Detroit: Wayne State University Press, 1991.

Hansberry, Lorraine. *A Raisin in the Sun/The Sign in Sidney Brustein's Window*. New York: New American Library, 1966.

Hatch, James V., and Leo Hamalian, eds. *Lost Plays of the Harlem Renaissance*. Detroit: Wayne State University Press, in press.

Hill, Errol, ed. *Black Heroes, 7 Plays*. New York: Applause Theatre Book Publishers, 1989.

Kennedy, Adrienne. *Adrienne Kennedy in ONE ACT*. Minneapolis: University of Minnesota Press, 1988.

―――. *The Alexander Plays*. Minneapolis: University of Minnesota Press, 1992.

King, Woodie, and Ron Milner, eds. *Black Drama Anthology*. New York: Columbia University Press, 1972.

Mahone, Sydne, ed. *Moonmarked & Touched by the Sun*. New York: Theatre Communications Group, 1994.

Nemiroff, Robert, ed. *Les Blancs: The Collected Last Plays of Lorriane Hansberry*. New York: Random House, 1972.

Oliver, Clinton, and Stephanie Sills, eds. *Contemporary Black Drama*. New York: Scribner, 1971.

Ostrow, Eileen, ed. *Center Stage: An Anthology of 21 Contemporary Plays*. Oakland, CA: Sea Urchin Press, 1981.

Oyamo [Charles Gordon]. *Hillbilly Liberation*. New York: Ujamaa, 1976.

Patterson, Lindsay, ed. *Black Theater*. New York: Dodd, Mead, 1971.

Perkins, Kathy, ed. *Female Black Playwrights*. Bloomington: Indiana University Press, 1989.

Richardson, Willis, ed. *Plays and Pageants from the Life of the Negro*, 2d ed. Jackson MI.: University Press of Mississippi, 1994.

Shange, Ntozake. *Three Pieces*. New York: St. Martin's Press, 1981.

Smalley, Webster, ed. *Five Plays by Langston Hughes*. Bloomington: Indiana University Press, 1963.

Turner, Darwin T., ed. *Black Drama in America*, 2d ed. Washington, DC: Howard University Press, 1994.

Walcott, Derek. *Dream on Monkey Mountain and Other Plays*. New York: Farrar, Straus & Giroux, 1970.

―――. *Three Plays*. New York: Farrar, Straus & Giroux, 1986.

White, Edgar. *The Crucificado: Two Plays*. New York: William Morrow, 1973.

―――. *Lament for Rastafari and Other Plays*. London: Marion Boyars, 1983.

Wilson, August. *Three Plays*. Pittsburgh: University of Pittsburgh Press, 1991.

Wilkerson, Margaret B., ed. *9 Plays by Black Women*. New York: New American Library, 1986.

Selected Bibliography of Authors in the Early Period

Bonner, Marita. *Exit, An Illusion*. In *Black Female Playwrights: An Anthology of Plays before 1950*. Edited by Kathy A. Perkins. Bloomington: Indiana University Press, 1989. This one-act experimental play concerns the psychological conflicts engendered by miscegenation.

―――. *The Pot-Maker*. In *Black Female Playwrights: An Anthology of Plays before 1950*. Edited by Kathy A. Perkins. Bloomington: Indiana University Press, 1989. This one-act folk play is a fatalistic melodrama about Elias, who is called to preach and who manages the death of his wife's lover.

Brown, William Wells. *Experience; or How to Give a Northern Man a Backbone* (1856). This play, never published or found, told the story of a white man from the North who was sold as a slave in the South.

Browne, Theodore. *A Black Woman Called Moses*. Unpublished script in the Hatch-Billoops Collection, New York City, 1937. A full-length play on the life of Harriet Tubman.

―――. *The Gravy Train*. A typewritten script in the Schomburg Collection, New York City, 1940. This is a full-length play about a sensitive young man trying to work, go to school, and keep his wandering wife happy.

―――. *The Seven Cities of Gold*. Unpublished historical fantasy, pre-1974. Based on the legend of Esteban (Stephen) Dorantes, a Moor, who explored the Southwest with the Spanish conquistadors.

―――. *Steppin' High*. Unpublished musical extravaganza with a book by Browne, pre-1974. The story of a Black entertainer's rise from a "tent show" to Broadway stardom. Said to be based on the life of Bert Williams.

Dunbar, Paul Laurence. *Clorindy, the Origin of the Cakewalk*. Paul Laurence Dunbar Papers, Ohio Historical Society, Columbus. A musical of slight plot explicating the show's title.

―――. *Robert Herrick*. Paul Laurence Dunbar Papers, Ohio Historical Society, Columbus. A comedy of manners in the style of Sheridan and Wilde.

Edmonds, Randolph S. *The Breeders*. In *Six Plays for a Negro Theater*. Boston: Walter Baker, 1934. A one-act drama showing slave resistance to breeding for more slaves.

―――. *Nat Turner*. In *Six Plays for a Negro Theater*. Boston: Walter Baker, 1934. A one-act play showing Nat Turner on the eve of his rebellion and in his defeat.

————. *Silas Brown*. In *Land of Cotton and Other Plays*. Washington, DC: Associated Publishers, 1943. A one-act play about a stingy, cruel father who drives his son from home and lives to regret it.

————. *Earth and Stars*. In *Black Drama in America: An Anthology*. Edited by Darwin T. Turner. New York: Fawcett, 1971. A full-length play that explores the Civil Rights Movement in the South before World War II.

Fuller, Charles H., Jr. *The Rise*. In *New Plays from the Black Theatre*. Edited by Ed Bullins. New York: Bantam Books, 1969. A historical drama based on the life of Marcus Garvey.

————. *In the Deepest Part of Sleep*. Unpublished manuscript. New York: William Morris Agency, 1974. A domestic drama concerning an emotionally disturbed mother and her young son.

————. *Jerry Bland and the Blandelles Featuring Miss Marva James*. Unpublished manuscript. New York: William Morris Agency, 1974. A musical about an aging blues singer trying to make a comeback.

————. *The Brownsville Raid*. Unpublished manuscript in the Hatch-Billops Collection, New York City, 1975. A drama based on historical facts about an army regiment dishonorably discharged after being falsely accused of participating in a riot.

————. *Zooman and the Sign*. New York: Samuel French, 1982. A Black Philadelphia teenager accidentally kills a young girl before witnesses too afraid to identify him.

————. *Jonquil*. Unpublished manuscript. New York: William Morris Agency, 1989. The play examines Ku Klux Klan activity during Reconstruction.

Grimké, Angelina. *Mara*. Manuscript in the Grimké Papers at the Moorland-Spingarn Collection, Howard University, Washington, DC. A four-act play set in the South and focusing on the southern Black woman's powerlessness in protecting herself against the white man's lust.

Hill, Abram. Burns Mantle, ed. NY: Dodd, Meade & Co., 1945. *Anna Lucasta*. Abridged in *Best Plays of 1944–45*. Hill's adaptation for a Black cast of Philip Yordan's play by the same title written about a Polish family.

————. *Walk Hard*. In *Black Theater USA*, 1st ed. New York: The Free Press, 1974. A young Black boxer has to fight racism and the mob as well as his opponents.

Hughes, Langston. *Simply Heavenly*. In *Five Plays by Langston Hughes*. Edited by Webster Smalley. Bloom-ington: Indiana University Press, 1968. A musical based on the adventures of Jesse B. Semple.

————. *Soul Gone Home*. In *Five Plays by Langston Hughes*. Edited by Webster Smalley. Bloomington: Indiana University Press, 1968. A one-act funeral monologue of a son for his prostitute mother.

————. *Tambourines to Glory*. In *Five Plays by Langston Hughes*. Edited by Webster Smalley. Bloom-ington: Indiana University Press, 1968. An evicted mother establishes a storefront church in Harlem.

————. *Emperor of Haiti*. In *Black Drama in America: An Anthology*. Edited by Darwin T. Turner. Greenwich, CT: Fawcett Publishers, 1971. A drama about Jean Jacques Dessalines, a Black rebel who rose to power as a general and an emperor during the Haitian rebellion against Napoleon Bonaparte.

Hurston, Zora Neale. *Color Struck*. In *Black Female Playwrights, An Anthology of Plays before 1950*. Edited by Kathy A. Perkins. Bloomington: University of Indiana Press, 1989. Emma, a dark woman, is driven insane by her jealousy of light complexioned women.

———— and Langston Hughes. *Mule Bone, A Comedy of Negro Life*. Edited by George Houston Bass and Henry Louis Gates, Jr. NY: Harper Perennial, 1991. Jim Weston, a Methodist and Dave Carter, a Baptist, are the best of friends until they quarrel over a woman, Daisy. They resolve the problem by leaving Daisy and going away together.

Johnson, Georgia Douglas. *Frederick Douglass*. In *Negro History in Thirteen Plays*. Edited by Willis Richardson and May Miller. Washington, DC: Associated Publishers, 1935. Drama of escape from slavery.

————. *William and Ellen Craft*. In *Negro History in Thirteen Plays*. Edited by Willis Richardson and May Miller. Washington, DC: Associated Publishers, 1935. Drama of escape from slavery.

————. *Blue Blood*. In *Black Female Playwrights: An Anthology of Plays before 1950*. Edited by Kathy A. Perkins. Bloomington: Indiana University Press, 1989. A drama of miscegenation with a happy ending.

————. *Blue-Eyed Black Boy*. In *Black Female Playwrights: An Anthology of Plays before 1950*. Edited by Kathy A. Perkins. Bloomington: Indiana University Press, 1989. A drama of miscegenation with a happy ending.

————. *Plumes*. In *Black Female Playwrights: An Anthology of Plays before 1950*. Edited by Kathy A. Perkins. Bloomington: Indiana University Press, 1989. One-act drama where a mother chooses between spending money for a doctor or for her daughter's funeral with "plumes."

————. *Safe.* In *Wines in the Wilderness.* Edited by Elizabeth Brown-Guillory. Westport, CT: Greenwood Press, 1990. A mother strangles her newborn boy while a lynching is taking place in town.

Mathews, John F. *Ti Yette.* In *Plays and Pageants from the Life of the Negro.* Edited by Willis Richardson. Washington, DC: Associated Publishers, 1930. A Creole brother kills his sister when she dates a white man during Mardi Gras.

————. *Black Damp.* In *Lost Plays of the Harlem Renaissance.* Edited by James V. Hatch and Leo Hamalian. Detroit: Wayne State University Press, in press. The story of a multiethnic group of coal miners trapped in a cave-in.

Miller, May. *Scratches.* In *Carolina Magazine* (April 1929). A one-act of life and love played out in a poolhall.

————. *Christophe's Daughters.* In *Black Female Playwrights: An Anthology of Plays before 1950.* Edited by Kathy A. Perkins. Bloomington: Indiana University Press, 1989. Historical drama about the fate of Haiti's Henri Christophe's daughters.

————. *Harriet Tubman.* In *Black Female Playwrights: An Anthology of Plays before 1950.* Edited by Kathy A. Perkins. Bloomington: Indiana University Press, 1989. A biographical drama depicting Tubman leading slaves to freedom.

————. *Riding the Goat.* In *Black Female Playwrights: An Anthology of Plays before 1950.* Edited by Kathy A. Perkins. Bloomington: Indiana University Press, 1989. A comedy about a doctor who is forced to participate in community rituals.

————. *Stragglers in the Dust.* In *Black Female Playwrights: An Anthology of Plays before 1950.* Edited by Kathy A. Perkins. Bloomington: Indiana University Press, 1989. A white veteran of World War I acts out his guilt at the monument to the Unknown Soldier because his life was saved by an unknown African American.

————. *Nails and Thorns.* In *The Roots of African American Drama.* Edited by Leo Hamalian and James V. Hatch. Detroit: Wayne State University Press, 1992. A drama depicting the effects of a lynching on a white family.

Richardson, Willis. *The Broken Banjo.* In *Plays of Negro Life.* Edited by Alain Locke and Montgomery Gregory. New York: Harper Brothers, 1927. A bad man with a good heart is guilty of an accidental homocide.

————. *Attucks the Martyr.* In *Negro History in Thirteen Plays.* Edited by Willis Richardson and May Miller. Washington, DC: Associated Publishers, 1935. The story of how Crispus Attucks was the first patriot killed in the American Revolution.

————. *The Chip Woman's Fortune.* In *The Roots of African American Drama.* Edited by Leo Hamalian and James V. Hatch. Detroit: Wayne State University Press, 1992. An old woman gives her savings to help a destitute family. This was the first drama by a Black author to be done on Broadway.

————. *The House of Sham.* In *Plays and Pageants from the Life of the Negro,* 2d ed. Jackson: University Press of Mississippi, 1993. A middle-class family, living beyond its means, gets a comeupance.

————. *A Pillar of the Church.* In *Lost Plays of the Harlem Renaissance.* Edited by James V. Hatch and Leo Hamalian. Detroit: Wayne State University Press, in press. A tyrannical father is outmaneuvered by his wife and daughter.

Séjour, Victor. *Richard III.* Paris: D. Giraud et J. Dagneau, 1852. A five-act play showing the bloody history of the English king.

————. *Les Noces Vénitiennes.* Paris: M. Lévy Frères, 1855. A five-act drama depicting the hatred and rivalry of two families in Venice.

————. *La Tireuse de Cartes.* Paris: M. Lévy Frères, 1860. A five-act drama of a mother who vows to kill her daughter's husband-abductor.

Spence, Eulalie. *The Starter.* In *Plays of Negro Life.* Edited by Alain Locke and Montgomery Gregory. New York: Harper Brothers, 1927. A one-act comedy about a young woman who tries to commit her boyfriend to a promise of marriage.

————. *Fool's Errand.* In *Black Female Playwrights: An Anthology of Plays before 1950.* Edited by Kathy A. Perkins. Bloomington: Indiana University Press, 1989. A folk comedy about busybody neighbors who assume that the unmarried daughter of a church member is pregnant.

————. *Her.* In *Black Female Playwrights: An Anthology of Plays before 1950.* Edited by Kathy A. Perkins. Bloomington: Indiana University Press, 1989. A mystery play about the ghost of a wife who had hanged herself.

————. *Episode.* In *Wines in the Wilderness.* Edited by Elizabeth Brown-Guillory. Westport, CT: Greenwood Press, 1990. A husband is more interested in his music and sports than his lonely wife.

————. *Hot Stuff.* In *Wines in the Wilderness.* Edited by Elizabeth Brown-Guillory. Westport, CT: Greenwood Press, 1990. The numbers racket, furs, silk stockings in the fast-paced life of a female con in Harlem.

Toomer, Jean. *Natalie Mann.* In *Wayward Seeking: A Collection of Writings by Jean Toomer.* Edited by Darwin T. Turner. Washington, DC: Howard University Press, 1980. Full-length play depicts a young, middle-class African American woman who achieves self-liberation.

———. *The Sacred Factory.* In *Wayward Seeking: A Collection of Writings by Jean Toomer.* Edited by Darwin T. Turner. Washington, DC: Howard University Press, 1980. An expressionistic drama revealing the monotonous birth-to-death cycle of a working-class family and the intellectual and spiritual confrontations that frustrate and defeat middle-class Black Americans.

Ward, Theodore. *Shout Hallelujah!* Unpublished manuscript in the Hatch-Billops Collection, New York City, 1941. A social drama about poverty and disease in a West Virginia coal mining town.

———. *Candle in the Wind.* Unpublished manuscript in the Hatch-Billops Collection, New York City, 1967. A historical drama concerning the murder of a Black senator from Mississippi during Reconstruction in 1875.

———. *Our Lan'.* In *Black Drama in America.* Edited by Darwin T. Turner. Washington, DC: Howard University Press, 1994. A story based on historical fact about the post Civil War struggle of Blacks to get and hold land of their own.

ABOUT THE EDITORS

JAMES V. HATCH is a professor in the Graduate Theatre Program of the City University of New York. He is the author of several books on African American theatre, including the prize-winning biography *Sorrow Is the Only Faithful One: The Life of Owen Dodson.*

TED SHINE received his Ph.D. in theatre from the University of California, Santa Barbara. He currently teaches and directs in the Department of Music and Drama at A & M University, Prairie View, Texas. He is the author of more than thirty plays, including *Contribution* and *Morning, Noon, and Night.*